Copyright Notices

Game Design:
Theory & Practice
Second Edition

Richard Rouse III

**Illustrations by
Steve Ogden**

**Foreword by
Noah Falstein**

Atomic Sam character designed by Richard Rouse III and Steve Ogden

Library of Congress Cataloging-in-Publication Data

Rouse, Richard.
    Game design: theory & practice / by Richard Rouse III ; illustrations by
    Steve Ogden.—2nd cd.
      p. cm.
    Includes bibliographical references and index.
    ISBN 1-55622-912-7 (pbk.)
    1. Computer games—Programming. I. Title.
    QA76.76.C672R69   2004
    794.8'1526—dc22   2004015102
                                        CIP

All inquiries for volume purchases of this book should be addressed to Wordware
Publishing, Inc., at the above address. Telephone inquiries may be made by calling:

(972) 423-0090

Dedication

In memory of Jamie.

Acknowledgments

Thanks to Steve Ogden for coming back to Atomic Sam and breathing life into the little kid once again.

Thanks to Noah Falstein, James Hague, Damion Schubert, Ian Parberry, and Margaret Rogers for looking over my work and providing me with invaluable feedback and support, which have improved this book tremendously.

Thanks also to Tom Hall, Katherine Isbister, Darius Kazemi, and Michael Eilers for their comments on this book and how it might be made better the second time around.

Thanks to Doug Church, Chris Crawford, Ed Logg, Jordan Mechner, Sid Meier, Steve Meretzky, and Will Wright for graciously subjecting themselves to my nearly endless questioning.

Thanks to Wes Beckwith, Beth Kohler, Martha McCuller, Alan McCuller, Denise McEvoy, Tim McEvoy, and everyone at Wordware for making this book once again become a reality.

For their help with this book, thanks to Jim Hill, Steve Crane, Ken Fedesna, George Gomez, Rob Gustafson, Reilly Brennan, Robin Hunicke, Matt Bertz, Scott Miller, Jenny Huldschiner, Tyrone Miller, Carol Quito, Rannie Yoo, Loretta Stevens, Jason Wonacott, Doug Zartman, Benson Russell, John Scott Lewinski, Ari Feldman, Laura J. Mixon-Gould, Jeff Buccelatto, Jayson Hill, Laura Pokrifka, Josh Moore, Lisa Sokulski, Dan Harnett, Steffan Levine, Susan Wooley, Chris Brandkamp, Kelley Gilmore, Lindsay Riehl, Patrick Buechner, Greg Rizzer, Lori Mezoff, Jenna Mitchell, Ericka Shawcross, Maryanne Lataif, Bryce Baer, Bob Bates, James Conner, Lisa Tensfeldt, Paula Cook, Donald Knapp, and Diana Fuentes.

Thanks to Jamil Moledina, Jennifer Olsen, Alex Dunne, & everyone at *Game Developer*/Gamasutra, Gordon Cameron, Tuncer Deniz, Bart Farkas, Andy Eddy, Brian Moriarty, Scott McCloud, Ed Magnin, Bernd Kreimeier, Andrew Rollings, George Broussard, Jason Della Rocca, Dave Astle, Tom Russo, Kevin Toyama, Greg Orlando, George Jones, Owain Bennallack, Matthew Percival, Dishad Husain, Julie Perkins, Angie Cox & everyone at Gamer.tv, Jon Goodwin, Christopher Erhardt, Jonathan Kay, Neil Morton, Stephen Granade, Jeff Vogel, Laura Heon, Kaarin Lemstrom-Sheedy & MassMOCA, Troy Dunniway, Clay Heaton, Rich Carlson, Iikka Keranen, Curt Feldman & everyone at E3, Alan Patmore, Nick Radovich & everyone at Surreal, David Zucker & everyone at Midway, Mark Bullock, the Leaping Lizard crew, Brian Rice, Lee Waggoner, Pat Alphonso, Peter Tamte, Nate Birkholtz, Al Schilling, Cindy Swanson & everyone at MacSoft, Alex Seropian, Jason Jones, Jim McNally, Jeff O'Connor, Ira Harmon, Gordon Marsh, Glenn Fabry, Derek Riggs, and Chuck Schuldiner.

Special thanks to Richard & Regina Rouse, Dave Rouse, Linda Rouse, Grayson Starner, Margaret Rogers & the Rogers clan, June Oshiro & Matt Bockol, Ben Young, Alain, Annalisa, & Alexandria Roy, Katie & Eric Pidkameny, Gail Jabbour, Amy & Jason Schigelone, Rafael & Belinda Brown, Eloise Pasachoff, Kristin Kane, and Christian & Logan Bell.

Contents

Contents

Foreword

Just a few years ago, books about computer game design were as rare on the bookshelves as silk ties in the wardrobe of a game programmer. Then, around the turn of the millennium, a trickle of new books began to appear. One of the early ones that caught my eye was the first edition of this book, *Game Design: Theory & Practice* by Richard Rouse III. I noted that Richard has design credits on published games and the hard-won insights that conveys, as well as the descriptive skills to articulate those insights. I also appreciated the literal truth of the title of the book; it covers both the underlying theories behind game design while providing practical guidance on how to put those theories to use. But my favorite chapters of the book were the interviews. Richard persuaded an impressive array of talented and influential game designers to answer his thorough and insightful questions. So when Richard asked me to review and comment on this latest revision of his book and write an introduction, I jumped at the chance.

Game design is still a young craft, but a rapidly maturing one. No longer in its infancy certainly, computer and video games have been around for over 30 years, and despite a generous helping of Peter Pan Syndrome they've achieved a virtual adolescence at least. This means that game designers have graduated from the trial-and-error stages of the early years and learned what works and what doesn't. In turn that has resulted in a growing shared knowledge base of universal principles of game design. My own quarter-century of experience in game development and research into the underlying rules of good game design have indicated that it is possible to both identify and teach the rules that have influenced every successful game for decades, and this book is a worthy contributor to that body of knowledge.

But the video games of the *Pong* era bear a pretty tenuous resemblance to the multi-million dollar extravaganzas of the current day, and many of the skills necessary to design a game have likewise changed and matured. Furthermore, games present a widely varied face to the world. Superficially, games like *Centipede* or *Tetris* are vastly different from *The Sims* or *Civilization*. So it is impressive that this book manages to identify many qualities that are common to all good games and the skills needed to create design documents for them, while doing a credible job of covering elements specific to certain types of games as well, such as storytelling, scripting, AI, and multiplayer design. The game analysis chapters dissect and appraise the internal qualities of games and so grant insight into both the games highlighted as well as the process of analysis itself. And the interviews delve into both the shared knowledge of renowned designers and their individual quirks and unique histories.

In short, I've found this book to be remarkable at revealing the range of the creative game design process, as well as just plain fun to read. And I hope you will as well!

Noah Falstein
Greenbrae, CA

Introduction to the Second Edition

It has been four years since the release of the first edition of the book you now hold in your hands. It is interesting to reflect on what has changed in the industry during the intervening time, or, more specifically, what has not changed. In many ways we have seen a continuation of the trends that were well underway when this book was first written. Games continue to get bigger and prettier but not necessarily any more fun. Licenses have become more prevalent than ever, whether in the form of a movie tie-in or just having a quasi-famous personality attached to a project. The line between a computer game and a console game has become more and more blurred, with the largest games typically coming out on both, some under the same name but in different forms, but most providing almost exactly the same experience. In general, boldly original titles have become fewer and farther between.

A lot has happened to me since the first edition, and where appropriate I have woven that experience into this revision. The game that I was working on during the writing of the first edition, a western called *Gunslinger*, died out from under me. Though it had a number of problems, in the end it fell prey to the industry's more and more risk-averse nature. Following that, I managed to do quite a bit of work on *Drakan: The Ancients' Gates* and then developed *The Suffering* from conception through to localization. New examples from the practice of game development on *The Suffering* are integrated throughout this edition's chapters. Also, in addition to the *Atomic Sam* document that appeared in the original book, the complete design document for *The Suffering* has been included as an appendix. I sincerely hope this design document will be of particular interest to readers since it was used for a title that actually shipped.

Since the first book came out, two games have achieved greater popular success than anyone could have predicted. Those games are *The Sims* (which was analyzed in the first edition) and *Grand Theft Auto III* (which is analyzed in this new edition). In the intervening time, all of the game designers who were interviewed in the original edition completed new works in the industry, with five out of the six shipping new games, while Chris Crawford released two books. For this edition, I was fortunate enough to talk once again with most of these designers to update their interviews to reflect their most recent accomplishments (with the notable exception of Sid Meier, who as of this writing is busily trying to ship the new version of *Pirates!*). Also, the second edition gave me the opportunity to do an in-depth interview with a game designer I quoted extensively in the first book, Doug Church. Church is one of the most forward-looking designers working today, and I hope reading his thoughts prove inspirational for any designer.

As well as adding more examples from the games of the last four years, for the second edition I wanted to improve on what the book did well the first time, while filling in a few of the gaps. Multi-player games have become significantly more prevalent since the first edition and were woefully underrepresented in the book before; now multi-player gaming is the subject of an entire chapter. Though the storytelling and artificial intelligence chapters are among the most expanded in the book, all of the chapters have been revised and updated significantly. Even the bibliography and glossary have been reworked and expanded.

When working on the second edition of *Game Design: Theory & Practice*, I revisited a lot of the feedback I received from the first edition, and did my best to address some of the concerns that were brought up. Nevertheless, I can say the views contained herein are still distinctly my own and represent my personal views on game development. Often my thoughts fall in line with the commonly held wisdom in the industry, but other times you will find I disagree with what everyone else seems to be doing. Who is right? No one is right, per se. In the creation of art there are no easy absolutes. As a game designer you need to balance going with the prevailing wisdom with what you feel in your heart. If you always make decisions based on popular opinion or on the flavor of the moment, you will always make average, predictable games. As a game designer, you should take what I say in this book, reflect on it, and decide where you stand and how you want to proceed on your own projects. It is my sincere hope that your views of game design end up substantially different from mine, so that when you make a game and I make a game we do not end up with exactly the same player experience. Variety, after all, is not only the spice of life, it is life.

One of the most frequent comments I heard about the first edition of the book was that it seemed dated. I would argue that it was not dated, merely that it attempted to look at game development over the entire history of the medium, not just the three years preceding the book's publication. The book contained examples and discussion of current games proportionate to classic games. Indeed, if I had focused more on what was current in the industry when I wrote it, the book might have seemed relevant on its release, but within a few years truly would have been horribly dated. If one looks at the first edition today, four years after it came out, one will find it is nearly just as relevant today as it was then. Thus, in making a new edition, I strove less to bring the book "up to date" and more to expand on what it was already doing. Yes, I've included references to newer games, since many great new games have come out since the book was first published, but I've kept just as many discussions of the classics from the last three decades. Anyone who has worked with me knows that, when in the heat of game development, I am as likely to pull inspiration from a game made in 1983 as a game made in 2003. I would argue that to be a great game designer, you need to understand the past just as well as the present. As a game designer, if you cannot see the value and lessons to be learned from a classic game made in 1983, then you have a long way to go before you truly understand our medium.

In truth, I have always seen this book as something of a history lesson for game developers and enthusiasts alike. In addition to the game analysis chapters, this especially comes through in the interviews, which I hope readers enjoy as much for what they tell us about game history as they do for their specific insights into game development. If a reader sees a reference in this book to a game that they are unfamiliar with, it is my hope that they might seek out that title in order to play it. Almost all the games I refer to in this book are titles that I consider to be worth anyone's time to play. That said, a big problem for game historians and developers alike is that actually playing a game from twenty or even ten years ago can be quite difficult. If you are an aspiring filmmaker, tracking down almost all the cinema classics stretching back a hundred years is fairly easy. Not so with computer and video games. Emulators have done a lot to help this, but many games that are quite well known and respected are all but unplayable for most people because the systems they worked on no longer run, because the games themselves are out of print, or both. I believe that our ability to grow as an industry is directly proportional to our ability to understand our past: if we cannot understand it because we cannot play it, our evolution may well be stunted.

Throughout this book I discuss what I believe a game designer should think about when developing a game. I have found that one way to improve your game design methodology is to write a book about it. Though I might not recommend this technique to everyone (after all, the bookstores can only bear so many different volumes on the subject), I can testify that it can be quite helpful to take your nose off the grindstone every once in a while and think about games and their development a step or two removed from the day-to-day process of making it happen. I should warn that one unfortunate side effect to writing a book is having your coworkers point out to you whenever you are failing to follow one of the techniques you advocated in print. And therein lies the fundamental problem: regardless of how much you think about game design or try to do everything the best way possible, at the end of the day modern computer games are still incredibly hard to create. I certainly don't pretend to have all the answers, but my hope is that this book will make things a little bit easier, not just for me, but for you as well.

Richard Rouse III
Seattle, Washington

Introduction

My earliest recollection of playing a computer game was when I stumbled upon a half-height *Space Invaders* at a tiny Mexican restaurant in my hometown. I was perhaps six, and *Space Invaders* was certainly the most marvelous thing I had ever seen, at least next to LegoLand. I had heard of arcade games, but this was the first one I could actually play. *Space Invaders*, I knew, was better than television, because I could control the little ship at the bottom of the screen using the joystick and shoot the aliens myself instead of watching someone else do it. I was in love. The irony of this story is that, at the time, I failed to comprehend that I had to stick quarters into the game to make it work. The game was running in "attract" mode as arcade games do, and my young mind thought I was controlling the game with the joystick when I was actually not controlling anything. But the idea was still mind-blowing.

This book is about developing original computer games that will hopefully have the same mind-blowing effect on players that *Space Invaders* had on my young brain. This book deals with that development process from the point of view of the game designer. Many books have been written about the programming of computer games, but I can remember my frustration in being unable to find a book such as this one when I was an aspiring game designer. In some ways, I have written this book for myself, for the person I was a decade ago. I hope that other people interested in designing games will find this book informative. In my humble opinion, it is the game designer who has the most interesting role in the creation of a computer game. It is the game's design that dictates the form and shape of the game's gameplay, and this is the factor that differentiates our artistic medium from all others.

What Is Gameplay?

I hear you asking, "But what is gameplay?" Many people think they know what gameplay is, and indeed there are many different reasonable definitions for it. But I have one definition that covers every use of the term you will find in this book. The gameplay is the component of computer games that is found in no other art form: interactivity. A game's gameplay is the degree and nature of the interactivity that the game includes, i.e., how players are able to interact with the game-world and how that game-world reacts to the choices players make. In an action game such as *Centipede*, the gameplay is moving the shooter ship around the lower quadrant of the screen and shooting the enemies that attack relentlessly. In *SimCity*, the gameplay is laying out a city and observing the citizens that start to inhabit it. In *Doom*, the gameplay is running around a 3D world at high speed and shooting its extremely hostile inhabitants, gathering some keys along the way. In *San Francisco Rush*, the gameplay is steering a car down implausible tracks while jockeying for position with other racers. In *StarCraft*, the gameplay is maneuvering units around a map, finding resources and exploiting them, building up forces, and finally going head to head in combat with a similarly equipped foe. And in *Civilization,* the gameplay is exploring the world, building a society from the ground up, discovering new technologies, and interacting with the other inhabitants of the world.

Though some might disagree with me, the gameplay does not include how the game-world is represented graphically or what game engine is used to render that world. Nor does it include the setting or story line of that game-world. These aesthetic and content considerations are elements computer games may share with other media; they are certainly not what differentiates games from those other media. Gameplay, remember, is what makes our art form unique.

What Is Game Design?

What, then, is game design? Having defined what exactly I mean when I refer to gameplay, the notion of game design is quite easily explained: the game design is what determines the form of the gameplay. The game design determines what choices players will be able to make in the game-world and what ramifications those choices will have on the rest of the game. The game design determines what win or loss criteria the game may include, how the user will be able to control the game, and what information the game will communicate to him, and it establishes how hard the game will be. In short, the game design determines every detail of how the gameplay will function.

Who Is a Game Designer?

By this point it should be obvious what a game designer does: he determines what the nature of the gameplay is by creating the game's design. The terms "game designer" and "game design" have been used in such a wide variety of contexts for so long that their meanings have become diluted and hard to pin down. Some seem to refer to game design as being synonymous with game development. These people refer to anyone working on a computer game, whether artist, programmer, or producer, as a game designer. I prefer a more specific definition, as I have outlined above: the game designer is the person who designs the game, who thereby establishes the shape and nature of the gameplay.

It is important to note some tasks in which the game designer may be involved. The game designer may do some concept sketches or create some of the art assets that are used in the game, but he does not have to do so. A game designer may write the script containing all of the dialog spoken by the characters in the game, but he does not have to do so. A game designer may contribute to the programming of the game or even be the lead programmer, but he does not have to do so. The game designer may design some or all of the game-world itself, building the levels of the game (if the project in question has levels to be built), but he does not have to do so. The game designer might be taking care of the project from a management and production standpoint, keeping a careful watch on the members of the team to see that they are all performing their tasks effectively and efficiently, but he does not have to do so. All someone needs to do in order to justifiably be called the game's designer is to establish the form of the game's gameplay. Indeed, many game designers perform a wide variety of tasks on a project, but their central concern should always be the game design and the gameplay.

What Is in This Book?

This book contains a breadth of information about game design, covering as many aspects as possible. Of course, no single book can be the definitive work on a particular art form. What this book certainly is not is a book about programming computer games. There are a wealth of books available to teach the reader how to program, and as I discuss later in this book, knowing how to program can be a great asset to game design. However, it is not a necessary component of designing a game; many fine designers do not know how to program at all.

The chapters in this book are divided into three categories. First are the thirteen core chapters, which discuss various aspects of the development of a computer game, from establishing the game's focus, to documenting the game's design, to establishing the game's mode of storytelling, to playtesting the near-final product. These chapters discuss the theory behind game design, and what a designer should strive for in order to create the best game possible. The chapters also include discussions of the reality of game development, using examples from my own experience, to delve into the actual practice of game design.

There are six analysis chapters included in this book, covering six excellent games in six different genres. One of the most important skills a game designer must have is the ability to analyze games that he enjoys in order to understand what those games do well. By understanding these other games, the designer may then attempt to replicate those same qualities in his own projects. That is not to suggest that good game designers merely copy the work of other game designers. Understanding the reasons why other games succeed will bring the designer a more complete understanding of game design as a whole. Every game designer should take the games that he finds most compelling and try to examine what makes them tick. The examples I include in this book, *Centipede*, *Tetris*, *Loom*, *Myth: The Fallen Lords*, *The Sims*, and *Grand Theft Auto III*, are all very unique games. And though a given project you are working on may not be similar to any of these games, a lot can be learned from analyzing games of any sort. First-person shooter designers have had great success in revitalizing their genre by looking at adventure games. Certainly, role-playing game designers have recently learned a lot from arcade game designers. *Grand Theft Auto III* improved over its predecessors by cribbing from racing games. Melding in techniques from other genres is the best way to advance the genre you are working on and to create something truly original.

This book also includes a group of interviews with seven of the most well-respected game designers of the industry's short history who have designed some of the best games ever released. These are lengthy interviews that go deeper than the short press kit style interviews one finds on the Internet or in most magazines. In each interview the subject discusses the best titles of his career and why he believes they turned out as well as they did. The designers also talk at length about their own techniques for developing games. Throughout my own career in game development, I have found interviews with other computer game designers to be exceedingly helpful in learning how to perfect my craft. There is much information to be gleaned from these chapters, ideas that can help any game designer, regardless of how experienced he may be.

At the end of the book you will find a glossary. Though it is far from a complete listing of game design terminology, it does cover many of the more esoteric terms I use in the book, such as a personal favorite of mine, "surrogate." Every game designer has a set of jargon he uses to refer to various aspects of his craft, and this jargon is seldom the same from one designer to the next. If nothing else, the glossary should help you to understand my own jargon. For instance, it will tell you the difference between gameplay and game mechanics. Furthermore, readers who may find the content of this book to assume too much knowledge may find the glossary helpful in sorting out what an RTS game is and what the two different meanings for FPS are. Often, discussions of game design can degrade into questions of semantics, with no two sides ever meaning exactly the same thing when they refer to a game's "engine." I hope that the glossary will help readers to avoid that problem with this book.

Who This Book Is For

This book is for anyone who wants to understand the computer game development process better from a strictly game design standpoint. As I stated earlier, there are plenty of books available to teach you how to program, or how to use Photoshop and 3D Studio MAX. This book will do neither of these things. Instead it focuses on the more elusive topic of game design and how you can ensure that your title has the best gameplay possible. Though solid programming and art are both central to a game's success, no amount of flashy graphics or cutting-edge coding will make up for lackluster game design. In the end, it is the gameplay that will make or break a project.

I have written this book in such a way as to encompass projects of different scopes and sizes. It does not matter if the game you are working on is destined for commercial release, if you hope to someday release it as shareware, or if you are only making a game for you and your friends to play; this book should be helpful to a game designer working in any of those circumstances. Furthermore, it does not matter if you are working on the game with a large team, with only a few accomplices, or going completely solo. In the book I often make reference to the "staff" of your project. When I refer to "your programming staff" I may be referring to a team of ten seasoned coders commanding massive salaries and pushing the boundaries of real-time 3D technology, or I may be referring to just you, coding up every last aspect of the game yourself. When I refer to "your playtesting staff" I may be referring to an experienced and thoroughly professional testing staff of fifteen who will pride themselves on giving your game a thorough going-over, or I may be referring to your cousins Bob and Judith who, like you, enjoy games and would love to play what you have made. Good games certainly do not always come from the biggest teams. Even today, when multimillion-dollar budgets are the norm, the best games still often result from the vision and determination of a lone individual, and he need not always surround himself with a massive team to see that vision through to completion.

Many places in this book make reference to you leading the design on the project on which you are working. Of course, not every designer can be in the lead position on every project, and even if you are the lead, you will often find yourself without the absolute final say on what takes place in the game. In this regard, this book is written from a somewhat idealistic point of view. But regardless of how much authority you actually have over the direction of the project, the important point is to always know what you would do with the project if you could do whatever you wanted. Then you should campaign for this direction with the other people on the team. If you are persuasive enough and if you are, in fact, correct in your instincts, you have a good chance of convincing them to do it your way. Projects are often led not by the people with the most seniority or who have the right title on their business card; projects are led by the people who "show up" to the task, who care about their projects and are committed to them, and who are willing to put in the time and effort to make the game the best it can be.

Theory and Practice

Every medium has a unique voice with which it can speak, and it is the responsibility of the user of a medium to find that voice. Computer games have a voice that I firmly believe to be as strong as that available in any other media. Computer games are a relatively young form when compared with the likes of the printed word, music, the visual arts, or the theater, and I think this currently works against the likelihood of computer games truly finding their most powerful voice. This book is an attempt to help readers find that voice in their own projects. This can come in both the more theoretical form of questioning why it is that players play games, but also in the entirely more practical form of how to most effectively work with playtesters. To have any chance of producing a great game, the game designer must understand both the theoretical aspects and the practical necessities of game design.

Chapter 1:
What Players Want

"But when I come to think more on it, the biggest reason it has become that popular is Mr. Tajiri, the main developer and creator of *Pokemon*, didn't start this project with a business sense. In other words, he was not intending to make something that would become very popular. He just wanted to make something he wanted to play. There was no business sense included, only his love involved in the creation. Somehow, what he wanted to create for himself was appreciated by others in this country and is shared by people in other countries. ...And that's the point: not to make something sell, something very popular, but to love something, and make something that we creators can love. It's the very core feeling we should have in making games."

— Shigeru Miyamoto, talking about the creation of *Pokemon*

It may seem too simple a question to even ask, but determining what players want out of a game is a question all game designers must contemplate if they want to make great games. Further complicating matters, understanding what is enjoyable about a game experience is not knowledge that can be taught; on some level it must be an innate sense that a designer possesses. Designers must have the ability to assess whether something is fun for themselves, combined with the ability to listen to the opinions of others. Frank Capra, one of the most popular film directors from the golden age of Hollywood, often said that he was simply making films that appealed to his own tastes, and that it was luck they were enjoyed by so many other people. Similarly, one cannot simply look at the problem of "what players want" purely from a market-driven standpoint and declare, "I don't understand it, but if they want it, I'm going to give it to them." In order to make a great game, you must first find it fun yourself, and hopefully this can be used to build something that appeals to others as well. But in the end, the spark must come from within.

Game designers spend a lot of time concerning themselves with what game players are looking for in a computer game. What can they put in their computer game that has not been done before and will excite players? Often game designers are so bereft of an idea of what will be fun and what gamers want that they instead only include gameplay ideas that have been tried before, rehashing what was popular with game players last year. Surely if players liked it last year, they will like it this year. But therein lies the rub. Gamers generally do not want to buy a game that is only a clone of another game, a "new" game that only offers old ideas and brings nothing original to the table. Nonetheless, successful games can be useful, not for cloning, but for analysis. As game designers, we can look at the games that have come out previously, that we have enjoyed in years past, and try to determine a set of directives that explain what compelled us to try those games in the first place, and why they held our interest once we started playing them.

Why Do Players Play?

The first question we should consider is: why do players play games? Why do they choose to turn on their computer or console and run *Halo* instead of visiting the art museum or going to see a movie? What is unique about computer games versus other human entertainment media? What do games offer that other activities do not? It is by understanding what is attractive about games that other media do not offer that we can try to emphasize the differences that separate our art form from others. To be successful, our games need to take these differences and play them up, exploiting them to make the best gameplay experience possible.

Players Want a Challenge

Many players enjoy playing games because they provide a challenge. This provides one of the primary motivating factors for single-player home games, where social or bragging rights motivations are less of an issue. Games can entertain players over time, differently each time they play, while engaging their minds in an entirely different way than a book, movie, or other form of art. In somewhat the same way someone might fiddle with a *Rubik's Cube* or a steel "remove the ring" puzzle, games force players to think actively, to try out different solutions to problems, to understand a given game mechanism.

When a person faces a challenge and then overcomes it, that person has learned something. It does not matter if that challenge is in a math textbook or in a computer game. Challenging games can be learning experiences. Players will learn from games, even if that learning is limited to the context of the game, such as how to navigate through the forest, survive a particularly hairy battle, or convince the duke that their intentions with his daughter are honorable. In the best games, players will learn lessons through gameplay that can be applied to other aspects of their life, even if they do not realize it. This may mean that they can apply problem solving methods to their work, use their improved spatial skills to better arrange their furniture, or perhaps even learn greater empathy through role-playing. Many players thrive on and long for the challenges games provide, and are enriched by the learning that follows.

Players Want to Socialize

I have a friend who maintains that games are antisocial. This is, of course, absurd, as nearly all non-computer games require a social group in order to function. Games arose as a communal activity many millennia ago out of a desire to have a challenging activity in which a group of friends and family could engage. Computer game designers need to remember that the origin of games is tied to a social experience, and that this communal component is central to their appeal.

For most people, the primary reason they play games is to have a social experience with their friends or family. I am not talking about computer games here, but rather board and card games like chess, *Monopoly*, bridge, *Scrabble*, *Diplomacy*, or *The Settlers of Catan*. People like to play these games because they enjoy spending time with their friends and want to engage in a shared activity that is more social than going to a movie or watching TV. It is true that lots of people enjoy playing solitaire card games as well, but there are many more multi-player games than there are single-player. This is because people enjoy a social gameplaying experience.

But how does this apply to computer games? If one considers all the computer games ever created, the majority of them are single-player only experiences. But of course there are plenty of multi-player games, ranging from the "death-matches" found in *Doom* and its legion of imitators, to the classic *M.U.L.E.* game of wheeling and dealing, to the persistent worlds founds in MUDs (Multi User Dungeons) or their commercial equivalent, massively multi-player games such as *Ultima Online* and *EverQuest*. It is telling about the popularity of multi-player games that from the very inception of gaming there were multi-player games, ranging from *Pong* to some of the very first games developed on university mainframes that eventually evolved into MUDs.

Many death-match style multi-player games are basically adaptations of single-player games into multi-player incarnations, such as *Doom*, *Half-Life*, and *Halo*. These games typically provide a single-player game in addition to a multi-player game, both played with nearly the same set of rules and game mechanics. But even in these single-player-turned-multi-player games, players like to socialize while playing. Anyone who has ever played one of these games over a LAN in a room with a bunch of their friends can testify to this. These LAN-fests are usually rich with conversation as players shout back and forth to each other, bragging over their most recent "frag" or proclaiming how close they came to being killed. Games such as *Unreal Tournament* can also be played over the Internet, where the experience is quite a bit less social, since players may be miles apart and are thus only able to communicate through the computer. Indeed, lots of death-match or *Counter-Strike* enthusiasts have been known to use their office telephone systems to allow players who are not in the same building or even the same state to talk freely to each other while playing. Those not so well equipped still try to communicate by typing messages into the computer. Unfortunately, the high-intensity, fast-action nature of these games doesn't leave players much time to type messages to their opponents, if they hope to survive for long. But these

Death-match style multi-player games are adaptations of single-player shooter experiences. *Halo* comes with both single-player and multi-player modes.

games do still provide chat functionality, and players, when they are in a safe corner, after they have died, or between games, can send conversational messages to each other. At more hectic points in the gameplay the messages are short and typed on the fly, consisting of only a couple of letters. The fact that players still try to chat with each other in these high-velocity games is testament to the players' desire to socialize.

A separate category of multi-player games is what has come to be called "persistent universe" or "massively multi-player" games. These games tend to be more in the style of role-playing games, where players wander around "virtual worlds" and meet and interact with the other characters in these worlds, characters that are controlled by other players. These games tend to be played over large networks such as the Internet, instead of over LANs, and as a result players only socialize with each other through what they type into the computer. Since these games are considerably slower paced than death-match games, there is a much greater opportunity for players to chat with each other while playing. MUDs were the first popular incarnation of this style of game, and were played primarily by college students from the late 1980s on. At the time, these students were the main group of people with ample free time who had access to the Internet. These games are text-only, and provide their players with quests to accomplish in mostly fantasy settings. The quests, however, take a backseat to the socialization and role-playing, with players spending the vast majority of their time chatting with other players. A lot of people are drawn into playing these games as a way to interact with their friends, despite the fact that these friends are people they met online and who they have never seen in person. Indeed, the persistent worlds, MUDs in particular, draw in a legion of players who are not interested in playing any single-player computer games. These people play games in order to meet and talk to other people. The games are merely a compelling activity these people can engage in together while socializing.

As multi-player games have become more and more common, many game developers have been quick to point out their advantages in terms of competitive AI. Human opponents are much more unpredictable and challenging than any AI that could be reasonably created for most games. This, they suggested, is why people are drawn to multi-player games. Though this may be true, the biggest advantage of these multi-player games is that they transform computer games into truly social experiences, which is one of the largest motivating factors for people to play games.

Players Want a Dynamic Solitary Experience

Perhaps I have confused the reader by saying first that players want to socialize and then suggesting that players want a solitary experience. Of course the two do not happen at the same time; some game players are looking for a social experience, while others are looking for something dynamic that they can engage in by themselves. Sometimes friends are not available to play, or players are tired of their friends, or simply are tired of having to talk to other people all the time. Similar to the difference between going to a movie theater with an audience versus renting a video alone at home, the antisocial nature of single-player games attracts a lot of people who have had enough of the other members of the human race.

But games are distinct from other solitary experiences such as reading a book or watching a video since they provide the players with something to interact with, an experience that reacts to them as a human would, or at least in a manner resembling a human's reactions. The players are always in control, and can start and stop playing at any time. Thus the computer game "fakes" the interesting part of human interaction without all of the potential annoyances. In this way, people are able to turn to computer games for a dynamic and interactive yet unsocial experience.

Players Want Bragging Rights

Particularly in multi-player gaming, players play games to win respect. Being able to frag all of your friends in *Unreal Tournament* will force them to have a grudging respect for you: "Bob isn't very good in algebra class, but he sure can annihilate me in a deathmatch." Even in single-player games, players will talk with their friends about how they finished one game or about how good they are at another. Players will brag about how they played the whole game through on the hardest difficulty in only a few hours. If one looks at arcade games both old and new, the high-score table and the ability to enter one's name into the game, even if only three letters, provides a tremendous incentive for people to play a game repeatedly. Players who may not have much to brag about in their ordinary lives, who may not be terribly physically coordinated at sports or bookish enough to do well in school, can go down to the arcade and point out to all their friends their initials in the *Centipede* game. Gaming forums are full of people bragging about how they beat hot new game X in only five hours, and then taking pride in doling out advice to those who have not made it as far. Even without telling anyone, players can feel a tremendous sense of self-satisfaction when they beat a particular game. When players are victorious at a challenging game, they realize they can do something well, probably better than most people, which makes them feel better about themselves.

Players Want an Emotional Experience

As with other forms of entertainment, players may be seeking some form of emotional payoff when they play a computer game. This can be as simple as the adrenaline rush and tension of a fast-action game like *Doom*. It can be the great satisfaction of having built up a massive metropolis in *SimCity*. Or it can be considerably more complex, such as players' feeling of loss when their friendly robot companion sacrifices himself for them in Steve Meretzky's *Planetfall*. The emotions that games are able to evoke in players are much stronger than what can be experienced in other media where the experience is less immersive and considerably less personally involving. Unfortunately, many games' emotional ranges are limited to excitement/tension during a conflict, despair at repeated failure at a given task, and then elation and a sense of accomplishment when the players finally succeed. It may seem strange that players would play a game in order to feel despair, but many people enjoy watching plays that are tragedies or movies that have sad endings, or listening to music that is out-and-out depressing. People want to feel something when they interact with art, and it does not necessarily need to be a positive, happy feeling. Perhaps the sense of catharsis people obtain from these works makes them worth experiencing. Many classic arcade games, such as *Centipede* or *Space Invaders*, are unwinnable. No matter what players do, eventually the game will beat them. These games are, in a sense, lessons in defeat — tragedies every time players play them. Yet the players keep pumping in their quarters. This is why players' feelings of hopelessness as a game repeatedly bests them are not to be ignored. The players are feeling *something*, and at the highest level that is the goal of all art.

Emotional range is not something computer games have explored as much as they could. The example from *Planetfall* I cited above is one of the very few examples in computer games of players becoming attached to a character in a game, only to have him killed later on. Many developers are wary of making a game too sad. But in the case of *Planetfall*, the tragic story twist of that game was exploited for all the pathos it was worth by designer Steve Meretzky. It is a moment of tragedy that has stuck in many gamers' memories. Game designers would be wise to concentrate on expanding the emotional experience in games beyond excitement and accomplishment, into more unexplored and uncharted emotional territory.

Players Want to Explore

One of the main motivating forces that propels players through many level-based games is the desire to explore new spaces and see new environments. Anyone who has played a progression-based game like *Super Mario 64* or *Morrowind* knows the feeling of getting to a new and different level and wanting to just look around for a few moments before taking on the objectives at hand. And game exploration is not limited to spatial exploration. There is the exploration of different strategic choices in a game like *Civilization*, different types of resources to manipulate and combine in a game like *Magic: The Gathering*, and the exploration of the personalities of the characters you meet in RPGs such as *Wasteland* or *Fallout*. Though exploration is not completely integral to a pure gaming experience, the investigation of a fantastic world on one's own terms can be a rich experience that games excel at in a way no other media can.

Players Want to Fantasize

A major component of the popularity of storytelling art forms is the element of fantasy. Whether one considers novels, films, or comic books, many people experience these works to "get away" from their own "mundane" lives and escape to an altogether different world, one filled with characters that engage in exciting, interesting activities, travel to exotic locales, and meet other fascinating people. Certainly not all storytelling works portray exciting and glamorous protagonists, but there is certainly a large segment of works that is labeled "escapist." Some critics deride such escapist pieces of art, and indeed a lot of very good books, movies, and comics deal with more realistic settings and topics to great effect. The fact remains, however, that many people want to be transported to a world more glamorous than their own.

Computer games, then, have the potential to be an even more immersive form of escapism. In games, players get the chance to actually *be* someone more exciting, to control a pulp-fiction adventurer, daring swordsman, or space-opera hero. While in books or films the audience can merely watch as the characters lead exciting lives, in a well-designed computer game players will actually get the chance to live those lives themselves. Even better, these fantasy lives are not weighed down with the mundane events of life. In most games, players do not have to worry about eating, needing to get some sleep, or going to the bathroom. Thus, a game can create a fantasy life without the tedious details. And, most importantly, the level of fantasy immersion is heightened from that of other art forms because of the interactive nature of gaming.

Another part of the fantasy fulfillment element of computer games is enabling players to engage in socially unacceptable behavior in a safe environment. Many popular games have allowed players to pretend they are criminals or assassins. *Driver* is a good example of this. Though the back-story explains that the player character is actually playing an undercover police officer, players get to pretend they are criminals who must evade the police in elaborate car chases. There is a devilish thrill to outrunning police cars, especially for anyone who has ever been pulled over by the police. Though most players would never consider participating in car chases in real life, there's something tempting and enticing about engaging in taboo activities. The massive popular success of the *Grand Theft Auto* series is another testament to gamers' desire to break society's rules during gameplay. Computer games provide a good medium for players to explore sides of their personality that they keep submerged in their daily lives.

Players may also fantasize about events in history. If the player could have been Napoleon, would Waterloo have turned out differently? If the player were a railroad baron in the twentieth century, would he be able to create a powerful financial empire? A whole line of historical games, from wargames to economic simulations, allow players to explore events in history, and see how making different choices than those made by the historical figures involved will result in wildly different outcomes. While many people spend their time dwelling on the past, wondering how events could have transpired differently if alternate decisions had been made, games can give players a chance to actually find out how history might have been different.

Even without the elements of excitement and glamour, even if another person's life is not actually that exciting, it can be interesting to spend time as that person. Good computer games can provide players with the otherwise unavailable opportunity to see the world through someone else's eyes. As millions of gamers can attest, it is fun to role-play and it is fun to fantasize.

Players Want to Interact

At the beginning of this discussion of what players want, I suggested that it was important to create an experience that players would choose over one of the many other entertainment options presented to them, such as watching television, reading a book, or going to a concert. The one common thread running through all of the "wants" I mentioned above is what our art form can do better than any other: provide an interactive experience. Though we may be envious of a film's special effects budget, a novel's ability to tell a gripping narrative, or the emotive power of a great piece of music, no other form allows the audience to be the guiding force in the experience they are having. Games have found their greatest successes when they have played up the interactive nature of the experience and provided our audience with something they cannot get anywhere else. Game designers need to constantly keep this in mind as they are developing their games if they are to have any chance of winning players' attention.

What Do Players Expect?

Once players have decided they want to play a given game because of one motivating factor or another, they will have expectations for the game itself. Beyond the game not crashing and looking reasonably pretty, players have certain gameplay expectations, and if these are not met, they will soon become frustrated and find another game to play. It is the game designer's job to make sure the game meets these expectations. Indeed, player frustration is the nemesis of every game designer, and it is important that game designers do everything possible to eliminate it. So once the gameplay begins, how do game designers minimize player frustration? Exactly what is it that players expect?

Players Expect a Consistent World

As players play a game, they come to understand what actions they are allowed to perform in the world, and what results those actions will produce. Few things are more frustrating than when players come to anticipate a certain result from an action and then the game, for no perceivable reason, produces a different result. Worse still is when the consequences of the players' actions are so unpredictable that players cannot establish any sort of expectation. Having no expectation of what will happen if a certain maneuver is attempted will only frustrate and confuse players, who will soon find a different, more consistent game to play. It is the consistency of actions and their results that must be maintained, for an unpredictable world is a frustrating one to live in.

Fighting games are a particularly appropriate example of the importance of predictable outcomes from actions. Players do not want a maneuver to work sometimes and fail other times, without a readily apparent reason for the different outcomes. For instance, in *Soul Calibur*, if players miss an attack, it has to be because their opponent jumped, blocked, was too far away, or some other reason that players can perceive. The players' perception of the reason for the move's failure is important to emphasize. It may be that the internal game logic, in this case the collision system, will know why the attack missed, but it is as bad as having no reason if players cannot easily recognize why the maneuver failed. Furthermore, if only expert players can understand why their action failed, many novices will become frustrated as they are defeated for no reason they can understand. If a sword slash fails in a situation that closely resembles another situation in which the same slash succeeded, players will throw their hands up in frustration.

Pinball games are another interesting example. Of course, a pinball game is a completely predictable game-world, since it is based on real-world physics. Expert pinball players know this, and will use it to their advantage. But a problem arises with novices. Inexperienced players will often fail to see what they "did wrong" when the ball goes straight between their flippers or rolls down one of the side gutters. These players will curse the pinball game as a "game of luck" and not want to play anymore. Of course, the fact that players of different skill levels will have radically different levels of success at a given pinball game proves that it is not just a game of luck. But only those players who stick with the game through numerous early failures will find this out. I am not suggesting that pinball games should be abandoned or radically simplified, but one of their shortcomings is that they alienate new players who cannot see the connections between their actions and the outcome of the game.

Players Expect to Understand the Game-World's Bounds

When playing a game, players want to understand which actions are possible and which are not. They do not need to immediately see which actions are needed for a given situation, but they should understand which actions are possible to perform and which are outside the scope of the game's play-space.

In *Doom II*, the player will not expect to be able to start a conversation with the monsters he is attacking.

For instance, in *Doom*, players will intuitively figure out that they are not going to be able to hold a discussion with the demons they are fighting. Players will not even want to initiate a conversation with a demon during which they suggest surrender as its best course of action. Players understand that such interpersonal discussion is out of the scope of the game. Suppose that *Doom* had included a monster late in the game, a foc that could only be defeated if players were friendly to it, winning it over with their witty conversation. Players would have been frustrated, since they came to understand, through playing the levels that led up to that level, that in *Doom* all that is needed for victory is to blast everything that moves, while avoiding getting hit. Talking is completely out of the scope of the game.

Of course, a chatty monster in *Doom* is an extreme example of a game having unpredictable bounds, but plenty of games break this design principle. These games have players performing actions and completing levels using a certain type of game mechanism, and then later on insert puzzles that can only be solved using an entirely new mechanism. The problem is that the players have been taught to play the game a certain way, and suddenly the game requires players to do something completely different. Once players come to understand all of the gameplay mechanisms that a game uses, they don't want new, unintuitive mechanisms to be randomly introduced.

Players Expect Reasonable Solutions to Work

Once players have spent some time playing a game, they come to understand the bounds of the game-world. They have solved numerous puzzles, and they have seen what sorts of solutions will pay off. Later in the game, then, when faced with a new puzzle, players will see what they regard as a perfectly reasonable solution. If they then try that solution and it fails to work for no good reason, they will be frustrated, and they will feel cheated by the game.

This sort of difficulty in game design is particularly true in games that try to model the real-world to some degree. In the real-world there are almost always multiple ways to accomplish a given objective. Therefore, a computer game set in the real-world must also try to allow reasonable and logical solutions to a problem to result in success. Of course, a designer always provides at least one solution to a puzzle, and that solution may be perfectly reasonable. But there may be other equally reasonable solutions, and unless the designer makes sure those solutions work as well, players will discover and attempt these non-functioning alternate solutions and will be irritated when they do not work. It is the game designer's task to anticipate what players will try to do in the game-world, and then make sure that something reasonable happens when players attempt that action.

Players Expect Direction

Good games are about letting the players do what they want, up to a point. Players want to create their own success stories, their own methods for defeating the game, something that is uniquely theirs. But at the same time, players need to have some idea of what they are supposed to accomplish in this game. Not having direction is a bit too much like real life, and players already have a real life. As I have discussed, many gamers are probably playing the game in order to get away from their real lives, to fantasize and escape. They usually do not play games in order to simulate real life on their computer.

Thus, players want to have some idea of what their goal is and be given some suggestion of how they might achieve that goal. With a goal but no idea of how to achieve it, players will inevitably flail around, try everything they can think of, and become frustrated when the maneuvers they attempt do not bring them any closer to their goal. Of course, without an idea of what their goal is, players are left to wander aimlessly, perhaps enjoying the scenery and marveling at the immersive game-world. Yet without something to do in that game-world, it has failed as a game. If players do not know what their goal is, the goal might as well not exist.

SimCity 3000 is the third in a series of city simulation "software toys," which let users play without giving them a specific goal.

The classic example of the goal-less game is *SimCity*. In fact, Will Wright, the game's creator, calls it a "software toy" instead of a game. *SimCity* is like a toy with which players can do whatever they want, without ever explicitly being told that they have failed or succeeded. In some ways *SimCity* is like a set of Legos, where players can build whatever they desire just for the thrill of creation. The trick, however, is that *SimCity* is a city simulator, wherein players are allowed to set up a city however they want. But since the game simulates reality (constructing and running a city), and players know what is considered "success" in reality (a booming city full of lovely stadiums, palatial libraries, and happy citizens), they will naturally tend to impose their own rules for success on the game. They will strive to make their idea of the perfect city, and keep its citizens happy and its economy buoyant. In a subtle way, players are directed by their own experience with reality. If *SimCity* had been a simulation of a system that players were completely unfamiliar with, it would certainly have been less popular. Indeed, Wright's games that are based in concepts average users are considerably less familiar with (such as *SimAnt* and especially *SimEarth*) have found considerably less popular success. Though *SimCity* does not explicitly have a goal, the very nature of the game and its grounding in a widely understood reality encourages players to come up with their own goals. And so, what starts out as a toy becomes a game, and thus players are compelled to keep playing.

Players Expect to Accomplish a Task Incrementally

Once players understand what their goal in the game-world is, they like to know that they are on the right track toward accomplishing that goal. The best way to do this is to provide numerous sub-goals along the way, which are communicated to players just as clearly as the main goal. Players are rewarded for achieving these sub-goals just as they are for the main goal, but with a proportionally smaller reward. Of course one can take this down to any level of detail, with the sub-goals having sub-sub-goals and so forth, as much as is necessary to clue players in that they are on the right track.

Of course, not every goal needs to be communicated to the players via text. For example, in a story-based shooter such as *Call of Duty*, there are macro-goals that are communicated via text to players on the "mission objectives" screen. There are an average of four objectives on any given level. Beyond that, though, the game is littered with sub-goals (such as "clear out the machine gun nests") that players intuitively figure out along the way. For accomplishing these goals, players are rewarded by congratulatory dialog from their fellow soldiers, the health and ammo they will be able to collect from the fallen German soldiers, and the ability to access a new area of the level. If one takes it to a truly micro level, each enemy that players must kill can be considered a mini-objective with tangible rewards such as seeing the foe fall over dead, the fact that he stops being a threat to players, and players' ability to collect his weaponry. Platformer-style games such as *Ratchet & Clank* are particularly good at providing incremental micro-goals, with all of the thousands of bolts players are able to pick up throughout the game each helping them a tiny bit toward their larger goal of buying the super weapon to use against the giant enemy. The great platformer games all use these incremental pick-up rewards to pull players through their levels.

Without providing feedback of this kind (no matter how small it is), especially if the steps necessary to obtain a goal are particularly long and involved, players may well be on the right track and not realize it. When there is no positive reinforcement to keep them on that track, players are likely to grow frustrated and try something else. And when they cannot figure out the solution to a particular obstacle, they will become frustrated, stop playing, and tell all their friends what a miserable time they had playing your game.

Players Expect to Be Immersed

A director of a musical I was once in would become incensed when actors waiting in the wings would bump into the curtains. She suggested that once the audience sees the curtains moving, their concentration is taken away from the actors on the stage and their suspension of disbelief is shattered. They are reminded that it is only a play they are watching, not real at all, and that there are people jostling the curtains surrounding this whole charade. Perhaps exaggerating a bit, this director suggested that all of Broadway would collapse if the curtains were seen shaking.

But she had a point, and it is a point that can be directly applied to computer games. Once players get into a game, they are progressing through various challenges, they have a good understanding of the game's controls, and they are role-playing a fantasy. They have forgotten that they are playing a game at all, just as a film audience may forget they're in a theater or a book's reader may become completely swept up in the lives of the story's characters. Commonly referred to as the "suspension of disbelief," this is the point when a piece of art can be its most affecting on its audience. Once their disbelief is suspended, players do not want to be snapped out of their experience. For starters, a game should never crash, as that would be the most jarring disruption possible. Beyond that, the littlest glitch in the game can immediately bring players out of their trance-like immersion. If a character that is supposed to be walking on the ground starts walking into the air for no recognizable reason, players will realize it is a bug and their suspension of disbelief will be lost. If players come to a puzzle, figure out a perfectly reasonable solution to it, and that solution does not work, players will again be reminded that they are "only" playing a computer game. If the game's GUI is not designed to be easy to read, transparent, and stylistically consistent with the rest of the game-world art, it will stick out and ruin their immersion. All of these pitfalls and countless others detract from players' feeling of immersion, and the more players are rudely awakened from their game-world fantasy, the harder it is to re-immerse them in it. Remember that many players want to play games in order to fulfill fantasies. It is very hard to fulfill a fantasy when the game's idiosyncrasies keep reminding players that it is just a game.

Despite all his fame, Mario does not have a very distinct personality. He is pictured here in *Super Mario 64*.

    Another important component of player immersion is the character that players are controlling in the game. Most all games are about role-playing to some extent. And if the character players are controlling, their surrogate in the game-world, is not someone they like or can see themselves as being, their immersion will be disrupted. For instance, in the third-person action/adventure game *Super Mario 64,* players are presented with a character to control, Mario, who does not have a very distinct personality. Mario has a fairly unique look in his pseudo-plumber getup, but he never really says much, and acts as something of a blank slate on which players can impose their own personality. On the other hand, some adventure games have starred characters that acted like spoiled brats, and players have to watch as their character says annoying, idiotic things over and over again. Each time the character says something that players would never say if they had the choice, they are reminded that they are playing a game and that they are not really in control of their character as much as they would like to be. In order for players to become truly immersed, they must come to see themselves as their game-world surrogate.

Players Expect Some Setbacks

Players tend not to enjoy games that can be played all the way through the first time. If the game is so unchallenging that players can storm right through it on their first attempt, it might as well not be a game. If they wanted something that simple they might as well have watched a movie. Remember that gamers are drawn to playing games because they want a challenge. And a challenge necessarily implies that the players will not succeed at first, and that many attempts must be made to overcome obstacles before they are finally successful. A victory that is too easily achieved is a hollow victory. It is not unlike winning a fistfight with someone half your size.

It is important to understand that players want setbacks because of their own shortcomings, not because of the idiosyncrasies of the game they are playing. When players fail, they should see what they should have done instead and they should instantly recognize why what they were attempting failed to work out. If players feel that the game defeated them through some "trick" or "cheap shot," they will become frustrated with the game. Players need to blame only themselves for not succeeding, but at the same time the game must be challenging enough that they do not succeed right away.

It is also a good idea to let players win a bit at the beginning of the game. This will suck players into the game, making them think, "this isn't so hard." Players may even develop a feeling of superiority to the game. Then the difficulty must increase or "ramp up" so that players start to fail. By this time players are already involved in the game, they have time invested in it, and they will want to keep playing, to overcome the obstacle that has now defeated them. If players are defeated too early in the game, they may decide it is too hard for them or not understand what sort of rewards they will receive if they keep playing. If a game allows players to win at first, they will know that success is possible and enjoyable and will try extra hard to overcome what has bested them.

Players Expect a Fair Chance

Players do not want to be presented with an obstacle that can only be surmounted through trial and error, where an error results in their character's death or the end of their game. Players may be able to figure out the proper way to overcome the obstacle through trial and error, but there should be some way to figure out a successful path on their first try. So, extending this rule to the whole game, extremely observant and skilled novice players should be able to progress through the entire game without dying. It may be that no players will ever be this skilled on their first time playing, and, as we discussed, ideally the designer wants players to have many setbacks before completing the game. However, it must be theoretically possible for players to make it through on their first try without dying. If players keep dying from each shot-in-the-dark attempt around an obstacle, they will realize that, due to short-sighted design, there was no real way to avoid all of these deaths. They will be frustrated, they will curse the game, and soon they will not waste their time with it any longer.

Players Expect to Not Need to Repeat Themselves

Once players have accomplished a goal in a game, they do not want to have to repeat their accomplishment. If the designer has created an extremely challenging puzzle, one that is still difficult to complete even after players have solved it once, it should not be overused. For instance, the same painfully difficult puzzle should not appear in an identical or even slightly different form in multiple levels of an action/adventure, unless defeating the puzzle is a lot of fun and the rewards are significantly different each time the puzzle is completed. If it is not a lot of fun to do, and players have to keep solving it throughout the game, they will become frustrated and will hate the game designers for their lack of creativity in not coming up with new challenges.

Of course, many games are built on the principle of players repeating themselves, or at least repeating their actions in subtly varied ways. Sports games such as *NFL Blitz* and racing games such as *Project Gotham Racing* are all about covering the same ground over and over again, though the challenges presented in any one playing of those games are unique to that playing. Classic arcade games like *Centipede* and *Defender* offer roughly the same amount of repetition. *Tetris* is perhaps the king of repetitive gameplay, yet players never seem to grow tired of its challenge. The key component of these games that makes their repetition acceptable is that these games are built purely upon their game mechanics and the enjoyment players derive from various permutations of them. In games where exploration is a key part of the players' enjoyment and in which the challenges presented in any specific playing are fairly static and unchanging, players do not wish to unduly repeat themselves. In these games, after exploring a game-world once, subsequent explorations are significantly less interesting. While every time players engage in a game of *Tetris, Defender, Project Gotham Racing*, or *NFL Blitz* the game is unique, every time players play *The Legend of Zelda: The Wind Waker, Doom*, or *Baldur's Gate* the challenges presented are roughly the same. Therefore, players do not mind the repetition in the former games while they will quickly become frustrated when forced to repeat themselves in the latter.

Game players' lack of desire to repeat themselves is why save-games were created. With save-games, once players have completed a particularly arduous task they can back up their progress so they can restore to that position when they die later. Players must be given the opportunity to save their work after a huge, tricky challenge has finally been overcome. Allowing players to save their game prevents them from having to repeat themselves.

Some games will even automatically save players' games at this newly achieved position, a process sometimes known as checkpoint saving. This method is somewhat superior since often players, having succeeded at an arduous task, will be granted access to a new and exciting area of gameplay, one that they will immediately want to explore and interact with. Often, in their excitement, they will forget to save. Then, when they are defeated in the new area, the game will throw them back to their last save-game, which they had made prior to the challenging obstacle. Now players have to make it through the challenging obstacle once again. However, if the game designers recognize that the obstacle is a difficult one to pass, they can make the game automatically save the players' position, so that when players die in the new area, they are able to start playing in the new area right away. Indeed, automatic saving provides players with a more immersive experience: every time players access a save-game screen or menu, they are reminded that they are playing a game. If players can play through a game without ever having to explicitly save their progress, their experience will be that much more transparent and immersive.

However, it is important to note that automatic saves should not be used as a replacement for player-requested saves, but should instead work in conjunction with them. This way players who are accustomed to saving their games will be able to do so whenever they deem it appropriate, while gamers who often forget to save will be allowed to play all the way through the game without ever needing to hit the save key. Many developers are concerned that allowing players to save anywhere removes a key element of tension for the player. Indeed, if players can save after each tiny, incremental step they make, the game will be significantly less challenging. However, it is important to remember two fundamental things. First and foremost, if players truly want to ruin their experience by saving constantly, we should allow them to do that, because games are supposed to be about empowering players to do whatever they want to do. Secondly, by not allowing players to save whenever they want, they will be forced to do ridiculous things such as leave their game system on overnight because a parent or spouse has demanded that bedtime has arrived but they do not want to lose their progress. If games are supposed to be the most interactive medium, game designers need to make sure they are at least as interactive as a DVD player or a book, and thus allow players to stop the activity and save their progress at any point they desire.

Players Expect to Not Get Hopelessly Stuck

There should be no time while playing a game that players are incapable of somehow winning, regardless of how unlikely it may actually be. Many older adventure games enjoyed breaking this cardinal rule. Often in these games, if players failed to do a particular action at a specific time, or failed to retrieve a small item from a location early in the game, they would be unable to complete the game. The problem was that players would not necessarily realize this until many hours of fruitless gameplay had passed. The players' game was essentially over, but they were still playing. Nothing is more frustrating than playing a game that cannot be won.

As an example, modern 3D world exploration games, whether *Metroid Prime* or *Super Mario Sunshine*, need to concern themselves with the possibility that players can get hopelessly stuck in the 3D world. Often this style of game provides pits or chasms that players can fall into without dying. It is vital to always provide ways out of these chasms, such as escape ladders or platforms that allow players to get back to their game. The method of getting out of the pit can be extremely difficult, which is fine, but it must at least be possible. What is the point of having players fall into a pit from which they cannot escape? If they are incapable of escape, the players' game-world surrogate needs to be killed by something in the pit, either instantly on impact (say the floor of the pit is electrified) or fairly soon (the pit is flooding with lava, which kills players within ten seconds of their falling in). Under no circumstances should the players be left alive, stuck in a situation from which they cannot continue on with their game.

One of the primary criticisms leveled against *Civilization*, an otherwise excellent game, is that its end-games can go on for too long. When two countries remain and one is hopelessly far behind the other, the game can tend to stretch on past the point of

Level designers for 3D action/adventure games, such as *Metroid Prime*, need to create maps that prevent the player from ever getting permanently stuck behind a piece of architecture.

interest while the dominant power tracks down and slaughters the opposition. Indeed, the less advanced country is not technically without hope. Players can still come from behind and win the game; it is not completely impossible. Players are not stuck to the same degree as players trapped in the pit with no exit, but the players are so far behind that it might as well be impossible; the luck they would need to have and the mistakes the dominant power would have to make are quite staggering. The solution to this is perhaps to allow the AI to figure out when it is hopelessly overpowered and surrender, just as players who are hopelessly far behind will do the same by quitting and starting a new game.

Players Expect to Do, Not to Watch

For a time the industry was very excited about the prospect of "interactive movies." During this period computer game cut-scenes got longer and longer. Slightly famous film actors started starring in the cut-scenes, and the budgets ballooned. Games became less and less interactive, less, in fact, like games. Then — surprise, surprise — gamers did not like these types of games. They failed to buy them. Companies collapsed, and everyone in the industry scratched their heads wondering what had gone wrong. Of course the gamers knew, and the game designers were soon able to figure out what was amiss. The problem was that players wanted to do; they did not want to watch. And they still feel the same way.

I am not completely against cut-scenes; they can be very useful tools for communicating a game's story, or for passing along to players information they will need in order to succeed at the next section of gameplay. That said, I do believe that cut-scenes should be stripped down and minimized to the absolute shortest length that is necessary to give some idea of the game's narrative, if any, and set up the next sequence of gameplay. Cut-scenes over one minute in length, especially those that fail to provide information essential for completing the next gameplay sequence, should be avoided. It does not matter if the cut-scene is text scrolling along the back of the screen, full-motion video with live actors, cel animation, or done using the game engine, the entirety of this break in the gameplay should not take longer than a minute. If there is gameplay involved in some way, such as players planning out troop placement for the next mission, then it is not really a cut-scene and can be as long is necessary. And certainly, if the cut-scene contains information critical to the gameplay, the designer will want to let the players replay the cut-scene as many times as they desire.

The quality of the cut-scene really does not matter either. There have been many games with the most atrocious "acting" ever witnessed, usually as performed by the assistant producer and the lead tester. There have been games with Hollywood-quality or better production and content. But in the end, if the game is any good, gamers are going to want to get back to playing and will skip the cut-scene.

In short, the reason people play games is because they want something different from what a movie, book, radio show, or comic can provide. They want to interact. I did not include among the reasons why people play games "because the library is closed" or "because the TV is on the blink." Gamers want a game, and game designers should give it to them.

Players Do Not Know What They Want, but They Know When It Is Missing

One of the biggest mistakes a designer can make at the start of development is to have a focus group with a bunch of gamers and ask them what they want to see in a new game. One could see this as an argument against focus groups, but that is not quite the point. Having playtesters is a very important part of game development. By playtesters, I mean people looking not for bugs in your game, but rather analyzing the gameplay and providing constructive feedback about it. A designer should have lots of people playing his game once it is at a stage in development where a majority of the gameplay can be judged. This may include using focus groups to obtain invaluable feedback about where the game is too challenging or confusing, but only once the game is ready for them to play.

On the other hand, having a focus group of gamers before a game has been created just to "bounce ideas around" is pretty much useless. Gamers are good, of course, at judging whether a game they are playing is any fun or not. They may not be able to explain in a useful way what exactly they like or dislike about a particular game, but they certainly know when they are having a good time, whether they are having their fantasies fulfilled, whether they are being appropriately challenged, or if a game gets them excited. When the game is failing to be any fun at all, gamers will be able to point that out to you but relatively few will be able to tell you what to do in order to fix the problem. Furthermore, just because gamers enjoy a wide range of finished games does not mean they are qualified to critique raw game ideas. Similarly, game ideas they come up with are not certain to be good ones. It is the rare person who can discuss the idea of a computer game and determine if is likely the final game will be fun or not. People with these skills are those best suited to become game designers. Not all game players have these skills, so when asked what sort of game they might be interested in playing, gamers may not really know what they want. But, as I say, they will be sure to tell you when it is missing from the final product.

A Never-Ending List

Of course, this exploration of what players want could fill an entire book. I encourage readers, whether aspiring game designers or those who have already had a number of games published, to create their own lists of what they think gamers want. Think of what frustrates you while you play a game and what parts of a given game give you the greatest satisfaction. Then try to determine why you react to a game mechanic as you do. What did it do right and what did it do wrong? This will allow you to establish your own list of rules, which you can then apply to your own designs. These rules will be part of what makes your games uniquely your own. Without feedback from playtesters it is often hard to determine whether your game is entertaining and compelling or not. But with a set of rules you can systematically apply to your design, you may be able to figure out whether anyone will like the completed game.

Chapter 2:
Interview:
Sid Meier

Sid Meier is certainly the most famous and well-respected Western computer game designer, and deservedly so. In his nearly twenty years of developing games, he has covered all manner of game designs and all types of subject matter. He co-founded Microprose and at first focused on flight simulators, culminating in his classic *F-15 Strike Eagle* and *F-19 Stealth Fighter*. Subsequently, he shifted to the style of game he is better known for today, developing such classics as *Pirates!*, *Railroad Tycoon*, *Covert Action*, and *Civilization*, this last game being one of the most universally admired game designs in the history of the form. In the late '90s Meier founded a new company, Firaxis, where he created the truly unique RTS wargame *Gettysburg!* Most recently he has continued to take on new gameplay genres with the amusing course manager *SimGolf*. What strikes one most when looking back over his games is their consistent level of quality and the fact that he almost never repeats himself, always preferring to take on something new and different for his personal projects. If anyone has a solid grasp on what makes a game a compelling experience, it is Sid Meier.

Your first published games were flight simulators. Eventually you drifted over to doing what you are now known for — strategy games. What drove you from one genre to the other?

It was not a deliberate plan. I think I've always tried to write games about topics that I thought were interesting. There are just a lot of different topics, I guess. A lot of things that I've written games about are things that, as a kid, I got interested in, or found a neat book about the Civil War, or airplanes, or whatever. I think the other thing that drove

F-19 Stealth Fighter

that a little bit was the technology. That at certain times the technology is ready to do a good job with this kind of game or that kind of game. Or the market is ready for a strategy game, for example, or a game that you've wanted to do for a while but you didn't think the time was right. The shift, specifically from flight simulators to strategy, came about for two reasons, I think. One, I had just finished *F-19 Stealth Fighter*, which included all of the ideas I had up to that point about flight simulation. Anything I did after that would be better graphics or more sounds or more scenarios or whatever, but I didn't feel I had a lot of new ideas at that point about flight simulation. Everything I thought was cool about a flight simulator had gone into that game. And the other thing was that I had spent some time playing *SimCity* and a game called *Empire* which got me to thinking about strategy in a grand sense, a game that really had a significant amount of scope and time and a lot of interesting decisions to be made. The combination of those two factors led me to do first *Railroad Tycoon* and then *Civilization* after that, as kind of a series of strategy games.

I find it dangerous to think in terms of genre first and then topic. Like, say, "I want to do a real-time strategy game. OK. What's a cool topic?" I think, for me at least, it's more interesting to say, "I want to do a game about railroads. OK, now what's the most interesting way to bring that to life? Is it in real-time, or is it turn-based, or is it first-person..." To first figure out what your topic is and then find interesting ways and an appropriate genre to bring it to life as opposed to coming the other way around and say, "OK, I want to do a first-person shooter; what hasn't been done yet?" If you approach it from a genre point of view, you're basically saying, "I'm trying to fit into a mold." And I think most of the really great games have not started from that point of view. They first started with the idea that, "Here's a really cool topic. And by the way it would probably work really well as a real-time strategy game with a little bit of this in it."

So when you come up with your ideas for new games, you start with the setting of the game instead of with a gameplay genre.

I think a good example of that is *Pirates!* The idea was to do a pirate game, and then it was, "OK, there's not really a genre out there that fits what I think is cool about pirates. The pirate movie, with the sailing, the sword fighting, the stopping in different towns and all that kind of stuff, really doesn't fit into a genre." So we picked and chose different pieces of

Pirates!

different things like a sailing sequence in real-time and a menu-based adventuring system for going into town, and then a sword fight in an action sequence. So we picked different styles for the different parts of the game as we thought they were appropriate, as opposed to saying, "We're going to do a game that's real-time, or turn-based, or first-person, or whatever" and then make the pirates idea fit into that.

I think it's interesting that *Pirates!* was designed with all those mini-games, but you haven't really used discrete sub-games so much since. Did you not like the way the mini-games came together?

Well, I think it worked pretty well in *Pirates!* It doesn't work for every situation. One of the rules of game design that I have learned over the years is that it's better to have one great game than two good games. And, unless you're careful, too many sub-games can lose the player. In other words, if you've got a good mini-game, then the player's going to get absorbed in that. And when they're done with that, they may well have lost the thread of what your story was, or if any game is too engrossing it may disturb the flow of your story. Frankly, the mini-games in *Pirates!* were simple enough that you didn't lose track of where you were or what your objective was or what you were trying to do. But I wrote a game a couple of years later called *Covert Action* which had more intense mini-games. You'd go into a building, and you'd go from room to room, and you'd throw grenades and shoot people and open safes and all that kind of stuff and you'd spend probably ten minutes running through this building trying to find more clues and when you came out you'd say to yourself, "OK, what was the mission I was on, what was I trying to do here?" So that's an example for me of the wrong way to have mini-games inside of an overall story.

I've read that *Covert Action* **was one of your personal favorites among the games you designed.**

I enjoyed it but it had that particular problem where the individual mini-sequences were a little too involving and they took you away from the overall case. The idea was that there was this plot brewing and you had to go from city to city and from place to place find- ing these clues that would tell you piece by piece what the overall plot was

Covert Action

and find the people that were involved. I thought it was a neat idea, it was different. If I had it to do over again, I'd probably make a few changes. There was a code-breaking sequence, and circuit unscrambling, and there were some cool puzzles in it. I thought that overall there were a lot of neat ideas in it but the whole was probably not quite as good as the individual parts. I would probably do a couple of things differently now.

So *Covert Action* **seems to have had origins similar to** *Pirates!* **You started with, "I want to do a covert espionage game…"**

Right, what are the cool things about that. And unfortunately, the technology had gotten to the point where I could do each individual part in more detail and that for me detracted from the overall comprehensibility of the game.

In *Pirates!* **and** *Covert Action*, **the player can see their character in the game, and the player is really role-playing a character. By contrast, in** *Railroad Tycoon*, *Civilization*, **or** *Gettysburg!*, **the player does not really have a character to role-play. I'm curious about that shift in your game design, where the player used to be a specific character and now is more of a godlike figure.**

It's good to be God. I think that's really a scale issue more than a specific game design choice. It's fun to see yourself, and even in a game like *Civilization* you see your palace, you do tend to see things about yourself. But the other thing is that a pirate looks cool, while a railroad baron doesn't look especially cool. Why go to the trouble to put him on the screen? I've never really thought too much about that, but I think it's probably more of a scale thing. If you're going through hundreds and thousands of years of time, and you're a semi-godlike character doing lots of different things, it's less interesting what you actually look like than if you're more of a really cool individual character.

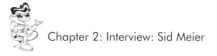

So how did you first start working on *Railroad Tycoon*?

Railroad Tycoon

Well, it actually started as a model railroad game with none of the economic aspects and even more of the low-level running the trains. You would actually switch the switches and manipulate the signals in the original prototype. It kind of grew from that with a fair amount of inspiration from *1830*, an Avalon Hill board game designed by Bruce Shelley, who I worked with on *Railroad Tycoon*. So, that inspired a lot of the economic side, the stock market aspects of the game. As we added that, we felt that we had too much range, too much in the game, that going all the way from flipping the switches to running the stock market was too much. We also wanted to have the march of technology with the newer engines over time, all the way up to the diesels. So there was just too much micro-management involved when you had to do all the low-level railroading things. So we bumped it up one level where all of the stuff that had to happen on a routine basis was done for you automatically in terms of switching and signaling. But if you wanted to, and you had an express or a special cargo or something, you could go in there and manipulate those if you really wanted to make sure that train got through on time, or a bridge was out and you had to stop the trains. But the origin of that was as a model railroading game and we added some of the more strategic elements over time.

It really was the inspiration for *Civilization* in a lot of ways, in terms of combining a couple of different, interesting systems that interacted continuously. The economic, the operational, the stock market, all interesting in their own right, but when they started to interact with each other was when the real magic started to happen. As opposed to *Pirates!* and *Covert Action,* where you had individual sub-games that monopolized the computer. When you were sword fighting, nothing else was going on. Here you had sub-games that were going on simultaneously and interacting with each other and we really thought that worked well both in *Railroad Tycoon* and later in *Civilization,* where we had military, political, and economic considerations all happening at the same time.

So in a way, you are still using sub-games; they just happen to all be in play all the time.

It's not episodic in the way that *Pirates!* was. Whenever you're making a decision you're really considering all of those aspects at the same time. That's part of what makes *Civilization* interesting. You've got these fairly simple individual systems; the military system, the economic system, the production system are all pretty easy to understand on their own. But once you start trading them off against each other, it becomes more complex: "I've got an opportunity to build something here. My military really needs another chariot, but the people are demanding a temple..." So these things are always in play and I think that makes the game really interesting.

In *Railroad Tycoon* you've got a very interesting economic simulation going, but at the same time the player has the fun of constructing a railroad, much as a child would. Do you think that contributed to the game's success?

It actually started there. And it was really the first game that I had done where you had this dramatic, dramatic change from the state at the beginning of the game to the state at the end of the game. Where, at the beginning of the game you had essentially nothing, or two stations and a little piece of track, and by the end of the game you could look at this massive spiderweb of trains and say, "I did that." And, again, that

Railroad Tycoon

was a concept that we carried forward to *Civilization*, the idea that you would start with this single settler and a little bit of land that you knew about and by the end of the game you had created this massive story about the evolution of civilization and you could look back and say, "That was me, I did that." The state of the game changed so dramatically from the beginning to the end, there was such a sense of having gotten somewhere. As opposed to a game like *Pirates!* or all the games before that where you had gotten a score or had done something, but there was not this real sense that the world was completely different. I think that owes a lot to *SimCity*, probably, as the first game that really did a good job of creating that feeling.

Were you at all inspired by the Avalon Hill board game *Civilization* when you made your computer version?

We did play it, I was familiar with it, but it was really less of an inspiration than, for example, *Empire* or *SimCity*. Primarily, I think, because of the limitations of board games. There were some neat ideas in there, but a lot of the cool things in *Civ.*, the exploration, the simultaneous operation of these different systems, are very difficult to do in a board game. So there were some neat ideas in the game, and we liked the name.

[laughter] But in terms of actual ideas they were probably more from other sources than the *Civilization* board game.

A lot of your games seem to be inspired in part from board games. But, as you just said, *Civilization* **would never really work as a board game. How do you take an idea that you liked in a board game and transfer it into something that really is a computer game instead of just a straight translation?**

Before there were computers, I played a lot of board games and I was into Avalon Hill games, et cetera. I think they provided a lot of seed ideas for games. Often they are a good model of what's important, what's interesting, and what's not about a topic. But once you get into mechanics and interface and those kind of things, really there starts to be a pretty significant difference between board games and computer games. There's a lot of interesting research material sometimes in board games. Often they're interesting for "we need some technologies" or "we need to think about which units," et cetera. There's that kind of overlap in terms of the basic playing pieces sometimes. But how they are used and so forth, those things are pretty different between board games and computer games. I would say board games provide an interesting review of topics that are available and topics that are interesting. But once it gets into the actual game itself there is a wide difference between computer games and board games, in my mind.

One of the most remarkable things about *Civilization* **is its addictive quality. I was wondering if that came about by luck or if you planned it from the start.**

We didn't really envision that. We intend for all of our games to be fun to play and hope that they are addictive to some degree. But *Civilization* had a magic addictiveness that we really didn't design, that we really didn't anticipate. I think any game where everything falls together in a really neat way is going to have that quality. I think that it's really a result of how well the pieces fit together and how I think

Civilization

we picked a good scale, a good complexity level, a good number of things to do. I think we made some wise decisions in designing that game. And the sum of all those decisions is addictiveness. And I think that it was a good topic. A lot of things were right about that game, and that all came together to create this addictive quality. It was not something that we designed in, but it was something that we were kind of aware of.

About halfway through the process we realized that, wow, this game really is a lot of fun to play. It was a pleasant discovery for us.

So you don't have any advice for how other designers can try to achieve that addictiveness in their own games?

I think in hindsight we know, or we think we know, why the game is addictive, or have our theories. One thing is what we call "interesting decisions." To us that means you are presented with a stream of decision points where the decisions are not so complex that you are basically randomly choosing from a list of options. A too-complex decision is one where you say, "Oh, I've got these three options. Yeah, I could spend five minutes analyzing the situation, but I really want to get on with the game so I'm going to pick B because it looks good." And on the other extreme there's the too-simple decisions: "It's obvious that I must choose A, because it is clearly better than all of the other options." In *Civ.* we try to present you choices where they are easy enough to under-stand, but in a certain situation you might choose A, in a slightly different situation B is a good choice, in another situation C is a good choice. So you're really saying, "Here are the three technologies that I can go for next." And you say to yourself, "Well, right now I'm about to get into a conflict with those no-good Romans. So I really need that tech-nology that gives me the next cool military unit. But, well, that map-making looks kind of interesting. Next time I might take that because I want to do some exploring." So if you can create decisions where the player is always saying, "Next time, I'm going to try that one, because that looks interesting too," that creates this whole idea that there's this richness there that you're only scratching the surface of this time.

The addictive quality, I think, also falls out of the fact that you've got multiple things happening or in process at the same time. On the one hand you've got your next technology churning away over there. Your scientists are working on that. And this city is making that first tank that you're looking forward to. Over here is a unit wandering around to the next continent, and pretty soon he'll find something interesting. You've got different things that you are looking forward to in the game, and there's never a time when those are all done. There's never a reset state. There's always two or three things happening in the game that you are looking forward to when they finish. So there's never actually a good time to stop playing. I think that really helps the "you can never stop playing the game" phenomenon.

I know *Gettysburg!* was not your first real-time game, but it seems to have been in part inspired by the big hit RTS games like *Command & Conquer* and *WarCraft*.

I think the technology had gotten to the point where you could have a whole bunch of little guys running around doing stuff on the screen in real-time. And what you call "real-time," it's kind of a weird term because we've done real-time games forever, but we didn't think of them as real-time because it just seemed a natural thing. But I guess when turn-based got to be its own genre, we had to make a distinction. I think *Gettys-burg!* is a game that I wanted to do for a long time, but the technology didn't really lend itself to being able to do it until fairly recently. We finally got to the point where we could have a bunch of guys marching around the screen on a realistic-looking battlefield, loading their muskets, shooting and wheeling in different formations, and doing all that sort of stuff that I had visualized as what was cool about a Civil War battle. The time came along when that was doable.

It seems like it takes what *WarCraft* **and the other, simpler RTS games did well, but then adds a deeper level of simulation, where you have flanking bonuses and other more traditional wargame features. Was it your goal to take a more complex wargame and merge it with the fast-paced RTS format?**

Again, the idea was to do a Gettysburg battle game, and then the genre of "real-time" made the most sense. I'd always had a feeling in playing any other board game that something was missing. The sense that I get from reading the histories, the stories of the battles, is not captured in a board game or in any of the games I had played about Gettysburg. The time pressure, the sense of confusion, the sense of these different forma-

Gettysburg!

tions, et cetera, didn't make any sense until you actually had to make the decisions yourself. And then all of a sudden you realize, "Boy, it wasn't quite that easy to do that obvious maneuver that would have won the battle if only they had tried it," or "Now I understand why they lined up in these formations that seemed pretty stupid to me before." A lot of things started to make sense when the battle came to life. And that was the idea, to include enough Civil War tactics like flanking, morale, and things like that to really capture the flavor of a Civil War battle without overwhelming the player with hard-core wargaming concepts. By representing the key factors that influenced the battle or that influenced tactics, you could naturally learn how to be a commander. You wouldn't have to follow a set of rules, but you would realize that, "Oh, if I give these guys some support they're going to be better soldiers, and if I can come in on the flank then that's a better attack." And you go through a learning process as opposed to being told how to be a good general. You learn that along the way. That was the intention.

I was wondering about the "click-and-drag" method you had the player use for directing his troops somewhere. It's very different from what other RTS games employ. Did you use it because you thought it was a better system, even though it was not the standard?

I'm not sure I'd do that the same way today. I think that click-and-drag made a certain amount of sense, especially since as you dragged we were showing with the arrow interesting things about the path that you would take. I'm also a big fan of standard interfaces, so if I had that to do today, I probably would try to go with more of the standard RTS interface. I think at the time that we were doing that, it was pretty early. *WarCraft* was out, but I don't think *StarCraft* was out, and *Age of Empires* came out at just about the same time. So the interface standard had not coalesced when we did that. I think that in recognition of that we gave the player the option to use the right-click/left-click way of doing things too. But if I had that to do today, I would probably make the standard RTS method the default and make the click-and-drag the option.

As opposed to *Railroad Tycoon* **or** *Civilization*, *Gettysburg!* **has discrete scenarios: you play for a while and then that battle ends, you get a new briefing, and your troops reset. Why did you opt for that style of gameplay progression?**

Gettysburg!

Well, I did that because the stupid Battle of Gettysburg had too many units! [laughter] I would have preferred a complete battle at the kind of level that the actual game turned out to be. Basically, to make the game fun, I have found that you need to have somewhere between ten and twenty-five discrete units that you can move around. Unfortunately the entire battle had seventy or eighty regiments, so it would have been totally out of control. We tried for a while actually fudging the scale, and saying, "You'll actually be given brigades but they'll act like regiments and then you can fight the whole battle." But it didn't feel right skewing the scale in that way. So, we got to the point where it was, "OK, the most fun and most interesting battles are of this scale. And that really means that it's a portion of the battle. And we have to accept that, and live with that, and make the best of that." And I think the scenario system was an attempt to do that.

I think that in an ideal world I could have picked the Battle of Hunter's Run or something where there were only three brigades and it was all capturable in a single scenario. But nobody's going to buy *The Battle of Hunter's Run*; they all want *Gettysburg!* So it's an unfortunate part of history that it happened to be such a large battle. And, I think it worked fairly well. But I understand when people say, "Well, I really want the whole battle." And we tried to give them that, and show them that they really didn't want that in this system. It was a case where history and reality didn't create probably the ideal situation for the game system that we had. But it was our feeling that, as opposed to either giving you the whole battle and overwhelming you with eighty units, or trying to play some pretty convoluted games to get the whole battle into that scale, we thought that the scenario system was the best compromise in trying to make it playable but also historically realistic. And I think there are some cool scenarios in there. It probably skews it a little more toward the hard-core, Civil War interested person but they can't all be *Civilization*.

So you are still working on your dinosaur-themed game. What are your goals with that project?

Well, the goal of the game is really the same as all the games that I've worked on: to figure out what is the really cool part, the unique part, the interesting part of this topic, and find a way to turn that into a computer game. I've thought that dinosaurs were cool for the longest time, and I think it's a topic that needs to be computer-motized. I try to take the approach of putting into the game a lot of things that are scientifically true or historically accurate, but that's not to be educational, it's to let the player use their own knowledge in playing the game. Most people know something about dinosaurs, or something about history, and if they can apply that knowledge to the game, then that makes it a lot more interesting and makes them feel good about themselves. It's not because they read the manual that they're good at the game, it's because of what they know. They realize that it's cool to have gunpowder and the wheel and things like that.

So in the same sense, people know that the *T. rex* is the baddest dinosaur. So we use things in the game to make it valuable to know some basic facts about whatever the topic is. We try and put that amount of realism and accuracy into the game. And then make it fun on top of that. In the same way that a movie gives you all the fun and the action sequences and all the important parts of a story and then jumps quickly over the boring things. I think the game has the same responsibility, to bring you to the key decision points and then move you on to the next interesting thing. We're trying to take that same approach with the dinosaur game, to bring them to life, to figure out what's cool and unique about them while cutting out all the dull parts. We're really in a "working that out" phase, and we don't have a lot to say about the specifics of that; hopefully in another few months we'll be able to talk a little bit more about how that's going to turn out. [Since this interview was conducted, Meier abandoned the dinosaur game, instead opting to develop *SimGolf*.]

Relatively speaking, you've been making computer games for a long time, since the early '80s. I was wondering how you thought the industry has changed over that time.

I think there's been a general, overall improvement in the quality of the games. I think there are some great games out there right now. I like *StarCraft*, *Age of Empires*, *Diablo*, *The Sims* I thought was really interesting, and *RollerCoaster Tycoon* was a hoot, a lot of fun. So I think those games compare very favorably to anything that's been done. I think they're overall better games than we were doing five or ten years ago. I think you can certainly see the improvement in presentation, graphics, video, and all that kind of stuff. The core of the games, the game design stuff, I think is a pretty slow evolutionary process. I think in terms of game design, games like *Pirates!* and *SimCity* and *Civilization* really stand up. I think they're really pretty strong designs, even today. I think they haven't been eclipsed by what's going on now. So I think that in terms of game design, the rule that says that things get twice as good every year, processors get twice as fast, et cetera, I don't think that applies. I think game design is a pretty gradual, evolutionary process, where we build on what's gone on before, and make it a little bit better, a little bit more interesting. Every so often a new genre comes along to open our eyes to some new possibilities. I think that will continue, but it's interesting to me that a three-year-old computer is completely obsolete, but a three-year-old game can still be a lot of fun.

As long as you can get it to run…

Right, as long as you have that three-year-old computer to run it on. There's a different pace, I think. Technology moves at one pace, a very quick pace, and game design evolution moves at a much slower pace.

Do you think that game design evolution has slowed since the early days of the industry?

I don't see a significant change. I think one phenomenon is that we only remember the good games from the past. The past seems like it had all sorts of great games, and the present seems like it has a few great games and a lot of crap. And I think there was a lot of crap in those days too, it has just all faded away. I think there is a lot of great game design work going on today. Before there was a lot more unexplored territory, and that gave us the opportunity to be a little more innovative. But with online technology and things like that, that opens up a lot of new areas for being innovative. So I don't see a substantial difference between the amount of good work being done today versus what was going on years ago.

You have worked at both small development studios, Microprose in the early days and Firaxis, as well as a big one, latter-day Microprose. Do you find that one environment is better at fostering the creation of good games?

I'm personally much more comfortable in the small environment. That may be more of a personal feeling than any kind of a rule about where good games happen. I think the trend certainly has been to bigger groups, bigger teams, bigger bigger bigger. And that may be just the way things are. If there's anything that makes me feel a little bit old, it is the fact that I'm not as comfortable in the big group environment as clearly some of the other developers. I think some of the younger developers who grew up in that mode are much more comfortable with the big projects. I was in Los Angles for the E3 show, and the winner of the Hall of Fame award was Hironobu Sakaguchi who designed *Final Fantasy*, which is a massive, massive, massive game. It would totally frighten me to tackle something that big. But there are designers who just thrive on that. I think it's a personal preference for designers, and I think since I started in the time when there was no such thing as a gigantic team that I am comfortable in that smaller mode, while other designers prefer the larger projects. Primarily it's a personal preference.

Since you started in game development, development teams have grown from one or two people to a standard number of twenty or more. Do you think that has made games less personal?

I think it did, but there are still games today that have that personal touch. And I think those are the good games. I think that a lot of the games that are not so much fun are those that have this "designed by committee, programmed by a horde" feeling to them. And, yeah they look good, and they are kind of reminiscent of maybe one or two other games that were good. But they don't have that personal spark. To me, *RollerCoaster Tycoon* is a good example of a personal game. It really feels like somebody thought that was cool. Nobody said, "That's goofy" or "That's stupid." A lot of the ideas there are very clever, but if you brought it up before a committee they would say, "Oh really, won't people think that's silly?" And even *Final Fantasy*, in spite of its massive team, is really the product of one person's vision. And if you can keep that going in a big team, that's great. But I think that it becomes harder and harder the larger the team is to keep that personal vision alive and not get watered down by the committee approach.

You still serve as both lead programmer and lead designer on your projects. Are you happiest filling both roles?

I cannot imagine working in another way. It's just much more efficient for me to have an idea and just type it into the computer than to try to explain it to somebody else and see what happens. So, again, it's my personal style, but to me it's the most efficient way to get something done.

On most modern projects at other companies, you have one person who's the lead designer, and one person who's the lead programmer, and they're both very busy. It would appear that performing both roles you would be completely overwhelmed.

Well, I think they probably spend half their time talking to each other, which is something I don't have to do. I would see a certain efficiency in cutting out all those meetings. But certainly it works both ways. Either way can work, but my personal preference is for the designer/programmer approach.

Now that you are working on a larger team, how do you communicate your game design vision to the rest of the team and get them excited about the project?

Our primary tool is the prototype. In our development, one of the advantages of being a programmer/designer is that within a week or two we can throw together something that feels like a game. That gives people the idea of what the game is going to be about, how it's going to work, the general parameters of it. Again, if we're working on a historical or scientific topic, most people are half-way into it already, they know something about the topic. And then just talking, saying here's the kind of game I want to do, and here are the three or four really cool things that are going to happen in the game that are going to be the payoffs. Putting those things together I think gives people a pretty good idea of what direction we're headed. At that point you want people not to get the whole picture, but to figure out where they fit in and can contribute their own things that hopefully you hadn't even thought of, in terms of cool art or cool sounds or neat ideas. In a way you don't want it to be so complete that it feels done, because you want people to feel that they can make their own contributions above and beyond what you've already thought of.

So if someone else comes up with some cool ideas to add to your game design, you're happy to incorporate those even though you didn't come up with them.

I'm happy to steal those and claim they were my ideas years later. [laughter]

With your prototyping system, do you ever try out a game and then it just doesn't work out as you had hoped?

Yup, I have a whole group of directories on my hard drive that fall into that category. And many of the games that turned out to be products started in a very different direction. *Civilization*, for example, was originally much more like *SimCity*, much more zone this territory for farms, and place a city here and watch it grow. Initially it was much more of a stand-back-and-watch-it-evolve approach; it only became turn-based after a couple of months. I mentioned that *Railroad Tycoon* started out as a model railroading game. A lot of times the prototypes will have to be radically modified to work. That's the whole idea of the prototype: to pretty quickly give you an idea of does the idea work, does it not work, and what are the major problems. It lets you focus on the big issues first, and hopefully straighten those out.

Your games seem very easy to pick up and learn to play. But at the same time they have very deep, interesting gameplay. How do you manage to accomplish both?

The easy-to-play part is pretty well understood. I think interface conventions, and again getting back to the idea of a familiar topic helps people to get right into it because they know a little bit of what they should be doing. You want to give the players a lot of positive feedback early in the game to give them the idea they're on the right track. In *Civilization*, pretty quickly the people add something to your

Civilization

palace, and you get a population milestone, and your first city is formed. You want to give the players, especially in the early stages, the idea that they're on the right track, that everything they do, the computer acknowledges it, recognizes it, and thinks it's

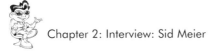

really cool. That gets the players into the game.

In terms of the depth, that's really because we play the games. The other advantage of prototyping is that if you have a game that takes two years to write, you spend one year and eleven months playing the game. You get pretty bored with the beginning of the game after a while. In one sense you are putting that depth in the game to keep yourself interested in writing this game. If there's twenty or forty hours of gameplay in a scenario, it's because we have played those scenarios for twenty or forty hours and found that, after about twenty hours, it gets a little thin. We have to come in with a new thing and make this problem a little more interesting, a little more complex at that point. So a lot of the depth comes out of the fact that we have intensively played the game for long periods of time.

Do you find that prototyping facilitates balancing as well?

Playing the prototype really facilitates balancing. It also really helps with writing the AI if you've played the game enough so that you really understand what are good strategies, bad strategies, and interesting strategies. Having played the game quite a bit helps to write the AI, it's good for the depth. The danger is that you lose sight of the beginning player. That's why we go back to playtesting at the end of the game's development. And we say, "Here's what we think the game is, try and play it." And we invariably find that they can't play it. There's just too much of that cool stuff in there. So we say, "All right, where are you getting stuck?" We're essentially unable to see the game in that light anymore. But you need to have both the depth and the ease of entry. Those are both important.

Your games all are grounded in history or real-life events, as opposed to many games which have fantasy or science fiction settings. Is this because you enjoy creating a game-world that the player is already somewhat familiar with?

I do think that's important. It does add a lot when you can apply your own knowledge to a game. I think that makes you feel better about yourself, and I think that's a positive thing. I think it also gives me a lot more to work with in terms of a historical or realistic situation. I probably grew up in a time also when there was less of the Middle Earth, the fantasy, the *Star Wars*, et cetera. Kids these days think these things are just as real as history. Spaceships, magicians, and wizards are as real to a lot of kids as airplanes, submarines, and things like that. It's kind of an evolutionary thing, but in my growing up it was things like airplanes, submarines, the Civil War, and the Roman Empire that were interesting and cool things, and I try to translate those things into games.

I am curious about how you balance historical realism with the gameplay.
Gettysburg! **seems to be one case where you had to break the gameplay up into scenarios to keep it both historically accurate and fun.**

That was one of the few times that we actually gave in to historical reality. In general our rule is if you come to a conflict between fun and history, you go with the fun. You can justify any game decision somewhere in history. Our decisions are made almost exclusively to the benefit, hopefully, of the gameplay as opposed to the historical accuracy. In *Gettysburg!* we came to a situation that we could just not fudge, though we tried. We tried as hard as we could to fudge that situation. In many other situations we come to an idea that we think is going to work well for the game and then we find the historical precedent or an explanation historically to justify it. In no sense do we try and stay slavishly accurate because, basically, we're trying to create a situation which is fluid where you're not just going down the path of history, you're creating

Gettysburg!

your own history. Even though the pieces are realistic, you can take them off in a completely different direction that never really happened. Certainly, part of the fun of *Civilization* is that the Zulus can take over the world, or the Mongols. Anybody can take over the world; it's not necessarily the Americans who are going to win in the end. We're not slaves to history.

At least since your days developing flight simulators, your games have not really been on the cutting edge of technology in terms of graphics. Was that a conscious decision on your part?

As I have said, in our prototyping process, things change almost up until the last minute. Most of the cutting-edge technologies are things that need to be researched from day one, and are gigantic investments in technology. And given that we're in a mode where things are changing constantly, it's practically impossible to merge those two approaches. The research project can't start really unless you know exactly what you want, or pretty much what you want. And we don't usually know that at the beginning. And we're not willing to put ourselves in that straightjacket in terms of game design. And I think a lot of times that's what it is. If you are committed to a first-person 3D viewpoint where you can see a certain amount, and you find out that to make your game fun you really need to see more, you really need to get more context for your location or whatever, you're kind of screwed at that point.

Often there's a conflict also between the functionality of the graphics and the loveliness of the graphics. A game that looks good but doesn't give you the information you need to play or doesn't give you the clarity, I think that's the wrong trade-off. We try and make games that we think look good. But in any good game the great graphics are happening in your imagination and not on the screen. If we tell you that the people have declared "we love the king day" in a certain town, if you're really into the game, that's a lot more meaningful, and you create a much more exciting image in your mind than anything we could show you on the screen. And vice versa, if you're not into the game, then anything that comes on the screen you're going to pick apart anyway. Our goal is to involve you in the game itself and have you create your own really cool mental images based on some suggestions that we give you on the screen.

You were one of the first game designers to get your name above the title on the box. I was curious how that came about.

Well, the way that happened goes back to *Pirates!* That was the first game that had my name on it. In those days I was working at Microprose and my partner was Bill Stealey who did the business/marketing side of things while I did the development/creative stuff. And the previous game before *Pirates!* was one of the flight simulator games, and I said to Bill,

F-15 Strike Eagle

"Well, I'm going to work on this game about pirates." And he said, "Pirates? Wait a minute, there are no airplanes in pirates. Wait a minute, you can't do that." "Well, I think it's going to be a cool game." And he answered, "Well, who's going to buy a pirates game? Maybe if we put your name on it, they'll know that they liked *F-15* or whatever, and they might give it a try. OK." There was a real concern that there was this pirates game coming out, but nobody's going to be interested, because who wants a pirates game? People want flight simulators. So it was to say, "Sure, you want a flight simulator, but maybe you might want to try this pirates game because it was written by the guy who wrote that flight simulator that you're playing." I guess it was branding in a very crude, early form. It was because we were making this big switch in the type of game that I was working on, and to try to keep that connection between the games.

So it wasn't your lust for fame?

[laughter] No, no. Even today, fame is not a computer game thing. I think it's good. It's still a pretty non-personality oriented business. I think that people remember great games, and they know to a certain extent who's involved. But there's not a cult of Robin Williams or, you know, movie stars who really have a cult of personality. I think it's good. Once we get the idea that we can get away with anything just because we're who we are, that's not a good thing.

But that sort of confidence led to *Pirates!*, didn't it?

[laughter] Well, it was a good game. Had it not been a good game, that strategy would not have worked.

A lot of your games have had sequels of one kind or another, but you have never been the lead designer on one of them. Why is this?

I think they are a fine thing to do in general, especially if they're done well. I seldom go back to a topic primarily because I haven't run out of ideas yet, so I'd rather do a dinosaur game than go back to an older title. I don't have a lot of energy to get too involved in the sequels. Some of them turn out well, some of them turn out not quite so well. As opposed to letting the topic fade away, I think doing a sequel is often a good idea. In an ideal world, I'd like to be involved in everything, but I can't really do that. So I tend to be more interested in being involved in a new product as opposed to a sequel. It's certainly gratifying that people want another *Railroad Tycoon* or *Civilization*, et cetera. I think that's great. I'm happy that it can be done. On *Civilization III*, since it's being done inside of Firaxis, I'm able to take a more direct part in that, which I think is good. I would have liked to have done *Railroad Tycoon II* and do a new *Pirates!*, et cetera, if I had an infinite amount of time. But it's just not feasible.

I hear a lot of people talking about storytelling in games. Usually by storytelling they mean using cut-scenes or branching dialog trees or devices like that. Your games have never been very concerned with that side of storytelling.

To me, a game of *Civilization* is an epic story. I think the kind of stories I'm interested in are all about the player and not so much about the designer. There are players that are more comfortable in situations where they're making small decisions and the designer's making the big decisions. But I think games are more interesting when the player makes the big decisions and the designer makes the small decisions.

Civilization

I think, in some sense, games are all about telling stories. They have a story created more by the player and less by the designer, in my mind. I think in *Civilization* there are fantastic stories in every game, they're just not in the more traditional sense of a story. We have, amongst our rules of game design, the three categories of games. There are games where the designer's having all the fun, games where the computer is having all the fun, and games where the player is having all the fun. And we think we ought to write games where the player is having all the fun. And I think a story can tend to get to the point where the designer is having all the fun or at least having a lot of the fun, and the player is left to tidy up a few decisions along the way, but is really being taken for a ride. And that's not necessarily bad, but our philosophy is to try to give the player as much of the decision making as possible.

Though *Gettysburg!* had a multi-player option, by and large your games have been single-player only for a long time. What do you think of the emerging popularity of multi-player gaming?

I think down the road I would like to get more into multi-player, perhaps even a game that is primarily multi-player. But I still enjoy essentially single-player games, so I'm not sure exactly when or how that's going to happen. Online multi-player gaming is probably the only revolutionary development in our technology we've seen since I started writing computer games. Everything else has been pretty much evolutionary. Better graphics, better speed, more memory, et cetera. But the multi-player online thing was a revolutionary change in the tools that we had to make games. I'm interested in doing something along those lines, but I'm not sure what it would be right now.

In an old *Next Generation* magazine interview, you said, "Games are going to take over the world. It's going to take a while, but there's something inherently more engaging about computer games than any other form of entertainment." Board games have certainly been around a long time, but have not yet taken over the world. I wondered what it is about computer games that you find so compelling.

Yeah, I think I stand by that statement. I think that it's the element of interactivity that makes them unique. They interact personally with you as a player, as opposed to movies, television, or music, which don't. There's this phenomenon of watching television and using the remote control to desperately try to make it an interactive experience, going from one channel to another... [laughter] But the interactivity of computer games is what differentiates it and makes it so very powerful. Now, we're still learning how to use that tool and in a lot of other ways we're not as good as television, movies, et cetera. But I think that as we learn to use the advantages that we have, they're more powerful advantages than the advantages of other entertainment media.

I think that board games are kind of interactive, but they require other players. The computer brings a lot of power to the equation that board games don't take advantage of. If anything, the advent of the Internet and multi-player play, that combined with interactivity seems to me like a really powerful combination. I think as we learn to use that element of our technology too, games can be very, very compelling. The question that pops up is do people want games that are that interesting to play? There was the whole *Deer Hunter* phenomenon, and there was *Slingo* and things like that and I'm still working to integrate that into my model of the world, and I haven't totally succeeded in doing that. But what that tells me is that there's a broader range of potential gamers than I am really familiar with. And part of our learning process is going to be to integrate them into the way that we design games and the way that we create games. But I still think we're going to take over the world.

Sid Meier Gameography

Hellcat Ace, 1982
NATO Commander, 1983
Spitfire Ace, 1984
Solo Flight, 1984
F-15 Strike Eagle, 1985
Decision in the Desert, 1985
Conflict in Vietnam, 1985
Crusade in Europe, 1985
Silent Service, 1986
Gunship, 1986
Pirates!, 1987
F-19 Stealth Fighter, 1988
Railroad Tycoon, 1990
Covert Action, 1990
Civilization, 1991
Colonization, 1994 (Consultant)
Civilization II, 1996 (Consultant)
Gettysburg!, 1997
Alpha Centauri, 1999 (Consultant)
Civilization III, 2001 (Consultant)
SimGolf, 2002

Chapter 3:

Brainstorming a Game Idea: Gameplay, Technology, and Story

"You know what's the number one dumbest question I get asked when I'm out at some great university lecturing? I'm always asked 'Where do you get your ideas?' For about forty years I've been yanking their chain when I answer 'Schenectady.' They stare at me, and I say, 'Yeah, Schenectady, in New York. There's this idea service, see, and every week I send 'em twenty-five bucks, and every week they send me a freshly picked six-pack of ideas.'"

— Harlan Ellison

Harlan Ellison might scoff at the idea of trying to explain where ideas come from. Certainly, if you are a novelist having trouble coming up with ideas, it may be time to wonder if you have chosen the right profession. Similarly, a good game designer, at any given moment, will be able to come up with no less than five solid ideas she would like to try to make into a computer game. There is no shortage of ideas in the gaming world. Aspiring game designers often think they can sell their idea to a development company. They seem to be under the impression that game developers are just sitting around waiting for a hot idea to come around so they can spend several million dollars to make it a reality. On the contrary, selling a game idea to a company is so rare that one should consider it an impossibility. Almost all of the challenge in game development is not coming up with a good idea, but in following through and being able to craft a compelling game around that idea. That's what the rest of this book endeavors to explore.

In the arena of computer game design, the process of coming up with a game idea that will work is complicated by a number of factors fiction authors do not need to worry about. In part this is because computer game ideas can come from three distinct, unrelated areas of the form: gameplay, technology, and story. These different origins are interconnected in interesting ways, with the origin of the game's idea limiting what one will be able to accomplish in the other two areas. So when a game designer starts thinking about the game she is hoping to make — thinking about it in terms of gameplay, technology, or story — it is important that she consider how that initial idea will impact all aspects of the final game.

Starting Points

Perhaps a quick example is in order. Say a game designer feels the need to create a game based around the specific stories of Greek mythology. This would be starting from a story. Immediately this limits the type of gameplay she will be going for. Chances are a *Civilization*-style strategy game is out, since that sort of game really has nothing to do with the classical stories of Zeus, Heracles, Ares, and so on. A real-time strategy game is out of the question as well, since it is not good at telling stories involving only a few protagonists. A high-end flight simulator is probably not going to work either. The designer could, however, still pursue it through an action game, a role-playing game, or an adventure game. Similarly, the technology is limited. In order to tell the story of the Greek gods, the designer will need some way to communicate a lot of back-story information to the player. Thus there will need to be technology in place that can allow this. Furthermore, if the designer chooses the technology to be employed by the game at this point, this will have still further impact on what type of gameplay will be possible. For example, choosing an isometric 2D engine will best lend itself to an RPG or an adventure game instead of an action game, unless one plans on being deliberately "retro" and opts for a 2D action-adventure in the spirit of *Crusader: No Remorse*. If a 3D technology is to be used, in order to tell the story of Greek mythology properly it will need to support both indoor and outdoor environments, which immediately eliminates a lot of 3D game engines.

For each decision the designer makes about the game she is hoping to create, she needs to understand how that limits what the game will be. If the designer tries to fit a type of gameplay around an ill-suited engine, the game will suffer in the end. Trying to do a *Populous*-esque "god-sim" using a first-person, indoor *Unreal*-style 3D engine is a big mistake. Just as if one tried to tell the story of the Greek gods through flight simulator gameplay, the game would simply fail to work. Herein lies the difficulty with many "high-concept" ideas, often the brainchildren of marketing specialists who want to capture disparate markets with one product. If the parts do not work together, it does not matter how many markets the concept covers — no gamers will be interested in playing the final game.

Starting with Gameplay

Beginning with gameplay is one of the most common starting points for game development, especially for designer- or management-driven projects. Thinking about a style of gameplay is often the easiest core for someone to latch onto, especially if that gameplay is similar to an existing game. "It's a racing game!" "It's a flight simulator!" "It's a 3D action/adventure like *Super Mario 64*!" "It's a first-person shooter like *Halo*!" Often a game developer will have enjoyed a game in one of these genres and will want to apply her own spin to it. With a general idea for a game that is interesting to her, the designer will want to work out what her particular game is going to accomplish in terms of gameplay. What type of racing game will it be? What aspects of racing are we trying to capture for the player? With a more specific idea of what type of gameplay she wants to create, the designer should start thinking about how that will impact the technology the game will require and what sort of story, if any, the game will be able to have.

Depending on the type of gameplay you are hoping to create for the player, you need to analyze what sort of technology that undertaking will require. Does the game need a 3D engine, or will 2D be enough or even more appropriate? What sort of view will the player have of the game-world? Will it be fixed or dynamic? Does the action transpire fast and furious with a large number of entities moving around on the screen at once? Are the game-worlds large or small? All of these questions and many more need to be analyzed to understand what the game's engine must accomplish in order to properly execute the gameplay idea. Of course the technology you choose to employ for your gameplay must actually run on the target system, whether it be a PC, console, or custom-made arcade cabinet. You must also ask if the game's programming team is up to creating the required technology. Technological feasibility may end up limiting the scope of your gameplay. Even worse, will the engine team's existing technology work or will they need to scrap it and start from scratch? Is there enough budget and time to trash it and start over? If you find that you need to adapt your gameplay to match the engine, you really are not starting out with gameplay as the origin of your idea, but instead with technology, as I will discuss next. If you are starting out with a gaming engine that must be used, it is in your best interest to not fight that technology with incompatible gameplay. Instead you should try to conceive of gameplay that is well suited to that engine.

The type of gameplay your game will employ similarly limits what type of story can be told. An RPG can tell a much more complex and involved story than an action/adventure game, and in turn an action/adventure can tell a more substantial story than an arcade shooter. Certain types of stories just will not fit with certain types of gameplay, such as the Greek mythology in a flight simulator example discussed previously. Similarly, a romantic story might not fit with a strategy game, and a tale about diplomacy would not fit so well with a fast-action first-person shooter. Since you made the choice to come up with your gameplay style first, you need to ask yourself what sort of story is best suited to that gameplay, and try to tell that tale. Sometimes a designer will have both a story she wants to tell and a type of gameplay she wants to explore, and will attempt to do both in the same game, even if the two do not go well together. Do not try to cobble an inappropriate story, either in terms of complexity or subject matter, around gameplay that is ill-suited to that type of narrative. Save the story for a later date when you are working on a title with gameplay that will support that story better. And while your technology is limited by what your team is capable of accomplishing in the time allotted, the story is limited only by your own ability to tell it. You should pick the story best suited to your gameplay and go with it.

Starting with Technology

Going into a project with a large portion of the game's technology already developed is also a fairly common occurrence. If this is not the development team's first project together at a new company, then it is likely that there will be an existing technology base that the project is supposed to build from. Even if the project is to use a "new" engine, this often only means an older engine updated, and as a result, the style of game best suited to the engine will not change significantly. Even if an engine is being written from scratch for the project, it is likely that the lead programmer and her team are best equipped to create a certain type of engine, be it indoor or outdoor, real-time or pre-rendered, 3D or 2D, with a complex physics system for object movement or something more simple. The programmers may be interested in experimenting with certain special lighting or rendering effects, and will create an engine that excels at these objectives. The designer is then presented with this new technology and tasked with coming up with a game that will exploit the sophisticated technology to full effect.

Other times it is predetermined that the project will be using an engine licensed from some other source, either from another game developer or a technology-only company. Though some of these licensed engines are becoming more and more robust and as a result can allow for a fairly broad number of games to be made with them (Criterion's RenderWare is certainly a good example of this), many licensed engines are still developed with one game genre in mind, and no engine is without its fundamental limitations. Sometimes the project leaders have enough foresight to consider the type of game they want to make first and then pick an engine well suited to that. Sometimes the engine licensing deal that seems to deliver the most "bang for the buck" will be the one chosen. Then, with an engine choice decided, the team is tasked with creating a game and story that will fit together well using that technology.

Just as starting with a desired sort of gameplay dictates what type of engine should be created, starting with set technology requires that the game designer consider primarily gameplay that will work with that sort of technology. If the engine is 3D, the designer will need to create a game that takes place in a 3D world and uses that world to create interesting 3D gameplay. If the engine is only 2D, a first-person shooter is out of the question. If the engine has a sophisticated physics system, a game should be designed that makes use of the physics for puzzles and player movement. Of course, the designer does not need to use every piece of technology that a programmer feels compelled to create, but it is always better to have your gameplay work with the engine instead of fight against it. Often, when a project is using a licensed game engine, that technology will have been chosen with a certain type of gameplay in mind. The designer needs to seriously consider how far she should deviate from that initial technology, for it is surely going to be easier to make the engine perform tasks for which it was intended instead of pushing it in directions its programmers never imagined. For instance, the oft-licensed *Quake* engine (in all its various incarnations) was created for handling an indoor, first-person perspective, fast-action game involving a lot of shooting. Though some teams that have licensed that engine have tried to push it in different directions, one of the most artistically successful licensees thus far, Valve, retained much of the standard *Quake* gameplay that the engine excelled at for their game *Half-Life*. Certainly Valve added a lot of their own work to the engine, technology that was necessary in order to do the type of game they wanted. But at the same time they did not try to do something foolish such as setting their game primarily outdoors or using only melee combat, at least not in their first title with the technology. When technology is handed to a game designer who is told to make a game out of it, it makes the most sense for the designer to embrace the limitations of that technology and turn them into strengths in her game.

The designers of *Half-Life* smartly used the indoor first-person shooter gameplay established by *Quake,* the engine licensed for the game's creation. Pictured here: *Quake II*.

The technology can also limit what sort of story can be told. Without a sophisticated language parser, it is going to be difficult to tell a story in which players need to communicate with characters by typing in questions. Without an engine that can handle outdoor environments reasonably well, it is going to be difficult to make a game about mountain climbing. Without robust artificial intelligence, it is going to be hard to make a good game about diplomacy. Without streaming technology that allows for the playback of large sounds, it will be hard to have huge amounts of dialog and hence hard to have characters whose dialects are important to the story. Without the ability to have large numbers of moving units on the screen at once, it will be impossible to tell a story where the player must participate in epic, massive battles between armies. The game designer needs to consider how the story line will be communicated to the player through the engine that she must use. Trying to tell a story with an inadequate engine is just as likely to compromise the game as tying a particular story to inappropriate gameplay. Again using the example of *Half-Life* mentioned above, if the team at Valve had tried to set their game in Death Valley and involve the player battling gangs of twenty giant insects at once, the *Quake* engine would have ground to a halt on the machines of the day and the game would have been miserable to play. In the Death Valley scenario, Valve might have been telling the story they wanted, but no one would have cared since the game would have been miserably slow and looked horrendous. For the greater good of the game, the story and the technology must be compatible with each other.

Something else to always keep in mind when considering how your technology will limit your gameplay and story is how you can creatively work around your limitations. For example, if you are trying to do a game about massive battles with thousands of individual units, do all of the units need to be represented in 3D, or will a 2D representation work just as well? Or, perhaps you never need to have all of the units in the world at the same time; you could tell the story of such a gigantic conflict from the viewpoint of a single soldier in that battle, with between-mission updates that show the larger picture. For an example out of my own past, my ill-fated game *Gunslinger* tried to capture the myths and storytelling of the Old West. We had a technology that was perfectly suited to rendering sprawling outdoor environments in 3D, so it was a natural fit to the game. But if we had only had a 2D engine, there is nothing to say we could not still have done a tale about the legends of the Old West in a 2D game with a god's-eye view of the proceedings. As a game designer, it is possible to get stuck in a rut of how a game "needs to be done" and forget the potential for alternate implementations that may be a better fit for your technology.

Starting with Story

Finally, it is certainly possible that the brainstorming for your game may start with a setting you want to employ, a story you want to tell, or a set of characters you want to explore. This is probably a less common starting point than technology or gameplay. Indeed, since many games have no story whatsoever, the very concept of a game starting with a story may seem strange. At the same time, it is not unheard of for a game designer to think of a story she wants to explore, and only then start exploring what sort of technology and gameplay will be best suited to telling that story. Frequently, a particular setting may inspire a game designer, such as the adventurous world of Errol Flynn or the dark and gritty crime world of *Sin City*. A designer may not care too much about the specifics of the plot, but may have a strong desire to work in a world filled with swashbucklers or grim private detectives. For my purposes in this chapter, I consider these inspirational settings to fall under the definition of starting with story.

Any good game designer who thinks up a story or a setting will have a tendency to think of it in terms of how it would translate into a game, how the player can interact with that story, and how the story may unfold in different ways depending on the player's actions in the game-world. Indeed, not all stories will translate very well into games, and thinking of gameplay possibilities early can help you rule out settings that simply will not work out in games. So a designer may not be thinking solely of the story but also of the gameplay. But the story can be the jumping-off point, the central vision from which all other aspects of the game are determined.

Of course the type of story to be told will have a dramatic effect on the type of gameplay the project will need to have. If the designer wants to tell the story of a group of friends battling their way through a fantastic world full of hostile creatures, a first-person shooter with teammates might be appropriate. Any sort of story that involves the player talking to a large range of characters and going on "quests" for those characters might be addressed with more RPG-style mechanics. Telling the story of the Battle of Waterloo could be perfectly addressed in a project with wargame-style strategic play, with the gameplay adjusted in order to best bring out the aspects of Waterloo with which the designer is primarily concerned. Does the designer want the player to have a general's-eye view of the game? In that case, gameplay that allows for the tracking of tactics and logistics should be used. Or does the designer want to tell the story more from the view of the soldiers who had to fight that battle? Then gameplay that would allow the player to track and manipulate her troops unit by unit would be appropriate. If conversations with non-player characters (NPCs) are an important part of communicating the story, the designer will need to design game mechanics that allow for such conversations, using typed-in sentences, branching dialog choices, or whatever will work best. The designer needs to find gameplay that will allow the player to experience the most important elements of whatever story she is trying to tell.

Of course, the technology will have to match up with the story as well, primarily in order to support the gameplay the designer decides is best suited to telling that story. If conversations are an important part of communicating the story, the programming team will need to be able to develop a conversation system. If world exploration and discovery are a big part of telling the story, perhaps a 3D engine is best suited to the gameplay — one that allows the players to look anywhere they want with the game camera. The designer may find that specifically scripted events are important to communicating aspects of the tale; players must be able to observe unique events that transpire at specific times in different parts of the world. In this case, the programmers will need to give the level designers the ability to implement these scenes. The technology is the medium of communication to the players, and thereby the story is directly limited by what the technology is capable of telling.

Maniac Mansion was the first of the story-centered adventure games from LucasArts to use the SCUMM system.

Good examples of story-centered or at least story-dominant game design are some of the adventure games created by Infocom and LucasArts. All of the adventure games from these companies used very standardized play mechanics and technology. The game designers worked with the company's proprietary adventure game creation technology, either the Infocom text-adventure authoring tool or LucasArts' SCUMM system. By the time the game designer came onto the project, her process of creation could start more naturally with creating a story she wanted to tell. Certainly the story had to be one that was well suited to the adventure game format and that could be implemented using the existing tool set. And of course, there was a lot of game design still to do, in terms of coming up with what the player's actions and choices would be in that specific story, what puzzles would be encountered, and so forth. Both Infocom's and LucasArts' tools were general purpose enough to allow the designer to create a wide range of games, with a good amount of variation in terms of storytelling possibilities, even though the core mechanics had to consist of a typing-centered text adventure in the case of Infocom and a point-and-click graphical adventure for LucasArts. Thus the game designers' primary driving motivation in the game's creation could be telling a story, with the designing of game mechanics and technology development much less of a concern. Just as film directors are limited by what they can shoot with a camera and then project on a 2D screen of a certain size at 24 frames per second, the adventure game designers at Infocom and LucasArts were limited by the mechanics of the adventure game authoring system they were using. Since the mechanics of the medium were firmly established well before both the film director and the adventure game designer began their project, they were freed up to think beyond the nuts and bolts of the audience or user's gaming experience.

Working with Limitations

Experienced game designers already understand the limitations placed on the creation of games by the technology, gameplay, and story. When they take part in brainstorming sessions, these game designers have a good gut sense of how making certain choices about the game in question will limit its creation further down the road. For each decision that is made about the game, many doors are closed. When enough decisions about the nature of the game have been made, it may be that there is only one type of game that can possibly accomplish all that the designers want. The stage for making major decisions is over, and now all that lies ahead are the thousands of smaller implementation issues.

For four of the games I have completed — *Odyssey: The Legend of Nemesis*, *Damage Incorporated*, *Centipede 3D*, and *The Suffering* — I began development from different starting points. Coincidentally, one game started with story, another with technology, the third with gameplay, and the final with a combination of setting and gameplay. Throughout each game's development I made every effort to remember where the game was coming from and what it was hoping to accomplish. The origins and objectives limited everything else about the experience, resulting in only one acceptable game that achieved the goals I had set.

Odyssey: The Legend of Nemesis

Odyssey started with a story. I actually inherited this project at a point where a significant part of the 2D technology and RPG game mechanics were in place. Some story existed but it was by no means complete, and I was not terribly excited by it. As my first game project that was actually likely to be published, I immediately set to work rewriting the story into something in which I was personally invested. For years I had been wanting to get into game development in order to tell interactive, non-linear stories, and so I immediately set to writing just such a story, wherein the player would be presented with moral choices beyond just "to kill or not to kill." I wanted to create a game in which the choices the players made would actually change the outcome of the story in a meaningful way. So I charged blindly forward, with the story as my only concern.

Levels in *Odyssey: The Legend of Nemesis* were designed around the game's story.

Fortunately, the technology and game mechanics that were in place by and large supported this story I wanted to tell. Where they did not, I changed the game mechanics as necessary. When NPC AI had to function in a certain way to support the story, I made the AI work that way. When forced conversations became required, where an NPC could walk up to the player and initiate a conversation with her instead of the other way around, I implemented the appropriate game mechanic. The levels were designed with no other goal than to support the story. Since I was primarily interested in the story, the game's levels were not designed with exciting battles in mind and combat situations in the game were not as compelling as they could have been. The constant conflict with strange, marauding creatures was something people expected in an RPG and so it remained in, but I made combat such that it was very much secondary to exploring the story. This ended up turning the game into almost more of an adventure than an RPG, but that was fine with me, since it was what supported the story best.

Looking at it today, I can see that *Odyssey* has many flaws. But I do not think that these problems arose because it was a game whose development started with a story. This may be a rare way to begin game development, but it can still be a viable starting point. If I had possessed a better sense of game design at the time, I could have taken

efforts to make the rest of the game as interesting as the story was, while never undermining or diminishing the impact of the game's epic tale.

Damage Incorporated

In the case of *Damage Incorporated*, the publisher, MacSoft, had obtained the license to a sophisticated (at the time) technology that they wanted to use for a game. It was the engine Bungie Software had created for use in *Marathon* and *Marathon 2*, two games I enjoy and admire. In particular, *Marathon 2* remains one of the best first-person shooters ever made, easily holding its own against its PC contemporary, *Doom*. What *Marathon 2* lacked in fast-action battles and the atmosphere of menace that *Doom* created so well, it more than made up for with a compelling and complex story line, superior level design, and a good (though simple) physics model. Indeed, Bungie's *Halo* built upon *Marathon*'s many innovations, finally bringing them to a wider audience. As a result of my having enjoyed the *Marathon* games so much, I decided to make my game embrace the technology and gameplay that *Marathon* had established. I would craft my game around the technology that had been licensed and use that technology to the greatest effect I possibly could.

Damage Incorporated (pictured) had its origins in the licensed Marathon technology.

With a starting point of technology, I crafted gameplay and a story that could succeed using the *Marathon* technology. Of course, we added features to the gameplay and engine. The primary addition to the game mechanics was the player's ability to order teammates around the game-world, thereby adding a real-time strategy element to the mix. We added to the engine numerous enhancements that allowed for swinging doors, moving objects, and other effects necessary to create a game-world that more resembled the real-world. I was still concerned with story in the game, though not to as great an extent as I had been with *Odyssey*. Since having conversations with NPCs did not really fit in with *Marathon*'s game mechanics, I worked interesting characters into the game experience through the player's teammates. These fellow marines would chat among themselves as the player maneuvered them through the game-world.

One of the game's weaknesses was that at the start of the project I did not fully understand the limitations of the *Marathon* engine. It was best suited to creating indoor environments, so outdoor areas ended up looking fake, especially when they were supposed to represent real-life locations on Earth. Modeling the exterior of an alien world in the engine, as *Marathon 2* had done, was one thing, but creating environments that looked like the woods in Nebraska was another. Around half of the levels in *Damage Incorporated* are set outside, and none of these outdoor areas ended up looking very good. If I had understood the technology better, I could have designed the game to take place in more indoor environments, thereby better exploiting what the engine did well.

Interestingly, at the same time I was using the *Marathon 2* engine to create *Damage Incorporated*, MacSoft had another team using the same engine to create a game called *Prime Target*. The members of that team did not like *Marathon 2* as much as I did, and wanted to create more of a *Doom*-style shooter, with faster, simpler, more intense combat. Instead of starting with the technology and running with the type of gameplay it handled well, they started with a type of gameplay they wanted to achieve and modified the engine to better support that. As a result, the *Prime Target* team spent much more time modifying the engine to suit their needs than we did. On the other hand, they were wise enough to set their game primarily indoors, an environment much better suited to the technology. Because of our different decisions in how to use the technology, *Prime Target* became a significantly different game from either *Marathon 2* or *Damage Incorporated*. Not a better or worse game, merely different. The differences can be traced back to the origins of the idea for their game, and the way they approached using a licensed engine.

Centipede 3D

The *Centipede 3D* project was started when the publisher, Hasbro Interactive, approached the game's developer, Leaping Lizard Software, about using their *Raider* technology for a new version of *Centipede*. Hasbro had recently found success with their modernization of *Frogger*, and wanted to do the same for *Centipede*, the rights to which they had recently purchased. Producers at Hasbro had seen a preview for *Raider* in a magazine, and thought it might be well suited to the project. Hasbro had a very definite idea about the type of gameplay they wanted for *Centipede 3D*: game mechanics similar to the classic *Centipede* except in a 3D world. The team at Leaping Lizard agreed. At the time, few games were utilizing simple, elegant arcade-style gameplay, and adapting it to a 3D world would be a unique challenge.

For the development of *Centipede 3D*, the origin of the game's development lay in gameplay. Recreating the feel of the original *Centipede* was at the forefront of everyone's minds throughout the project's development. When Hasbro set out to find a company with a technology capable of handling the game, they knew to look for an engine that could handle larger, more outdoor areas, because those were the type of locations a modernized *Centipede* would require. They knew not to go for a *Quake*-style technology in order to achieve the gameplay they wanted. Leaping Lizard's *Raider* engine was a good match with the gameplay, but not a perfect one. Much work was required to modify it to achieve the responsiveness of a classic arcade game. *Raider* employed a physics system that was by and large not needed for *Centipede 3D*, and so

The new, 3D version of *Centipede* was based on the classic "bug shooter" gameplay found in the original *Centipede*.

the majority of it was stripped out. Thus the technology was molded to fit the gameplay desired.

Centipede 3D's story was the simplest of any of the games I have worked on. In part this is because one of the traits of a classic arcade game is its lack of any real storytelling. For games like *Centipede*, *Pac-Man*, and *Space Invaders*, setting was enough; all the games needed was a basic premise through which the gameplay could take place. Furthermore, everyone working on the *Centipede 3D* project realized that it was the simple, addictive gameplay that would draw players into *Centipede 3D*, not the story. The classic arcade style of gameplay simply did not call for it. The primary effect of the meager story line was to provide a setup and to affect the look of the game, to explain why the player is flying around blasting centipedes and mushrooms, and why the game-worlds change in appearance every few levels. Just as the original *Centipede* used the setting of a garden and bugs to justify the game's gameplay, so did the remake. In the end, *Centipede 3D* was all about the gameplay.

The Suffering

My most recent game, *The Suffering*, had its origins in a combination of setting and gameplay. The game's publisher, Midway, suggested to the game's developer, Surreal Software, that they wanted an action game, preferably a shooter, set in a horror milieu. Surreal was excited at the prospect of working in a horror space, but we were not big fans of the game mechanics that up until then had dominated the genre. Games such as *Resident Evil* and *Silent Hill*, though very good games, relied on scaring the player by limiting their ability to look around the environment with the camera, by having awkward and unresponsive controls, by strictly limiting the available ammo, and by using fairly weak central protagonists. This had the effect of distancing players from the game, forcing them to think about the camera and controls, and making them realize that they definitely were not playing themselves. In short, these games were not as immersive as they could have been, and being big first-person shooter fans we knew that immersion was fundamental to truly frightening someone. Making the game more of a shooter got us a more action-oriented experience and increased the game's potential for immersion.

The Suffering originated with the idea of combining shooter gameplay with a distinctly disturbing horror setting.

So our origins were truly in a combination of gameplay and horror, with both dependent on the other. It was only through the combination of these two elements that we were going to differentiate ourselves among the many games that were available for the PlayStation 2 and Xbox. Certainly, there were many shooters on the market, and also plenty of horror games, but no game that combined both. Without considering both setting and gameplay simultaneously from the very beginning, our game design would not have evolved into a game that accomplished what we wanted.

Though *The Suffering* was built on existing technology that Surreal had most recently used for *Drakan: The Ancients' Gates*, that engine was significantly stronger at outdoor environments and thus was ill-suited to the dark and shadowy confined spaces of a horror game. From the beginning of the game we knew we wanted to include outdoor environments as well in order to add much-needed variety to the game, but we also knew we would have to rework our technology significantly to pull off our action/horror ambitions. Thus our technology was significantly reworked to use portals that allowed us to include complex and detailed indoor spaces in addition to outdoor ones. Since our primary starting point for the project was gameplay and setting, our technology was forced to change and adapt.

Embrace Your Limitations

In many ways, developing a game is all about understanding your limitations and then turning those limitations into advantages. In this chapter I have discussed how the designer must understand where her game idea is coming from: gameplay, story, or technology. With this understanding, the designer must recognize how this limits the other attributes of the game — how a certain gameplay calls for a certain type of story and technology, how one story requires a specific technology and gameplay, and how technology will lend itself to specific types of games and stories. One designer may consider these requirements to be limitations, while a more positive designer may consider them to be simply constraints. Indeed, many people do their best work when operating inside constraints; having limitless options can be quite intimidating and confusing. It is the designer's job to establish what constraints the project has, find the perfect parts that fit within those limitations, and finally make all the pieces fit together in a compelling game.

It is a very rare case indeed for a designer to be able to think of whatever game she wants and then search out the perfect implementation of that idea. In almost all cases, the designer is limited by the situation that is presented to her. The limitations may come in the form of the technology available, the team she has to work with, the budget available to develop the game, and the amount of time allowed for its creation. Though the producer is primarily responsible for making sure the game is on time and on budget, the designer must concern herself with all of the limitations she is faced with if she hopes to create a good game in the final analysis.

Established Technology

Often a designer at a larger company is required to work with whatever technology that company has. This may be an engine left over from a previous game, or it may be that the programming team only has experience working in 2D and as a result the only technology they will be able to viably develop in a reasonable time frame will be 2D. Even if the designer is fortunate enough to be able to seek out a technology to license for a project, that designer will still be limited by the quality of the engines that are available for licensing and the amount of money she has to spend. Engines are becoming increasingly versatile and affordable, but it will be some time before they can be used for all game types on all budgets.

If the developer is a lone wolf, working solo as both designer and programmer on a project, one might think the designer could make whatever she wants. Of course this is not the case, as the designer will quickly be limited by her own skills as a programmer and by the amount of work she can actually accomplish by herself. Except in rare cases, no single programmer is going to be able to create a fully featured 3D technology to rival what can be built by the large team at Criterion or John Carmack and his id Software cohorts. It is simply not possible. Functioning as the sole programmer and designer on a project has many benefits, but it certainly limits what one will be able to accomplish.

Even if a programmer is able to create the perfect engine for her game, what if it is simply too slow? If a large number of fully articulated characters in an outdoor real-time 3D environment are required for your gameplay and the technology is not specifically built to support this, the frame rate is going to be languid. Throw in some truly sophisticated AI for each of those creatures and your game will slow to 1 FPS, becoming, in essence, a slide show. If she must make that game, the designer has to wait until the processing power required is available, which may not be for years to come. Unfortunately, suggesting that a project be put on hold until the technology improves usually has the direct result of causing the publisher to stop making milestone payments.

Of course, if a designer is truly committed to making a certain game, before giving up she may need to be more clever in how she implements it. Are there tricks that can be employed to make a large group of AI agents look like they are working independently when really they are using a relatively cheap flocking algorithm? How high-poly do the environments truly need to be? Or the really big question: does the game truly need to be 3D at all, or will a 2D implementation be just as good? Resourceful and determined designers will be able to find clever solutions to what at first seem like unsolvable problems.

The Case of the Many Mushrooms

When working on *Centipede 3D*, we were constantly troubled by our frame rate. Remember, for that game, our primary concern was to achieve gameplay that was in the spirit of the original arcade classic. But *Centipede*'s gameplay hinged on the presence of a lot of mushrooms on the screen at once, with similarly large numbers of other insects, arachnids, and arthropods flying around the world, threatening to destroy the player's little "shooter" ship. Furthermore, the gameplay necessitated a top-down view, which provided a fairly large viewing area of the game-world so that the player would be able to see the maneuverings of those deadly creatures. The end result was that there could be several hundred 24-polygon mushrooms, twelve 40-polygon centipede segments, and numerous other creatures all on the screen at once. On top of that, Hasbro wanted *Centipede 3D* to be a mass-market title, so the product's minimum system requirement had been predetermined to be a 133 MHz Pentium with no hardware graphics acceleration. On top of all that, *Centipede*'s fast-action gameplay required a similarly fast frame rate to be any fun at all.

While working on the project, we were constantly confronted with the problem of escalating polygon counts, with artists always attempting to shave a few polygons off of the much-used mushroom model. At one point, one artist suggested that perhaps if we could reduce the mushroom to two pyramids sitting on top of each other, we would have the absolute minimum representation of a mushroom, while using only six or eight polygons. Indeed, it was suggested, if all of the game's models went for a minimalist representation, we could use the polygon limitation to our advantage, creating a unique game-world filled with objects that looked as if they were created by a cubist. It would certainly be a unique look for a game, and would fit in quite well with *Centipede 3D*'s already somewhat surreal game-world. "Embrace your limitations!" I proclaimed in the midst of this discussion, not unlike a weary scientist might finally shout, "Eureka!" All present thought my proclamation to be quite funny, but thinking about it later I decided it was actually quite true for game development. Unfortunately, we were too far along in development to convert all of our art to the minimalist implementation we had thought of, not to mention the potential troubles of trying to sell the publisher on the idea of a minimalist game.

But in general I still believe that game developers need to embrace their limitations as soon as they discover them. When presented with an engine that must be used for a project, why go out of your way to design a game that is ill-suited to that technology? Your game design may be fabulous and well thought out, but if the technology you must use is not capable of implementing it well, you will still be left with a bad game in the end. It is better to shelve an idea that is incompatible with your technology (you can always come back to it later) and come up with a design better suited to the tools you have. Once you have identified the limitations that the engine saddles you with, it is best to embrace those limitations instead of fighting them. This is not to suggest that a designer should always design the simplest game that she can think of or that sophisticated, experimental designs should not be attempted. If a shrewd theater director knows a given actor is interested in working with her, she will pick the best play to show off the particular skills of that actor. Similarly, a designer should consider what the technology lends itself to and use that as the basis for the game she designs and the story she sets out to tell.

The Time Allotted

Limitations that I have not discussed much in this chapter but which are nonetheless very important in game development are the budget and schedule with which a designer may be presented. Though these are primarily the concern and responsibility of the project's producer, the game designer needs to know how these factors will limit the project just as the technology, gameplay, or story may. When choosing the technology to be used, the designer must ask herself: can it be completed in the amount of time scheduled for the project? Can it be completed in time for level implementation and balancing? Does the suggested design call for the creation of such a large number of complex levels and heavily scripted behaviors that they cannot be completed in eighteen months by only one designer? Just as the timeline will limit the amount of time that can be spent on the project, the budget will affect how many people can be working on the project during that time. It may be that, given double the budget, the game design could be easily completed in a year and a half, but with only half the budget the designer will need to scale back the design to come up with something feasible. Again, if development is running six months late with no end in sight and as a result the publisher pulls the plug, it does not matter how brilliant your game design may have been in theory. No one will get to play your game because you failed to fully consider the logistics of implementing it. And if you fail to allocate enough time for fine-tuning and balancing the gameplay, your publisher may demand you ship a game you consider unfinished. What might have been a great game will be a bad one because there was not enough time to really finish it.

Lone wolf developers have it a bit easier in terms of time constraints and budgetary limitations. If a single person is creating all of the art, code, and design for the game, and is developing the game on her own time without relying on income from its development in order to survive, she is much more free to follow wherever her muse takes her, for as long as she likes. Of course, she is still limited by her own talents, by the quality of the art she can create, and by the limits of her programming skills, but at least these are the only limitations. When creating art, there is a lot to be said for not being beholden to the person writing the checks.

If You Choose Not to Decide, You Still Have Made a Choice

So often producers, programmers, artists, and designers fail to consider the limitations of the game idea they are planning to develop. Whether it springs from notions of gameplay, suggestions of technology, or thoughts about a story, as soon as a game idea takes on form it begins limiting what the game can be if it is to be successful. Game developers need to understand that not every technology will work with every game design, nor every design with every story, nor even every story with every technology.

Often developers will try to take a bunch of compelling concepts and attempt to stuff them all into one game. The lead programmer may be interested in developing a cutting-edge human body physics system. The lead game designer might have wanted to try a real-time strategy game ever since she played *Age of Empires* for the first time. The game's writer may think there's entirely too much violence in computer games and therefore wants to write a tale of romance. If the producer is a fool, she may even be thrilled that the members of her team are so excited about what they are developing and that, by combining physics, RTS, and romance, the result will be a breakthrough game.

Of course anyone with a whit of sense knows this game is doomed to fail. Without a consistent and unified vision, no game will have a fighting chance. Though each member of the team may have a valid case for pursuing her idea, if the ideas do not work together, at some point the group will need to pick one and go with it. If, at the brainstorming session, the team decides which idea they want to concentrate on, the team can work to make the game as a whole as good as possible. Suppose they choose physics as their most promising strength. Then the designer can mull it over and realize an RTS is probably not ideal but a circus-themed game could be an inventive use of the human body physics simulator. It could include launching performers out of cannons, having acrobats create human pyramids, and allowing players to perform complex trapeze stunts. From there, the writer could come up with a love story about two aerialists whose relationship is tested by the arrival at the circus of a stunning new strong man, with everything coming to a climax during a complex high-wire act where the safety net has been removed. This game has a fighting chance of being fun to play because all of the components are working together. In the end, you do not want your game to consist only of an excellent technology or a compelling story or a brilliant game design. If none of these components support each other and you lack a unified vision, your game will be just as bad as if you were working with a hackneyed story, a thin game design, and an incomplete technology.

Chapter 4:
Game Analysis: Centipede

Designed by Ed Logg with Donna Bailey
Released in 1981

One can think of the classic arcade game as a form of the computer game in the same way that a silent slapstick comedy is a form of film or the hard-boiled detective novel is a form of literature. The classic arcade game form fell out of favor with the commercial gaming companies pretty much as soon as the technology was available to move beyond it. However, many independent game developers still work on classic arcade games either for their own amusement or to be released as freeware or shareware titles. Many of these labors of love are imitations of established classic arcade games, but many others are interesting experiments in new gameplay. There remains something uniquely compelling about the form, and the fact that one does not need to have a sophisticated 3D engine to make a wonderfully entertaining classic arcade game helps to make the form an appealing one in which to work.

It bears mentioning that when I refer to the classic arcade game, I do not mean to imply that all classic arcade games are classics. Many of them are quite bad. As with any media, the old arcade games that are remembered and talked about decades after their release tend to be the best ones, thus creating the false impression of a "golden age." The bad arcade games have fallen between the cracks of history. The term "classic arcade game" refers to the form as a classic one, not to the games themselves, just as one might refer to "classical music." Surely the term "arcade game" is not limiting enough, since this would seem to include every game found in an arcade, including modern racing, gun, and fighting games, none of which are what I consider to be part of the form I am concerned with here.

The classic arcade game form had its commercial and creative heyday in the late 1970s through the early 1980s, when machines exhibiting the form lined the arcades. Looking at the games as a whole, one can come up with a series of traits that they all shared. Some of these aspects of the form may have been arrived at because of the commercial considerations of the arcades. The thought was to get players to easily understand a game, so that by the end of their very first game they had a good sense of how the game worked and what was necessary for success. Second, the players' game, even the game of an expert, could not last very long, since any one player had only paid a quarter, and if the game only earned a single quarter in a half hour, it would not be profitable to operate. The manufacturers of coin-op games wanted average play time to be 2.5 minutes. Players needed to be sucked in to replay the games, to keep plunking in quarters. As a result, in some ways the arcade games had to be more refined than home games are today. Once the players have purchased a home game, often for at least a hundred times the cost of a single arcade game play, the sale is completed. If they are not completely disgusted with the game they are unlikely to return it. Features such as scoring and high-score tables only served to increase the arcade game's addictive nature and encourage players to keep spending money.

In addition, the technical restrictions of the day limited what the games could do, and thereby influenced what the game could accomplish in terms of gameplay. Had the designers had the RAM and processing power to include fully scrolling game-worlds that were many times the size of the screen, they probably would have. If the games had been able to replay full-motion video of some sort, perhaps the designers would have incorporated more story line into the games. But the fact remains that a unique genre of computer games emerged, and if the commercial and technical limitations shaped the form, so be it. Just as early films had to work with the limitations of silence and short running times, computer game designers were limited in what they could create, and were able to come up with brilliant games nonetheless. Often, a series of strict constraints forces artists to focus their creativity in a fashion that leads to better work than if they could do anything they wanted.

One key ingredient to many classic arcade games was their wild variation in gameplay styles. *Centipede*, *Missile Command*, *Pac-Man*, and *Frogger* are as different from each other as they possibly could be. Many classic arcade games featured variations on a theme: *Centipede*, *Space Invaders*, *Galaga*, and *Tempest* all revolved around the idea of shooting at a descending onslaught of enemies. However, the gameplay variations these games embraced are far more radical than the tiny amount of variation one will find in modern games, which are more content to endlessly clone already-proven

Tempest is one of many classic arcade games that is centered on shooting at enemies which keep getting closer. *Tempest* is memorable because of the many unique twists included.

gaming genres. Despite the wild variety of gameplay that can be found in classic arcade games, one can still look back on these games as a collective and view them as an artistic movement in the brief history of computer games. By analyzing the form's shared traits, modern game designers can learn a lot about how they can make their own games more compelling experiences for players.

Classic Arcade Game Traits

- Single Screen Play: In a classic arcade game, the bulk of the gameplay takes place on a single screen, with players maneuvering their game-world surrogate around that screen, sometimes only in a portion of that screen. This was done, no doubt, in part because of technological limitations, but it also has very important artistic ramifications on the game's design. Players, at any time, are able to see the entire game-world, and can make their decisions with a full knowledge of the state of that game-world. Obviously, empowering players with that kind of information seriously impacts the gameplay. Many of the games in the classic arcade game form would include more than one screen's worth of gameplay by switching play-fields or modifying existing ones to create additional "levels." Examples of this include *Joust*, *Pac-Man*, and *Mario Bros*. Though these games may have included more than a single screen in the entire game, at any one time the game-world still consisted of just that one screen.

- Infinite Play: Players can play the game forever. There is no ending to the game, and hence no winning it either. This was done in part to allow players to challenge themselves, to see how long they could play on a single quarter. Players can never say, "I beat *Asteroids*," and hence players are always able to keep playing, to keep putting in quarters. At the same time, having an unwinnable game makes every game a defeat for players. Every game ends with the player's death, and hence is a kind of tragedy. Having an unwinnable game also necessitates making a game that continuously becomes more challenging, hence a game design with a continuous, infinite ramping up of difficulty. With the advent of the home market, game publishers no longer wanted players to play a single game forever. Instead they want players to finish the games they have and buy more. This is one reason why it is now rare to see a game with infinite play.

- Multiple Lives: Typically, classic arcade games allow players a finite number of tries, or a number of "lives," before their game is over. Perhaps derived from pinball games, which for decades had provided players with three or five balls, multiple lives allowed novice players a chance to learn the game's mechanics before the game was over. Given adequate chances to try to figure out how the game works, players are more likely to want to play again if they improved from one life to the next. The ability to earn extra lives provides another reward incentive for players and also sets up a game where dying once is not necessarily the end of the game, which in turn encourages players to take risks they might not otherwise.

- Scoring/High Scores: Almost all classic arcade games included a scoring feature through which players would accumulate points for accomplishing different objectives in the game. For example, in *Centipede*, players get 1 point for destroying a mushroom, 10 points for a centipede segment, 100 points for a centipede head, and 1000 points for a scorpion. Another classic arcade game component with origins in the world of pinball, the score allows players to ascertain how well they did at the game, since winning the game is impossible. The high-score table was introduced in order to allow players to enter their initials next to their score, which would then be ranked in a table of scores so players could have a point of comparison to see just how good they really were. The game would remember the table as long as it stayed plugged in, with some games, such as *Centipede*, even remembering the high-score list or some portion of it once unplugged. The high-score table enabled the classic arcade games to exploit one of the key motivations for playing games — "bragging rights." Players could point out their name in the high-score table to their friends as a way of proving their mettle. Friends could compete with each other (almost all of the games included two-player modes, where players switch off playing) to see who could get the higher score.

- Easy-to-Learn, Simple Gameplay: Classic arcade games were easy for players to learn, impossible (or at least very difficult) to master. Players could walk up to a game of *Centipede*, plunk in their quarter, and by their third life have a good idea of how the game functioned and how they might play better. Why players died was always completely apparent to them. There were typically no "special moves" involving large combinations of buttons that players had to learn through trial and error. There were few games with tricky concepts such as "health" or "shields" or "power-ups." Again, commercial considerations were probably a factor in making these games simple to learn. At the time of their initial introduction, there was no established market of computer game players and there were few arcades. The games wound up in pizza parlors and bars, where any regular person might walk up to one and try it out. These novice players might be scared away if the game were too complex or baffling. Of course, simple does not always mean "limited" or "bad" gameplay; it can also mean "elegant" and "refined."

- No Story: Classic arcade games almost universally eschewed the notion of trying to "tell a story" of any sort, just as many modern arcade games continue to do. The games always had a setting players could easily recognize and relate to, many of them revolving around science fiction themes, though others dabbled in war, fantasy, and sports, among others. Many, such as *Pac-Man* and *Q*Bert*, created their own, unique settings, keeping up with the rampant creativity found in their gameplay. The classic arcade game designers did not feel required to flesh out their game-worlds, to concoct explanations for why players were shooting at a given target or eating a certain type of dot, and the games did not suffer for it.

Even though the action in *Sinistar* did not take place only on one screen, it is still considered to be an example of the classic arcade game form.

Of course, some games broke some of the above rules of the form, yet they can still be considered classic arcade games. For example, *Sinistar* and *Defender* both included scrolling game-worlds for players to travel through, with players unable to see all aspects of the game-world at any one time. Indeed, on first inspection, *Battlezone* seems entirely the odd man out among early classic arcade games. Yet, if one looks at the traits above, one will discover that it featured infinite play, multiple lives, scoring, was easy to learn, and had almost no story. All three of these games included mechanics which, by and large, were adherent to the classic arcade game form. Thus we can still group them with games like *Space Invaders* and *Asteroids*, which follow all the rules laid out above.

Centipede, one of the defining games of the form, follows all of the characteristics of the classic arcade game listed above. Though not a very complex game by today's standards, the marvel of *Centipede* is how all of the different gameplay elements work together to create a uniquely challenging game. It is easy enough to make a game ramp up in difficulty by adding more and more enemies, but *Centipede* naturally increases the challenge by the interplay of its few elements so that the game organically becomes more difficult over time. Nothing in *Centipede* is out of place, nothing is inconsistent, nothing is unbalanced. To analyze *Centipede* is to attempt to understand how to design the perfect game.

Input

One of the great advantages to working on a game for the arcades is that the designer has complete control over the type of device players will use to control the game. On the PC, the designer can only count on players having a keyboard and a mouse, and on a console, the designer must work with the standard controller that comes with that particular console. The arcade designer (budget constraints notwithstanding) is able to pick the best type of control for the game and provide players with that control system. The designer can then create the game around those controls, precisely balancing the game to work perfectly with that input method. *Centipede* does this expertly, providing players with an extremely precise analog control device in the form of a trackball. This is ideally suited to moving the player's shooter ship around on the bottom of the screen. Players can move the ship quickly or slowly, whatever the situation calls for. For many fans of *Centipede*, the excellent controller is one of the first things they remember about the game.

The player's shooter in *Centipede* is more mobile than in *Space Invaders*, since it can move up and down in addition to moving sideways. Pictured here: *Centipede*.

The shooter is extremely responsive to the players' manipulation of the trackball, with players being able to easily and intuitively understand the relationship between their manipulation of the trackball and the shooter's movement. *Centipede* was no doubt inspired by other classic arcade games, such as *Space Invaders*, which feature the players' game-world surrogate locked at the bottom of the screen, allowed only to move left or right and shoot. *Centipede* takes that idiom one step further: players are still trapped at the bottom of the screen, but the shooter can move within a six-row vertical space. This allows players to avoid enemies that might be on the bottom row. At the same time, the shooter can still only shoot forward, so enemies that get behind the ship cannot be destroyed. Aside from the trackball, the only other control players have is a button for firing the shooter's laser-type weapon. The game allows an infinitely fast rate of fire, but only one shot can be on the screen at a time, which means players have to think beyond just holding down the fire button constantly. If players move the shooter directly below a mushroom, they can hold down the fire button and quickly

Physical Processing	Order Type: Firm Order	Sel ID/Seq No:

Cust/Add: 401800008/01

Cust PO No. WP06003908   EWOU   UNIVERSITY OF WOLVERHAMPTON

BBS Order No: E785023   Ln:1   Del:1   **Cust Ord Date:** 19-Jan-2007

1556229127-10469133   **BBS Ord Date:** 22-Jan-2007

(9781556229121)   **Sales Qty:** 1   **#Vols:** 001

Game design

Subtitle:theory & practice

PAPERBACK   **Pub Year:**2005   **Vol No.:**   Stmt of Resp:by Richard Rouse III

Rouse, Richard.   Edition:2nd ed.

     Ser. Title:

Wordware Publishing

Acc Mat:

Tech Services Charges:

  Kapco UK   Property Stamp UK

  Accession Stamp UK   Security Device UK

  Base Charge Processing

  Date Due Slip UK

Cust Fund Code: 071   **Cust Location:** WV

Stock Category: Long Loan   **Cust Dept:**

STOCK CAT: Long Loan **

Order Line Notes

Notes to Vendor

     COPY ID: 1097270 1097271 1097272

95130

/11

O4F

shoot the mushroom four times, thus destroying it. But at the top of the screen, where players cannot maneuver the ship, destroying a mushroom takes much longer, since players must wait for each shot to hit the mushroom before another shot can be fired. Shooting the ever-approaching enemies creates a similar situation. If their last shot is in the midst of traveling to a faraway target, players will be unable to shoot again in order to take out a dive-bombing enemy. Thus, when the enemies are far away, they are less of a threat, but players have trouble killing them. As the critters get closer, players can kill the bugs more easily, but their chance of dying goes up. This keeps the game perfectly balanced, and requires players to plan their shots carefully, a design element that adds more depth to the game's mechanics.

Interconnectedness

One of the great strengths of *Centipede* is how well all the different elements of the gameplay fit together. Consider the different enemy insects that try to kill players. The centipede winds its way down from the top of the screen to the player's area at the bottom, moving horizontally. The centipede appears as either a lone twelve-segment centipede or as a shorter centipede accompanied by a number of single heads. At the start of a wave, the number of centipede segments on the screen always totals twelve. Next is the spider, which moves in a diagonal, bouncing pattern across the bottom of the screen, passing in and out of the player's area. Then comes the flea, which plummets vertically, straight down. There is nothing terribly sophisticated about any of the movement patterns of these insects. Indeed, the flea and the centipede, once they have appeared in the play-field, follow a completely predictable pattern as they approach the player's area. The spider has a more random nature to its zigzagging movement, but even it does nothing to actually pursue players. Therefore, once players have played the game just a few times, they have a completely reliable set of expectations about how these enemies will attack them. Fighting any one of these creatures by itself would provide very little challenge for players. Yet, when they function together they combine to create uniquely challenging situations for players. With any one of these adversaries missing, the game's challenge would be significantly diminished, if not removed altogether.

Each of the insects in the game also has a unique relationship to the mushrooms, which fill the game's play-field. The primary reason for the existence of the mushrooms is to speed up the centipede's progress to the bottom of the screen. Every time a centipede bumps into a mushroom, it turns down to the next row below, as if it had run into the edge of the play-field. Thus, once the screen becomes packed with mushrooms, the centipede will get to the bottom of the play-field extremely quickly. Once at the bottom of the screen, the centipede moves back and forth inside the player's area, posing a great danger to players. So, it behooves players to do everything they can to destroy the mushrooms on the play-field, even though the mushrooms themselves do not pose a direct threat. Further complicating matters, every time players shoot a segment of the centipede it leaves a mushroom where it died. Thus, wiping out a twelve-segment centipede leaves a big cluster of mushrooms with which players must contend.

As the flea falls to the bottom of the play-field, it leaves a trail of new mushrooms behind itself, and the only way for players to stop it is to kill it. The flea only comes on to

In *Centipede*, fleas drop toward the bottom of the screen, leaving mushrooms behind them, while spiders eat whatever mushrooms block their movement.

the play-field if less than a certain number of mushrooms are on the bottom half of the screen. This way, if players destroy all the mushrooms closest to them, the flea comes out immediately to lay down more. The spider, the creature that poses the biggest threat to players, has the side effect that it eats mushrooms. This then presents players with a quandary: shoot and kill the spider or just try to avoid it so it can take out more mushrooms? Finally, the scorpion, a creature that travels horizontally across the top half of the screen and hence can never collide with and kill players, poisons the mushrooms it passes under. These poisoned mushrooms affect the centipede differently when it bumps into them. Instead of just turning down to the next row, the centipede will move vertically straight down to the bottom of the screen. So when a centipede hits a poisoned mushroom, the centipede becomes a much more grave threat than it was before. Once a scorpion has passed by, players must now expend effort trying to shoot all the poisoned mushrooms at the top of the screen or be prepared to blast the centipedes as they plummet vertically straight toward them.

So we can see that each of the creatures in the game has a special, unique relationship to the mushrooms. It is the interplay of these relationships that creates the challenge for players. The more mushrooms the flea drops, the more mushrooms the scorpion has to poison. The spider may take out mushrooms along the bottom of the screen, getting them out of the way of players, but it may eat so many that the flea starts coming out again. If players kill the centipede too close to the top of the screen, it will leave a clump of mushrooms that are difficult to destroy at such a distance and that will cause future centipedes to reach the bottom of the screen at a greater speed. However, if players wait until the centipede is at the bottom of the screen, the centipede is more likely to kill them. With the mushrooms almost functioning as puzzle pieces, *Centipede* becomes something of a hybrid between an arcade shooter and a real-time puzzle game. Indeed, some players were able to develop special strategies that would work to stop the flea from ever coming out, thus making the centipede get to the bottom of the screen less quickly and allowing players to survive much longer. It is the interplay of each of the adversaries with these mushrooms and with each other that creates a unique challenge for players.

Escalating Tension

A big part of the success of *Centipede* is how it escalates tension over the length of the game. The game actually creates peaks and valleys in which tension escalates to an apex and, with the killing of the last centipede segment, relaxes for a moment as the game switches over to the next wave. One small way in which the game escalates tension over a few seconds is through the flea, which is the only enemy in the game players must shoot twice. When it is shot just once, its speed increases dramatically and players must quickly shoot it again to avoid being hit. For that brief speed burst, tension escalates. In terms of the centipede itself, the game escalates the tension by splitting the centipede each time it is shot. If players shoot the middle segment of an eleven-segment centipede, it will split into two five-segment centipedes that head in opposite directions. Sure, the players have decreased the total number of segments on the screen by one, but now they have two adversaries to worry about at once. As a result, skilled players will end up going for the head or tail of the centipede to avoid splitting it.

Most of the game's escalating tension over the course of a wave is derived from the centipede's approach toward the bottom of the screen and players' often frantic efforts to kill it before it gets there. Once a centipede head reaches the bottom of the screen, a special centipede head generator is activated, which spits out additional centipede heads into the player's area. If players are unable to kill the centipede before it reaches the bottom of the screen, which has already increased tension by its very approach, that tension is further escalated by the arrival of these extra heads. And those extra heads keep arriving until players have managed to kill all of the remaining centipede segments on the screen. The rate at which those extra heads come out increases over time, such that if players takes their time in killing them, additional centipedes will arrive all the faster, making players still more frantic.

Once players kill the last segment, the game goes to its next wave, and the centipede is regenerated from the top of the screen. This provides a crucial reprieve for players, a moment of rest. Players will feel a great rush at having finally defeated the centipede, especially if the extra centipede head generator had been activated. In addition, the newly generated centipede at first appears easier to kill, since it is generated so far from the player's area.

Over the course of the entire game, the mushrooms inevitably become more and more packed on the play-field. Once there are more mushrooms toward the bottom of the screen, players feel lucky if they can just clear all of the mushrooms in the lower half of the play-field. They have no chance of destroying the mushrooms toward the top, since the lower mushrooms block their shots. Similarly, if the scorpion has left any poisoned mushrooms toward the top of the screen, players have no chance whatsoever of destroying them, and as a result the centipede dive-bombs the bottom of the screen on every single wave. Far into a game, the top of the play-field becomes a solid wall of mushrooms. As the mushrooms become more and more dense, the centipede gets to the bottom of the screen faster. When the centipede can get to the bottom of the screen extremely quickly, the game is that much faster paced, and players are that much more panicked about destroying the centipede before it reaches the bottom of the screen. This increased mushroom density has the effect of escalating tension not just within a

Over the course of a game of *Centipede*, mushrooms become more and more tightly packed on the play-field.

wave as the extra centipede head generator did, but also from wave to wave, since the mushrooms never go away unless players shoot them.

Centipede also balances its monsters to become harder and harder as players' scores increase. And since the score can never decrease, the tension escalates over the course of the game. Most obvious is the spider, whose speed approximately doubles once the score reaches 5000 (1000 if the game's operator has set the game to "hard"). The spider also maneuvers in a smaller and smaller area of the bottom of the screen as the score gets really high, eventually moving only one row out of the player's six-row area. With the spider thus constrained, it is both more likely to hit players and less likely for players to be able to shoot it. Recall that the flea drops from the top of the screen based on the quantity of mushrooms in the bottom half of the screen. When players start the game, if there are less than five mushrooms in that area, the flea will come down, dropping more as it does so. As the score increases, however, so does the quantity of mushrooms needed to prevent the flea's appearance. Now players must leave more and more mushrooms in that space to prevent the flea from coming out and cluttering the top of the screen with mushrooms.

At the start of each wave, the game always generates a total of twelve centipede segments and heads at the top of the screen. This means that if a twelve-segment centipede appears at the top of the screen, it will be the only centipede. If a seven-segment centipede appears, then five other centipede heads will appear as well, thus totaling the magic number of twelve. The more centipedes that appear, the more challenging it is for players to shoot them all, and the more likely one will sneak to the bottom of the screen. The game starts by releasing a single twelve-segment centipede. In the next wave, a slow eleven-segment centipede appears along with one head. In the following wave, a fast eleven-segment and one head combination arrive. Then a slow ten-segment and two heads appear. With each wave there are a greater number of individual centipedes for players to keep track of and a greater escalation of tension. The game cycles around once twelve individual heads are spawned, and then becomes harder by only spawning fast centipedes.

The player's death also provides a brief respite from the tension. When the player's ship is destroyed, the wave starts over and hence the centipede returns to the top of the screen. Before this, however, all of the mushrooms on the screen are reset. This means that all the partially destroyed mushrooms are returned to their undamaged state and all of the mushrooms poisoned by the scorpion are returned to their unpoisoned state. Many waves into the game, the increased mushroom density makes shooting poisoned mushrooms all but impossible, and with those poisoned mushrooms in place, players are bombarded by centipedes hurtling toward them in every single wave. Thus, players are almost relieved when their shooter is destroyed and all those poisoned mushrooms are removed from the top of the screen. This causes the game to be much more relaxed, at least for a time.

Centipede's frantic gameplay keeps the player tense most of the time, though it provides some breaks in the action during which the player can relax.

Centipede is marvelous at creating and maintaining a tense situation for players, while still providing brief "breathing periods" within the action. Designers of modern games, who are always concerned with ramping up difficulty for players, could learn much by analyzing how *Centipede* keeps players constantly on their toes without ever unfairly overwhelming them.

One Person, One Game

Many may scoff at *Centipede* almost twenty-five years after its creation. There is no question that it is a less technically astounding accomplishment than more modern works, and those who do not examine it closely are likely to dismiss it as more of a light diversion instead of a serious game. But what *Centipede* does, it does with such facility, featuring game mechanics so precisely and perfectly balanced and gameplay so uniquely compelling, that it is truly a marvel of computer game design. One must remember that *Centipede* was created in the days of the one-person-one-game system, when the development team for a game consisted primarily of one person, in this case Ed Logg. By having one person in total control of a project, where a single talented individual fully understands every last nuance of the game, the final product is much more likely to come out with a clearness of vision and brilliance of execution. Of course, one person can create a terrible game just as easily as a large team, but one must wonder if the lone wolf developer does not have a better chance at creating the perfect game.

Chapter 5:
Focus

"Feel the flow... To become one with the flow is to realize purpose."
— Warrel Dane

Developing a game for two years with a team of twenty people typically more resembles war than the creation of art. Many would say that a decent amount of conflict can lead to great art, especially in collaborative forms such as modern commercial computer games. A stronger game may arise from the ashes of team members arguing over the best way to implement some aspect of gameplay. If the game merely becomes unfocused as a result of these squabbles, then a good game is not likely to emerge. Over the course of the many battles you must fight, skirmishes you must endure, and defeats you must overcome in the course of a game's development, with conflicts potentially arising with other team members or from within yourself, it is far too easy to lose track of just why you were creating the game in the first place. Is it possible that at one point the game you are working on captivated your imagination? Was there some vision you had for why this game would be fun, compelling, and unique? Is it possible that at one point you actually liked computer games at all?

Sometimes in the middle of a project it is easy to get sidetracked — sidetracked by technological obstacles that are thrown in your path, sidetracked by altercations between team members, or sidetracked when your publisher tells you features A, B, and C simply have to be changed. It is at these junctures where you come to doubt that your game will ever be fun, or whether it will even be completed. These periods of doubt are the ones that separate the good game designers from those who are merely passable. Good game designers will be able to overcome these difficulties and stay on track by remembering their focus.

The technique I explore in this chapter is certainly not one that all game designers use, but I think it is one that all game designers could benefit from. Many designers may use the technique but not realize it or have a different name for it. Others may have entirely different methods for assuring their game comes together as a fun, consistent whole. You cannot expect to go up to any game designer and say, "What's your focus for your current project?" and expect them to produce an answer in line with the method I explore in this chapter. But if you start being rigorous in maintaining focus in your projects, I think you will see very positive results in the final quality of your games.

Establishing Focus

A game's focus is the designer's idea of what is most important about a game. In this chapter I encourage designers to write their focus down in a short paragraph, since putting it down in writing can often clarify and solidify a designer's thoughts. Furthermore, having it in physical form opens it up for discussion with the development team. However, it is the idea of the focus that is of paramount importance. In a way, a game's focus is similar to a corporation's "mission statement," assuming such mission statements are actually meaningful and used to guide all of a corporation's decisions.

As a game designer you should start concerning yourself with your game's focus from the very beginning of the project. When the project is in its infancy, before work has started on the design document and the project exists primarily as an idea in your head, you should ask yourself a series of questions about the game you are envisioning:

- What is it about this game that is most compelling?
- What is this game trying to accomplish?
- What type of experience will the player have?
- What sort of emotions is the game trying to evoke in the player?
- What should the player take away from the game?
- How is this game unique? What differentiates it from other games?
- What sort of control will the player have over the game-world?

By going over these questions, you should be able to determine the core nature of the game you are planning to create. If you have trouble answering these questions, now is the time to think about the game until the answers to these questions become obvious. Now — before there is anyone else working on the project, before "burn rate" is being spent and driving up the game's budget, before the marketing department starts trying to influence the game's content and direction — is the time to focus. Only by firmly establishing the vision of the game early on will you have any chance of seeing it carried out.

If you do not have too much trouble divining answers to these questions, you may have written an entire page or more delineating the game's points of differentiation. But a page is too much. The focus that we are striving for needs to be succinct — a few sentences, a short paragraph at the most. Some would go so far as to say it should be a single sentence, though I personally prefer something slightly longer than that. What is most important is that it be something you can quickly read to your colleagues without their eyes glazing over. You should take whatever notes you have in answer to these questions and whittle them down until they are short enough to fill only a few sentences, a mid-sized paragraph. Keep only your most compelling ideas. You do not need to list every single feature of the game, or even everything it does differently from other games. Keep only what is most important to your vision of the game, only those points which, if you took them away, would irreparably weaken the game.

You do not need to include the fictional setting of your game if that is not inherent to the actual focus of the project. It may not matter if your game has a fantasy, science fiction, or 1920s crime fiction setting if what is really at the heart of your game is exploring the relationships between characters in a stressful situation or the subtleties of siege warfare. If the setting is not vital to what you want to do with the game, leave it out. Of course, your primary motivation for working on a project may be hopelessly intertwined with the setting. If you actually started with a setting you wanted to explore in a game, such as costumed superheroes in small-town America, and your vision of the gameplay formed around the idea of these characters in a certain environment, then you will want to include it in your focus. The focus is exclusively for the concepts that are most central to the game you are hoping to develop. All that should remain in your focus are the elements without which the game would no longer exist.

Your focus should be something that grabs you viscerally, stirs your creative juices, and makes you feel absolutely exhilarated. If it is not something that thrills you, even at this early stage, it is going to be hard for you to muster enthusiasm when your deadlines are slipping, your budget is skyrocketing, you still have three levels to create, and your lead artist just left for another company. Chris Crawford touched on the idea of a game's focus in his book, *The Art of Computer Game Design*, as he was discussing what he called a game's goal: "This is your opportunity to express yourself; choose a goal in which you believe, a goal that expresses your sense of aesthetic, your world view… It matters not what your goal is, so long as it is congruent with your own interests, beliefs, and passions." If you do not believe in your game, it is not going to be the best game you can make.

Even if you are working under the constraints of a license, a domineering publisher, or a prima donna lead programmer, make your own goals for the project. If the game you have been assigned to work on is not one in which you are interested, figure out some way to transform it into something you can get excited about. No situation is so bad that, given enough time, you cannot make something out of it that you find personally compelling. You want your focus to be something you will fight for intensely until the game finally ships.

Much of this chapter is written in a fashion that implies that you are in charge of your project, at least from a game design standpoint. Of course, this may not be the case. You may be one of several designers on the project. You may even be one of seven and you were just hired last week, so you are at the bottom of the seniority ladder. This does not excuse you from determining what your game's focus is and doing everything you can to keep the game on track. Hopefully the lead designer has already determined what the project's goals are and should have included this information in the introduction to the design document. If you cannot find it there, you may wish to go talk to your lead. Ask him what the project is really trying to do, not in a confrontational way, but just so you get a good idea of where the project is going, and how your contribution to the game can be properly aligned with that direction.

If it turns out the design lead does not really have a focus in mind, it may be held by another member of the team, say a lead programmer or lead artist. However, if despite your best research efforts, the project seems to be goal-less, you may need to take matters into your own hands. Try to figure out where the project seems to be heading, and start talking with people about it. Chat with the other designers, artists, programmers, and producers. Try to talk to them about what the game is all about, and try to get everyone to agree. Meetings may be a good place to do this; when everyone is present, any conflicts between different perspectives or personalities on the team can be found and addressed. You do not need to be in a lead position in order to keep your project on track. As a designer in any capacity on a project, it is ultimately your responsibility that the game always has a clear direction and that a fun game emerges at the end of the tunnel.

An Example: Winter Carnival Whirlwind

Let us suppose you have a vision for a game involving a winter carnival. What is it about winter carnivals that excites you? Is it the ice sculptures? Taking a block of ice and converting it into a snow-themed mammal? No? Perhaps what is really exciting to you is going to winter festivals, with their combination of frozen art, ice skating, snowman competitions, skiing, snowball fights, and championship ice fishing. Indeed, you always wondered how they kept those festivals going so long even with the threat of warmer weather constantly looming on the horizon. Since the winter carnival component seems fairly central to your idea, you will need to include it in the focus. So your focus can start with a sentence that explains this: "The player's experience will revolve around running an ice carnival, with the player responsible for maintaining as long a season as possible, despite uncooperative weather."

Now, what is it about running an ice carnival that grabs you? You see a relentless battle against the elements, racing against spring to keep your operation running as long as possible. Something about harnessing the cold is uniquely compelling to you. Perhaps you enjoy the feeling of running around in the snow, not quite being in control of how fast you can stop and the slapstick moments that may result. This particular appeal of the elements may be unique to you and may not be the most commercially promising new game to come along, but at this stage you're trying to capture your personal thoughts about the game. Do not self-censor your ideas until it is absolutely necessary. So include a few more sentences that serve to illustrate the feeling of your game: "The game will capture the excitement of playing in the snow, including the simple physics that make that fun, through a central character who must move around a somewhat hazardous environment and keep multiple displays, rides, and other attractions operating smoothly. The player's main source of conflict will be the weather itself. Throughout, the tone will be light and whimsical."

What else about your winter festival game is a central part of your vision? Do you want to realistically simulate the injuries one might sustain by falling down on ice? Is going to the hospital and waiting for your surrogate to heal an intrinsic part of your game? Not really; it seems that though that feature could be added to the game, it is not absolutely essential to your vision. Indeed, such a level of "simulation" might detract from the light and whimsical tone. Will the game be in 3D or in 2D? Well, actually, the game could work in either. To be commercially viable in today's marketplace it will probably need to be 3D, but that is not central to your vision. In your focus, do not include aspects of your game that are more about getting the project funded and published than making the game you want to make. You can worry about commercial considerations later. As I stated before, right now you are concerned with your vision, and if you start compromising your vision before absolutely necessary, at the end of the day you are going to be blind. So you do not need to specify 2D or 3D. Indeed, maybe you have everything you need for the focus. Remember, the focus should not be very long.

Now is the time to put your two sentences together in a paragraph and name the game. Though it may seem premature, naming the game is actually a good idea at this point. You want other members of your team, the marketing department, and the business people to start liking your game as soon as possible, and having a name they can refer to it by is fairly important to that process. Can they really discuss it seriously as "this game idea Richard had"? Giving your game a name makes it real instead of just an idea, as ridiculous as that may seem.

Try your very best to come up with a name that you like and that could end up being the final name for the game. Often whatever name is given to a game early on will end up sticking with the game forever. It is especially important not to pick a purposefully idiotic name, since those are the kind most likely to stick. For instance, let us say you name it *Egyptian Rumba*. As your team keeps referring to the game as *Egyptian Rumba*, they will start to associate your cool game with this idiotic title, and your idiotic title will start to sound pretty good through association. Someone working on the art team may start giving the characters an Egyptian color scheme. Team members who are working on the story might spend a lot of time trying to figure out why the game should be named *Egyptian Rumba*, and will develop an especially clever story line around the name. If later try to change the name they will be sad and possibly angry that their story no longer makes any sense. Even the "suits" will start to like your *Egyptian Rumba* title. They will think of how they can capture both the adventuring archeologist market and the Cuban dance market. And soon, if you even remember, you will say it is time to change the game's title, and everyone will say, "Why? We like *Egyptian Rumba*! It's a great name!" And then you will really be stuck. Then the public will see it on the shelves and will think, "What the heck is that? It sounds stupid," and quickly pass on to games with more reasonable titles.

So you finally choose *Winter Carnival Whirlwind*. Perhaps a more exciting name will come up later, but you can live with this one. Now, assemble the pieces of your focus into one paragraph, and try to write it cleanly and succinctly. Refer to your game in the present tense, as though your game already exists. "*Winter Carnival Whirlwind* is an exhilarating…" instead of "*Winter Carnival Whirlwind* will be an exhilarating…" This lends your game a more concrete existence in the minds of those who read your focus. It is not just a game that may come about at some point in the future; it already is a game, if only in your head. Something else to avoid is using generic descriptions that do not actually provide the reader with any useful information. For instance, "*Winter Carnival Whirlwind* is a high-quality, fun game that…" Of course it is supposed to be fun. Does anyone set out to create a boring or low-quality game? Edit out any sections of your focus that do not communicate important information about your game.

Putting together the parts of your focus, you will end up with the following:

> Winter Carnival Whirlwind *is a fast and furious character action and theme park management hybrid game. The player's experience revolves around running an ice carnival, with the player responsible for maintaining as long a season as possible, despite uncooperative weather. The game captures the excitement of playing in the snow, including the simple physics that make that fun, through a central character who must navigate a somewhat hazardous environment and keep multiple systems operating smoothly. The player's main source of conflict is the weather itself.* Winter Carnival Whirlwind *has a light and whimsical tone throughout.*

The Function of the Focus

Try to keep your focus from referring to other games. You want the focus to describe the essence of your game, and if your focus is, "*Voltarr* is like *Tomb Raider*, but set on the whimsical planet Dongo and featuring many intense laser gunfights," it is hard for someone looking at your focus to understand immediately what parts of *Tomb Raider* you are hoping to emulate. Take a look at *Tomb Raider* itself and determine what you think its focus may have been. Then take that focus, remove whatever parts are not necessary for your game, and add in whatever new ideas your game will incorporate. Chances are your idea of what was compelling about *Tomb Raider* will be different from

Your game may be similar to another game such as *Tomb Raider*, but in your focus you want to describe the game on its own terms and avoid making comparisons to other games.

someone else's understanding. When members of your team read, "It's like *Tomb Raider*," they are probably reminded of some different aspect of that game's gameplay than you are. That's assuming that they have played *Tomb Raider* at all. Since the focus is designed to guide your team members as well as yourself, it needs to communicate the same ideas to everyone who reads it. Even if the focus is primarily for your own use, the process of analyzing *Tomb Raider* to determine what about it you want to replicate will help you to better understand your own game. You need to have a properly stream-lined focus that can stand on its own, without demanding that the person who is reading the focus understand any other particular games. All the relevant information that is important to your focus must be contained within the focus itself, without outside references. Often when designers set out to create "It's like *Game X* but with…" games, they tend to lose sight of what made the game they are imitating so compelling in the first place. Then they proceed to make their own game top-heavy with tacked-on features that exist only to hide the fact their game is just like *Game X*. Removing references to other games from your focus will help expose the true nature of the project you are undertaking. If you add sufficient description revealing what it is about another game that you are trying to capture in your new design, it may be OK to leave in the reference to that original game since it can provide a helpful starting point for readers. This is a matter of individual preference when writing your focus, and I personally prefer to leave out other game references of any kind if at all possible.

Establishing a focus for your project does not need to limit the scope of your game, and is not intended to do so. Your game can still be a massively complex game with an epic sweep. In fact, if appropriate, this complexity and depth should probably be mentioned in your focus, but you should still be able to describe the game in a few sentences in order to succinctly communicate what is most important about your undertaking. Your game can even include multiple styles of gameplay within the same game. Suppose your goal is to simulate the life of a pirate. You might want to include an exploration mode for navigating the seas, a tactical mode for engaging another ship in battle, a sword-fighting mode for fighting an enemy captain one-on-one, and even a trading mode for selling off booty. (Indeed, Sid Meier already made this game; it is called *Pirates!*) But having this multiple game structure does not mean that the focus could not still consist of, "This game recreates the many different facets of a pirate's life through numerous different campaign modes, all designed to evoke the spirit of being a cutthroat. The player is able to explore the nature of being an outlaw, including the economic and physical risks involved." If your game is to have multiple separate modes, your focus should apply to all of the different sub-games within your project.

If you are working on a project solo or with a small team, you may think it unnecessary to actually write down your focus. After all, if you can just explain it to everyone who needs to know, what's the sense in writing it down? I would argue that writing it down is key to truly coming to grips with the nature of the game you are planning to develop. There is a world of difference between an idea that is kicking around in your head and one that is written down on paper in front of you. When it is on paper you can look at it and make sure that what is typed is really the core of your idea, and that those sentences represent everything that is most important to you about the project. Unlike when you describe the project to someone, on paper you cannot say, "Oh, yeah, and there's this part, and this other aspect over here, and I really mean this when I say that." If it is not down on the paper, it is not part of the game's focus. Someone who reads the focus on paper should be able to understand your vision without further explanation. I find that writing the focus down really helps to clarify and solidify what the game is attempting to achieve.

Though I did not know it at the time of the game's development, Odyssey's focus was centered on telling a specific story.

When I worked on my first game, *Odyssey*, I had no grand plan to have a focus. Nor did I sit down and purposefully think it out. On the other hand, I recall the primary goal revolving around a story. It was the story of a mad scientist-type character, a powerful sorcerer who performed experiments on hapless humanoid creatures. These were not biological experiments, but rather social ones — experiments where he would see how these humans would treat each other when placed in certain circumstances. Really, he was exploring the evil side of all sentient creatures. So *Odyssey*'s focus was to explore the mean and vicious ways different groups of people can treat each other in certain situations and to set up scenarios where the players witnessed this first-hand and would have a chance to make a real change in their lives. Non-linearity and multiple solutions were also at the forefront of my mind, so I set out to make sure players would be able to pursue different tactics to solve the problems they were presented with, with no solution being designated as the "right" one. And so I had my focus. Without really thinking of it in terms of a focus or vision, I had determined what I wanted to do with the game, and I was able to stick with that for the duration of the project. Since I was basically developing the project solo, I did not have to communicate this focus to anyone else, and if I had needed to I doubt that I could have without considerable reflection. Though I knew in my head what I wanted in the game, at the time I could not define my goals in terms someone else could understand. Now, looking back, I can come up with the following:

> In Odyssey, *the player explores a rich story line about the evil nature of mankind, and sees under what circumstances groups will treat each other in morally reprehensible ways. This is a simple RPG/adventure game. Though sword-and-sorcery combat will be involved, it never overtakes the*

story line. The story line allows for multiple solutions and non-linearity whenever possible, with the player able to effect real change among the NPCs he encounters in the game.

Maintaining Focus

Once you have a focus down on paper and can read it over and say with confidence, "Yes, certainly, that's what I'm going for," it is time to share it with the other members of your team. It is important that you get everyone on your team to "sign on" to your focus. You want them to acknowledge that, yes, this is the direction the team is taking, and to agree that they see a compelling game coming out of it in the end. If no one on your team thinks your focus is very captivating, and despite your best efforts to campaign for it no one can get excited about it, you can come to one of two conclusions. First, perhaps your game idea is not all that good. Hard as this may be to admit, it could be that your focus statement and possibly the game it describes are simply not original or enticing. If the idea in your head is still exciting to you, maybe you did not capture the correct focus properly on paper. You should go back and try to figure out what about the game excites you but did not come across in your focus.

If you persist in thinking your game is compelling and that your focus properly reflects why, it may be that people on your team are not excited by it because they were not involved in creating it. When working in a team environment, it is important to include people in early brainstorming sessions so that they can feel that they contributed to the birth of the idea. Even if not everyone's ideas end up being used, if you honestly listen to people and use not only your own ideas but the best ideas regardless of their source, you will end up with a happier team that respects your leadership. In the end, all projects can benefit from a strong central vision that is maintained by a single person, but that does not mean you need to lock yourself into a room to be "brilliant" all by yourself. It is often said that the best lead designers on large projects act primarily as filters, taking in ideas from all sources and molding them to fit into a single, unified vision. It may be that the focus you have come up with is quite strong and will produce a great game, but selling people on it will be trickier if they feel like they were needlessly excluded from its creation.

It may also be the case that the team assembled is simply the wrong one to develop the game you have come up with. Not every team can develop every type of game. A team that has been making sports games for years, likes working on sports games, and knows how to make a sports game fun is probably not the best team to enlist to create your nineteenth-century economics simulation. If you have the option of finding a new team for your game, you probably should. If not, you may need to come up with an idea that most of your team is going to find compelling. It is important that everyone on your team sees the value in your focused idea. Because of the collaborative nature of modern, high-budget computer games, it is virtually impossible to create a good game if you do not have the majority of your team excited to be working on it.

If you are working on a project largely by yourself with others contributing significantly less to the game than you, you may not need to sell your focus at all. Indeed, games created by lone wolf designer/programmer/artists can be among the most focused of computer games. Since one person is creating the vast majority of the game's content, he is able to exert absolute control over every nuance. Solo game development is typically not something at which one can earn a living these days, but I know of a few who manage it. Of course, the fact that a game was created largely by one individual does not assure that the game is going to be focused. If that individual is scatterbrained and unfocused himself, chances are good the game will not be very focused either. Even if he is a more sane, organized person, if he does not keep track of his game's focus over the course of the project, his game may end up being just as unfocused as the most uncoordinated, over-budgeted, fifty-developer game.

If you are working as a designer on a game with a team, it is essential to make sure the other people on your project, whether artists, programmers, or producers, understand the nature of the game's focus. Without a strong focus to guide their actions, programmers and artists may have a misunderstanding of what the game is supposed to accomplish, and may be thinking of some other type of game as they work on yours. Through no fault of their own, their work may deviate from what needs to happen for your game to become a reality, and you will be forced to say, "No, that doesn't fit, redo it." If the team has a focus to follow, a focus they have signed on to, then they are far less likely to create work that is inappropriate for your game. Having a strong focus does not get you out of keeping a watchful eye on the artists' and programmers' work, of course, but it will save you the trouble of having to redirect them too frequently.

Fleshing Out the Focus

Once the team is enthusiastic about the project, has signed on to the focus, and has a clear understanding of what the game is supposed to be, you can proceed to more fully flesh out your idea through a complete design document. You may even want to make your focus the beginning of your document, as a sort of summary of the nature of the game that people can read quickly. (The nature and creation of design documents is more fully explored in Chapter 19, "The Design Document.") The design document should take the game suggested by your focus and expand on it, detailing how the goals in your focus will be accomplished by gameplay and precisely how that gameplay will function. You will also be sketching out the flow of the game, what the game-world will be like, and what sort of entities the player will encounter. Of course, while you are working on the design document, there will be countless points at which you have to struggle to come up with the correct solution to a given problem. Should the control system use method A or method B? In what sort of environments will the player be interacting? What sort of challenges do the enemies present? A properly designed focus will allow you to refer back to it to answer many of the questions you encounter during the design process. As these elements of the game are fleshed out, you should continually refer back to your focus to see if the additions you are making match with that focus. Through the focus, you can carefully consider if you are adding gameplay that takes the game in a new direction. It is important to identify which additions to your game cause it to deviate from the focus, and then to change or eliminate those erroneous elements.

You want to avoid having your game become too bloated with features, components that may be "cool" in some way but that do not support the game's main focus or that distract the player's attentions. Using your focus as a tool, you can prevent this overexpansion by cutting away the chaff in your game design to leave only the core gameplay for which you were striving. Many of the ideas you or members of your team have may be fine concepts, but if they do not fit the game you are currently working on, they are not worth exploring or implementing. Do not throw these incompatible ideas away, however. Write them down in your notebook for the next time you are working on a game design. If they are good ideas, there is probably some game with which they will work well. If they are very good ideas, you may even want to design an entire game around them. But for the current project, by referring back to your focus you should be able to determine whether these extra, cool features are helping or hurting your game as a whole.

Once the design document is finished and other elements of preproduction are completed, full production can start on your game. Your team of programmers, artists, and other personnel will begin attempting to implement what you have set out to accomplish in your design document. As the project proceeds, there will be countless times where questions arise. Your design document will not cover everything needed to actually make the game playable; it cannot possibly. Questions will come up about how to implement a feature, in addition to new ideas about how to improve the game. For each of these, again, you should refer back to your focus to clarify your team's direction. Is the implementation that is being suggested going to keep the game on track with the focus or will it distract from the main thrust of the game? Is the distraction going to be too much of a diversion? Using your focus statement wisely throughout the course of the project will keep the game on the right course, and will result in an end product that is better because of it. Players will know the difference between a game that is properly focused and one that is not, even if they do not communicate their feelings in so many words. They will play and enjoy a focused game and will quickly cast aside one that is unfocused.

Changing Focus

Of course, either while working on your design document or when the game is in full production, it may become apparent that the goals of your game need to change. This can happen for a variety of reasons. You may come to see shortcomings or failings in your original focus. Through the act of creating your game, you may come to recognize a more compelling experience that the game can provide that is outside the scope of your original focus. Depending on where you are in the project's development, you may want to change your focus. This is particularly painless to do when you are still in the preproduction phase and the design document is not yet complete. In fact, you should expect your focus to change several times, if not on a daily basis, while you are working on the design document. There is nothing like trying to write down all the important information about your game to expose holes and failings in your original concept.

Even beyond the design document, when you are working on your game's first level you may begin to see weaknesses in your design, holes you had not anticipated when you were just working with an idea of the gameplay in your head instead of a playable game on the screen in front of you. At this point making changes to the focus is still not catastrophically damaging to your schedule and will not involve redoing much work. Better to fix problems in the game and your focus now than to be stuck with them for the rest of the project and end up with an inferior game.

When changing the focus, you should take the same care as you did when you initially came up with it. Make sure the focus fully represents your new vision for the project. Of course, if your focus changes radically, you will need to tell the team about the change and make sure they all agree with it. Remember, the team needs to be behind the project in order for it to succeed, and if you change the focus in such a way that the team is no longer interested in working on the project, you need to rethink that change or rethink your team.

For whatever reason or in whatever way you may change your focus, it is important to examine what parts of the game may already exist and see how far they diverge from your new focus. Look over the design document and realign it to your new goals. Consider whatever game mechanics may be in place and see if they are sufficient to carry the new focus. Look over whatever levels may exist (hopefully not too many have been created at this point) and see if they fit with the new focus. Whether it is in documentation, code, level design, or art, anything that does not fit will need to be reworked so that the new focus is properly supported.

If too many assets need to be reworked, or if it is too close to the ship date to change them, or if there is not enough funding available to get them changed, you may need to rethink changing your direction. Is it really necessary? Often, after you have been working on a project for a long time, you may want to change your game just to keep it interesting to yourself. What seemed fun to you a year ago may seem dull now, not because it fundamentally is not fun but because you have been buried in the project too long. Avoid changing things just because you are tired of them, since your players, seeing it for the first time, will think it is fantastic and throwing out all the good work of your team would be a tragedy.

However, even late in the project you may find out that your game truly is not what you had hoped, and a refocus is necessary to fix it. At this point you need to move into a damage control mode. Can you make the change in direction less drastic while still solving the problems, such that the old assets can still be used? The worst decision you can make is to create whatever new assets the game needs following a new focus, while the old assets still follow the inferior focus you had embraced previously. Instead of focusing the game, your two focuses will end up creating a game with a split personality, one that is entirely unfocused. Try your very hardest to come up with a refocusing plan for your project that will not put you over budget or schedule, if these are pressing concerns (as they almost always are). Realizing your project is not as good as it could be, but lacking the time or money to fix it properly is a tough position to be in. Finding the best solution in such difficult situations can be extremely challenging and frustrating.

When I worked on *Centipede 3D*, we ended up changing our focus near the beginning of the project. This resulted in some amount of work needing to be redone, but it also led to a significantly stronger game in the end. *Centipede 3D* was something of a special case since it was a remake of a classic and much-loved game, the original Atari *Centipede*, created by Ed Logg. When doing a remake or a sequel, it makes sense to take a look at the original game you are working from, and get a clear understanding, for yourself, of what its focus was. This is necessary so you will have a good idea of what exactly you are remaking. Of course I was not present when Logg was making the original *Centipede* in 1979 and 1980, but I can try to guess what his focus might have been:

> Centipede *is a fast-action shooting game involving a variety of adversaries that the player must kill in order to avoid being killed by them. The enemies move in completely predictable, predetermined patterns, but the combination of the movement of these creatures and other objects in the game-world creates a challenging experience for the player. The player can attempt to change the game-world to make the adversaries' movements less threatening, and the player can see the entire game-world at once. The game continues until the player dies a specific number of times, with points accumulating to represent how well the player did in that particular game; there is no winning or finishing* Centipede.

That focus is probably too long and too detailed to be a proper game focus, but it is hard for me to read Ed Logg's mind to know what his core concerns were when making *Centipede*. So I have included all of the crucial parts of the game I can find. Of course, the focus he used may bear no relationship at all to the one above, if he used a focus at all.

The focus of the 3D version of *Centipede* was to create a game that captured the arcade game-play of the original *Centipede* in a three-dimensional, level-based environment.

When development of *Centipede 3D* initially got under way, the idea was to take only the most basic characters of *Centipede* — the player's shooter ship, the centipedes, spiders, fleas, and mushrooms — and have them interact in a 3D world. The decision to move the game to 3D was already a foregone conclusion when we started working on the project. It was a choice whose appropriateness was certainly debatable given the fundamental mechanics of the original. Indeed, from conception through the earliest versions of the game, not much attention was paid to the game mechanics and behaviors of the original. The elements from the original *Centipede* were being used more for aesthetics than anything else. When our initial game prototype turned out not to be very fun, we decided to try to emulate more of the original game's gameplay in the new 3D version, wherever possible imitating and updating whatever the 1981 *Centipede* did in a 3D, level-based world. As we started pursuing our new focus, we found that the more we emulated the classic, the more fun the new game became. Though it was not written down at the time, you could say our focus was along the lines of the following:

> Centipede 3D *is a remake of the arcade game* Centipede, *and attempts to take what that original game did well and transplant it to a 3D environment. The original* Centipede *featured fast-action shooting combat in waves, with the player's deft maneuvering of the ship being the key to success, and with enemies that moved in completely predictable patterns. Instead of being on one level for the entire game as* Centipede *was,* Centipede 3D *takes the player through a progression of levels. The new game also embraces certain gameplay norms of modern console games, such as replayable levels, bonus objectives, and obstacle navigation. The action and combat portions of* Centipede 3D, *however, will be extremely reminiscent of the original game, employing identical AI wherever possible, and thus retaining the gameplay feel of the original.*

With our new focus, the game assets we had developed thus far were readdressed, and a number of levels had to be discarded, while others were significantly reworked. A small amount of coding that had been done had to be modified, but fortunately no change in the artwork was necessary. All told, our refocus resulted in some loss of work. However, in the end this lost work was worth it because the final *Centipede 3D* had a consistent, focused style of gameplay. And as a direct result, it was fun to play.

It is important to note that our focus for *Centipede 3D* was not a standalone focus as I advocated earlier in this chapter. The focus for *Centipede 3D* refers to another game, the original *Centipede*, and thereby does not stand completely on its own. Of course, *Centipede 3D* is a remake, and as such it makes sense to refer to the game the project follows. For either a remake or a sequel, the game you are making has a direct relation to the other game you refer to in the focus, and a large part of whether the game is deemed a success or not will rest on how well it follows up its predecessor. As such, throughout the game's development, the team members should be asking themselves how their work relates to the original game, and whether what they are trying to accomplish in terms of gameplay is a logical and worthy successor. Since this is such a central concern, it belongs in the focus. In working on a sequel or a remake, your entire team should have played the original game through, and hence can be expected to understand it reasonably well. Note, however, that the focus for *Centipede 3D* includes a brief description of the primary appeal of the original *Centipede*, so that the focus can stand by itself better than if the central concerns of the classic game were assumed. If the focus must refer to another game, it is important to make sure everyone involved with the project understands the focus of that other game as well.

Sub-Focuses

It may be advantageous to take the focus technique to another level by including sub-focuses. Though not absolutely necessary, this will allow you to start to flesh out your game idea while keeping track of your overall focus. A sub-focus is distinct from the main focus, and should be designated as such when presented alongside the main focus. You can see a sub-focus as a concept that supports your main focus, and one that will help your game attain that central focus. A sub-focus alone cannot be used to design a game. It serves primarily to support your main goal, to break apart other objectives your game will strive for in an attempt to accomplish the central focus.

For an example of using sub-focuses, I will return to the *Winter Carnival Whirlwind* example. As you may remember, you had come up with a focus for a game that puts players in charge of a winter carnival. Now that you have the central focus for *Winter Carnival Whirlwind* squared away, you can consider what other goals the game may have. What other aspects of the game should the development team focus on to assure that our gameplay vision is implemented in the best way possible?

Now might be a time to explore what type of player you are thinking will want to play your game. Are you appealing more to the hard-core gaming crowd, or to people who maybe do not play computer games quite so often? This will have a direct effect on many aspects of the game, including what level of simulation will need to be created (the hard-core gamers will demand a more involved and complex gameplay experience), as well as the control system the game will use (hard-core gamers can put up with a more obtuse and convoluted control scheme if that provides a deeper play experience in the end, while more casual gamers will need something they can pick up quickly).

Perhaps it has long been your desire to make a game that all of your non-gamer friends could enjoy. Thus you decide you want to go for the more casual gaming crowd. This means you can create a sub-focus explaining what you will do to skew the game toward this audience: "*Winter Carnival Whirlwind* appeals to more casual gamers." It makes sense to explain just what you mean by making the game appeal to casual gamers. Probably the biggest issue is control; you want *Winter Carnival Whirlwind* to allow people to get in and play the game quickly, without confusing them with a lot of keys to remember to control the main character. Your focus could read: "The game provides the simplest control scheme possible, with a player needing to use a small number of easily remembered keys to successfully play the game. Novice players can figure out how to play the game without reading the manual or playing the tutorial, though a training mission will be provided." Note that you do not actually want to go into what the controls are at this point. Save that for the design document. Here you are just working on your goals for the game, not so much the specifics of how they will be implemented. You may also want to say something about the game's difficulty level. If you are aiming at casual gamers, you are probably going to want to make the game easier than it would be if it were aimed more at the hard-core market. You may want to specify that the game will play at various difficulty levels: "*Winter Carnival Whirlwind* is of a relatively low overall difficulty, with the player able to specify difficulty levels in the game. Even marginally skilled, poor players will be able to play the game to completion on the easiest difficulty level, given enough attempts."

It might make sense to talk about what type of engine and graphics your game will have in one of the sub-focuses. We discussed previously whether the game should be 2D or 3D, but decided that aspect was not central to our vision of the game. Therefore it was left out of the primary focus. It may, however, fit well as a sub-focus, something that will help further define how the game's development will carry out the initial vision. Now might be a good time to explain the visual style of the game as best you can, to give your art team an idea of what direction they should pursue, as well as your programming team what sort of technology your game will need to support. Furthermore, you may want to consider our previous sub-focus here. It states that this game is supposed to appeal to the casual gaming audience, and that the game is supposed to be fairly easy to play. Thus you will want your statements about the game's graphics to support this if appropriate. *"Winter Carnival Whirlwind* features a visually lush, high-contrast environment. Despite being set in a somewhat monochromatic snow and ice environment, specular effects will be used to clearly differentiate different types of ice. The player character along with the patrons of the winter carnival will be brightly colored in their cold weather gear in order to set them off from the environment and make them easier to see." You may decide you want to pursue a 3D engine technology that handles physics well, since that can best help capture the out-of-control nature of running around in snow and ice, and since the nature of the marketplace demands a 3D game. As part of the 3D engine, perhaps a variable-zoom third-person view is the one that will work best to allow the player to control their harried carnival manager while keeping an eye on all the attractions. So your focus statement could include: "The game uses a 3D engine that allows for the player to easily zoom in and out on the micro or macro events taking place at the winter carnival, with the technology capable of rendering the entire carnival at once when necessary."

Of course, there could be numerous other sub-focuses for *Winter Carnival Whirlwind*, covering everything from gameplay mechanics to what sort of story line the game will have, to how long an average game should last. Always try to avoid putting in too much detail, however. That is for the design document. Here you are merely setting the project's direction, not actually implementing it. But for the purposes of our example, we have enough sub-focuses now, leaving us with a focus and sub-focuses that look like this:

> Winter Carnival Whirlwind *is a fast and furious character action and theme park management hybrid game. The player's experience revolves around running an ice carnival, with the player responsible for maintaining as long a season as possible, despite uncooperative weather. The game captures the excitement of playing in the snow, including the simple physics that make that fun, through a central character who must navigate a somewhat hazardous environment and keep multiple systems operating smoothly. The player's main source of conflict is the weather itself.* Winter Carnival Whirlwind *has a light and whimsical tone throughout.*

> ### Audience
> Winter Carnival Whirlwind *appeals to more casual gamers. The game provides the simplest control scheme possible, with a player needing to use a small number of easily remembered keys to successfully play the game. Novice players can figure out how to play the game without reading the manual or playing the tutorial, though a training mission will be provided.* Winter Carnival Whirlwind *is of a relatively low overall difficulty, with the player able to specify difficulty levels in the game. Even marginally skilled, poor players will be able to play the game to completion on the easiest difficulty level, given enough attempts.*

> ### Visuals
> Winter Carnival Whirlwind *features a visually lush, high-contrast environment. Despite being set in a somewhat monochromatic snow and ice environment, specular effects will be used to clearly differentiate different*

types of ice. The player character along with the patrons of the winter carnival will be brightly colored in their cold weather gear in order to set them off from the environment. The game uses a 3D engine that allows for the player to easily zoom in and out on the micro or macro events taking place at the winter carnival, with the technology capable of rendering the entire carnival at once when necessary.

Notice how the sub-focuses are set off by separate headings from the primary focus. This way, readers of the focus can easily see the primary and most important focus and how the sub-focuses go into detail about specific parts of the game.

As you are working on your sub-focuses, it is important to always make sure that they jibe with your primary focus, as well as any other sub-focuses you may have. For instance, it makes sense that the Visuals sub-focus talks about the game providing a game-world that is simple to understand visually, since the Audience sub-focus talks about making the game easy to pick up and get into. If you are already contradicting yourself in the writing of your focus you are going to have a very hard time writing a whole design document that makes any sense at all. Keeping all the components of your focuses supporting each other should not be a problem, however, since properly written focuses should be short, concise, and easy to understand.

Using Focus

It is important to realize that your focus statement is not a marketing tool. It is not created to sell your game to the executives. It is not written with the hope of printing it on the back of the box or showing it to the people in charge of purchasing for large retailers. It is first and foremost written as a development tool for your team. Writing a statement that clearly establishes the goals of your game will be hard enough without also trying to craft something that will work for the marketing folks. Nevertheless, you may be able to take your focus and change it into something to get your marketing department excited about your game. If generating a significant number of sales is one of the items on your agenda (let us presume it is not your primary motivation for working in games, for surely there are more profitable careers to pursue), then having the marketing people get excited about your game when they try to sell it is almost as important as having the programmers excited during the game's development. Marketing people will try to sell games they believe in and that they think are cool concepts, and a modified and adapted version of your focus statement can serve to quickly explain to them what is so thrilling about your idea. Of course, marketing people also love comparative descriptions, such as, "The game's basically *Bejeweled* meets *Max Payne*." Thus, you may want to come up with some direct comparisons that place your game within the context of known popular games, games that the marketing specialists already know how to sell. Of course, you can use the content of your focus to back up such superficial comparisons and to make the marketing folk understand why your game is unique and will appeal to gamers. With this knowledge in hand, hopefully they can make an ad campaign that is an appropriate representation of your game and not something that you will be embarrassed by when you see it in the magazines.

Regardless of what other applications you may find for it, always remember that you wrote down your focus in order to help your game's development. Many game designers do not have a focus when they are working on a game, and it shows. Some fear it because they do not want to become "locked" into any one idea. Such trepidation is unfounded since you have the freedom to change your focus whenever you want. Indeed, without writing it down, you may not even realize that a change of course is warranted. Of course, it is possible to make a good game without really having any idea of what your game is all about. It is also possible to win the lottery. When your livelihood, reputation, and the quality of your final game are on the line, however, you want something more than luck to determine if your game works or not. Using a focus is one tool that will help you to create a solid, entertaining, and compelling game.

Chapter 6:
Interview: Ed Logg

Asteroids, *Centipede*, and *Gauntlet*. If there was ever an impressive track record for a game designer, that is it. Throw in some lesser-known classics such as *Super Breakout*, *Millipede*, *Gauntlet II*, and *Xybots*, and you have a truly unequaled career. Ed Logg designed and developed all of those titles at Atari back in the heyday of the arcades. Before the collapse of the coin-op market, Logg had already switched to working in home game development, adapting popular Atari arcade games such as the *San Francisco Rush* series to consoles. Subsequently, Logg took on an original home game for the first time, serving as lead programmer on the unique platformer *Dr. Muto*. Today Logg has returned to his roots, working on games for mobile phones. To look at them, the classic arcade games seem quite simple, but it is that simplicity which forced their designers to refine them to the point of perfection. Logg's classic coin-op games remain some of the best computer games ever made, and the insight designers can gain from studying them is enormous.

What was it like working at Atari in the late '70s and early '80s?

We were young and energetic. I imagine it is very similar to the atmosphere at most Internet start-ups these days. We were a relatively small group in the Coin Operated Games Division. This allowed everyone to know everyone else. Ideas and pranks flowed freely. Since we were working on a new medium we could do anything and it would be "new." Even games like *Lunar Lander*, done by Rich Moore, which had been done originally years before, were new to our audience.

Where did most of the ideas for the games come from?

The ideas came from many sources. For example, Owen Rubin, another engineer at Atari, told me Nolan Bushnell had suggested to him an extension of *Breakout*. I took his idea and added many of my own to create *Super Breakout*, my first commercial success. The idea for *Asteroids* came from Lyle Rains, who was in charge of engineering at the time. He got the idea from a previous coin-op game. *Xybots* came from a challenge by Doug Snyder, a hardware engineer at Atari. We wanted to do a multi-player *Castle Wolfenstein*-like game but we had no "bit-map" hardware. So I created an algorithm based on 8 by 8 stamps and he did the hardware. *Centipede* came from a list of brainstorming ideas. Atari would go off-site each year to think up new ideas. One of those ideas was "Bug Shooter," which was used as a starting point for *Centipede*.

Asteroids

Management had reviews where they would come in and play the game and give feedback. Sometimes the consensus was negative and a game could be killed. Most often it would continue until it could be "field tested." This meant it was left to the players to determine how much and for how long the game earned. However, sometimes good suggestions came from these reviews. The most important one of all was a suggestion made by Dan Van Elderen, who was in charge of engineering. He asked me why we could not shoot the mushrooms in *Centipede*. Yes, the mushrooms were originally static. It was his suggestion that led to the breakthrough that made this game fun.

Were you excited to get into game development at Atari?

Actually, I had been doing games for many years on the side, while in high school, at Berkeley in the '60s, and also at my first job at Control Data Corp. I ported *Star Trek* and the original *Dungeon* game between Stanford's and CDC's computers.

I had built a home computer a year or two before joining Atari, just to create and play games. I had been to a Pizza Time Theater and played *Pong* and *Breakout*, so I was well aware of the coin-op business. I had also played games and was very inspired by a prototype of the Atari VCS (2600) at a Christmas party in 1977. So the change in employment seemed natural for me. At the time I thought it was great for them to pay me to create and play games.

Dirt Bike **was your first game for Atari, but I understand it didn't make it into production. What sort of game was it?**

This game was started by Dennis Koble who went on to do many consumer titles. It was a game similar to *Sprint* except you drove a dirt bike and the control was a set of handlebars that could be used to steer the bike instead of a steering wheel.

We field tested the game and it earned enough money to make it good enough not to kill outright but not good enough to make it into production. However, I had made *Super Breakout* at the same time I was working on *Dirt Bike*. No one at Atari had ever worked on two games at once before. *Super Breakout* had earned a large amount of money, and this probably led to the decision not to build *Dirt Bike*. I was not disappointed considering the success of *Super Breakout*.

What was the genesis of *Super Breakout*?

The original idea included six variations on *Breakout*. I envisioned three released games with two variations in each game. However, in actual play there was one overall favorite: *Progressive Breakout*. In the end we put three variations in one game: *Progressive*, *Double*, and *Cavity Breakout*. The variations that did not make it were more vertically oriented and I had to agree they were not as fun.

Were you given a lot of creative freedom on *Super Breakout*, or were you constrained since it was a sequel to a previous hit?

To me, *Super Breakout* was not a sequel. Remember, the original game was not done in software. The code had to be created from scratch and the gameplay was completely different from the original even though we used the same controls.

I was given freedom because I was doing the title without any official sanction. It was not the last time I would do that, either. Games could be done in a short time in those days, which meant you could make something fun before anyone even noticed you were doing anything different.

Maybe I should explain how we were developing games in those days. We had one main Digital computer which had the cross assembler for our 6502 based games. We had several gals who would enter our handwritten pages into our programs and

Super Breakout

give us back a computer printout and a paper tape. Yes, you heard that right. We would then feed the paper tape through our development system into the RAM replacing the game ROM on the PCB. We would debug this using primitive tools and a hardware analyzer and write our changes on the paper printout. Since this process left time between the debug session and the next version, I used this time to develop a second game. I would just swap the graphics PROM (yes, we created the graphics by hand ourselves), and load the new paper tape.

That's really astonishing that you ever developed a game using such primitive methods. How did you manage to fine-tune your game with such a long time between versions?

Well, actually, I was very good at just patching RAM with new instructions, so it was easy to see what small changes did to the game. We also had an HP analyzer that we could use to trap on many conditions, which allowed us to find many bugs that many development systems cannot even do today. Actually it was possible to do some new coding while you were waiting for your last changes to be made, so less time was lost than you think.

But you would certainly agree that modern development tools have made game development easier?

There are several issues here. First, back then we often knew everything about the target hardware, which made it easier to see what was going wrong. Today, the target hardware is often hidden from us and there are several layers of software, which can make debugging or doing what we really want to do difficult. So in this sense it is much harder now. Also, these modern software or hardware layers are often not documented, documented incorrectly, or just getting in our way. Second, the hardware has gotten very complex with interactions between the many bytes causing all sorts of problems. Third, the processors have become very complex, causing all sorts of debugging nightmares, especially in dealing with the caches. Fourth, today there are many programmers working on a game and it is easy to mess up one of your coworkers.

Surprisingly, the development environment has not gotten any faster over the past few years despite the great increases in the computing power and RAM. As an example, some of my files on my 25 MHz Mac IIci with 6 MB of RAM compile and link in the same time or faster than files on a 550 MHz PC under NT with 512 MB of RAM. Even the same project on my 150 MHz Indy builds faster than my 550 MHz PC. I firmly believe that every tool developer should be given the slowest possible system to use to develop their software! Otherwise, we are doomed to continue to run no faster with each new upgrade.

The modern tools are so much better than the old method, it is hard to imagine how I could have done so well, but you mustn't forget how much time is spent learning each new software tool, processor, and operating system these days. In addition, the amount of time wasted chasing after bugs on new systems because I did not understand some other hardware or software is quite large. But I would not want to go back to the old tools unless the processors, hardware, software, game concepts, and team sizes were much simpler.

I've never seen your next game, *Video Pinball*. How did it play?

It simulated pinball by using a half-silvered mirror with a monitor below the mirror and the graphics for the play-field above the mirror. The monitor would show the flippers and ball, which gave the impression the white ball was on the play-field. The play-field actually had LEDs controlled by the program which simulated lit targets. In addition, the control panel was hinged, which allowed the player to "nudge" the cabinet to give the ball some English. I did not think this game up. I believe it was Dave Stubben's idea.

How did you hope to convince players to play *Video Pinball* instead of the real thing?

I did not believe *Video Pinball* would be successful and I was asking that exact question. However, there were places video games could go that a large pinball game could not. In the end, the game earned more than I had expected and it was a commercial success. I must say I was wrong on my first impressions, and that does not happen often.

Was it hard to work on a project that you did not think would be any fun? Did the final game turn out to be entertaining?

The gameplay was fun but no comparison to a real pinball game. I was surprised that it sold as well as it did. Yes, it was hard to work on an idea that I did not think would work well. But I was young and motivated… What else can I say?

Where did the idea for *Asteroids* come from?

Lyle Rains had suggested to me the idea of a game where the player could shoot asteroids because there had been an earlier coin-op game with an indestructible asteroid that the players kept shooting instead of pursuing the intended goal. I told Lyle we would need a saucer to force the player to shoot the asteroids instead of wasting time. I also suggested breaking the rocks up into pieces to give the players some strategy instead of just shooting the larger rocks first.

Asteroids

Lyle gave me the idea. People often attribute the success to one or the other of us. I would probably not have come up with the idea on my own, and if someone else had done the game it would most likely have been totally different. So in truth, we should both be given credit for this idea. Come to think of it, without the vector hardware, *Asteroids* would not have been a success either. So there are many people and events that led to its success. I am very glad to have been there at that time and place.

The game changed very little in development from the original idea. I did make two saucers, one dumb and one smart. I made one fundamental change near the end of the project that had far-reaching implications. Originally, the saucer would shoot as soon as the player entered the screen. Players complained — and I agreed — this seemed unfair. Often the saucer was not visible just off the edge, and if it started next to your ship you had no defense. So I added a delay before his first shot. This, of course, led to the "lurking" strategy. While testing, I had actually tried to lurk at one point and decided it was not going to work, which shows you how well the game designer can play his own game.

Were you surprised by *Asteroids'* success?

I was not surprised by its success. It sounded like a fun game when I played it in my mind. Even after the first few weeks, people would come by and ask when they could play. That was a sign your game was fun!

Even when we field tested the game for the very first time, I saw a player start a game and die three times within 20 seconds. He proceeded to put another quarter in. This tells me the player felt it was his fault he died and he was convinced he could do better. This is one of the primary goals a game designer tries to achieve and it was clear to me *Asteroids* had "it."

Back there you mentioned that you played the game out "in your mind." Do you find that to be an effective technique for predicting whether a game will be fun or not?

It is a skill which I find works well for me. I also play devil's advocate with my ideas. I ask myself, "What can go wrong?" or "Will players be confused by what I am presenting?" I find that some designers often are so married to their ideas that they will not accept the concept that maybe it just won't work. I cannot tell you the number of great ideas I have had that I "played out" in my mind that turned out to be bad ideas.

Asteroids

I am one of the few designers I have ever met that has actually killed many of his own games. I think this is a good trait. Why waste another year to two if the gameplay does not play like you expected?

Did you work on the sequel, *Asteroids Deluxe*?

I did not do *Asteroids Deluxe*. It was done by Dave Shepperd. I was promoted around that time into a supervisor role. I believe I was also leading the four-player *Football* project. So I was busy. I have no problem doing sequels if that is the best course of action. I had some new ideas, so I wanted to do *Millipede*. *Gauntlet II* was a logical choice since Bob Flanagan, my co-programmer, and I knew the code and this was the best game concept we came up with.

After *Asteroids* you didn't make another vector-based game. Did you not like working with the hardware?

Actually, I loved vector hardware for the reason it allowed me to put up high-resolution 1024 by 768 graphics. However, the industry was just moving over to color monitors at the time. Dave Theurer did do *Tempest* as a color vector game, but the color mask on color monitors did not permit high resolution. Besides, you could not fill the screen with color on vector-based games, so that medium died with the advance of color games.

Wasn't *Asteroids* the first Atari game to have a high-score table?

Actually, *Asteroids* was not the first game; there was another game that used it just prior. I thought the idea was a great way to preserve your score and identity for the world to see. So I added it to *Asteroids*. I see it as filling the role of graffiti. Now it is standard, of course, and the industry has added battery-backed RAM or EEROM to save it permanently.

Around this time you created the *Othello* cartridge for the Atari 2600. I understand you studied AI while at Stanford. Did the *Othello* project grow out of your interest in AI?

No, actually *Asteroids* showed more influence from my Stanford experience. While I was at the Stanford AI Lab, I had played *Space War* on their PDP machines. I had also played a coin-op version of this in the Student Forum coffee shop. In my mind, this was the first video game. *Pong* certainly was the first commercial video game. Anyway, the spaceship design in *Asteroids* was a copy of the original *Space War* ship.

I had played *Othello* as a board game and I was intrigued by possible strategies. So I worked on this game at home and developed an idea that the game could be played by pattern matching without any AI. In other words, the computer does not look ahead at your replies to any of its moves, which was the standard AI approach at the time. So really the *Othello* game I did had no AI. It was good enough for the beginner and average player. It was not an advanced game by any means. Besides, the 2600 had only 128 bytes of RAM so there was not much space to look ahead.

In fact, Carol Shaw had done the hard part by providing me the kernel which drew the pieces on a checkerboard. The 2600 was extremely difficult to do anything complex on. It was intended to do *Pong*-style games. You spent all of active video counting cycles to draw the screen. This left Vblank to do any thinking or other work. There was limited RAM so nothing complex could be saved in RAM. *Othello* was 2,048 bytes. Most of this was the kernel. So I often spent time trying to eliminate a few bytes to add something new.

Was *Centipede* your next game?

No, as I mentioned I was a supervisor at the time. I was project leader on four-player *Football* and a kit to upgrade the plays on the original *Football* game.

On *Centipede*, I thought up the idea of the centipede segments and the way the legs moved. I do not believe it was mentioned in the original "Bug Shooter" brainstorming idea. In fact, no one has ever stepped forward to claim "Bug Shooter" as their idea.

Maybe it was due to the finished product being so much different from the original idea. I had assigned a new programmer, Donna Bailey, to do the programming on *Centipede*. Partway through the project, I quit being a supervisor (I didn't like the job and it took me away from doing games) and spent time working on *Centipede*.

So Bailey was pretty important to the game's development?

I would guess she did about half the programming. The game design was left to me because she was working on her first project.

It seems that *Centipede* appeals to women more than most arcade games. Do you think Bailey had something to do with that?

I wish I knew the answer to that question. Someone could point out that no other game I have done appeals to women as much as *Centipede*.

Many theories have been suggested. One is that is was created by a woman. Another is that destroying insects fits well with a woman's psyche. I believe this game appeals to women because it is not gender biased like fighting games or RPGs or sports games. Other examples like *Pac-Man* and *Tetris* are notable.

Centipede

I do know *Centipede* fits the basic criterion for a game that appeals to a wide audience. It has a new, appealing look (to get players to try it), an obvious goal (shoot anything), clear rules, an easy set of controls, a sense of accomplishment (kill the entire centipede before he gets you), dynamic strategies abound (trap the centipede and kill spiders or the blob strategy or channel the centipede or just plain straight-up play), enough randomness to make the game different each time, a goal to keep you going (a new life every 12,000 points), a clear sense of getting better with more play, and a sense that any death was the player's fault.

So you mentioned that *Centipede* grew out of a brainstorming idea. How did the brainstorming process work at Atari?

The brainstorming ideas came from anyone in the company. They were usually gathered weeks before the actual meeting which was held off-site, away from Atari. Often the ideas were just a theme. Most submittals had sort of a sketch or art to give the reader a little more info. Occasionally a full game description was submitted which explained the hardware, controls, art, and gameplay.

During the brainstorming session, each idea would be presented and then suggestions would be made for improving it. In addition, marketing would give a rundown of what was selling and the state of the industry. We would also break into smaller groups to discuss a specific type of game or talk about specific games themselves. In the end we would meet again to present any additional ideas from these smaller meetings and vote for the popular ideas. I would say we would get a majority from programmers and designers, but there were a significant number of ideas from artists and others in the company. I found many of the ideas needed a lot of work, so it was not uncommon for the original brainstorming idea to get a major overhaul.

Atari Games Corp., now Midway Games West, still uses this process each year. But quite honestly, many of the recent coin-op games are just remakes of older games. For example, more versions of *Rush* or *Cruisin'*. The reason is often market driven: these are the games that have done well in the past and the company does not often want to risk taking a chance on a new theme.

How did *Centipede* change over the course of the game's development?

I mentioned that Dan Van Elderen asked why the player could not shoot mushrooms. I realized early I would need some means to create new mushrooms. This led to one being left when a centipede segment was shot. I also created the flea which left a trail of them when he dropped to create more randomness in the pattern. In other words, I did not want the player to create the only pattern of mushrooms. The spider was always planned to be my "*Asteroids* saucer" which kept the player moving; the spider also had to eat mushrooms to keep the player area somewhat free of mushrooms. The scorpion was added to add a randomness to the centipede pattern and create a sense of panic when the segments would come rushing to the bottom of the screen.

Centipede

Do you try to create games that allow different players to use different strategies to succeed?

I do strive to give the players as much freedom to create as many strategies as possible. So in a sense, yes, I guess I do encourage players to experiment and try different strategies. I do try to make sure that none of them work all the time or make the game too easy. But I want to leave the player with the impression that if he was only a little bit better he could pull it off.

Why did you choose to use the trackball for *Centipede?*

I believe we used the trackball from the start. I had experience with the trackball on *Football*, but I wanted something that was not as heavy and physical to move around. That is how the *Centipede* trackball came about. The trackball, just like the computer mouse, provides a means for inputting arbitrary direction as well as speed. No other controller comes close. It was the clear winner for player controllability.

In my opinion, *Centipede* is one of the best balanced games ever. Was there a lot of experimentation to achieve such a balance?

I would not use the term experimentation in this case because nothing was tried and discarded. There was a grasshopper that we intended to add to hop onto the player, but the spider was sufficient in forcing the player to move so the grasshopper was never even tried. Of course, you can still see the graphics for the grasshopper if you look at the self-test graphics.

There certainly was a lot of tuning. The timing and speed of when things happened certainly was changed over the course of the project. The balance comes from the inherent rules of the game and the art of knowing when to leave the play alone and when to change something. This art is something that some people have and others just don't. I cannot define it other than to use the term "game sense."

Were you given freedom to do whatever you wanted for *Millipede*?

With my past record I was given more freedom than anyone else. Something most people do not understand is that half of the games I started did not make it into production. No one ever hears about the failures. Some of the games I actually killed myself. That's something I believe no one else at Atari did. Of course, there are a few I tried to kill but was not allowed to that eventually died. These days you would probably see them come out in the consumer market anyway just to get back some of the development cost. But in the coin-op market there is no chance to sell anything that isn't a clear winner.

Millipede

***Millipede* allowed players to start farther into the game, at 45,000 points, for example. Was this an effort to shorten the games of the expert players?**

It was a way to increase the cash box. It allowed the good players to start at a higher score where the gameplay was on a difficulty level that was probably just above his level of skill. This often meant shorter game times but would allow higher scores. In a sense I was doing this for marketing reasons. This was not a first for *Millipede*. *Tempest* had this feature back in 1981.

I particularly like the "growth" of the extra mushrooms in *Millipede*. Was this done using a "life" algorithm?

Yes, it is based on the game of life where two or three neighbors would create a new mushroom and anything more or less would kill the mushroom. This has an interesting history. Mark Cerny asked why I didn't do a life algorithm on the mushrooms. I told him I was busy but if he wanted to add it to the game he could. Of course, Mark, being the sharp guy he is, looked at my code and quickly created this feature. He also added the attract mode to demonstrate all the creatures.

During the *Asteroids* to *Millipede* period, almost all your games were being ported to a wide variety of systems: the 2600, the Apple II, and so forth. How did you feel about these conversions?

It was good business for the company so it made business sense. Of course it always made me proud to see my game in many new places. I did have some concerns about several of the ports. I understand the limitations of some of the systems but I wanted to make sure the company released the best possible conversion. In many cases I was involved in making sure it had all the features but unfortunately not often enough.

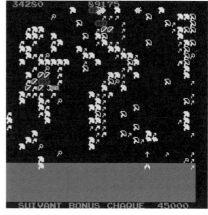

Millipede

Some of the conversions made improvements that were not possible in the coin-op market. For example, in *Gauntlet* they made a quest mode with a limited amount of health. This would not be possible in coin-op where the object is to get more money added on a regular basis. Another example would be to look at the number of variations of *Pong* included on the Atari 2600 cartridge. It just makes good sense to add value for a consumer title.

Was *Maze Invaders* the next game you worked on after *Millipede?* I know it never went into production.

It was a cute puzzle-like game. I was not sad it didn't make it; it did not earn enough on field test. My son loved the game though and I still have one of the two prototypes in my garage. The other was purchased by an operator in Texas, I believe. He loved the game so much he talked Atari into selling it to him.

I believe I mentioned earlier that nearly half of my games did not make it into production. There were engineers that had a higher percentage, Dave Theurer in particular. But there were others who never had a game in production.

The name *Maze Invaders* suggests perhaps something inspired by *Pac-Man*. Was it?

Yes, in a way. It was a maze-like game but the maze changed dynamically. The main character was very *Pac-Man* like; he was cute. There were some parts that I found frustrating, such as when the maze would temporarily block me off. I could not resolve this frustrating aspect, which is probably why it failed.

I understand in 1983 you also worked on a *Road Runner* laser disk game. Was it based on the Warner Bros. cartoon character?

Yes, it was based on Road Runner created by Chuck Jones. The player played the part of the Road Runner who would try to have Wile E. Coyote fall prey to some trap. I had Time Warner send me all of the Road Runner cartoons. I watched every one and selected the best shorts to be included on a laser disk. So when you succeeded in getting Wile E. destroyed, the game would cut from the action to a similar scene from a cartoon where Wile E. met his usual fate.

I always loved the Road Runner and I thought I could bring him to a video game. When I started I had a vision of something unique. The game certainly met that criterion but it was not as fun as I had hoped. I certainly enjoying seeing all the old cartoons and meeting Chuck Jones but…

So the game was killed?

Laser disk games were failing in the coin-op world because of reliability problems. The game actually earned enough to warrant interest but not as a laser disk game. So when they asked me to port it to their new "System I" hardware, I declined, saying I had another idea I wanted to pursue. I am glad they let me pursue this new idea because this idea became *Gauntlet*. *Road Runner* was converted over to System I and actually was released.

Did *Gauntlet* follow your initial vision fairly closely, or did it change a lot in development?

Gauntlet

I went back recently and looked at the original game design document and I was surprised how closely the graphics and gameplay matched the finished product. Of course, what did change during development was the hardware. I created an algorithm which would allow me to deal with 1,000 objects without burdening the processor or slowing down the frame rate. I asked Pat McCarthy, the electrical engineer, if he could extend the existing hardware and he found a way to do this which would allow me to display all the objects I needed. In the end there were five patents issued for *Gauntlet*.

Because of the size of the PCB and the restrictions on PCB size for Japanese kits, we decided to use a four-layer PCB for *Gauntlet*. Atari had never laid out such a board nor had they ever used traces as small as we required. But in the end we paved the way for all future PCBs at Atari. So besides the success of the game in the industry, *Gauntlet* also made a giant leap in the way we did engineering and manufacturing at Atari.

To my memory of arcades in 1985, *Gauntlet* seemed to be one of the first action games to allow four players to play at once.

This was the first multi-player game which allowed players to end or leave at any time and the screen scrolling was controlled by their actions. This was not the first game to have multi-players. *Tank 8* allowed eight players on one monitor. But all the players had to start at the same time. The idea of using four players was designed into *Gauntlet* from the start. I suspect it was due to the fact that I could only put four players around an upright monitor.

I believe *Gauntlet* was the first game that allowed the player to buy in any time he wanted. I did not want the players to wait, like in *Tank 8*, for everyone to coin-up at the same time. The only solution was to have players come and go at will. Health was always planned from the start. I believe this idea came from *Dungeons & Dragons*, which was very popular at the time. So it was logical that money just bought more health. Since it is every coin-op designer's wish to have the players put as much money as they can into their game, I saw no reason why I would not have the players just increase their health with each coin. In hindsight, this is a wonderful idea because losing 2000 health was not as painful psychologically as inserting another quarter. Besides, the players would not need to reach into their pocket to find another quarter to insert before their character was lost.

Where did the idea to have the game say things like "Red Warrior needs food, badly" come from?

I do not remember. I suspect it was not my idea. It may have come from my co-programmer Bob Flanagan or from someone else at Atari. In any case we had a large list of phrases we wanted the "Dungeon Master" to say to taunt the player. There are several phrases that seem to stick in everyone's mind. My favorite is "the Wizard (me) seems to be eating all the food lately."

Many think the Valkyrie was the most powerful of the four characters.

Actually, the Hulk or the Wizard could be used to play forever. This was demonstrated first by players in Japan playing a one-player game. This was fixed later by reducing the amount of food on subsequent levels if the player had not lost enough health during the last level. The Valkyrie was designed to be the most balanced of the characters but shot power, shot speed, and strength proved to be more important than other attributes. This is why the Hulk and Wizard seemed to be the most powerful. Of course, the Elf was fun to play with for many players because you could always get more food or treasure than the other players.

***Gauntlet II* allowed four players to all be playing Valkyries, or Elves, or whatever combination they wanted. Did this mean the character classes had to be more equal than in the first game?**

No, we actually did very little that I can recall to equalize the characters. This feature was added because some players wanted to play a particular character and I did not want them to wait until the desired position was open. So in essence I eliminated another reason for not entering the game right away.

Was *Xybots* your next project after *Gauntlet II*?

Bob Flanagan and I actually started another game, which I quickly killed after the initial gameplay turned out to be less fun than I had expected.

Xybots, as I mentioned earlier, started out as an idea to do *Castle Wolfenstein.* I started the game as a two-player split-screen *Gauntlet III.* Partway through, marketing said they wanted something other than *Gauntlet.* So I changed the characters and enemies to be more like *Major Havoc.* I still regret changing the theme and wish I had kept my original game concept.

Gauntlet II

Was it a great engineering challenge to create the game's 3D look?

I developed a very interesting algorithm for doing the 3D rotation using just 8 by 8 pixel stamps, as we call them. I don't know how to explain how this worked without getting my original sketches to visually demonstrate it. I could have had the player rotate other than in 90-degree increments, but it made the gameplay simpler to just allow only 90-degree rotations.

If I recall, the game had interesting and unique controls.

The controller was very unique because it provided the standard eight-way joystick as well as a knob on top which could turn left or right to indicate a rotation. This control made the game more difficult, which is often the kiss of death in the coin-op market. As with any 3D game, players could not easily visualize where they were despite the map available to them. In addition, it was possible to get shot in the back, which added to the frustration factor.

Xybots

How did you get involved working on the Atari *Tetris?*

I played a version of *Tetris* and was quickly addicted. I asked our legal counsel, Dennis Wood, to get the rights. Since I had just worked on reverse engineering the Nintendo Family Computer, which soon became the Nintendo Entertainment System in the U.S., I decided to create a version on the FC and NES and sell it through Tengen, which was

Atari's consumer publisher. Dennis Wood got the rights and we showed *Tetris* first at the June Consumer Electronics Show. It was decided to improve the game so I redid the visuals and we released it at the following CES in January.

I should point out that I was working on another game at the time I was doing this, so I could not devote all my time to the *Tetris* project. It was this fact that made me need to turn over *Tetris* to Greg Rivera and Norm Avellar for the coin-op market. I did get my original code to run on the coin-op hardware before going back to my project. This is why my name appears on the credits of the coin-op version.

What did you like so much about *Tetris*?

It was just so addicting I knew we had to have it. In hindsight, I could explain why this game worked so well but I am not sure that would prove anything. Besides, the real question is "Why didn't I think of this idea?"

Was Tengen *Tetris* your only NES project?

I had *Centipede* and *Millipede* running on the FC before the lawsuit with Atari Corp. resulted in the ruling that they owned the rights to all our games prior to the sale of Atari to Tramiel by Time Warner. So we had to drop the work I did. So my previous work made *Tetris* very easy to do on the NES. I also added the two-player simultaneous feature, which made this game better than all the other versions. Later you would see Tengen versions selling for $150 or more.

Why was Tengen *Tetris* eventually withdrawn from circulation?

You can read several versions of the story but I suspect the bottom line is the Hungarian who had the rights did a poor job of covering all the bases. The Russians accepted money from Nintendo when Nintendo created a new category of rights. Despite the fact we had the rights to computer systems, Nintendo claimed their Family Computer was not a computer even though they sold Basic and a keyboard and other services in Japan just like any other computer. I was certainly disappointed to see my work lost.

Why did you want to work on conversions of someone else's game?

As with many of my games, this was the best idea I could think of at the time. However, in this case, because I enjoyed it so much, it was an easy decision. What better way to play the game you like so much and make sure it comes out the way you like?

What did you work on next?

I eventually killed the game I was working on during the "*Tetris* Affair." I believe *Steel Talons* was my next project. I wanted to do a 3D Red Baron flying/shooting game but marketing thought World War I planes were not cool enough for teens, who were the prime coin-op target audience. Marketing wanted jets and I thought that was a dumb idea because who wants to see dots at a distance shooting at each other. I wanted something close where you can see the detail of the enemy you are shooting at. Helicopters were the logical choice.

Wasn't *Steel Talons* a fairly authentic helicopter simulator?

Steel Talons had all the regular helicopter controls: a rudder, a collective for controlling height, and a stick for turning. Of course flying a helicopter is difficult without some assistance, so I had computer assist just like real military helicopters. I added automatic collective control so the player would maintain level flight and any landing would be smooth. It would also increase height if the ground was sloping in front of the height. The "real" mode just disabled this helping code and increased the player's acceleration to compensate. This was a unique feature and Atari was issued a patent on this idea.

The game had another interesting feature that had never been used on a video game before. We installed a pinball thumper, often used to indicate a free game, under the seat. This was used whenever the player's helicopter was hit by enemy fire. During the first field test, the voltage for this thumper was higher than it should have been and the first players to use it nearly jumped out of their seats when it fired. The noise could be heard over the entire arcade.

The first field test also introduced a new problem that we never had before. I went out to check on collections and I tried to remove the coin box. If you have ever seen *Steel Talons*, you will see that the coin box is located at a strange angle, requiring the operator to lift the box with his arms fully extended. Not the easiest position to lift any weight. Well back to the story. I tried to lift the box out but could not budge it. I thought it was jammed. I soon discovered that the box was so full and was so heavy it was nearly impossible to remove. This led to the strange instructions in the manual asking the operators to empty the coin box every couple of days.

On *Steel Talons*, didn't you work with *Battlezone* creator Ed Rotberg?

Yes I did. He was at Atari during the golden days of *Battlezone*, *Asteroids*, et cetera. He left Atari to do a start-up called Sente, before returning to Atari a few years later. He had just finished working on a *Tube Chase*-like game using the same 3D hardware that *Steel Talons* used. This hardware was a cost-reduced version of the *Hard Drivin'* PCBs. So it was natural for Ed to work with me on this project. Another interesting feature of this game was fog. The original *Hard Drivin'* team did not believe me when I told them I could add fog to the world. I am still proud of this effect and they were surprised that it worked.

How did the *Space Lords* project come about?

I wanted to continue my ideas of multi-player play that I started on *Gauntlet*, and then continued on *Xybots* and *Steel Talons*. So I chose a 3D space environment with up to four cabinets linked together. Each cabinet had two monitors similar to *Cyberball*. I tried to keep the cost down by using Atari's "growth motion object" hardware, which was cheaper by far than the 3D hardware used on *Steel Talons*. It could not draw 3D polygons, but it could grow or shrink flat textures.

I understand *Space Lords* did not do too well financially.

Space Lords had some strange earning patterns. At some arcades it earned more than $1,000 per week for two double cabinets. But at some small arcades it earned only $75 as a single cabinet. The bottom line is we had a difficult time selling it because of its cost and the limited number of locations it could be sold into. It was definitely hard to make a coin-op game using the concept of one player per monitor. Even though I added a second player as a gunner at half price, it was felt by many to be not as fun as being the pilot.

And *Space Lords* came out right around the time the fighting games were taking off.

The fighting games made *Space Lords* difficult to sell because they were often "kits," which sold much cheaper than a large dedicated upright. *Street Fighter II* had great earnings and continued to earn good money for a long time.

In fact, since the early '90s most arcade games have been in one of a very few, limited genres. What do you think of many of the arcade games that come out these days?

You are right, the coin-op market seems to be all driving, fighting, and shooting with an occasional sports title, like golf. There are reasons for this. Driving has universal appeal and usually earns for long periods. So it is often the most accepted game theme. Besides, most home units do not have steering wheels and gas pedals or give you the feel of being inside a car. So you cannot get this experience in the home. Fighting games are now difficult to sell in the arcades, and I believe this is because you can get the same experience on most advanced consoles. At the time, they were cheap and earned big bucks. Shooting games are still viable because guns are not the standard controller on consoles or PCs. So the only way a game player can get this experience is in the arcade.

So the bottom line is, most arcade games these days are not unique and fit very limited categories. I don't think the arcades are completely dead but they are not the destination places they used to be.

Did *Space Lords* turn out to be your last coin-op?

I was working on a shooting game prior to my departure from Atari. That game died but the gun was used later on *Area 51*. I joined Electronic Arts who were trying to start up their own coin-op group. My intention was to start doing consumer games. But EA had some old Atari friends and I decided to join them. I had done one puzzle game, which I killed, and was working on a shooting game when they decided to drop out of the coin-op market. Then I was even more determined to enter the consumer games business.

How did you come to start doing N64 programming?

I was looking for a project to work on, so I contacted many companies to see what they had to offer. I was planning to work with another programmer from EA but he decided to join some friends to start up a new company. Atari wanted the coin-op *Wayne Gretzky 3D Hockey* done on the N64 and I was looking forward to doing something on that platform. This was partly because the game promised to look better than the PSX but also because it looked like we could be the first hockey title available. So I joined a group at Atari and we started work on *Wayne Gretzky 3D Hockey*. This turned out to be more work than I expected partly due to the state of N64 development systems but also due to the fact the coin-op was not going to be done until just before we released.

As you mentioned, a lot of the appeal of playing an arcade game like *San Francisco Rush* **seems to be sitting in the chair, having the gearshift, the steering wheel, the force feedback, and so forth. How do you try to capture that for the N64, which has none of these niceties?**

You are right. The home does not have the environment of the arcade cabinets but we can do things on the home games we can never do in the arcade. We can provide more choices for the player, more tracks for them to learn, and more things to discover.

San Francisco Rush: Extreme Racing for the Nintendo 64

I try to keep the basic play the same but I always try to add value to the product. This is one thing I made clear when I joined Atari. Atari wanted me to just do a straight port. That had always worked for them in the past. I did not believe this would work and told them I would be adding additional "stuff." For example, on *Gretzky* we added a full-sized rink, a new AI, instant replay, more players, full seasons, et cetera. In general, home games require considerably more work. I also believe we can do different games for the home market that we could never do in the arcade. So for me, this opens up new possibilities.

Arcade pieces must be easy to learn with rules that are obvious and provide entertainment that lasts ninety seconds. The home market is not bound by these rules. Instead, you must provide more life for your product. Often this means it takes the player longer to "finish" the game. Even when the player has finished it, there must be reasons why he will want to go back to do it all over again.

Do you like the engineering challenges of doing home conversions?

I actually enjoy the "old style" of trying to get everything to fit. I also enjoy adding tricks to get the frame rate as high as possible. It was very interesting to get all of *SF Rush* into 8 MB, which includes around 3 MB of audio and all the graphics.

How did the *Dr. Muto* **project originate?**

I am not sure of all the details, but I believe the basic concept came from our producer, Scot Amos. I was very intrigued by the idea of playing as a mad scientist, so I thought the game idea was a good one.

There is actually an interesting story that goes along with this. When we proposed the game to the management committee, their main complaint was that no one would want to play a mad scientist. To prove their point they wanted to do a marketing survey to see if a mad scientist was a good choice. Of course, the engineering team thought this was a waste of time. Imagine if they were to ask anyone if a purple hedgehog or an Italian plumber would make a good main character. Of course, the answer came back that the mad scientist was not a good idea because they had no point of reference as to how it would be used. In the meantime we did a small demo with a couple of rooms to show off our rendering engine, basic look and feel, morphing, and some basic humor. When management saw this, they knew exactly what we had in mind and we got a unanimous decision to go ahead with the project.

Dr. Muto

I always thought that *Dr. Muto* was fairly unique for a platformer in that its main character was older and not particularly cute or furry. Where did the desire to have such a different character originate?

The character design concepts came from our lead artist, Steve Caterson, whom we call Scat. We definitely wanted to do something different than everyone else was doing. Having a cute and fuzzy mad scientist just did not sound right. Besides, we wanted to look different than everyone else.

***Dr. Muto* was the first game you developed for the home market that wasn't an adaptation of an existing game. How was the development different from your previous experiences?**

This game was so different from any other game I have attempted to do. The market of course had changed, requiring better rendering, special effects, and movies. But the most important point was, this was a platformer and the standards for this type of game are very high indeed. We needed to match anything that was currently on the market or planned to be on the market.

The other most significant point is the sheer number of people, the cost, and the time required to do this project. *Dr. Muto* was by far the largest project I had ever been part of. There were more than twenty-five people on the team plus a tools group and video production people. The game design alone was orders of magnitude larger than anything else I have ever been associated with.

For *Dr. Muto* you were just the lead programmer and not the lead designer, correct?

The lead designer, Mark Simon, came in later on the project, around April 2002, I believe. This was his first large-scale project where he was lead designer, and I think he was a little over his head on this one. I would not have made a good choice as lead designer either because this type of game was unfamiliar territory for me. Besides, I like to program and I would not have been able to do anything except design as the designer. Even then I would have had to have several others assisting me in laying out levels, tuning, et cetera. But I was not even leading all the programmers because there

Dr. Muto

was a tools group doing the rendering engine and all the work making sure the game ran on the Xbox and GameCube as well. Scot Amos, our producer, served as project lead. He was really good at motivating people and even better at enthusiastically pushing our product — much better than I could do. He did a marvelous job.

But there were things I would have done differently. I certainly would have pushed our original idea for a sidekick. She was called Eyesore. She was to add sex appeal and humor to complement our bumbling mad scientist.

Why do you think *Dr. Muto* didn't fare better commercially?

I wish I had a good answer to this. I am afraid that we just did not get critical mass in the market. There were many platformers coming out at Christmas 2002 and we were up against some very well-done and well-advertised products. The industry claims that platformers did not do as well in 2002 as they had done in previous years. However, I believe the reason has to do with the game *Grand Theft Auto*. Because this game had such huge sales it naturally took sales away from other games. I contend this game is really a platformer, shooter, and a driving game all in one. If you lump this game into the platformer category, then you will see that platformers actually did quite well.

What are you working on these days?

I am doing cell phone games for a start-up called GenPlay Games. There are several of us from Midway Games West (originally Atari Games Corp.) working together now. I have just finished my second game, which will be out shortly on Verizon and Sprint.

I like the cell phone game industry in that the games are smaller and more arcade like. By that I mean the audience is looking for a more casual gaming experience. I also like the fact I can get back to doing programming and game design without managing other programmers. This industry will of course change as the cell phones become more powerful. 3D chips are already on their way into cell phones. It will not be long before we see the latest console games running on cell phones. The marketing of games is already getting to the stage where licenses or some name recognition are needed to get the attention of the carriers and players.

You have been involved in game development for almost twenty-five years. How do you explain your longevity?

Longevity comes from doing what I like. Working on games requires something which many people do not have. Many cannot take the constant pressure to perform, the long hours, and the thought that their "baby" that they have been working on may get killed after eighteen months of hard labor. Others are programmers or artists who have found more interesting things to do.

I must admit I have often thought of doing something else. I just have not found anything else I want to do more than what I am doing now. That could change or I may find myself doing games until I retire.

How did you feel about the closing of the old Atari offices?

This is like asking me how I feel about an old, dear friend passing on. I was very sad. We were the only project at Midway to be on time but in the end we were all let go. Such a waste of technology and the really great people we had working together.

In recent memory, *Asteroids*, *Centipede*, and *Gauntlet* have all been remade. How do you feel about the remakes?

Many are doomed to fail just like most game ideas. *Gauntlet* was a good case of a remake that worked very well. *Arkanoid* was a remake of *Breakout* that worked very well. So remakes can work, but it is difficult.

The real failure comes from comparing the gameplay to the original. For example, making a 3D version of *Centipede* makes the gameplay harder because the 3D information is not as easy for the player to process. Remember,

Gauntlet Legends

designers have had twenty years to play these old games and come up with a new twist to make a new great game. The fact that they haven't done it yet seems to indicate that it is unlikely. Not impossible, but unlikely.

Which one of your games might you want to remake?

If I had the answer to that, and if I believed it was the best idea I had, I would be working on it. Besides, if I told you, then someone else would be doing it now, wouldn't they? In other words, I don't have any idea how to take some old classics and make them new and interesting in today's market.

How has the game development industry changed over the years?

The games industry has definitely changed, but it is still a video game industry. Video games were not a $7 billion industry when I started. With big business comes big money and that invariably brings with it control over how it is spent. So there is definitely more politics at the corporate level. The interference from management comes from their need to control the costs, but the real reason, I believe, is due to the evolution of the games themselves. By that I mean, we could design and program a game in three months in the early years. In three months you did not spend enough money for them to interfere. Games have evolved to the point where you cannot do a game with just one person in a realistic amount of time. It takes several programmers, several artists, an audio specialist, and someone to manage the project over a period from twelve to twenty-four months. The console market has changed too. You did not need to spend $1 billion to launch a new console in the early days, but it costs that much now. So with evolution comes longer periods for development and higher costs to produce a product. With the higher costs comes more money and hence more control (i.e., interference) over how it is spent.

When working on home games, what have you changed in how you design your games versus your work in coin-op?

This depends on the type of game. For example, it is not sufficient to have a driving game with a dozen cars and a similar number of tracks. Now we would expect to see a large number of licensed cars, perhaps licensed drivers or tracks, or better yet a movie license. Of course we expect even better graphics and special effects than before. But aside from this point the basic idea is to add enough gameplay to make the purchase of a console game worthwhile. Remember, players can rent the game at the video store. If the gameplay is too short or does not meet their expectations or does not merit replays, then you can be sure the game will not sell well.

Now that I am on the subject, I have been really disappointed to see that nearly ninety percent of the top one hundred games are licenses or sequels. It is the single most overwhelming concern for any new game. It is sad to think game design cannot proceed without some tie-in with a movie or some other easily recognized title.

Do you miss doing more simple, classic arcade game designs?

Yes, I do miss the old game designs, which is why I am glad to be working on cell phone games. 2D worlds are so much easier for the player to understand. I also like the idea of creating a game with a fixed set of rules and enough randomness so that the player can create different play-styles and their own strategies.

I am not sure I could sell a game with an "old design" to the console market. Players have different expectations now. They would expect 3D designs or Internet play or high-resolution textures and pre-rendered movies or highly developed characters… Besides, just about anything I do now will just elicit comments like "It is just a twist on game xxx with a little of game zzz." For the record, many of the old designs were based on previous game ideas. Remember, *Asteroids* came from a previous game with a little of *Space War* thrown in, even though many thought of this as an original design.

For most of your original designs, you served as both designer and lead programmer. Do you enjoy working in both capacities?

Working as game designer and programmer is a good idea if you can pull it off. There are very few people who are good at both. So it is not a strategy I recommend today. For example, for today's complex multi-character and multi-level games, I am not as good a designer as I would be on other styles of games. So I would be willing to give up this role to someone else.

The programmer has to implement the design and if the designer's ideas are not communicated well enough, then the game is programmed differently than the designer expected. I believe it is often the programmer who can make or break the "feel" of a game.

You seem to have missed one point. I was also project leader on many projects. This is a role I am very good at but receive no acknowledgment. My projects are almost always on time and if there are problems, management is often told well in advance. No one outside Atari probably is aware of this. Unfortunately, I do not enjoy this role so I try to spend as little time as possible actually managing a project.

You even served as artist on your early games, didn't you?

Early on it was a good idea. There is no reason to train an artist to create a rock on graph paper and provide me with the coordinates so I could enter them into my game. When there was so little in the way of graphics or audio required, it makes no sense to have another specialized person doing this. Today, it is an entirely different matter. Today it is absolutely required.

Asteroids

Do you feel that any of your games are underappreciated?

As a game designer, no, I do not feel I have any games that were underappreciated. If the game design works, then the gameplay is fun and the game sells. As a programmer, yes, there are probably some game ideas or algorithms or programming speed which are underappreciated. Many programming tricks I do for personal enjoyment so I am not looking for external recognition.

In the early days you were pretty limited by the technology available to you. Did the technology limitations foster creativity?

Yes, I would have to agree. There were many times I spent thinking about how to do something on a given hardware and that turned into a game. *Xybots* was certainly one of those games. On *Gauntlet* we created new hardware to make the gameplay possible.

Do you think that gaming technology is stabilizing to the point where future games will be less about cutting-edge rendering and more about new game ideas?

As I mentioned earlier, marketing forces will drive games more than technology from the standpoint of getting the financing to get started. Since games have gotten so much more expensive and take so long, I suspect technology and new game ideas will take a backseat. This is not to say that there will not be even more improvement in the quality of the video and audio. I can assure you technology will be used to help sell the game in the end and will be a factor for the players. I can also assure you that new ideas will be tried but I doubt that any major studio will pin the hopes on the technology or game idea by itself.

In a way I agree that gaming technology is leveling out, as it were. By that I mean if the number of polygons that can be drawn increases by ten I would not expect to see much improvement in the quality of the video. Yes, you can add bump mapping or per-pixel shaders, but the basic TV has only so many pixels and covering the screen with more than one polygon per pixel will not improve the quality of the final video.

When working with an original game design, where do you start?

First, I try to come up with the game and then look at all the aspects of the play. From the market perspective: will it sell, is the timing right, licensing requirements, competition, et cetera. From the player's perspective: what makes this game fun and what is unique that will make it interesting. From the development side: what will it take to do this game in terms of people and equipment and will it be fun to do. Ideas themselves come from just about every possible source. I have mentioned how some come from previous games, brainstorming ideas, technical challenges, and other people's suggestions.

So, once you have your idea, do you start coding right away, or do you spend a lot of time thinking it through ahead of time?

With the large budgets and large teams these days, it is necessary to do a game design document and technical design document before the game gets too far into development. However, I try to start work on some critical aspect while the design documents are being drawn up. I believe it is extremely important to work on the aspect of the game that will make or break the concept. The front-end movies, story line, front and back end screens can all wait until the gameplay has been proven. Sometimes this prototyping phase is quick but often it can take several months.

Once you have proven the gameplay concept in a prototype, how does the rest of development progress?

Games go through four phases for me. The high at the beginning of a project of doing something new and the feeling that this will really be a great game. The project often makes giant leaps in short periods. The middle part of the project is mundane. The concept has been proven but there is often so much work to do and the game does not appear to change much for all your effort. The third phase is often full of panic and stress. This is the part just before release when you just want the project to end. The fourth phase is one of satisfaction after the game has been released.

With the current long projects I often feel I am getting diminishing returns for my effort, so I am happy to have the game end. In my case, almost everything I had planned for my game has been implemented, so I am happy to call it done. Except for finding those irritating last-minute bugs…

So after the prototype is functional, you don't really enjoy the development process?

Yes, I would say the bulk of the game is done after the core game concept has been proven. However, there are often parts that prove rewarding during the long development before the game is finished. But after doing so many games over the past thirty years, working on, say, the user interface just does not get me all excited.

No, I would like to do a prototype and leave it to someone else to finish. But I feel I still have the vision for the gameplay and I do not believe another person or group would continue the gameplay as I envision it. So in the end I would feel that the game was not what I expected, not mine anymore. I would always have the feeling that if I had worked on it to the finish, the game would be better than what anyone else could have done. I guess I would feel differently if I had not been as successful as I have.

Do you think focus groups or playtesting accomplishes for home games what field testing accomplishes for coin-op?

Field testing served as a means to make sure the software and hardware was bug free but this was a secondary benefit — this was not the real reason why it was done. Field testing for coin-op games gives you a good idea how well the game stacks up against other current games. It is easy to predict from the earnings and sales price how well it will sell. Focus groups rarely gave any clear indication of how well the game would sell either in coin-op or the consumer market.

For the consumer games, I do not believe there is any direct equivalent. The playtesting or focus group gives you some idea how well the game will be perceived, but in the case of *Dr. Muto* the ratings did not translate into the sales expected. I believe the reason is when a player goes to an arcade he can expect to see only a few new games. So it is likely your game will be seen. In the current consumer market there are numerous titles and it is

Dr. Muto

not easy to find the new games. In many cases your local games store may not even carry the game because they have reduced the number of games they will put on shelves. Even more important, coin-op games have a sample of gameplay, which players can glimpse to see if it interests them. The best you are going to get from the consumer store is a few screenshots on the box. I know this is not really accurate because we expect to see TV time for consumer games, but you need to be one of the top games to warrant that kind of marketing money and not all games do.

For *Dr. Muto* this point was rather moot for another reason. The finish date was selected for the team. We were told when it would be released, so we cut many of the features and gameplay we would like to have seen. More importantly, player testing was of no use because if they suggested a change there would be no time to add it or change the game.

What role do you think AI plays in games?

In the old games AI had no involvement. Often the enemy would follow a fixed set of rules with some randomness thrown in if necessary. These days it is entirely a different matter. It is becoming very important for modern games. Some people have recommended that, when appropriate, each project have one specially trained person dedicated to doing the game AI. And for some games, I would agree.

Why do you think games require more sophisticated AI now?

I believe the theme and gameplay of most new games require more AI. The sim games, the shooters, et cetera, all try to give the real sense of intelligent life competing against you. If games do not try to mimic real life, then a set of rules may do just fine.

How important do you think it is to make the AI in a game "real"? That is, to provide the AI only with the information the player would have in the AI agent's position?

It is not necessary but may lead to more believable enemy AI, so I would recommend it in some cases. For example, in *Steel Talons,* the enemy gunners would not turn or fire until they could see you visually. If there was a hill in the way or you were hugging the ground at the end of their range, then they did not see you. This is one case where it was necessary.

Lately, a lot of attention is being given to combining games and stories. Many arcade coin-ops, perhaps as part of their nature, have almost no story. What do you think about telling a story within a game?

I have never been high on stories. I feel it is absolutely necessary to have the player grasp the theme: setting, ambience, and goals. Sometimes stories help to make the goals easier to understand. Some games are made like a movie, so a story makes good sense: the player feels he is the main character that he is controlling. In a coin-op game, a story makes no sense unless it is shown in the attract mode. We do not want the player wasting his time watching something when he could be playing or putting in more money.

You mentioned before that you specifically wanted to get into doing games for the home market. Why was this?

I wanted to do home games instead of coin-op games because I saw more opportunity to do something new in the home market.

Do you not see any future for coin-op arcade games?

I suspect coin-op games in the arcades will tend toward cheaper simulation rides (physical movement or encompassing environment), just like you see now. They provide something you cannot get at home and are cheaper than the rides at Disneyland. I believe the coin-op arcade market is already there. The coin-op street market will always need to be inexpensive. So I see a consumer platform in a coin-op box or cheap PCBs with simple games that do not require long development times.

The arcade version of *San Francisco Rush 2049*

The consumer market already dominates over the coin-op industry. I do not have the numbers, but it is clear to me by looking at sales numbers of hit games and the dollars they represent. It is sad to see the changes in the coin-op industry. I am sure glad I was a part of the industry. I feel I was definitely in the right place at the right time.

Ed Logg Gameography

Super Breakout, 1978
Video Pinball, 1979
Asteroids, 1979
Othello (for Atari 2600), 1979
Football (four-player conversion), 1979
Centipede, 1981
Millipede, 1982
Gauntlet, 1985
Gauntlet II, 1986
Xybots, 1987
Tetris (conversion to NES), 1988
Steel Talons, 1991
Space Lords, 1992
Wayne Gretzky 3D Hockey (conversion to N64), 1996
San Francisco Rush (conversion to N64), 1997
San Francisco Rush 2 (conversion to N64), 1999
San Francisco Rush 2049 (conversion to N64
    and Dreamcast), 2000
Dr. Muto, 2002
GenPlay Stack'um, 2004
GenPlay Pool Pro Online, 2004

Chapter 7:
The Elements of Gameplay

"We ended up with a game that I didn't know how to win. I didn't know which were the best strategies or tactics, even though I designed all the game's systems. That is what makes a good strategy game."

— Julian Gollop, talking about his game *X-Com: UFO Defense*

What are the game design elements that make up a really good game? Of course, there is no definitive answer to such a question. Nonetheless, as a game designer you will be expected to intuitively know the answer. Understanding game design, as with any art form, is very much an internalized understanding, a "gut" reaction, a "feeling" you might have. It may be that you will not be able to form that answer into words, but you will need to understand what aspects of a game are strong and which are weak, and how the latter can be replaced with more of the former. Experience plays a big part in understanding what makes a game fun, experience both as a game designer and as a game player.

Over my years of playing and creating games I have come up with my own answers for what makes a game great, and in this chapter I discuss some of those qualities. Some of these topics may seem fairly distinct from each other, yet to my mind they all play a crucial role in making a good game. Certainly I cannot hope to list all of the knowledge I have, since, as I mentioned, much of my understanding is more akin to a "sixth sense" than anything I could hope to write down. But the ideas contained in this chapter should provide a solid foundation.

Unique Solutions

For me, one of the most exciting moments of being a game designer is when I hear someone talking about playing one of my games, and they explain a successful tactic for a given situation that I had never considered. This could be a solution to a specific puzzle, a new strategy to incapacitate challenging enemies, or a method for maneuvering a perilous canyon. I see the games I develop as creating situations in which game players can utilize their own creativity to succeed. When players' creativity can lead them to solutions that I had not envisioned, it shows me that the players and I are sharing in the creation of their experience, instead of my dictating everything. And when the players and I share in the authorship, I feel my game is doing its job.

Anticipatory versus Complex Systems

Good designers will try to guess what players are going to attempt to do and make certain their game responds well to those actions. For instance, take an RPG that features a puzzle that involves placing weights on a series of pressure plates. (Having put such a puzzle in a game of my own, I would like to implore game designers to be a bit more creative than that, as pressure plates are surely one of the most overdone puzzle devices. But I digress.) Suppose the designer leaves a conspicuous pile of rocks a few rooms over from the pressure plate puzzle. The obvious solution to the puzzle is to use those rocks on the pressure plates to achieve the desired results. But what if players try dropping their various weapons on the plates instead? This is a perfectly valid solution that should work equally well, provided players have weaponry of the appropriate weights. What if players have the Summon Minor Threat spell, which allows them to summon a variety of different small monsters? If players summon those monsters onto the pressure plates, they might do the trick too.

Now the designer, having thought through the puzzle fully, can have the programmer add in code where the game reacts correctly if rocks, weapons, or monsters are on the plates. This is the anticipatory school of game design, where the designer thinks of what players might do and hardwires the game to work well with those actions. I agree that this tactic is surely better than allowing for just one solution. However, what if players think of some other weight they can place on the pressure plates? What if players use their Berkshire Blizzard spell on the pressure plates, causing snow to fall on them? Enough snow could conceivably pile up on the plates to have a significant weight. However, if the game has been hardwired only for rocks, weapons, or monsters, the game will not react appropriately. Players will have thought of a perfectly reasonable solution and the game will fail to recognize it.

Instead of hardwiring, however, what if the designer had the programmer come up with a system where every object in the game had a weight associated with it? This would include rocks, weapons, monsters, weather effects, blood, and any other dynamic objects found in the game-world. If the programmer then made the pressure plates simply measure the weight of all of the objects on top of them, regardless of their type, then this global solution would work for all objects. If each object was set up with a reasonable weighting, it would not matter what objects players tried to place on the pressure plates, as they would all work automatically.

This latter method is less of an anticipatory technique of game design; it is more holistic and systems-based in its approach. It relies more on creating reliable, consistent systems with which your game will function. With these systems in place, the game becomes more a simulation and less of a hard-coded puzzle. A game need not be a flight simulator or a *SimCity*-style game to include some level of simulation; indeed almost all games include some degree of simulation, however crude it may be. The more designers recognize the value of simulation over hard coding and emphasize these complex and interconnected systems in their games, the deeper their games become. In a game with a more simulation-based approach, containing a puzzle such as the pressure plate one described above, the designer and programmer come up with a series of success conditions for that puzzle. Instead of "the puzzle is solved if players use rocks, weapons, or monsters to offset the plates," the rule is "the puzzle is solved when the plates are offset by the correct weight being placed on top of them." Certainly the example of this puzzle is a simple one, but the same techniques can be applied to much more sophisticated and interesting systems that engender a wide variety of successful playing styles.

Emergence

The *Civilization* games are some of the best examples of complex gameplay emerging out of multiple consistent systems running in parallel. Pictured here: *Civilization II*.

It is the development of numerous robust and logical systems that leads to player-unique solutions to situations in the game. One could describe these solutions as "emergent" from the systems design of the game, a popular buzzword in game design circles. Establishing a game universe that functions in accordance with logical rules players can easily understand and use to their advantage allows those same players to come up with their own solutions to the problems the game presents. Nothing is more rewarding for players than devising some obtuse, unobvious method for solving a puzzle or a combat situation and then having it actually work. The more complex systems work correctly and concurrently with each other, the more interesting and varied the solutions to situations become. Consider the game *Civilization*, with its numerous systems running in parallel. These systems work together to create some of the most compelling gameplay ever pressed to disk.

At the same time, many designers fear players discovering emergent strategies they can use as exploits: tactics that will allow players to finish a game too easily, skipping a lot of the fun. With its complex systems design, *Civilization* was a prime candidate for player exploitation. In the original game, players were able to exploit a rush strategy where they would never build cities of a size larger than two while staying in the most primitive form of government, quickly sweeping over the world and winning the game prematurely. This strategy was so effective it was clearly the best strategy to use and allowed players to miss 90 percent of the game. Sid Meier ended up patching the game to increase the citizens' unhappiness when this strategy was used, fixing the exploit. In this case the emergent tactic revealed a shortcut through the game that needed to be fixed.

Another example of this sort of emergent strategy that might be regarded as an exploit can be found in the original *Centipede*. Anyone who has ever played the game knows that the piling up of mushrooms is one of the greatest impediments to a long game, and many players understand the importance of keeping the play-field as clear as possible. As the devotees of the game pumped quarter after quarter into the game, they began to notice some patterns. First, they recognized that the flea is responsible for dropping most of the problematic mushrooms, though destroyed centipede segments also drop them. Second, they saw that the flea does not come out on the game's first wave. Third, it was observed that the flea is triggered by the absence of mushrooms in the bottom half of the screen. Thus the famous "blob" strategy was developed, one that the game's designer, Ed Logg, never anticipated. To use the blob strategy, players would clear all of the mushrooms from the board on the first wave, and then allow mushrooms to survive only on the bottom-right quadrant of the screen. If, through careful destruction of the centipede, the players only allow mushrooms to be created in that section of the screen, the flea will never come out, making the game much simpler indeed. This is an emergent solution to racking up a high score at *Centipede*, one which players no doubt felt quite proud of when it was discovered. It was a tactic that Logg, as the game's creator, did not even know was there to be found. Unlike the *Civilization* rush strategy described above, the blob strategy was so hard to pull off that it was not truly an exploit, merely an alternate tactic that required a good deal of player skill. Though some designers become distressed whenever an unanticipated strategy emerges in their game, it is important to look at the given tactic and determine if it ruins the player's experience or if it is a technique equally or even more fun than what the designer had planned. If such emergent strategies do not completely break the game, they need to be viewed as a boon to the game's depth and the direct result of good game design.

Non-Linearity

Non-linearity is another buzzword in the game industry, but like emergence, there is a lot of value to the concept. Non-linearity is what interesting gameplay is all about, and many game developers forget this in the heat of production. Non-linearity gives interactivity meaning, and without non-linearity, game developers might as well be working on movies instead. The more parts of your game that you can make non-linear, the better your game will be. Unfortunately, on the flip side, the more non-linearity your game has, the more time consuming and difficult it will be to develop.

In general, when someone says something is linear they mean that it follows a line. A line is a series of points connected in either two- or three-dimensional space, where one can find any point on that line using a specific equation, such as, in a 2D case, $y = mx + b$. In layman's terms, this means that a line must be straight. If one considers any two points on that line, say A and B, there is only one way to navigate that line from A to B. There are no choices to be made; one simply must navigate all of the points between A and B. Outside the world of mathematics, we can consider reading a book to be a linear experience. If one is reading a 323-page book and if one does not skip pages or chapters, there is only one way to read the book: by starting on page 1 and reading all of the pages leading up to page 323.

Games, however, are non-linear works. In the game of chess, there are multiple ways to capture the opponent's king, to move from the game's predetermined starting state to its conclusion. Indeed, there are a vast number of different ways to be victorious in chess, and that variety is what keeps the game interesting. These choices make chess non-linear. Suppose the chessboard were one-dimensional instead of two, each player's pieces could only move in one direction, and each player had only one piece. This version of chess is a linear one, since there are no meaningful choices for players to make and the outcome of every game is completely predetermined. And, as a result, it would not be any fun to play.

Types of Non-Linearity

So when we say we want our games to be non-linear, we mean we want them to provide choices for players to make, different paths they can take to get from point A to point B, from the game's beginning to its end. We can mean this in a number of ways: in terms of the game's story, in terms of how players solve the game's challenges, in terms of the order in which players tackle the challenges, and in which challenges players choose to engage. All of these components can contribute to making a game non-linear, and the more non-linearity the developer creates, the more unique each player's experience can be. Furthermore, the different non-linear components can interact with each other to make the whole far greater than the sum of its parts.

- Storytelling: I discuss non-linear storytelling in more detail in Chapter 11, "Storytelling." Of course, a non-linear story line is necessarily tied to non-linear gameplay, and no one would bother to try to make a story non-linear if the game itself offered players very little in the way of meaningful decisions. Storytelling is perhaps one of the most neglected parts of games in terms of non-linearity, with many developers allowing for non-linear gameplay while constraining their games to a completely linear story.

- Multiple Solutions: I discussed above how a well-designed game will enable players to come up with their own solutions to the challenges the game presents. Not every player will go about solving a situation in the same way, and, given that these alternate solutions are reasonable, almost any challenge must have multiple ways for players to overcome it. Having multiple solutions to the individual challenges within a game is a big part of non-linearity; it enables players to have multiple paths to get from point A (being presented with the challenge) and point B (solving the challenge).

- Order: Beyond being able to figure out the solutions to challenges in unique ways, players will appreciate the ability to pick the order in which they perform challenges. Many adventure games have made the mistake of being overly linear by allowing players access to only one puzzle at a given time. In order to even attempt a second puzzle, players must complete the first one. That is a linear way of thinking, which proves especially frustrating when players get stuck on a particular puzzle and, due to the game's linear nature, can do nothing else until that puzzle is solved. Giving players choices of different puzzles to solve allows them to put aside a troubling puzzle and go work on another one for a while. After completing the second puzzle, players may return to the first refreshed and revitalized, and thereby have a better chance of solving it.

- Selection: Another way of making a game non-linear is to allow players to pick and choose which challenges they want to overcome. Say that between point A and point B in a game there lies a series of three challenges, X, Y, and Z, which are non-order dependent, that is to say, players can do these challenges in any order they wish. What if, once players surmount challenge X, they do not have to go back and solve challenge Y or Z, they can simply move on to point B in the game, perhaps never returning to Y or Z? The same is true if players initially choose to tackle Y or Z instead of X. Any one of the choices will allow players to proceed. The advantage is that if players find challenge X to be insurmountable, they can try challenge Y or Z. This greatly decreases the chance of players becoming permanently stuck. It need not be the case that Y is easier than X; the mere fact that it is different may allow players a better chance of getting through it, depending on their strengths. Other players may find X to be easier than Y or Z, but giving players a choice of which challenges they take on allows them to exploit their own personal skills to get through the game. Of course, after completing challenge X, players may still have the option of going back and completing the Y and Z challenges, perhaps just for the fun of it or because overcoming those challenges somehow improves their chances down the line. Perhaps completing Y and Z gives their player character greater overall experience or riches. This type of non-linearity can also be used to add totally optional side-quests to the game. These challenges are not strictly required for players to get to the end of the game, though they may make it somewhat easier or merely provide an interesting diversion along the way. Whatever the case, these optional challenges provide an extra degree of non-linearity, further customizing players' experiences.

Implementation

Odyssey is an extremely non-linear game, allowing the player to solve puzzles in whatever order he chooses and to select which quests he wants to go on. The game almost always provides more than one solution to any given puzzle.

My first game, *Odyssey: The Legend of Nemesis*, is without doubt the most relentlessly non-linear game design I have ever done, and includes examples of all the types of non-linearity described above. *Odyssey* is an RPG and takes place on an archipelago that includes seven primary islands for players to explore. Though players are required to complete at least one quest on the first island before moving on to the rest of the game, there are two quests, each with multiple solutions from which players may choose. Indeed, clever players can skip the quests entirely if they figure out how to rob a particular townsperson. (In fact, this was an emergent behavior that I had not anticipated, but which fortunately made sense and did not derail the game significantly.) From there, players are able to move freely about the next five islands, picking which ones they want to explore and which they prefer to just pass through. Indeed, all that is required for players to reach the seventh island and the end-game is successful navigation of each island, killing the monsters that get in their way. Of course, killing those creatures is made significantly easier if players receive the rewards for completing the quests. But if players so choose, they can skip the entire middle of the game. Of course, few players have done this, preferring instead to explore the different quests and situations they encounter there. Nearly every one of these quests has multiple ways for players to solve it, with their actions having a direct impact on how each of the island's mini-stories resolves. Finally, the game itself has multiple endings for players to explore, endings that suit the different overall goals players may have: survival, revenge, or a sort of justice and harmony. Though the game had a very definite story, I am happy to say that I doubt very much that any two players ever experienced it in exactly the same way.

Overall, my game *The Suffering* was significantly less non-linear than *Odyssey*, but still I applied many of the same non-linear storytelling techniques in order to give the game's story depth. *The Suffering* makes each player's experience unique through its morality system, which assesses how the game is being played and then determines

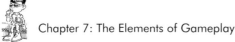

the player character's past and changes how the characters in the present speak to him. As a horror game, the plot was kept somewhat vague on purpose, with players needing to fill in many of the blanks themselves. Furthermore, each player was likely to have a different subsection of the overall story, since much of the story is contained in optional side areas. Indeed, players who blaze through the game full speed ahead will miss a lot of the plot, while those who play normally will probably see about half of what there is to be found. This means there are many different ways to experience the story and players will have different impressions of it depending on how they play. Indeed, during development there was a lot of concern about players missing too much of the game by running through it quickly since there are relatively few bottlenecks to block progression. In the end, though, through gameplay testing and the feedback we received after the game shipped, we realized that almost all players will explore the game more than is required of them merely because they are interested in it. Similarly, players will fight creatures they don't strictly need to. It is important to remember that players want to play a game to have fun, and only the most masochistic will deliberately ruin their play experience. Thus you don't need to worry about the game's exploits quite as much as making sure the game is fun if played by cooperative players.

On the puzzle side of things, *The Suffering* is somewhat less successful in terms of non-linearity: many of the puzzles have multiple solutions, but an equal number do not. Though most of the objectives were planned to have multiple ways of completing them, we had several situations where one solution would involve an exciting payoff while the other did not. Our producers were concerned gamers would miss too much by choosing the alternate solution, and thus we ended up cutting some of the less exciting alternatives. This leads to an important rule of thumb: if you want to have multiple solutions or paths, they should all be equally compelling so players will not feel cheated at having picked the much less spectacular path. Another failed bit of non-linearity in *The Suffering* involved a particular level that was initially designed to be extremely non-linear. In this level, there were originally three separate paths leading to the level's end. Through our gameplay testing we learned that players were extremely confused by the three paths, with almost all players looping back to the beginning of the level and then being confused as to where they were. Admittedly this particular problem was due to poor level design, but this is a case where non-linearity ended up hurting the player's experience, and we ended up reworking the level flow in the final game.

Non-linearity is an extremely powerful tool to use in designing a game, and the above descriptions of the types of non-linearity a designer can employ may seem obvious to the reader. What is astonishing, then, is how many games fail to provide any substantial non-linearity for players, instead insisting that players play through the game on a single line from point A to point B. One reason for this is that creating all of these non-linear elements can be quite time consuming. Consider that between point A and B, we have the aforementioned challenges X, Y, and Z, but players only have to overcome one of these challenges in order to progress. Players can then continue playing through to the end of the game having never interacted with challenge Y or Z. As a non-linear game, that is the players' prerogative. The problem arises when a cost accountant looks at the game and tries to figure out where the game's budget can be trimmed. Well, obviously, if Y and Z are not strictly necessary, why bother having them at all? Why spend a lot of money on the programming, art, and design necessary to get Y

Working meaningful non-linearity into *The Suffering* proved quite challenging.

and Z working when there's a chance players will never see them? Unfortunately, accountants are often not in touch with the finer points of game design, and when you say, "But non-linearity is what makes this game great!" they are likely to dismiss you as "unreasonable" or "difficult."

Non-linearity is also often hard to pull off from a design perspective, certainly harder than simple linearity. This may be another reason why so many designers shy away from it at the first opportunity. Designing numerous obstacles that are different enough to provide variety for players and apply roughly the same challenge is not an easy task. In the X, Y, and Z challenges example, if Z is significantly easier than X or Y, it is quite likely no one will ever bother with X or Y. In a way, a game with poorly designed choices for players is nearly as linear as a game without any choices at all. The non-linearity your game provides must be meaningful and useful to players or it is a waste. Designers who think too highly of their own design skills may also avoid non-linearity in their designs because they want players to experience every single element of the game they decide to include. "Why spend a lot of time on portions of the game that not everyone will see?" say these somewhat egotistical designers, missing the point entirely. If enough people play your game, some people will surely see what you have created, and each one of the players will have a somewhat different experience because of it. Just as a great novel will have multiple layers to its story and different meanings that different readers will take away, even more so a game should allow players to find their own way through the game-world and empower them to craft their own unique experience.

The Purpose of Non-Linearity

It is important to always remember that non-linearity is included in the game to provide players some meaningful authorship in the way they play the game. If they are forced to stay on a specific line to get from the beginning of the game to the end, the game will feel constrained. The challenges along that line may be brilliantly conceived, but if players have no choice but to take them on in order, one by one, the fun they provide will be greatly diminished.

Non-linearity is great for providing players with a reason to replay the game. Replaying a game where players have already overcome all of the challenges is not that much fun. In replaying a more non-linear game, however, players will be able to steer away from the challenges they succeeded at the last time they played and instead take on the game's other branches. However, it is important to note that replayability is not the main motivation for including non-linearity in your game designs. I have heard some game designers complain that replayability is unnecessary since so many players never manage to finish the games they start playing. So if they never finish, why add replayability? These designers do not realize that the true point of non-linearity is to grant players a sense of freedom in the game-world, to let players have a unique playing experience, to tell their own story. If players want to replay the game again, that is fine, but the primary goal of non-linearity is to surrender some degree of authorship to the players.

Furthermore, the contention that players seldom finish games and hence the games do not need to be non-linear is a self-fulfilling prophecy. The reason players fail to finish games is often because they become stuck at one particular juncture in the game. This may be a boss-monster that is too difficult, a puzzle that is too confounding, or merely failing to find the exit from a given area. If the game were more non-linear, however, players would have much less chance of getting stuck at any point in the game, since the variety of paths available would increase the likelihood that players' unique talents would be sufficient for them to make it successfully through one of the paths.

At a Game Developers Conference talk entitled "A Grand Unified Game Theory," Noah Falstein suggested that when non-linearity allows players to tackle a series of required challenges in whatever order they desire, completing one challenge should make the others easier for players to accomplish. In the case of a collection of puzzles, this can be done by providing players with a hint about the other puzzles once one is completed. In the case of a collection of battles of some sort, this can be done by providing players with additional weaponry with which to survive the other battles. Whatever the case may be, using this technique increases the chance that players will be able to overcome the challenges at hand and get on with the game.

A note of caution: all designers should understand that non-linearity is not about having players wander around the game-world aimlessly. If the game is non-linear to the point where players have no idea what they are supposed to try to accomplish or how they might go about it, the non-linearity may have gone too far. Often game designers talk up their in-development games by making statements like "In our game-world, players can do anything they want; there are no restrictions. The game is completely non-linear!" Such a game would likely be completely annoying as well. Of course, by the time these "completely non-linear" games have shipped, most of the non-linearity has been stripped out and players are left solving puzzles on a rail. Somewhere between "on a rail" games and total freedom lays an ideal middle ground, where players are left with a sense of freedom accompanied by a sense of guidance.

Modeling Reality

The desire to model reality in computer games is one that has driven game development for a number of years. The more real we make the games, proponents say, the more compelling and immersive gamers will find them. But is this always the case? What would a greater degree of reality add to a game like *Tetris* or *Centipede*? Surely they could not be much more immersive than they already are. Consider a game such as *Age of Empires*, which is already modeled on reality. Would adding more reality to it make it any more fun? Actually, quite the opposite is true: adding a more realistic economic model or combat system would detract from the game's strengths as a macro-strategy game and quite possibly make the game more annoying than fun.

The trouble with modeling reality in games comes when titles get mired in reality to the point where they come to resemble real life a little more than players actually want. Alfred Hitchcock described films as "Life with the dull bits cut out." Indeed, games can be seen as modeling life or some aspect of life while leaving out the tedious and boring parts. If the designer, in an attempt to achieve a greater degree of reality, decides to include too many unnecessary and dull details, the game will likely become tedious to play. My favorite example of this is the use of food in RPGs. Many RPGs of the '80s were perpetually on a quest to make themselves more real than other RPGs, to up the ante with each new game that was released. One way designers attempted to do this was to add a basic hunger simulation, and to require players to remember to feed their party members periodically, lest they starve to death. Here was a "dull bit" that did not need inclusion, especially as eating regularly scheduled meals is not the first thing that jumps to people's minds when they think of adventuring in fantastic worlds.

Using reality as a basis for your game has its advantages, however. First and foremost, it provides players with a world they are instantly familiar with, a world in which they have some idea of what actions are reasonable and which are out of the question. Whether in *Civilization*, *SimCity*, *Deadline*, or *Grand Theft Auto*, a properly executed realistic setting gives players an instant "in" to your game-world. They understand or at least think they understand how it works and what they can do to be successful in it. Players can start playing the game and instantly have some idea of what they are supposed to accomplish. A more abstract game like *Centipede* or *Tetris*, on the other hand, has such abstract goals that players must be taught what it is they are supposed to do, either through reading the directions or by experimenting with the game-world.

Beyond the gameplay advantages, in terms of story and setting, placing your game in a real-world setting can be much more meaningful to players, allowing the actions that take place in the game-world to resonate with them more deeply than if your game were set in abstract worlds. *The Sims* works in part because of its well-balanced gameplay and simulation, but also because of its real-world setting that allows players to feel that their actions have real meaning to the simulated people they are guiding. My game *Damage Incorporated*, though it admittedly had a somewhat implausible premise, was set in the real-world and dealt with real-world issues that made the missions and their outcomes more relevant to players than if the game had been set in outer space. Similarly, *The Suffering*, despite having supernatural creatures spawning out of every nook and cranny, was set in a believable prison environment populated by recognizable

Having a believable and recognizable environment was a big part of *The Suffering*'s appeal.

and plausible characters. Thus it was able to deal with weighty and serious themes in a more resonant fashion than if the game had taken place in some demonic netherworld.

A potential downside to having a realistic world is that, since the game mimics a reality players are familiar with, players will expect certain game-world elements to work in certain ways and will be very quick to notice when something fails to do so. For example, many of the early first-person shooters, such as *Doom* and *Marathon*, did not allow the player character to jump. The worlds of these first-person shooters were more "realistic" than those game players were accustomed to finding in computer games, so real that players' expectations were raised and many were quick to complain that they could not jump over even waist-high obstacles. So the next generation of FPS titles added the ability to jump, then to crouch, then look up and down, and so on and so forth, making the games still more complicated with each element of reality added. Now, as the worlds possible with RT3D engines look more real than ever, players are constantly asking questions such as "Why can't I lie flat on the ground? I can do that in real life; why not in the game?" Indeed, many of the more complex first-person shooters have added this very feature. Some would say that, certainly for novice players, these FPS games have grown too complex as a result of their attempt to model reality. Bringing in a certain level of reality raises players' expectations in a way that the totally abstract world of a *Centipede* or *Tetris* never does. Players never question their capabilities in these worlds because the boundaries were completely arbitrary in the first place.

At the same time, players are particular about the type of reality-based improvements they want in their games. For example, if FPS games added a more realistic modeling of player movement, players would be irate. If suddenly you were able to trip over low-lying obstacles or always fall down to your knees whenever falling from more than five feet, the experience of running around the game-world would be considerably more aggravating. These are the tedious parts of real-world movement, and therefore can and should be ignored. In the end, most players only want more realism if it means they get to do more interesting and fun things, not if it makes their game experience more frustrating.

So is there a definitive answer to whether or not you should model reality in your game? Of course not, just as there are no easy answers in all of game design, and as there are no easy answers in art. As a game designer you must strike the balance between reality and abstraction, weighing what your game needs from a gameplay standpoint with what your story and setting require and with what your engine can reasonably handle. What is vital to remember, and what many designers often forget, is that more reality is not always a good thing. At the same time, saying that reality does not matter and that fun is the be-all and end-all may prevent you from creating a world that resonates with your audience.

Teaching the Player

Attempting to model reality may be one way to give players an advantage going into your game-world; through their own life experiences, players will know to some extent what to expect of your game-world. However, even with the most realistic game, players will need time to learn how to play your game, and this learning experience is often a crucial time in a player's overall experience. The first few minutes players spend with your game will often make the difference between whether they want to continue playing it or not. Whenever players tell friends about your game, they will often remember those first few minutes and say, "Well, it was a little weird to get used to" or, preferably, "It was great. I jumped right into the game and found all this interesting stuff."

In the past, many computer games relied on manuals to teach players how to play them. With some titles players literally had almost no chance of success in the game without first reading a large chunk of the manual. Today many games try to get away from this reliance on players' reading ability, realizing that often the last thing players want to do when they have just purchased a new game is to sit down and read an extensive instructional manual. Players definitely have a strong desire to just pick up the controller and start playing the game. Now that so many games allow players to do just that, the importance of allowing players to "jump right in" has increased. If your game is too difficult to get a handle on within the first minute, players are likely to put it down and try something else.

This does not mean that your game has to be dumbed down or simplified, merely that you must introduce the complexity of your game-world gradually through the gameplay instead of through the manual. For example, at first your game should start out requiring players to perform only the simplest of actions. Say you are creating a third-person over-the-shoulder action/adventure game akin to *Tomb Raider*. It makes the most sense to first teach players how to move the player character around correctly on the ground. Then, after players have had a chance to become accustomed to the horizontal movement controls, you might introduce a section where the player character has to jump to cross a canyon or climb up a cliff. After enough of that, you might want to introduce some simple combat challenges, where players will learn how to use their character's weapons.

It is important that during the introduction of these controls players are in a safe environment that engenders learning. If players already have to worry about dying at every step and the game is generally unforgiving of players' mistakes, chances are good that players will become frustrated quickly. Designer Sheri Graner Ray has studied

Prince of Persia carefully taught the player what to expect of traps such as collapsing floors and sharp spikes.

how players prefer to learn a new game and has found that some players, typically males, prefer to try out and experiment with each game mechanic as it is introduced. Thus, allowing players to try out new mechanics in a safe space is very important. *Half-Life* did this particularly well, with an introduction to the game that provided a safe yet interesting environment and allowed players to become accustomed to the controls without immediately threatening them. The original *Prince of Persia* was another game that was particularly good at introducing challenges to players in a way that taught them through example instead of by punishing them. For instance, when the players first encounter a breakaway floor in *Prince of Persia*, falling through it is non-lethal. Similarly, spikes are introduced in such a way that players are very likely to notice them and to be able to survive them. Subsequent encounters with spikes will not be so forgiving, but by then players have learned of the threat they pose to their game-world character, and if they are clever they will be able to survive them.

During this learning period in the game, it is important to reward players for even the simplest of accomplishments. This makes players feel that, indeed, they are on the right track with the game and encourages them to keep playing. It is true that players do not want their games to be too simple and too unchallenging, but punishing them for blunders from the very start of the game is not the right way to produce this challenge. The key is to give players success early on, to draw them into the game, to make them think that they know what the game is all about, and that they are better than it. "Ha-ha, this game is easy! I rule!" they may say. And then, when the game becomes suddenly more challenging, players will already have been drawn into the game and will be much more likely to see the challenge as a reasonable one, one that they can surely overcome. After all, this game is easy, right?

Tutorials

Recently, many complex games have started introducing players to the gaming world through a tutorial level that exists outside of the game-world proper. Players can access this tutorial world through the main menu as an alternative to starting a "real" game. These tutorial levels are generally a good idea and are certainly an improvement over teaching players about the game in the manual. The tutorial levels do one of the things

Deus Ex integrated its training into the game fiction in a very believable way.

that computers do best: provide an interactive learning experience. These levels tend to lead players by the hand through the game's mechanics, teaching them what they will need to know bit by bit. Sheri Graner Ray has found that some players, typically females, tend to prefer actually being led through the game for a bit until they get the hang of it, and structured tutorial levels are perfect for this. The one problem with tutorial levels is that they are seldom much fun to play, and as a result many players will skip them and head straight for the actual game. Beyond the learning of the controls, there is often little of interest in them. There is a feeling among players that the tutorial level is not part of the "real" game, and many players want to start playing this "real" game as soon as possible. If the designer includes a tutorial level because she wants to make her game difficult from the very beginning and avoid teaching players how to play through the gameplay, players who skip the tutorial will become frustrated. Tutorial levels are good for players who want that sort of educational prelude to the game, but they must not replace making the beginning of the game itself somewhat of a well-disguised tutorial that is easy to play. Again, *Half-Life* provided a tutorial level that taught players about the game-world, but the tutorial worked in conjunction with the beginning of the actual game itself, which was quite easy to play and had a friendly learning curve. Of course, making the tutorial level as entertaining as possible goes a long way toward encouraging players to actually play it. *Deus Ex* made some improvements on this front, setting the tutorial firmly in the game-world fiction and then having the training unexpectedly malfunction toward its end, suddenly thrusting players into a threatening situation. *Halo* took this same concept and executed it particularly elegantly without making the level feel like a tutorial level at all. Players were only stuck in a strange state for a brief time at the very start while they became accustomed to using the two-analog-stick control scheme. Then, suddenly, the spaceship the player character is on is overrun by hostile aliens. The first level players then play introduces them to the game's mechanics one by one in an area that looks dangerous but is actually pretty safe. Here was a training level completely camouflaged in the game-world that was a good deal of fun to play.

Console titles such as *The Legend of Zelda: Ocarina of Time* are good at teaching the player how to control the game.

Usually these tutorial levels include instructions that explain what keys or buttons players are supposed to press in order to achieve certain effects. Often on-screen text appears, sometimes accompanied by voice-overs that tell players to "Press the Spacebar to fire your primary weapon" or "Press and hold down the blue X for a super jump." *Halo*, again, had a very nice implementation of non-obtrusive help text that showed up during gameplay. The key with such automatic in-game help is that you want the players who do not need it to be able to ignore it fairly easily (or even have an option to turn it off completely), while it needs to show up and stay around long enough for those who do need it to see it. You need to make sure novice players will not miss it and will get a chance to apply it before it disappears. Well-implemented help text can be quite a boon to making a complex game easier to pick up. Beyond that, however, games like *Spyro the Dragon* and *The Legend of Zelda: Ocarina of Time* go so far as to have actual game characters tell the player character what the controls for the game are. In the former game, the friendly elder dragon says, "Spyro, press and hold the blue button in order to glide." I think this goes too far and totally shatters the player's suspension of disbelief. The in-game characters should not know anything about the player and certainly nothing about a PlayStation controller. However, I do think it is helpful to remind players of the game's controls while they are playing through more removed GUI displays and non-game character voice-overs. Many modern games include such sophisticated controls that they are likely to alienate non-hard-core gamers, and reminding novice players of what they need to do in order to perform a certain move is a good idea.

I would say that, in retrospect, most of my games have been too difficult, and certainly too hard for players to get into. The exception to this is *The Suffering*, which far and away did the best job of introducing mechanics to players gradually over the first level. Indeed, it was specifically designed to do this from the beginning of development. Though players get the impression that monsters are swarming all around the level, killing everything they encounter, in fact it is impossible to die for the first 10 to 15 minutes of the game. This gives players a safe place to learn the controls. During this safe period and throughout the first level unobtrusive help text shows up on the screen to help players learn the different actions they can perform. However, *The Suffering's* biggest failure was not ramping up the difficulty over the course of the game, making the game too easy overall. But that is less a training issue and more of a balancing problem. In terms of training, one game that erred in the opposite direction is *Odyssey*, my turn-based RPG. In it players start off shipwrecked on an island, without any weapons or possessions of any kind. I wanted players to immediately be frightened and need to find a safe place to hide in a nearby cave. I achieved this by having a few monsters start charging in the players' direction a few turns after the player character arrives on the beach. Players had no chance of defeating these creatures on their own, and needed to enter the nearby cave to survive. Originally, I had the cave hidden in the woods, making it hard for players to find and thereby making the game even more unforgiving. Fortunately, my playtesters convinced me that the introduction was too hard, and I moved the cave out into the open where players could easily see it. However, the problem remained that, before players even had a chance to become familiar with the controls, they were assaulted by strange monsters, with no real idea of what they were supposed to do about it. I often wonder how many players were frightened away by this overly challenging introduction and never played the rest of the game as a result.

Input/Output

Your game's input and output systems are two of the primary factors that determine how steep the learning curve for your game is and whether players will find it intuitive to play. Using the input/output systems you design, players must be able to control and understand the game effortlessly. Designing these systems is one of the hardest aspects of game design, since, if they are designed well, players will not even know they are there. But if they are designed poorly, players will become easily frustrated, complaining that the game's controls prevent them from doing what they really want to do in the game. Designing input and output systems is an "invisible" art in that the goal of their creation is for them to be transparent to players. This can sometimes lead to designers failing to fully consider how to best make the I/O work in their game, a mistake you must avoid if you want your games to be any fun to play.

Controls and Input

Nothing is more frustrating to players than knowing exactly what they want their game-world character to do but being unable to actually get her to do that because the controls will not let them. Good gameplay is never about trying to figure out the controls themselves; though you may want puzzles in your game-world, your control scheme should not be a puzzle players need to figure out. The controls are the players' interface between the real-world and game-world. In order for players to experience true immersion in the game they must be able to manipulate the game-world almost as intuitively as they manipulate the real-world. Every time players have to think, "Now, what button do I have to press to do that?" that immersion is destroyed.

Though the controls for many computer games seem to be getting more and more complex, particularly those for 3D action games, there is a lot to be said for keeping your controls simple. Indeed, a lot of the success of games like *Diablo*, *Command & Conquer*, and *The Sims* can be attributed to the fact that players can play these games one-handed, controlling everything with only the mouse. The mouse is an extremely

The *Diablo* series' extremely simple controls make them some of the easiest games to learn available. Pictured here: *Diablo II*.

powerful input device when used correctly. Its great strength is that it is a control device with which most non-gamer computer users are already familiar. This makes mouse-only games very easy to jump into, since they minimize the time the user must spend learning controls.

A big part of designing a good mouse-based interface is making a system that does not look as sterile and business-like as the Windows file manager yet retains its ease of use. Making the interface look attractive is mostly a matter of well-conceived art, but making it attractive without losing any of its intuitiveness and functionality can be quite challenging. Whenever an artist suggests making a button look a certain way, the designer must consider if the new design takes away from the player's ability to understand how that button works. Often, you can borrow clearly understood icons from other interfaces, either from other games or from real-world devices such as VCRs or CD players. For example, everyone knows what a "fast forward" symbol on an audio device looks like, and using this appropriately in your game will mean that players instantly know what a given button does. Making buttons in your game that players can intuitively understand and that also look attractive is equal parts creativity and playtesting. If a majority of the people playtesting your game tell you your buttons are unobvious and confusing, they almost definitely are, and you need to return to the drawing board.

A common game design mistake is to try to include too much. This applies to all aspects of gameplay, but particularly to controls, where sometimes the cliché "less is more" really holds true. Every time you add a new button or key to your game, you must ask yourself if the complexity you have just added to the game's controls is worth the functionality it enables. When designing a PC game, the temptation is particularly great, since the keyboard provides more keys than any game would ever need to use. Unfortunately, some games have tried to use nearly all of them, binding some unique function to practically each and every key. Complex keyboard controls favor expert players while alienating the novices, leading to a radically decreased number of people who might enjoy your game. Due to the limited number of buttons they provide, console control pads are much more limiting in what they will allow the designer to set up.

Unlike many other designers, particularly those making the switch from PC to console, I often feel that this limitation is a good one. Control pads force the designer to refine her controls, to cut away all that is extraneous, and to combine all of the game-world actions players can perform into just a few, focused controls. This leads directly to games that are easier to learn how to play. Indeed, many of the most accessible console games do not even use all of the controller's buttons. Because of the massive keyboard at their disposal, designers of PC games are not forced to focus the controls of their games in the same way, and I think their games may suffer for it. As I mentioned above, some of the most popular PC games have managed to squeeze all of their core controls into the mouse.

Much of the increasing complexity of game controls can be attributed to the increasing dominance of RT3D games. These games, by trying to include the ability for the player's game-world surrogate to move forward and backward, up and down, sideways left and right, turn left and right, and pitch up and down, have already used a massive number of controls while only allowing players to move in the game-world and do nothing else. In many ways, the perfect way to simply and intuitively control a character with total freedom in 3D space is still being explored. This is why for some time very few of the successful 3D games released allowed players total freedom to control their character. With the console success of complex first-person shooter-style games such as *Halo* and *Medal of Honor: Frontlines*, players seem to have grown accustomed to the intricacies of freely moving and looking around in an elaborate 3D environment. Nevertheless, in order to allow players a fighting chance, the most popular 3D games, such as *The Legend of Zelda: The Wind Waker, Max Payne, Grand Theft Auto III*, and *Tomb Raider*, continue to restrict player character movement to a ground plane.

StarCraft provides the player with a very elegant interface which allows her to issue orders to her units using a variety of techniques.

One technique that can be used to make your controls intuitive to a variety of players is to include multiple ways to achieve the same effect. For instance, if one looks at the interface used by the RTS game *StarCraft*, players are able to control their units by left-clicking to select the unit, then clicking on the button of the action they want the unit to perform, and then left-clicking on a location in the world where they want the unit to perform that action. Players can also left-click on the unit to select it and then immediately right-click in the game-world, causing the unit to do the most logical action for the location the players clicked, whether it means moving to that point or attacking the unit there. Furthermore, *StarCraft* also allows players to access a unit's different actions through a hot key instead of clicking on the button. This has the pleasant side effect of keeping the interface simple enough for novice players to handle, since it is all point-and-click, while the expert players can spend their time memorizing hot keys in order to improve their game. In many console action games, different buttons on the controller will perform the same action. A common choice to make, particularly on PlayStation games, is to allow players to control character movement through either the left directional pad or through the left analog control stick. *Crash Bandicoot*, for instance, allows players to move with either the directional pad or the analog stick, and also allows players to access Crash's ability to slide by pressing either a trigger button or one of the buttons on top of the controller. Providing multiple ways for players to achieve a single game-world action helps to ensure that a given player will enjoy using one of the ways you have provided.

There is a lot of room for creativity in game design, but control design is not one of the best areas to exercise your creative urges. Your game should be creative in its gameplay, story line, and other content, but not necessarily in its controls. Some of the most successful games have taken control schemes that players were already familiar with from other games and applied them to new and compelling content. Sometimes the established control scheme may be weak, but often it is not weak enough to justify striking out in an entirely new direction with your own control system. As a designer you must weigh what is gained through a marginally superior control scheme with what is lost because of player confusion. For example, Sid Meier's fine RTS game *Gettysburg!* included as its default method for ordering troops around a "click-and-drag" system instead of the established "click-and-click" system found in other games. His system was quite creative and actually may have been a better way of controlling the game than the established paradigms. However, it was not so much better that it outweighed the confusion players experienced when first attempting to play the game, a fact he admits in the interview included in Chapter 2 of this book. Console games are particularly good at providing uniform control schemes, with fans of games in a particular genre able to pick up and immediately start playing almost any game available in the genre, even if they have never seen it before.

During the course of the development of a game, as you are playing the game over and over and over again, it is very easy to get accustomed to bad controls. Though the controls may be poorly laid out or counterintuitive, as a game's designer working on a project for several years, you may have used the controls so much that they have become second nature. However, as soon as others play the game for the first time, they will quickly be frustrated by these controls and are likely to stop playing as a result. Indeed, when I ran *Drakan: The Ancients' Gates* a few years after it shipped, I was immediately stunned at how bizarre and disorienting the controls were, particularly the ability to look left and right on the PS2's right analog stick. Other members of the team I showed it to were similarly shocked. "We shipped it like that?" they said incredulously. Over the course of three years developing the game, we had grown familiar with the game's oddities and the controls seemed fantastic. With some distance between ourselves and the game, we were able to see its glaring control problems. Ideally, a proper playtesting phase will include many players playing the game for the first time, and witnessing their initial reaction to the controls is crucial to understanding how intuitive your controls really are. Do not think, "Oh, she'll get used to it," or "What an idiot! These controls are obvious; why can't she see that!" or "Well, *I* like them the way they are." Instead think, "Why are my controls bad and what can I do to fix them?"

Designing controls that players will find intuitive can be quite challenging, especially with such a variety of control setups for different games, particularly in the PC market. For example, back when the FPS genre was first establishing itself, it was hard to determine what the "standard" controls for an FPS should be since the last three successful FPS games had all employed unique control schemes. Thankfully, over time, the controls became standardized, and now fans of shooting mayhem are easily able to jump into almost any FPS they come across. Almost every PC action game released in the last decade allows players to configure the controls however they desire, and this is an absolute must for any PC game that demands players manipulate a large number of buttons. That said, many players never find or use the control configuration screens, either because of a desire to start playing the game immediately or a general lack of savvy with the computer. Many, many players will be left playing with whatever the default keys are, and this is why it is the designer's job to make sure these default settings are as playable as possible. Here, following the standard set by most other games is very important. You should never use a strange or confusing set of default controls for your game merely because the programmer in charge likes it that way or the team has grown accustomed to them. Always make sure the default controls are as intuitive as possible, and if this involves shameless imitation, so be it.

When the attempt to have unique controls did not work out as planned, *The Suffering* was changed to emulate control systems from other games.

Making a game in an established genre is one thing, but when it comes to developing a game that tries to do something substantially new with what actions players can perform, there is no way to avoid spending a lot of time on the controls. After you get them so you like them, you must put them in front of players to see how well they work in practice instead of theory. Trying out brave new control styles is a noble endeavor, but you will need to make sure players actually prefer them to more traditional methods. And as you gather their feedback, long-term iteration is all but unavoidable. One example of this happened on my game *The Suffering*. The game was a shooter and we wanted to make it as console-friendly as possible, and thereby took *Devil May Cry* as a source of inspiration. At the same time, we wanted players to have the freedom to move through the environment and position and orient their camera like in first-person shooters or, specifically, *Syphon Filter* and our own *Drakan: The Ancients' Gates*. So we developed a hybrid targeting system that provided players with intuitive movement through the world with a single thumb stick, but then allowed for simple targeting of enemies. We spent a long time developing this system and iterating on it, and felt we had done a pretty good job. Then we started hearing grumblings from fellow developers we showed the game to that the controls seemed odd. When we finally put the game in front of players their feedback almost universally mentioned the controls as what they liked least about the game. We tried tweaking it a bit more, showed it to some more players, and found that the controls still seemed odd. At this point we were fairly far into development and realized that the innovative control scheme we had attempted simply was not working out. Since it was the control system we were having a problem with, we decided it made the most sense to imitate some existing control schemes. We wanted something powerful that we knew players would be familiar with, so we copied the two-analog-stick scheme that most of the other current console shooters, including *Max Payne* and *Halo*, were using. At this point we were imitating instead of innovating, but when we put the game in front of players again with our new control scheme they almost all praised the quality of our controls and then were able to focus their complaints on other aspects of the game.

Particularly in action games, when your controls are perfect, the wall separating players from the game-world will disappear and they will start to feel like they truly are the game-world character. This is the ultimate sign of an immersive game, and achieving this effect is impossible without strong controls. In a game where that level of immersion is possible, the controls must be completely invisible to players. This can be frustrating to a designer. Why work so hard on something that, if implemented perfectly, will be completely invisible? The designer must realize that it is the transparency of controls that allows players to enjoy the rest of what the game has to offer.

Output and Game-World Feedback

While the player's ability to intuitively control the game-world may be key to a successful game, outputting vital information about that game-world to players is just as important. Computer games contain numerous complex systems, commonly performing more calculations than a human would ever be able to track. Indeed, that is the area where computer games excel. Condensing that massive amount of data into its most instructive form and communicating that information to players is key to a well-designed output system.

Consider a strategy game in which players have a number of units scattered all over a large map. The map is so large that only a small portion of it can fit on the screen at once. If a group of the players' units happen to be off-screen and are attacked but players are not made aware of it by the game, players will become irritated. Consider an

RPG where each member of the players' party needs to be fed regularly, but the game does not provide any clear way of easily communicating how hungry their characters are. Then, if one of the party members suddenly keels over from starvation, the players will become frustrated, and rightly so. Why should players have to guess at or go digging for such game-critical information? In an action game, if players have to kill an enemy by shooting it in a particular location of its body, say its eye, they need to receive positive feedback when they successfully land a blow. Perhaps the enemy reels back in pain or screams in agony once an attack damages him. If players do not receive such feedback, how are they supposed to know they are on the right track? Of course, all computer games conceal a certain amount of information from players, and cannot possibly communicate all of the information they have about the game-world to players. But they must communicate what is reasonable and important for the players to know, and communicate that data effectively.

Almost all games present players with a view of the game-world as the central part of their output system. Through this view players see the object they are currently controlling and its location and state in the game-world. Your game should try to communicate as much information through this view as possible. Consider a third-person 3D action game. Certainly players see the environment and position of their game-world surrogate, but what about the condition of the player character? Perhaps as its health goes down, the character's animations change to a limp or hobble instead of moving normally. Similarly, the strength of the current armor can be represented by texture changes on that character, with the armor appearing more and more deteriorated as it takes damage and nears destruction. The game can represent the character's current weapon by showing that weapon equipped on the character. If players have a spell of protection currently in effect on their character, perhaps the character should emit a certain glow to easily communicate that. Though the designer may also want to include this data in a heads up display (HUD) of some sort, communicating it through the game's primary game-world view makes it that much more transparent and easy for players to understand.

What the game-world view cannot represent is typically contained in some sort of a GUI, which usually borders the game-world view or is overlaid on top of it like a HUD. This GUI may be simple, such as the high-score and lives remaining display on *Centipede*, the small potion-health display at the bottom of the screen in the original *Prince of Persia*, or the score/moves display in almost any Infocom game. For more complicated games, the GUI is also more complex, such as the button bars used in any of Maxis' *Sim* games, the elaborate status display in the original *System Shock*, or the extensive party data provided in many RPGs, such as the *Bard's Tale* games. Many GUIs in older games were created in order to block off a large portion of the screen. This was not because of any sort of design decision, but instead because the game's engine was not fast enough to handle rendering the game-world full screen. As engine technology has improved, games have attempted to make the game-world view take up the majority of the screen, with the GUI minimized as much as possible.

A few games try to work without any GUI whatsoever. *Crash Bandicoot*, for instance, only displays the lives remaining GUI if players press a button to bring it on the screen; otherwise a completely unobstructed view of the world is displayed. Another example is *Oddworld: Abe's Oddysee*. The game's director, Lorne Lanning, felt

Oddworld: Abe's Oddysee did away with an in-game GUI entirely, giving the player an unobstructed view of the game-world.

very strongly that any sort of GUI would distance players from the game-world. As a result, Abe's health is communicated to players through the way he animates. Since the game grants players infinite lives, there was no need for a lives remaining display that so many console platformer games of the time included as their only HUD element. Certainly, as technology has allowed it, the trend has been to get away from on-screen HUDs as much as possible, allowing the game-world view to take over the screen. The advantages of the immersion gained by a minimized GUI are obvious, and if the game-world can effectively communicate all of the information the players need to play, there is sometimes no reason to use a GUI at all.

On the other hand, it is important to not go too far in the quest to eliminate a GUI. In general, a small, unobtrusive HUD is a game convention that players have grown accustomed to and thus are very unlikely to be bothered by. Though having no HUD worked pretty well in the *Oddworld* games, *The Getaway* is an otherwise fun game that suffered because of the developer's decision to avoid a HUD. Driving around London was needlessly difficult because, instead of having a map HUD, players were forced to navigate to their destination by making turns based on hints from the blinking turn signals on their car. This was a particularly imperfect and infuriating system when navigating the labyrinthine streets of London. Similarly, the game has no health meter, and players are required to use a considerably less precise and quite subtle player texture change to figure out their character's health status. Given the game's shooting and driving mechanics, leaving out the HUD hurt the gameplay far beyond the immersion that was gained.

The most important part of designing a GUI is to try to keep it as visual as possible. In fast-paced action games in particular, the GUI is designed to communicate information to the players very quickly, whether this is the players' current health, ammo available, or nearby monsters (through some sort of radar). If anything, the ascendancy of the graphical user interface as the dominant mode of controlling a computer, first through the Macintosh and subsequently through Windows, shows that most people think visually instead of in numbers or words. As a result, a well-designed graphical HUD in your game will be easier for players to glance at and understand than one that contains a lot of numbers or words. This explains the superiority of the health bar over a health number or percentage. The artists will like a graphical HUD as well, since a health bar can look a lot more attractive than a big, ugly number. Though some amount of fine precision will be lost with a less precise health bar, players are willing to sacrifice this because the bar is so much easier to read quickly.

The head at the bottom of the screen in *Doom* is a well-designed interface element because it communicates the player's current health visually.

A game element that is particularly well designed is the "head" used in *Doom* and *Quake*. This face, which appears at the center of the bottom of the screen, represents the players' approximate health completely visually. The face starts out healthy and snarling, ready to take on the world. As the players progress and they lose health, the head starts to look bruised and bloodied, eventually looking all but dead when players have almost run out of health. At any point during the game players are able to glance down at the head and instantly get a sense of how much health they have remaining. If the health had been represented instead by a number, it would have been much more difficult for players to comprehend their current health level just by glancing at it. The difference in time may be milliseconds, but in a fast-action game, that may be the difference between life and death.

Of course, the visual representation of data can also have a negative side effect if that representation is too obtuse for players to easily understand. For instance, in *WarCraft*, the buttons for the different actions that a unit can perform are all represented by icons, which I would generally encourage. However, some of the buttons can be a little difficult to figure out at first. Fortunately, the game also displays text at the bottom of the screen when the players' mouse cursor hovers over a particular button, communicating what that button will do if clicked. What would have been even better is if the icons on the buttons were just a bit more obvious. Admittedly, representing a real-world action such as "guard" through a 32 x 32 icon can be quite a challenge. The GUI for your game needs to balance the superiority of visual representation with the clarity of text, possibly using a combination of both as needed.

Audio output as a communication device to players is something that is often underused in games. Not all of the information about the game-world needs to be communicated to players through visual stimuli. For instance, in *The Sims*, players gain a good sense of whether their character is enjoying a particular conversation based on the tone of the participants' voices. In *Command & Conquer*, players know that a unit has received a particular order by an audio cue provided by that unit: "I'll get right on it!" Similarly, when units off-screen are being attacked, the game communicates this to players by saying "Unit attacked" or "Unit lost." Audio cues can provide an excellent supplement to on-screen information, or can work quite effectively as the sole way of communicating critical information.

A good output system for a game is both powerful and intuitive. It allows players to jump right into the game and understand what is happening in the game-world, but it also provides expert players with all the information they need to play the game effectively. Over time, the data the game communicates to the players should become transparent, just as the players' controls should become invisible once players are familiar with them. Players should not have to think about understanding the state of the world; they should just retrieve what they need by quickly looking at the screen, and then be able to react to it just as quickly through intuitive and responsive controls. As I have stated before, it is important not to get too creative in developing your input/output systems. The dominant paradigms from other games are often dominant for a reason: they work. The expression that "good artists borrow but great artists steal" is nowhere more true than in I/O design in games.

Basic Elements

In this chapter I have discussed just a few of the elements of good gameplay: unique solutions, non-linearity, modeling reality, teaching players, and input/output. I feel that each of these components deserves serious thought as you set out to develop a game. Of course, this is far from a complete list, and as you work as a game designer you will accumulate your own personal list of elements that you feel contribute to good gameplay. No one can say for certain what the elements of good game design are. Each game designer must decide that for herself. This personal preference is part of what makes each game bear the distinct stamp of its author and lends the best games the individuality that makes them great.

Chapter 8:
Game Analysis: Tetris

Designed by Alexey Pajitnov
Released in 1987

Few games are as universally well respected by game developers as *Tetris*. Often when a game becomes as popular as *Tetris* has, with versions for every system imaginable and untold millions in sales, gaming professionals start complaining about what a poor game it is. *Myst* is a good example of this. On its release, the title received near universal praise from the gaming press for being a fun adventure game in a beautifully conceived world. Game developers themselves, though not quite as enthusiastic, still thought it was a good game. Multiple millions of copies later with years spent on the best-seller charts, the same gaming press found reason to start hating the game and its amazing continued popularity. Game developers are particularly loud in voicing their dislike for the game. Is the game worse now? No, of course not. Do gaming professionals, press and developers alike, resent the game for its sales? It would appear so.

But this is not the case with *Tetris*. *Tetris* conquered the world in terms of popularity, yet one is hard pressed to find anyone with a negative comment about the game. What is it about *Tetris* that makes the game immune to criticism? It would appear something about the game's simplicity and clearness of design vision makes even the most cynical game developer concede the game's greatness. Contrary to what happened with *Myst*, when *Tetris* was first released, most of the gaming press dwelled on the game's origins in Russia and seemed underwhelmed, or at least unexcited, by the title's gameplay. The game was so simple, its technology so lacking in razzle-dazzle that, perhaps, the press found themselves incapable of writing enthusiastically about the game — at least at first. Now that the game is an undisputed classic, any game critic will be happy to tell you about the hundreds of hours he spent blissfully lost in the game.

Gameplay in *Tetris* is exceedingly uncomplicated. The game-world is a tall, rectangular, 2D box. Blocks appear at the top of the box. The blocks are made up of four squares arranged in every possible pattern where all the squares share at least one side with another square. The blocks then slowly fall to the bottom of the box, and players are able to move these blocks to the left and right, or rotate the piece in 90 degree increments. Once the block hits an obstruction, either the bottom of the box or another piece, the block stops moving, players lose control of the block, and another piece that players can now control appears at the top of the screen. When the blocks at the bottom of the screen form a horizontal line across the rectangle, that line of squares disappears, and any squares above that line move down one row. The players' game is over once incomplete rows of the blocks fill up the game-world rectangle and subsequent pieces are prevented from entering the play-field.

Puzzle Game or Action Game?

Tetris is often referred to as a puzzle game, and for good reason. *Tetris* has elements obviously reminiscent of a puzzle, with players needing to find how blocks best fit together. In this way the game is similar to a right-angle jigsaw puzzle, or any number of other "organize these geometrical shapes in this small space" puzzles. An even better comparison would be the traditional game pentomino, from which Alexey Pajitnov, *Tetris*'s designer, is supposed to have drawn inspiration. In pentomino, one must take twelve different shaped pieces, each made out of five squares, and fit them into a square box. One can see the similarities, but at the same time *Tetris* changes the game into something entirely different, something entirely more challenging and compelling. Pajitnov could have just as easily made a direct adaptation of pentomino to the computer, as many other developers have done for jigsaw puzzles or "sliding number"-type puzzles. This might have been an entertaining program, though perhaps not as fun as the actual game itself since part of the fun of pentomino is the tactile nature of manipulating the blocks. But by taking the puzzle and changing it into a game that could only happen on the computer, Pajitnov ended up creating a unique new game that is far more entertaining than the original.

Many times when members of the computer game intelligentsia refer to a game as being a puzzle game, they do so with derision. For them a puzzle game is one that

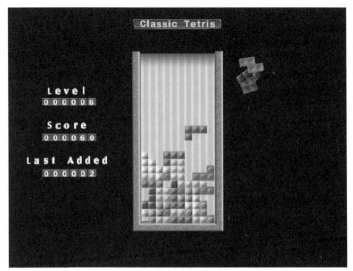

Classic Tetris

Level
0 0 0 0 0 6

Score
0 0 0 0 6 0

Last Added
0 0 0 0 0 2

Tetris carefully balances action and puzzle elements to create a unique gameplay experience. Pictured here, and throughout this chapter: classic mode in *The Next Tetris*.

presents a series of static puzzles to players, puzzles that never change and never react to the players' actions. They argue that a game must provide a reaction to the players' actions and an opponent for players to compete against. Hence, the critics would say, these so-called "puzzle games" are not really games at all, but just puzzles. Furthermore, often the puzzles found in these games have only one solution, further limiting the players' interactive experience. Examples would include most all adventure games, such as *Zork*, *Myst*, or even *Grim Fandango*, games that, though they provide players with a world to explore and challenging puzzles to complete, do nothing to create a unique experience for players.

But *Tetris* is never criticized for this shortcoming because it so brilliantly combines the mechanics of a puzzle game with the mechanics of an action game in order to create a truly compelling gameplay experience. Thus everyone who plays *Tetris*, each time they play it, has a unique experience. One action game mechanic *Tetris* uses is the sense of an ever-approaching threat that players have to address in a limited amount of time. Just as most fiction revolves around dramatic tension, so do games, and *Tetris* is no exception. In *Centipede* this threat is the arthropod winding its way down from the top of the screen. In *Tetris* it is the block dropping from above. If players do not move and rotate as well as determine an optimal placement for the piece before it reaches the bottom of the screen, it may get stuck in a location that blocks off lower rows from being completed, and players get one or more lines closer to ending their game. As gameplay progresses, the speed at which these blocks fall from the top of the screen increases, thus increasing the challenge for players and ramping up the difficulty over the course of the game.

Another similarity between *Tetris* and action games that further distinguishes it from other puzzle games is the variety of gameplay situations *Tetris* can create: each game played is unique. The play mechanics set up an infinitely large number of unique games, with each move players decide to make influencing the rest of their game. The way a piece is positioned into the blocks already at the bottom of the screen directly impacts where the next piece can be placed. Should players fill up the four-block-long slot with only two blocks from an upside-down "L"-shaped piece? Or should they hold out, waiting for that desperately needed "I"-shaped piece? The "L" will not fill the slot completely, but no one knows how long it will be until the "I" piece arrives. In other cases players may have a number of different positions in which to put a piece, and must think ahead, figuring out if they put a piece in a given slot what sort of slots that will leave available for later pieces. Players constantly have to consider where future blocks will or will not be able to fit. Players may learn to recognize certain piece configurations, but every game is sufficiently unique that no players can be completely prepared for the challenges they may face.

Tetris as a Classic Arcade Game

Despite being developed years after classic arcade games had fallen out of style, *Tetris*'s gameplay embodies many of the design principles of that genre of games.

There are many indications that *Tetris* is an example of what I call the "classic arcade game" form. This is despite the fact that it was not originally conceived for gameplay in the arcades (though its rampant popularity eventually led to its arrival there), and that it was created years after the classic arcade game form had stopped being used by professional arcade game developers. Looking over the list of classic arcade game qualities described in the *Centipede* analysis in Chapter 4, we can see just how Tetris fits the guiding principles of the form.

- Single Screen Play: Of course, *Tetris* takes place on only one screen. Players are able to view the entire game-world at one time and make informed decisions about what they want to do with a given piece based on that. There is no exploration component to the game, no way to really surprise players (beyond what piece appears next), so players have all the information they need to be successful at the game, and have nothing to blame but themselves for failure.

- Infinite Play: *Tetris* allows players to keep playing until, through their own bad decisions, the blocks reach the top of the box. Every game ends in defeat, and no one can truly say they have "beaten" the game. Players can always find ways to improve their *Tetris* playing ability. This is a crucial difference between *Tetris* and a traditional puzzle. Once players have solved a puzzle, if they remember how they did it the first time, the puzzle will no longer present any challenge to them. People usually do not enjoy doing puzzles multiple times, whereas a well-designed game can be replayed forever. *Tetris* is just such a game.

- Multiple Lives: Unlike most classic arcade games, the original *Tetris* implementation only offers players one life. Once the blocks reach the top of the box, the players' game is over. The design of the game, however, allows players to see that they are doing poorly while not defeating them instantly. As the blocks stack up at the bottom of the rectangle, players see the mistakes they are making and have time to figure out how to better line up the blocks before their game is over. So, while *Tetris* does not offer players multiple lives, it does give them a chance to learn the game well enough to achieve some minor successes before forcing them to start over.

- Scoring/High Scores: *Tetris* uses a model for giving players a score and recording it in a high-score table, which is directly taken from the system used in games like *Asteroids* or *Galaga*. Indeed, since the game cannot be defeated, it is the possibility of achieving a higher score that can become the players' true impetus to play the game again.

- Easy-to-Learn, Simple Gameplay: *Tetris* truly excels in how simple and obvious its game mechanics are. Players really only need three buttons in order to play the game successfully, and these all translate into obvious results on the screen. This means that virtually anyone, regardless of how familiar they are with computer games, can walk up to the game and start playing it immediately. However, players will never be able to fully master the game due to the game's ramping-up difficulty and the potential for infinitely long games.

- No Story: *Tetris* has even less story than most classic arcade games, and is the case most often cited by people who want to point out that games do not need stories to be compelling for players. The only sort of setting *Tetris* has is its origins in Russia, which has been used for various aesthetic effects in the different incarnations of the game. The first PC version of the game, as published by Spectrum Holobyte, included backdrops behind the gameplay that involved different scenes from Russian life, and the music sounded vaguely Slavic in origin. But once people learned what a great game *Tetris* was, subsequent implementations of the game, such as the one for the Nintendo GameBoy, had no Russian theme to them and had no setting or story at all. The game did not suffer one bit for this lack of story. Indeed, *Tetris*'s total lack of setting may actually be something that separates it from the classic arcade games, which all made an attempt to be grounded in a fantasy world of some sort, whether it was outer space in *Galaga*, insects in a garden in *Centipede*, or funky ghosts chasing a little yellow man around in *Pac-Man*. *Tetris* has no such pretensions, and thus stands out.

The Technology

Another similarity between *Tetris* and classic arcade games is that none of those games relied on their technology to impress players. For CAGs, the graphics the arcade machines in the early '80s could produce were so lackluster compared to what players would find in other media, such as movies or television, that players had to be drawn in by something else. As a result, the gameplay had to be truly captivating for these games to survive. Despite the fact that much more sophisticated graphics were available by the time *Tetris* was released in the West in the late '80s, the game did not need fancier graphics and stuck to a very simple 2D implementation. *Tetris*'s gameplay is so strong that it does not matter how technologically simple its implementation may be, the game is still wildly entertaining.

The implementation of *Tetris* is so simple that many aspiring game programmers start out by making a *Tetris* clone. Indeed, numerous companies have attempted to add fancy graphical effects to the game, including making it 3D. The first of these was probably *Welltris*, a sequel of sorts to *Tetris*, designed by Pajitnov. In *Welltris*, a 3D "well" takes the place of the *Tetris* box. *Tetris*-style pieces (though not always of four blocks) fall down along the sides of the well and must be lined up into rows on the bottom. The gameplay was considerably more complex without being particularly more fun or challenging. As a result, players were uninterested, and went back to the simplicity of the original. Many subsequent *Tetris* knockoffs attempted to make "improvements" on the original, either through fancy effects or special pieces of various sorts. None of these attempts were particularly successful, and players continued to want to return to the original.

The attempts to add technological sophistication to *Tetris* failed, not just commercially but also artistically. The enhanced technology added to these knockoff products was actually detrimental to the original game design, polluting its purity and making the game lose its elegance and fun in the process. Of course, the moral to the story is that enhanced technology is not necessarily beneficial to a given game, and game designers must be wary when the whiz-bang engine effects start to get in the way of what makes the game entertaining in the first place.

While *Tetris* may have not needed much in the way of computer technology to function, it is worth pointing out that there could be no *Tetris* without a computer. *Tetris* is not a game adapted from a pen and paper or board game, but rather something that only can exist in a world carefully controlled and governed by a computer. As mentioned previously, Pajitnov is said to have drawn his inspiration from the non-computer puzzle game pentomino. In adapting it to the computer, Pajitnov changed it into a form that could exist only on a computer. The descending of the pieces from the top of the screen at a steady rate, the way they can interact with the pieces already at the bottom of the screen, and the random way in which pieces become available to players are all operations only a computer program could provide while still allowing for an entertaining experience for players. These are all tasks the computer performs expertly, and it was brilliant of Pajitnov to think to add them to his game.

Artificial Intelligence

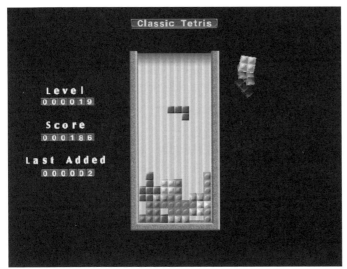

Tetris has a very limited artificial intelligence that randomly picks the blocks which fall into the play-field. Despite its simplicity, this AI provides the perfect challenge for the player.

All the game has in terms of AI is the random number generator that picks the next piece to enter the play-field. However, the game mechanics are such that this random number is enough to completely change each game, presenting players with unique challenges after every piece is dropped. Since the randomness ensures that players never know what the next piece will be, they are forced to play the piece in a way that is optimal for whatever one of the seven pieces comes along next. (Many incarnations of *Tetris* include a "next" feature, which shows players the next piece that will come onto the play-field, a feature that does make the game a bit easier. Even when using this, however, players still do not know what the next-next-piece will be, hence they are still just making an educated guess as to where to stick the currently falling block.) If gameplay is about opposition, meaning an opponent providing a challenge to which players must react, and if in solitary computer games that opponent is the computer, then the fact that a random number generator provides all the challenge in *Tetris* demonstrates an important point. The AI the players face only needs to be as smart as the game mechanics require. An AI needs to present players with a situation that will challenge them, and it really does not matter how the AI establishes that challenge. It could be as complicated as the AI for a deep strategy game like *Civilization*, or it could be as simple as the random piece picker found in *Tetris*. What matters is that the AI matches up with the game mechanics to sufficiently challenge players.

The random nature in which pieces arrive at the top of the screen might suggest to the reader that success at *Tetris* is just luck. If the pieces players get are random, how can different players' scores be compared against one another? The key point to realize here is that, over time, the randomness of the pieces evens out. Just as die rolls in a board game even out over the course of the game, the random pieces passed to players in *Tetris* end up functioning as if they were not random at all. Since there are only seven types of pieces, none with more than four blocks, and since players (at least initially) have a large space in which to manipulate them, the randomness keeps the game from becoming predictable while still making one player's game comparable to another's. Over the course of a game, players will get a few hundred pieces. The number of times players get just the piece they were looking for is evened out by the times they do not get the piece they want. It may be that players will fail to get exactly the right piece at the right time and that, since the box is already full of pieces, the game ends as a result. However, in order to get to a situation where they could not use whatever piece was given to them, players have already made a number of mistakes. In the end, the random piece picker found in *Tetris* provides a fair, consistent challenge to all players.

Escalating Tension

Tetris is very ruthless in the way it escalates tension throughout the game. Unlike a game such as *Centipede*, *Tetris* players get no reprieve when a wave ends, nor do they get the ability to "start fresh" when they lose a life. In *Tetris* players "die" when the box fills up with pieces that fail to make complete rows, and their game is over, period. This means that players must be constantly on their guard, constantly considering what to do with a piece before it reaches the bottom of the screen. Even a fast-paced game such as *Doom* provides players with plenty of respites from the action. In that first-person shooter, there are safe corners to hide in and rooms where, once all the threats have been eliminated, players can wait indefinitely without being threatened. *Tetris* never lets up and constantly confronts players with a new challenge that must be addressed.

The only reprieve players find in *Tetris* is when they "battle their way back" from a tricky situation. Say players have dropped some blocks in bad locations, thereby blocking off uncompleted rows below. Now the game is harder because they have less space and time to manipulate their pieces before they are stopped at the bottom of the screen. The game's tension has escalated as a result of the players' mistakes. Players may be able, through careful placement of subsequent pieces, to erase the poorly placed bricks and finally complete the rows below. Now the game's tension has decreased and players are back to where they were, with more space and time to manipulate the falling pieces. Players feel a sense of accomplishment and relief. They are able to relax momentarily, knowing they have a "clean slate" to work with once again. Of course, this only lasts until other mistakes are made, and then the game's tension increases once again.

Further escalating the game's tension is the acceleration of the speed at which the pieces fall over the course of the game. When the players' score increases above certain specific amounts, the pieces in the game start moving at a faster rate, which makes the game more nerve-racking for players. Since the pieces fall down the board more quickly, players have less time to figure out the best position for a given piece, and also less time to manipulate the piece into that position. At the game's fastest speed, most players will be incapable of placing a piece in an ideal location, and with a piece in the wrong place the game only gets harder. Just before the speed increases, players might start to feel that they have mastered the game and could play *Tetris* indefinitely. But when the speed increases, whatever sort of rhythm players had established is thrown off. Now players need to do everything they were doing before, only faster.

Once players start making mistakes in *Tetris*, these mistakes compound, making the game harder and harder to play. As players fail to complete rows at the bottom of the screen, they have less and less space in which to manipulate their pieces. When players accidentally drop a piece in the wrong location, that piece may block rows below from being completed, and will make it harder to maneuver subsequent pieces around that ill-placed piece. When players try to hold out for an "I"-shaped piece to fill a narrow column of empty spots, players will have to keep placing other pieces in perhaps less-than-perfect locations until that piece randomly arrives. In all these ways, *Tetris* penalizes players for failure. Instead of giving players a chance to catch up as some computer games do, *Tetris* just punishes them, making it even harder to come back from errors made previously. Further complicating matters are the bonus points players receive for removing four rows all at once with an "I" piece. With this tactic, the game tempts players into taking potentially game-ending risks.

Simplicity and Symmetry

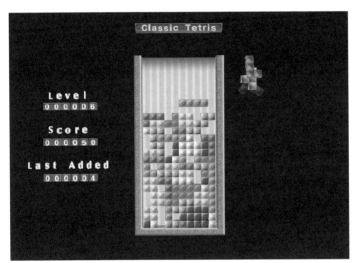

All of the pieces in *Tetris* are composed of four squares, each of which shares at least one side with another square. This gives the game an inherent consistency and balance.

    Tetris, as has been discussed, is a very simple game. A big part of its success is due to its simplicity and that it is so easy to learn while being so relentlessly challenging. Players do not need to learn any special moves in order to play the game. There are a very small number of keys used by the game, and those keys produce very obvious results on the screen. It is interesting to look at the pieces used in *Tetris*. They are all composed of four squares, and, in fact, the seven different types of pieces used in the game represent every possible combination of four squares, where each square must share a side with another square in its group. Since players can rotate the pieces to whatever orientation they want, there are only seven truly unique combinations of squares possible.

    It has been reported that Pajitnov, in creating *Tetris*, originally considered using pieces consisting of five squares combined into twelve unique pieces. Indeed, the pentomino game from which Pajitnov drew his inspiration used twelve five-square pieces. Pajitnov soon realized that this was too many different pieces to have to manipulate in *Tetris*'s high-pressure setting, where players have a limited amount of time to find a perfect fit for a given piece. Certainly a game using five-square pieces could have been challenging in its own way, and perhaps a slower falling speed and larger play-field could have compensated for the added complexity of the larger pieces. But would it have been *Tetris*? No. Would it have been as fun and addictive as *Tetris*? Probably not. At some point a complexity level begins to stifle the core nature of a game and confuses players instead of challenging them. Using five instead of four squares ruined the simplicity Pajitnov was striving for, and as a result he reduced the number of squares a piece could have. Similarly, if he had used only three squares, the game would have been too simple. It would appear *Tetris* expertly follows the adage that everything should be as simple as possible but no simpler.

There are actually thirteen unique combinations of five squares possible, where each square shares a side with another square. So it would appear that the original pentomino game, with its twelve blocks, did not use a complete set of pieces. I have never tried pentomino, so I have no idea how much fun that puzzle may be. Part of what makes *Tetris* so elegant is the completeness of its pieces. Every possible permutation of four squares with squares sharing sides is used in the game. Remove any one of the pieces from *Tetris* and the game's balance would suffer. When playing, players will find themselves presented with situations that cry out for certain pieces. Certain arrangements of the blocks on the bottom of the screen leave holes that can only be perfectly filled by a specific *Tetris* piece. Part of what lends *Tetris* its balance is the fact that Pajitnov was wise enough to include each piece possible, thus providing a piece for every type of gap. The natural completeness and symmetry of the pieces available to players in *Tetris* is a crucial component of its balance.

Fifteen Years On, Who Would Publish Tetris?

One must wonder, if *Tetris* were created today, what publisher would be willing to publish it. Originally *Tetris* was sold as "the game from Russia" and featured art and music of a similar nature, almost as a gesture to our new friends in what was then the U.S.S.R. Had *Tetris* been dreamed up by a kid in a garage in Iowa one wonders if it ever would have been published at all. (One would like to be optimistic and think that he would have been able to code it up, release it as shareware or to the casual games market on the Internet, and the game's fame would still have been assured.) *Tetris* is the ultimate in low-technology gameplay, and many game publishers simply refuse to publish games that do not utilize the latest in computer graphics wizardry. After all, where will they find the pretty screenshots for the back of the box? The game lacks any sort of story or even setting, another absolute must for the people in marketing. What sort of copy will they write in their ads? Indeed, it is a testament to *Tetris*'s brilliant gameplay that it cannot be adequately described in any amount of words, much less in a catchy one-liner. Even looking at a static screenshot of *Tetris* is a thoroughly unexciting experience, one which cannot hope to communicate the game's sublime art. Gameplay is an elusive subject for manipulators of the written word; it must be experienced to be understood.

Chapter 9:
Artificial Intelligence

"I'd basically watch the game play until I saw the AI do something stupid, then try to correct that and repeat ad infinitum. Over a long enough period that produced a pretty darn good AI. I have always tried to teach the AI the same successful strategies that I use in playing a game."

— Brian Reynolds, talking about the creation of the artificial intelligence for his games *Civilization II* and *Alpha Centauri*

Artificial intelligence can mean a variety of different things in different contexts. In an academic context, artificial intelligence is sometimes defined as a system that can reliably pass what is called the *Turing test*. In the Turing test, humans are presented with computer terminals into which they can type various sentences and can then see responses printed on the screen. If the users believe that the responses were provided by a human, even though they were actually provided by the computer, then that computer would have passed the Turing test and could be said to possess artificial intelligence.

One could apply a similar test to computer games. If one is playing a game of *Unreal Tournament* and cannot tell if the opponent one is playing against is a human opponent or a 'bot, then one could say that the game passes a limited version of the Turing test and therefore possesses some sort of artificial intelligence. However, in actual practice, even if the game had failed that test, people would have said that the game has artificial intelligence, just not really good artificial intelligence. When game developers talk about artificial intelligence, they do not mean the computer's ability to trick players into thinking they are playing against actual human opponents. Instead, game developers refer to whatever code is used to control the opponents that players battle as artificial intelligence. In AI research, the end goal is to simulate the human mind. In a game, the ultimate goal is to make sure the game experience is fun. How the game reacts to players' actions is determined by the game's AI, and thereby the quality of the AI determines how fun and challenging the game is. The reactions of the game may be completely random or completely logical; in either case the code that controls those reactions is referred to as the game's artificial intelligence.

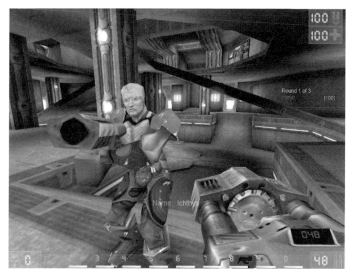

If a player plays a game of *Unreal Tournament* and cannot tell whether the opponent is a 'bot or a human, the 'bot's artificial intelligence has passed the Turing test.

Consider a game like *Centipede*. The AI for this game is completely predictable, with the various insects moving in predetermined patterns, with a small amount of randomness thrown in. Some people would say that the game does not really have any AI. Indeed, the behaviors of the creatures in the game are exceedingly simple to implement. But at the same time, the game provides a great deal of challenge for the player. The difficult part of creating the AI for a game like *Centipede* lies entirely in the design of those creatures' behaviors and in coming up with the movement patterns that will provide an interesting challenge for the player. The AI is more design than implementation. *Tetris*, perhaps, is an even more extreme example. The only AI the game could be said to have is the random number generator that determines which piece will drop into the play-field next. Yet *Tetris* is designed such that this is the only AI the game needs.

The reader may be wondering why I am talking about game AI in a book about game design. Surely AI is a programming task, and since this book is not about programming, the discussion of AI contained in this chapter may seem out of place. But determining what the AI will do and actually programming that behavior are two fairly distinct tasks. The first primarily involves creativity and the second consists of a whole lot of hard work. A game's designer should be intimately concerned with making sure the game's AI behavior is as well conceived as possible and performs the actions most likely to provide players with a challenging and compelling gameplay experience. Part of designing a good game is designing good AI for that game, and a designer who just leaves the creation of the AI up to programmers better hope that they are good AI designers. If they are not, the game will likely not be much fun to play. As with many of the programmers on a development team, the AI programmer needs to have a good game design sense in order for the final AI to be sufficiently challenging, interesting, and entertaining to the player. The more the designer works with the AI programmer, the more likely the two of them will be on the same page in terms of what the AI needs to accomplish.

If a computer game is like improvised theater, where players get to be directors of the primary character or group of characters, then all of the other actors in the play are controlled by the artificial intelligence. As the game's designer, you want to direct those AI-controlled actors to create the most stimulating experience possible for the player. These AI agents are not just the opponents players might battle, but also any characters with which players interact. How will a town full of people behave? How will they react to players' actions? Designing the AI is a big part of designing a game.

Goals of Game AI

The Sims' success is completely dependent on the strength of its artificial intelligence.

Players have different expectations of the AI they find in different types of games. Players do not expect much of the AI in an arcade game like *Centipede* or a puzzle game like *Tetris*. As I have discussed, these games provide plenty of challenge to players while using various simple-minded or outright stupid opponents. In a wargame like *Close Combat*, however, players expect a lot more from the intelligence of the opposing forces. In an RPG, players expect to move into a simulation of a living world, where

154 Chapter 9: Artificial Intelligence

characters move around in a town more or less "realistically." In a game like *The Sims*, the AI more or less is the game; with weak AI the game would simply not be worth playing.

So different games provoke different expectations in players of how smart the AI agents in those games need to be. However, we can still construct a general list of goals for any computer game AI, goals that change in importance as the design goals for a given game vary.

Challenge the Player

Providing a reasonable challenge for players must be the primary goal for AI in any computer game. Without setting up a worthy adversary of some sort, a game becomes unchallenging and therefore too easy to defeat. Worse still, a game that provides no dynamic challenge stops being a game entirely and becomes more of a puzzle or an interactive movie.

In a classic arcade game like *Robotron: 2084*, the challenge comes from the sheer number of opponents the player must fight.

In a classic arcade game like *Robotron: 2084* or in a first-person shooter like *Doom*, the challenge mostly comes from players being overwhelmed by adversaries and by the powerful abilities those adversaries have. For instance, in my oft-used example of *Centipede*, the bugs can kill players by touching them, while players must shoot the creatures in order to kill them. This puts players at something of a disadvantage. The fact that there are multiple insects attacking players at once does not help matters. As a result, the AI for these creatures can be fairly simple and predictable, yet players are still challenged by them.

The same imbalance holds true in *Doom*, where players may run out of ammo but their enemies never do, where players are much more helpless in the dark while the enemies can detect players just as easily as in the light, and where often the enemies, such as flying creatures, can go where players cannot. The fact that the creatures far outnumber the player character also tends to compensate for the reality that none of the creatures is very smart. The AI in *Doom* has to appear more sophisticated than the *Centipede* insects because the *Doom* world seems more real than the *Centipede* world, as I will discuss in a bit. The fact remains that primarily the AI provides a challenge for players by being more powerful and numerous than the player character.

Creating a challenging AI for a real-time strategy game like *StarCraft* is an entirely more difficult proposition. The expectation in games of this sort is that players are competing with opponents equivalent to them in strength. In your average real-time strategy game, both sides have a large number of troops to manipulate and the ability to build more as needed. Both sides usually need to mine a resource of some kind and use that to build more structures or troops. Basically, the AI in an RTS has to do everything players do and seem smart while doing it. Often the AI is given an advantage by being able to see the entire level while the players cannot, and possibly having a larger number of starting units, an easier method for obtaining more, or a bigger pool of resources from which to draw. Nonetheless, creating a challenge for players in an RTS game is quite difficult since it requires the AI to coordinate the movement of the units beyond the individual unit level, making the units appear to work collaboratively, as players would use them.

Developing a challenging AI for a turn-based strategy game such as *Alpha Centauri* can be quite difficult since the player is supposed to be fighting opponents with roughly the same strengths and weaknesses as himself.

The difficulties presented in creating a challenging AI for an RTS game are only magnified in a turn-based strategy game such as *Alpha Centauri*. Here the AI is supposed to operate just as players do. Of course turn-based strategy games are some of the most thought-intensive games available, so that only amplifies the problem of creating a compelling opponent AI. Furthermore, the computer does not get to benefit as much from its extremely fast processing power; since the game is turn-based, players have as long to think about a move as they like. The computer's analytical nature does give it a leg up on remembering the exact status of all the units it has at its command, an ability at which human minds are significantly less skilled. Often turn-based strategy AIs create a challenge for players by cheating in various subtle ways, though I would certainly be the last to accuse any particular game of doing so. In the end, I certainly have no problem with such a tactic, since the end goal is to challenge the player without appearing too unfair in the process.

Regardless of the game type, the AI must present players with an interesting challenge. Without good AI, a game may become similar to playing chess with your (much) younger brother: somewhat pointless. The difference is, when you play chess with your kid brother, you hope to teach him the nuances of the game so that one day he may become a good player. You may also enjoy socializing with him, making an otherwise pointless game of chess worth it. Sadly, the computer game AI you battle has no hope of improving and is woefully inadequate when it comes to providing companionship. In order for a game AI to justify its existence, it must provide players with a challenge. At the same time, it is important to keep in mind that you do not want to punish the player too severely with your game's AI. Getting into a "It's me versus the player!" mind-set when you, as the game designer or AI programmer, hold all the cards is similar to savagely trouncing your little brother at chess every time you challenge him to a match. It is not a fair fight, and pretty soon your brother or game players in general will not want to play with you anymore.

Not Do Dumb Things

AI for a computer game must not appear overly stupid. Players love laughing at AI when it does something completely foolhardy. Nothing breaks a player's suspension of disbelief more than when an AI agent fails to navigate around a small obstacle such as a fire hydrant or a tree, or when an agent charges right off a cliff to its doom like a lemming. To the player, it is completely obvious what the AI should do in each situation. But what may look obvious to players can actually be a fairly complex action for the agent to perform or understand. Nonetheless, for the game to avoid becoming a laughingstock, the game's AI must have a solid mastery of what seems obvious to human players.

When fighting aliens in a game such as *Marathon 2*, the player has lowered expectations of how smart these enemies will be.

The number of dumb things the AI will be able to get away with has a direct relationship to what sort of intelligence the AI is supposed to represent. For instance, in my first-person shooter *Damage Incorporated*, players are supposed to be almost exclusively battling human opponents. In *Marathon 2*, however, players are battling a variety of alien species mixed with some robots. The enemies in *Marathon 2* are able to get away with appearing stupid since they are non-human creatures. In *Damage Incorporated*, conversely, since the enemies are all humans they must look much smarter. For another example, in *Damage Incorporated*, according to the game's story and the appearance of the levels in the game, the action is supposed to be transpiring in a real-world environment. On the other hand, *Centipede 3D* takes place in a whimsical fantasy world that bears only a tangential relationship to the real-world. Therefore, while the guards in *Damage Incorporated* need to appear to be tracking players like real human soldiers would, in *Centipede 3D* it is less absurd that the centipedes are unable to make a beeline for the player character and instead have to wind back and forth between mushrooms. AI stupidity is acceptable relative to the type of world the computer game is supposed to represent.

Be Unpredictable

Humans are unpredictable. That is part of what makes them good opponents in a game and one of the primary reasons that people enjoy playing multi-player games; a skilled person will be challenging to fight in a way that a computer never will. A large part of that is the unpredictability of a human opponent. The same should be true of the AI opponents in a computer game. When the game gets to the point where players feel with certainty that they know exactly what the enemy forces are going to do at any given second, the fun of playing the game quickly wanes. Players want the AI to surprise them, to try to defeat them in ways they had not anticipated. Certainly multi-player games still have the advantage of including a social component, which is a major factor in their success, and the AI in your game will never be able to be a friend to players in the same way another human can. Since you cannot provide the social component of multi-player games, you can at least strive to make the AI agents provide much of the same challenge and unpredictability that is provided by a human opponent.

In all art, viewers want to see something they have not been able to anticipate, something that challenges their expectations. When, within the first ten minutes, you know the exact ending of a movie, book, or play, a big part of the thrill of experiencing that work is removed. The same is true for computer games. Of course, games can surprise players with their predetermined story, or what sort of environment the next level will take place in, or what the big boss robot will look like. But if the AI can also contribute to this unpredictably, the game gains replayability. Players will keep playing a game until it no longer provides them with a challenge, until they no longer experience anything new from playing the game. An AI that can keep surprising them, and thereby challenging them, will help keep their interest high.

Successful unpredictability can take many different forms in games. It can be as simple as the random number that determines what piece will drop next in *Tetris*. Surely this is a very simple case, and optimally we would hope many games could provide deeper unpredictability than that. But at the same time, one must realize that for *Tetris*, it is the perfect amount of unpredictability. If players knew what piece was coming next, the game would lose a lot of its challenge. Indeed, with the "next" feature on (which displays the next piece to drop on the side of the screen) the game becomes somewhat easier. Pure randomness is often a really good way to keep players

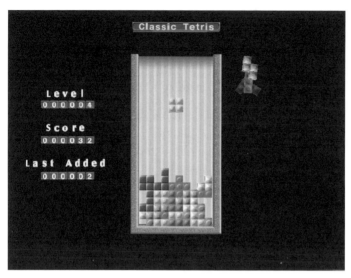

The only AI *Tetris* needs is a random number generator. Pictured here: classic mode in *The Next Tetris*.

interested in the AI, to make them wonder, "What's it trying to do?" when in fact it is just being random. The randomness in *Tetris* provides the unpredictability required to keep players challenged for hours.

Sometimes the goals of computer game AI can get confused, and in a quest for the holy grail of realism a designer or an AI programmer can end up making a very dull opponent for a game. Sure, the agent always makes a decision that "makes sense" given its current situation; it may even make the decision most likely to win the current battle. But if that logical decision is completely obvious to the player, how much fun is it going to be to fight that AI? If every time you run into a room in a first-person shooter, the orc you find there is going to spin around, heave its club above its head, and charge at you while swinging wildly, the next time you play that room the situation will be much less challenging and interesting. What if sometimes the orc is startled by the player's sudden arrival? Then the orc might flee down the hall or go cower in a corner. What if sometimes the orc decides to hurl his club at the player character instead of trying to use it as a melee weapon? That would certainly provide enough spice to keep players on their toes. You must remember that each human being is different and that many humans are known to act irrationally for any number of reasons. That irrationality keeps life interesting. If players are battling humans or human-like monsters/aliens in a computer game, a little irrationality will result in making the opponents seem that much more real, believable, and interesting to engage.

"Fuzzy logic" is one method AI designers and programmers may use to keep the AI agents unpredictable and interesting. Essentially, fuzzy logic takes a logical system and inserts some randomness into it. In fuzzy logic, when the AI is presented with a given situation, it has several worthwhile courses of action to choose from instead of just one. Say players are at a certain distance with a certain weapon while the AI agent is at a certain health level and is equipped with a certain type of weaponry. There may be three reasonable things for the agent to do in this case, and each can have different numerical values or "weights" representing their relative quality. Say that running up and attacking the player character makes a lot of sense, so it rates a 5. Doing a threat display in order to frighten the player makes a bit of sense, so it rates a 2. And maybe trying to circle around the player character in order to disorient him is also plausible, so it rates a 3. Using these different weights, the agent can simply randomly pick a number from 1 to 10 (the total of the weights). If less than or equal to 5, the agent will run up and attack. If 6 or 7, the agent will try to frighten the player, and if 8 through 10, the agent will do its best to disorient the player. The weights represent the chance that the AI will make a given decision. If the AI has enough different plans at its disposal, players will never be able to know exactly what the AI will do, thereby making the AI unpredictable. In the final analysis, basing AI decisions on randomness makes the agent look like it is performing complex reasoning when it is not. Players will never know that the AI in question just picked its action out of a hat. Instead, if the agent's action does not look too stupid, players will try to imagine why the AI might have chosen to do what it did, and may end up thinking the agent is pretty sly when really it is just random.

Of course, the unpredictability of an AI agent in a game must not conflict with the other AI goals I have listed here. If an agent is so busy being unpredictable that it cannot put together a solid plan of attack against the player, it is not going to be much of a threat to players and they will not be challenged. Ideally, unpredictability enhances the challenge the AI presents, instead of proving a detriment. If the AI randomly chooses to do something completely foolish when what it was doing was about to lead to victory, players cannot help but wonder, "Why would the AI do such a stupid thing?" When working on the behaviors of the creatures in a game, it is always important to keep an eye on the bigger picture of what that AI is trying to accomplish.

Assist Storytelling

Game AI can be used to further a game's story. For example, in an RPG, players may travel to a certain town that is home to a number of fearful residents who dread the arrival of outsiders. If players only observe these people, they can be seen to be navigating the town, going to the stores, restaurants, and factories just as people in a real town would. This sets the scene for the town and makes it seem real to players. But whenever players approach these people, they turn away, fleeing to safe areas to avoid interacting with the players. Why is this? What does it say about the town and the people who live there? Why are they frightened? What can players do to make the townspeople trust them? Players want to know the answers to all of these questions, and will start exploring the game's story as a result. English teachers are notorious for telling their students that it is better to show than to tell. This is especially true in a visual medium such as computer games. Instead of just seeing that the town's inhabitants are frightened of strangers in a cut-scene, a properly designed AI can actually show players this interesting information during gameplay. And when players are able to interact with these characters, their involvement in the story goes beyond being shown to actually being active in it. Players are able to be part of the narrative in a way no other medium makes possible.

Even the adversaries that players might fight in a battle can be adjusted to aid in the storytelling process. Suppose that in a wargame players are supposed to be fighting a general who is known for being compassionate about the welfare of his troops, perhaps more than is logical in a combat situation. Players could send in a few snipers to pick off several of the opposing force's troops that are serving as guards along the border between two contested areas. If the AI for the enemy general was properly designed, the slow drain of troops in that manner would start to enrage him. Once infuriated, the general would try a foolhardy attack to get back at the enemy forces, thus putting him at the disadvantage. Here again, a bit of the game's story has been told through the AI.

In *Damage Incorporated*, the AI the player's teammates exhibit plays a crucial role in telling the game's story.

In my game *Damage Incorporated*, the player is a U.S. Marine Corps sergeant in charge of a fire-team of four men. Together with their men, players storm through numerous missions against a variety of heavily armed opponents. The men each have different strengths and weaknesses. Some are headstrong and will charge bravely into a fight. Some of the squad members are more careful about firing their weapons than others, and as a result are less likely to hit the player character or the other teammates. These personality traits are all communicated through the AI that these teammates use. Before each mission, players get to choose their team from a selection of thirteen different soldiers, each with a dossier players can read. The dossiers provide a psychological profile of each of the teammates, which gives some insight into their personalities. Furthermore, when actually on a mission, the teammates are constantly speaking, either in response to the players' orders or just to comment on a given situation. This gives further insight into their personalities and how they will behave on the battlefield. If players read the dossiers and pay attention to the squad members' personalities carefully, they will notice warnings that some of the teammates may not be completely balanced psychologically. For some teammates, if they are taken on too many missions they will "crack" or become "shell-shocked" and attempt to run away from the battle. Other teammates, if taken on specific missions that they do not agree with ideologically, will turn against the sergeant and his men. The AI, of course, handles these "shell-shocked" situations, which thereby helps to tell the story of these characters.

One area where AI is often avoided entirely by designers but where it can be quite useful is in dynamic storytelling. All too often designers cobble a story around a game instead of integrating the story with the gameplay. Furthermore, often designers want to tell static stories in which how a given character will react to players is entirely pre-determined, regardless of the game-world actions or how the players treat that particular character. While designers often strive to keep the battles and action sequences as dynamic and unpredictable as possible, they almost always want to keep the stories exactly the same every time the players experience them. Why not have players be able to affect the mood of the different NPCs they encounter? Maybe if players say all the right things and do not ask questions about sensitive subjects, the NPC becomes friendly toward the player character. Maybe players can only coax crucial information out of a character after first becoming his friend. Perhaps the players' reputations precede them, where the actions players have performed elsewhere in the world directly impact how that NPC will treat the player character. If players have performed less-than-good actions earlier in the game, maybe the players have to redeem themselves in the eyes of a character before they can proceed in the game.

In my game *The Suffering*, players determine what ending they get based on how they treat the friendly human characters they meet in the game. Players have the option to help these AI-controlled humans, kill them, or ignore them completely. I deliberately made the characters a wide variety of personalities, and made their AI reflect these traits. One character is extremely frightened by the creatures in the game-world, and thus spends most of his time frantically fleeing from them. Later in the game, players meet a corrections officer named Ernesto who hates all inmates, including the player character, Torque. When they first meet in the game-world, Ernesto immediately threatens Torque, pointing his machine gun at him but not firing it. If players shoot Ernesto early in this encounter, Ernesto will immediately become hostile to Torque. If players wait, however, Ernesto realizes that he and Torque must work together to survive against the monsters. Now if Ernesto is shot by players, he does not immediately become hostile but instead warns Torque that he needs to watch what he is doing. Thus Ernesto's AI changes based on how he is feeling about Torque. Of course, if Torque shoots him two more times, Ernesto will still become hostile; he's no fool. In the end it is to the players' advantage to keep Ernesto around, as his AI is set

In *The Suffering*, the AI for the companion NPCs changed their behavior based on the actions of the player character.

up such that he is the most effective combat companion in the game, enabling him to help players dispatch the countless creatures that keep rearing their ugly heads.

Of course, there is a wide range of different effects that can be achieved using the game's AI to create interesting interpersonal relationships. Sadly, this is something that has been all but unexplored in commercial games to date. Instead of telling static stories, we could be telling ones that, though not entirely procedurally generated, were subtly different depending on how players played the game. Using AI to spice up and vary the story from game to game may make telling a story much more difficult, but what it can add to the game's non-linearity and replayability is enormous.

Create a Living World

In many games, the AI does more than just provide a threat and a challenge to the player. A game may even include AI agents that players do not directly interact with at all. The AI can instead be used to inhabit the living world the game creates. A game-world may be infinitely detailed in terms of the objects it contains and how it looks and sounds, but players are used to a real-world that also contains living organisms that think for themselves and behave in interesting ways. Therefore, creating a sterile game-world filled with inanimate objects is not going to be a very believable space for the player. One does not need to go overboard in filling up the game-world with complex ambient AI agents; a little can go a long way. Whether this means a few birds that fly around in the sky, insects that crawl around on the ground, or humans that go about their daily business, adding ambient life to a world can do a lot to make the game-world seem more real to the player. The *Grand Theft Auto* games have featured cities full of humans going about their daily lives, most of whom are not directly needed for the main story. These pedestrians make the city seem more real, and the more real the game-world is the more likely that players will be able to immerse themselves in it.

There is a close connection between filling the game with ambient life and using the AI to tell the game's story. Creating these inhabitants does a lot to establish the setting for your game, and setting is a key part of telling any story. But ambient life in a game goes beyond just establishing that setting; it helps make players feel less lonely in the game-world. How many times have you played a game where you felt like you were walking around a sterile wasteland, as if an exterminator had come through previously to eliminate any signs of life? Players love to see that the world has ambient life in it, creatures they can just look at rather than kill, and the depth it adds to the world can be invaluable.

The Sloped Playing Field

Often when programmers get together to talk about AI for computer games, they concentrate their discussions on how they want their AI agents to be on equal footing with the player. This was certainly the case at the AI roundtables I have attended in years past at the Game Developers Conference. These AI specialists want their AI systems to know only what players would know, see what players can see, and so forth. This, they suggest, will make the conflict between the AI and players more realistic and therefore more interesting.

Of course, for years games have been giving the AI agents unfair advantages over the player. They have made the AI have more hit-points than the player character. They have outnumbered the player a hundred to one. They have made the AI agents have a practically psychic knowledge of every location in the game-world, which allows them to know exactly where the player character is at any given second, certainly an unfair advantage. Some game AIs have even been known to cheat. Surely this is unfair to the player, the AI programmers will say. They proclaim the AI should be on equal footing with the players and should triumph through its wits alone.

But is it really better to put the AI and players on a level playing field? First and foremost, this is quite likely to lead to AI that fails to provide much of a challenge for players. The fact remains that shrewd players are going to be able to outsmart even the most sophisticated game AI without that much difficulty. Trying to put players and AI on equal terms will create a much larger challenge for your AI programmers. They will need to invest countless more hours in developing an AI that has even a slight chance of beating the players, time that cannot be spent improving other parts of the game. In the end they may well end up with an AI that does not provide a captivating gameplay experience. In the worst case, the AI is too busy being "real" to avoid performing blatantly stupid actions.

A big part of what drives AI programmers to attempt a level playing field for players and AI agents is the programmers' own egos. These programmers pride themselves on their work and will assert that they can come up with an AI that will be able to challenge players without having to resort to superior numbers, greater strength, or any sort of cheating. The programmers want the bragging rights of being able to say that their AI is as smart as a human. Often hours and hours are spent trying to come up with the sophisticated algorithms required for such equal versus equal competition, and in the end something has to be hacked together to make the game actually function. The goal of game AI is to support the game and enhance players' experiences, not to serve as a test-bed for artificial intelligence techniques.

Besides, there is something romantic for players when they manage to defeat an AI opponent despite the fact that the AI's forces greatly outnumber their own, were better armed and equipped, and even had the benefit of prescient knowledge of the map. Just as the Hollywood action hero triumphs over countless foes, players want to overcome seemingly insurmountable odds for their own victories. Tipping the scales in the AI's advantage only makes players' eventual victory all the more sweet. Unless, of course, the design ends up making the game too hard.

How Real Is Too Real?

Another potential AI programming pitfall is creating an AI that, though it actually performs like a "real" person, ends up detracting from the gameplay as a result. In terms of the stories they tell and the settings they employ, games are often contrivances, strictly unreal situations that are specifically set up because they are interesting, not because they are authentic, and the AI must support this.

Consider the James Bond movies. These films are like many popular games in that they feature a lot of action and exciting situations with less of a focus on character development or meaningful stories. In nearly every film, Bond is captured at some point and tied down to a particularly hideous execution device. This device does not kill

Bond instantly, but instead employs some slower method, such as a laser steadily burning a hole down the middle of the table to which James is strapped. Why does the villain not simply shoot Bond? Or simply aim the laser straight at him? Why does the villain almost always leave before the execution has actually been completed? And why does the villain reveal to Bond his entire mad scheme for world domination before he starts the execution device in motion? None of these choices are indicative of especially smart behavior, but it is fun to watch, and fits with the overall style of the movie. It entertains the audience, which is the primary goal of the Bond films. Realism is much less of a concern.

And so it is with games. If the enemy AI is so smart, surely it should realize that it has no chance against the player and should lock itself away in a safe bunker, refusing to open the door for anyone. It has, in fact, saved its own life by doing this, which is the smartest decision possible. But what has it done to the game? Now players are stuck, since they have no way of getting to the enemy and continuing on with the game. Another example might be a cowardly AI that runs from players when sufficiently wounded. This is used to great effect in many games. But what if the agent was faster than the player character and better at dodging into safe locations? When quite wounded, the AI agent will start fleeing from the battle, with players left with no other option but to chase after it. If the AI is speedier and better at navigation, players will have a hard time catching up with it. What may have been a fun action game now becomes a tedious chase with a foregone conclusion, since the agent is mortally wounded and has no chance of recovering its health. And what of the deadly serpent boss players must battle? With its protective armor coating, it is impervious to players' attacks, and can only be damaged by being shot when its mouth is open. So the strictly logical choice might be to always keep its mouth closed whenever players have any chance of getting off a shot. This is a decision it can make very easily. But now, of course, players have no chance whatsoever of winning the battle. Is that fun?

The point again is that the AI must never overshadow the gameplay, and it must never distract the development team from the true goal of the project: to make a fun, playable game. If the AI is really very sophisticated but, as a result, the game is unplayable or extremely frustrating, players are not going to remark on the intelligence of the game's combatants. AI and gameplay are too closely entwined for one to succeed if the other fails.

AI Agents and Their Environment

Computer game AI cannot be designed or developed in a vacuum. For a game AI to turn out well, it needs to be developed in close association with the game's gameplay and the environments in which that gameplay is going to take place. The simple fact is that no AI agent is going to be smart enough to prevail in all situations. While an AI may be exceedingly good in wide-open spaces, when it is thrown into a narrow canyon it will encounter problems its programmer never anticipated. If the AI programmer comes up with an AI that can handle the confined spaces, chances are it will not be as successful out in the open. The best one can hope for is that the AI has a fighting chance in a specific type of gameplay situation. If the levels and AI are not developed synchronously, then there is little chance that the opponents the players face will appear very smart at all.

This creates special problems in terms of how to best produce a game. Level design is often one of the last tasks to be carried out on a game, before it goes into final balancing, then testing, and finally ships. Similarly, AI is usually only worked on after the core engine is firmly in place, most of the mechanics for the player's movement are fully functional, and many of the other more critical programming tasks are mostly complete. Now, if the same person who is designing the levels is also creating the enemy AI, it might be simple to integrate the development of the two, but this is rare if not unheard of in modern game development. As a result you have two teams — the programmers and the level designers — working in parallel. Unfortunately, the usual case is that each charges forward with their work without fully considering the other. The level designers do not have the AI yet, so they cannot tailor their levels to support it. It is just the opposite on the other side of the equation: the programmer does not have the levels yet, so it is hard for him to make an AI that will function well in those levels. The situation is a catch-22. Once the levels are done in terms of architecture, the AI is finally added to them, and then it turns out that one or the other needs to be radically reworked if the game is going to be any fun. In the worst-case scenario there is no time to rework either the levels or the behaviors, and the gameplay ends up suffering as a result.

Of course, the level designers will protest that the AI should be designed to fit the levels they create. And, similarly, the AI programmers will complain that the levels simply must be reconceived to work with the AI they developed. Since I have worked as both a level designer and an AI programmer, I may be in a special position to arbitrate this dispute. In my opinion, neither party is entirely right, and a little give-and-take is required on each side. I would advocate trying to make a simple, playable AI first. It does not need to be bug free or work perfectly in every situation. If it works fairly well in some situations, level designers can start making levels that facilitate what the AI is known to do well. As the level designers take this direction, the AI programmer can keep working on his AI, getting rid of any bugs while always keeping an eye on what shape the game-world is taking. The AI programmer must communicate to the level designer when he sees a problem emerging in a level, such as a situation the AI is unlikely to handle well. At the same time, the design of the levels may give the AI programmer new ideas about what tricks the AI can pull off. Maybe ledges start showing up in the game-world that would be ideal locations for snipers. Or perhaps the structure of the game-world's architecture is suited to coordinated team movements. If the AI programmer can then add functionality to his algorithms to allow the agents to identify these locations and behave accordingly, the AI will become stronger as a result. Both sides of the designer/programmer equation must be ready to compromise. Often a designer may have to compromise for the good of the project, modifying something he may like as is but which horribly confuses the AI. Similarly, the programmer may need to add some ugly special-case code to accommodate a problem that occurs in a majority of the maps that have been created. The designer and AI programmer must trust each other such that when one of them tells the other something needs to change, they believe the other and make it happen.

Getting the AI agents in *Damage Incorporated* to work properly required many changes to the levels.

For example, in my game *Damage Incorporated*, players are responsible for not only controlling their own character, but also for directing four teammates in a 3D environment. When I was working on that game, one of the greatest challenges I encountered was getting the teammate AI working in a way that appeared intelligent to players. Fortunately, I had a rudimentary form of this AI working before any real level design began. This way I realized ahead of time that the teammate AI would not be smart enough to jump or swim to areas. This meant that the levels had to be designed accordingly, or the teammates would not be able to reach the end of a level with the player character. Also, the teammates performed badly in tight, constrained spaces, often running into each other or blocking players' progress. The levels had to be made with large, open areas so that the AI agents could have a decent chance of performing well.

But even with foreknowledge of the sophistication of the game's AI, once *Damage Incorporated* entered testing, endless problems arose with the AI. The teammates constantly seemed to be able to get wedged in tiny little spaces they were not supposed to enter. The end solution turned out to be about 25 percent code fixes and 75 percent reworking parts of the levels to eliminate the little nooks into which the AI agents jammed themselves. There were countless sections of levels that I had wanted to look a certain way but that needed to be scrapped because the AI simply could not function in those areas. I was sad to see those sections go, but not as sad as players would have been when they managed to get a teammate stuck in a crevice. The AI and levels had to work together if the final game was going to be any fun to play.

In *The Suffering*, I had a much smoother experience getting friendly AI characters to navigate through the game world, though a few snafus arose. It was not originally in the plan to have the human characters be able to climb ladders, open doors, or jump across chasms. As we built the world, we realized that there was no way around getting them to navigate the ladders. We had relatively few scenarios where it was necessary, but there was no way to easily remove them or to script or "can" the AI agent's ladder movement. Without the ability to open and close doors, the AI agents simply looked too dumb when you slammed doors in their faces, so we ended up adding that as well. We had a few cases where NPCs were going to need to jump across small gaps, but we quickly realized we did not have enough to justify the programming involved in getting the NPCs to jump. Analyzing the situations where jumping was required, we were easily able to rework areas to eliminate a few jumps. The ones we could not remove, we were able to solve with a scripted jumping action for the NPCs that could be performed in those spots only. This required some tedious debugging on the design side, but in the end was much simpler than implementing a general-purpose jump behavior.

How Good Is Good Enough?

Damage Incorporated and *The Suffering* suggest another interesting point about the sophistication that will be required of AI in different games. What made the work on these games so challenging was the fact that players were counting on the AI to perform certain actions for them. In *Damage Incorporated*, if players ordered a teammate to move to a certain position, they expected that trooper to reach that position and defend it. If the AI failed to do so, players might die as a result, and would curse the AI for failing them. Even worse, if players ordered the AI to relocate to a specific position and the trooper had difficulty getting there, players would become frustrated, especially when the appropriate path to that location was completely obvious to players. But if an enemy AI agent had trouble finding a path to a location, players would never be the wiser. If an opponent got stuck in a corner on rare occasions, players would be all too happy to exploit the AI agent's stupidity by mowing down the stuck foe with a blast of machine gun fire. However, if a teammate got stuck in a corner, he would be unable to follow players to the end of the level. Since players could not finish a level unless their entire squad was in the "Extraction Zone" for that level, the AI's mistakes would end the players' games prematurely. Nothing frustrates players more than dying because of faulty teammate AI.

In a game with teammates, such as *Damage Incorporated*, the failure of the AI agents to work as the player expects seriously impedes the player's ability to play the game.

One can take a couple of lessons away from the problems I had with the AI implementation on *Damage Incorporated*. The first is to never do a game with teammates in a complex 3D environment. This is a lesson I apparently missed entirely, since I subsequently included companions in *The Suffering*. Thankfully, my experience with *The Suffering* was much smoother, in part due to the lessons I had learned the first time around. The other conclusion is that the amount of AI sophistication a game requires is dependent on how much the failure of that AI will impact the player. If the AI screws up and the player's game ends as a result, that is very bad. If the AI makes mistakes and the only consequence is that the player's game gets slightly easier, then it is a failing the players can probably live with, as long as it is a rare enough occurrence. So when a designer is working on an AI system or critiquing a programmer's work, he should always keep in mind how important it is that the system function correctly. It is perfectly acceptable if only the development team knows of the AI's stupidity while players are completely ignorant of its shortcomings.

It would be nice to make every system in a game as smart as possible, but the realities of the production cycle dictate that there is only so much time that can be invested in any given part of a game. Rare is the case that a programmer has finished all of the work needed for a game and still has time to "polish" everything that he would like. As such, spending a lot of time on overly sophisticated AI systems will directly take time away from other tasks that desperately need work. The reader will notice that when I listed the attributes that a game's AI needs to have, I did not list "be a respectable, academic-quality artificial intelligence." The AI for a game only needs to be good enough to challenge players while not appearing overly foolish in its actions.

In his fascinating Game Developers Conference talk "Who Buried Paul?" Brian Moriarty discussed the concept of "constellation" in games. This theory is of particular relevance to game AI. Roughly stated, the theory is that humans, when presented with some seemingly random data, will try to make sense of it, to put it into order, and to try to find meaning where there may, in fact, be none. For game AI, then, Moriarty suggested that having your AI perform seemingly random actions will cause players to think the AI has some grand, intelligent plan. Players might think something along the lines of the following: "Why did that platoon of tanks suddenly storm over that hill? There does not seem to be any reason for it. Maybe they know something I do not. Maybe they are regrouping with a force I cannot see." Players who are not game developers themselves will have a tendency to try to believe that game AI agents make intelligent choices. Of course, there is a fine line. If players see an AI agent pointlessly ramming into a wall they will know something is amiss. It is important to remember that players do not want to find bugs in your game, and will do their best to believe in the intelligence of the characters they see therein. By throwing in some random behavior, your AI agents may come out looking smarter than they really are.

Scripting

Of course, game AI does not need to spontaneously think up every behavior that is performed in the game. In some games, a combination of dynamic AI with predetermined paths and scripted behaviors may create the most exciting experience possible for the player. Usually scripted behaviors work best in games that have predefined locations and where players are not likely to play through those levels repeatedly. In these games, players are likely to come into a given area from a certain location, and therefore the designer can make assumptions about what plan of attack will provide the most interesting challenge for the player.

First-person shooters are a good example of a game genre that works well with somewhat scripted AI behaviors. *Half-Life* was one of the first games to show how complex scripting could be used to make opponents that were a lot of fun to fight. That game was widely praised in the gaming press for the strength of its AI, while in fact much of that perceived intelligence was accomplished using scripted paths that the AI agents would move to in specific situations. RTS games such as *StarCraft* have used extensive scripting in their single-player scenario maps for as long as they have been around. In these games the AI receives instructions from the script about what to do when players finally reach a certain location or after they have built a certain number of units. This makes each level present a more unique challenge to the player than if all the maps were run off of a purely general-purpose AI.

Setting up scripted behaviors that are specific to a level is very much the concern of the level designer. The level designer already needed to concern himself with where the opponents should be placed to create maximum gameplay effect. But with scripted behaviors the designer needs to repeatedly play an area to figure out the most devilish places for the AI to hide, where it should retreat to when low on health, and how it should best reposition to have the greatest chance of defeating the player. Of course, the AI agent cannot only be on a path, at least not if the player is likely to interact with it. The AI must still be used to enable the agent to determine which location it should try to get to in which situation. Furthermore, the AI must be able to realize when the scripted plans are not working out and when to try an unscripted, more general behavior. One might think that having AI agents that use scripted, predetermined behaviors will fail to produce the unpredictability I discussed earlier. One might wonder how a scripted behavior can be anything but predictable. For just this reason, scripted behavior should be used just to give the AI agent hints as to where good locations to duck and cover might be, not to specify where the agent must always go, regardless of the situation. The agent must still be able to react to the player's tactics in order to avoid looking too foolish.

The Suffering used a lot of scripted AI actions to make the enemies and companions appear more intelligent than they actually were.

Of the games I have worked on, *The Suffering* relied the most on scripted AI behaviors to make its characters appear smart and to create a compelling gameplay experience for the player. This scripting took a number of forms. Frequently, we would use some light scripting to introduce a creature into the environment. For example, when the player runs through a trigger along the top of a wall, we then activated a number of creatures to jump up onto the wall and run down it toward the player. After the creatures landed on the wall, they would follow a path toward the trigger the player hit, breaking off from that path as soon as they took damage or when they detected the player as a viable target. One particularly crafty creature early in the game was scripted to rip a door off its hinges (which happens in a cut-scene), and then run to the various dark corners of the room until the creature either takes damage or a timer runs out. This gives it the illusion of playing cat and mouse with the player. This only happened until the player was able to damage the creature, since after that it seemed foolish to continue taunting. There were a number of places in the game where players were able to attack NPCs with ranged weapons from a high and inaccessible position where the melee combat based NPCs were unable to retaliate. Unfortunately, the creatures were unable to figure this out on their own, so without some type of scripting they would tend to fruitlessly attempt to navigate to the player's position and ended up looking fairly stupid doing so. In these situations, we added scripting that would switch the NPCs between a hostile and a flee behavior depending on whether the player was in the sniper spot or not.

The human companions the player encounters throughout the game were heavily scripted. Some of these characters lead the player from location to location over the course of a particular level. These destinations were specifically mapped out by the level designer ahead of time. Sometimes they were set to be on the watch for hostile creatures while moving to those positions, while other times they are set to blindly move to a location and only then become hostile to whatever threats they might find. Typically the AI agent would then stay hostile until a certain success condition was met in the environment, such as all the creatures in an area being killed or the player having solved a particular puzzle. Only then would they be triggered to move to the next destination. Typically, only the specific destination point is specified by the level designer, with the AI dynamically figuring out the best path to get to that location based on its current position. These friendly NPCs also tended to be big talkers, and hence said specific dialog at different points throughout the level, all integrated into the more active behaviors they performed as part of their scripting.

Beyond event-based scripting, *The Suffering* also used a lot of NPC "helper" objects that were set up by hand by level designers. These took primarily two forms: flee positions and targeting positions. The NPCs would know to use the former when they needed to flee from combat in a room, and we placed these positions in little nooks, behind pillars, and in other places that it would look intelligent for an NPC to hide. Before actually using one of these positions, the AI agent would need to analyze all the locations within a certain radius around it, picking the one where its enemies did not have line-of-sight to it and where, in order to reach that position, it would not need to pass too close to any active threats. Even once the AI picked a particular flee location to use, the AI would continually reevaluate its decision, potentially moving to a different position if an enemy ran too close to a given location and thereby made it significantly less desirable. Targeting positions used essentially the same concept, except these helpers would be placed in locations where the AI would want to go in order to look smart while shooting at a target; while flee positions would be placed in good locations for hiding, targeting positions were placed on top of ledges, at junctions in hallways, and other locations where the AI was likely to be out in the open and able to get a shot off at a variety of targets. Some targeting positions were tied to other targeting positions around a particular piece of low-level geometry that could be used as cover. The AI knew to pick one targeting position from a group that would make it appear to hide behind the desk, rock, or other low object while blasting away at its target.

The Suffering combined dynamic AI behaviors with scripted ones to create agents that look much smarter than if they were all dynamic or all scripted. It is through this combination that we were able to pull off some of the most exciting scenarios in the game, where AI agents appear to have dynamic battles with each other but where these situations have actually been very carefully set up by the level designer for optimal effect. The trick is to maintain that precarious balance between too much scripting and too little so the game is still fun, challenging, and dynamic while also providing complex and memorable scenarios in which players can participate.

Artificial Stupidity

The fact that games are often referred to as having not artificial intelligence but rather artificial stupidity is quite telling about the quality of AI present in many games. It is certainly true that the AI in almost all games is not something that in and of itself is impressive. However, when considered in terms of what it is intended to do — challenge the player — many of the best games really do present well-designed computer opponents. While multi-player games provide many avenues for interesting gameplay design and production, a large segment of the gaming population is still going to desire single-player games. Solitary games provide a unique experience, and the game's AI is crucial to making that experience as fun as possible. It is the designer's responsibility to carefully conceive this artificial intelligence, and to make sure those who implement it have a clear understanding of what the AI must do to successfully challenge and entertain the player.

Chapter 10:
Interview: Steve Meretzky

In the early 1980s, Infocom's games were quite unique — so much so that the company preferred to call them something else entirely: interactive fiction. Infocom's titles were totally separate and distinct from the arcade game clones and derivatives that so many other computer game companies were publishing at the time. Infocom's interactive fiction appealed to an entirely different and more sophisticated group of computer game players. The games' content was surprisingly literate and professionally made, with a consistent level of quality that has never been matched. Their text-only nature gave them a literary quality that lent them some degree of respectability, enough to garner a review of the game *Deadline* in the *New York Times Book Review* and the admission of two of Infocom's implementors, Steve Meretzky and Dave Lebling, into the Science Fiction Writers of America as interactive authors. The *Book Review* has certainly never reviewed a computer game since, and the SFWA subsequently changed its rules to prevent the inclusion of any more interactive authors. Steve Meretzky remains one of Infocom's greatest talents, having worked both on one of Infocom's best-selling games, *The Hitchhiker's Guide to the Galaxy*, and on one of its most respected, *A Mind Forever Voyaging*. Since the demise of Infocom, Meretzky has continued the literary tradition in adventure gaming — first with a string of titles for Legend Entertainment and subsequently with his own company, Boffo Games, which produced the lovely *The Space Bar*. Currently, Meretzky is involved with the Internet game company WorldWinner.com. Of late, adventure games have fallen out of favor with publishers, game audiences, or some combination of both. One cannot help but wonder: what happened to the adventure game fans that made Infocom such a huge success?

What initially attracted you to computer games?

In the late '70s and early '80s, I was actually pretty repelled by computer games and, in fact, by all things computer-ish. I considered them nerdy and antisocial, and it seemed that whenever the talk turned to any computer-related subject, English went right out the window. Lots of people in my dorm were playing the original mainframe *Zork*, since it was being written at the Lab for Computer Science, and I found their preoccupation with the game pretty distasteful. I played a little bit of *Maze Wars* at the Lab, and I had a brief fling with *Space Invaders*, but that was about it.

Until, in '81 my roommate Mike Dornbrook was Infocom's first and, at the time, only tester. He started testing *Zork I* on an Apple II on our dining room table. When he wasn't around, I started playing a little and was soon very hooked. *Zork II* soon followed *Zork I* into our dining room "test lab." I reported all the bugs that I found, even though Mike was getting paid to find bugs and I wasn't.

So that led to employment at Infocom?

At MIT, I majored in Construction Project Management, and that's the work that I did for the first couple of years after I graduated in June of '79. It was awful: tedious work, boring people, far-from-cutting-edge companies. So, in the fall of 1981, when my roommate Mike Dornbrook went off to business school in Chicago, Marc Blank (VP of Development at Infocom) needed a new tester for his forthcoming mystery game, eventually named *Deadline*. Since I had proven myself an able tester while testing *Zork I* and *II* for free, he hired me on an hourly basis as the replacement tester for Mike. At this point, Infocom still had no office, and just one or two full-time employees. I continued to test at home on the Apple II.

In January of 1982, Infocom moved into wonderful office space at the edge of Cambridge, and I started working out of the office, testing *Deadline* and then later *Zork III* and Dave Lebling's first post-*Zork* effort, *Starcross*. In June, I began as a half-time employee, having been just a contractor up to that point.

Even at this point, I didn't really have any plans to become a game author — I was just having a good time doing something fun for a change and waiting to figure out what I wanted to do with the rest of my life. I had minored in writing at MIT, and had submitted some science fiction stories to various magazines, but didn't get anything published.

So how did you come to make the jump from tester to author? Did you have to prove yourself first?

Sometime late in the summer of '82, Marc Blank asked me if I'd be interested in writing a game. I agreed right away, pretty much thinking that, while testing games was quite a bit of fun, writing them was probably going to be even more fun. I didn't have to prove myself, for a few reasons. First, I'd known Marc for a few years at MIT; we were both involved with running the campus film program, so he knew that I was a pretty hard-working and creative person. Second, Infocom was still quite small and informal, with virtually no bureaucracy involved in such decisions. And third, in making suggestions while testing games, I'd shown that I understood the game and puzzle design process.

So what was your inspiration for *Planetfall*?

My main interest as a reader, and as a writer, was science fiction, so it was a foregone conclusion that the game would be SF. And since character interaction was what the Infocom development system was weakest at, an environment like a deserted planet seemed like a good idea. Beyond that, I can't really say.

What were your design goals with the Floyd character?

The idea of having a single, very well fleshed-out non-player character was a very early design focus of *Planetfall*. The Infocom games up to that point had usually had half a dozen characters each, such as the wizard, genie, dragon, princess, and gnomes in *Zork II*. Because of the large number of such characters, all were rather thin. I thought that by having just one other character (not counting the extremely brief appearances by Blather and by the alien ambassador during the opening scene) I'd be able to make that character more interesting and more believable.

I can't remember how I got from that point to Floyd, although "cute robot" was a very early decision. Perhaps the influence was the *Star Wars* trilogy, which was then between *Empire* and *Jedi*. The character of Willis, a cute alien in Robert Heinlein's book *Red Planet*, may have been another influence.

Did you always plan to force the player to allow Floyd to be killed in order to win the game?

No, that decision definitely came midway in the game design/implementation process. Floyd was turning out to be somewhat more humorous than originally conceived, and he was also turning out to be somewhat more sentimental a character than originally conceived: rubbing his head against your shoulder, getting his feelings hurt, discovering the remains of his old friend Lazarus, et cetera. It was clear that people were going to be very attached to him, and at some point the idea just clicked that I could create this really emotional moment.

Also — and this is a relatively minor influence on the decision, but still worth mentioning — at the time Electronic Arts was just getting started. They were running a series of ads meant to establish their stable of game designers as artists. One of the ads quoted one of their designers as saying something like, "I want to create a computer game that will make people cry." There was a little touch of a budding rivalry there, and I just wanted to head them off at the pass.

The Hitchhiker's Guide to the Galaxy **was an adaptation from an already much loved radio series and book. How did you go about adapting a piece of linear fiction into interactive form?**

It was actually quite ideal for adaptation, because it was a fairly episodic story line, and because it was an environment filled with all sorts of great characters, locations, technologies, et cetera, while the story line wasn't all that important. It was challenging, but good challenging, not bad challenging.

How was it working with Douglas Adams?

On the plus side, Douglas was already an Infocom fan and had played several of our games, so he understood what an adventure game was and he understood the abilities and limits of our system. On the other hand, he had never written non-linearly before, and that's always a difficult process to get a handle on. Also, I was somewhat awed to be working with him, and didn't assert myself enough at the start of the process. So I think you'll see that the beginning of the game is quite linear, including the destruction of Arthur's house and the scene on board the Vogon ship. Later, when Douglas became more comfortable with interactive design and when I got over my sheepishness, the game became one of the most ruthlessly non-linear designs we ever did.

It was quite wonderful to collaborate with Douglas, who passed away in 2001 at the too-young age of 49. He was a very intelligent and creative person, and humorous as well. He's not a laugh a minute, as you might expect from his writing, but more wry with lots of great anecdotes. He was constantly coming up with ways to stretch the medium in zany ways that I never would have thought of on my own: having the game lie to you, having an inventory object like "no tea," having the words from a parser failure be the words that fell through a wormhole to start the interstellar war, et cetera.

How evenly was the work divided between you two?

The original goal was that we'd do the design together, Douglas would write the most important text passages and I'd fill in around them, and I'd do the implementation, meaning the high-level programming using Infocom's development system.

Douglas came to Cambridge for a week when we got started. Then we exchanged e-mails daily, and this was in '84, when non-LAN e-mail was still pretty rare. We also exchanged phone calls approximately weekly.

However, Douglas' single overriding characteristic was that he was the world's greatest procrastinator. He was slipping further and further behind on his schedule, and at the same time, his fourth *Hitchhiker's* book, *So Long and Thanks for All the Fish*, was about a year late and he hadn't written a word.

So his agent sent him away from the distractions of London and forced him to hole up in a country inn out in the western fringes of England. So I went over there to stay at this inn, which was an old baronial estate called Huntsham Court which had been converted into a delightful inn, and spent a week there completing the design. Then I returned to the U.S. and implemented the entire game in about three intense weeks, just in time for an abbreviated summer of testing. Douglas came back over in September for some final rewriting of key text portions, and it was done in time for a late

October release. The game quickly shot to number one on the best seller lists, and stayed there for months.

I've seen *Hitchhiker's* referred to as a particularly hard Infocom game. Was that your intention?

Douglas and I both felt that adventure games were becoming a little too easy, that the original *Zork* had been much harder than more recent offerings, and the 24/7 obsessive brain-racking was what made these games so addictive. So we might have overreacted and gone too far in the other direction. Certainly, Infocom's testing staff was strongly urging that the game be made easier.

On the other hand, the game's most difficult puzzle, the babel fish puzzle, became a revered classic, and Infocom even began selling T-shirts saying, "I Got the Babel Fish." So it's possible that, while some people were turned off by the level of difficulty, others were attracted by it. My feeling was, and continues to be, that people who find the game too hard can get hints, while people who find the game too easy are screwed because there's no way for them to make it harder.

Another contributor to the difficulty may have been the abbreviated testing schedule for the game, because an already aggressive schedule was made even more so by Douglas' spell of procrastination. More time in testing generally results in an easier game, because the inclination is that if even a single tester found a puzzle too hard it should be made easier.

***A Mind Forever Voyaging* is almost completely missing the humor you are so well known for in your other titles, yet I think it is one of your best works. Was your goal with that project to make a more serious game?**

Yes, partly that was a reaction to having just completed a purely comedic game (*HHGTTG*), and partly the feeling that interactive fiction was such a compelling medium that really "took over" someone's life for days at a time, it was an ideal way to put out a political/social message. It was my attempt to change the world, as it were. The goal was not just to make a work that was more serious and that had a message, but also to create a work that moved away from puzzles and relied more on its story.

The pretense for the player's existence in *AMFV* is very interesting and a change from other Infocom games. Did you feel the need to "break the mold" with this title?

I'm not sure what the inspiration was for the main character in *AMFV* being a self-aware computer, although I can remember the moment when the idea came to me, just sitting at my dining room table with one of my roommates, eating dinner. The navigational and interface differences just seemed like a natural extension of that initial decision. "Breaking the mold" in that way wasn't in my mind as much as "breaking the mold" in the game's content, as I mentioned earlier.

Did you meet much resistance from within Infocom to do the title, or did the success of your previous games grant you the freedom to do whatever you wanted? Were there fears that the game would be too different?

No resistance at all, and sure, the fact that my games to date had been both critical and market successes certainly helped. But the Infocom philosophy at the time was to do a mixture of games aimed at our core audience — the *Zork* games and *Enchanter* games, for instance — along with a few more experimental games aimed at pushing the envelope creatively and attempting to expand the audience for interactive fiction. Another example of this latter category were the "junior level" games like *Seastalker* and *Wishbringer,* which were an attempt to bring interactive fiction to a younger audience. There were some slight concerns that the game was a little too puzzle-less, and in fact we beefed up the puzzles in the last section — not in the epilogue section, but where Ryder comes and occupies the complex.

AMFV also pushed the envelope in the technical direction, being the first game in the "Interactive Fiction Plus" line, requiring 128K of memory rather than just 64K. It was also about twice as large as any other Infocom game to date.

As you mentioned, the moral implications of the game are particularly strong. Why have you not made a serious game since?

I would like to because I really enjoyed creating *AMFV,* and I still feel that computer games can have as much of an artistic component as books, movies, theater, et cetera. And I've gotten so much feedback over the years from people who were impacted by *AMFV.* A couple of people have mentioned to me that they went into the computer games industry because of playing it.

Unfortunately, even though *AMFV* had a pretty significant impact on the people who played it, there weren't that many people who played it or bought it compared to other Infocom games: about thirty thousand. And the sort of creative freedom that I had at Infocom has not been present since. With game budgets soaring into seven figures, publishers are not interested in anything that is in any way unproven or experimental.

A couple of years ago, I was involved in a group that was attempting to put together an adventure game whose purpose, in addition to entertainment, was to expose the plight of Chinese-occupied Tibet. One of the people involved was Bob Thurman, a Columbia University professor who is one of the leaders of the Free Tibet movement. He also happens to be the father of Uma Thurman, who would have been in the game and would have brought along a number of other Hollywood celebrities. Not just actors, but people like Philip Glass to do the score, et cetera. There was even the possibility of a cameo by the Dalai Lama. Even with all that marquee value, we couldn't find a publisher who was interested.

But it seems that serious works are allowed to exist in other media, alongside more "fun" or "light" works. Why do you think this is not the case in computer games?

I think one problem is that the games industry tends to be less profitable than other media. I've heard, for example, that it's very rare for a movie to lose money once everything is said and done, including foreign distribution, video, and all that. The vast majority of computer games lose money. So I think that as difficult as it is in cinema to get something made that is kind of experimental or a little bit different, it's way harder in the computer games industry. The executives in my industry are much more afraid of doing anything to shatter expectations.

I think another difference is that there is a path for the less expensive, artier films. There's really no similar path like that in the computer games industry. There are sort of signs that maybe something might be developing on the Internet. It's very encouraging that the Game Developers Conference has been running the Independent Games Festival, and I'm also encouraged by the work that's been coming out of Garage Games in Oregon. But for the most part there's nothing like a *Blair Witch Project* or a *Crying Game* that the computer games industry can really point to.

So, I think without an avenue for that kind of more experimental game, and with publishers being even more conservative than in other industries, the bottom line is publishers want the "safe game." And the safe games tend to be the ones that aren't serious or message-oriented.

So you think Internet distribution might lead to the creation of more serious works?

Well, I think that it may happen if a distribution channel coalesces, and the Internet does seem to be the best bet for that. And it's really not just distribution, it's also on the PR side. All the major magazines pretty much ignore everything except for the major publishers' games. In fact, I remember one tiny little blurb, and I think it was really just in somebody's column. It wasn't the magazine reviewing a game, but just one of the columnists mentioning that he'd run into a game that he liked and had maybe three column inches on it. And it was this very low production value game that was being distributed over the Internet as shareware, and it sounded really good, like the kind of game I would like. So I went ahead and I downloaded it. And it just really stuck out as a real rarity for a computer gaming magazine to have any mention of a game of that sort.

And certainly, in addition to having the distribution for something like that, you've also got to have some method for getting the word out to people. You can have a perfectly good distribution system, and if no one finds it, so what? But I think if something like that does coalesce, there will be an avenue for someone to do a relatively inexpensive game, something that could be done in a garage but that does have something really interesting, that does push the envelope in some way other than really high production values. It might be something that creates a new genre, like a *SimCity*.

How did *Leather Goddesses of Phobos* come about?

Quite a funny story. When Infocom was still pretty young and small, a few months after moving into its first Cambridge offices, it was decided to have a small beer-and-pizza party for our handful of employees and consultants, the board of directors, local retailers, and people from companies we were working with such as our ad agency or our production warehouse. It was a very informal gathering of just a few dozen people, but it was Infocom's first social function, and Joel Berez, Infocom's president, and Marc Blank were extremely hyper about seeing it come off perfectly.

The party was held in the large central room of Infocom's office space, which doubled as a meeting room and the "micro room" where we had our one Apple II, our one Atari 800, our one TRS-80, et cetera. One entire wall of this room was a single enormous chalkboard with a permanent handwritten table of all version numbers in release. Something like this:

	TRS-80 Model I	TRS-80 Model III	Apple II	Atari 800	IBM PC	DEC PDP-11
Zork I	42	42	44	45	42	45
Zork II	17	17	17	19	17	17
Deadline	31	31	29	30	33	33
Zork III	10	12	12	10	13	13
Starcross	28	29	30	28	28	31

That is, every time a new version of a game was compiled in-house, it was given a new version number. When a given version number was released on a given machine, that number would be written up on the board. If the supply of, say, Apple II *Zork III*s ran out, we would order more with the latest approved version, and that particular number on the board would be updated.

So, to get back to the point of this story, shortly before this party I quietly went over to the board and added a line for a game called *Leather Goddesses of Phobos*. It was just a hack, and I just picked the name as something that would be a little embarrassing but not awful. As it turns out, Joel spotted it before anyone arrived and erased it in a panic. However, the name stuck, and for years thereafter, whenever anyone needed to plug the name of a nonexistent game name into a sentence, it would be *Leather Goddesses of Phobos*.

Then, at some point in 1985, I came around to the idea of actually *doing* a game by that name. After all, everyone loved the name, and had been loving it for years. I brought it up as a project that would be a little racy, but that was really more of a take-off on — and loving tribute to — SF pulp of the '30s. The idea was instantly accepted by Marc and the other game writers, as well as by Mike Dornbrook, my ex-roommate, who by this point had graduated business school and returned to Infocom to head up marketing.

Upper management took longer to convince, particularly our humorless CEO Al Vezza, who was really only interested in the business products side of the company and found doing any games at all distasteful, even though they were wildly successful and were financing the database project. In fact, a year later, when *LGOP* was nearly done, and Infocom had been bankrupted by the business products effort, Infocom was in the process of being acquired by Activision. Activision's president, Jim Levy (who understood games and game development), was being shown around the offices by Al Vezza. *LGOP* came up, and Al quickly and nervously said, "Of course, that's not necessarily the final name." Jim roared, "What? I wouldn't call it anything else!" Naturally this made everyone feel a lot better about the acquisition. Unfortunately, Jim was axed by Activision's board of directors about a year after that.

How did you come to work on *Zork Zero*?

It was my idea to do a prequel to the game, and everyone loved the idea of calling such a prequel *Zork Zero*. It poked fun at the whole sequelitis syndrome that gripped and continues to grip the computer game industry. I had written *Sorcerer*, the second game of the *Enchanter* trilogy that can be unofficially considered to be *Zork V*. It was in the same universe as *Zork*, and as part of writing the game I compiled the first compendium of *Zork* history, dates, places, characters, et cetera, by combing through the *Zork* games and the first *Enchanter* game, and then attempting to tie them all together with a comprehensive geography and history. There was some initial resistance to this from the original authors, but it quickly became apparent how necessary — and later, how popular — a step it was.

So, I was pretty versed in the *Zork* milieu when *Zork Zero* began to be discussed. In fact, I think it's safe to say that I was more of an expert on *Zork*-related details than the original authors. *Zork Zero* had been on my list of potential next projects for a couple of years, and probably would have been my game the year that I did the *Planetfall* sequel, *Stationfall*, except that Brian Moriarty had just finished an adventure-RPG hybrid that we had decided to place in the *Zork* universe called *Beyond Zork*, and two *Zork* games in such close proximity wouldn't work.

As an aside, after finishing *Stationfall*, the decision was between *Zork Zero* and an idea that I had been tinkering with for years: an adventure game set on the Titanic during its maiden voyage. But Infocom's management finally decided — and I heard this many times over the next few years as I pitched this project to many publishers during my post-Infocom days — "people aren't interested in the Titanic." So when the Cameron movie came out and became the most popular movie ever, it was something of a bittersweet moment for me.

When the decision came down to go ahead with *Zork Zero*, the first thing I did was convene a brainstorming session with the original "implementors," or three out of four, at any rate. Marc Blank (who had long since left Infocom and moved to the west coast), Dave Lebling (still a game author at Infocom), and Tim Anderson (still a "senior scientist" special-projects programmer at Infocom) were all there. The fourth original author, Bruce Daniels, had long since moved on. The only thing set in stone going into this session was that the game would be a prequel, and that it would end "West of a white house." This session produced the very general framework for the game: the setting of Dimwit's castle, the reasons for the destruction of the Flathead dynasty, and the collection of artifacts belonging to each of the twelve Flatheads.

***Zork Zero* is a strange hybrid of a game: it's almost all text, with just some snippets of graphics thrown in. What was the general idea behind the design?**

At the time, Infocom was undergoing some stress and soul-searching. Our sales had been dropping for several years. Going into the 1987 product cycle, the thinking from Infocom/Activision management was "There are n thousand hard-core adventure game fans who'll buy any Infocom game no matter how many we put out. Therefore, the strategy should be to put out as many games as possible." We put out eight games during 1987, whereas in any previous year we'd never put out more than five. And all of them did pretty badly. So, going into the 1988 product cycle, the thinking was "Text adventures are a dying breed; we need to add graphics to our games."

Throughout Infocom's existence, we had always denigrated graphical adventures, and during the early and mid-'80s, this was pretty correct. While the early micros were pretty good at arcade-game-style graphics, they were pretty awful at drawing pictures, as seen in the graphic adventures of that time period. But then the Macintosh came out, providing much better black and white graphics than had been seen to date, followed by the Amiga, which did much better color graphics than anyone had seen before. IBM-PC graphics cards were also getting better. So graphics were starting to look reasonable and give all-text a run for its money. Infocom was a bit slow to come around to this truth.

So, in late '87 and early '88, Infocom's development system was being completely overhauled to handle the addition of graphics. At the same time, the game authors were collectively and individually wrestling with the issue of how to use graphics in games. Some people decided just to use them to illustrate occasional scenes, the way a book with occasional illustrations might use pictures. This is what Dave Lebling did with his IF version of *Shogun*.

Since the goal for *Zork Zero* was to be a classic puzzle-based adventure game on steroids, I decided that I primarily wanted to use graphics for puzzle-based situations, so I created five graphical puzzles: a rebus, a tower of Hanoi, a peg-jumping game, a pebble-counting game called nim, and a card game called double fanucci. But I didn't want the game to just look like an old-fashioned text adventure the rest of the time, so I designed the three different decorative borders: one for outside, one for inside buildings, and one for inside dungeons. I also gave every room an icon, and then used those icons for the on-screen graphical maps, which was a pretty good mnemonic device. Finally, I used graphic illustrations in the Encyclopedia Frobozzica, a book in the library that was basically an in-game version of the *Zork* universe compendium that I'd begun compiling while working on *Sorcerer*.

But none of the graphics games sold any better than the previous year's all-text games, and by mid-'89 Activision decided to shut Infocom down.

They didn't improve sales at all?

I would say that during the previous year, '87, all the games sold around twenty thousand. And the four graphical games that came out in late '88 and early '89 also sold around those same numbers.

So why do you think that was? LucasArts and Sierra seem to have been quite successful with their graphical adventures around that time.

Yes, at the time Sierra was selling several hundred thousand copies of their games. But certainly not Lucas nearly as much. Lucas was in fact quite frustrated that they were putting out games that they felt were technically pretty identical to the Sierra games and in terms of writing and content were really superior to them, and yet only selling a fifth or a third as many copies. And I don't really know what to think about that. It might just be that Sierra was doing a really good job producing games that were very well aimed at a middle-brow audience, at kind of the broadest audience. And much like many of the Infocom games, Lucas games tended to appeal to a somewhat more sophisticated and therefore smaller audience.

So that's why you think the Infocom graphical games didn't take off?

Well, no. I think it was much more that by that point the graphical games had become pretty sophisticated in terms of being not just graphical adventures but animated graphical adventures, like the Sierra and Lucas games of that period. And the Infocom games weren't really more than illustrated text adventures. Even though the graphics were introduced, I don't think it was perceived as being that much of a new animal from what Infocom had been producing up until that point.

So do you think Infocom might have been more successful using graphics if they had made them more integral to the design of the games?

It's hard to say what might have happened in '87 if Infocom had said, "We're going to go out and exactly imitate the Sierra adventure game engine the way Lucas did." On the one hand, it has always seemed to me that whoever gets to a market first kind of owns it. And I think that's another reason that Sierra really dominated Lucas at that point. There were certainly a lot of companies that came in, did text adventures, put a lot of effort into it, and did some pretty good text adventures. For example, Synapse Software, in the mid-'80s, with their BTZ engine did a few pretty good games. But they got virtually no sales. It's just pretty hard to go head to head with a market leader, even with games that are just as good, because it's hard to make up for that head start. On the other hand, Infocom certainly had a name that was pretty synonymous with adventure games, so if there was anyone who could have made headway against Sierra's head start it probably would have been Infocom. But at this point it's completely academic, obviously.

The Infocom games all ran off of pretty much the same storytelling system, using nearly identical game mechanics from game to game. Do you think this shared technology and design worked well?

It worked extremely well for its time. It allowed us to get our entire line of games up and running on a new computer within weeks of its release. This was a tremendous commercial edge during a time when the market was fragmented between many different platforms and new, incompatible platforms were coming out all the time. For example, there was a time when there were about twenty-five games available for the original Macintosh, and fifteen of them were Infocom games. This annoyed the Mac people at Apple to no end, since we didn't use the Mac GUI.

Also, the type of games we were doing lent themselves well to a "line look," both in the packaging and in the games themselves. It gave them a literary feel: Infocom games all look similar in the same way that all books look similar.

But even today, engines are usually used for several games, particularly if you include expansion packs. And even though the final products appeared to be pretty similar, the Infocom library actually represents several generations of the ZIL engine. There was a pretty major revamping when the "Interactive Fiction Plus" line came along, starting with *AMFV*, and then another pretty major revamping around '87 with the introduction of an entirely new, much more powerful parser. And then, of course, there was a major overhaul for the introduction of graphics in '88.

A lot of effort was put into the Infocom parser, and it was well respected as the best in the industry. Did it ever get so good that you thought it couldn't get any better?

Certainly, by the time of the new from-the-ground-up parser circa 1987, I thought we had a parser that, while it could certainly be improved, was about as good as we'd ever need for a gaming environment. After all, we weren't trying to understand all natural language, just present-tense imperative sentences. The only area where I would have liked to see continued improvement was in the area of talking to NPCs. But the main problem with making NPCs seem more deep and real wasn't due to parser limitations, it was just the sheer amount of work needed to give a character enough different responses to keep that character from seeming "canned," even for a short while.

I personally loved and still love the text-based interface, both from a player and a game writer point of view. But I don't mind either reading or typing, and some people dislike one or the other or both, and that tended to limit our audience, especially as non-reading, non-typing alternatives proliferated. But I find the parser-based input interface to be by far the most powerful and flexible, allowing the user to at least try anything he/she can think of, and allowing the game writer to develop all sorts of puzzles that wouldn't be possible with a point-and-click interface. So many point-and-click adventure games became a matter of simply clicking every object in sight in every possible combination, instead of thinking through the puzzle.

What do you say to criticisms that the parser interface often proved more frustrating than intuitive, and that though the player may know what they want to do, he or she may have trouble finding the correct words for that action?

I think that's simply a poor parser. I can remember playing one Sierra game where there was what I thought was a horse on the screen, and I was trying to do all sorts of things with the horse, and it later turned out it was a unicorn. In those days, when the resolution was so grainy, I was simply not noticing the one pixel that indicated a horn. And so when I was saying stuff like, "Get on the horse," it wasn't saying, "There's no horse here," which would have tipped me off that maybe it was a unicorn. Instead it was responding with, "You can't do that" or something much less helpful. So to me, the fault wasn't that the game had a parser interface; the fault was that the game was not well written to begin with or well tested.

Certainly when someone sits down with even the most polished Infocom game, there tends to be, depending on the person, a one-minute or a half-hour period where they're kind of flailing and trying to get the hang of the syntax. But for most people, once they get past that initial kind of confusion, a well-written parser game isn't particularly frustrating. Even in the later Infocom games, we were starting to introduce some things that were really aimed at making that very initial experience less difficult: trying to notice the sorts of things that players did while they were in that mode, and make suggestions to push them in the right direction. The game would try to catch if they typed in an improper kind of a sentence, such as asking a question or using a non-imperative voice. It would try to notice if they did that two or three times in a row and then just say, "The way to talk to the game is," and then give a few examples.

And I think that the really critical thing about the parser interface has nothing to do with typing, it is being able to use natural language for your inputs.

Did you ever feel limited by the Infocom development system?

The system was extremely powerful and flexible, and could grow to meet the need of a particular game fairly easily. A minor exception was any change that required a change to the "interpreter." Every game sold consisted of the game component, which was machine independent, and an interpreter, which was a machine-specific program which allowed the game component to run on that particular microcomputer. Since there were twenty or more interpreters (one for the Apple II, one for the Mac, one for the DEC Rainbow, one for the NEC PC-800, et cetera) a change to the interpreter required not changing just one program, but changing twenty-plus programs. So that could only be done rarely or when it was extremely important, such as changing the status line in *Deadline* to display time instead of score and moves.

A more stringent limit was imposed by the desire to run on the widest possible array of machines, so we were always limited by the capabilities of the smallest and weakest of those machines. In the earliest days, the limiting machine was the TRS-80 Model 1, whose disk drive capacity limited the first games to an executable size of 78K. As older machines "dropped off" the to-be-supported list, this limit slowly rose, but even when I wrote *HHGTTG*, games were still limited to around 110K. Generally, this limit would be reached midway through testing, and then every addition to the game, to fix a bug or to handle a reasonable input by a tester, would require ever more painful searches for some text — any text — to cut or condense. At times, this was a good discipline, to write lean, to-the-point text. But often it became horrible and made us feel like we were butchering our own children. OK, that's a slight exaggeration.

How did the development process work at Infocom? Were you fairly free to choose what games you made?

In the early days, things were pretty informal, and decisions were made by fairly informal consensus. In the later days, particular after the acquisition by Activision, decisions were much more mandated by upper management. Generally, the choice of a game was left up to the individual author. Authors with more of a track record, like Dave Lebling and myself, had more leeway than a greenhorn implementor. Of course, there were marketing considerations as well, such as the strong desire to complete trilogies or the opportunities to work with a licensed property such as *HHGTTG*.

One thing that was standard over the whole seven-plus years that I was at Infocom was the "Implementors' Lunches," or, for short, "Imp Lunches." These were weekly lunches at which the game writers would get together to talk about the games in development, share ideas, critique each other's work, et cetera. It was probably the most fun couple of hours of the week.

There wasn't too much oversight during the first few months of a game's life, while the implementor was working pretty much alone, other than at the Imp Lunches, any impromptu brainstorming, or requests for help/advice. But once the game went into testing, first among the other writers, then with the internal testing group, and then finally with outside "beta testers," the game was under the microscope for months on end. During this time, bugs and suggestions would often run into the thousands.

How fluid and changing was the design of an Infocom game?

This varied from implementor to implementor. My own style was to do a little bit of on-paper design before starting, mostly in creating the geography and any "background universe" documents such as a time line in the case of *Sorcerer*, or the rules of the deserted planet's language in *Planetfall*. But for the most part I would just jump right in and start coding with most of the characters and puzzles living only in my head.

The Infocom development system was terrific, compared to the graphic-based systems I've worked with since those days, because just the game writer working alone could implement an entire section of the game in only a couple of days, and then try it out and see how it worked. If it had to be scrapped because it wasn't working, it was no big waste of time or resources. This allowed for a lot of going back and rewriting big sections of the game, which is inconceivable nowadays, where such a decision might mean throwing away a hundred thousand dollars worth of graphics.

Was there a lot of playtesting on Infocom titles?

Lots of testing. Since the development system was quite stable during most of Infocom's life, the testing was able to concentrate on game-specific bugs and game content. There would ideally be about two weeks of "pre-alpha" testing where the other game writers would play a game, followed by two to three months of alpha testing with our in-house testers, followed by a month of beta testing with a couple of dozen outside volunteers. If time allowed, there was also a month of "gamma" testing, which was just like beta testing except that the idea was not to change a thing unless a really major problem was found.

Testing for both game-specific bugs and game content went on pretty much concurrently, although more heavily weighted toward content during the early days of testing and more toward bugs in the later days, when it became increasingly less desirable to make any significant changes to game content.

The early testing period was probably the most fun and exciting time in the game's development. For one thing, after months and months of working alone, not having any idea if a game was any good other than my own instincts, all of a sudden a bunch of people are playing the game, usually enjoying it, and giving tons of feedback. It's a real rush. Also, we had an auto-scripting feature where our network would automatically make a transcript of each player's sessions, which I could read to see what everyone was trying at every point, so I'd often find things which were wrong, but which testers didn't necessarily realize were wrong. Or I'd find things that they'd tried which were reasonable attempts to solve the puzzle at hand and I'd try to reward such an attempt with a clever response or with a hint, rather than just a default message like, "You can't put a tablecloth on that."

It was during the testing period that games became great. Going into the testing period, the game was more like a skeleton, and the testing period, as one of our testers once said, "put meat on the bones." Lots of the humor, the responses to wacky inputs, the subtle degrees of difficulty, the elimination of unfair puzzles — these were all the products of Infocom's excellent testing group.

The packaging for Infocom games was really unique. Why did the company go above and beyond what so many other game publishers did?

When Infocom started, the standard for computer game packaging was something similar to a Ziploc bag. It was just a clear plastic bag with a Ziploc top and a hole to hang on a pegboard in stores; the bag would hold a floppy disk and an often cheaply photocopied manual. In fact, the early Radio Shack versions of *Zork* were in just such a package.

The original publisher of *Zork I* was a company in California called Personal Software. In fact, the product manager for the *Zork* line at Personal Software was Mitch Kapor, who went on to found Lotus. Shortly after they starting publishing *Zork*, Personal Software hit it big-time with a program called Visicalc, the first successful piece of business software for computers. They changed their name from Personal Software to Visicorp, and decided that they didn't want to waste their time dealing with games, and they gave *Zork* back to Infocom.

Rather than find a new publisher, Infocom decided to be its own publisher, and hired an agency to design the packages. The result was the "blister pack" packages for *Zork I* and *Zork II*, the first time such packages had been used for computer games. This is the type of package in which a clear piece of molded plastic is glued to a cardboard back, with the contents visible through the clear plastic, in this case the contents being the *Zork* manual with the disk out of sight behind it.

When it was time for the packaging design on Infocom's third game, *Deadline*, Marc Blank went to the agency with a series of out-of-print books from the 1930s, written by Dennis Wheatley. With names like *Murder Off Miami* and *Who Killed Robert Prentiss?*, the books were a portfolio of reports and clues, just like a police detective would be given when investigating a case: interviews with witnesses, typed letters, handwritten notes, railway tickets, newspaper clippings, a used matchstick, and lots more. The idea was that *you* were the detective, and after sifting through the evidence, you should decide who the murderer was and how they did it, and then open a sealed section of the book and see if you were right.

Marc was very influenced by those books in creating *Deadline* — in fact the original working title was *Who Killed Marshall Robner?* — and he wanted the agency to be very influenced by them in creating the packaging for *Deadline*. Marc wanted the player to feel like they were a detective being placed on a case from the moment they opened the package. Also, because of the strict limits on game size, having lab reports and suspect interviews in the package freed up space in the game for more interactive content. The *Deadline* package that resulted is very reminiscent of those Dennis Wheatley books, with a photo of the crime scene, interviews, fingerprints, lab analyses of things like the teacup found near the body, and even a bag of pills labeled "Pills found near the body." Those were actually white-colored SweeTARTS.

The *Deadline* package was a huge hit, even though we charged $10 more for it, $50 MSRP instead of $40 MSRP. We decided that great packaging was fun, was a great value-added, was a great way to "raise the bar" and make it harder for new competitors to enter our market space, and most importantly, it was a way to discourage pirating of our games. It was more difficult and less cost effective to need to copy a bunch of package elements as well as the floppy disk. Also, because the packages were so neat and so integral to the experience of playing the game, many people wouldn't have felt they owned the game unless they owned the complete original packaging.

The next games were *Zork III* and *Starcross*. *Zork III* just went in a blister pack to match its brethren, but *Starcross* was placed in a large plastic flying saucer, along with an asteroid map of your ship's vicinity. This package, while problematic for some stores because of its size and shape, was phenomenally eye-catching and popular. Recently, a still-shrink-wrapped copy of *Starcross* in this original packaging sold for *three thousand dollars* on eBay.

My favorite package of all the ones that I worked on was *LGOP*, with its scratch 'n' sniff card and 3D comic. The comic was a collaboration between me, a comic book artist, and a guy who specialized in translating conventional 2D comic drawings into 3D layers. For the scratch 'n' sniff card, I got several dozen samples from the company that made the scents. Each was on its own card with the name of the scent. So one by one I had other Infocom employees come in, and I'd blindfold them and let them scratch each scent and try to identify it. That way, I was able to choose the seven most recognizable scents for the package. It was a lot of fun seeing what thoughts the various scents triggered in people, such as the person who was sniffing the mothballs card and got a silly grin on his face and said, "My grandmother's attic!"

We, the implementors, had pretty wide latitude on the choice of package elements, as long as we stayed within budgetary parameters. But marketing often had good ideas too, suggesting that my idea for a book in *Zork Zero* become a calendar, and suggesting things like the creepy rubber bug in the *Lurking Horror* package. But most of the best ideas came from the writers.

The best package pieces were those that were designed in from the beginning of the game, rather than tacked on as an afterthought once the packaging process started in mid-alpha. Most other game companies had anti-piracy copy protection in their packages, but it was often completely obvious and mood-destroying, such as "Type the seventh word on page 91 of the manual." With the better Infocom package elements, you never even realized that you were involved in an anti-piracy activity, because the package elements were so seamlessly intertwined with the gameplay. And, of course, in the all-text environments of our games, the package elements were a great way to add visual pizzazz to the game-playing experience.

There seems to have been a clear difference between Infocom games and the games the rest of the industry offered, especially in terms of a consistent level of quality. Why do you think this was? How was this quality maintained?

Partly, it was the very early philosophy of Infocom, and even before Infocom, in the creation of *Zork*, which was to take a fun game, *Adventure*, but do it better. So there was always a strong desire to be the best. Also, partly it was because the people who made up Infocom were just a really smart and talented group of people. And partly it was luck. We had early success, so when we created each new game we could invest a lot of time and money into it, knowing that its sales would justify the investment, while many other companies couldn't assume that level of sales and therefore couldn't afford the same level of investment.

Our always improving development environment, parser, et cetera, was a big reason for the high level of quality. The talented testing group, and the time we scheduled for testing, bug-fixing, and general improvement, was another big factor.

Did Infocom's consistent quality level allow it to weather the "crash" of the mid-'80s pretty easily?

The mid-'80s crash began with a crash on the video games side, and then spilled over into the PC market. Many companies had a mixture of video game and microcomputer SKUs, but Infocom was entirely in the PC market. Also, our games were as un-video-game-like as possible. Another reason why the mid-'80s slump had little effect on Infocom's game sales was that we were on so many machines, and we could quickly get onto any new computers that were released. For example, the Mac came out in early 1985, and our games were extremely successful on the early Macs. And, of course, the high quality helped, because during any slump it's always the schlocky products that die first.

To me, it seems that Infocom games are the only titles from the early '80s that don't seem at all dated. Why do you think that is?

Well, graphics from games in the early '80s look awful, but text just looks like text. So time is kinder to text adventures. And, as we've already covered, the games were of a very high quality, which helps them hold up over time. And, once you've eliminated technical obsolescence as an issue, ten to twenty years isn't a very long time for a creative work to age well or not well. Think about books, movies, TV shows, et cetera from the same period. Only a very few that were unusually topical would seem dated today, and Infocom games certainly weren't topical, with perhaps *AMFV* as a lone exception. And it's certainly not unusual for people to continue to enjoy the best works long after their creation: *I Love Lucy* is forty years old, *Gone With the Wind* is sixty years old, the films of Charlie Chaplin and Buster Keaton are eighty years old, *Alice in Wonderland* is one hundred fifty years old, and Shakespeare's plays are four hundred years old.

Did the Infocom team think that text adventures would be around forever?

We certainly thought they'd evolve, in ways foreseeable and unforeseeable. While everyone had their own ideas, I'd say that around 1985 a composite of the thinking at that point would be something like this: graphics will improve to the point that they're worth putting in adventure games, there will be a growing emphasis on story over puzzles, games and game-worlds will get larger, there will be more realistic, believable characters in adventure games, many people who have been successful storytellers in other media, such as fiction writers and movie auteurs, will gravitate toward adventure games as the storytelling medium of the future. Looking back, only the first of those points came to pass.

But despite anticipated changes, I think everyone thought that adventure games would be around indefinitely in some form. I don't think anyone thought that by the end of the century all forms of adventure games would be virtually defunct as a commercial game type.

It's interesting that books seem to be able to coexist alongside television and film. Why do you think text adventures cannot seem to do the same thing?

There is still a fairly vigorous marketplace for text adventure games. There are still people writing them and people playing them, it's just not an economic market. The people writing them are not writing them for pay, they're just writing them for the joy of it, and the people playing them are mostly not paying for the experience. And I think one thing that's similar between writing text adventures and writing books is that it tends to be a one-person operation, assuming that you use an existing text adventure writing system. One person without too much specialized training can go off and in a few months write a text adventure game, just like someone with a typewriter, word processor, or big stack of paper and a pen can go off and write novels.

Perhaps it's just a matter of scale, as you mentioned before. The total number of people interested in playing a computer game is just a lot less than the number of people interested in other, traditional, non-interactive media.

I think that's probably true, though I don't know the numbers offhand. But I imagine a best-selling book is probably not much more than a million copies or something. I seem to recall that at the time we did the game, an aggregate of the *Hitchhiker's* books had sold seven million copies, so maybe a couple of million each? And certainly the number of people who watch television is certainly dozens of times more than that.

The interface for the *Spellcasting* series was interesting. It allowed the games to function exactly like the Infocom text adventures, but then added the ability for the player to use only the mouse to play by clicking on the list of verbs, nouns, and so forth. What was the idea behind this new interface?

This interface came from the folks at Legend, particularly Bob Bates, who had begun working on this interface for his post-*Arthur* Infocom game *The Abyss*, based on the still, at the time, unreleased movie. The game was canceled when Infocom was shut down by Activision, and when Legend decided to start publishing their own adventure games, they continued developing that interface.

Spellcasting 101: Sorcerers Get All the Girls

The impetus for the interface was not a particular feeling that this was a good/useful/friendly/clever interface for playing adventure games, but rather a feeling that text adventures were dying, that people wanted pictures on the screen at all times, and that people hated to type. I never liked the interface that much. The graphic part of the picture was pretty nice, allowing you to move around by just double-clicking on doors in the picture, or pick things up by double-clicking on them. But I didn't care for the menus for a number of reasons. One, they were way more kludgey and time-consuming than just typing inputs. Two, they were giveaways because they gave you a list of all possible verbs and all visible objects. Three, they were a lot of extra work in implementing the game, for little extra benefit. And four, they precluded any puzzles which involved referring to non-visible objects.

Also, the *Spellcasting* games went beyond *Zork Zero* by having full-on graphics. Did you make any changes to the way you wrote and designed your games as a result?

Not much. I think I could take any of my graphic-less Infocom games, get an artist to produce graphics for each room, and retrofit them into Legend's graphical engine. The menu-driven interface would be more problematic than the graphics. Conversely, all the games I did for Legend had a hot key which allowed you to turn off graphics and play them like a pure old-fashioned text adventure. So the graphics were always just an extra, not a mandatory.

In terms of the overall gameplay experience, what do you think was gained and lost by the addition of graphics to the text adventures?

There's the unending, passionate, almost religious argument about whether the pictures we create in our imagination based on a text description are far more vivid than anything created on even a high-resolution millions-of-colors monitor. My own feeling is that there are probably some people who create better images in their

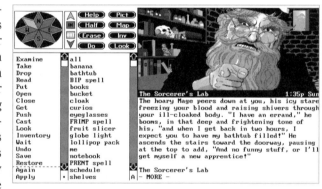

Spellcasting 201: The Sorcerer's Appliance

imagination, and some whose imaginations are pretty damn feeble. Still, the change resulted in adventure games moving in a somewhat lower-brow, less literary direction.

Second, there were some puzzles precluded by graphics. For example, puzzles that relied on describing something and letting players figure out what it was by examination and experimentation. An example from *Zork I*: the uninflated raft that isn't called that, it's called a "pile of plastic." You have to examine it and find the valve and figure out to try using the air pump, and only then do you discover that it's a raft. In a graphical game, you'd be able to see instantly that it was an uninflated raft.

Thirdly, and most importantly, graphics cost way way *way* more than text. As Brian Moriarty puts it, "In graphic adventures, you have to show everything — and you can't afford to show anything!" As a result, graphic games have far fewer of everything, but most important, far fewer alternate solutions to puzzles, alternate routes through the game, interesting responses to reasonable but incorrect attempts to solve a puzzle, fewer humorous responses to actions, et cetera. In other words, graphic adventures have a whole lot less "meat on the bones" than the Infocom text adventures. You get a lot more of those infuriating vanilla responses, like, "You can't do that" or your character/avatar just shrugging at you.

How did *Superhero League of Hoboken* come about? Had you wanted to tackle that genre for a while?

Well, I'd been wanting to make an RPG for many years, and at the time, the early '90s, RPGs were generally outselling adventure games. This was before the "death" of RPGs that lasted until the release of *Diablo*. But I thought that the usual Tolkien-esque fantasy setting and trappings of RPGs had been done to death, and it occurred to me that superheroes was an excellent alternate genre that worked well

Superhero League of Hoboken

with RPG gameplay, with superpowers substituting for magic spells.

I originally planned to make it a full RPG, but Legend had never done anything that wasn't a straight adventure game and were therefore nervous, so the only way I could convince them was to make it an RPG/adventure game hybrid.

It's the only superhero game I am aware of that was not dreadful. Why do you think so few superhero games have been done?

I think that the dearth of superhero games is mostly a legal/licensing issue. Most companies probably feel that only one of the well-known superheroes is worth creating a game around, and such licenses are hard to come by. And even if a license is obtained, the cost of obtaining it means a lot less money in the development budget, which is why all licensed games, not just superhero games, are often so mediocre. I was able to get by with original content in *Superhero League* because it was a satire. I don't think I ever would have been able to convince Legend to do a "straight" superhero game in the same style and engine.

Superhero League is your only RPG. What made you want to try a game design in more of an RPG direction?

I enjoyed and still enjoy playing RPGs a lot, and I always try to make games that would be games I'd enjoy playing myself if someone else created them. And I always prefer to do something that I haven't done before, whether it's a new genre as was the case here or a serious theme like *AMFV* or adapting a work from another medium like *Hitch-hiker's* or a larger scale like *Zork Zero*. Of course, that's just my preference. Publishers often have other ideas!

The game seems to automatically do a lot of things for the player that other RPGs would require the player to do for themselves. Was one of your design goals to make the RPG elements very simple to manage?

Because it was an adventure/RPG hybrid, we guessed that a lot of the players would be RPG players who were pretty inexperienced with adventures, and a lot of the players would be adventure gamers who were pretty inexperienced with RPGs. So I tried very hard to make the puzzles pretty straightforward, and we tried to keep the interface as simple and friendly as possible, given the highly detailed nature of RPG interactions.

Superhero League of Hoboken **seemed to be pretty popular. I was wondering why you haven't done another RPG since.**

Superhero League of Hoboken

Well, it actually didn't sell all that well. I don't think it sold more than twenty, twenty-five thousand copies. And it was certainly pretty disappointing, because I spent somewhat longer on it, certainly longer than any of the other games I did for Legend. And it got quite good reviews, so the sales numbers were pretty disappointing. I think it was Accolade who distributed that, but at the time Legend was not doing all that well financially, so they didn't really do that great a job on the marketing side. As the publisher but not the distributor, their job was to handle all the advertising and PR, and they couldn't really afford to do all that much on either front. And Accolade as a publisher was certainly not as strong a publisher as someone like an EA might have been.

And I think something that really hurt *Superhero League* a lot was that the game was delayed about a year from its original release date. That was partly due to the delay of the previous games in the Legend pipeline ahead of it, and partly due to the fact that the game was trying to do some things that couldn't be done in the Legend development system, and this required some extra support. They hired a programmer to do that, and he kind of flaked out, and therefore it had to be rewritten by internal resources. So this served to delay the game, and it ended up coming out middle of '95 instead of middle of '94. And it was a regular VGA game. So, in the meantime, everything had become Super VGA. So by the time it came out it looked very dated. In fact, I remember another game that came out around the same time was *Colonization*. And I remember playing *Colonization* and being shocked at how awful it looked. I'm sure the experience was very much the same for people looking at *Hoboken* for the first time.

So would you ever want to do another RPG?

Certainly a lot of the projects that I started working on at GameFX were role-playing games, but of course none of those came to fruition. I certainly very much enjoyed working on *Hoboken* and I like playing role-playing games, so I definitely wouldn't mind working on another one.

***Hodj 'n' Podj* was certainly your most different game up to that point. Were you trying to appeal to a new audience with the game?**

Well, I wasn't really trying to appeal to a new audience. As with all my designs the audience was basically me. I always just hope that there will be enough other people with the same likes as me to make the game a success.

Hodj 'n' Podj

The idea for *Hodj 'n' Podj* was at least five years old when it finally became a real project. I originally conceived of the game as a way to bring back all those fun, simple games which had pretty much disappeared, because the hard-core gaming audience which was driving development decisions wouldn't be satisfied by such simple games. This, of course, was before those classic games became ubiquitously available via CD-ROM "game packs" and more recently via the Internet.

At the time, I felt that a collection of such games would need a framework to tie them together to make them an acceptable economic package, thus the overarching board game and fairy tale back-story/theme. Of course, in the meantime, many companies released game packs with no connecting theme or mechanisms, and did quite well with them. Still, I'm very happy creatively with the decision to make the *Hodj 'n' Podj* mini-games part of a larger structure.

It was only after the game was well into development that we began to suspect that it was going to appeal to a very different gaming audience. This was before the phrase "casual gamers" had really entered the industry vernacular. As outside testers, employees' friends and family, et cetera, began playing early versions of the game, we were surprised to find it appealing to people who didn't normally like computer games. We were particularly pleased and surprised to find how much female players liked it. And finally, we discovered that the game was appealing to another niche that hadn't really been identified yet at that time, "family gaming": that is, parents and children playing together. And, thanks to the difficult leveling mechanisms, parents could compete on a relatively level playing field with children, without having to "play down" to a child's level. It's still the only game I've ever written that I've been able to play myself for fun, and I still play with my kids every now and then.

How did *The Space Bar* project come about and what were your design goals for the project?

That's another idea that had been brewing for a long time. I think the genesis was actually back around 1986 or '87, when the *New York Times* threatened to sue Infocom because of our customer newsletter being called the *New Zork Times*. Our lawyer completely poo-pooed the threat, but when Activision began negotiating to buy Infocom, they insisted on all such "clouds" being removed, and thus we were forced to change the name of the newslet-

The Space Bar

ter. There was a naming contest open to customers, plus tons of discussions within the company, and the newsletter ended up being renamed *The Status Line*. But in the meantime, I suggested *The Space Bar* and giving the newsletter the ongoing fiction that it was being written by denizens of such a bar and populated with ongoing characters who were "regulars" in the bar. I'm not sure exactly how, but at some point the idea made the leap from newsletter idea to game idea.

The main design goal for the project was to create an adventure game which was composed of a lot of smaller adventure games: a novel is to a short story collection as a conventional adventure game would be to *The Space Bar*. In addition to just a desire to want to try something different, I also felt (once again reflecting my own needs and wants in my game design) that people had increasingly scarce amounts of time, and that starting an adventure game required setting aside such a huge amount of time, many tens of hours. But if, instead, you could say to yourself, "I'll just play this 'chapter' now and save the rest for later," it would be easier to justify picking up and starting the game. Secondary design goals were to create a spaceport bar as compelling as the one in the first *Star Wars* movie, to create a Bogart-esque noir atmosphere, to be really funny, and to prove that you could make a graphic adventure that, like the Infocom text games, could still have a lot of "meat on the bones." As with *Hodj 'n' Podj*, I felt that just a collection of independent games was too loose and required a connecting thread, thus the meta-story involving Alias Node's search for the shape-shifter, Ni'Dopal. Empathy Telepathy was just a convenient device for connecting the "short stories" to the meta-story.

At the very beginning of the project, Rocket Science was really interested in "synergies" to "leverage" their projects in other media: movies, action figures, board games, books, et cetera. I suggested that a great companion project for *The Space Bar* would be to commission an anthology of short stories by SF writers, with each one selecting one of the characters/races we created for *The Space Bar* and writing an original story about that race or character. Thus, it wouldn't be a conventional "novelization" of the game but an interesting companion piece. But, despite initial enthusiasm on their part and repeated reminders on our part, Rocket Science never did anything about it.

Correct me if I'm wrong, but it seems that *The Space Bar* **was certainly your biggest budget project. Were you eager to work with such lavish production values?**

Yes, it was more than twice the budget of *Hodj 'n' Podj*, which was my largest budget up to that point. But it was still a relatively small budget compared to other graphic adventures of that time; Boffo was a pretty lean operation that really got a great deal of bang for Rocket Science's buck, and the same is true for our primary art subcontractor for the game, Dub Media.

The Space Bar

Even though it was a big budget, it certainly wasn't lavish, because there was never nearly enough money to do everything we wanted to do, so we were always cutting corners. Just one example: Alias' PDA was supposed to be an actual animated face, not just a disembodied voice. So in terms of what we wanted to do versus what we could afford to do, it was actually my most financially tight project. This is the big problem with graphic adventures, as discussed earlier, and the main reason why the medium is basically financially dead at this point.

But the project, while extremely stressful from a budgetary standpoint, was still a great time. Working with Ron Cobb as the conceptual artist was one of the real thrills of my career. *The Space Bar* team was the largest team I'd ever directed, which, of course, goes hand in hand with it being the largest budget, and it's pretty exciting having so many people contributing because almost everyone contributes beyond their narrow areas of expertise/responsibility. And I felt that despite the cut corners we substantially met every design goal, which was quite gratifying.

What led you to WorldWinner.com?

After about a year of canceled projects at GameFX/THQ, I was looking to get out and was working with a recruiter, and she steered me toward WorldWinner. The individual games will be very reminiscent of the kind of games in *Hodj 'n' Podj*, which was definitely one of the main attractions. Also, working in a multi-player online environment was a big lure, because I haven't done that before.

So do you think the Internet provides new possibilities for a wider breadth of games than is currently available?

Yeah, well I definitely think so in terms of providing an outlet for the more personal or more experimental kind of games. Other than that, for now, there are certainly negatives about it in terms of bandwidth. With the games I'm doing now, while there are really interesting and really fun things about them, it's certainly kind of annoying to be back in the days where 100K is really big, and in some cases too big. I had gotten away from that as we got into the CD-ROM days, where the size of things became, in most cases, completely inconsequential, and now all of a sudden it's back in spades. But yes, overall, there are certainly positives and negatives, but overall the positives are very promising and the things that are negative about it, like there are certain kinds of games we can't do because of bandwidth — well, people can still do those games via the normal, traditional channels.

Do you find writing or playing games more fun?

Playing. Writing games is sometimes a lot of fun, and sometimes a lot of drudgery, and sometimes it's really brutally painful, like when your company goes out of business. But playing games is always fun. Of course, the funnest parts of making games are more fun than the funnest parts of playing games.

So much writing in games is dreadful. What do you think is important to keep in mind when writing for a game?

All types of writing are different, and there are plenty of excellent novel writers who couldn't write a screenplay or vice versa. And writing for games is at least as different as those two. Of course, there are exceptions also. It helps to be a game player. You wouldn't expect a novelist to succeed as a screenwriter if he hadn't seen any movies! So a lot of the writing in games is bad because it's being written as though it is for another medium. Of course, some of the writing is bad just because the writers doing it are untalented. As with game design, programmers and producers often incorrectly feel that they're capable of doing the writing.

One thing that makes the writing in games so different is that it often comes in little disconnected chunks, one-word or one-sentence responses to various actions by the player. There is a difficult trade-off between keeping such snippets interesting and keeping them terse. Also, writing has to be so meticulously crafted for gameplay and puzzle purposes — give away just enough clues, not too many, don't mislead — that the quality of the writing often has to take a backseat. And the non-linear nature of games is another obstacle to good writing. If you don't know whether Line A or Line B will come first, there often has to be a duplication of information, giving the appearance of being sloppy or overly wordy. And finally, there's the issue of repetition. In adventure games, you often see the same piece of writing over and over again, with familiarity breeding contempt for even very good writing.

How organic is the design process for your games? Did the onset of graphics end up limiting how much you could change your game?

Very organic, but you're right, graphics games are far more limiting in terms of how much the game can change once it gets beyond the original design stage. Of all my games, *AMFV* was probably the one that changed the most as the game's production progressed. Originally, it was a much more ambitious, much less story-oriented game, almost a "future simulator" where the player would be able to set parameters in the present and then travel *n* years in the future to see what world would result from those decisions.

I also think that development works best when the game grows during implementation, rather than mapping/plotting out the entire game to a fairly high detail level and then starting implementation. That is another big advantage of text adventures over graphic adventures. It allows me, in a game like *LGOP* or *Hoboken,* to find and then hone a voice/style while a lot of the game is still on the drawing board, resulting in better, more unified work.

A big issue for adventure games seems to have been difficulty. For instance, if the game is too hard, you are likely to frighten away new players. But if the game is too easy, the hard-core players will dismiss your game. Do you have any idea what a solution to this problem might be?

Difficulty was a constant problem. Our games got consistently easier, which didn't seem to help attract any new players, and definitely seemed to turn off our hard-core fans. Hint books and later in-game hints were definitely considered ways to keep the games pretty hard without discouraging newer, less sophisticated, less masochistic players. It's a pretty good solution, because if the game is too hard, hints can help make the game a good experience for a weaker player, but if the game is too easy it's pretty much ruined for a stronger player. Another solution is to have multiple difficulty levels, with more in-story clues in the easier levels, but this is obviously a lot more work to design, program, and balance.

A frequent complaint one sees about adventure games is that they don't have a lot of replay value. As a designer, what do you do to add that replayability, or do you not consider it a big issue?

Yes, that became increasingly a big issue as my games were competing not so much against other adventures and RPGs, but against strategy games like *Civilization* and RTS games like *WarCraft.* To some extent, you can have replayability in adventure games. For example, *Suspended* was an extremely replayable Infocom game, as you strove to finish the game with the lowest possible casualty levels. Even with *Zork I*, I remember a New Jersey couple who used to write to us constantly with new ways to win the game in ever-fewer numbers of moves. Alternate puzzle solutions and "meat on the bones" responses to wacky inputs are other ways to extend playtime. But for the most part, it's just a matter of making sure that it takes thirty or forty hours to play the game, and hoping that that's enough to get a person to spend forty or fifty dollars on it.

Did you ever want to forget about the puzzles and have a game that mostly focused on story? You seem to have done an "all puzzles" game with *Hodj 'n' Podj*.

My desire, and I think this goes for most adventure games writers, is to do more story and less puzzle, but puzzle is necessary to keep that thirty- to forty-hour playtime goal. Of all my games, *AMFV* was certainly the most in the story direction, and *Zork Zero* was probably the most in the puzzle direction. I certainly don't agree that *Hodj 'n' Podj* was all puzzles, as the board game certainly has a well-developed opening and closing story, and the gameplay fills in a little more between those bookends: prince rescues princess, prince confronts brother, et cetera.

Did you ever add puzzles to a game solely to make the game longer?

I have definitely added puzzles simply to prolong the gameplay. I'd say the whole third section of *AMFV* was partly that, and partly feeling scared that the game was too different and too puzzle free and that people would rebel if at least there weren't some puzzles in the game. I think *Planetfall* and *Stationfall* were definitely cases where, as the game went into testing, there was kind of an impression that the game was too easy and over too quickly. Some more needed to be put in to keep people from finishing the game in ten hours and feeling that they hadn't gotten their money's worth.

Do you ever fear that some people who might like the story elements of adventure games are scared off by the really hard puzzles?

Well, it is kind of a conundrum, because it seems like what makes adventure games so compelling and obsessive are really difficult puzzles that have you up all night, thinking about them even when you're not sitting down playing the game. Then, when you're away from the game, you're thinking about it and all of a sudden "Oh my God, the kumquat over in the hay shed seven rooms over, I've never tried that!" And you can't wait to run home and boot up the game to your save and run over to get the kumquat, bring it back, and try whatever. And maybe it works and it's the greatest feeling, or maybe it doesn't work and it's the worst feeling, or maybe it doesn't work but at least it gives you some new direction or hint or something. And in a game with no puzzles or pretty easy puzzles you just don't get that same rush. But, on the other hand, particularly as time went by, it seemed there were more and more people playing adventure games who really, really disliked very hard puzzles. It's very hard to satisfy both audiences. Attempting to satisfy the people more interested in the casual gaming experience seemed to, over time, dribble the audience away, because it resulted in a less compelling gameplay experience.

Did you also serve as a programmer on all of your games?

Through *Hoboken*, I did both design and programming, and since then just the design. I certainly prefer to avoid programming if possible; doing so was always just a necessary evil. Of course, it certainly has some great advantages in terms of efficiency and one hundred percent perfect communication between programmer and designer. But even if I loved programming, games these days are too complex for one programmer anyway, so I'd never be able to do all the design and programming myself anymore.

In adventure games and, in particular, text adventures, limiting what the player can do is a major part of the game. Players can become frustrated from seeing "you can't do that" too often. How hard do you work to eliminate this problem?

Part of this is limiting the geography of the game. The original choice of setting helps. This is why so many games are set inside a geography with very well-defined boundaries like a cave, castle, island, zeppelin, et cetera. It's less frustrating to not even perceive a boundary than to reach a boundary and be told "There's nothing interesting in that direction" or "You'd probably die of thirst if you tried crossing that desert."

Part of it is just rolling up your sleeves and putting in as many non-default responses as possible, based on initial guesses of what people will try, augmented by suggestions from testers and even more ideas from reading the transcripts of testers' game sessions. Adding such responses was only limited by time and, more often, by disk space. This was also a good way to put in hints; a player tries something which isn't the "Right Answer" but which is a "Reasonable Thing to Try." I'd make the response an explanation of the failure, but perhaps a clue for what to try. For example:

>GIVE THE SANDWICH TO THE OLD MAN
He looks too tired to eat right now.

And part of it is making the default responses as flexible and fun as possible. For example, in *Hitchhiker's*, the default response for the verb FILL was "Phil who?" Phil was Zaphod's alias during the party scene. For another example, in *Zork I* the default response to many "impossible" actions was chosen from a table, giving you a variety of responses.

So instead of:

>TAKE ALL
loaf of bread: Taken.
knife: It's stuck firmly into countertop.
countertop: You can't take that!
sink: You can't take that!
stove: You can't take that!
oven: You can't take that!

you'd get:

>TAKE ALL
loaf of bread: Taken.
knife: It's stuck firmly into countertop.
countertop: What a concept!
sink: Think again.
stove: Not bloody likely.
oven: Think again.

Do you have a particular starting point when creating a new game?

Varies from game to game. *AMFV* started with the game's theme/message. *Sorcerer* started with the complex time travel, meet-your-own-self puzzle and built from there. I've explained earlier what the seed ideas were for *Planetfall* and *The Space Bar*. Generally, I don't do all of one thing before moving on to the next. I don't write the entire story line, and then start on the geography, and then when that's done start writing some puzzles. Instead, I'll rough out a story line, then design the core part of the geography, start populating it with characters and puzzles, refine the story line, add a new scene with resulting geography, add in the two puzzles I thought of in the meantime, combine two characters into a single character, add a couple more rooms to that Laboratory section of the game, add a new puzzle to flesh out the end-game, figure out why Esmerelda ran away from home in the first place, and so forth.

Why do you think that adventure games are so commercially unviable these days?

Simply, the cost-revenue model for the average adventure game is so far from being profitable that almost no publishers will touch them, since almost all publishing decisions these days are being made on a purely commercial rather than creative basis. It's just one of the most expensive types of games to make, and the top n adventure games sell less than the top n games in almost any other category.

Of course, it can be argued that the adventure game isn't dead, but has simply evolved into action/adventure games, e.g., *Tomb Raider*, and platform games, e.g., *Mario, Crash*. Personally, I don't consider any game that relies on even a relatively small degree of hand-eye coordination to fit the bill of an adventure game.

I suspect that a major technical innovation could revive the genre, but I don't know whether that will be a voice recognition interface, Turing-proof NPCs, 3D-surround-VR environments, or what.

It's particularly distressing when a well-budgeted game that everyone agrees is well done doesn't sell very well. In particular I'm thinking of *Grim Fandango*.

Yes, *Grim Fandango*. I don't know the exact numbers, but I don't think it broke a hundred thousand. And that was everyone's pretty much unanimous choice for adventure game of the year. It was a wonderful game. I didn't think from a puzzle point of view it was that great, but from an art direction point of view it was probably the best adventure game I'd ever seen.

It seems strange that adventure games used to be among the best-selling games, and now they don't sell well at all. Maybe my numbers are off...

No, that's really true. Around the time of the *King's Quest* games of the very late '80s and early '90s, they really were the best-selling genre at that time. And the Infocom adventure games, from circa '83 to '85 were too. There was a point when we had five of the top ten selling games for a given month.

So what happened to the players of adventure games?

Well, there are certainly genres that exist now that didn't even exist then. And there are other genres that may have existed then but have certainly come along quite a ways. So it may be that the people who were playing then liked an interactive experience, but they would have been playing the sort of games that are popular today if they could have then. And in 1985 there wasn't anything like a first-person shooter, there wasn't anything like a real-time strategy game.

It might be that there are still quite a few adventure game people out there but simply that the critical mass of them has dropped a little bit to the point where the ones who are left can no longer support the same degree of game. An adventure game that would cost two million dollars to make now would require ten times as many people to be interested in it as an adventure game that might have cost two hundred thousand dollars fifteen years ago. And maybe the market has even doubled since then, but it hasn't gone up ten-fold. So it has dropped below the critical mass that would make that kind of game economically viable.

What has kept you interested in games for as long as you have been? Have you ever considered writing a novel or writing for other non-interactive media?

I have often considered writing a novel or screenplay, particularly at the most discouraging moments in my game writing career: canceled projects, a company going under, a game selling very poorly. But game writing has always paid the bills, so other writing projects would have to be a moonlighting thing, and with parenting and other outside interests there just isn't a lot of free time for non-paying writing. But any frustrations and unhappiness with making games has been completely on the business side; I've never found the creative process of making games to be anything less than a blast. It's still a growing/developing medium, so it's pretty exciting to be helping to invent a new "art form." Because the pay in the industry is relatively low, everyone you work with tends to be really motivated and love what they're doing, and it's just a pretty cool way to earn a living. For example, how many dads can give their kids T-shirts for a canceled *WarCraft* adventure game?

Steve Meretzky Gameography
Planetfall, 1983
Sorcerer, 1984
The Hitchhiker's Guide to the Galaxy, 1984
A Mind Forever Voyaging, 1985
Leather Goddesses of Phobos, 1986
Stationfall, 1987
Zork Zero: The Revenge of Megaboz, 1988
Spellcasting 101: Sorcerers Get All the Girls, 1990
Spellcasting 201: The Sorcerer's Appliance, 1991
Spellcasting 301: Spring Break, 1992
Leather Goddesses of Phobos II: Gas Pump Girls Meet the Pulsating Inconvenience from Planet X, 1992
Superhero League of Hoboken, 1994
Hodj 'n' Podj, 1995
The Space Bar, 1997
Tile City, 2000
Word Cubes, 2001
Hangmania, 2002
Catch-21, 2002
SwapIt!, 2003
Blockwerx, 2004
Triv!, 2004

Chapter 11:
Storytelling

"The danger for designers is that they get hooked into their story, and they forget that storytelling is a linear narrative-type thing. And the more you flesh out the story, the more you remove the interactivity and the more you remove the player from the game. It's kinda like 'Oh, the outcome has already been determined. So what's the point?'"

— Eugene Jarvis

Strictly speaking, computer games do not need to tell stories. Over the years there have been plenty of fabulous games that offered very little in the way of storytelling. Consider *Tetris*, which had no storytelling whatsoever, or *Centipede* and *SSX*, where the only story found is in the game's setting. But other games, such as *Halo*, *Command & Conquer*, and *Thief*, have taken a story and made it work as a key part of the gameplay, creating tales so rich that players find themselves sucked into the game-world more than if the games had been storyless. And still other games, such as *A Mind Forever Voyaging*, *Myst*, *Ico*, and the *Ultima* series, have made the story such an integral part of the game that one can hardly imagine them otherwise. So games certainly do not need stories, but it seems that when employed properly, stories can make games that much stronger.

The story is so central to *Myst* that it is hard to imagine the game without it.

In fact, the dream of interactive stories is what drew me into game development in the first place. Imagine all of the power of a story in a novel, with its ability to grab hold and captivate the reader, to make her care about the characters in the story, to change her perception of the world, and, in some special instances, to change the way she lives her life. Now imagine how much more powerful that would be if, instead of reading about the actions of other characters, the reader was the main character in the story and was able to make choices that would affect the shape, direction, and outcome of the story. This interactive reader could see the ramifications of different choices made in different situations, and since it was her own choices that determined the nature of the story, the interactive story's draw would be that much more compelling than a traditional story. The mind boggles at the possibilities. Of course this dream is still a long way off, with no available game close to achieving this ideal. But it does provide a compelling reason to keep experimenting, with the hope of one day achieving a truly interactive story.

Designer's Story Versus Player's Story

So what do we mean when we talk about a game's story? Many game developers consider a game's story to be a predetermined series of dramatic events, much like the story one would find in a novel or a film. These events are static and unchanging, regardless of players' actions in the game-world, and the story is typically conveyed to players between gameplay sections. For example, in *Command & Conquer*, players are told the story of the conflict between the GDI and Nod forces through cut-scenes between the different missions. The story determines in part where the missions take place and what players have to do in them, but typically once players have completed a level, the story can proceed in only one direction. The only potential endings to the story are success and failure, with success coming after players have completed all of the predetermined goals in all the levels, and failure coming at any point where players let their forces be overwhelmed by the opposition. Some games allow some simple branching in their story lines, but each branch is still predetermined by the game's designer, and usually the branches are fairly limited in scope.

But there is an altogether different type of a story associated with a game. If what I have just described is the designer's story, we can call this other type of story the player's story. Returning to the example of *Command & Conquer,* each time a specific player plays the game, she generates a new story unique to her. Indeed, each level makes up a mini-story of how the player won or lost that level. For instance, let us say that the player started out her game on the GDI side, building a large number of Minigun Infantry, Grenade Infantry, and Humm-Vees. These forces, however, were nearly wiped out by an early Nod attack, during which the enemy's Flamethrower Infantry proved to be too much for the player. The player, however, was able to exploit a vein of Tiberium she found nearby and build an Advanced Power Plant and some Barracks. The player then concentrated on building only Rocket Infantry and Mammoth Tanks. When the Nod Flamethrower Infantry next attacked, the player was easily able to run them over with her tanks. A number of the infantry started retreating, and the player directed her tanks and Rocket Infantry to follow them back to their base. There the GDI infantry were able to bombard the Nod structures from a distance, with the Mammoth Tanks taking out any resistance they encountered. Thereby, the player won the level. This is the player's story.

Now, when many game designers talk about storytelling in games, they are most likely not talking about the player's story such as the one told above. However, the player's story is the most important story to be found in the game, since it is the story the player will be most involved with, and it is the story in which the player's decisions have the most impact. This is the story they will share with their friends when they talk about the game. Though the story may not be very interesting to others, it will be extremely interesting to the person telling it, who lived through it. In most cases, once players have defeated the level using cunning tactics, they will be much less interested in the pre-scripted, full-motion video (FMV) designer's story that comes up between the levels, explaining the next level to be played. There are certain advantages to having a designer's story, of course. It can contain interesting characters and situations and employ traditional storytelling devices such as building to a climax, creating tension, foreshadowing, and so forth. The designer's story can add meaning and relevance to the actions the player performs in the game. For example, taking the One Ring to Mount Doom to be incinerated and taking your trash to the incinerator are roughly equivalent activities, except in the former case the story gives the action meaning and importance, while in the latter the banality of the activity makes it thoroughly uninteresting. Unfortunately, the use of these devices is often at the expense of the interactive nature of the story. On the other hand, depending on how a given player plays the game, the *Command & Conquer* player's story told above may not have much drama or narrative tension to it, and as a result may be somewhat limp as a storytelling experience.

The ideal for interactive storytelling is to merge the designer's story and the player's story into one, so that players can have a real impact on a story while the story retains its dramatic qualities. There are two good examples of the ideal interactive storytelling experience. The first is an example Chris Crawford is fond of using: that of a parent telling a child a story. The parent has in mind a story to tell including what characters it will involve, what surprises it will contain, roughly how the story will unfold, and approximately how it will end. But as the child asks questions about the story, the parent will change the tale accordingly. The parent may use a book as a guide, but will stray from that guide as necessary. For example, the story might begin: "As the princess wandered through the dark forest, she was frightened by many different things she saw, including a large newt, a dark cave, and an old shack." As the parent tells the story, the child may ask questions. "What color was the newt?" "The newt was a strange shade of yellow, a color the princess had only seen in the royal spiced mustard." "What about the cave?" "From within the cave came a terrible smell, reminiscent of the smell of sulfur burning." "Maybe there's an old sorcerer in there, making potions. Does she go into the cave?" "She did enter the cave, taking each step carefully in order to avoid stumbling in the dark. And as she went deeper into the cave, she started to see a light, and a voice shouted, 'Who is it that enters my cave?' And as she got closer, the princess saw an old wizard with tattered robes…" There may not have actually been a sorcerer in the story as the parent had initially intended to tell it, but as the child asks questions, instead of answering "you can't go that way" or "there's nothing special about it" as a poorly designed computer game might, the parent adapts the story to the child, adding detail and introducing new characters and situations as necessary. The overall story arc and its main protagonists may not change that much, but the child has had a real role in determining what exactly happens in the story.

Another example of truly interactive storytelling is found in many pen-and-paper role-playing games, such as *Dungeons & Dragons*. In a game of *D&D*, the Dungeon Master (DM) leads the game, guiding the other players through the game-world and telling them the story as it happens. The Dungeon Master plans out in advance the locations the players will be exploring, has some idea of what characters the players will meet in what locations, and probably knows what major conflicts will be presented. The players, though, are in control of what parts of the level they investigate, and how they conduct themselves with the different NPCs they may meet. For instance, the DM probably does not have a script of what the different NPCs will say when approached. Instead, she knows what their personalities are like, and how they are likely to respond. When players ask an NPC a question, the DM is able to come up with a reasonable response on the fly. A clever DM will never have to say, "The NPC does not understand your question." As with the parent-child storytelling experience, the DM will be able to keep the players on track with the overall story she wants to tell, while allowing the players a considerable amount of freedom in how that story unfolds and perhaps even in how it resolves.

Of course, the problem in creating a computer version of an interactive storytelling experience such as the ones described above is that both require a human to be telling the story, since a modern computer will never be able to dynamically come up with story developments as well as a human can. So the best a game designer can do currently is try to recreate such an interactive storytelling experience, but, in lieu of dynamically generating the story line, anticipate all of the questions players might ask, places they might go, and lines of dialog they might want to say. Of course, this is a Herculean task, and no matter how much anticipation the designer employs, she will never be able to think of everything players might try. At the very least the designer must try to allow for different playing styles and levels of inquiry into the story-world, instead of pigeonholing players into one way of playing the game and exploring its story. If a designer is interested in truly interactive storytelling, it is her responsibility to make the designer's story flexible enough to allow it to become the player's story as well.

Places for Storytelling

There are a number of ways in which a game can tell a story. Customarily, games use a number of different storytelling devices to communicate their story, with different games relying on some devices more than others. The type of story you hope to tell, what technology you will be using, and the gameplay of your game will determine what storytelling devices will work best for your project.

The simplest distinction one can make is in what context the storytelling takes place:

- Out-of-Game: This is any storytelling that is done on the computer while the game is running, but when the players are not actually playing the game. This includes any cut-scenes during which players lose control of their character, such as the cut-scenes or mission briefings that occur between levels in *Command & Conquer* or brief non-interactive sections in *Super Mario 64*.

- In-Game: Logically, this is the opposite of the above, and covers any storytelling that occurs while players are actually playing the game. This includes the setting of the game-world, the behavior of the players' opponents, any dynamic conversations players may have, and any interactive pre-mission planning players may do.

- External Materials: This includes any storytelling done completely outside of the computer, such as in an introduction written in the manual or any paraphernalia that may come with the game, such as a map or a collection of gems.

Though *Max Payne* used in-game storytelling through its settings and mission design, much of the story line was effectively communicated through the out-of-game, non-interactive cut-scenes and comic book interludes.

A given game may use only one or all three of the above types of storytelling. *Half-Life* is an example of a game that included only in-game storytelling; players never lost control of their character from the beginning to the end of the game. The Infocom games are good examples of games that used both in-game and external materials to tell their stories. In addition to the conversations and descriptions of the game-world players had in the game itself, the Infocom games always came with extra documents and knickknacks, which served to enhance the players' understanding of the game-world, in addition to sometimes being required to complete the game's puzzles. *Max Payne* used in-game storytelling through its settings and combat design, while much of the story line was communicated through the out-of-game, non-interactive cut-scenes and comic book pages. *Tekken* is an example of a game that tells its story, as insubstantial as it may be, almost entirely through out-of-game cut-scenes: one precedes the gameplay and one plays after players have defeated the single-player game using a specific character. The settings of the various arenas have nothing whatsoever to do with the story line, and the characters themselves exhibit nothing of the personalities described in the scenes either, though their fighting styles usually relate to their nationalities. Indeed, it is unclear why the designers of *Tekken* felt compelled to include a story line at all. Perhaps they wanted to give players something to reward them for defeating the game, and a cut-scene was the only suitable prize they could imagine.

Out-of-Game

Out-of-game storytelling is perhaps the most prevalent form currently in games, and it comes in a variety of forms. One can attribute the popularity of out-of-game storytelling to its similarity to storytelling in other media. For example, a cut-scene is very often like a film and uses established cinematic techniques, while a text briefing for a level is not unlike what one might read in a novel. These are both types of media that have been around for much longer than computer games, and both have an established syntax that allows them to tell stories very effectively. In a way, it is much easier to tell a story through these methods than it is through gameplay. But as a designer you must ask yourself, are non-interactive cut-scenes what games are supposed to be about? If your gameplay is any good at all, players will want to get back to playing instead of sitting through long cinematics. Players play games in order to interact. If they wanted a more passive experience, they would have gone to a movie theater or gotten a book from the library. Non-interactive storytelling may have its place in games, but designers need to be aware that it must supplement and not detract from an exciting gaming experience.

As I have discussed, there are a number of different methods that can be used to tell a story outside of the gameplay. The major methods are:

- Cut-Scenes: What are commonly referred to as cut-scenes use cinematic techniques to communicate a narrative to players. These may take place in 2D or 3D, and often involve cuts, pans, the "180 degree rule," and other devices that anyone who has watched movies or television will be familiar with. They are in essence short films interspersed with the gameplay itself.

- Text: Many games use text to describe the story or to give players goals for the upcoming mission. The text may fill the entire screen and then flip to another screen as necessary, or text may scroll by at a slow enough speed that players have time to read it.

- Images: Sometimes players are presented with simple images that communicate some part of the story line. These do not qualify as standard cut-scenes precisely, since they do not include camera cuts or other cinematic techniques, though a simple camera pan may be used to sweep across an image that does not fit on the screen. The image may be a map of an area, an "establishing" image of the challenges to come, or a recap of those the players have just accomplished. Images are often mixed with text, sometimes using comic book techniques but usually without word balloons (with the notable exception of *Max Payne*).

- Audio: Sometimes players are given directives that are spoken dialog or other audio. This is usually when the budget did not exist to create FMV to go along with the dialog or when the dialog is presented over other information players are supposed to be looking at, such as maps, dossiers, or a list of objectives.

One of the most important goals to have when working with cut-scenes is to establish a consistent visual appearance between the cut-scenes and the gameplay. If at all possible, the same engine should be used for the cut-scenes as for the rest of the game. In the mid-'90s, as games switched to CD-ROM as the distribution medium of choice, for the first time games were able to include actual video playback, even if these movies often could not fill the entire screen. Thus came into being the dreaded FMV game, such as *The 7th Guest*. Typically, these games presented long FMV clips with mini-games between them, resulting in products that were more movies than games. In these games the vast majority of the players' time was spent not actually playing the game but instead watching totally non-interactive cut-scenes, with these cinematic sections usually amateurish and somewhat worse than what one would find on even the cheapest TV show. This serves to explain why the genre quickly fell out of favor with players. Other games, such as the aforementioned *Command & Conquer* and *Dark Forces*, used FMV sections between the levels that made up the actual game. These games were fortunate enough to actually include viable and compelling gameplay and thereby stood up as games regardless of the inclusion of FMV. However, the FMV sections of these games were created using live actors in worlds that looked nothing like the worlds in which the gameplay took place. Other games, such as *MechWarrior 2* and my own *Centipede 3D*, used super high polygon, pre-rendered 3D environments to handle these cut-scenes, creating an environment that looked nothing like the ones generated by the real-time 3D engines used for the gameplay. The result is a disjointed visual experience for players, something that breaks whatever suspension of disbelief players may have established. The use of cut-scenes is in itself already a very jarring experience for players; one minute players have an active role in the proceedings, the next they have to be passive, content to sit back and watch instead. Using cut-scenes that look nothing like the game-world only exacerbates matters.

Many games have successfully incorporated cut-scenes that use the same graphics as the in-game visuals, going back to 2D games such as *Pac-Man*, *Karateka*, and *Maniac Mansion*, up to such modern RT3D titles as *The Legend of Zelda: Ocarina of Time* and the *Drakan* games. In these games, though players may lose control of the game briefly, at least they have a completely seamless visual experience. The artists may complain

Cut-scenes in *Karateka* are all handled using the game engine, resulting in a seamless visual experience for the player.

that the cut-scenes do not look as good; after all, they can only play with the number of polygons that can be rendered in real time. But what may be lost in terms of visual quality is more than made up for by the overall consistency of the game.

Another strange aspect of cut-scenes in many computer games is their non-interactive nature, which is indicative of the inability of the designer to understand the capabilities of the computer as an interactive device. Consider spectators at a movie or a play, or the nationwide audience watching a television show. The audiences for those productions are unable to interact with the proceedings in any way: the performance occurs and then it is over. On the other hand, someone reading a book, watching a video, or being told a story is able to experience the medium at whatever speed they want. Pages can be reread in a book, videotapes can be rewound or fast-forwarded, and a child can ask her parent to further explain or reread part of the story she did not understand. The key difference here is that the audience of the first set of non-interactive media is a large group of people, while the audience for the latter set is a single person.

Consider the audience for a computer game. Is it a group or a sole individual? Obviously, for multi-player games the audience may be more than one, but multi-player games almost never bother with cut-scenes of any sort. No, the storytelling games that require cut-scenes are almost all designed as single-player experiences. Why, then, when the text scrolls by in the mission briefing for a game, is the user unable to rewind it? Indeed, why is it scrolling at all? Computers are excellent tools for giving users control over their experience, and since players are usually playing the game by themselves, who would mind if they read the text at their own speed, as controlled by a scroll bar or arrows on the keyboard? Similarly for cut-scenes: why can users almost never rewind to watch the cut-scene again? What if they missed a part of the story they want to hear, or just want to enjoy the presentation again? Even worse, many cut-scenes cannot even be paused, only skipped. Perish the thought that someone might actually want to take a break at some point during a long cut-scene. The prevalence of only-skippable scenes leads to a distressing confusion among users from game to game, as they wonder, "If I hit the Start button, will it pause the scene or skip it?" It seems that the out-of-game sections of computer games are less user-friendly than almost any other solo experience medium. It seems likely that game designers may be thinking that they are movie directors and therefore want to create a movie theater-like experience, despite the extremely different nature of the medium with which they are working.

Rewind

The Last Express' clever save game system allows the player to turn back game-time in order to rewatch cut-scenes or play parts of the game again.

Some games are smart enough to allow the users to control the playback of cut-scenes. *The Last Express* in particular springs to mind, with its unique "egg" save-game feature that allows the users to go back to any point in their game and re-experience it. The game prided itself on transpiring in real-time or close to real-time, and hence players were able to turn back the hands on a clock to any particular time they were interested in and the game would return them to that point, a feature that was essential for understanding the game's complex story. Numerous games have started letting players view all their pre-rendered videos via an option on the main menu, once they have seen the movies during the course of normal gameplay. This allows players to easily replay parts of the videos that they may have missed the first time around. My own game *Damage Incorporated* used extremely interactive mission briefings in order to make sure the players understood what they had to do on a level. Players could use the arrow keys to flip back and forth between text and image documents. During these mission briefings there was also spoken dialog that supplemented the material printed on the screen. Players could pause, rewind, and fast-forward this spoken dialog as they desired using tape deck controls displayed on the bottom of the screen. In this way players were able to read the text at whatever speed they wished and re-listen to portions of the dialog that they may have missed.

Unfortunately, the only interaction with the cut-scenes that many games include is the ability for players to skip them entirely. This is essential, since many players will want to skip over the non-interactive sections of the game, as any playtesting session will reveal. Forcing players to watch cut-scenes is a totally unnecessary limitation no game should attempt to enforce. As I explained above, better than complete skipping is to allow players to skip forward and back through cut-scenes as they desire.

If one stops for a moment to consider the nature of out-of-game devices for story-telling in games, one will be struck by what a strange concept it is to disrupt the interactive experience with a non-interactive one. For instance, when you go to a movie, do the theater workers ever stop the film, bring up the lights, and direct the audience to read a book that they handed out? Sometimes text is shown on the screen, but never in a way that requires the audience to read more than a few words at a time. Instead, films present a consistent media experience for the audience. Games, on the other hand, still mix media in seemingly unnatural ways, forcing users who may just want to play a game to have to read a bit of a book or watch a movie, and only then actually get to play. Surely there is a better way to tell a story, convey a plot, and introduce characters from within the game itself that is far superior to out-of-game storytelling, at least in terms of maintaining a fluid experience for players.

On the other hand, the use of cut-scenes in games has been so prevalent that they are now an accepted gaming convention, and players have come to expect them. They have also evolved in how they are integrated into the gameplay to be much better than simply tacked on, and have been used in games without completely ruining the experience for players. Indeed, we originally attempted to avoid cut-scenes entirely in my game *The Suffering*, but found that, since it was primarily a third-person perspective game, the player was often too far away to see all the elements of a complex story scene clearly. This was in part because we did not appropriately plan our scenes to play well from such a distant view, which is not an easy task for a team accustomed to using cut-scenes and close-up camera views on such events. When we decided to use cut-scenes, we specifically chose to keep them to an absolute minimum and to use them only for fairly frightening and intense moments or key storytelling events. In the end, I feel that the use of cut-scenes in the game was reasonable and did not overly hurt the game, and certainly no press or fans have complained about it. But to this day I am not certain it was the right choice. What we gained in having "cooler" scenes we lost in player immersion.

Though *The Suffering* did use a lot of in-game storytelling techniques, it also included cut-scenes when necessary.

But including cut-scenes will not completely destroy your game, and certainly plenty of games that I love have used them. Indeed, lots of media have employed equally bizarre suspension of disbelief-shattering conventions, such as the total lack of

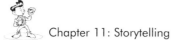

normal conversation in operas, the ability to learn what a character is thinking in a novel, or a movie camera seemingly floating in midair above a given scene in a film. When trying to add storytelling to a game in order to increase its emotional impact, it is extremely difficult to weave all of that story into the game itself without ever falling back on out-of-game techniques, and trying to do so will almost certainly alter the type of story you are able to tell. For example, in *The Suffering* we wanted to have the human characters you meet throughout the game impart important information to the player. However, in the end this information could not be too important since all the scenes happen in-game when the player has the option to kill the characters at any time. This makes sense, since the player is heavily armed, and though many games do not allow you to use your weapons on friendly NPCs, we thought this was an even worse decision than using more cut-scenes. Of course there were some ways to have human characters that were believably invulnerable until after they had conveyed their crucial information, such as having them talk over a PA system, putting them behind bullet-proof glass, or having them be far away from the player (where it could be reasonable that the player would miss if he shot at them). These, of course, had their own downsides, which could make the story seem quite convoluted. Indeed, once we decided to use cut-scenes, in a few cases they solved a number of difficulties we had with story elements that the player could interrupt, problems we had not yet found an answer to. But we still tried to keep the number of cut-scenes to an absolute minimum. For storytelling outside of cut-scenes, we used a number of undead and thereby invincible characters to convey key plot points. This worked for us because it was a horror game and it fit. If we had been doing a crime game such as *Grand Theft Auto III* or *Vice City*, we would have probably needed to resort to cut-scenes to convey key story components, which is exactly what those games did. They too kept their scenes as short and limited as possible (more successfully in *Grand Theft Auto III* than in *Vice City*) and implemented them such that they minimized the disruption to the player's immersion in the game. Though not ideal, cut-scenes can be a useful storytelling tool when they are not abused.

In-Game

There are numerous powerful techniques for telling a story during gameplay. *Half-Life* was universally praised in the gaming press for the strength of its story. However, if one looks at the game's story, it is not actually all that compelling, perhaps even hackneyed. Many other games, even many other first-person shooters, have contained stories just as compelling. What *Half-Life* did well, however, was to tell its story entirely from within the gameplay. Players never lose control of their character, Gordon Freeman, even if he is locked in an observation room, stuck on a tram car, or thrown in a garbage compactor. The story is communicated through a combination of level settings, chatty scientists, announcements over the PA system, and NPC scripted behaviors. By the game's end, players are under the impression that the story was excellent because of the compelling way in which it was told.

Some of the different techniques one can use to tell a story through gameplay are as follows:

- Text: A lot can be communicated to players through text placed around the game-world. These can be signs explaining directions to locations, pinned-up notes left by previous inhabitants of a given area, graffiti on the wall, or books left lying around for players to read.

- Level Settings: Almost all games use this technique, regardless of whether they attempt to tell a story or not. Consider the garden setting of *Centipede*, the hell-like setting of *Doom*, or even the art deco real estate setting of the board game *Monopoly*. What little story these games have is told entirely through setting, but setting can also be key to telling more complex game stories. The players' exploration of the game-world can lead to discoveries about the type of people that inhabit a given area, or inhabited it in years past. Instead of reading in a cut-scene that the land is run-down and decayed, players can simply see that truth by navigating the game-world. When the dam breaks because the evil overlord has broken his promise, the players can see this by the water flooding the ground around them. Setting is a perfect example of showing a story instead of telling it.

- Dialog: Dialog with NPCs during gameplay is another massively powerful tool that designers can use to great storytelling effect. This dialog can be spoken during gameplay through conversations players have with NPCs, where players get to choose their character's response to the NPC's dialog, either through a multiple choice of responses or by typing in their own response. Dialog can also happen non-interactively during gameplay with NPCs, either friendly or unfriendly, speaking to players during the game and thereby communicating more of the game's story. Dialog can also come from computer terminals, PA systems, or tape decks, to name just a few plausible devices.

- NPC Behaviors: Of course, the NPCs should not just talk to the player; they should perform actions that back up the story line. For instance, say that players fight two different races of aliens in the game, and according to the story line the two races bitterly despise each other. If players ever battle both at once, they should be able to trick them into fighting each other. In a peaceful village, if the player character approaches the NPCs with her weapons drawn, perhaps the NPCs will flee from the player. In a more hostile town, the NPCs might draw their own weapons and threaten to attack the player character if she fails to stand down. NPCs can also be engaged in scripted behaviors that communicate to players the nature of the game-world. For instance, say the people of a town live in fear of the Gestapo-like police force. As the player character enters, she may observe a townsperson receiving a harsh and unjust beating from a member of the police.

The *Marathon* games used text expertly to communicate their story line while never taking players out of the game. The game featured computer terminals scattered throughout the levels the players navigated. Players could walk up to one of these terminals and hit the "action" key to activate them. Then the players' view of the game-world would be replaced by a close-up view of the terminal. Players could then use the arrow keys to flip back and forth between different text screens, which revealed more details about the plot and told the players what their objective was for the current level. The great thing about these terminals was that while players were reading them, though they could no longer see the game-world, the game-world was still very much active and players could be attacked by aliens or drowned by rising water. This sometimes gave the reading of the terminals a certain urgency, keeping the players' game-world tension active. Of course, players were able to control the text by flipping forward and backward through the screens, rereading the text at whatever speed they wanted. Bungie's subsequent game, *Halo*, drew a lot of its strengths from ideas first introduced in *Marathon*. *Halo* also featured excellent in-game storytelling through the teammates that accompany players on various missions, the computer AI that speaks to players through their body armor, and events that happen in the game-world. Unfortunately *Halo* did not include anything as novel as *Marathon*'s computer terminals, an in-game technique, but instead featured cut-scenes, an out-of-game technique.

The *Marathon* games allow players to log onto computer terminals scattered throughout the levels, where they can read more about the game's complex story. Pictured here: *Marathon 2*.

Damage Incorporated used a combination of NPC behaviors and dialog to give players some sense of character about the teammates who accompany them through the game's various missions. Players were able to pick from among thirteen different marines the four they wanted to accompany them on a given mission. Each of these marines had a distinct personality and would communicate this through the dialog he spoke during the missions themselves. This dialog might include the response to a directive from players, a comment about the nature of the mission itself, or a response to the players' particularly effective killing of an enemy. Furthermore, different teammates could react differently to being taken on different missions. Some of the marines were less mentally sound than others and if taken on too many missions they would become "shell shocked" and run around the level at random, muttering gibberish all the while. Other marines would have moral objections to some of the missions on which the team was sent. As a result, these rogue teammates would rebel against players and their other teammates in certain circumstances, shouting their disapproval for the task at hand as they went on a murderous rampage. Thus, a combination of dialog and NPC behaviors created a group of teammates with real personalities, almost all of which was communicated during the gameplay itself.

One of the big concerns some people have with in-game storytelling is that players may miss some of the story. What if players fail to see the story being told? Since players never lose control of the game with in-game storytelling, this makes it possible for players to avoid talking to characters, witnessing scripted NPC behaviors, or reading signs. It is true that locking players in front of a non-interactive cut-scene or scrolling text is one way to guarantee that they see exactly what the designer wants them to see. But, as I have stated previously, one needs to remember that games are an interactive form, and the fact that players do not experience every last element of the story is part of the nature of interactivity. If players are interested in getting the entire story, it is their responsibility to seek it out. If players would prefer to just charge through the game focusing solely on the gameplay, that is their choice to make. Indeed, having different layers of the story that can be discovered on playing the game a second time can be a significant incentive for replaying the game.

In *The Suffering* we used a number of in-game storytelling techniques. These included simple methods, such as voices coming over the PA system, haunted telephone calls the player would receive, notes you could pick up and read at will, scripted scenes involving supernatural creatures, and the human companions players would meet as they explored the game-world. All of these techniques stood on their own without triggering a cut-scene or doing anything else to break the player's immersion. One of our more innovative storytelling devices was what we called in-game "environmental flashes." These were basically visions of events from the game's back-story, typically played in slow motion with various screen effects overlaid on top of them, but with the player maintaining control of the main character and still having the freedom to look around the environment. Indeed, sometimes an environmental flash would be set up to trigger when the player was literally standing in the middle of the apparitions, and thus would want to rotate the camera around himself to see everything before the vision suddenly came to an end. We found that, both for the environmental flashes and other in-game scripted scenes, though players might miss them if they happened to look away once the scene had started, the majority of players would see the scenes to completion if they were oriented in the correct direction when the scenes started. Thus, getting the scenes to have a good chance of being seen was a level design challenge where we had to place them where players naturally tended to be looking as they ran through a level. Furthermore, we used special triggers that were not just based on the player's position, but also on where he was looking. These triggers would only activate once the player had a certain portion of the environment in a certain place on the screen, further ensuring that the scripted event would be seen as we intended, all without actually breaking the player out of the game. Finally, we were careful to include far more story content in the game than you would need to get the gist of what was happening with the plot. Thus, if players only saw 75 or even 50 percent of it, they would still understand the story and enjoy their experience.

Almost everyone has had an English teacher who emphasized the importance of showing instead of telling in creative writing. Instead of being told that the people are wealthy, readers should be able to read the author's description of an area and from that deduce that the region is populated by a prosperous people. For games, in-game storytelling is the equivalent of showing, while out-of-game cut-scenes and other methods are telling. Taking the idea one step further, Noah Falstein is fond of saying that the

Though *The Suffering* did use some cut-scenes, a lot of storytelling was done using in-game storytelling techniques.

gaming equivalent of the "show, don't tell" rule is "do, don't show." In games, you want to keep players actively involved in the story, "doing" actions instead of being "shown" them. In-game storytelling is a key part of that. In addition to maintaining the players' immersion in the game-world, in-game storytelling makes the players active participants in the game's story instead of just flashing it in front of their eyes.

External Materials

Many games have used external materials to tell their stories. This was particularly true in the 1980s when disk space was severely limited and designers could not fit all of the story they wanted to include onto a single 400K or smaller floppy disk. Some designers used manuals to communicate the game's back-story, writing a narrative that would lead players up to the point where they would start playing the game. Some games, such as the classic *Wasteland*, even used "paragraph" books, where the game would play for a while, and then when players got to a storytelling juncture they would be instructed "Now read paragraph 47." Sometimes this referencing of the manual was used as a form of copy protection, in that players would be unable to play the game without having a copy of the manual.

Arcade games also used external materials. Often the names of the game's characters were written on the side of the cabinet instead of in the game. Some cabinets even included a few sentences further explaining the game's setting and the mission at hand. The artwork featured on the sides of arcade game cabinets used superior graphics to add a small amount of depth to what meager story lines the games may have had.

These days storytelling in manuals and other materials is generally frowned upon, and rightly so. We are certainly no longer presented with the technological limitations that necessitated storytelling through external materials. Furthermore, often the stories told in the manuals were not written by the game's designers or even with their consultation. Therefore these stories can hardly be considered a part of the game itself, but rather the marketing department's attempt to create a game-world they could hype on the back of the box. Sometimes a few text pieces that set up the game's action are included in the game's manual, but these are almost never fundamental to the player's understanding of the game's plot. I would certainly never use a manual to be the sole place to convey the story in one of my own games since I believe it detracts from the continuous experience of playing the game on the computer or console. *The Suffering* did include some back-story pieces in the manual, but these were purely supplemental and enhanced the game's story for players who sought them out, without detracting anything from players who did not.

That said, some games have used external materials extremely effectively. In particular, the Infocom games always included materials in the boxes that added to the players' gameplay experience in meaningful ways. Often the games referred to these materials, saying something to the effect of, "The magazine you find is the same one as came in your game package." These materials were customarily prepared by or in conjunction with the game's author, thereby making them valid parts of the game itself. For more information on how Infocom used its packaged materials to add depth to the story and their motivations for doing so, consult the interview with Infocom author Steve Meretzky found in Chapter 10.

Linear Writing Pitfalls

One of the primary story problems that many computer games have is that their stories are written by people who wish they were writing in a more linear medium. Sometimes moonlighting screenwriters or novelists are hired to work on game projects. These writers often feel disappointed to have to work in games and see their game work as something they do strictly for the money, while simultaneously viewing themselves as above gaming as an art form. As a result of their training in linear writing and distaste for interactive writing in general, these writers use all of the linear writing techniques they have honed over the years and try to apply them to games, where they fail miserably.

Sometimes the game developers themselves secretly or not-so-secretly wish they were working in another medium and make their story writing choices accordingly. After all, for as long as games have existed, film has been a more respected, popular, and financially rewarding medium to work in, with mammoth cults of personality surrounding actors, directors, and sometimes even writers. Game designers can be sucked in by this allure and become envious of filmmakers. These designers often start emphasizing the cinematic nature of their games, sometimes attempting to deny that they are games at all by calling them "interactive movies." The games' cinematic cut-scenes become longer and longer, with the predetermined story line dominating the gameplay completely.

And in a way, the mistakes game developers make putting story into their games are forgivable due to the youth of the medium. For example, when the technology that enabled filmmaking was introduced, many of the first films that were made were documents of stage plays. A camera was placed in a fixed position on a tripod and the actors considered its frame to be their stage, just as if they were working with a live audience. There were no cuts, pans, or camera movement of any kind, because the language of film had yet to be invented. As time went on, however, filmmakers learned that their films could be more than straight transcriptions of stage plays, and they could instead take advantage of the strengths of their new medium. In some ways, games still suffer from the same problem, where established mediums, film in particular, are taken and just thrown into games without considering how a story might best be told in a language suited to interactivity.

What results from these frustrated linear writers are projects that try to be both games and movies, usually with the end result that they do neither very well. Taking a plot and adapting it to work in a game is a lot like taking a plot that works in a novel and adapting it to work in a film. A novel's strength is in allowing the readers to truly get inside the heads of its protagonists, to read what they are thinking. In a movie, a lot of the audience's understanding of a character comes from being able to read the subtleties of expression on the actor's face. When a screenwriter adapts a novel, he has to re-imagine how it could work in a film, replacing what worked well in the book but won't translate well to the screen. Compared to either novels or films, games need to be significantly more active, with the character the player is controlling having plenty to do in the story. This is especially true given the current status of game development, where making dialog with other characters fun is all but impossible. Until technology advances to the point where games are able to simulate conversations significantly better than they do currently, game stories need to center around actions that games do well. This is one of the many reasons why writing stories for games is significantly different than for non-interactive media. In addition, writing a story that is suited to an interactive experience is extremely hard because we have so little experience with it, certainly when compared with the centuries of human experience that have been invested in linear storytelling. But telling a story that is suited to a playable space will reflect on the quality of your final game. There are a number of symptoms that arise when inappropriate stories are used, and recognizing these problems as they come up is crucial to preventing them from ruining your game.

The first problem is forcing players to experience the story in only one predetermined path. The linear writer often feels that there is only one way for the drama to unfold, and if players try to pursue anything else they, or at least their character, should be killed. The linear writer does not want to allow players to discover different ways of navigating through the story space when there is only one path that makes for the most powerful narrative. What the linear writer fails to realize is that games are about letting players find their own path through the game-world, even if the story suffers a little as a result. What the path may lose in drama it makes up for in players' feelings of ownership. It is the player's story instead of the designer's story.

Player Character Personality

Linear writers also often try to force the player's character to have a strong personality. There is a popular trend in game design that says gamers want to have main characters with strong personalities for them to control, particularly in adventure and action games. But if one looks at the most popular entries in these genres, one will quickly notice that the player character's personality is often kept to a minimum. Look at Mario in *Super Mario 64* or *Super Mario Sunshine*. Though Mario has a fairly distinctive look, what really is his personality? He does not actually have one, leaving him undefined enough for the players to imprint their own personality on him. What about Lara Croft in *Tomb Raider*? Again, a very distinct appearance but a very undefined personality. And

Despite being perhaps the most famous computer game character in existence, Mario has a relatively undefined personality. Pictured here: *Super Mario Sunshine*.

if one looks at the Space Marine in *Doom* or Gordon Freeman in *Half-Life*, one will find no personality whatsoever.

The reason for this is simple: when players want to play games, often they want to play themselves. If the character they are controlling has a very strong personality, there is a distancing effect, reminding players that the game is largely predetermined and making them feel like they are not truly in control of what happens in the game. Particularly frustrating are adventure games that feature strongly characterized player characters who keep speaking irritating lines of dialog. I remember one adventure game in particular where players had to control a spoiled brat who constantly said annoying, idiotic things to himself and to the characters he met. Who would want to control such a character? The dialog for the character was actually amusing and quite well written, but not to the players who were forced to go through the game using that obnoxious character as their game-world surrogate. It would appear that the game's writer got carried away with this interesting characterization without realizing the detrimental effect it would have on players' gaming experience.

Of course there are a number of popular games that have succeeded while having extremely well-defined main characters. *Duke Nukem 3D*, the *Monkey Island* games with Guybrush Threepwood, *No One Lives Forever* with Cate Archer, any game featuring James Bond, the *Oddworld* games, *Max Payne*, and any of the later *Final Fantasy* games all contained extremely well-defined player characters who had piles of dialog in cut-scenes and during gameplay. When gamers play these games they are definitely acting as the guide to another character instead of becoming that protagonist themselves. Thus these games focus less on immersion and more on entertaining players at a simpler narrative level and do that quite well. In these games, players feel more like they are playing the game to unlock a predetermined story, that the adventures of these strong characters are already known, and that they are just uncovering them by playing the game. The most recent game in the *Prince of Persia* series, *The Sands of Time*, defined the main character more than any of the previous games in the series, and took the "player discovering a story" concept one step further. In the game, the main character acts as the game's narrator, and each time the player fails to accomplish an objective the player character is heard saying, "No no, that's not what happened." In terms of story these games really are more interactive movie than game. They emphasize the designer's story as the definitive story and do little to foster the player's story. These games prove to be successful because they contain such well-written designer's stories and feature extremely good gameplay mixed in with it.

Prince of Persia: The Sands of Time featured a very well-written and strong designer's story, making it more important than the player's story.

It is interesting to note, though, two games that deliberately went out of their way to have main characters who stayed mute and were thereby more iconic: *Grand Theft Auto III* and *Jak & Daxter*. What's most interesting is that for the sequels to both of these games, both of their respective developers decided to make their main characters talk, thereby diminishing the potential for player immersion. *Grand Theft Auto III* of course was a massively popular hit and featured a character who never said a word throughout the game. The game was still filled with well-written and interesting characters that the player met as he moved through a seamy underworld milieu, but the main character was specifically designed to have an everyman quality to him and never spoke. Through his actions he exuded a street tough and cool attitude, but his lack of dialog made it easier for players to project themselves into him. In the next game in the series, *Grand Theft Auto: Vice City*, the game was improved in nearly every way with tighter game mechanics, better graphics, resonant licensed music, and a more colorful and well-written cast of supporting characters. In this game, however, the main character talks quite a bit, both during cut-scenes and occasionally during gameplay. Though I would say the cut-scene dialog works much better than the in-game dialog, neither did anything to improve the popularity of the game with fans or critics, and overall the game did about as well as its predecessor. (This may be unfair since the first was so popular that it would be very difficult to be more popular.) A game that was somewhat less of a hit though still quite popular was *Jak & Daxter*, which also contained a mute main character. Commenting on the first game, Naughty Dog co-founder Jason Rubin stated, "[Jak] doesn't speak much either, so you don't feel like you're playing Gex, and you don't want to play that character — you don't feel turned off by it." When the first game failed to sell up to expectations, many elements were changed for the sequel, including adding a voice to Jak. Interestingly, the game proved to be a bit less popular than the first, both with fans and the critics. Of course there are a myriad of reasons for this and one can hardly attribute it solely to the decision to make Jak talk, but making that change was not something that was seen as a substantial improvement to the game.

In *The Suffering*, immersion was one of our primary design goals, and having the main character, Torque, not talk was a big part of that. In particular, the game hinged on the player determining what kind of person Torque was and whether or not he was guilty of the heinous crime that landed him on death row at the start of the game. It seemed odd to have a game where you were determining the main character's moral nature where you did not actually get to become that character. During development there was discussion about making Torque's personality stronger by having him talk, but in the end we decided that supporting the players' ability to become Torque was extremely important in terms of players caring about the game's story. If Torque had been more strongly defined as a character, players would have been left feeling that everything about him was already predetermined and that they could not control his fate at all, or that whatever they could control was strictly canned.

The quest to have a character that players can project themselves into is something that is far more important in games, where the player is supposed to be in control of what happens, than in any other media. In Scott McCloud's great book *Understanding Comics*, he spends a chapter discussing the iconic representation of characters in cartoons and how this allows readers to project themselves into the characters much more than in photo-realistic works. Throughout the book McCloud draws himself as the narrator and host and uses a very abstract and cartoony style. Explaining this choice, he states: "That's why I decided to draw myself in such a simple style... I'm just a little voice inside your head. You give me life by reading this book and by 'filling up' this very iconic (cartoony) form. Who I am is irrelevant. I'm just a little piece of you." The more abstract the notion of the character, the more the audience will be able to fill in the blanks with themselves. McCloud states that this is why cartoony imagery is so pervasive in our culture; people can become much more involved with iconic imagery than they can with more detailed and thereby specific representations of reality. Similarly, this is why abstract characters are so prevalent in computer games.

Whether or not to have a specifically defined central character in your game is a personal decision and depends on what you are trying to accomplish. You can tell a richer conventional story if you have the player control a very distinct character, but you can suck the player into the game much more if you keep the main character iconic and allow players to feel like they are in charge of determining that character's personality and fate. Personally, I believe that the advantages of having players feel that they are the hero outweigh the advantages of having a strong character. Keep in mind, your game can still have terrific characters in it, and indeed, without strong characters your game will fail to have much of a story at all. Instead of trying to imbue the main character with a lot of personality, make the NPCs players encounter in the game memorable and interesting. If players find these characters annoying, that is acceptable; it means that they have enough personality for players to feel strongly about them. But the players' character should be sufficiently amorphous and unformed that players can think of that character in whatever way they see fit. And fear not, after spending forty or more hours with that character, players will come up with their own ideas of what motivates and drives their game-world surrogate. The character they create in their mind will be one whom they like and with whom they will want to continue to play.

Game Stories

As I have discussed, when writing a story for a game, it is important to stay away from the conventions of linear media, such as forcing players to follow only one narrative and instilling too much character in the players' game-world surrogate. Beyond the pitfalls to avoid when creating the game's story, the game's scriptwriter should worry less about the overall plot and more about the situations in which players find themselves and characters with which they interact. Indeed, many film directors are keenly aware of this technique. For instance, in talking about his notoriously confusing film *The Big Sleep*, director Howard Hawks said: "Making this picture I realized that you don't really have to have an explanation for things. As long as you make good scenes you have a good picture — it doesn't really matter if it isn't much of a story."

I have played countless games where the overall plot was completely lost on me; I simply did not care to follow it. Often in these games, I enjoyed the gameplay, the situations the game placed me in, and the interesting and amusing characters I met there. Since the characters and situations were interesting, it did not really matter if I knew who did what to whom and when. All I knew was that I was having fun playing the game. Often when games try to hit me over the head with their plot through long cut-scenes that go into minute detail about the reasons for the state of the game-world and the character's motivations for every last action, it becomes tedious. Remember that players want to play games. If the story enhances that experience, that is good, but if the story starts to get in the way of the gameplay, that is bad. Spelling out too much of the story is also a common failing of novice writers. Readers, viewers, and players alike are able to figure out much more than novice authors give them credit for. It makes sense for the author of the story to have all of the character's motivations figured out in detail, with all of the nuances of the different twists and turns of the plot detailed in her notebook. Indeed, having a rich back-story or story bible can be a fantastic way to ensure consistency and allow for later changes or additions to still fit with the overall game fiction. But does every last element of this story need to be included in the game? No, what is more important is that pieces players are presented with are consistent and could be used to put together the complete story. Players will not mind if every last plot point is not explicitly spelled out.

In Chapter 9, "Artificial Intelligence," I talked about Brian Moriarty's concept of "constellation" and how it could help to create more interesting AI. Constellation is a natural tendency that game storytellers can also use to their advantage. Moriarty has described constellation in media as the ability of an audience to fill in the holes or inconsistencies present in a storytelling experience, regardless of what form that story may take. For instance, if a storyteller only hints at the true appearance of an evil foe, the image conjured in the mind of an audience member may be far more frightening than what the storyteller might be able to describe to the audience. One can also look at the fan base for a TV show such as *Star Trek*. The slightest hinting at a bit of story by the writers of the show will lead to endless speculation among the audience members as to what the implications of that subtle hint are, and the fans will come up with their own explanation for what it might mean. This may or may not be the explanation the writer originally intended, but what is important is that it involves the audience in the work to a much greater degree, switching them from a passive mode to an active one. Of course, games are already much more interactive than television, and therefore it makes sense that game storytellers would not tell the audience every last detail of a plot. This will involve the players still more in the game as they try to figure out what exactly the story is all about. And above all, they will be delighted to avoid long expository scenes and get back to the game.

Non-Linearity

Much talk is made of non-linearity in games, and storytelling in particular is a key area where non-linearity can be used to enhance players' gaming experience. I feel the goal of game storytelling is to create a story in which players feel they can play a significant role that may affect the outcome. Non-linearity is an essential tool for accomplishing that goal. In a way, in-game storytelling is non-linear. In-game storytelling allows players to talk to some characters and not to others, to choose which signs to read and which to ignore, and to explore the game-world in order to reveal its relevance to the story line, exploration over which players have control. With players empowered to explore the story-space in their own way, some degree of non-linearity is unavoidably created. This was certainly true in *The Suffering* and with *Odyssey* before it, where I put a lot of story into the games that many players would not necessarily find, making players' exploration of the story-space somewhat non-linear or at least unique to them.

Much of the story in *The Suffering* needs to be found by player exploration.

One popular way to add non-linearity to the storytelling experience is through a branching story. With a branching story, at various points the decisions players make will have a significant effect on how the story progresses. This may mean if players succeed in defeating a certain adversary, the story will progress differently than if the players fail to kill that foe. In the latter case, it may be that players will have to kill that foe later, or that the foe will summon a force to help him that players will have to confront. Of course, branching stories increase the amount of content that will need to be created for a game, at least in terms of game design and dialog, if not also in art assets.

This can sometimes make this technique unpopular with the cost accountants, who see the creation of such assets as wasted money. What they fail to see is that if the branching story line is implemented properly, the gameplay payoff will be tremendous, thereby making the game more popular and profitable.

Another technique that can be used to inject some non-linearity into the game's story is to allow players to determine the order in which different story components occur. Suppose there are three sections of the story you need to tell. Perhaps the order in which players experience those components is not so important. With a little extra work, you may be able to give players the choice of which section to do first, which to do second, and which to do last. If one thinks of this in terms of the "chapters" of a game's story, often designers find that, though the first and final chapters of the narrative must happen at the beginning and end of the game respectively, the other chapters in the game can happen in any order. Of course, issues with the difficulty of the sections may arise, since ideally designers want the difficulty of their games to ramp up continuously. This, however, is more of a game design question, and one that clever designers will be able to solve. It also presents problems with the story itself, where the writer must keep those plots discrete so that they can be experienced in any order and still make sense. This may have the negative side effect that you cannot have each of these interchangeable story chapters build on each other in the same way as you could in a completely linear story. Often this is not a problem, however, and the advantage of having players craft their own experience outweighs the drawbacks.

Of course non-linear storytelling in games goes hand in hand with non-linear gameplay; one can hardly imagine one without the other. Non-linearity is explored more in Chapter 7, "The Elements of Gameplay."

Working with the Gameplay

One of the most important parts of creating a story for a computer game is to match the story with the gameplay as much as possible. Earlier, in Chapter 3, "Brainstorming a Game Idea," I discussed how a game's development might start with technology, gameplay, or story/setting. If you are starting your game development process with gameplay or with technology, these are going to directly dictate which kind of story you can tell. If you try to fight the gameplay or technology with a story that is not suitable, you are going to be left with a poorly told story in a poorly executed game. There are infinitely many stories to be told, and infinitely many ways to tell a given story. Your job as game designer is to find a story and a telling of that story that will work with the game design and technology that you will be using. It is reasonable to alter the gameplay somewhat in order to support the story you are trying to tell. There should be a fair give and take between the two, but in the end you will need to remember that it is a game that you are developing and that gameplay must almost always take precedence.

For me, stories seem to naturally fall out of gameplay. I seldom think of a story independently and try to fit it into some gameplay. Instead, I see the constraints of the world with which I will be working, and start thinking of the most interesting content possible for that space. I do not see these constraints as a limitation on my ability to tell a story, but more as guidelines or even sources of inspiration. For example, in *Damage Incorporated*, long before the game had a story there was a technology and a game design in mind. From the game design, which centered around players controlling

Damage Incorparated's story was created to fit around the gameplay and technology.

teammates in an FPS environment, sprung the idea for the different teammates that would accompany players, and how each one of them would have a distinct personality. What sort of men would be in the Marine Corps of the 1990s? How would they react to a combat situation? What would their reaction be when they saw their commander killed? These were the questions that ended up driving the development of the game's story. And these questions arose directly out of the limitations imposed by the game design.

Similarly, in *The Suffering* we wanted to keep the player as immersed in the game as possible, and therefore wanted to have a continuous game-world where the player ran through every inch of it on foot. We also wanted a space where the player could be reasonably constrained without it seeming contrived. Thus setting the game on a relatively small island made perfect sense and acted as a natural and believable physical limitation to where the player could go. In writing the story, I used this to my advantage, building up the mythos of the game around its island setting, to the point where, from a story standpoint, the game is inconceivable anywhere else. Similarly, since we were building an action game, we knew we had to have a fairly large body count, and thus the game's fiction was written to support an endless supply of hideous creatures springing forth from caves beneath the island's surface. In the end the creatures and the island seem to be a natural and appropriate part of the story, but originally they were decisions that were fully dictated by the gameplay.

The Dream

One could say that the goal of gameplay is to allow for different player strategies to lead to variable types of success, to reward player experimentation and exploration, and to empower players to make their own choices. All of these factors allow players to craft their own unique stories when playing your game. If in addition you want to tell a more predetermined story through your game, it is important to do everything possible to make players feel that it is their own unique story. Players should feel ownership over the actions in their game, and thereby ownership in the story that is being told.

Marketing people and game reviewers in part like storytelling in games because stories are much more easily understood and discussed than game design concepts. Writing about game mechanics and how much fun a game is to play is really hard to do. A story makes easy copy for either the back of the box or the text of a review and is much easier to describe than gameplay. These days, game reviewers will be frustrated if your game does not have much of a story, regardless of whether it needs one or not. Games without stories are considered passé and archaic. But reviewers are generally wise enough to recognize that gameplay is essential as well, and games that focus on story at the expense of gameplay will tend to get panned, and rightly so. Unfortunately, the marketing people truly will not care if your story is non-linear or allows for the players to make the story their own. Indeed, the business types will love a main character with a strong personality since it will be more likely to lead to licensing opportunities for action figures and Saturday morning cartoon shows. Never mind that the character's strong personality may alienate players from the game.

Titles like *SimCity* allow players to truly tell their own story, with barely any guidance from the designer.

But as a game designer your ambitions must be higher than creating entertaining box copy or simplifying the job of game reviewers. Many great games dispense with traditional storytelling entirely. *Civilization* and *SimCity* immediately spring to mind as indisputably great games that allow players to tell their own story, with the designer providing only a starting place from which the tale can unfold. Although games do not require pre-scripted stories, a compelling story can give the players' actions meaning and make players feel like their decisions are important. Furthermore, a truly interactive story, where the narrative can change radically depending on the players' choices, while retaining the emotional resonance and power of a story told in a novel, is a very compelling idea. It is so compelling that it is hard to imagine any truly ambitious game designer who would not hope for it to someday become a reality.

Chapter 12:
Game Analysis: Loom

Designed by Brian Moriarty
Released in 1990

For 1990, the year it was released, *Loom* was a decidedly different type of adventure game. Though it had many gameplay similarities to graphical adventure games that had been released previously by LucasArts, *Loom* endeavored to reduce the adventure game to its core mechanics from a storytelling standpoint and to cut away all that was extraneous. Looking in the manual, one finds that the game's authors were keenly aware that they were creating something different, as the following excerpt from the "About *Loom*" section indicates:

> *Loom* is unlike traditional "adventure games" in many ways. Its goal is to let you participate in the unfolding of a rich, thought-provoking fantasy. It is neither a role-playing game (although it incorporates elements of role-playing), nor a collection of brainteasers. Its simple mysteries are designed to engage your imagination

and draw you deeper into the story, not to frustrate you or increase the amount of time it takes to finish.

Later on in the manual is a section titled "Our Game Design Philosophy," which contains a statement reprinted in a number of LucasArts adventure game manuals of the time. In it one finds still more references to how unique *Loom* and the LucasArts games were:

> We believe that you buy our games to be entertained, not to be whacked over the head every time you make a mistake. So we don't bring the game to a screeching halt when you poke your nose into a place you haven't visited before. Unlike conventional computer adventures, you won't find yourself accidentally stepping off the path, or dying because you've picked up a sharp object.

> We think you'd prefer to solve the game's mysteries by exploring and discovering, not dying a thousand deaths. We also think you want to spend your time involved in the story, not typing in synonyms until you stumble upon the computer's word for a certain object.

Reading the above, one gets the idea that perhaps *Loom* was a reaction by the game's author, Brian Moriarty, to what he saw in other adventure games as detrimental to the players' enjoyment. Though only the first statement was written specifically about *Loom*, it seems likely that they both represented Moriarty's feelings on the subject accurately. *Loom* was going to retain the positive storytelling elements of adventure games and remove everything that conflicted with players' enjoyment of the story. It succeeded admirably, resulting in a game that seemed to earnestly want players to complete its interesting story.

Prior to coming to LucasArts to work on *Loom*, Brian Moriarty had worked at Infocom for a number of years, a company renowned for the unsurpassed quality and depth of their text adventures. There he had created two text adventures, *Wishbringer* and *Trinity*, and one text-only adventure/role-playing hybrid, *Beyond Zork*. While *Wishbringer* was designed from the start to be an easy-to-play game for beginners, both *Trinity* and *Beyond Zork* were massive and terrifically difficult games to complete. *Loom*, then, seems to be a change in direction from those titles, a return to a game that does not challenge players merely for the sake of challenging them, but instead includes only those challenges that are critical to the story. Furthermore, *Loom* was Moriarty's first game to not involve a text parser, an input method that he was all too happy to do away with, if one believes that the sentiments expressed in the manual are his own. Again, the simplicity of *Loom* seems to be a reaction to the needless complexity of older adventure games, both in general and Moriarty's own. In *Loom*, the story was king, and whatever stood in its way was removed.

Focused Game Mechanics

Loom seems to be a perfect example of a game that is completely focused in what it wants to accomplish. Instead of trying to include all of the game mechanics he possibly could, it appears that Moriarty thought long and hard about what were the minimum game mechanics necessary for the telling of his story. He then eliminated everything that did not truly add something to that story. This had the result of greatly simplifying

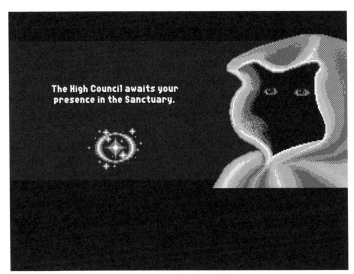

The High Council awaits your presence in the Sanctuary.

Loom's game mechanics are focused on telling the game's story.

the game, while at the same time making it considerably more elegant and easy to navigate.

The game was developed using the SCUMM Story System, which most of LucasArts' adventure games have used in one form or another. Credited to Ron Gilbert and Aric Wilmunder, SCUMM stands for "Script Creation Utility for Maniac Mansion," so named after the first game to use the system. Indeed, if one looks at the other LucasArts adventures, one will notice that nearly every one has much more in the way of gameplay mechanics and user interface than *Loom*. Both *Maniac Mansion* (1987) and *The Secret of Monkey Island* (1990, the same year as *Loom*) include inventories for players to manipulate, in addition to allowing players to click on a variety of verbs that can be used on various objects in the game world. Both games were created using the SCUMM system, indicating that inventory and verb systems were readily available to Moriarty via SCUMM if he wanted to use them. Indeed, inventories and verbs were a very common element of nearly all of the adventure games released prior to *Loom*. (Many adventures released since *Loom* have done away with both verbs and inventories, most notably *Myst* and its many imitators.) So Moriarty was making a tremendous break from both the SCUMM system and tradition when he left these mechanics out. Including an inventory and verbs could have added a lot of depth to the game if the story was reconceived to take advantage of them. But as it stands, the game functions perfectly without them.

Many other adventure games also feature branching dialog trees. In this sort of system, when the player character is talking to another character, players are presented with a list of different sentences their character can say. Players can then pick from those choices and some level of interactivity is achieved during the conversations. Again, *The Secret of Monkey Island* featured exactly such a system, used by the game's creator, Ron Gilbert, to enormous gameplay payoff, particularly in the classic sword-fighting sequences. But, as with the verbs and inventory, there are no branching dialog trees to be found in *Loom*. Instead, when the player character talks to someone, players just watch the conversation unfold as a non-interactive cut-scene, unable to control it. On one level, this would appear to remove a degree of player interaction with the game. But, in the final analysis, the branching conversation tree systems always contain a finite number of branches, and hence most such systems devolve into players simply clicking on each of the options, one by one. (*The Secret of Monkey Island* is one of the few examples of a game that actually adds depth to the gameplay with branching conversations.) For *Loom*, Moriarty went with the cut-scene conversations since they were the most effective system for conveying his story. Again, Moriarty was focused on his storytelling goal, and he let no adventure game conventions stand in his way.

User Interface

The interface in *Loom* is the epitome of simplicity, requiring players only to use their mouse and a single button. This, of course, makes the game very easy to learn and play for anyone at all familiar with a point-and-click system. This is in sharp contrast to many other adventure games, particularly the text-only adventures that had their hey-day in the 1980s, including those that Moriarty had worked on. Nearly all of these games include a text parser which, ideally, allows players to enter whatever they want their character to do using natural language. "Get book," "Northwest," "Open door with red key," and "Look at painting" are all examples of common commands from such text adventures. The limitation, unfortunately, was that many text parsers did not fea-ture a complete set of the words in the English language, nor could they properly parse complex sentences. In fact, Infocom, the company that published Moriarty's *Wishbringer, Trinity*, and *Beyond Zork*, had the best text parser available by far. Yet the parser could still be challenging to use. Especially frustrating was when players knew exactly what they needed to do in the game, but they could not find the correct words to say it. Not to mention the fact that, for the system to work, players are required to spell everything correctly, a task at which few people excel. At the very best, one could become familiar with the idiosyncrasies of a text parser over time, but to a beginner the dominant feeling was one of frustration.

Loom keeps its interface as simple as possible by having the player interact with the game-world by using only the mouse.

Indeed, in the excerpt from the manual included earlier, the text parsers of old are derided. It seems that Moriarty was ready to move on to a more intuitive and easy-to-learn interface. Of course, one of the primary requirements of any interface is that it be easy to learn. The challenges players face should be in the game-world itself, not in the controls they have to manipulate in order to affect that game-world. *Maniac Mansion* had already used an entirely point-and-click interface, and *Loom* borrowed a lot from that game's mechanics, at least in terms of world navigation. Players could move their character, Bobbin Threadbare, through the world simply by clicking on the location where they wanted him to go. This seems quite obvious to modern gamers who have seen countless point-and-click movement systems in games ranging from *Diablo* to *Grim Fandango* to *Command & Conquer*. Part of the beauty of the system is its obviousness; once one has seen it in action, one cannot imagine how else you would direct a character using a mouse.

However, *Maniac Mansion* and other graphical adventures had still included verbs for players to click on. These verbs were basically a holdover from the text parsers; players would click first on an object and then on a verb in order to manipulate that object accordingly. Some other graphical adventures had replaced these verbs with icons that functioned identically to their text counterparts. Of course, in many cases there was only one verb/icon that would have any useful effect on a particular object, hence making the functionality of the icons largely extraneous. *Loom* eliminated the verbs entirely to allow users to simply double-click on a given object and then have the game figure out what they wanted to do with the object. If players double-clicked on a person, Bobbin Threadbare would talk to him or her. If it was an object with text on it, Bobbin would read it. If it was a sheep, he would poke it. The game works with players instead of against them, allowing players to perform only the actions that will be useful to them. The double-click is an obvious extension of the single click. The single click moves Bobbin to that object; a double-click has him attempt to use it. Obviously, this input system is also identical to how point-and-click is used on the Macintosh and Windows platforms, so it has the added advantage that players are likely to understand it before they even start playing. The lesson to be learned here is that copying input ideas from established standards is almost always better than making up something new. Whatever slight gain one might achieve with a new input method is almost always negated by the frustration players experience while trying to learn it.

The Drafts System

While the game may do away with an inventory, verbs, and branching conversations, it does add a unique and well-designed game mechanic accessible through the main character's distaff. This system allows players to cast the equivalent of spells on various objects in the world. This system is quite different from spell-casting systems in any other games, and was especially revelatory in 1990. Again, the interface is entirely point-and-click, and it is a system that is very easy to learn.

The system is based around players hearing different tones in different situations and then repeating those tones on their staff, in a manner reminiscent of a game of simon says. If players double-click on a particular spinning wheel, a series of four tones will be played. These tones will also be reflected on the players' distaff, which is displayed at the bottom of the screen. Below the distaff are a series of musical notes that correspond to positions on the distaff: c, d, e, f, and so forth, up to a full octave. When players hear the tones for the first time, these notes light up to show players visually what the different notes are. Players must then remember this series of tones (usually by writing it down), and then can repeat the tones in order to cast a particular "draft" or spell on a different object. Players repeat the notes simply by clicking on different locations of the distaff, a beautifully intuitive interface.

If the player plays *Loom* in the expert setting, the musical notes on the distaff disappear, making the game significantly harder.

If players play the game in the expert setting, the learning of drafts becomes significantly more difficult. The musical notation is no longer present on the screen, and now players only hear the notes; they no longer flash on the distaff. This forces players to "play it by ear" in order to succeed. This, coupled with the fact that the tones required for a draft change with every game, gives the game significantly more replayability than many other adventure games. The musical nature of the drafts and of the entire game is a tremendous break from most other games that can be played with the sound completely off. Instead of just using music for sonic wallpaper, *Loom* beautifully makes the music an integral part of the gameplay.

The order of the tones can also be reversed to cause the opposite effect of playing the tones forward. The objects players double-click on to originally learn the tones all correspond to the drafts they teach players: double-clicking on a blade teaches the "sharpen" draft, double-clicking on water dripping out of a flask teaches the "emptying" draft, double-clicking on a pot full of bubbling dye will teach the "dye" draft, and so forth. Spinning drafts with the distaff is the primary method for performing actions on objects in the game. Sometimes the draft learned is not entirely obvious, and some creative thinking is required of players in order to figure out which draft to use where. Drafts that are learned for use in one application will turn out to have related but different applications later. For instance, a draft that at first hatches an egg actually turns out to be quite handy for opening doors. A draft that heals a human can also be used to heal a rip in the fabric of the universe. All the connections are subtle yet logical. The manipulation of these drafts makes up the primary source of puzzles in the game, and they are used in such a way that the puzzles are never overly convoluted. *Loom* is one of the few adventure games where, once a puzzle is completed, players never feel that the puzzle was arbitrary or capricious.

Difficulty

Once again, from the comments in the manual, one can infer that *Loom* was made from the start to be an easy game to play. One definitely gets the sense that the game truly wants players to succeed and hopes players will see the end of its lovely story. Traditionally, adventure games prided themselves on vexing players and making them play the game again and again until, after much suffering, a reward was doled out.

The LucasArts games made a dramatic break from other adventure games by, for the most part, preventing players from ever being killed or from ever getting stuck. Many prior adventure games included countless ways to die, thereby punishing players who had forgotten to save their game. Some adventure games would also allow players to progress in the game even though they may have forgotten to do something fundamental earlier in the game. Then players would get to a location, not have the object needed there, and have no way of going back to get it. In effect players were dead, since they could not progress in the game, but this was a worse kind of death: it was death masquerading as life, where players could still interact with the game-world but had no chance of actually winning the game. The LucasArts games set a standard that many subsequent adventure games have emulated: do not be unfair to players.

If the LucasArts games in general tried to eliminate player frustration, *Loom* went one step further in making the game as player-friendly as possible. Some cries were made by players that *Loom* was too easy. Indeed, the adventure game enthusiasts who had been hardened on the adventure games that came before *Loom* found it very easy to finish. They were used to dying around every corner and spending hours bashing their heads against nearly incomprehensible puzzles. Indeed, many adventure gamers were accustomed to not being able to finish the games at all, at least not without buying a hint book. But the problem with making games that only appealed to the veteran enthusiasts was that it made it hard for any new players to start playing adventure games. If players were not already experienced with these twisted and convoluted exercises in masochism, there was a good chance an adventure game would frustrate players so much that they would feel no desire to try another one.

Story

With the game mechanics focused in order to emphasize the game's storytelling component, the entire game would be for naught if the story Moriarty wished to tell was not of the highest quality. Fortunately, it is. The story of Bobbin Threadbare, the chosen "Loom-Child" whose task is to restore the fabric of reality, is one of simple beauty and great poignancy. On his seventeenth birthday, Bobbin is summoned before the elders, only to watch in amazement as they are transformed into swans. Dame Hetchel, the weaver who has been like a mother to Bobbin, explains to him the dire situation: the young weaver must discover what is slowly destroying the Loom and save it before it is too late. Thus Bobbin's adventure begins, with his trips to the various guilds of the land

Much of *Loom*'s success rides on the strength of its fantastic and whimsical story.

of *Loom*, drawing to a unique climax complete with a bittersweet ending. Along the way bits of the trademark, wise-cracking LucasArts humor are included (a style of humor found at its most intense in *The Secret of Monkey Island*), though never so much that it dominates the story. Some players might see the story as strictly aimed at children, but *Loom* is a children's game in the same way *The Hobbit* is a children's book, *The Dark Crystal* is a children's movie, or *Bone* is a children's comic book. All contain enough sophistication and intelligence that one does not need to be a child to enjoy them, merely childlike.

The story is ideally suited to the gameplay that *Loom* includes, with navigation and the spinning of drafts being players' only actions. The gameplay and story are so well integrated that the gameplay ends up involving the player in the story far more than if the story were told in a non-interactive format. At the same time the story never seems contrived for the sake of the gameplay, as many adventure game stories do. The text in the story is kept to a bare minimum, never going into excessive detail about anything, allowing the players' imaginations to fill in the holes. It is a story that is told well visually, with the players' exploration and experimentation with the distaff matching the emotional temperament of the character they are playing, Bobbin Threadbare. Since Bobbin first acquires the staff at the beginning of the game, it makes logical sense that he would not yet be an expert at it. Thus players' many failed attempts to use the drafts fit perfectly with Bobbin's character. This is in contrast to many adventure games where, though players are controlling an intelligent, experienced character, players must complete idiotic puzzles such as figuring out their character's password to log onto a computer system, when obviously the character being controlled would already know this information.

One problem with third-person adventure games, games where players see their character in the game instead of just seeing what that character would see, is that often the character in question has such a strong personality and appearance that it may be difficult for players to feel properly immersed in the game. If the character is too much of a departure from one players could see themselves being, players may become frustrated when that character speaks lines of dialog they would not say themselves or performs other stupid actions. *Loom* works around this problem by putting Bobbin Threadbare inside a cloak, with players only ever seeing his eyes. This keeps the main character anonymous enough that players could believe that, in fact, it is themselves inside that cloak. At the one point in the game where Bobbin takes off his hood, the game quickly cuts away to a different scene, almost poking fun at the continued anonymity of the main character. And Bobbin's dialog is kept level and anonymous enough that he never says anything that might annoy players. Many game developers and publishers speak of creating strong characters, perhaps ones that can be used for action figures and movie rights later on. But what often keeps a game enjoyable for players is a more anonymous character — one players can sculpt in their minds into their own idea of a hero.

Loom as an Adventure Game

For all of its strengths, *Loom* is still an adventure game, and indeed a fairly linear one. Adventure games are the genre of computer games most concerned with traditional storytelling, while at the same time often being the least encouraging of player creativity. The story being told in an adventure game is the designer's story, one that was clearly established ahead of time and one that allows players only to experience it without really being able to change its outcome. The critics of adventure games are quick to point out that, really, adventure games are not games at all, but merely a series of puzzles strung together with bits of story between them. The puzzles, regardless of their form, serve as locked doors between the different parts of the story, and in order to experience the rest of the story, players must unlock that door by completing the puzzle. Games, they say, are required to react to players, while a puzzle provides a more static challenge, one that, once solved, is not nearly as much fun to try again. These critics suggest that once the story is experienced, because of its static nature it is hardly worth experiencing again.

Loom's gameplay centers on the player solving simple yet elegant puzzles. Once solved, the puzzles do not provide much replay value.

And *Loom*, for all its beauty and strength of design, still succumbs to some of the problems of adventure games. During the conversation cut-scenes, the game is completely linear and players have no control of the game whatsoever. This might be more acceptable in smaller doses, but some of the cut-scenes in *Loom* go on for a significant amount of time. The game can also sometimes degrade into players trying to click everything on the screen, just to see which objects can be manipulated. There is a good chance that, if an object can be manipulated, players will need to do something with it to complete the game. This is both good and bad: good in that it limits players' actions to useful ones instead of leading them down a false path after red herrings and pointless diversions; bad in that it severely limits the interactiveness of the world. And sometimes the game's landscape art is drawn in such a way that it is difficult to figure out where Bobbin can navigate and where he cannot.

But, truly, these are minor complaints. Is it so bad that *Loom* is a storytelling experience with a predetermined story? The game is only as worthwhile to play again as it is to read a book or see a movie a second time. Of course, repeat reading and viewing is something many people enjoy, if the work is good enough to warrant it. *Loom* may not be as interactive as *Civilization*, but does every game need to be that interactive? A game of *Civilization* may tell an interesting story of the rise of an empire and the advancement of technology, but to me there has never been a game of *Civilization* with a story as compelling and touching as *Loom*'s. Critics might ask, why not tell *Loom*'s story as a book or an animated feature? Sure, the story could work in those forms, but would players be so drawn in as when they are allowed to explore and interact with the story-world in question? Through an adventure game like *Loom*, players gain a certain emotional attachment to and involvement in the events that transpire that is impossible in other media. Perhaps it is not a game by an exclusionary definition, but that does not make it any less worthwhile.

Chapter 13:
Multi-Player

"No one on their death bed ever said, 'I wish I'd spent more time alone with my computer.'"

— Dani Bunten Berry

As the above quote suggests, few computer gamers would care to admit to their families just how much time they spend playing their games. One might think this shame is because single-player video games are such a solitary pursuit. What's interesting is how other pursuits that are equally solitary — reading books, listening to music, or studying math — are not seen as embarrassing ways to spend one's time. Besides their often-puerile nature and immature content, one key difference between games and other pursuits is that single-player computer games present the illusion of interaction with another human, though no other human is actually present. Though the AI agents take the place of the other players required to play a non-computer game, in many ways it is truly the designer who takes the place of the other players. Unfortunately, the designer can only take their place to the extent he can put himself into digital form on a CD or DVD. Of course, in the end the dynamic interaction that single-player games provide is far more limited than what can be provided in multi-player games.

But to the non-gaming world multi-player online games are seen as just as antisocial as single-player games, if not more so. Indeed, with an online game, the user is still alone in a room with the computer, but if the game is well designed it allows the computer to project the other players onto the screen in a way that greatly exceeds the expressive potential of, say, a telephone. Yet to the outside world these interpersonal interactions are not seen as "real." To them the world players are battling or cooperating or simply socializing in is not a worthwhile place to be. The millions of fans of multi-player gaming know that this space becomes real because of the people filling it. The realness of the other players makes the experience of playing a multi-player game have a much greater importance than any single-player game can ever manage.

Though commercial multi-player online games have had a rocky history over the lifetime of the industry, there is no doubt that as a more mass medium they truly started to take hold in the early 21st century. These multi-player games attract such a particularly devoted following and create such compelling experiences that many cannot help but wonder: as soon as the rest of the world catches up in terms of technology and playing habits, are the days of solo-play games numbered? Indeed, if one looks at non-electronic games, multi-player games are as old as games themselves, with single-player games such as solitaire being in the extreme minority of available choices. If one looks at the classics, such as chess, *Monopoly*, *Scrabble*, *Dungeons & Dragons*, *Cosmic Encounter*, *Magic: The Gathering*, or *The Settlers of Catan*, one will see the incredible breadth and depth of multi-player games. Throw in all forms of sports and one will see a form whose popularity still greatly exceeds computer games. Though the legacy of computer-based multi-player games is more limited than their single-player brethren, the history of human experience with multi-player games gives a rich history upon which to draw.

Motivations

The popularity of multi-player games makes perfect sense given that they satisfy many of the player desires laid out in Chapter 1, "What Players Want." Many developers see the most immediate advantage of multi-player games as the ability to replace AI opponents with real humans in order to provide much deeper and more unpredictable adversaries. This increases the amount of challenge a game can provide, and allows a game to stay compelling for a much longer period of time. Unlike game AI agents, player opponents will learn as they play. As players improve, so too do their opponents, and thus the players' desire to be challenged is met. An even more significant advantage to having human opponents is the ability for the players to socialize; anyone who has played a board game can tell you how important socializing among the players is to that experience. Indeed, many people play multi-player games exclusively because they want to socialize with the other people playing, not because of a fundamental love of gaming.

The presence of real players for opponents brings with it a tremendous change in the players' perceived importance of playing the game; instead of just winning or losing the game in private, through their social component multi-player games make each win and loss a public affair and thus significantly more meaningful. The potential for bragging rights goes up tremendously for a multi-player game since players now have someone to brag to, as does the potential for shame at a resounding defeat. Regardless of whether they win or lose, the potential for glory and shame can make playing a multi-player game a much more emotional experience than engaging in a single-player experience. Regardless of win or loss, the players' ability to socialize in a collaborative and social game such as a massively multi-player RPG can lead to emotionally charged alternate realities, where players can get married and will mourn the passing of a friend when they stop playing the game.

Finally, having real people playing the game with you can help make the game significantly more interactive since dealing with other humans is always a much more dynamic experience than interacting with a computer alone. Looking at all the "wants" that multi-player games satisfy makes the success of these games hardly surprising. They provide for players a challenge, a social experience, the potential for bragging rights, a significant emotional payoff, and a deeply interactive experience. When working on multi-player games, it is important for game designers to keep these strengths in mind and make sure their designs play up the qualities that players are looking for.

Multi-player games are so strong at satisfying what players are looking for that they open up entire new areas of game design and development, allowing the use of mechanics that simply do not work in single-player games. Even if an AI is incredibly smart and challenging to play against, players will still not want to socialize or role-play with it in the same way they will with a human. Indeed, when creating a multi-player game, taking a single-player game and forcibly converting it to multi-player can be extremely limiting and will prevent the final game from achieving its full potential. It is important to remember that a multi-player component is not always an improvement for a given game: some titles are ideally suited to being single-player, just as other games can only work as multi-player experiences.

The Forms

When looking at multi-player computer games, two groups of games immediately present themselves: games that are played by a number of gamers all in the same location and huddled around the same computer or console, and games that are played online by multiple players who are in significantly different locations. Though both are definitely multi-player experiences, these two types of games are extremely different and each present their own design challenges.

Single System Multi-Player

Due to the limitations of networking, multi-player games that occur around a single computer system have been popular and commercially viable for a good while longer than online games. These originally took the form of multiple players controlling their game-world surrogates in a shared view of the game-environment, with the earliest example being *Pong* and progressing through arcade games such as *Mario Bros.*, *Gauntlet*, *Smash TV*, many sports games, and all fighting games. These games are limited in that both players have to be constrained to relatively the same portion of the game-world so that they can both stay visible. Multi-player single-screen play can be further problematic when players have to wait for one another to perform certain actions. For example, in cooperative mode in *Baldur's Gate: Dark Alliance*, the other player must sit idle while one player manipulates his inventory. Some PC games, such as *M.U.L.E.*, used a single screen with each player taking a turn at playing while the

Many early multi-player games, such as *Smash TV*, confined two players to the same portion of the game-world.

other players waited, referred to as hot seat play. A solution for the problem of constraining two or more players to the same location came with the advent of split-screen gaming, where each player has a section of the monitor devoted to displaying the portion of the game-world that is relevant to them at any given time. This includes such classics as *Mario Kart*, and continues today for games such as *Centipede 3D* or *War of the Monsters*. This last title is one of the latest in a long line of games to dynamically switch to non-split-screen when both players happen to be in the same location in the game-world.

Split-screen is used even more extensively for single-machine adaptations of games that were originally designed to be played over a network, such as the death-match modes in *Halo*, *Syphon Filter*, or *SOCOM*. For these games, there is the distinct disadvantage that all players can see the location and status of the other players simply by looking at their portion of the screen. This may be unethical, but is hard to avoid when their view is right next to your own world-view. This is not detrimental to a game such as *Mario Kart*, but can often weaken the experience in a game like *Halo*, whose death-match gameplay is modeled after online, blind-play competition. However, split-screen play cannot be considered unfair since all players have access to the same information about the other players' status; the fact that it is split-screen simply makes it a different type of game. Some single-system games have tried to allow some degree of blind-play through various devious techniques. *Robot Rascals* included a deck of special cards that dictated the victory conditions for each player, with the cards kept secret until the end of the game. The Sega Dreamcast included a display in the controller that allowed players of football games to make their play selections without the other players seeing their choices. Despite the potential disadvantages in terms of blind-play, multi-player games that take place around one system have a tremendous advantage in terms of the social interaction they engender. Whenever you cluster a bunch of people, presumably already friends, around a single screen, they are guaranteed to talk to each other and play differently than if the other players were in another room or building. Anyone who has watched the verbal and physical interaction between players around a cart racer or a sports title can testify to this and how much fun players derive from such interaction. Though networked voice communication and other advances can help make players who are far away seem closer, nothing can compare to the physical proximity of your opponent for real human communication and camaraderie.

Online Multi-Player

Of course networked games provide a significantly more immersive player experience for the very reason that the other players are invisible to each other. For online games, players each have their own computers and are situated in separate locations and thus need to project themselves into the game-space much more, since none of the other players can see what they look like, hear what they are saying, or observe how they are acting. First-person shooters such as *Unreal*, *Quake*, *Counter-Strike*, and *Battlefield 1942* work extremely well over networks, since the separation of the players enables blind-play in a way split-screen cannot, thus making these games much more challenging. Air combat simulations such as the classic *Air Warrior* are one of the oldest forms of networked multi-player games, and in spirit work mostly the same as shooter games. Many sports-style games — including racing games and fighting games — provide networked multi-player support in addition to their single-system multi-player games. Though this was originally true primarily on the PCs, the success of Xbox Live has made including a multi-player mode de rigueur in console games, at least where such gameplay makes sense.

Massively multi-player persistent online games such as *Dark Age of Camelot* create elaborate virtual worlds in which players can fully immerse themselves.

Massively multi-player persistent games (MMPs) such as *Ultima Online*, *EverQuest*, and *Dark Age of Camelot* have become increasingly popular in recent years, though the MUDs (multi-user dungeons/domains) that inspired them have existed for nearly three decades. These games provide the ultimate in immersive online gaming, with players spending an exceedingly large amount of time in complex virtual worlds. There they interact and form strong bonds with other players they have often never met in the physical world. Though these games are almost always engaged in by players alone in separate locations, the social ties that form between players make these games extremely social experiences. Indeed, playing MMPs can be such a lifestyle choice that many couples will play together, with women tending to enjoy them more than most games. These games are much more open-ended in their design, emphasizing multiple paths to success and allowing players to spend their time how they choose. Players can go on quests, get a job and build up a home, or just spend all their time socializing with the other people they meet there. Indeed, some have charged that these MMPs are really just cleverly disguised chat rooms. However, *Ultima Online* and *Star Wars Galaxies* lead designer Raph Koster is quick to point out that players will not play these games solely for the social experience. Since they can do that over e-mail or ICQ, there will be no incentive for them to keep playing the game (and paying the monthly subscription fee that most of these games charge) if all they are doing with the game is socializing. For it to be successful in the long term, the game must provide an interesting enough game that facilitates socialization in conjunction with other rewards.

Each of the different forms that multi-player games can take determine the kind of interaction players will have with each other while playing. This in turn dictates which type of games will best succeed in those forms. Having both players share a single view of the game-world demands cooperation between the players if they are going to progress to new areas. Having a split-screen means that, if the game is competitive, players will be unable to avoid seeing what the other players are doing. Having players at separate systems means they will be able to have proper blind-play but will be significantly hindered in their ability to interact with each other while playing the game, no matter what the game designer does to facilitate socialization. All these types of games can be fun if, from the start, the designer is fully cognizant of the strengths and weaknesses of the type of multi-player game he is building and designs the game to work optimally within that paradigm.

Design Considerations

Of course multi-player games present significantly different challenges in their design than do single-player games. For example, the pacing of multi-player games needs to be more varied than it is in single-player games, for the simple reason that in a multi-player game players cannot pause the game, since the other players would need to simultaneously pause as well. Though most single-player games provide a variable curve with peaks at high tension and valleys in calmer moments, getting this curve right is even more important in a multi-player game since players are unable to create their own valley by hitting the pause button. Without being able to pause their game, players run the risk of being slaughtered by the other players if they let their guard down for even a moment. It is human nature (at least, for everyone except for the most hard-core) to need breaks from any activity, and a designer should plan his game so it is possible for players to tend to the needs of the real world without needing to quit the game. This may mean letting them choose how long to wait to respawn after dying, providing safe places in the world for them to hide without the immediate threat of death, or having a short enough game duration that wanting to pause is not a major issue.

If possible, you want to predetermine how long it will take players to play your game, at least on average. You want to pick a time that will be a reasonable investment for your target audience, and then try to make the design of your game support that length. Most players want to know how much time they need to play your game, since all but the most hard-core have a variety of things to do with their lives other than playing games. It is a very different decision to play an online game of hearts versus going on an epic adventure in *EverQuest* or starting up a multi-player game of *Civilization III*. In board games, *Monopoly* is a good example of a game that many people refuse to play because they know how long it can take in the worst cases. Games can drag on for days. *Risk* and *Diplomacy* provide even more extreme examples of this same problem. If players find a game is going on too long for them (either as an aberration or standard operating procedure) they are likely to drop out in the middle of the game, something that can be very frustrating to the other players. Letting players know what they are getting into before they start up a game is a good way to encourage them to play games all the way through.

Similarly, if at all possible you want your game design to allow players to feel that they still have something of a shot at success even when they are losing. Games that allow one player to get extremely far ahead of the other players but still require a long and tedious end-game for that player to complete the win will encourage the losing players to drop out, essentially forfeiting. Though this does not need to be disastrous, it is better if your game is designed so that players never feel like all hope is lost. One way to accomplish this is through employing negative feedback systems to give players who are falling behind a better chance of catching up. At a talk at the Game Developers Conference, Marc LeBlanc discussed how positive feedback systems can push the player who is ahead in the competition even farther ahead, while negative feedback will keep the competition close. For example, in a racing game, if there are guns mounted on the front of the vehicles, players who are behind can shoot at the players who are ahead, thus closing the gap. If the guns are mounted on the back of the cars, however, the feedback is positive, allowing the winner to take out the opponents who are already behind it. Therefore, with its front-mounted guns, *Mario Kart* is a good implementation of negative feedback that helps keep the races closer and thereby more exciting.

With its front-mounted weapons, *Mario Kart* is an excellent implementation of negative feedback keeping races close between competing players. Pictured here: *Mario Kart: Double Dash.*

Of course, players will still drop out of your game regardless of how much you try to discourage them. Indeed, due to the somewhat chaotic nature of the Internet, some players may get dropped from the game in the middle through no choice of their own. Your game will need to handle these dropouts in an elegant way such that the remaining players can continue playing if at all possible, with the now-missing players having essentially forfeited their slots. You may wish to allow them to reclaim their spots in the game if they reconnect quickly enough, to forgive unavoidable Internet flakiness. If having players drop out in the middle is not handled well by your game, you are almost surely doomed to frustrating the players who want to keep playing.

Allowing players to customize their avatar in the game-world is also key to making players feel that they are actually putting themselves into the game. This can be as simple as picking their name or "handle," or choosing their color. Players will also enjoy picking the base talents of their character, whether this means deciding between infantry, medic, or engineer in *Battlefield 1942* or between paladin, ranger, and sorcerer in an RPG. Different players will gravitate to different classes based on their skills and personalities. For those who want to take it a step further, empowering players to alter their body type, skin color, and clothing can go a long way to helping them immerse themselves in the experience. Just as people enjoy dressing up in real life as a way of communicating to others what type of person they are, they will also fancy it in an online space. Interestingly, however, players will primarily enjoy adjusting those traits of their avatar that will not actually impact their success in the game. They'll love to pick eye color or hairstyle, but it will take players with a fervent interest in role-playing to play a gimpy character with weakened stats to match its physical impairments.

In Chapter 7, "The Elements of Gameplay," I talked about emergent gameplay and allowing for multiple player tactics to lead to success. While these sorts of significant player choices are important in single-player game experiences, in multi-player they are absolutely essential. In a multi-player game, players are not thinking "What does the designer want me to do here?" but instead "What tactic can I come up with that will allow me to win against these equally clever other players?" If your game design does not allow for a flexible enough space for players to develop unique tactics to counter other players' moves, all but the newbies will quickly lose interest in your game. With multi-player games you have the advantage of not needing to come up with ways to directly challenge players, but you need to provide the palette of potential actions that will empower players to challenge each other. For example, rocket jumping may not have been planned as part of the design of *Quake* or its rocket-jumping predecessor *Marathon*, but the robustness of the technology and design of these games supported the players' innovative tactic. Fundamentally, multi-player designers have much less dictatorial control over players' experiences than do single-player designers, and it is in their best interests to recognize this and work to empower players instead of constraining them.

Playing to Strengths

Often when designers move from single-player games to multi-player, the first thing they think of is replacing their AI adversaries with human ones. This is a choice that is guaranteed to lead to a more challenging and dynamic experience for the user. But at the same time, it fails to truly explore the full potential of multi-player games. For years, single-player games have been built around the limitations of what an AI could and could not do. Many action games, for example, have balanced their gameplay by throwing a large number of fairly dumb AI agents at players. When these same games became death-match online games, designers typically replaced these dumb AI creatures with human players but, in order to balance the game, drastically decreased their number and made the players fight for themselves. Whereas there were two factions previously (the player and the enemies), now there were as many adversaries as there were players. These simple choices managed to rebalance the game experience fairly well. But these combat games were still not close to exploring the full potential of multi-player games, because these human players could just as easily still be really smart 'bots. In Chapter 9, "Artificial Intelligence," I talked about how an artificial intelligence can be considered to pass the Turing test if players mistake it for a human. For multi-player games, the goal should be somewhat different: players could never mistake their adversaries for anything but other humans.

To create a distinctly multi-player game experience, it can be valuable to take a cue from the rich history of multi-player non-computer games, particularly games that require more than two players. For example, many of the more sophisticated board games involve negotiation between players via trading and bartering or establishing alliances. Excellent examples of both mechanics can be found in any playing of seminal multi-player games like *Diplomacy*, *Cosmic Encounter*, and *The Settlers of Catan*. In many three or more player board games, deciding who the various players will gang up on at any given time is a key part of the play experience. This can help to fix whatever balancing issues the game design may have, since as soon as one player gets significantly ahead of the other players through luck or an exploit, the other players will quickly gang up on him. In such games, the personalities of the gamers inevitably come into play, whether through going easy on the less skilled player who gets upset easily or a hidden vendetta against a spouse that does not manifest itself except during gaming sessions. *Dungeons & Dragons* and other RPGs allow players to play together in a group, with the Dungeon Master creating a dynamic game experience for the other players in a way a computer never can. An online game with players located miles away from each other and who are most likely real-world strangers will probably never recreate the in-person multi-player experience. Nevertheless, the more successful online games include components that force players to socialize as part of the game mechanics, and thereby make the social interplay in the game that much richer. This includes seasoned players coordinating their tactics in team-based multi-player games like *Counter-Strike* or *Battlefield 1942*, or the recreation of the Dungeon Master experience in *Neverwinter Nights*.

Though the potential for players to cooperate should be a key part of almost any multi-player game, getting players to actually do it is another problem entirely. *Battlefield 1942* lead programmer Johan Persson has lamented at how infrequently most players exploit the game's more cooperative features, such as one player scouting and providing coordinates to another player who fires artillery. One way to improve the chances of player cooperation is to make sure that players who work together have a significant advantage over those who do not. It stands to reason that if there is a complex cooperative option available that does not provide significant benefit over what one can accomplish alone, most players will choose to just do it all themselves. An early

Battlefield 1942 requires players to work together to be truly successful, creating a unique experience that cannot be replicated in a single-player game.

example of this comes from *Joust*, which had "survival" levels where two cooperative players received a large score bonus only if both of them did not lose a life during that level. When there is a significant advantage to cooperating in a team versus team style game, there may be the unfortunate side effect that more casual players will get crushed by the opposition and thus may never live long enough to enjoy the game. Of course, for all but the most sadistic, crushing weak opponents is only fun for so long, so most cooperative gamers form clans and fight against other clans on servers that are labeled and restricted accordingly.

Protect Newbies

Newbies are the most vulnerable players, and it is the game designer's job to do everything he can to keep them protected long enough for them to become familiar with the game's mechanics and tactics. This is essential to your game's long-term success. Unlike in a single-player game, where the designer has ultimate control over the players' learning experience, in a multi-player game your new players are immediately at the mercy of the more experienced players who are likely to show newbies no quarter. When I first started work at Surreal Software, the company was close to shipping the original *Drakan* game. They were spending a lot of time testing the multi-player code, and I was quickly sucked into playing multi-player games with the development team. Of course, they had been playing the game for many hours a day for at least a year, and had been focusing on the multi-player game for several months. As a result, they knew it backward and forward, while I had no idea what was going on. The game's melee combat system was particularly unforgiving to new players, so I was soundly beaten again and again without ever even realizing why I was getting killed. I recall breaking several mice in frustration. If I had not been getting paid to do this testing, I surely would have quit the game and never played it again.

Though my problem was an extreme one, this is approximately the experience of many newbies who do not have time to properly prepare for an online player-versus-player encounter. For a more disastrous example of newbies getting beaten off before they have a chance to really become familiar with the game, one needs to look only as far as the history of the online combat flight simulator market. These are some of the oldest online combat games, and seem to be ideally suited to multi-player gaming. But the community never grew beyond the super-hard-core flight simulator buffs. One reason for this was that the controls for these flight simulators were so challenging to learn and the physics so difficult to wrap your head around that most players had trouble even keeping their planes in the air for very long. Throw in seasoned players who showed no mercy in taking out these newbies, and you have a market that never extended beyond a certain limited size. In the end, the games were simply too unforgiving toward new players.

The original *Ultima Online* had many hostile users known as "player-killers" who made the game especially challenging for newer players.

To make matters worse for newbies, it is a rule of thumb in online game development that some fixed percentage of players, say one percent, are complete jerks (or at least become jerks when playing online games) and love to prey on new players who do not stand a chance against them. Though this may only be one percent of your audience, unfortunately they are typically the most tenacious and tireless of players. Many of the multi-player combat games have tried to partially solve this problem by including single-player training areas in their games. *Ultima Online*, the first commercially successful massively multi-player game, was particularly plagued with player-killers when it launched. This despite the fact that the game, unlike death-match style games, was not designed to emphasize players killing other players. To many players this resulted in a significant barrier for entry. Almost all subsequent MMPs fixed this problem in various ways. One solution requires player-killers to register as such and then allows them to only attack other player-killers. Another technique involves segregating new players in safe zones for a time before allowing them to go to more hostile locations. Indeed, even *Ultima Online* eventually fixed the problem by creating a mirror of the world that was safe and then allowing the players who were looking for a less hostile environment to migrate over to it.

Protecting newbies is a concern online game designers will always need to deal with and for which there will probably never be a perfect solution. As I mentioned previously, offline training areas can be extremely helpful for players to practice without the shame of being crushed by human opponents repeatedly while they try to get up to speed. Instead of always rewarding players for killing other players, Dani Bunten Berry suggested that a mentoring system may be appropriate, where more veteran players are appropriately rewarded for watching over the newer players. Indeed, *Asheron's Call* implemented just such a system through allegiances, which worked quite well in giving players a large incentive to help each other, particularly newbies.

Keeping features to a minimum and controls as simple as possible will also help. The more complex and hard to understand the controls are, the longer it will take someone to get used to them, and then the further ahead the experienced players will be from the novices. The air combat flight simulators are a perfect example of too complex controls creating a hard-core-only gaming community. Having simpler controls but combining them with a deep range of actions and tactics helps keep the barrier to entry reasonably low while providing the experienced players with raw materials with which to experiment. Finally, if your game design supports something more complex than "I win, everyone else loses" gameplay, the game will be a lot more inviting to new players. Massively multi-player games have become particularly good at this, allowing all players to go on all the quests and supporting players succeeding in a variety of equally satisfying ways. Many death-match games show the ranking of players at the end of the match instead of just reporting the winner. This way, though it may be a while before a newbie moves to first place, he can see himself crawl out of sixteenth place and up to higher ranks over time. To players, there is less shame if they come in fifth out of eight than if all they know is that they failed to win.

Socialization

One of the primary reasons that players engage in multi-player games is to socialize with other players. This is true both in computer games as well as non-computer games. Anyone who has played board games with his family can attest to the fact that one person is always suggesting they play a game while some others will go along just to have something social to do, not because they are particularly captivated by the gameplay itself. Indeed, when I first started playing *Dungeons & Dragons* I was not very interested in the game at all (indeed, I would have much rather played *Champions*). But *Dungeons & Dragons* was what my friends wanted to play, and rather than stay home and do nothing I joined in. I only came to appreciate the gameplay after playing with them for some time. Similarly, I knew people in college who became so wrapped up in a given MUD that friends of theirs would start playing the MUD just so they could socialize with them again. Certainly a large number of people playing massively multi-player games such as *EverQuest* today primarily do so in order to socialize. This also explains why these games have attracted a larger female fan base than, say, first-person shooters: the commonly held wisdom is that women enjoy socializing more than men. At the very least, females are looking for a social experience a little more involving than a game that revolves around kill-or-be-killed mechanics.

With a board game or a non-computer role-playing game, the players' ability to socialize mostly comes free. Nevertheless, a game like chess is far less social than a game that requires players to cooperate or backstab each other. In a multi-player computer game with all the players playing around one screen, such as *Mario Kart* or a split-screen death-match game like *Halo*, socialization also comes largely for free, though if the game is too frantic and intense in its pacing then the players' ability to socialize may be more limited.

With a split-screen multi-player experience, as found in *Mario Kart: Double Dash*, you are almost guaranteed a very social experience for players.

For an online game, the designer will need to go out of his way to facilitate player socialization. The first step is providing an interface with which players can chat among themselves. Almost all online games do this, though some of the earlier death-match and "casual" games did not. Similarly, some online games aimed at children have been forced to leave out chat options for fear of adults abusing such a system to obtain a child's address. For example, the children-oriented MMP *Toontown Online* allowed communication only through a symbol-based language. Assuming you are not legally prevented from adding full chatting, you want to facilitate conversation in all parts of the game, not just during active gameplay. For short-duration combat games, if there is a lobby where players wait for the game to start once all the players have joined up, this is a perfect place for conversation since players otherwise have nothing to do. You should also enable conversation on any post-game screen where player rankings are displayed; players will want to be able to talk here in order to discuss what just happened, either to brag or to congratulate and vow revenge in the next game.

Of course, chatting via keyboard is significantly inferior to the expressive potential of actual human speech, with the obvious advantage that players can talk while continuing to play the game. Indeed, the use of "emoticons" and creative punctuation may do their best to imbue text with the emotional depth of speech, but only go so far. Speech communication between your players comes for free if your game is not online and your players are all playing around a single screen. Anyone who has ever played a first-person shooter over a LAN with all the players sitting in close proximity to each other (such as after hours in a campus computer lab) can attest to how much fun playing against players who are close by can be, with players screaming in surprise when they are killed unexpectedly, cursing each other for cheap shots, taunting each other that their time left to live is limited, or proclaiming their vast superiority over their opponents. This type of socialization has proven so popular that players who are either in separate parts of the same building or in separate offices entirely have been known to teleconference themselves together in order to recreate a space where they can socialize via voice. This also explains the burgeoning popularity of headset support for online games on the consoles; players really want to be able to talk to each other while playing. The largest downside to adding voice support to your game is the negative impact it can have on the sense of immersion you get from playing the game. Despite its simplistic "Indiana Jones" version of World War II, playing *Battlefield 1942* can often be an extremely immersive experience with its combination of planes flying overhead, explosions going off all around, and battles for control points truly seeming like important skirmishes in an epic struggle. This immersion can be dashed if you hear a twelve-year-old on the other side of the headset screaming complete nonsense or nonstop obscenities. In the end, though, most players are likely to find the loss of immersion to be well worth it for the improved ability to communicate and play cooperatively, as well as the sheer pleasure of hearing their fellow players screaming their way through the battle.

At times, waging multi-player war in *Battlefield 1942* can be extremely immersive.

Another important part of facilitating player communication is giving players time where they feel safe enough that they can talk without being killed. This is particularly true in intense death-match style games, where there is hardly enough time to compose a five-word sentence before a grenade lands in your lap. Of course, including voice support will help this, but anyone who has played a truly intense action game can testify to how mesmerizing and frantic it can become, often to the point where talking and playing may be too much to ask. Thus the importance of pacing the game such that players have opportunities to talk. Similarly, the higher the glory to shame ratio in your experience, the less likely players are to be willing to talk, since each defeat is so tremendously humiliating, particularly when the winner will not stop bragging about it.

Just adding the ability for players to talk via text or even full voice support and making sure players have free moments in which to compose at least partial sentences will not guarantee a social play experience. A large part of the reason why players enjoy playing non-computer board games or RPGs is that they are playing with friends that they are familiar with and whose company they enjoy. Playing with random people over the Internet is much less likely to be enjoyable if you only know these players for the duration of a death-match game and then switch to a totally new set of people with every new match. Players will never get a chance to know each other. Therefore, having a game experience that encourages players to form clans or guilds that need to work together to succeed will be essential to creating a more social experience for your players. Fostering relationships between players that last beyond the time they are playing the game will not only benefit the players themselves but also the long-term success of your game. Those players who became friends playing your game are likely to get together to play as a social event in the future, assuming they still enjoy the game and it allows them to strengthen their friendship while playing. These players are also more likely to talk to each other on forums dedicated to your game, which can help build up your community and attract other players to your game in the future. The community surrounding an online game is even more important than the community for a single-player game, and allowing players to have a rich social experience in your game can help build this community better than anything else you could possibly do.

Every feature or play mechanic you add to your multi-player game should be examined to determine how it impacts the players' social experience. Though not every feature needs to be a social one (it is still a game, after all, and most likely a competitive one), any feature that actively disrupts the players' ability to socialize and work together needs to be carefully considered to make sure the impact it will have on the game will be worth the cost. Indeed, having features that do nothing to improve the game mechanics directly but do help the players socialize will often end up improving the players' overall experience with your game. Allowing players to communicate with each other is one of the most compelling aspects of multi-player games and is something that a single-player game will never be able to provide in any sort of meaningful way.

Development Issues

Beyond the unique design considerations that are raised by multi-player games, there are also a number of development issues that teams need to be aware of. First and foremost, development teams need to decide what type of game they are making: multi-player or single-player. With an online-only game such as a massively multi-player RPG, the answer to this question is obvious. But for an action game that includes a single-player level-progression based game, adding a multi-player component can be approached in several ways. Many games have suffered when they opted to add multi-player support midway through development. This is a decision that may seem like it is not that big a deal, but in the end it may necessitate rewriting large chunks of the code or reworking the game mechanics themselves to be more appropriate for multi-player games. If the single-player game is significantly under way when this change happens, this may result in redoing a lot of work that was perfectly fine when the game was single-player only. On *Centipede 3D*, we were encouraged to add multi-player fairly late in development, but beyond the programming required to get it working, we did not have the art or design resources to make it fun. Since it was not a major priority for us, we ended up adding a cooperative mode and doing nothing to tweak or balance it. We specifically decided not to compromise the single-player experience, either through changing the mechanics or taking our time away from working on that primary part of the game. Interestingly, the multi-player in *Centipede 3D* did actually function and was not a complete failure from a creative standpoint; it worked as an amusing diversion for a short period of time. But it was not a great enhancement to the title since the game had never been planned for it and we lacked the design time it would have required to make it a truly worthwhile experience.

Some games that have added multi-player midway through development have ended up with mechanics that are significantly different in the multi-player and single-player games. This is unfortunate, since the idea of having a game with both modes is that players who are fans of the single-player experience can easily switch over to the multi-player game to continue playing the game they already enjoy. If the game is extremely different they may become frustrated and give up. Of course, some differences are certainly fine, such as slight variations in how the inventory functions or how long a given power-up lasts. But players should feel like they are playing largely the same game.

When developing *Halo*, Bungie concentrated on developing the multi-player game first, before moving on to the single-player levels.

Thankfully, tacking multi-player gaming onto an existing single-player game is no longer acceptable to critics or gamers. In Chapter 15, "Getting the Gameplay Working," I encourage designers to keep the game development process as organic as possible for as long as they can. But for the above reasons, it is very important to decide from the very start if your game will include multi-player. This is important not just so your code can be architected correctly and your game mechanics can be designed to work for both types of games, but also because you can use the multi-player game to actually greatly aid you in development. Assuming your networking code is working early enough, you can actually get your development team playing the multi-player game and start iterating on your game mechanics early to get them as tight and fun as possible. Assuming you keep making progress and the multi-player game is fun, this can be great for team morale and help people see how the game they are working on is coming together. And once your mechanics are a known quantity, building a fun single-player experience will be much simpler. Also, personally I feel that developing a fun multi-player game is a much bigger challenge than building a single-player game, since you as a designer have so much less control over the experience. Thereby, developing a fun multi-player experience fundamentally takes longer than an equally fun single-player experience. In some ways, designing a good multi-player game is all about realizing what players will attempt to do after playing your game for a while and how you can better support that with deep game mechanics. The longer you have players playing your game, the more you can balance the play experience. Thus, focusing on your multi-player experience early on will give you a better fighting chance of developing a solid game at the end of the day. Both Ensemble with the *Age of the Empires* series and Bungie with *Halo* are known to have deliberately focused on getting their multi-player experience right from the start, before working on the single-player experience. Thereby, they have both managed to deliver titles that have very well-balanced multi-player experiences while also including peerless single-player games.

Playtesting and User Feedback

As you develop your multi-player game and observe people playing it, you will quickly find that you never can anticipate what players will attempt to do. Anticipating what players in a solo play game will do is hard enough; doing the same thing for a multi-player game is all but impossible. For example, in *Centipede 3D* we saw the multi-player experience as strictly collaborative, where players would be able to play through the various levels together. Thus the two players the game allowed were immune to each other's weapons fire. But as soon as we got the multi-player code working and started playing the game, the first thing players tried to do was shove each other into the water, since the water is deadly to the players' "shooter" ships. Due to the game's light but robust physics, pushing the other player around was an enjoyable experience made even more amusing when it led to the other player's death. I had certainly never imagined this outcome, but it is hardly surprising given players' tendencies to take a cooperative experience and make it adversarial as quickly as they can. Another interesting emergent behavior that players quickly discovered was the ability for one player to jump on top of the other and ride him around, rotating whichever direction he wanted and acting as a turret. As I mentioned, on *Centipede 3D* there was literally no time dedicated to designing the multi-player gaming experience so there was nothing we could do to fix, adjust, or even encourage these interesting behaviors since we only discovered them a week before we were scheduled to ship.

Even more so than in single-player games, playtesting your multi-player game for as long as possible before it is released to the general public is essential. However, that testing can only tell you so much. For this reason nearly every massively multi-player game has included an "open beta" as part of its development. During this period, the developers take a large though still limited number of the general public and let them play the not-quite-finished game for free. The number of people attracted during such a test is much greater than the number of players that can possibly play as part of an in-house testing effort, and thereby provides a much closer simulation of what the game will be like when it is finally released to the world. The players who sign up for such open betas are typically particularly dedicated and mischievous gamers, and as a result will push your game's systems to the limit. Obviously, this is a good thing.

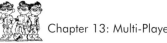

However, the flip side of this is that, since they are such hard-core gamers who are so into gaming that they are willing to play a buggy and unfinished product, these testers do not necessarily represent the views of more casual players. Therefore the feedback you get from them will not necessarily match what you will see when the game finally comes out. Furthermore, sometimes these testers may be tempted not to report all the bugs they uncover if they are able to exploit them to their own benefit; they may hope to continue to reap the rewards from these oversights in the final game. There is little that can be done to remedy this, but it is important that designers recognize it and know there is surely more balancing work to be done once the game goes live.

Even with an open beta, when your game is unleashed on the masses, issues will come up that you failed to anticipate. This is true for smaller scale multi-player games (such as death-match games) and these problems are often addressed in patches that come out shortly after the game is released. Patches are so common that gamers have come to expect them. If you do not actively try to track what problems people are having, both with the networking code and with the play mechanics, and fail to tweak the game to fix at least the most glaring problems (and there will be glaring problems), players will quickly abandon your game in favor of another game whose developers take better care of their end users.

In the world of massively multi-player persistent games, the duty of maintaining the game after it ships is even more important. With these games, players are typically paying a monthly subscription fee and, in addition to adjustments to the player mechanics and balancing, expect a steady stream of new content to keep them challenged and a certain level of customer service to fix their problems. Indeed, most of the developers of these games consider reaching launch as only about half of the work, with the game needing constant care and tweaking on a day-to-day basis, much as a theater troupe that just launched a new play will refine and rewrite it based on how it goes over with each night's audience. Richard Garriott has gone so far as to encourage developers of MMPs to ship "feature thin" and then add features to the game that players have shown interest in or even demanded.

Adjusting the game in any significant way after it has shipped can be a delicate process. First and foremost, before starting to make any adjustments you need to do your best to understand the current state of your game and what players are enjoying and what they are not. It is easy to guess at what you should fix only to break a feature that players love. One obvious way to track what players enjoy in your game is to listen to their direct feedback, but this can be problematic for a few reasons. First of all, the players who do provide feedback may not be representative of the average person playing your game, and may be part of an outspoken minority. One saying goes, "The happy ones are playing the game, the unhappy ones are on the boards." Also, players are not game designers, and as such do not understand the ramifications of some of the features they are demanding. Indeed, designers are often much better served by looking at the root problem that is causing players to suggest a feature. In the end, the designer may be better off coming up with his own solution to that problem. Art Min, project leader on the online tactical strategy game *FireTeam*, stated that the project became derailed when they spent too much time listening to the participants of their open beta test. Min pointed out that the members of an open beta test are most frequently younger gamers with massive amounts of time on their hands. Developers, who have actual work to do, do not have time to deal with all of their suggestions or demands, and if they devote too much time to placating everyone they are liable to lose track of their own design vision. For this reason, many online games hire community managers whose sole job is to listen to and communicate with the players and synthesize their feedback into useful information that the development team can then use to refine the game.

After *The Sims Online* had launched, the team at Maxis used player metrics to uncover player exploits.

The fact remains that, though invaluable, the feedback offered by players, whether in a beta test or after the game has launched, is problematic at best. A more reliable technique is to look at player metrics, though this data can be quite challenging to understand. Sometimes referred to as data mining, analyzing player metrics is the process of tracking what players are actually doing in the game and using that data to adjust the play experience. So if you find that 90 percent of your players are using one particular type of object, it might suggest you should make more objects of that type. Similarly, if players are never using a certain feature you put in, it might be worth your time to try to determine why players are never using it and then address their issues. If it turns out the feature simply is something they do not need, it may be wise to cut that feature instead of maintaining it. Furthermore, you can learn from this mistake by avoiding similar unwanted features in the future. The value of player metrics is that the data cannot lie or exaggerate and it is a fair representation of what all of the players are doing, not just the ones who take the time to talk to the developers. Just as surveys in general can be colored by people's desire to make themselves look good in various ways, so too can feedback from players about their game experience. On *The Sims Online*, the developers used player metrics to uncover player exploits, since shortly after one player found an exploit, soon the whole world would know and everyone would be using a particular object for their own benefit. Analyzing player metrics is essential to assessing the true state of the world before making any changes and adjustments to your game.

A World of Their Own

The future for multi-player gaming looks bright indeed. The genre's hard-core fans are so enthralled with it that they often have no interest in single-player games. Indeed, MUDs and the massively multi-player commercial games they have inspired have attracted a whole group of fans that were never interested in single-player experiences. It cannot be disputed that multi-player games, through their inclusion of multiple intelligent players, contain a combination of emergence, novelty, and unpredictability that single-player games will never achieve, regardless of how much artificial intelligence improves. At the same time, multi-player designers have much less control over this game-space and thereby the games can be quite hard to get into, especially when a player finds himself a late arrival among a sea of veterans. The glory/shame balance in a multi-player game can be intensely satisfying for the winners, but just as intensely depressing for the losers. Furthermore, once other players are involved in a game the level of immersion players can experience is severely diminished. As soon as one player in the game-world discusses what he saw on TV last night, the other players' suspension of disbelief is shattered and they are reminded that they are not really running around an enchanted forest or a World War II battlefield. This is all but impossible to prevent, yet in the end, though developers may lose sleep worrying about the suspension of disbelief being shattered, the players of the games are just happy to be talking to each other. Players of multi-player games are mostly looking for a fun, social experience, not an all-consuming immersive journey with a rich narrative. This means that, for all the advantages and untapped potential of multi-player games, single-player games will probably continue to be more popular for years to come because they can provide a highly tailored experience that gamers can start and stop whenever they want. Anyone who has played a multi-player game for long enough can tell you that hell truly is other people. But for the ardent fans of multi-player gaming, the drawbacks are more than worth the unique experiences that only social gaming can provide.

Chapter 14:
Interview: Chris Crawford

Today, Chris Crawford is probably best known for his contributions to the dialog of game design, including his founding of the Computer Game Developers Conference, publishing the *Journal of Computer Game Design*, and writing the book *The Art of Computer Game Design*. In particular, *The Art of Computer Game Design*, though written in 1983, remains the best work ever published on the subject, and served as the inspiration for this book. The brilliance of Crawford's games cannot be denied either, including such undisputed classics as *Eastern Front (1941)*, *Balance of Power*, and Crawford's personal favorite, *Trust & Betrayal: The Legacy of Siboot*. For most of the '90s Crawford devoted himself to his labor of love, the interactive storytelling system called the Erasmatron, a tool that shows great promise for transforming interactive stories from mostly prewritten affairs into truly dynamic experiences. Most recently he has continued to contribute to the dialog of interactive design, having authored two new books, *Understanding Interactivity/The Art of Interactive Design* and *Chris Crawford on Game Design*.

What initially attracted you to making a computer play a game?

That actually started back in 1966, when I was a high school sophomore, and a friend of mine named David Zeuch introduced me to the Avalon Hill board wargames. We played those, and I thought they were a lot of fun. I played them into college, though I didn't have a lot of free time during my college years. When I was in graduate school, I ran into a fellow who worked at the computer center, and he was trying to get *Blitzkrieg*, an Avalon Hill game, running on the computer. I told him he was crazy. I said, "That can't be done, forget it." But that conversation planted a seed. I thought about it, and about a year later I decided I was going to attempt it. So I went to work and it turned out to be nowhere near as difficult as I had feared. So I ended up putting together a little program on an IBM 1130 in FORTRAN. It actually ran a computer game, a little tactical armored simulation. The debut of that game came early in 1976 when I showed it off at a little wargame convention that we held. Everybody played it and thought it was a great deal of fun. So then I bought myself a KIM-1 and redid the whole thing around that system. That design was unmatched for many years, because you had genuine hidden movement. I had built little tiny terminals, as I called them, and each player had his own little map and little pieces, and a screen to divide the two players. Two guys played this wargame, each one unaware of the position of the other. It was a lot of fun, and that was 1977 or '78.

What made you at first think it would be impossible?

The difficulties of organizing the artificial intelligence for it. I thought, "That's just going to be impossible." And the hex-grid motion, I figured that was probably computable, and in fact it turns out it's not that difficult. But I figured that doing armored tactical planning on the computer, at the time, seemed ridiculous. Now, you have to remember that was twenty-five years ago, and given the state of AI back then, I was really on rather solid ground thinking it impossible. But as it happens I solved that problem, marginally, within a year.

What made you think it would be worthwhile to put games on the computer?

I was driven by one thing and that was "blind" play. I was very concerned that, no matter how you looked at it, with board games you could always see what the other guy was up to. And that always really bothered me, because it was horribly unrealistic. It just didn't seem right, and I thought the games would be much more interesting blind. And, in fact, when we did them, they were immensely powerful games, far more interesting than the conventional games. And as soon as I saw that, I knew that this was *the* way to go. And board-play technology has never been able to match that simple aspect of it. It was so much fun sneaking up behind your opponent and, as they say, sending 20 kilograms up his tailpipe. It was really impressive stuff, very heady times.

So from that early work, how did you come to work at Atari?

Well, actually a bit more transpired first. I got a Commodore Pet and programmed it in BASIC with some assembly language routines to handle the hex-grid stuff. I had shown my tactical armored game at some wargame conventions and everyone had been very impressed. So then I actually made *Tanktics* into a commercial product and sold it on the Commodore Pet for fifteen bucks. And then I did another game called *Legionnaire*, also on the Commodore Pet. And based on that I got a job at Atari, doing game design there. Actually, I was one of the few job candidates they had ever had who had any experience designing computer games. It's hard to appreciate just how tiny everything was. The very notion of a computer game was, itself, very esoteric.

What was the atmosphere like at Atari then?

It was heady. Again, it's very difficult for people nowadays to appreciate how different things were just twenty years ago. I remember a conversation with Dennis Koble. We met one morning in the parking lot as we were coming into work, and we were chatting on the way in. And I remember saying, "You know, some day game design will be a developed profession." And he said, "Yeah, maybe someday we'll be like rock stars!" And we both laughed at how absurd that thought was. There were, in the world, a couple dozen game designers, most of them at Atari. And everybody knew each other, at least everyone at Atari, and it was all very cozy. And many of them did not consider themselves to be game designers.

For example, I remember a meeting where the department manager said, "All right everybody, we need to print up new business cards for everybody, and we need to select what kind of title you want." And there was something of a debate among the staff whether they wanted to be listed as "Game Designer" or "Programmer." I remember people saying, "Gee, you know, if we put our titles down as Game Designer, we may not be able to get another job." And I think we ended up going with "Game Programmer." But game design was nowhere near the thing it is today, it was just a very obscure thing. I remember telling people when they'd ask me, "What do you do?" And I'd say, "I design games for Atari." And they'd say, "Wow. That's really strange. How do you do that?" It was a very exotic answer back then.

Were you able to do whatever you wanted in terms of game design?

It depended on what you were doing. If you were doing a VCS [Atari 2600] game, then you talked your games over with your supervisor, but there was considerable freedom. The feeling was, "We need plenty of games anyway, and we really need the creativity here, so just follow your nose, see what works, see if you can come up with anything interesting." And in general the supervisor gave you a lot of latitude, unless you were doing a straight rip-off of somebody else's design. So in that area we had lots of freedom. But once you got your design complete, there would be a design review where all of the other designers would look it over and make their comments. This wasn't a marketing thing, it was a design level review.

Everybody wanted to program the computer [the Atari 800] because it was so much more powerful than the VCS. So at the time I started, in 1979, the policy was that you had to prove yourself by doing a game on the VCS first. And only then could you go to the computer. Well, I mumbled and grumbled; I didn't like that idea at all. But I learned the VCS, and I did a game on it. However, another policy they had was that all games had to be done in 2K of ROM. They were just coming out with the 4K ROMs, but at the time those were rather expensive. And so the feeling was, "You can't do a 4K ROM. You've got to prove yourself, prove that you're a worthy designer if we're going to give you all that space. We've got to know you can use it well." So I had to do a 2K game.

And I did one called *Wizard*, which I think was rather clever and worked in 2K. Although I got it done in record time, I finished it just as Atari was starting to get its 4K games out. Everybody started realizing that the 4K games were not just a little better, but immensely superior to the 2K games. So there was a feeling that anything that was marketed is going to be compared against the 4K games, and my design as a 2K game just couldn't compare with a 4K game. So the other designers ended up saying, "This is a very nice design, for 2K, but it just doesn't cut it." They wanted it redesigned for 4K. I could have redesigned it for 4K and gotten it published, but my feeling was, "OK, look. I've done my game on the VCS, now I'd like to move on to the computer. So let's not screw around here." So I argued that, "Look, this was designed as a 2K game, we're not going to simply add features to it. If you want a 4K game, we start over; that's the only way to do it right." And mumble-mumble, I was able to sneak past it and be allowed to go straight to the Atari 800. So that game was never published. And I had no regrets.

So your biggest commercial success while at Atari was *Eastern Front (1941)*. But I understand that you had trouble convincing people that a wargame would be successful. Were you confident a lot of people would like it?

No no, I didn't really care. My feeling was, this is the game I wanted to design, so I did it in my spare time. This was nights and weekends. Meanwhile, I was doing plenty of other stuff at work. In October or November of 1980 I was promoted away from game design. I was basically the first hardware evangelist. I did for the Atari what Guy Kawasaki did for the Macintosh. And, actually, I was successful at that. I did a very good job of attracting people to work on the Atari, because it was so much better than the Apple and all it needed was a good technical salesman. So I traveled the country giving these seminars, handing out goodies, and so forth. And I generated a lot of excitement among the programmer community, and the Atari really took off. There was this explosion of software about a year after I started that task. I take primary credit for that.

So anyway, I started that task in October or November of 1980, and as part of that I was putting out these software demos to show off the various features of the Atari. And I told myself, "I'm finally going to take the time to teach myself this scrolling feature that everybody knows is in there, but nobody has actually gotten around to using." So I sat down and started messing around with it, and within a couple of weeks I had a very nice demo up and running. I built a big scrolling map and I thought, "Boy, this is pretty neat." And by the standards of the day this was revolutionary. It went way way way beyond anything else, just mind-blowing. And I remember taking that to S.S.I. which, at the time, was the top wargame company working on the Apple. And I showed it to the fellow there, and he was very unenthusiastic. He said, "Whoop-de-do, this will never make a good wargame." I think it was some kind of prejudice against Atari, that "Atari is not a real computer." I was kind of disjointed, and I thought, "Jeez, what a narrow-minded attitude." So I decided, "I'll do it myself." I did this game in the classic way that many games are done nowadays: I started off with a cute technical feature and said, "How can I show off this wonderful graphics trick?" So I said, "Let's build a game around the scrolling." I went to work and built *Eastern Front*. I had it working by June of '81, but the gameplay was awful. It took me about two months to finish up the gameplay.

We released it through APX [the Atari Program Exchange] in August of 1981 and it was a huge success. It was generally considered to be the second definitive Atari game, the first being *Star Raiders* of course.

So you actually made the fancy graphical effects first, and then built the game around that?

That's a phase every designer has to go through. You start off designing around cute techie tricks, and as you mature as a designer you put that behind you.

So you ended up releasing the source code for *Eastern Front (1941)*. What motivated you to do that?

It was an extremely unconventional act. My feeling was, this is a fast-moving field. I'm good. I'll have new, wonderful technological discoveries by the time other people start using this. I'll be on to something else. I didn't feel any sense of possessiveness: "This is mine, I don't want anybody else to know." My feeling was and continues to be that we all profit more from the general advance of the industry. But I'm not an intellectual property anarchist. I do believe people have rights to claim certain things as theirs. I just feel that this should be done with great restraint, and only in situations where there is something very big which took a *lot* of work. I felt this was just a little techie stunt, no big deal. So I gave it away.

It's funny. There were a number of technologies that I gave away that nobody really used. The scrolling one was a good example: there were a couple of attempts to use it, but they were all half-hearted. Then the other thing, I never could get anybody to learn a wonderful graphics trick that was shown to me by Ed Logg, and I sort of picked it up and ran with it. I did a number of extensions which took it well beyond what he showed me. But it was a wonderful thing for doing dissolves, a variety of transitions, and it was beautiful. Very clever code. You applied this to a bitmap and, wow, you could get fantastic things happening. And I used that a number of times and nobody else ever seemed to bother to use it. But I think lots of people did look at the *Eastern Front* source code as a way of realizing that games aren't that hard to write.

So did your evangelism work take away from the amount of time you were able to spend developing games?

Well, I was software evangelist for only a year. I was then asked by Alan Kay to join his research team. In fact, I was the first guy he invited. For about three months the Atari Research Division consisted of Alan Kay, myself, Alan's administrative assistant, Wanda Royce, and my employee, Larry Summers. And the only place they could put us back then was in the executive suites, there was a spare room there. And there were Larry and I doing programming in the executive suites. Ray Kassar, the Atari president, was a very stuffy, straightlaced guy. And he really resented our being up there. I mean, it really bothered him. So we got a new building real quick.

I'm curious about another game you did during your Atari days, *Gossip*. Was that game ever released?

Yes, it was released, but it was released just as Atari was going down in flames, so nobody had any opportunity to see it. *Gossip* was an immensely important game in that I tackled interpersonal relationships. I had realized very early that computer games had an emotional sterility about them, and I spent a long time thinking about that. I finally decided that the crucial factor was the absence of characters, of people. And I remember writing an essay, way back then, entitled "People not Things," arguing that computer games were very thing oriented, and that we had to focus our energies on people. So I attempted to design something around people and interpersonal interaction. And *Gossip* is what I came up with. A very simple design, but way ahead of its time in terms of its goals.

So what was the gameplay like?

It was solely about what I call circumferential relationships affecting radial relationships. Basically the idea was that you had a group of eight people, and your goal was to be popular. This was just before the high school prom, and you wanted to be elected king or queen of the prom, and so you were doing your politics. And the way you did this was by calling people up. It had a really cute interface. There were eight people sitting in two rows of four; they looked like panelists on a game show. You were the one in the upper left corner. And you would use the joystick to select one of the other seven players, and then you pushed the button and the telephone would ring at that person's station. He'd pick up the phone. Then you would use the joystick to point at another person. And then, once you'd selected that other person, you'd push the joystick up or down to show a facial expression ranging from a big smile and nodding your head up and down all the way to a big frown and shaking your head from side to side. These were expressions of how much you liked or disliked this person. So you'd point to someone and say, "I like them this much," and then your interlocutor would say, "Well, I like them this much." Then your interlocutor would tell you things about what other people were saying: "This person likes him this much, and that person likes him that much." And the idea was, you would try to read the social clustering and decide which clique are you going to join so as to ingratiate yourself to everyone else. To some extent this involved a certain amount of deception. You'd tell everyone, "Oh, I like you very much" and you'd say, "Oh, if you hate him, then I hate him too." But you could get caught at it, and that would really hurt; you did have to be quite careful in all of this. It was a very interesting little game.

What was the mind-set like at Atari during the video game crash?

There was a sense of catastrophe. It turns out that it was solely a matter of momentum. That is, all that really happened was that Atari went bust. Atari did a lot of things really wrong, and those are what led to its going bust. It's just that in going bust, it discredited an entire industry, and so many companies that hadn't done anything wrong and were perfectly healthy, they went bust too. It was just a matter of an industry collapsing because its lead company was greatly discredited. It was kind of silly in many ways.

Everyone just convinced themselves that bust was upon us and everyone decided, "Oh, we're all going to die, so let's just die." The underlying forces had not changed by much.

So things were able to pick up. Unfortunately, the recovery surprised everybody by its shape. The initial collapse discredited video games, but not really computer games as much. Unfortunately, at the time, most computer games were just copies of video games. Hence, many computer game companies that were deriving all of their sales from video games collapsed. It was really bad for a while there. I couldn't get a job, I couldn't get

Balance of Power

anything. There were two new things for me: *Balance of Power* and the Macintosh. I had some serious discussions with the people at Amiga as to whether I wanted to do software evangelism for them. And really this boiled down to a choice between platforms. Which platform am I going to run with — the Mac or the Amiga? I gave that a lot of thought, because I realized you hitch your star to a platform. I chose the Macintosh, which turned out to be the right decision.

I went to work on *Balance of Power*. My big hope then was that we could maybe rebuild the industry along more rational lines. And, you know, there was a real chance there. That was the crucial moment of truth for the computer games industry, the period from '85 through '87. And it took the wrong turn. Actually, 1990 was when the fate of the industry was sealed. And if anything sealed it, it was Chris Roberts' *Wing Commander*. But we had a real opening there for a while; it looked like we might pull it off.

How do you think *Wing Commander* sealed the fate of the industry?

The big question for the industry in 1985 was what, if anything, will sell? Nobody seemed to know for sure, but there were a few strands. The fact that *Balance of Power* was a huge hit suggested to people that perhaps serious games might have a future, or at least games that weren't video games. And there was a lot of excitement about exploring some of those ideas. The other games that were a big success back then were the whole series of Infocom games, which continued to do well right through the crash.

Because they were clearly different from video games.

Yes. And you put those two together, and it pointed strongly in one direction. So there was a lot of effort in that direction. The industry was still torn because it was so much easier to design the video games, and they did seem to sell to a group of people who weren't affected by the crash. We really teetered on that fence: which way are we going to go — video games or a broad range of game possibilities? What sealed it was *Wing Commander*, for two reasons. The main thing that *Wing Commander* did that doomed the industry was that it bought market share. That is, *Wing Commander* was a hugely expensive program to write. It's funny; Chris Roberts has denied that it cost much, but that's because of some creative internal accounting. Back in those days, around 1990, a typical budget for a game would be $100,000 to $200,000. There were some done cheaper, but $300,000 was a very expensive game. *Wing Commander* probably cost about $1,000,000. By the standards of the day that was considered absurd. And in fact, I've been told by an Origin insider that *Wing Commander* by itself never paid back its investment, but that the follow-ups and add-ons did. But what they were really doing was spending so much money that it would only work if it became the top hit. It did. The problem then was, they've raised the bar for the whole industry, we all have to produce $1,000,000 games, and unfortunately they can only work if each one is the number one game. And you can only have one number one game. So that, in turn, forced the industry to become much more conservative. We've got these huge expenses, we simply can't make money turning out a number twenty game. Anything less than being in the top ten will lose money. So very quickly it became a hit-driven business. That was already starting in the late '80s, but *Wing Commander* sealed it. So once it became a hit-driven industry, the whole marketing strategy, economics, and everything changed, in my opinion, much for the worse. The other thing was that *Wing Commander* also seemed to reestablish or reconfirm the role of the action game as the wave of the future. And basically that's where the industry solidified, and the cement has now set.

It was right before the crash that you wrote *The Art of Computer Game Design*, **wasn't it?**

Yes, actually I started that as soon as I joined Atari Research. It's funny, one of my goals at Atari Research was, "Let's really sharpen up the whole field of game design." So I, in essence, tried to create a computer game developer's conference within Atari. I tried to set up a Friday afternoon seminar. And some politics got in the way. I sent out invitations to all the designers throughout Atari, and some pig-headed guy who was running the software group at coin-op was furious that I didn't route it through him. I didn't follow the hierarchy properly, and he therefore sent out a memo forbidding any of his employees to go. That's one of the reasons why Atari collapsed; there was a lot of pig-headed ego crap going on. So the seminars never really came off. I therefore decided, "OK, I'll write these ideas down." I started working on the book. I finished it in 1982, but Ray Kassar, the CEO, was also pig-headed and insisted that he personally approve the manuscript before we sent it out to a publisher. So I sent it to him, and he sat on it for a year.

Do you still look back on the book positively?

I certainly have come a long ways. Had I known that fifteen years later people would still be reading it and deriving some benefit from it, I would have been flabbergasted, and I simply would not have believed it. I still get e-mails referring to it. There's no question it's still providing people with some benefit. And that says some very bad things about the whole games industry and the games community, how little thinking there is going on. It's shameful.

There's really no other book like it at all.

Yes, all the other attempts just turn out to be programming books. It is shameful that no one has gone beyond that book.

Ever since you published that book, you have been very concerned with sharing your thoughts about game design with the community. I'm curious why that is.

There are two very separate reasons. First, sharpening my own thinking through writing, which I do a great deal of. And second, communicating ideas to others. There is some overlap. Most of the time I write for myself. I have reams and reams of little design essays on particular designs, where I muse with myself on design issues. However, I will sometimes write an essay solely for public consumption, put it up on the web or something, and that is done with a very different purpose. But I often write with both purposes.

So did your writings about game design lead to your establishing the Computer Game Developers Conference?

I had started off by founding the *Journal of Computer Game Design*. That turned out to be quite a success; it rose up to one hundred to one hundred fifty subscribers rather quickly. And by the time it reached that level, I realized that it really would be possible to have a conference, there were enough people out there. So I decided to have a little miniature conference at my home. I just put a little notice in the *Journal*, saying, "I'm going to put together a conference, it's going to be at this date. And anybody who wants to come, contact me." We ended up having twenty-six people show up to this conference, one day long, and we all sat in the big room upstairs and talked about game design. It was a very exciting experience! Everybody agreed, this is great, this is wonderful, we've got to do this again. They all turned to me and said, "Chris, do it again." I said OK. I thought about it for a while and then I decided it would be really good if I broadened participation in this by recruiting some other people to help me. I decided the only way they were going to be really involved was if they had a sense of ownership. If I brought them in as assistants to me, it would never really work. So I decided to create a corporation with a board of directors, and I invited five other people to be on the board. And to give them a sense of ownership, even though I owned the whole thing free and clear and had gotten it rolling with my own money, I basically just gave away ownership. Everybody had an equal share in the conference. We set up the conference, and it was a huge success, and it just grew and grew every year.

Did you foresee it growing to be the mammoth event it is now?

No, and to some extent that reflects a violation of my initial intentions. We had some clear disputes within the board: is this a show, like E3, or is this an academic conference, like AAAI? My feeling was that the core of this is the exchange of ideas among developers. We can have a show, but it's got to be a sideshow. It's always tucked away in a corner. This conference is designed around people sharing ideas, and that's why I came up with the idea of the roundtables. Unfortunately, it is now a show, and the conference is now a secondary activity.

So after Atari you became an independent game developer. Why did you do that instead of opting to return to a big company?

Well, at first it was forced on me. But then, once I got going, I was working on *Balance of Power* and it was an independent project. It was more inertia than anything else.

Do you prefer being independent?

Yes, I am very much a solitary worker. I am very concerned with my efficiency and how much I get done. When you're working with other people, you spend a lot of time just holding their hand, explaining things to them, helping them out, rather than actually getting anything done. I felt I had a lot of ideas, and if I really wanted to explore them I had to explore them alone.

So what originally started you working on *Balance of Power*?

It was a sort of a culmination. My interest in wargames arose because I was part of the Vietnam generation. While a lot of people wanted to resist the war, I wanted to understand war so that I could ultimately do something about it. I felt that protesting in the streets was very ad hoc, a very temporary solution, and not very effective either. I was asking questions like, how do wars get started? All through the early '70s and early '80s, I was very

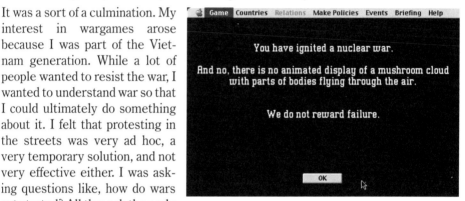

Balance of Power II: The 1990 Edition

much a student of warfare, learning everything I could about military history. Finally, by 1984, I felt I had figured that out well enough that I could design a game around some of those concepts. I would say that the emotional support for the game was the Bob Dylan song "Blowin' in the Wind." You know, "How many times must the cannonballs fly before they're forever banned?" That was the thing that gave me the emotional inspiration to continue with the project even though there were many points where it looked impossible. I was taking a completely different approach to design and exploring new territory and there were many times when it looked hopeless. It took a lot of emotional toil to get over those problems and carry on.

But you thought the concept was compelling enough to be worth it?

Yes. I really wanted to do an un-wargame. We have plenty of wargames.

And in *Balance of Power* when you get to the point of having a war you have lost.

Yes, that was very much the point of the game. I don't know if you remember, but if there was a war, the screen would go black, and it would say, "We do not reward failure." That was very much a surprise to many people.

At any time were you concerned that the game was too different?

I did not expect it to become a hit, but I felt it was important to do. This was exactly the same thing that happened with *Eastern Front*. I did *Eastern Front* for myself and then, lo and behold, everybody loved it. Well, that's very nice. I did *Balance of Power* for myself and, gee, everybody loved it. But I also did other games for myself that were dismal failures, commercially speaking.

How did you go about balancing realism with the gameplay in *Balance of Power?*

People talk about realism versus playability as if it's a dilemma. I see it more as a matter of sharpening things. An artist, painting a portrait, will deliberately accentuate certain components of the face that he feels bring out the character of the subject. They don't see that as realism versus playability, they see that as art. In the same way I felt that I needed to sharpen up, editorially and artistically, those elements that I thought clearly showed the issues at stake. So I certainly made the world a much more dangerous place. I took out a lot of the boring complexities, simplified it down, and sharpened it up to a game about pure, direct geopolitical rivalry between the two superpowers. And that's all it was, clearly showing that conflict.

I've read that *Trust & Betrayal: The Legacy of Siboot* **is your favorite of your games. Why is that?**

Every game I have done has been original, with the exception of the second *Balance of Power*, which I did at the urgent request of my publisher. With that one exception everything I have done has been a new design. But with *Siboot* I went much further out than with any other game, that is, in terms of just how far I took the design beyond the conventions of game design. *Siboot* was easily the most advanced. I explored ideas with *Siboot* that

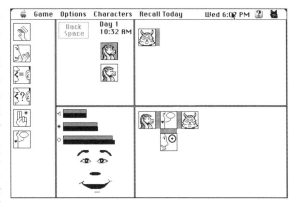

Trust & Betrayal: The Legacy of Siboot

people still have not even come close to. We were talking about *Gossip* as in some ways ahead of other games. *Siboot* went way, way beyond *Gossip*. The other thing about *Siboot* was it wasn't just one good idea. There were at least three major ideas in *Siboot*, each one of them worthy of a game all by itself.

And then there were lots of other little ideas. Here's an example of a little idea. There's now a user interface concept called "tool tips." If you put the cursor over something and leave it there for a few seconds, it pops up some descriptive text. I anticipated that and came up with something vaguely similar, where you could click and hold on a button to see its functionality. That was four years before tool tips were first noted as a user interface item in the PC world. That wasn't a major idea on my part; I considered it to be just a minor little thing, but at the time, nobody had anything like that.

So what were the three major innovations?

First, the language, use of language as the primary interface element. You talk to the other creatures. I see this as completely different than the text parser approach, because I really don't think that's linguistic communication, that's something very different. Second, it used an inverse parser. Actually, the core concept behind the parser was patented by Texas Instruments in 1979. I didn't know that at the time. However, my implementation was different enough that we were never concerned with any patent infringement issues. TI's approach was more menu driven. Mine, in the end, boiled down to being functionally similar to a menu, but technically it's called a palette. So I didn't invent that concept, but I developed its implementation and showed very clearly how to do that kind of thing. That was a major innovation, and I'm sad to say that nobody seems to have run with that concept. The third major game innovation was the use of non-transitive combat relationships, which has been used in some games since then. That was basically just an extension of the rock-scissors-paper idea. That basic concept of non-transitive relationships has enormous potential for development; you can build whole games out of extensions of that. And there's no reason why non-transitivity has to be applied to three components. You can have a ring that has twelve components and then the implications of victory or defeat in the non-transitive ring can be interpreted many, many ways. It's a huge area of game design to explore. This would be easy to implement. It's just that nobody is thinking along lines that unconventional.

Do you think the unconventionality of the project hurt *Siboot*'s popularity?

Well, yes and no. Actually, it was only sold on the Mac. There was never a PC version done. I think we sold about four thousand copies on the Mac, which by the standards of the day was disappointing but not horrible. The general rule back then was that you'd sell five to ten times as many on the PC as you'd sell on the Mac. So we're talking twenty to forty thousand copies if there'd been a PC port. But the publisher opted against doing so.

So, as with *Gossip*, was your goal to put people in the games?

Yes. And I took that concept of "people not things" much, much further with *Siboot* than with *Gossip*. Another innovation was the interstitial stories that pop up. They weren't irrelevant, they actually did tie into the overall game.

So you did *Balance of Power II* solely at the insistence of the publisher?

Yes. I had done *Siboot*, and they had published it, and it was obvious that it wasn't going to make money for them. They were obviously disappointed. They'd been asking about a sequel. They pressed me hard this time, and I felt I owed them one. So I did the *Balance of Power* sequel.

So you didn't have great hopes to better the original?

No, and in fact I felt that *Balance of Power II* was little more than a clean-up of *BoP I*. It's funny, though. By the standards of the industry, it was a major new version and deserved to be called "Second Edition." But by my standards it was just tidying up, adding some bells and whistles, but in terms of gameplay it didn't do much.

Balance of Power II: The 1990 Edition

So where did the idea for *Guns & Butter* come from?

At about the same time, the three best game designers in the world, independently, all got the same idea. Each of us said, "I'm going to do a conquer-the-world game, an *Empire* game." (Those three were Sid Meier, Dan Bunten, and myself.) It is interesting how each of us took a completely different route. We all know how Sid took his, and it was an immense success. Sid, Dan, and I got together at one point to discuss how the three of us approached our designs. Sid had a very clear notion: he was going to make it fun. He didn't give a damn about anything else, it was going to be fun. He said, "I have absolutely no reservation about fiddling with realism or anything, so long as I can make it more fun."

My approach was to make it educational, and Dan's approach was to make it social. Dan came up with this wonderful little game, *Global Conquest*, where you really interacted with the other people playing. I think that game was an undiscovered jewel. It bombed even worse than *Guns & Butter*. He had endless trouble with Electronic Arts. I don't see why he stuck with them, because they kept wanting him to put shoot-'em-up elements into his games, especially *M.U.L.E.* I consider *M.U.L.E.* to be, probably, the greatest game design ever done. That is, in terms of the platform he had to work with, and the design expertise of those times, *M.U.L.E.* was definitely the greatest ever done. And it is a brilliant game, it is loads of fun, and it has never been ported onto a modern machine. That's a tragedy. And the reason why is that Electronic Arts insisted that the players be able to go shoot each other up. Dan refused, just said flat out, "That will not happen." And *Global Conquest* was the same way. It was not so much about shooting as about teamwork.

Guns & Butter

My conquer-the-world game, *Guns & Butter*, was really more about macro-economics. In fact, during development, it was called *Macro-Economic Conquest*. I think it's reasonably successful as a game to teach about how history really develops, but that's all. It was certainly one of my poorest games, no question. It really didn't have that much creativity. There were some cute ideas, but where that game had cute ideas, *Siboot* had thunderclaps of genius. For example, *Guns & Butter* had this nifty little algorithm for generating continents. I also developed a wonderful algorithm for giving names to states and provinces, and I'm very proud of that algorithm; it's very clever. But this is mere cleverness, not creative genius.

***Guns & Butter* has some interesting ideas about balancing complex systems. But you think it did not work?**

No, it didn't work, largely because I completely blew the handling of trade and alliances. That was a disaster. I think if I'd given that game another six months it probably would have worked out just fine, but I rushed it.

***Balance of the Planet* seems to be an extremely educationally oriented game. Was that your intent?**

Oh, absolutely. I had no intent whatsoever to make something that was fun. My feeling was, "OK, there are all of those shoot-'em-ups and so forth, and I'm not going to try to compete with those things. I'm going to do a game that taps into another area of humanity. So I'm going to do pure simulation, and I'm going to make that simulation very realistic and very educational as well." We knew Earth Day 1990 was coming up, and we thought, "We're going to release this thing in time for Earth Day." And I felt that would be one of my contributions. Again, Vietnam generation, Earth Day, and all that jazz. *Balance of Power* was about the Vietnam War, and *Balance of the Planet* was about Earth Day.

Balance of the Planet

Will Wright's *SimEarth* came out just shortly after *Balance of the Planet*. It's interesting to compare the two. Of course, his is more of a toy and yours is much more goal oriented.

SimEarth was not one of Will's better efforts. He's done brilliant stuff, but I think he didn't have a clear purpose with *SimEarth*. It was kind of, "OK, here's this planet, and here are these geological processes, and here are these life forms, and ..." There was no design focus to it. He seems to have said, "Let's take *SimCity* and do it to the whole Earth." That kind of extrapolatory approach to design never works well. And it didn't work well for him. It was certainly more successful than *Balance of the Planet*, because it was a lot better looking and had plenty of cute features. But it was not as educational as *Balance of the Planet*.

SimEarth had a lot of interesting systems in it, but it was difficult to understand what was going on.

It was more that all of the different systems, they sort of didn't add up to anything. He had all of these simplifications, but they weren't purposeful simplifications. They were simplifications to make the internal systems accessible, but they didn't really add up to anything. The model for the way living systems develop didn't seem to make any sense to me, even though it was easy to see its results.

I've heard *Balance of the Planet* criticized for not being a lot of fun. Do you see fun as the sine qua non of game design?

That's exactly the problem. Many people do see fun as the sine qua non. That's one way that the game design industry has gone down the wrong path. Basically, computer games and video games are now one, and in fact they're all video games in the sense of cute shoot-'em-ups, lots of graphics, splendiferousness, and emphasis on fun in the childish sense. I see no reason why computer games needed to constrain themselves in this fashion. It's rather like some-

Balance of the Planet

body saying, "I went to go see the movie *Das Boot*, but it wasn't any fun, so it's a crummy movie." Well, I'm sorry, but *Das Boot* was not meant to be fun. I think we could agree that *Saving Private Ryan* is not a fun movie, but it is a damn good one. And the same thing goes for *Schindler's List*. And, sure, there are plenty of fun movies. *Star Wars* was lots of fun. But Hollywood doesn't constrain itself the way the games industry does. I suppose that was the whole thrust of my efforts all through the '80s and into the early '90s, to help the games industry become a broad-based entertainment industry, rather than a kiddie, fun industry. I failed at that. It is now most definitely not an entertainment industry, and never will be. They've painted themselves into a corner from which they can never extricate themselves. It's rather like comics. It's a shame to see the medium of comics used brilliantly by people like Spiegelman and McCloud, yet it is relegated to the comic book stores where the kids chewing bubble gum come. Not enough adults take graphic novels seriously. Some progress is evident, but it's a slow, slow process. I'm not sure they'll ever pull themselves out of that dump.

So you think the games industry has reached that same point of stagnation?

Yes. Only they're not even trying to get out; they haven't even realized yet that there's a problem.

So I guess that's what led to your leaving the games industry and starting work on the Erasmatron.

Well, there were two factors in that. Yes, I had been steadily drifting away from the games industry. The hallmark of that was the "Dragon Speech" I gave. That lecture was... I'll just tell you how it ended. In the lecture, I'd been talking about "the dragon" as the metaphor for this artistic goal. And, right at the end of the speech, in essence I stopped talking with the audience and had a conversation directly with the dragon. I said, "And now that I have finally devoted myself heart and soul to the task of pursuing the dragon, all of a sudden, there he is, I can see him brightly and clearly." I began talking to the dragon, and that was intense. I can't remember it exactly, but I said something like, "You're mighty, you're powerful, you're beautiful, but you're oh so ugly. Yes, yes, you frighten me," and then I screamed, "You hurt me! I've felt your claws ripping through my soul!" I wasn't lecturing any more, this was much more acting. I let out that line "you hurt me" with great passion, and it frightened the audience. They weren't used to that level of passion in the technical lectures that they were familiar with. And then I said, "I'm not good enough to face you, I'm not experienced enough, so I'm going to do it now. I've got to go face to face with you, eyeball to eyeball, and I'm going to do it now, here." I reached over and I pulled out a sword and I kind of hunkered down and shouted in a battle cry, "For truth, for beauty, for art, charge!" I went galloping down the center aisle of the lecture hall, and I never came back.

This was at the Computer Game Developers Conference?

Yes. A lot of people thought, "Well, Chris gave his swan song, he'll never come back." But in fact I came back the next year, and I had every intention of continuing to lend my expertise: "I'm going off in this other direction, but you guys need my help, and I will still be there." Unfortunately, a whole ugly incident with the conference board members put an end to that. What was so hurtful was not just the behavior of the board members, but also the attitude of the community, which was, "Hey, this is Silicon Valley, you just gotta fight to get yours. If they play hardball, what's the big deal?" My reaction was, "I just don't want to be a part of this nasty community." It was so bitter an experience that moving to Oregon was an imperative. I had to get out of Silicon Valley. And it's funny, every time I go down there now, I can see the Silicon Valley greed all around me. It really bothers me.

So that drove you into working on the Erasmatron?

I had been evolving in that direction. But what made it a negative move was A, the industry was editorially going in directions I did not like, and B, the industry was going in moral and social directions that I did not like.

So how did the Erasmatron project come about?

I set out to do interactive storytelling. I said, "I'm going to go back, and I'm going to do my King Arthur game now." Because I had done a King Arthur game at Atari that I was proud of, that had a lot of good ideas, but I felt it did not do justice to the legends, so I felt that I owed something to those legends. I started all over to do a completely new approach. That led me up to the storytelling engine. However, everything was hand-coded and it was enormously difficult. We had gone the rounds to all the big companies trying to interest them in it and nobody was interested.

Just about that time, I ran into a lady named Edith Bjornson, who was with the Markle Foundation. She suggested that I take the technology in a different direction, as an enabling technology to permit non-technical people to create their own story-worlds. I very much liked the idea. So Markle funded me, and the fundamental strategy of the project was expressed in the slogan "Unleash a tidal wave of creativity." Thus, I was building three pieces of software. The Erasmatron, which is the editing software for the engine, the engine, which actually ran everything, and finally the front end, which delivered it to the user. It was a huge project and I had to do it in two years. Unfortunately the problem turned out to be much bigger than I anticipated. What I got working after two years was nice, and indeed technically adequate, but I don't think it was commercially adequate.

How do you mean?

It takes too much effort to create a sufficiently entertaining end result. Laura Mixon worked on *Shattertown Sky* for nearly eighteen months. But *Shattertown* just didn't work. It was not entertaining, it was not even finished. There were places where it would just stop. Yet she worked longer and harder on it than she was expected to. There wasn't any failure on her part. The failure on my part was underestimating the magnitude of the task. I thought that a year would be sufficient. Well, first, she didn't get fully operational software for at least six months. And second, the tool she had was so weak that she spent a lot of time doing busywork. The conclusion was that the Erasmatron needed to be souped-up, and there were a few embellishments to the engine that came out of that. But they were actually comparatively minor. Most of the work I have been doing since that, on the Erasmatron 2, has been to make the whole process of creating a story-world easier.

So you haven't concluded that making a story-world is just an inherently hard task? You've found ways to make it easier?

Well, there's no question in my mind that creating a story-world with Erasmatron 2 is immensely easier than with Erasmatron 1. Erasmatron 2 dramatically cleans up the process of creating a story-world, cutting the time required roughly in half. You see, with Erasmatron 1, we were shooting in the dark. I had no idea of what the process of creation would look like. I don't feel bad that Erasmatron 1 was a bad design; in fact it was much better than the original design document. I'd made quite a few improvements, but they weren't enough. I think that, using Erasmatron 2, people can create excellent story-worlds with an adequate commitment of time, which I consider to be at least six months and probably a year, but I haven't proved that. That is what's stopping the whole project: I need proof.

Is that something you're hoping to provide with the *Le Morte D'Arthur* project?

I don't know. I've had some kind of writer's block with that project and I don't understand why. I think one factor is a sense of demoralization. I've put nine years into this project, and so far it's been a failure. With the exception of the Markle funding, nobody's interested. There are always a few pots bubbling. Right now there are three separate groups who have expressed interest in this. So it's not as if I ever reach a point where I can say "it's dead." There's always something going on, and there's always the hope that it will go somewhere, but these things never go anywhere. I'm definitely getting discouraged.

What would an ideal Erasmatron storytelling experience be like?

I'll describe it in two ways — tactical and strategic. Tactical being what the audience experiences moment to moment, and strategic being the overall experience. Tactically, the audience will see a static image on the screen representing whatever has just happened. It will show the face of the person who just did whatever happened, as well as anybody else who's on the same stage. It will have some text explaining what has happened. The other thing I want to use is something like a comics technique. That is, comics show action between frames very well. So it might require two frames. But I want to use the artistic styles that have developed in the comics. In Scott McCloud's book, *Understanding Comics,* he has that triangle that represents the amount of abstraction.

With the smiley face in one corner and the photo-realistic face in the other.

Right. My guess is we would want to move on that triangle far away from the photo-realism corner. We'd want to be somewhere much closer to abstraction and representation. So I think we're talking about a more abstract type of display. And then there will be your menu of choices, expressed as complete sentences. This is what the player is permitted to say or do. Strategically, the big difference is that all story-worlds have a very meandering character to them. "Barroom Brawl" doesn't, because it's a single scene. "Corporate Meeting" is a single scene and even it meanders a bit. We have figured out how to cope with that problem. I had thought that plot points would do enough, but Laura and I have now come up with a scheme. I don't want to describe this as a new discovery; rather this is a concept that has been slowly brewing for several years now. We're putting flesh on its bones and I think it will work.

The idea is that there is something like a core plot that is beyond the control of the player. However, the player does control lots of interactions that will not just influence but ultimately determine the final outcome of the plot. For example, consider a murder mystery, such as *Shattertown*. Basically at some point, time is going to run out, and either the clans are going to go to war or Sky will unmask the murderer or Sky will get caught by the murderer. That ending has been established, and events will force that ending. The thing is, what ending you get depends critically on all the things you have done up to that point. Same way with *Le Morte D'Arthur*. The basic design says, very clearly, that the end game is going to have Mordred revolt. No matter what happens, Mordred is going to revolt at some point. And when he does, all the other actors are going to choose up sides. Some of them will go with Mordred, and some will stay with you. There will be a big battle, and the side with the bigger battalions wins. The decision to go with Mordred or stay with you will be based on all the things you've done up to that point.

I've come up with another concept for *Le Morte D'Arthur* that I'm tempted to go with, which would incorporate some of the elements of the current *Le Morte D'Arthur*. In this one, you're not playing as Arthur, you're playing as Merlin, and you're a transplant from the future. Your task is to modernize Arthurian society and thereby prevent the Dark Ages from happening. You're trying to build up this society and get it operating on a more efficient basis and teach them a little bit about sanitation and education and so forth. Along the way all the nobles are developing their resentments against you, and they try various plots to discredit or kill you. And, once again, Mordred revolts. The end result feels more purposeful, less meandering.

So the player is led in a direction more than in the current version.

We're not asking you to be creative or come up with new social innovations, we'll simply present you at various points with opportunities to initiate new innovations, to say, "All right, do you think it's time to teach these people sanitation, or do you think it's time to teach them how to use the stirrup?" And each one takes time. And there's still this steady plot that develops as you help this society pull itself up by its bootstraps. But there's still an awful lot of interaction going on. What we're developing here is a concept of "semi-plot" or "pseudo-plot" or a "skeletal plot" that can proceed in the way that a plot is supposed to. You still have a plot, but it doesn't hijack the whole story and dominate it as it does in a conventional story.

So the player has more involvement than they would reading a book, but not total freedom either.

Yes. The idea is that you want to use dramatic constraints, not artificial constraints. This is a drama. It's got to evolve by certain rules. We're going to apply those rules here. It should not incur resentment on the player's part that he can't pick his nose while talking to Arthur. That's not dramatically reasonable. Some argue that if you don't give the player full freedom to be creative, it just doesn't work. I disagree with that entirely. So long as you give him all dramatically reasonable options, or even most of them, you're doing fine.

So you're quick not to call your Erasmatron system a game of any kind. Why is that?

The differentiation is two-fold. The first reason is marketing. Right now, computer games mean *Quake, Command & Conquer*, or something like that. The associations with that term are all about shoot-'em-ups, resource management, and those associations are very clearly defined in the public's mind. If I call this a game, they're going to apply associations that are misleading. Moreover, the term "game," if you look it up in the dictionary, has more column inches than most words. I compared it with words like "do" and "eat" and "have" and I found that it's bigger. Because that word is a semantic imperialist, it just goes everywhere. It can be used for many, many different meanings, all completely different. But then there's sort of a switcheroo that happens. You can apply the word "game" to a whole bunch of products and activities, but then as soon as people associate it with a computer they say "computer game!" and all the semantic meaning collapses down to this little bitty point. Maybe I should call it a web game, get the whole thing on the web. Or if I do it on the Mac maybe I can call it an iGame. But I don't dare call it a computer game or a video game.

Why do you think facial expressions are so important for storytelling?

Because facial expression is one of the fundamental forms of human communication. It's funny; other people think graphics where I'm thinking communication. What goes on between user and computer is primarily a matter of communication. I am deeply desirous of optimizing that communication. That means designing the computer display to most closely match the receptive powers of the human mind. And the two things that we are very good at are facial recognition and linguistic comprehension. Accordingly, those are the two things that computers should emphasize. Computer games have neither and that appalls me. Facial expression and linguistic comprehension are the two most important areas of development for the time being. Nowadays you can get excellent 3D facial models, although the expressions on them are still crappy. This is largely because the people who design them aren't artists, they're engineers, and they've come up with these anatomically correct heads. Every cartoonist in the world knows that you never, ever draw a face the way it really is. For this type of thing we've got to use cartoon faces and not real faces.

The *Corporate Meeting* story-world in the Erasmatron

When I was playing with the Erasmaganza, sometimes it would present me with three different actions to choose from, and I wouldn't want to do any of them. In that way, it feels a bit like an old adventure game with a branching dialog tree. Do you see that as a problem?

The real issue is not "Gee, you only get three things." The real issue here is that you're not permitted to say dramatically reasonable things, and that's a flaw in the design of the story-world. Both of the demo story-worlds have that problem, because they're very tiny story-worlds. If you want to get away from that you must have a much larger story-world. "Brawl" has about fifty or sixty verbs and "Meeting" has about a hundred. I used to think that five hundred verbs was the threshold for entertainment value. I now think it's more like a thousand verbs. But "Meeting" just doesn't give you very many options because it's so tiny.

As to whether the user will ever be satisfied with the finite number of options he's given, I don't see a problem there at all. Certainly you're not permitted nuance in such an arrangement. But you should have all dramatically reasonable options. Besides, if we gave you some system where you could apply nuance so that you could say, "I'm going to say this with a slightly sarcastic tone of voice," the infrastructures for that would be ghastly. It would make the game very tedious. So I feel that the only way to do this effectively is to confine it to a menu structure. In fact, there are some games that have implemented nuance as their primary modality of interaction. In these games you're interacting with someone and you've got these sliders: one is for forcefulness, one is for humor, and another is for charm. But that's all you get. You respond to some- one with this much forcefulness, this much charm, and that much humor. I've been tempted for quite some time to build something like that into the Erasmatron. But the problem is, first, coming up with some generality, and second, keeping the interface clean and usable. Right now, with the simple menu you need merely look, see, and press. I think that's important for a mass medium. The sliders for tone are for game aficionados.

The system that *Siboot* uses to construct sentences with icons and the inverse parser is an interesting one. Why did you opt not to use a system like that for the Erasmatron?

Trust & Betrayal: The Legacy of Siboot

Because the vast number of sen- tences in *Siboot* are self- completing. In *Siboot*, you could click on just one icon and often the rest of the sentence would fill itself in because that's the only option available. The way to do that nowadays, by the way, is with pop-up menus. I could do this with the Erasmatron. For example, suppose you had a con- ventional menu item that said, "I'll give you my horse in return for that six-gun." The words "horse" and "six-gun" could be in pop-up menus providing other options for the trade. This would require some expansion of the Erasmatron system, but nothing very seri- ous. The only reason I haven't done it yet is my unwillingness to add complexity. I believe that the system has all the complexity it needs and then some. It's always easy to add complexity to the design, but I'm thinking in terms of simplification.

Have you had a chance to play *The Sims*? It seems that a lot of people succeed in using that game as a sort of tool for interactive storytelling.

The Sims is not an attempt to produce interactive storytelling. I had some e-mail with Will Wright about *The Sims*, and he acknowledges that it isn't an interactive storytelling platform, but he pointed out that many people use it that way. *The Sims* is exactly what it claims to be — a simulation, not a drama. No drama simulates the real world. In Shakespeare's play, in the middle of Henry V's speech to the soldiers at Agincourt, he doesn't say, "Just a minute, guys, I have to take a pee." However, in *The Sims*, he does. Once when I was playing *The Sims*, a little girl couldn't get to sleep because there were spooks coming and frightening her. The spooks are a very nice touch, by the way. They kept her awake all night long, and she wandered all around until she fell asleep, because a sim who stays up too long is overcome with drowsiness. She happened to fall asleep on the floor of her parents' bedroom. Morning came, mommy woke up, stretched, got up out of bed, and walked to the bathroom, stepping over the inert body of her daughter! This is a good simulation of the physical processes of daily living. It is an atrocious simulation of the emotional processes of daily living.

Will built an excellent physical simulator. But it has no people content. It's a direct violation of my "people not things" argument in that it focuses on the things aspect of life, on all the mechanical details. Going to the bathroom is a major module in that program, whereas emotional processes simply aren't there. I don't want to criticize a brilliant product: Will set out with a clear goal and he achieved it, and that's wonderful. But he didn't set out to do what I'm doing and, lo and behold, he didn't achieve it. I refuse to criticize *The Sims*, because as a design it is magnificent. It has a clear purpose and it achieves that purpose brilliantly. It's just a different product, and it's not interactive storytelling.

So what makes you want to pursue interactive storytelling?

It's a hell of a lot more relevant. Furthermore, I think it's a hell of a lot more interesting than game design. The design problems of computer games nowadays bore me, because they're not very involved problems. They tend to be very small models, quite easy to calculate. I continue to be appalled at the low level of intelligence in a lot of these games. The computer opponent is really stupid, and that's about the only element that still interests me. I might like to do a game with some really good AI, where the computer opponent can really outsmart you, and I don't mean that in the sense of chess, I mean that in something complicated like a wargame. But wargames themselves are obvious. I feel that I have mastered that form and so why should I continue to indulge in it? There are so many other, more important tasks, such as interactive storytelling. This is a challenge! Something I can really sink my teeth into. Unfortunately, it appears I have sunk my teeth into the tail of a tiger.

Do you ever fear that you will always be dissatisfied with the Erasmatron?

I consider this to be my life's work. This is the culmination of everything I've been leading up to. I have no doubts that if I continue working on this I can continue to improve this technology. I have major doubts as to its commercial feasibility right now. That is, I'm quite certain that twenty years from now people will realize that interactive storytelling is a commercially wonderful thing and, golly gee, we ought to do it. I believe we can make products that people will find far more entertaining than computer games, because they'll be about drama instead of resource management. Unfortunately, I don't think people quite see that yet. Certainly the games industry does not and will not. They will feel that *The Sims* represents the correct step in that direction. They can continue to get more polygons in the faces and have them dance better and so forth. But in terms of dramatic resolution, they haven't even begun.

Maybe it would be good if they go down that path, leaving the real problem area free for me and the other people who are serious about interactive storytelling. There are indications of a hankering for dramatic content. For example, Sony calls the chip in the PlayStation 2 "The Emotion Engine." Well that's bull, total bull. It's a graphics processor and has nothing to do with emotional modeling. But it shows that they would sure like to have some honest emotional content. They're just not willing to make the product-level commitment. Then there's the twin factors of the Internet and Hollywood. Between them, there's a strong desire to establish an identity untainted by computer games. So between the Internet and the Hollywood people I think that we really ought to get interactive storytelling. There are lots of indications in that direction. Six years ago, when I went hat in hand to almost all the majors in Hollywood trying to get them interested, and I struck out, that was because they had all just recovered from the experience of getting burned by having their own games divisions. So nowadays they're starting over with web-based things that have a completely different outlook, and they might be interested.

I wonder if you have an answer to the critics who say that telling a story interactively is somehow at odds with the fundamental structure of storytelling. Obviously, you don't find this to be an issue.

Not at all, and in fact I'm surprised at the shallowness of that argument. The easy refutation is the example of grandpa sitting down with his little granddaughter to tell her a story: "Once upon a time, there was a girl who had a horse." And the little girl says, "Was it a white horse?" And grandpa does not say, "Shut up, kid, you are ruining my carefully constructed plot!" He says, "Oh yes, it was very white, white as snow." He develops his story and the little girl interacts with him. He embraces her participation and incorporates it into the story, which makes the story that much better. This kind of storytelling has been around since the dawn of human existence. We've long since proven that, yes, you can have the audience intervene in the story without damaging it.

In your games work, you created both the content and the technology, whereas with the Erasmatron you're focusing on creating just the technology, which will allow other people to create the content. Why did you shift your efforts in that direction?

There are lots of people who could provide artistic content, but I'm the only person who can provide the tool. I therefore have a moral obligation to concentrate on the talent that is unique to me. However, there are still some other things I want to do. There's so much going on, I have to very carefully allocate my time, and a lot of good projects are sitting on the back burner.

So as a result you don't get much chance to work on *Le Morte D'Arthur*.

Right, I have to just let it burble around in my subconscious for a while longer. And it may never come out, I don't know.

So what's next for the Erasmatron technology?

Well, the basic technology is, I feel, ready to go commercially right now. We still need to build a front end and so forth, but we are ready to begin the commercialization process immediately. My next primary task is to commercialize this technology. I'm not sure how to proceed on that point.

Would you ever be interested in working on a more traditional game again?

At this point I would be interested and willing to consult with people on various game designs. That is, I wouldn't mind going in and looking at a project and identifying fundamental design problems in it, or assisting. But I don't think I would want to accept responsibility for creating a commercial product for the games industry at this time. I'm happy to help somebody else do it. But that's such a political and nasty process, and less and less time is spent on the creative aspects and more on the political aspects that don't interest me.

Chris Crawford Gameography

Tanktics, 1978
Legionnaire, 1979
Energy Czar, 1981
SCRAM, 1981
Tanktics (updated for Atari 800), 1981
Eastern Front (1941), 1981
Legionnaire (updated for Atari 800), 1982
Gossip, 1983
Excalibur, 1983
Balance of Power, 1985
Patton vs. Rommel, 1986
Trust & Betrayal: The Legacy of Siboot, 1987
Balance of Power II: The 1990 Edition, 1988
The Global Dilemma: Guns & Butter, 1990
Balance of the Planet, 1990
Patton Strikes Back, 1991

Chapter 15:
Getting the Gameplay Working

"Those who wish to be must put aside the alienation, get on with the fascination, the real relation, the underlying theme."

— Neil Peart

Hollywood has a system. It is a well-known system with a well-defined goal, where the largest unknown is "Where is the money coming from?" not "How will we ever make this film?" Hollywood producers and talent know how to go from a treatment to a script, through multiple revisions of that script, then how to bring together the personnel that will shoot the film, and finally a smaller team that will edit it, culminating in the completion of the film on time and on budget (usually). Hollywood as a whole has much less of a handle on whether the final film will be any good or not, but they do at least know how to get the film made. Seldom does a film already in production have its script completely rewritten, its personnel trimmed, or more people added willy-nilly to its cast and crew. Customarily, films are completed months and months before they are scheduled to be released. Granted, sometimes the film may never make it beyond the script stage or, once completed, may not get released as originally intended. But, overall, Hollywood has an efficient system for creating films.

On the other hand, computer game developers have no such system. The development of a game design is a chaotic and unpredictable process filled with problems not even the most experienced producer, designer, or programmer can foresee. Customarily, development on computer games continues until the absolute last possible second, with changes made right up to the time the gold master disc is shipped to the duplicators. For PC games, usually a patch follows shortly thereafter, since the game was never properly finished in the first place. Why is computer game development so unpredictable while film production is so predictable? Granted, Hollywood has been making movies for a lot longer than the computer game industry has been making games, which gives them a leg up. But beyond that, Hollywood is making a much more predictable product. Different movies may have unique stories and characters, and may even use a variation on cinematic techniques, but much of filmmaking is a known quantity.

Doom offered gameplay so different from any game that came before it that the game's development was something of a bold experiment.

Original games, on the other hand, are a totally new animal every time. Part of the problem is the shifting technology targets, where programmers must learn about new consoles, operating systems, and 3D accelerator cards for each project. Add to that the fact that so many games feel the need to have a cutting-edge graphics engine. But purely from a design standpoint, a truly original game is far more unique compared to other contemporary games than a movie is to other films being made at the same time. Consider games like *Civilization, The Sims*, or *Doom*. The gameplay contained in these games was radically different from anything that came before them. Granted, many games are far less experimental and innovative than the games I just listed, and games that have followed more of a formula have had a much better success rate in terms of coming out on time and on budget. This includes titles such as the Infocom adventure games, the Sierra adventure titles, the annual revisions of sports games, or the new versions of arcade driving games. However, these are games that, though including new content consisting of new stories and graphics, offer gameplay very much the same as the previous year's offerings. When a game tries to implement a new form of gameplay, even if it is only a variation on a proven theme, all hope of predictability in its development is thrown to the four winds.

Only truly talented designers have any hope of predicting what is going to be fun or not in a game, and even the most experienced designers will tell you that they use a lot of prototyping, experimentation, and general floundering around until they come up with the gameplay they want. These talented veteran designers do not have crystal balls; they only have an improved chance of anticipating what will make for compelling gameplay. They do not truly "know" more than anyone else.

The closest thing game development has to a reliable system for developing an original game is to get some small part of the gameplay working first, before moving ahead to build the rest of the game. This may be called a prototype, a demo, a proof-of-concept, a level, or simply the current build of the game. This is not merely a demo to show off the game's technology. Instead, it is something that shows off the game's gameplay, which incorporates preliminary versions of all the features described in the game's focus, as discussed in Chapter 5. This demo should be something any member of the development team can pick up, play, and say, "Yes, this is fun, I want to play this." By concentrating on getting a small piece of the game fully functional and enjoyable, the developer can get a much better sense of whether the final game is going to be any fun or not. If the gameplay just does not turn out as anticipated, the prototype provides an early enough warning that the game needs to either be redirected in a more promising direction or, in the worst cases, aborted entirely.

The Organic Process

In the games I work on, I prefer to keep the development process as organic as possible and I try not to plan anything out beyond what is necessary at that stage in development. This may be the opposite of the approach many development studios prefer, but I find it to be the most effective method for developing the best game possible. Due to the highly unpredictable nature of game design, which I discussed above, a more organic process leaves me room and time to experiment with how the gameplay will work. Instead of writing a mammoth document, I can first try to get some portion of the game to be fun before I start adding detail and length to the game. Of course, keeping the process organic needs to be balanced with concerns about budget, schedule, and keeping a large team of developers occupied. Indeed, having too many developers too soon on a project can be a real problem, as they will have to move forward on creating content before you are sure what that content should be. Adding too much content to the game too early can be very wasteful, if not actually restrictive. This excessive detail can take the form of an elaborate design document, a script for the game's dialog, detailed maps of the various areas players will explore, or even fully built levels for the game. It makes no sense whatsoever to create these elements of the game until you have a firm grasp on what the gameplay will be, and have a working prototype that proves the gameplay to be fun.

Too Much Too Soon

The problem with creating scripts, documents, or levels without a prototype is that these assets will make assumptions about how the gameplay will function, assumptions that may turn out to be incorrect once the gameplay is actually functional. If a designer builds an elaborate game design on principles that turn out to be flawed, the entire game design will probably need to be reworked or, more likely, thrown away. But if people have devoted large amounts of time to creating these flawed assets, they are going to be understandably reluctant to throw them away. If a designer gets too attached to those ideas, even if they later prove to be unworkable, she may try to cling to them. This is an understandable natural human tendency. After all, a lot of work went into planning the game in advance via a long design document — how can it all just be thrown away? Cannot the assets be reworked to be usable? If you are not bold enough to throw away your inappropriate content, in the end you run the risk of producing a game that is patched together after the fact instead of built from the start with a clear sense of direction.

When I set about working on my first published game, *Odyssey: The Legend of Nemesis*, admittedly I had little idea of what I was doing. I had inherited a game engine and some portion of the game's mechanics from the previous developer. At the time, the project was very meagerly funded, and as a result, the publisher only requested a meager amount of documentation about where the game was going. I drew up a six-page document that briefly described all of the adventures players would go on. First of all, since the document was not very detailed, with just one page per major island in the game, that left me lots of room to maneuver. Second, by the time I had implemented the first two islands, I had learned enough about how the game truly worked that I decided to throw away the last three islands and design them over again. Since I had only written brief outlines of the gameplay in the first place, I did not actually lose much work.

Keeping the development documentation light and using placeholder art kept *Odyssey's* development extremely organic.

Another interesting aspect of *Odyssey's* creation was that I developed the game entirely using placeholder art. Along with the game's engine, I had inherited a fair amount of art from another project, and kept using that as much as possible. Since the project was underfunded, I did not have an artist to work with during most of the game's development, so this decision was made more out of necessity than foresight.

However, it did mean that by the time I had the money to hire artists to finish the project, all of the game's design was done and fully playable, and as a result the artists created almost no art for the game that went unused. Using the placeholder art had not hindered the game's development in the slightest. I concentrated first on getting all of the gameplay working, and then was able to focus on the visuals. Since I was not constrained by the thought of losing already created art assets if I changed the design, I was able to take the design in whatever direction seemed most appropriate while I was working on it.

On *Centipede 3D*, a significant amount of work was done before the gameplay was actually fun, and almost all of that work had to be thrown out as a result. The original idea for the gameplay had little to do with how the original *Centipede* functioned from a gameplay standpoint, and featured a more meandering, less-directed style of play. Using this original gameplay conception, six levels were actually built and numerous other levels were planned out on paper. For various reasons, the gameplay simply was not much fun, and we began to look at what could be done to fix that problem. In the end, we made the enemy AI function more like the original game's enemies and adjusted the gameplay accordingly. When we tried it we were not sure if it would work, but that gameplay style turned out to work quite well. Unfortunately, much of the level design work that had been done was lost. All of the levels that had been designed on paper were thrown away because they were incompatible with this new style of gameplay. Of the six levels that had been actually built, three had to be discarded in order to support the new gameplay, while the others had to be changed significantly in order to play well.

Looking back, if we had focused on making the gameplay fun before making a large number of levels, we could have avoided a lot of extra work and wasted effort. With the gameplay functional, we were able to draw up documents describing how the rest of the game would function. For the most part, we were able to hold to those documents throughout the remainder of the development process, with only minor changes necessary. Of course it would have been catastrophic to the project if we had been unable or unwilling to throw away the work we had already done. If we had tried to keep all of the levels without changing them significantly, the game would have shown it and those levels would have been greatly inferior to the ones made with the proper gameplay in mind. If we had been foolish enough to stick to the initial design completely, the entire game would have suffered and the end product would not have been as fun as it turned out to be.

Keep It Simple

Early in development, it makes sense to work with only your focus instead of a long design document. The focus is short enough that it can easily be completely rewritten if your game changes direction. Yet, at the same time, the focus will give you a clear direction for what you are trying to achieve with the gameplay you are endeavoring to implement. In the prototyping stage, the focus may change many, many times as you shift the game's goals to match what you find to be working out in terms of gameplay. When your prototyping is done, you will have a solid focus that you can reasonably hope to follow for the rest of the game's development.

Unfortunately, you may not always have the option of keeping the game design process organic. If you are working for an established company, you may have a fully staffed team working on your project from the very beginning, and those people need to be kept busy making art, building levels, or coding up systems, even though there may not yet be a functional and fun gameplay prototype. It does not take a large team to get the initial gameplay working, and indeed such a large team may only get in your way as you try to keep them busy while experimenting with how the gameplay will work. You may also have demands from those funding your project's development, whether it is your employer or the publisher. Whoever is paying the bills may want to see a complete design document or script up front, before a prototype of the game has been developed. You may be forced to abandon those documents later as the gameplay turns out to work differently than you had anticipated. Obviously, crafting these documents prematurely can be quite wasteful, yet you are forever beholden to whomever is providing the funding for your project. In some ways, if at all possible, it may make sense to self-fund the project until you have a fully functional prototype. Work on it "under the radar" if you are at a large company, or work on the gameplay prototype before you try to find a publisher. Besides, a playable demo will make the game easier to sell to a publisher or a green-light committee. Nothing proves to the financiers that your game is moving in the right direction better than a compelling prototype.

Building the Game

The best way to build your game is incrementally. Instead of working a little bit on all the different components of the game, you should try to complete one system before moving on to the next. Work on the most basic and essential systems first, and then build the systems that depend on that system. This allows you to implement a system, test it out, see if it "feels" right, and only then move on to the next system. That way, if you must change the underlying system to get it to work properly, your subsequent systems can be changed accordingly, before you have gone to the trouble of implementing them. It can often lead to disaster when you have a number of programmers concurrently working on coding up a variety of systems that work together. If one system has to change, other systems may need to be radically reworked. Better to build a solid foundation before trying to build on top of it. Programmers often enjoy working on their own isolated part of the code without fully considering how it will have to interface with the rest of the project. It is important for your programming team to be constantly focused on the big picture of making the game playable and fun.

Core Technology

Of course, all computer games rely on an underlying technology that has very little to do with the gameplay, usually referred to as the game's engine. Certainly you need to make sure that this underlying technology functions at a certain level before any work can be done on the gameplay. However, you do not need the engine to be perfect or feature complete before you can start building your prototype. Indeed, on a project with a cutting-edge engine, waiting until the engine is truly finished may mean it is too late to spend enough time refining the game itself. The peril of working with unknown technology is designing around projections of the capabilities of the technology. If you design your game thinking you will be able to have ten enemies on the screen at once and your engine turns out to be able to handle only three, you will need to radically alter your design to accommodate this restriction. It should be no surprise that the best-designed games are often ones that did not use the most cutting-edge technology available when they were released.

If the technology is simply not ready, I know a number of game designers who start off prototyping their game using technology from a previous project. It is rare that technology will actually make or break a game design, though it may make or break the game itself. But technology, as unpredictable as it may sometimes be, is still more of a known quantity than game design, so it makes sense not to worry about it when you are first prototyping your game. Since the first few areas you create should probably be thrown away later anyway, it is not that wasteful to get them working using a technology that you will eventually throw away as well.

Licensing technology can be a tremendous boon to game development, and is becoming increasingly common. Pictured here: the oft-licensed *Unreal* engine being used in *Unreal Tournament 2004.*

In recent years engine licensing has become much more common in the industry. This takes the form of using technology from a specific game such as *Half-Life* or *Unreal* or from a technology-only company that creates more robust engines designed to work for a variety of projects on a variety of platforms; examples include Criterion's Renderware and NDL's Gamebryo. The proliferation of licensed engines means that the majority of projects no longer need to wait for their technology to be built and more and more game developers have the luxury of starting out knowing what they will and will not be able to accomplish technically.

Incremental Steps

Once your technology is to a point where you can start developing the gameplay as I mentioned earlier, try to break down the game design into the most fundamental tasks that need to be accomplished and then the tasks that build on those. For example, suppose you are building an action game in which players navigate a humanoid character around the game-world, fighting insurance agents with a flyswatter while collecting kiwi fruits. Getting the player's navigation system working is a logical first task to tackle. First, get the character moving forward and backward and turning, allowing for basic navigation of the world. Work on this movement until it feels pretty good, until you find yourself enjoying playing the game in this simple, navigation-only way. Now you can build on that by adding more movement options, such as strafing, crouching, and jumping. As you add each new movement type, make sure that it does not break any of the previous types of movement and that they all work well together. Only once that is firmly in place should you try adding the ability for players to use the flyswatter. With the flyswatter fun to use, at least in some limited way, it makes sense to add the insurance agents into the game. The AI functionality can be broken down into building blocks just like the players' movement was. First, get the AI agents in the world so that players can whack them with the flyswatter. Next, get the agents moving around the game-world before finally adding the ability for them to do their "audit" or "excessive paperwork" attack. Finally, you can add the kiwis to the world and the ability for players to pick them up and launch them with their flyswatter. What is essential in this step-by-step process is that at each step along the way the game is still playable and fun. When you add something to the game that breaks a previous portion or simply makes it less fun, you must address this problem immediately. Now is the time to alter your design as necessary, before the game swings into full production.

Throughout the project's development, I think it is important to always keep a version of your game playable. You should get your game playable in some primitive form as soon as possible, ideally from day one, and keep it that way until you ship. Often programming teams will go for a long time coding up various pieces of the game without having a functional version that someone can sit down and play. It is very easy to lose sight of your gameplay goals when your game languishes in an unplayable state for much of the time. Certainly the game can be broken in many ways, with various components that do not yet work as they are supposed to and with placeholder art used in many locations. But as long as you always have a playable game, team members are able to pick it up and play it, and see what they are working on and how it impacts the game. And if anything added or changed makes this playable version of the game less fun, you can immediately discover this problem and rectify it.

A Fully Functional Area

Once you have many of the elements of your game mechanics working and you are happy with them, the next step is to make an entire section of the game that functions just like you want it to play in the final game. In many game genres this means one particular level of the game. You may think you have all of the components of your gameplay functional, but once you actually try to make an entire area playable you will quickly discover what you forgot to implement or failed to anticipate. Concentrate on getting this one level as close to a final state as possible before moving on to the creation of other levels. If you are observant you will learn many lessons about how level design must work for your particular game through the creation of this one level, lessons that will help to eliminate the element of guesswork from the creation of the other levels in the game. Once you are done with this level, it will no longer be the best you can do; you will have learned a lot, and subsequent levels you create will be better planned from the beginning. Though you do not need to throw away this prototype level yet, keep in mind that you should probably scrap it before the game ships.

The first network level made for *Damage Incorporated*, pictured here, was also the worst one in the game. It would have been better to scrap it and construct a new one.

One example of this is from the development of my game *Damage Incorporated*. The very first level I created for the single-player game was done before I fully understood the game mechanics or the level creation tools I would be using. As a result it was far from fun to play and was quickly thrown away. The next level I made, though certainly not the best in the game, was good enough to make the final cut. For this level, I had deliberately picked a map from the middle of the game, so that it would not be the very first content players would see since I knew my mapmaking ability would improve after I had a few more under my belt. It is often a good idea to start developing your content from the middle of the game. Early parts of the game need to be at the highest level of quality possible, so you want them to represent your more seasoned efforts, while levels at the end of the game will often tend to be more atypical and hence will not represent the "regular" gameplay that you want to have working first.

Damage Incorporated also included death-match style multi-player, which used a completely different set of levels. Due to time constraints, I spent significantly less time balancing the network play than I would have liked. In particular, the first level I created for the network game, "My Mind is Numb, My Throat is Dry," ended up not being much fun to play. It had a number of cool areas but they did not flow together very well and a number of sections in the level were unfair and unbalanced death traps. One of my playtesters even suggested it would be best to throw it away and start a new level from scratch. Unfortunately, I did not have the time to make a replacement and it ended up shipping with the game. Fortunately there were seven other network levels that were significantly more fun to play. Nonetheless, it would have been better if I had completely scrapped my first attempt at a network level and made a new one instead.

On *The Suffering*, the first level we built was the first level of the game. Interestingly, it ended up shipping in a form fairly close to how it was originally planned, and was one of our strongest levels. In part this was because we were a fairly experienced team working with a relatively known gameplay mechanic (a shooter). An equal part of the level's success was luck. Though it succeeded from a game design standpoint, from a technological standpoint that first level was built in such a way that it was a nightmare for level designers to edit and constantly pushed the limits of our technology. It was also one of the more complex levels in the game, with the player able to return to it later in the game-flow, thus making it contain double the amount of logic found in most levels. Because of the lessons learned from that level, subsequent levels were far more conservative. Though building the first level first worked out creatively in the case of *The Suffering*, the many problems we faced with it from a production standpoint demonstrate the problems with building the first level first.

Something you must be conscious of as you are building the first fully playable section of your game is how difficult the game is to play. Often difficulty can be adjusted and tweaked later in the development process, during playtesting and balancing. However, games also have a fundamental difficulty, which is more intrinsic to their nature and which cannot be easily adjusted late in the development cycle. As you are working on getting your gameplay prototype working, try to look at it honestly in terms of how difficult it will be for novice players to get into. Bring in some friends or coworkers and have them play the game. Observe how easily they manage to pick up the controls and mechanics. It is much simpler to make a game harder than to make it easier. If you find that your game is turning out to be harder to play than you had hoped, now is the time to alter the game design in order to make the game easier to play, before it is too late. I encountered an instance of this problem in *Centipede 3D*, a game that was far more difficult than we had hoped when it shipped. This was in part because it was based on a coin-op arcade game that was designed to kill the player within four minutes of play, and partly because we developers had played the game so much it did not seem difficult to us. By the time we realized the game was too hard it was too close to shipping to fix it. Because of the game's simple mechanics (the player and her adversaries all are killed by a single hit from adversaries) there was little that could be easily tweaked to make the game easier, short of redesigning the way the AI agents worked. If we had identified our difficulty problem earlier, we could have made fundamental changes to the game to make it easier to play.

Going Through Changes

A big part of the organic process of game design is being able to throw away your own work and, potentially, that of the rest of your team. This includes art, code, levels, and even general design itself; all of the game's content may need to change as your gameplay evolves. A particular asset may not be flawed in and of itself, but if it does not gel properly with the way the gameplay is working out, you may need to abandon that asset and start from scratch. Many developers are unwilling to do this, and it shows in their games. Either their games are shackled to an initial design document that turned out not to work as well in practice as it did in theory, or their games retain a hodgepodge of components from before their direction was finalized. Once a designer decides that the game's direction needs to change, all of the assets of the game must be assessed to see if they can fit with that new direction. If they cannot, they must be reworked or remade.

As I have discussed, *Centipede 3D* changed course significantly in the middle of development, which caused us to throw away a large amount of work. Fortunately, no one on the team was unhappy to do so, since we all realized it was in the best interests of the project. With other projects I have worked on, I have been more stubborn and ignored the pleadings of coworkers and friends when they said something needed to be reworked or changed. I was reluctant to throw away perfectly good work, even though it no longer fit with the game. Thus I can say from my own experience that sometimes the first step in fixing the problems with your game design is admitting that you have a problem.

Of course, you have to be careful not to go too far in the other direction by discarding usable content. As you work on a project, you are likely to become overly familiar with some of the content you have created, and familiarity can breed contempt. For example, after working with a level for a long time, a designer is likely to become sick of looking at the same geometry day after day. The designer may then feel the need to rework that level, not because it really needs it, but simply because it will be something new. This is wasted effort, since for first-time players, the level will be new and exciting. Changing your game's content just for the sake of changing it can lead to extra debugging time, delays in shipping your project, and general frustration for team members who do not know why perfectly good work is being thrown away and redone.

First impressions are very important, especially in game design. Always try to remember how you first felt when you played a level or tried to pull off a particular move. Was it too hard or too easy? Was it intuitive or confusing? Another big problem with working on a project for a long time is that the designers can grow accustomed to flaws in the design. Maybe the controls are unintuitive or a particular enemy attacks players in an arbitrary and unfair way. As they play the game repeatedly, designers will learn to overcome and avoid these problems in the game design, giving them the false impression that nothing is wrong with the game. Playtesting is an essential tool for revealing the weaknesses in the game design that the development team has grown accustomed to, as I discuss in Chapter 25, "Playtesting." However, before you get to the playtesting stage, try to always remember your first impression of a particular aspect of the game. It may even be appropriate to take notes when you first play a mechanic or section of the game; do not assume you will remember your impressions later. You may not fix everything in these notes right away, but for problems you keep in the back of your mind as needing improvement in the future, the notes will prove invaluable. As you near the end of development, ask yourself if the problems you saw back when you first played the game have been fixed or if they are still present, creating frustration for others who experience the game for the first time. Whenever possible, even if you do take notes, it is best to fix these problems as soon as you observe them because over time you are likely to forgive the game's subtler problems.

Programming

This chapter is written from the point of view of someone who is a designer and a programmer, as I have been on all of my projects. Being in such a position has many unique advantages, especially in terms of being able to experiment with gameplay. A designer/programmer is able to have an idea for some gameplay and then can instantly attempt to implement it exactly how she wants it. A designer who does not program is forced to first communicate her idea for the gameplay to the programmer and hope that the design is understood. Often the communication will break down and the designer will not get exactly what she wanted or the feature in question may have an inferior implementation than what the designer had in mind. As a result, either the game is weaker or the designer must go back to the programmer and try to explain how a particular feature is actually supposed to work. Since game design is such an iterative and experimental process, there must be a constant circle of feedback between the designer and the programmer. Obviously, this process is greatly simplified if the designer and programmer are the same person.

I often find that, as a designer who programs, I can try out ideas much more easily. In fact, many of the ideas I have I would feel bad trying to get someone else to work on, since I lack the confidence in them myself to waste someone else's time with them. But in the end some of these strange ideas turn out to work quite well in the game, and if I had never been able to experiment with the code myself, the ideas might never have been attempted.

A designer/programmer will also often be able to better understand the technology involved in a project, and be more able to see what is easily accomplished and what is not. Often a designer who is not a programmer or who is not technologically savvy will suggest gameplay that is very difficult to implement in the engine. It may be that a different, though equally functional type of gameplay will work better with the game's technology, and if the designer/programmer (or at least a designer with programming experience) notices that, she will be able to greatly simplify the game's development. Say a designer wants a certain sword to have a particular behavior to communicate to the players that it is enchanted. The designer may request that the sword physically appear to bend somewhat within the player character's hand. The programmer assigned to set up this functionality curses the designer, knowing this is a practically impossible task given the constraints of the engine they are using. The designer does not realize that creating a fancy particle system around the sword is much easier to do, though she would be perfectly happy with that solution. As a result, the programmer, not wanting to seem difficult by resisting the designer's request, spends a lot of time on a challenging implementation, when a much simpler one would have satisfied the designer had she understood the technology better and requested it. Understanding the feasibility of ideas is a skill that comes with understanding how game programming fundamentally works, and how the engine you are working with is architected. Even if you are not actively programming on the project you are developing, you can better understand what can be easily accomplished with the technology and what feature will suck away resources for months without adding that much to the game.

Another problem arises when the designer and programmer have different ideas of what the gameplay for the project should be. I have heard one designer refer to this as the "pocket veto." A designer may come to a programmer with an explanation of how gameplay for a particular section of the game should work, and if the programmer does not agree, she can simply not implement what the designer has requested. She may even pretend that the designer's request is very hard or actually impossible to implement when it is not. Fortunately, programmers who pull these kinds of tricks do not tend to last long in the industry. Nonetheless, a designer who cannot program will be beholden to the talents and inclinations of her programmers, which can be eternally frustrating.

I am of the opinion that it is worth learning to program if you want to be a designer, even if you never manage to program up to professional standards and will never do any coding on the games you ship. Indeed, I originally pursued programming because I wanted to design computer games. It is beyond the scope of this book to actually teach you to program, and there are certainly plenty of books available to help you learn what you will need to work on games. Much of effective programming is a matter of discipline. And you do not even need to be a terribly good programmer to have it help your design out immensely. Indeed, almost all the designer/programmers I know will insist that they are not very good programmers, but that they are persistent enough to get what they want out of their games. As I have mentioned, knowing how to program will give you a better sense of what is easy to do in a game and what is hard, and programmers will respect you for attempting to better understand their side of game development. Furthermore, learning how to program will help teach you how to think logically and abstractly, a talent of vital importance to both programmers and game designers.

Of course, with modern projects and fifty-person development teams, it is often difficult to be both a designer and a programmer, simply due to the amount of time designers will need to spend on their own work and conveying their vision to the team. If you are not going to be programming on your project, it is essential that you have a lead programmer with a good sense of gameplay, someone whose opinion you can trust. Indeed, you will be well advised to only have programmers on your team who have a good sense of what makes games fun. In the end, there are an infinite number of small decisions that programmers make that will have a profound impact on the gameplay, details that no designer can anticipate. These little details have an enormous impact on the final game and determine how the game "feels" to play. Often, unmotivated or disinterested lead programmers can be found to be behind games that seem like good ideas in theory but just do not turn out to be any fun. Many projects have gone from promising starts to dissatisfying final products as the result of programmers who merely implement various features from a specification and never take a moment to look at the whole game and see if it is any fun.

This book includes interviews with seven people who are indisputably some of the most talented game designers in the history of the industry. It is interesting to note that of those seven, all were programmers at one point in their careers and programmed in some capacity on their most respected games. Indeed, back in the early days of the computer game industry, the development process was of a small enough scale that one person was doing all the work, so there was no need to separate the role of designer and programmer. Nonetheless, several of the interview subjects still serve as the lead programmer on their own projects. This is not to say that one cannot be a great designer without being a programmer, but I think designers who are able to program have a leg up on those who cannot, an advantage that allows them to make better games.

When Is It Fun?

Getting your gameplay working is one of the most essential parts of game design, yet it is also one of the most difficult to try to explain or teach. A lot of the process involves understanding what is fun about a game in a way that no book can ever explain. Indeed, a game's design changes so often during the implementation stage that I do not believe a designer who is not actively working on the game during that period can truly be considered to have designed it. If this so-called designer simply typed up a 200-page design document and handed it to the lead programmer to implement while the designer frolicked in Bora-Bora, the lead programmer was then responsible for making the fundamental decisions that made the game fun or dull, stimulating or insipid, enjoyable or tedious. When the designer is AWOL during the implementation process, the lead programmer is probably the one who is actually designing the game.

Game developers do their best work when working on games they care about and enjoy. The excellent *Grim Fandango* appears to be a perfect example.

So much of implementing your game design relies on personal "gut" reactions that it is no wonder people have great difficulty designing games for people other than themselves. This is why so many games that are aimed at the "mass market" but which are designed by people who are hard-core gamers turn out to be so terrible. The hard-core gamer doing the design wishes she was working on *Grim Fandango* but instead is stuck working on *Advanced Squirrel Hunting*. Even if she can overcome her contempt for the project itself, she will probably have no idea what the audience who may be interested in playing *Advanced Squirrel Hunting* wants in its games. Often features will be added to a game at the behest of marketing, over the protests of the development team. These features are always the worst in the game, not necessarily because they are bad ideas, but because the development team does not understand why they need to be added to the game or how they might improve the gameplay experience. In the end, it is very hard to design a good game that you yourself do not enjoy playing. If you do not like playing it, it is unlikely that others will either, even if they technically fall into the demographic you were so carefully targeting.

The first step in designing a game is to get some portion of the gameplay working and playable. Once you have a prototype that you can play and find to be compelling and fun in the right quantities, you should step back and make sure that you have a firm grasp on what makes it fun and how that can be extended to the rest of the game. With that prototype as a model, you can now move on to make the rest of the content for the game, replicating the fundamental nature of the gameplay while keeping the additional content new and interesting. Now that you know that your game design is a good one, it may finally make sense to craft a thorough design document that explains that gameplay and explores what variations on it may be used for the rest of the game. This will provide a valuable guideline for the rest of the team in fleshing out the game. In some ways, once the prototype is working, the truly creative and challenging part of game design is done, and the rest of the game's development is simply repeating it effectively.

Chapter 16:

Game Analysis: Myth: The Fallen Lords

Designed by Jason Jones
Released in 1997

Designer/programmer Jason Jones' games have always exploited technology in ways no one else has quite managed. His first title, *Minotaur*, was a network-only game before such things were fashionable (1992). It created a uniquely stimulating game by using networked human opponents who could not see each other's screens. *Pathways into Darkness* took simple 3D technology and applied it to an action/adventure hybrid to create an immersive, story-driven world. *Marathon*

and *Marathon 2* improved that 3D technology and applied it to an action game setting, but with a more thought provoking game-world than was found in other first-person shooters of its day. Most recently, *Halo* refined a lot of the concepts introduced in *Marathon*, taking the crude physics found in the older game and bringing it to a new level, while also incorporating vehicles, massive indoor/outdoor environments, and keenly smart AI characters, and finally wrapping it all in an intelligent and captivating science fiction setting. Between the first-person action of *Marathon* and *Halo*, however, Jones went off in an entirely new gameplay direction with the strategy game *Myth*, immersing players in epic battles of strategic combat as no other game had. What is most important to note, however, is that in none of these games does the technology come to dominate the gameplay, as is so often the case when a game uses cutting-edge technology. Instead, in Jones' games, technology and game design work together to accentuate each other's strengths and create uniquely compelling experiences.

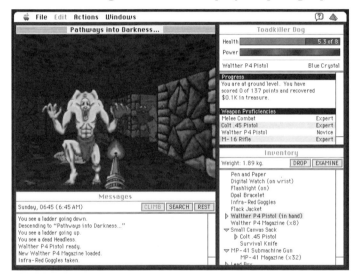

All the way back to his second game, *Pathways into Darkness*, Jason Jones' games have exploited technology to create new gameplay experiences.

Use of Technology

Myth is a good example of taking an established genre and then adding new elements to it in order to transmogrify it into something new and unique. The original genre in question here is real-time strategy games such as *WarCraft* and *Command & Conquer*, which had risen to tremendous popularity a year or so before development on *Myth* began. The games were so popular and seemed simple enough to develop from a technological standpoint that suddenly every publisher had to have one. A sea of clone games soon flooded the market. Most of these games attempted to function nearly identically to *WarCraft* and *Command & Conquer*, with minor improvements such as waypoint systems for unit movement and production queuing. These changes were far from revolutionary, however, and as a result, these games failed to offer any compelling reason for the public to purchase them. Consequently, they disappeared without a trace.

In a way, *Myth* was a part of the real-time strategy bandwagon, but Jones was too smart to just clone the success of RTS games. Instead, it would appear, he examined the games differently and questioned how they could be altered and improved on a more fundamental level. What if, instead of the 2D graphics technology that all of the games to date had used, a game used a truly 3D engine? With the sole exception of his first game, *Minotaur*, Jones' games to date had all been 3D, so it made sense for him to continue to use that technology for his new project. The 3D component would not be added merely for visual flair, however. As with id Software's *Wolfenstein 3D*, which years earlier had taken a relatively simple action game and, by incorporating 3D technology, dramatically changed the nature of the game design itself, *Myth* took strategy gameplay and molded it to suit the new technology. The result was an entirely new game design, not merely another clone.

However, it appears that the 3D technology used was not completely dictating the game's design direction. The 3D engine developed is one uniquely suited to modeling outdoor environments, and hence supporting RTS gameplay. Instead of taking the technology from his previous game, *Marathon 2*, and trying to make that work with a real-time strategy game, Jones wisely started over with a whole new engine. *Marathon 2* had used a *Doom*-style BSP engine, a technology suited for simple indoor, non-organic environments but not so conducive to the needs of RTS games, which require wide-open, outdoor environments to play well. So a new terrain engine was created that was uniquely suited to the gameplay requirements of a 3D RTS project.

Using its 3D terrain engine, *Myth* added new gameplay elements to the real-time strategy genre.

With the 3D technology in place, certain game design changes could be made to the fundamental RTS form as established by *WarCraft* and *Command & Conquer*. In *Myth*, the elevation of the terrain where combat took place would have a dramatic effect on how well players' units fared. Place the archers at the top of a hill for maximum effectiveness. Place them in a gully and watch them get slaughtered. *Myth* also uses a simple but effective physics system that serves to emphasize the 3D nature of the landscape. When players send a dwarf scurrying up a hill to throw one of his Molotov cocktails at an enemy atop that hill, they should be prepared for the bottle to possibly roll back down the hill before detonating. Should the projectile hit its intended target, players can marvel as the ground at the explosion point ripples in a visually interesting way, altering the landscape for the rest of the game. Of course, if the target is killed, players can expect the body parts of that destroyed enemy to roll back down the hill toward the dwarf.

Another significant improvement that results from the 3D engine is the ability of players to see the battlefield at a level of detail not possible in a top-down or isometric 2D game. Players can rotate the camera in order to see past objects that might obstruct their view or merely to find the perfect angle for a given battle. Furthermore, players can easily zoom in and out on the action. The zooming in has little gameplay benefit, and is almost exclusively useful for the visceral thrill of seeing a battle close-up, immersing players in the action in a way 2D RTS titles simply cannot. The angle of view is significantly different as well, being at a much lower angle relative to the battlefield than any strategy game that preceded it. The camera's position was no doubt chosen partly for aesthetic reasons and partly for gameplay considerations. Regardless of the motivations, the result of *Myth*'s close-up view of the battle is a decidedly more intimate experience for players, where the individual units become more important and more real than they ever do in an RTS game with a more removed perspective. Thus, the intimacy of a first-person shooter such as *Marathon* is married to the tactical gameplay of a strategy game, resulting in an entirely new type of gameplay experience.

The 3D engine employed by *Myth* is not all that sophisticated, especially by modern standards. The characters on the landscape, for instance, are simple sprites instead of being fully 3D polygonal beasts. This was no doubt important so that a great number of units could be on the screen at once. What fun would an RTS game be if one could only have three units on the screen at any one time? At the time, rendering a large number of fully 3D, humanoid creatures on the screen at once would have brought PCs to a crawl, and even today can be an extremely challenging undertaking.

In *Myth*, every bit of technology is used to its greatest gameplay effect, as is typical of projects run by designer/programmers such as Jones. This hybrid developer understands what the technology can do perfectly while also understanding what would be compelling in terms of gameplay, making for very economical game development. Thus, when the technology does something that can enhance the gameplay, the designer/programmer instantly notices it and is able to exploit it to its maximum effect. This differs greatly from so many projects where programmers implement complicated functionality that is never used because the designers never fully understand it.

Of course, adapting gameplay from 2D to 3D is not without its drawbacks. For instance, despite being able to zoom in and out in *Myth*, one is never able to zoom out from the action quite as much as one would like. This is in part because of the precedent set by other RTS games, which, because of their 2D engines, can have a much more distant viewpoint, a viewpoint that lends itself to tracking and moving large numbers of units. A patch was released for *Myth* shortly after its publication that allowed players to zoom the camera out farther, but with the side effect of decreasing their frame rate, since more landscape and hence more polygons are now in view. Of course, the engine could probably support viewing the landscape from still farther away, but the amount of polygons on the screen would quickly become prohibitive, decreasing the game's overall speed unacceptably. Thus, the limitations of a 3D engine come to constrain the gameplay choices the designer can make. Another gameplay drawback that results from the technology is the often confusing camera. Though the camera is able to rotate to view whatever side of the action is desired, this camera rotation can often become jarring and disorienting, causing the players to lose track of different locations and units on the map. It is as if previous strategy games had used a skilled cameraman who generally showed players what they wanted, but for *Myth* the job was handed off to the players, who could then look at exactly what part of the world they wanted. Unfortunately, most players were not quite up to the challenge of framing the action themselves. For a novice, a casual gamer, or anyone without a good sense of direction, the camera's movement would probably be altogether unmanageable.

Game Focus

Myth's gameplay is entirely focused on tactical combat, leaving out the resource management found in many other RTS games.

Myth is also a good example of a well-focused game design. As mentioned previously, *Myth* came out several years after the success of two other RTS titles, *Command & Conquer* and *WarCraft*. In both of those games, players build structures that exploit the terrain's natural resources in order to create additional units. Players are then able to direct these units against their opponents in a combination of ways. Thus, those trend-setting RTS games are a mixture of gameplay — part resource management and building, part combat. Many of the subsequent RTS titles, both the successes and the failures, copied this general model, dividing players' efforts between unit creation, resource exploitation, and strategic unit deployment.

But *Myth* does not feature any resources to be mined or structures to be built. Instead players are focused entirely on the tactical side of the game, on the combat experience. Players start out on a level with a given quantity of units, and for most of the levels in the game those are the only units they get for that entire level. In some scenarios, additional units are acquired later in the level, but those scenarios are the exceptions rather than the norm. *Myth* does away with everything except for the combat elements of RTS games, which gives its gameplay a unique focus.

This tactical emphasis has several ramifications on the overall game design. First, by not needing to worry about developing a resource exploitation system, Jones was able to focus on making the combat model as good as it could be. This resulted in more sophisticated and detailed combat than was found in any other RTS game at the time. In *Myth*, unit facing, formation, and placement matter more than they had in other strategy titles. Because the developers did not have to worry about how players would use resources, more time could be spent on the physics system and other technologies that would enhance the combat experience. For example, this attention to detail meant that archers needed to worry about finding a clear shot through the trees, how the weather would effect the trajectory of their arrows, and how their vertical placement on the landscape would impact the distance they could shoot.

Players' inability to build additional units also affects the care with which they use the units at the start of a level. In *WarCraft* one can make a very substantial blunder early on in a level and still be able to win by wise resource usage and unit creation. In *Myth*, such an error is often fatal, with the levels becoming less and less forgiving as the game progresses. Players' only recourse when their plan of attack fails is to reload the level. This makes for a very different kind of gameplay than is found in *WarCraft*. In *Myth*, players must think through their actions fully instead of just trying whatever first pops into their heads. The units are much more precious and, as a result, players start caring for their welfare. Since more can be made easily, the units in *WarCraft* may seem like just so much cannon fodder. Conversely, in *Myth* a particular unit may be crucial to finishing a level, and there is no way to bring him back once he is killed.

Storytelling

Despite its exemplary game design, a large component of *Myth* is its storytelling, which is conducted using a number of well-integrated devices. First are the cut-scenes, which appear sporadically throughout the game, outlining major plot points and setting up certain levels. These are often used more as "teasers" than to really advance the story significantly. Second are the mission briefings, which precede each level. These contain a large amount of detail about the progression of the war between the Light and the Dark (the game's two opposing forces). They also give meaning to the upcoming level, making the mission objective more than just some arbitrary task picked by the level designer.

Third, and most interesting, are the in-game storytelling devices that are used. Of course, the levels are set in locations that match the needs of the story line, whether it is a frostbitten, barren mountain area or a smoldering lava pit. The battles and missions contained in the level match up with the story as explained by the mission briefings. But players can also see and hear exchanges between different characters within the game. For instance, a townsperson may advise the players' units of the location of a traitor. Players' troops may provide advice such as, "We'd better get back to the bridge!" Though players never lose control of their units, the game is able to trigger these bits of dialog at different key points in the levels. In one mission, as the players' troops approach an insurmountable mass of Myrmidons, the Avatara that players have been guarding steps forward and says, "Let me handle this." He begins a conversation with the Fetch leading the opposing forces and the story line unfolds right there in the game-world during game-time.

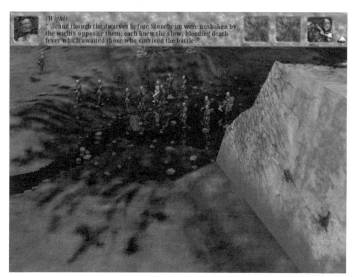

Myth tells a compelling story through a combination of mission briefings, level design, and gameplay.

In contrast to the majority of games that use storytelling as little more than an add-on to an already existing group of levels, *Myth* makes the story line, levels, and gameplay dependent on each other, strengthening each as a result. Players enjoy games because they enjoy the gameplay, not because the games are accompanied by long, non-interactive cut-scenes. Yet players do enjoy having stories in their games, since they can give the gameplay meaning. The best way to communicate a deep story is by making it integral to the gameplay and by revealing a little bit of it here and there during actual game-time, something *Myth* does expertly. Of course, the fact that *Myth*'s story line is top-notch, the script is well written, and the voice acting is professional certainly helps. Telling a story line through gameplay will not do a game a bit of good if the plot is hackneyed, the dialog is contrived, or the voice acting is amateurish.

Hard-Core Gaming

Myth is a game design by hard-core gamers for hard-core gamers and makes no apologies about it. Far from trying to capture the "mainstream" or "casual" gamer market that so many companies have tried to court, *Myth* is a game that would quickly frighten away anyone who is not already familiar with other RTS games and who does not have the quick-clicking skills required by *Myth*. There is nothing wrong with this, of course, and it is pleasing to see a game that has the artistic conviction to know its audience and to stick to it. Indeed, since the game's developers are among the ranks of the hard-core gamers, it only makes sense that they will best know how to make a game that this audience will like. Often, when hard-core gamers try to make a game that the mythical casual gamer will enjoy, they end up making a game they themselves do not like very much, and that the casual gamer does not care much about either. It is very hard for an artist to make art that appeals to sensibilities that are at odds with his own, the end result often being works that are without appeal to any group or demographic.

But *Myth* did not have this problem; its developers created a game that no casual gamer would ever be able to pick up. One reason for this is the incredibly sophisticated and challenging set of controls. For instance, consider the control of the 3D rotating camera. As opposed to other RTS games at the time, where the camera could only move horizontally along with the terrain, *Myth*'s camera can move horizontally, zoom in or zoom out, rotate around a point, or orbit around a point. Even experienced game players find it somewhat challenging to get used to this system. However, once the camera's movements are mastered, one finds that they are expertly designed and provide all of the freedom one could reasonably expect given the technology the game uses. The game is also littered with special keys for different commands, such as formations, special actions, and alternate attacks. Again, these commands, once mastered, provide players with a large degree of control over how their units move and attack, but do take some time to learn. Indeed, these keys make the game impossible to play with only the mouse, something almost all other RTS games focus on. The "gesture-clicking" is another interesting feature, used for pointing units in a certain direction when they reach a given location. The system for gesture-clicking is quite powerful yet nearly impossible to learn without being taught in person or by practicing a great deal. Nonetheless, for the hard-core players who are willing to put in the time to learn the controls, the end result is an extremely enjoyable game-playing experience.

Myth is also an inherently hard game. Even for players experienced at RTS titles, the game will prove to be extraordinarily difficult from the get-go. Customarily, games include a few simple levels toward the beginning of the game, in order to give players a fighting chance while they are still learning the controls. *Myth* does not. Immediately, players are presented with barely accomplishable goals, where one mistake may make the level virtually unwinnable. By streamlining the game to focus on the tactical experience, players have much less of a chance to come back from behind since there is literally no way to rebuild their troops. The loss of a particular unit will often cause seasoned players to conclude that the level is now too hard to beat, so why bother? They will just restart the level instead. The sad thing is that, despite their great difficulty, the levels toward the beginning of the game are the easy levels, with the levels becoming exponentially harder from there. However, this is the sort of challenge that truly hard-core game players thrive on. It is not that the challenges are unfair, arbitrary, or unpredictable, at least not always. In most cases, players can beat the levels on their first time through; it is just extraordinarily difficult to do so.

Myth is the kind of game that many publishers would demand be simplified so that non-hard-core gamers would not be frightened off by its complex controls or sadistic level of difficulty. But if the game were simplified significantly, would it still be as compelling as it is now? Probably not. For whatever small number of casual gamers might be gained, large numbers of hard-core gamers would be lost.

Multi-Player

As with the *Marathon* games before it and the *Halo* games after it, Bungie created *Myth* to excel both as a single-player game and as a multi-player experience. What is most notable about this is that Bungie manages to do both so well. Many games are criticized for emphasizing one over the other. *Quake* and *Quake II*, for instance, were both praised for their solid network play while being lambasted for their lackluster single-player games. Many other games seem to add multi-player support as an afterthought, hoping to get another bullet point on the back of the box. *Centipede 3D* is a good example of this, where multi-player was added late in the project as a marketing consideration, and almost no design time was spent making it any fun.

Bungie's well-publicized strategy for making a game that excels in both the single- and multi-player arenas is worth noting. After they have established the core engine technology for their game, getting the networking functional is the next step. Once it works, the entire team starts playing network games, and keeps playing them until they are fun. At this point no work has begun on the single-player game, and the team is entirely focused on enhancing the network play experience. Only after the networking game's core design is completed does the team start work on the single-player game. However, this is not to say that the single-player game is rushed. Instead, this technique forces the team to have rock-solid preproduction completed before time is spent on the single-player game. This means that the entire team knows what "works" and makes the game fun before any solo levels are even created, resulting in less rework on those levels and leading to more entertaining levels in the final product.

It is because the team has spent so much time playing the multi-player game that the net games have the depth to hold up over time. If the team were creating a shallow experience, they would quickly grow tired of it. *Myth*'s multi-player allows for many different game types with a variety of goals, all of which require different playing styles. The interesting pre-game unit trading system allows players to think up their own "killer" team, much like players of *Magic: The Gathering* spend time developing the perfect deck of cards. Team play, where multiple players control one set of allied units and go up against another team, opens up many possibilities for strategies too complex for a single person to pull off. It is because of the time Bungie's development team spent playing the multi-player game that it has such impressive staying power.

A Cohesive Whole

Myth is also littered with little design touches that add a certain luster to the solid foundation of the core design. Whereas missions in other RTS games exist as separate, self-contained play-spaces, in *Myth* the missions become a part of the whole due to the use of "veteran" units. These units, if they survive a given battle, will be available for players to use on the next level, and their skills will be noticeably stronger than the greenhorn units. This makes players treat those units with special care, expending the greenhorns on more dangerous explorations. Another nice touch is the ability of the units to leave footprints in the terrain, which adds an interesting element to tracking down enemies on snow-covered levels. The variety of missions available provides a much more diverse set of goals than many other RTS games, causing players to modify their gameplay style drastically from level to level.

Of course, *Myth* is not without its problems, even if one can accept the challenging controls and staggeringly difficult levels. Clicking around the overhead map sometimes causes the camera to rotate in ways players do not expect, possibly throwing off their orientation in the world and completely breaking their immersion. The overhead map is

Duri *(Dwarf)*
"The early Dwarven eddas always speak of heroes 'having gone north into the mountains to slay Ghôls', but most repeated is the tale of Dvalin son of Alfrigg, third ephor of Stoneheim ..."

Myth's developers paid a lot of attention to detail, which helped to create a deep gameplay experience.

actually translucent and drawn over the play-field, which can sometimes cause players to click in it by accident. The desire to see more of the play-field at once is a valid one, even if it is a limitation of the technology. Nevertheless, these are truly minor flaws in an overwhelmingly impressive design. *Myth* represents how a great game can grow out of the marriage of technology and gameplay. This is not a shotgun wedding, however, but instead one where the bride and groom have carefully thought out how they can happily live together, enhancing each other's strengths, thus creating something new and exciting in the process.

Chapter 17:
Game Development Documentation

"Omit needless words. Vigorous writing is concise. A sentence should contain no unnecessary words, a paragraph no unnecessary sentences, for the same reason that a drawing should have no unnecessary lines and a machine no unnecessary parts. This requires not that the writer make all his sentences short, or that he avoid all detail and treat his subjects only in outline, but that every word should tell."

— William Strunk in his book *The Elements of Style*

Many a game designer will proclaim himself better than development documents, and will make them only to suit the managers who demand their creation. Game design, these obstinate designers may insist, is something one cannot write down on a piece of a paper. And these designers are partly correct; writing quality development documentation is very difficult. Much of the development documentation you may come across seems to have been written merely for the sake of it, perhaps to placate a publisher who demands to see something on paper. Nonetheless, documentation does have a legitimate place in the creation of modern computer games, and it is the designer's job to make sure those documents are created, maintained, and used effectively.

The necessity of game development documentation is a side effect of the increasing size of game development teams. In the early days of game development, when a development team consisted of one multi-talented individual, documenting the functionality of the game was less important. If that one person was able to establish and implement a vision for the project's gameplay, it did not especially matter if he wrote it down or not.

As development teams grew from one to five, from five to ten, from ten to twenty, from twenty to thirty, and onward and upward, maintaining the project's focus became more and more of an issue. As members of the team became increasingly specialized in certain areas, a reference document they could turn to in order to see how a given system was supposed to function and how their work fit into the project became necessary. And so, various pieces of documentation came to be used, such as the design document, the art bible, the technical design document, and numerous other reference works for guiding the creation of a game's content. Development documents can be a key way of "holding the reins tightly" on a project, to make sure it does not spin out of control because of the impractical ambitions of team members. Writing down ideas and story components is a helpful way to quickly realize when a game is being overdesigned and whether the project can be completed on time.

Good documents have benefits not just for the production side of game development, but also for improving the game design itself. Chris Crawford has written more about game design than probably anyone else, as a visit to his web site (www.erasmatazz.com) will reveal. Crawford uses documents to refine and sharpen his own ideas and to track how a project evolves over the course of its development. Personally, I use a steno pad to keep all of my thoughts for a given project. I find that I can later go back and review these notes to see how I arrived at a particular design decision, and to recall good ideas that I have long since forgotten.

Of course, it is entirely possible to go too far in the other direction, to spend all of your time working on the documentation and none of it actually developing the game. And having a massive amount of repetitive documents is certainly not beneficial, especially if the team feels as though they are adrift in a sea of documentation, with none of it actually practical to their work. It is also possible to make games without any sort of documentation, but with a team of any size it will be extremely difficult. If one hopes to work at a development house or for a publisher that makes commercially viable, professional computer games, getting used to working with documentation is an absolute necessity.

Document Your Game

As a game designer, you will be primarily concerned with what is commonly called the design document, which I will explore in detail in Chapter 19. However, there are many other pieces of documentation used in the creation of modern computer games. Even though you may not work with all of these documents, it is important nonetheless to understand what each of them is supposed to contain and how the different documents are interrelated. So before delving into the nature of design documents, a survey of the different types of documents is appropriate. Different people at different companies or in different situations will invariably use a variety of different names for the documents listed below. You should realize that the naming convention I employ here is not universal, but the types of documents used are quite common throughout the game development industry.

Concept Document, Pitch Document, or Proposal

These are usually the first formal documents created for a given game. Often they are written in order to sell the idea of a game to a publisher (if the author works for a developer that does not publish its own work) or to upper management (at a company that publishes internally developed projects). In short, this document is shown to the green-light committee, the money, the suits, the decision makers, or whatever one may call them, in order to convince them to spend a lot of money on the idea, thereby funding its development. Concept documents are the seeds that have the potential to grow into a full game but all too often never get the opportunity. Concept documents are usually short in length, customarily no longer than ten pages, and in their more snazzy form include plenty of concept art. Often concept documents focus exclusively on high-level design issues, exploring the unique gameplay the title will provide, detailing the game's story, and generally pulling out all the stops to get the reader excited about the project. Writing a concept document can be quite a lot of fun, since the writer gets to focus on the most exciting parts of the game and does not have to worry about all the messy details of actually implementing the game. At the same time, it is important not to go overboard and promise the unattainable with your pitch document, since the more astute readers will quickly be able to pick up on the implausibility of your idea.

Concept documents can sometimes go a bit beyond the high-level ideas to become significantly more elaborate. In this case, they are often written by committee, typically involving the game's producer, lead designer, lead programmer, whatever marketing people may be on hand, and the lead artists who contribute a variety of sketches, conceptual pieces, and screen mockups. Concept documents discuss all aspects of the game idea in question, including how it might be positioned in the marketplace, budgets and development timelines, what technology will be used, what the art style of the game will be, mini-bios of the team members who hope to work on the game, and some broad description of the gameplay. These documents are not much use in the game's actual development, though they can be a springboard for creation of other documents, such as the design document or the art bible. Since concept documents do not apply very much to the game's actual development, I will not go into further detail about them.

Competitive Analysis

When writing a competitive analysis, you will need to include a discussion and potentially screenshots from the leaders in your title's genre. For an RTS title, you'd almost certainly want to discuss *WarCraft III*.

The competitive analysis is another document used in trying to sell your game. Sometimes competitive analyses are written in the early stages of a game that has already been green-lit, in order to clearly show the marketing department how the game will fare in the marketplace. It typically includes a shorter, more condensed version of the pitch document, and specifically lists the unique features of the game being developed. The competitive analysis then lists a number of other games that have shipped in the recent past that are similar to the proposed game, provides a brief synopsis of the fiction and gameplay of each, and then describes how each of these games performed (via average review score, quotes from various reviews, and sales figures, if available). For each of these previously released games, the document will go on to describe how that game compares to the new game being developed. For example, if you were writing a competitive analysis for a proposed real-time strategy game, you would probably want to include the more recent games from the major RTS franchises, such as the latest addition to the *Command & Conquer* series, the *WarCraft* series, and the *Age of Empires* series. Competitive analysis documents typically do not help very much with development, but can provide a useful reality check to help you realize that the game you are hoping to create really is exactly the same as another title that shipped six months ago.

Design Document

In other parts of the software development industry, the equivalent of the design document is often called the functional specification. Indeed, some game developers refer to the design document as the functional specification. I prefer "design document" because it is the more widely used term and because it better represents the content of the document. The design document's goal is to fully describe and detail the gameplay of the game. For large team projects, the design document serves as a vital reference work for how the different aspects of the game need to function, with, ideally, team members referring to it throughout the game's development. Producers will often use the design document as a springboard from which to schedule the project. A well-written and complete document can also be of vital importance when a game is subsequently converted to another platform by a different development team. The document can serve as an ideal reference tool for this new team to understand how the game is supposed to function as they start porting it to a new system, assuming it is kept up to date over the course of the project.

Whereas a functional specification for, say, a spreadsheet application can be extremely detailed and complete, a design document for a game is necessarily less complete because of the more organic, dynamic, and iterative nature of game development, as I discussed in Chapter 15, "Getting the Gameplay Working." As a designer working on a large team project, the design document will be the primary specification with which you will need to be concerned. The guts of a design document are the detailing of game mechanics: what the players are able to do in the game-world, how they do it, and how that leads to a compelling gameplay experience. Design documents typically also include the main components of whatever story the game may tell and a detailing of the different levels or worlds the players will encounter in the game. Also included will be lists of the different characters, items, and objects the players will interact with in the game-world. One can think of the important aspects of the design document as not dissimilar from what a journalist looks for in a news story: what the players do (which actions the players can perform), where they do it (the game's setting), when they do it (at what time and in what order the players must perform different actions), why they do it (the players' motivations), and how they do it (what commands are used to control the game).

The design document can also be defined by what it does not include. Most of the content contained in the other documents listed in this chapter should not be found in the design document, including the bulk of the information found in the script, the technical design document, and the art bible. In particular, a design document should not spend any time describing the game's development from a technical standpoint. Platform, system requirements, code structure, artificial intelligence algorithms, and the like are all topics that should be covered in the technical design document and therefore avoided in the design document. The design document should describe how the game will function, not how that functionality will be implemented.

Similarly, discussions about the marketing of the game, explorations of how it will be positioned compared to other games in the marketplace, and sales projections are all inappropriate in the design document. In addition, schedules, budgets, and other project management information should be left out. This information should certainly be recorded in some documents, such as the pitch document or project schedule, but it should be strictly excluded from the design document. I would think that such an exclusion would be obvious to anyone undertaking a design document, but I have seen many design documents that spent half their pages considering how the game will be sold. The design document needs to describe how the game functions so that someone working on the development team can see exactly what he needs to create. Including materials that are more about the business side of the game's development will only get in the way of more appropriate information.

The design document and its creation are discussed in more detail in Chapter 19, "The Design Document." You can find sample design documents in this book's two appendixes.

Flowcharts

Flowcharts may often be included as part of the design document or as separate documents. In game development, flowcharts have two primary uses. The first is to track the players' navigation of out-of-game menu options, such as those players use to start a new game or load a saved one. Flowcharts can also be used to chart the areas the players progress to and from in the game, particularly in level-based games. Beyond these most obvious applications, flowcharts can be quite useful for visually representing the results of any decisions players may get to make in your game. Flowcharts are a means for visually representing a chunk of gameplay, whether micro or macro, and can often evolve into full decision trees with lots of branches, each representing a player choice that leads to new choices or loops back to previous decisions. These visual representations can be helpful not only to a designer trying to figure out what the consequences of a player's actions will be, but also for communicating the sequence of events and choices to other members of the team. With complex scenarios involving a lot of branching, a flowchart representation will be much more effective at getting your ideas across than what you will be able to convey with text alone. Flowcharts can be either handmade or developed using various flowchart creation tools, such as Visio.

Story Bible

For games that tell stories, some amount of that story must be included in the design document. Certainly a summary of the game's overall story is essential, and a thorough description of the game-flow will need to include parts of the story, but the design document often cannot include it all. This is especially true if the game being developed involves a complex story line with a variety of characters and locations, or if the game takes place in a universe with a specific history. A story bible may be the best place to document this information. Often the author of a game's story will have in his mind a vision for the universe and its inhabitants beyond the scope of the game, such as where game characters come from and what their motivations are, and how the game-world came to be in the state it is in when players encounter it. What the players experience may be only the tip of the proverbial iceberg, with the story's author having in mind ten times more detail about the game-world than is actually communicated to the players through the gameplay. Other aspects of the universe may only be hinted at. By having a complete plan for the game's back-story, even if the players do not directly learn all of it, the story's writer will have a much better chance at keeping the game's narrative consistent and plausible.

A story bible, then, is a good place to document a game's potentially extensive back-story. Separating this information from the design document proper avoids burdening it with a lot of information that is less central to the game's creation. Weighing down a design document with a lot of back-story is an easy way to give it perceived depth and completeness, but can hide the fact that the specification fails to fully cover game mechanics and other more vital information. Nonetheless, the back-story is still important, and hence the value of its documentation in the story bible. Once a story bible has been created, when an artist wishes to learn more about the character he is modeling, he can turn to the bible and find out about that character's childhood. He can make his art better by making it fit with the back-story. When a voice actor wonders how he should play that same character, if he has read the story bible he will be working from the same information base as the artist. Properly used, a story bible can add to a game's consistency.

Should there ever be a sequel or spin-off made from the game, the game's story bible becomes all the more useful when the development team for the derivative project tries to understand what sort of new story line can be crafted. Since the story bible included more content than was actually used in the original project, it will provide the new team with plenty of unexplored areas of the game's universe. If the story bible is followed properly, the new game will fit in perfect continuity with the original. As that team creates the new game, the bible can be expanded and updated so that future projects will be just as consistent.

The format for a story bible is fairly open, and the bible's author should make the format best fit the information he is planning to include. Often the story bible consists of a number of different historical narratives of varying lengths. One narrative might describe the history of the game-world, detailing the major events that have led the world to the state it is in when the players start their game. Similarly, the document could include narratives for the different major characters the players encounter in the game. Topics discussed would include the character's childhood, how he rose to whatever position he has in the game, and what motivates the character to act as he does. By having a sense of the character's background, when it comes time to write the game's script, the game's writer will be better equipped to create compelling and believable dialog for the different characters. Of less importance but perhaps still appropriate for the story bible are the histories of the various major items or locations the players find in the world. A powerful sword might have a colorful history that NPCs may hint at when they talk of the object to players. A particular shrine might have a dark secret of its own. However, the author should always be careful to try to keep in mind how much information is actually going to be useful to the game's creation, and should not feel obligated to fully explain the lineage of every last character and object in the game. Include only the information that you think will be important to the game's creation.

The writing style of the story bible should be in more of a prose style than the bullet-point style of the design document itself. A team member using a story bible is more likely to want to sit down and read a few pages at a time, and will appreciate bible content that reads and flows nicely. Breaking the document down by character, item, or major event is still useful to the reader, so using a good quantity of appropriately titled headings is a good idea. You may also wish to include various diagrams in the document to supplement the written content, such as timelines, event flowcharts, or character-relationship trees. These charts can prove useful in allowing the reader to understand a particularly complex game-world.

On the other hand, even with a complex game-world, you may not need a story bible at all. If the author of the game's script is able to keep track of characters and their motivations in his head, and if the likelihood of a sequel worked on by another team is low, the creation of a complex story bible may not be a good use of anyone's time. It all depends on the working style of the team, particularly the lead designer and script-writer, who may or may not be the same person. Certainly many great authors have managed to write novels far more complex than your game is likely to be without keeping more than a few scribbled notes to themselves, if that. Many complex films have only had a script to go on for their stories, with the actors responsible for interpreting their characters' motivations based only on the lines they are supposed to speak. It may be that the script's author created a story bible for his own personal use, and never saw fit to share it with anyone else. The story bible is a tool that can help in the creation of the game's story, but it may not be a tool that every scriptwriter or game designer feels the need to use.

Script

If a game has a story, it is quite likely that at some point players will be asked to listen to narration, hear characters talking, or read information about upcoming missions. This dialog and the accompanying descriptions of the situations during which the dialog occurs (stage directions) should be contained within the game's script. A game's script may be written by a variety of people: a designer, an artist, the game's producer, or someone whose only role on the project is to write the script, someone who was specifically hired for his dialog writing skills.

The script may take on different forms depending on what type of game events the dialog will accompany. For instance, if the game has film-style cut-scenes, the script may closely resemble a movie script, with descriptions of the actions the players witness and rough indications of what the camera is looking at for any given instant. Or the script for these cut-scenes may be more like that of a play, focusing primarily on the dialog. For in-game conversations, the script will focus primarily on the dialog, since players are still in control of the game and thereby in control of what direction the game's camera is pointing. But a script for the in-game cut-scenes might include "stage directions" or "set directions" along with descriptions for the accompanying character animations to assist the artist in creating the appropriate motions to accompany the dialog.

For instance, here is an excerpt of a script that could be used for a cut-scene in an adventure game:

> When the PLAYER approaches PAUL and SANDY after resurrecting the TREE OF PLENTY, PAUL will be visibly thrilled at the player's arrival. He immediately bursts into effusive praise for the player's accomplishments:
>
>> PAUL: That's just the solution we have been praying for! You have saved our great Tree, and nothing we can do could ever thank you enough. Please accept this token of our appreciation...
>
> PAUL tosses a BAG OF FLIMFLAMS at the player's feet. SANDY steps forward:
>
>> SANDY: [Apologetically] We know it's not much, but...
>>
>> PAUL: [Interrupting] It's all we have!
>>
>> SANDY: [Cowering] Please do not hate us for our poverty...

The non-linear nature of games demands that the script be organized and presented differently from a play, movie, or television script. If players have branching conversations with NPCs, as they might in an RPG or an adventure game, the script will need to take on a special form conducive to the non-linear nature of the interchange. Here a script might use small amounts of pseudocode, using IF-THEN-ELSE or SWITCH-type syntax to communicate when the players would hear different pieces of dialog.

Returning to our adventure game example, here is one possible layout for a more non-linear conversation. This game uses the old "keyword" conversation system, where the players type in a word and the character being talked to may or may not have information about that subject:

IF the player asks about "FLIMFLAM":

> PAUL: A FlimFlam is a drop of dew, fallen from the morning sky, carefully wrapped in a baby leaf from the Tree of Plenty. It has special curative properties for Humanoids, when rubbed on the back of the neck.

IF the player asks about "TREE" **OR** "PLENTY":

> PAUL: The Tree of Plenty has been my people's source of life since before any of us can remember. Without the shade it provides, my people grow exhausted in the noonday sun. Without its leaves, we have nothing to eat. Without its strength, my people are weak.

DEFAULT, if the player asks about anything else:

> PAUL: I do not know of what you speak, stranger. We are not the most intelligent of peoples; we are not as wise as a great traveler, such as yourself.

In-game dialog may be randomly varied between a number of expressions that communicate the same information but say it differently. Simple OR statements between different lines of dialog can communicate to the reader of the script that the game will randomly choose between several different lines of dialog.

Once again returning to our adventure game, here we have a sample of dialog that players might hear during actual gameplay:

When the player bumps into PAUL, he says:

> "Oh, excuse me, begging your pardon."

OR

> "Oh dear, I seem to be blocking your way."

OR

> "My mother always said I was born to get in her way."

There is no industry-standard syntax that dictates the form of an interactive script. It is up to the designer, producer, and scriptwriter to come up with a form that best documents the dialog they will need to use in their game. Some RPG games, such as *Deus Ex*, involve so much conversation and branching dialog trees that they employ fairly robust and advanced scripting languages for the designer or writer to use to implement the dialog. Designers will often want to write their interactive script to match the syntax found in such an editor, so that when it comes time to implement the dialog the process will be greatly simplified.

Games that feature a lot of branching conversations, such as *Deus Ex*, often include a scripting language specifically for implementing the dialog.

The game's script is also where one might find the text of what the character reads in a mission briefing or in a book they might find. Any text that is contained in the game, from signs and posters on the walls to the commands issued to the player character from an off-screen commander, is included in the game's script.

As games try to incorporate more and more story, scripts documenting all of the dialog they include have become necessary. The most important thing to remember when working on the script for your game is that people are usually playing your game not for the dialog but for the gameplay. If they had wanted to watch a movie, they would have done so. Instead they booted up your game. They may enjoy hearing some clever dialog while they are playing, but they are usually not so interested in listening to long, drawn-out cut-scenes that delve into endless back-story. If the gameplay is any good at all, players are going to want to get back to it as quickly as possible. If players find themselves more captivated by the dialog in your game than in the gameplay, you need to wonder why you are bothering to make a game at all.

Art Bible

The art bible is often composed primarily of concept sketches and other resources that artists can refer to as they are working on creating various visual assets for the game. Sometimes text accompanies these images, whether in the form of handwritten notes on concept sketches or text descriptions describing the parameters artists should follow when coming up with new elements for the game. The art bible is usually not compiled or written by the designer, but instead by the lead artist working with his team. Of course, the information contained in the art bible needs to correspond and be consistent with the story and characters described in the game's other documents, including the design document, script, and story bible. Therefore, when constructing the art bible, the artist will work closely with the designers, writers, and producers to make sure his work is going to fit with the overall vision for the game.

The art bible is the place where the look and feel of the game is comprehensively established in detail. Descriptions of the art style to be employed in the game (art deco, animé, Warner Bros. cel animation, neo-realism, and so forth) will be found in the bible accompanied by sketches that communicate the game's style better than words ever could. It is important to keep the descriptions of the game-world's art style in this document instead of in the design document in order to allow each document to stand on its own as a comprehensive reference tool. Of course, designers on a project should read over and be familiar with the art bible, if for no other reason than to make sure it is on track with the rest of the game. An art bible may also contain technical guidelines that artists need to follow to create assets that will work with the game's engine, as detailed in the technical design document. This may include polygon limitations to be followed or the duration and number of frames involved in different animations.

The Game Minute

The game minute is typically a one- to three-page document that describes in detail a short section of gameplay. These documents are often written very early in development, when what exactly the gameplay consists of is still fairly nebulous. These documents can be used to communicate to the team or to upper management what direction the game is going and to serve as a reality check to make sure everyone is fully on board with how the game's high concept will actually play out. For this reason, the gameplay described in the game minute should be representative of a relatively average gameplay experience, not a boss battle or the training mission. Since in many ways the game minute is supposed to function as a reality check, it really needs to describe your "meat-and-potatoes" game experience. Game minutes are written in a prose style and go into specific detail about what exactly the player is doing from moment to moment in the game. Some game minutes even go so far as to list each button or key press the players would make to accomplish the various objectives in the game.

Game minutes can be very useful, but they can also be somewhat problematic since they represent a single way of playing out a scenario. This problem can be somewhat ameliorated by writing the text in such a way that it suggests what the player might do differently in a given situation. For example, in an action-adventure game, the player might see: "Rounding the corner, the player sees an intimidating Blugbatter Beast. The player contemplates charging up and attacking it with his cattle prod, but then recalls that the Blugbatter Beasts are immune to electricity, except in a weak spot at the base of their neck. Since the Beast has not yet seen the player, the player quickly backs up around the corner and waits there quietly. Knowing the Beast should soon be patrolling in this direction, the player hopes to surprise him and attack him from behind..." In addition, a designer may want to consider writing up several different versions of a game minute to show how significantly different approaches to a given scenario might play out. However much the designer tries to fix this problem, he is still stuck with a narrative that only describes one particular sequence of events. Sometimes team members who do not understand what a game minute is supposed to accomplish may even become confused when they read it, wondering, "Is that all the player can do?" Nevertheless, if used properly and if the team is made fully aware of the document's function, a game minute can be a very useful tool when the game is not yet in a playable state because the project is still very early in development.

Storyboards

Storyboards are an established film and television device for sketching or mocking-up shots before they are actually filmed. Storyboards may be included as part of the art bible or can stand alone as their own separate document. Storyboards are most handy for mapping out non-interactive cut-scenes, which are quite cinematic in nature and are thereby well suited to storyboarding. This allows members of the development team to provide feedback and corrections on those cut-scenes before someone goes to the trouble of filming or rendering them. Storyboards can also be used as concept sketches or mock-ups for how the game-world will appear to players if the game's engine is not yet ready to be used. Such storyboards can be useful both for making the entire team understand at an early stage where the game is heading, as well as convincing financiers to fund the project's development. Much like the game minute document described above, storyboards can be problematic because they necessarily represent a single way of playing a given area. Since they have their origins in film, traditional storyboards are completely linear and may suggest to readers that the game is more cinematic than it really should be. Indeed, when people fall in love with what they see in a storyboard they may try to limit the player's choices to doing only what has been drawn out. It may be advantageous to use some kind of branching storyboards, where the consequences of major player choices are drawn and then laid out like a flowchart or decision tree. Unfortunately, sometimes when people get overly excited by storyboarding a game it can be another case of movie envy, where developers actually wish they were filmmakers. Storyboards can be helpful, but only up to a point. In the end, they cannot replace actually prototyping gameplay on the computer, getting the game to a somewhat playable state, and then refining it until it is truly fun and all the player's choices are available for playtesters to explore.

Technical Design Document

A technical design document (TDD) is the sister specification to the design document. Whereas the design document focuses on how the game will function, the technical design document discusses how that functionality will be implemented. You can also think of it this way: the design document communicates how the player experiences the game, while the technical design document goes into how that experience will be implemented. Sometimes called the technical specification, the technical design document is customarily written by the lead programmer on a project, and is used as a point of reference by the programming team. Here is where the code's structure is laid out and analyzed. The technical design document is where programmers on the project can turn to figure out how they should implement a specific system. The document may include the overall code structure, what major classes will be used, descriptions of the rendering architecture, details of how the AI will function, and any amount of other implementation-side information. Pseudocode is appropriate, though not required, in the technical design document. Though the technical design document may be a good idea, in the past many projects have managed to undergo perfectly successful development cycles without a technical design document ever being created. On the other hand, with today's ever more complicated projects, escalating budgets, and the resultant increase in scrutiny placed on all titles, most all games developed now use one or more TDDs. Whether that TDD ends up being followed or not is another issue. In part to help fix the problem of useless TDDs, many developers avoid writing a massive and highly detailed TDD at the beginning of the project and write more of an outline or framework document up front. Then, as development progresses, they write smaller TDDs as each feature of the game is about to be implemented.

As I have mentioned, technical design documents are used primarily by the programming team. Nonetheless, it is very important that a designer with any sort of programming experience (or even one without any) look over technical design documents for his project, since they will certainly contain general descriptions of how AI and other algorithms will function, along with other information critical to the gameplay. Just as looking through the art bible is important for a designer to do, reading through the technical design document or documents, even if he cannot understand all of them, will give the designer a chance to make sure the programming team is on the right track.

Schedules and Business/Marketing Documents

I include these in my list of game development documents in order to emphasize that schedules, budgets, and marketing projection information does not belong in the design document. On many occasions, I've read design documents that had whole sections about how the game might be sold. Indeed, some so-called design documents are little more than dressed-up marketing plans. Such business-oriented information is neither appropriate in the design document, nor does it belong in any of the other documents I have discussed here, except for the concept document. The design document is about the game's functional design, not how it will be advertised or sold at retail. It is best to separate out such marketing plans and business data into distinct documents, where the people concerned with such information can best review it.

When working on a large-budget project that hopes to at least recoup its capital investment, it is important to have well-thought-out marketing projections, budgets, schedules, and any number of other documents that will assist press relations people, sales representatives, and advertising artists when they are working on your project. The lead designer on a project should offer his services to help in the creation and maintenance of these documents in whatever way he can, though the writing of these documents usually falls on people more attuned to selling and managing rather than creating. Often it is the responsibility of the game's producer to develop and maintain these documents. Still, it is the designer's moral responsibility to make sure that the people funding the project know what sort of a game they are getting. This makes them less likely to become upset down the road when the game is done and it fails to match the advertisements and box art they have already spent large amounts of money creating. And when the suits understand what makes your game good, they are far less likely to demand changes or, even worse, cancel it. If the business people are really happy with the finished product, they are much more likely to be enthusiastic about promoting and selling the game, which can only mean more people will end up playing it.

No Standard Documentation

Different companies may have different standards for what documentation they create in order to assist and guide a game's development. Though they may have different names for the documents than those I have used above, I think these categories cover the vast majority of documents that companies will create. Some teams may split the design document into two documents, one containing only gameplay information and the other containing only story and level progression descriptions. Some development teams may create only a design document, having no need for a story bible. Some programming teams may find that they do not need a technical design document. Some art directors may make it through a game's development without a formal art bible. Some teams working on multimillion-dollar projects may even get through them without any documentation at all, though this is increasingly unheard of as publishers demand documentation so that they have some idea of exactly what game they are financing. Furthermore, publishers like to have some tangible proof that the development team has a good idea of what it is doing. Usually, how much documentation a publisher requires is inversely proportional to how trusted and experienced you and your team are as developers. The newer and more unproven your team, the more assurances the people funding your project will want to make sure you are not throwing money away.

The Benefits of Documentation

Beyond making the suits happy, good documentation really can help make your game better, regardless of whether you are developing it alone in your basement or with a team of thirty other developers. I have listed a number of separate documents above, and over the course of the project it may become difficult to keep them all straight, organized, and accessible to the team members who need them at any given time. To assist with this, some developers have started using Wiki, a web-based system for organizing documents and allowing members of the team to easily modify or update any document, all while maintaining version control and history for each file. Though not without its drawbacks, a Wiki system will allow you to keep your documents organized while also allowing them to be kept up to date as the project changes and evolves.

As a game designer, you should be involved and interested in the creation of all of the documentation described above. As a lead or senior designer, the creation and maintenance of the design document, story bible, and script are all your responsibility. Each document may be written by an individual or worked on collectively by a number of people. For example, you may not actually write the script yourself if there is a writer available more qualified to compose compelling dialog. Yet as the lead designer, you must still be concerned that the story, script, and gameplay all fit together. Making sure that all of the documents are consistent with one another and are in line with the vision and focus of the project is something the designer needs to take very seriously.

Chapter 18:
Interview: Jordan Mechner

The only complaint one could have about Jordan Mechner's work in computer games is that he has not made more of them. Each of the games he has designed and spearheaded — *Karateka*, *Prince of Persia*, and *The Last Express* — has had a unique elegance and sophistication that one seldom finds in the world of computer games. But the game industry has had to do without Mechner for several periods of time while he pursued his other great love, filmmaking. Indeed, it is Mechner's knowledge of film that has helped to contribute to the quality of his games. But this quality does not come through the epic cut-scenes and barely interactive game mechanics that so often come about when developers attempt to merge film and gaming. Instead, Mechner has blended film and game techniques in unique and innovative ways, helping his titles to tell stories visually while still retaining the qualities that make them great games. This is the most apparent in his most recent work, the amazing *Prince of Persia: The Sands of Time*. This interview was originally conducted around the release of *The Last Express* for *Inside Mac Games* magazine. For inclusion in this book, Mechner was kind enough to fill out the interview a bit, expanding it to cover the full breadth of his twenty years in computer game development.

What initially attracted you to computer games?

Well, it was 1979, and I was a sophomore in high school. The first computer that I ever got a chance to play with was the PDP-11 that we had in our high school. But it was very hard to get any time on it, and the teacher who was in charge wouldn't let the students read the manuals, for fear that would give us the ability to go in and change grades and stuff like that. So it was this guessing game of trying to learn how to get the computer to do anything. So when a friend of mine showed me his new Apple II, it was just like a dream come true — to have a computer in your own house that you could use whenever you wanted. And it was completely open; you could pop open the top and see how it was made and you could read all the manuals that came with it. And of course, the irony was that at that time I didn't know of any manuals that explained assembly language. So I was just kind of looking through the assembly code of the computer's operating system to try to figure out what the different commands meant. Over the years I picked that up, and more books came out. It was just this great toy.

Did you always want to make games with the computer?

Well, I guess games were the only kind of software that I knew. They were the only kind that I enjoyed. At that time, I didn't really see any use for a word processor or a spreadsheet. I played all the games that I could find, and in my spare time I tried to write games of my own. That was just the first use that occurred to me.

So that was the origin of *Karateka?*

It took a few years to get there. The first really ambitious project I did was a game called *Asteroids*. That was my attempt to do for *Asteroids* what a game called *Apple Invaders* had done for the other most popular coin-op game of the time. I figured that if *Apple Invaders* was a big hit because it was exactly like the coin-op game, then I could do the same thing for *Asteroids*. But my timing was a little off. I actually finished an assembly language, high-resolution version of *Asteroids* and signed a deal with a publisher. But just about then Atari woke up to the fact that these computer games were ripping off its hugely profitable arcade franchises, so their lawyers scared everybody off and that *Asteroids* game was never published.

So then you did *Karateka?*

No, then I did a game that bore a strong resemblance to *Asteroids* except that instead of rocks you had brightly colored bouncing balls, and instead of wrapping around the edge of the screen they bounced off, hence its name: *Deathbounce*. I sent it to Broderbund (this was 1982, I was a freshman in college) and got a call back from Doug Carlston, who was at the time handling submissions as well as running the company. I was very excited to get a call from someone in the computer games industry. He said, "It looks like it's well programmed, we're impressed with the smoothness of the animation and so on. But it feels kind of old-fashioned. Take a look at our new game, *Choplifter*." Doug was kind enough to send me a copy of Dan Gorlin's *Choplifter*, which was the number one selling game at the time, along with a joystick to play it with. That was the game that really woke me up to the idea that I didn't have to copy someone else's arcade games, I was allowed to design my own!

Karateka came out of a lot of ideas all kind of converging at the same time. *Choplifter* showed me what was possible in terms of smooth scrolling and an original game design. Meanwhile, I was getting megadoses of exposure to cinema; Yale had about a dozen film societies and I was trying to see in four years every film ever made. *Seven Samurai*

Karateka

was my new favorite film of all time. My mom at that time was heavily into karate, and I had taken a few lessons during the summer down at the local dojo. Finally, I was taking film studies classes (always dangerous) and starting to get delusions of grandeur that computer games were in the infancy of a new art form, like cartoon animation in the '20s or film in the 1900s. So all those sources of inspiration got rolled into *Karateka*. What made the big difference was using a Super 8 camera to film my karate teacher going through the moves, and tracing them frame by frame on a Moviola. It was rotoscoping, the same trick that Disney had used for *Snow White* back in the '30s. That made the animation look a lot better than I could have done by hand and better than the other games that were out there. I worked on *Karateka* for a couple of years between classes, and sent it to Broderbund at about the end of my sophomore year. They were pleased and published it.

So one of your goals was to merge cinematic techniques with an action game to create a unique hybrid?

Very definitely. The accelerating cross-cutting to create suspense had been used by D.W. Griffith in 1915; I figured it should be tried in a computer game. The horizontal wipe for transition between scenes I lifted from *Seven Samurai*. The scrolling text prologue at the beginning. And silly things, like saying THE END instead of GAME OVER. I used the few techniques that I could figure out how to pull off in hi-res graphics on an Apple II.

***Karateka*'s actually quite short. Was that a deliberate decision, to keep the game focused?**

Well, it didn't seem short to me at the time. Actually, when I submitted it to Broderbund it only had one level: you'd enter the palace and have the fight. One of the first things they suggested to me was to have three different levels: you're outside, you're in the palace, then you're down below. I wasn't thinking in terms of hours of play, I just wanted to make it cool.

The ending is a pretty devious trick, where if the player approaches the princess in the "attack" stance she'll kick him. How did you come up with that?

It seemed like a fun little trick. You only have one life in that game: you get as far as you can, and if you're killed, it's "The End" and you have to start the movie from the beginning again. So I figured that most players, when they finally got to the end, would just run right into her arms. But it's not a total cheat, there's a little clue there, where she puts

Karateka

her arms out to you, and then if you run toward her she lowers her arms. So that's a sign that something's not right.

But I don't know that anybody ever played that game and did it right the first time.

Yeah, in retrospect that was pretty nasty. I don't know if we could get away with that today. The other thing that we got away with on *Karateka* was that if you played the flip side of the disk, if you put the disk in upside down, the game plays upside down. I was hoping at least a few people would call Broderbund tech support and say, "The screen is upside down, I think something's wrong with my monitor or my computer." That way the tech support person could have the sublime joy of saying, "Oh, you probably put the disk in upside down." And the customer would happily hang up thinking this was true of all computer software. I thought it was extremely brave of the publisher to increase the cost of goods by twenty-five cents just for a gag.

So did *Prince of Persia* grow out of your experiences on *Karateka*?

Well, there was a big gap between *Karateka* and *Prince of Persia* in terms of my own life. I finished school and I took a year off. I wasn't sure that I wanted to do another computer game. The most direct inspiration there was a game by Ed Hobbs called *The Castles of Doctor Creep*, which didn't get too big a circulation, probably because it was only available on the Commodore 64. My college dorm mates and I spent a lot of hours playing that game. It had these ingenious puzzles of the Rube Goldberg sort, where you hit one switch and that opens a gate but closes another gate, and so forth. So the one-sentence idea for *Prince of Persia* was to do a game that combined the ingenuity of *The Castles of Doctor Creep* with the smooth animation of *Karateka*. So when you ran and jumped you weren't just a little sprite flying through the air, your character actually felt like it had weight and mass, and when you fell on the spikes it felt like it really hurt.

Another inspiration was the first eight minutes of *Raiders of the Lost Ark*. I wanted to make a game with that kind of action feeling to it. And then there was the *Arabian Nights* setting. I was looking for a setting that hadn't been done to death in computer games, and a couple of animators at Broderbund, Gene Portwood and Lauren Elliot, suggested this one. I went back and reread the *Arabian Nights* and it seemed to offer a lot of promise. It had all those great story possibilities which have been absorbed into our collective unconscious — genies, the voyages of Sinbad, Aladdin's cave. It was just crying out to be made as a computer game.

You said you had taken some time off before making *Prince of Persia*. **What finally made you want to come back and do another game?**

That was the year I wrote my first film screenplay. It was optioned by Larry Turman, a very nice man who had produced about fifty films including *The Graduate*. We had a year of meetings with directors and studios and came close to getting it made, but in the end it didn't come together. Later I found out that for a first-time screenwriter, that's not considered a bad start at all. But I'd been spoiled by computer games, and I thought, "My God, I've just spent six months here in Los Angeles waiting for something to happen, and the film isn't even getting made." In comparison, I knew that if I finished *Prince of Persia,* it would get published. So I figured I'd better stick with that. At the point when all this good stuff had started to happen with the screenplay, I was about six months into *Prince of Persia*, and I'd put it aside for almost a year to focus on screenwriting. It was pretty scary going back to programming after so much time off; I was afraid I wouldn't be able to remember my own source code. But I went back, picked it up again, and finished it.

One thing about *Prince of Persia* **is that it takes this finite amount of game elements and stretches them out over all of these levels. Yet it never gets dull or repetitive. How did you manage that?**

That was really the challenge of the design. It was modular in that there were a finite number of elements that could be recombined in different ways. It's the same thing you try to do in a movie. You plant a line of dialog or a significant object, and fifteen or thirty minutes later you pay it off in an unexpected way. An example in *Prince of Persia* would be the loose floors. The first time you encounter one it's a trap: you have

Prince of Persia

to step over it so you don't fall. Then later on, it reappears, not as a trap but as an escape route: you have to jump and hit the ceiling to discover there's a loose ceiling piece that you can knock down from below. Later on, you can use one to kill a guard by dropping it on his head, to jam open a pressure plate, or — a new kind of trap — to accidentally break a pressure plate so that you can never open it again.

It was necessary to make *Prince of Persia* modular because the memory of the computer was so limited. The smooth animation of the character, with so many intermediate frames and so many moves, was taking up a huge percentage of that 64K computer. When efficiency is not an issue, you can always add production value to a game by throwing in a completely new environment or special effect or enemy, but when you're literally out of RAM and out of disk space, you have to think creatively. Which in turn forces the player to think creatively. There's a certain elegance to taking an element the player already thinks he's familiar with, and challenging him to think about it in a different way.

Prince of Persia is really a simple game to control, especially compared to modern action games. Was that a design goal of yours?

Absolutely. That was a very strong consideration in both *Karateka* and *Prince of Persia*, and I spent hours trying to figure out how to integrate certain moves. Should it be up with the joystick or up with the button? Personally, I have a strong prejudice against games that require me to use more than one or two buttons. That's a problem, actually, that I have with modern action games. By the time I figure out whether I'm using A, B, X, O, or one of those little buttons down at the bottom of the controller pad that you never use except for one special emergency move, I've lost the illusion that it's me that's controlling the character.

Ideally, you want to get the player so used to handling the joystick and the buttons that the action starts feeling like an extension of him or herself. The trick there, obviously, is that when you bring in a new movement that you haven't used before, you want the player to somehow already "know" what button or what combination of actions is going to bring off that move. In *Prince of Persia* there were moves where I thought, "This would be great, but I don't have a button for it, so let it go. It would be cool, but it doesn't help the game overall." A major constraint was keeping the controls simple and consistent.

Prince of Persia

As far as game design, it seems that _Prince of Persia_ was a logical extension of what you did in _Karateka_, and _Prince of Persia 2_ was in turn an extension of that. But _The Last Express_ seems to be off in a completely new direction. What provoked you to do something as different as _Last Express_?

I guess I don't think of _Last Express_ as being off in a new direction. I was still trying to tackle the same problem of how to tell a story and create a sense of drama and involvement for the player. There are a number of proven action game formulas that have evolved since the days of _Prince of Persia_. Part of what interested me about doing an adventure game was that it seemed to be a wide open field, in that there hadn't been many games that had found a workable paradigm for how to do an adventure game.

So it wasn't the inspiration of other adventure games?

No, on the contrary in fact. If you look at the old Scott Adams text adventures from the '80s, it's surprising how little adventure games have progressed in terms of the experience that the player has: the feeling of immersion, and the feeling of life that you get from the characters and the story. So I guess it was the challenge of trying to revitalize or reinvent a moribund genre that attracted me.

What inspired you to set the game on the Orient Express in 1914?

In computer game design you're always looking for a setting that will give you the thrills and adventure that you seek, while at the same time it needs to be a constrained space in order to design a good game around it. For example, things like cities are very difficult to do. A train struck me as the perfect setting for a game. You've got a confined space and a limited cast of characters, and yet you don't have that static feeling that you would get in, say, a haunted house, because the train itself is actually moving. From the moment the game starts, you're in an enclosed capsule that is moving, not only toward its destination — Paris to Constantinople — but it's also moving in time, from July 24th to July 27th, from a world at peace to a world at war. The ticking clock gives a forward movement and drive to the narrative, which I think works very well for a computer game.

The Orient Express, of course, is the perfect train for a story that deals with the onset of World War I. The Orient Express in 1914 was the "new thing"; it was an innovation like the European Economic Community is today, a symbol of the unity of Europe. At the time it

The Last Express

was possible to travel from one end of Europe to the other, a journey that used to take weeks, in just a few days, without trouble at the borders and so on. On that train you had a cross-section of people from different countries, different social classes, different occupations — a microcosm of Europe in one confined environment. All these people who had been traveling together and doing business together, found themselves suddenly separated along nationalist lines for a war that would last four years and which would destroy not only the social fabric but also the very train tracks that made the Orient Express possible. To me the Orient Express is a very dramatic and poignant symbol of what that war was all about. And a great setting for a story.

So would you say your starting point for *Last Express* was: "I want to make an adventure game; what sort of story can I tell in that form?" Or was it: "Here's a story I want to tell; what type of game will allow me to effectively tell it?"

Definitely the latter. Tomi Pierce [co-writer of *The Last Express*] and I wanted to tell a story on the Orient Express in 1914 right before war breaks out: how do we do that? I didn't really focus on the fact that it was a switch of genre from *Prince of Persia* or what that would mean for the marketing. It just became apparent as we worked out the story that given the number of characters, the emphasis on their motivations and personalities, the importance of dialog and different languages, that what we were designing was an adventure game. I consciously wanted to get away from the adventure game feel. I don't personally like most adventure games. I wanted to have a sense of immediacy as you're moving through the train, and have people and life surging around you, as opposed to the usual adventure game feeling where you walk into an empty space which is just waiting there for you to do something.

Was this your reason for adding the "real-time" aspect to *Last Express*, something we're not used to seeing in adventure games?

Of course, it's not technically real-time, any more than a film is. The clock is always ticking, but we play quite a bit with the rate at which time elapses. We slow it down at certain points for dramatic emphasis, we speed it up at certain points to keep things moving. And we've got ellipses where you cut away from the train, then you cut back and it's an hour later.

But still, it's more real-time than people are used to in traditional adventure games.

Or even in action games. I'm amazed at the number of so-called action games where, if you put the joystick down and sit back and watch, you're just staring at a blank screen. Once you clear out that room of enemies, you can sit there for hours.

You mentioned filmmaking back there, and I know in 1993 you made your own documentary film, *Waiting for Dark*. Did your experience with filmmaking help you in the making of *Last Express*?

It's been extremely helpful, but I think it can also be a pitfall. Film has an incredibly rich vocabulary of tricks, conventions, and styles which have evolved over the last hundred years of filmmaking. Some have been used in computer games and really work well, others are still waiting for someone to figure out how to use them, and others don't work very well at all and tend to kill the games they get imported into. The classic example is the so-called "interactive movie," which is a series of cut-scenes strung together by choice trees: do this and get cut-scene A and continue, do that and get cut-scene B and lose. For *Last Express*, I wanted the player to feel that they were moving freely on board a train, with life swirling all around them and the other characters all doing their own thing. If someone passes you in the corridor, you should be able to turn around, see them walk down the corridor the other way, and follow them and see where they go. If you're not interested, you can just keep walking. I think of it as a non-linear experience in the most linear possible setting, that is, an express train.

All of your games have featured cut-scenes in one way or another, and in *Karateka*, *Prince of Persia*, **and** *Last Express* **they've all been integrated into the game so as to be visually indistinguishable from the gameplay. Was this a conscious decision on your part?**

Absolutely. Part of the aesthetic of all three of those games is that if you sit back and watch it, you should have a smooth visual experience as if you were watching a film. Whereas if you're playing it, you should have a smooth experience controlling it. It should work both for the player and for someone who's standing over the player's shoulder watching. Cut-scenes and the gameplay should look as much as possible as if they belong to the same world. *Karateka* used cross-cutting in real-time to generate suspense: when you're running toward the guard, and then cut to the guard running toward you, then cut back to you, then back to the shot where the guard enters the frame. That's a primitive example, but one that worked quite well.

Same idea in *Last Express*: you're in first-person point-of-view, you see August Schmidt walking toward you down the corridor, then you cut to a reaction shot of Cath, the player's character, seeing him coming. Then you hear August's voice, and you cut back to August, and almost without realizing it you've shifted into a third-person dialog cut-scene. The scene ends with a shot of August walking away down the corridor, and now you're back in point-of-view and you're controlling it again. We understand the meaning of that sequence of shots intuitively because we've seen it so much in film. A classic example is Alfred Hitchcock's *Rear Window*. The whole film is built around the triptych of shot, point-of-view shot, reaction shot, where about half the movie is seen through

The Last Express

James Stewart's eyes. That's the basic unit of construction of *Last Express* in terms of montage.

On the other hand, in *Prince of Persia 2*, the cut-scenes were actually painted pictures that looked quite a bit different from the actual gameplay. I seem to recall not enjoying those quite so much...

I agree with you about that. There's a distancing effect to those cut-scenes, they make you feel like you're watching a storybook. But it was the effect we were going for at the time.

Right now there seems to be a trend away from full-motion video cut-scenes in computer games...

And rightly so, because the full-motion cut-scenes sometimes cost as much as the whole game and it's debatable whether they really improved the gameplay. Also, there's the problem that the quality of the cut-scenes in most cases was pretty low, if you compare it to good TV or good movies.

So you made a conscious attempt to do something different in merging a filmmaking style with a game-making style?

My hope is that *Last Express* offers something that hasn't really been offered by any other adventure game, or actually a game of any genre, which is to really find yourself in a world that's populated by people. Interesting, well-rounded characters, that are not just physically distinguishable, but have their own personality, their own purpose in the story, their own plans of action. And through the fairly conventional point-and-click mechanism, you're actually interacting with a world that's not just visually rich but richly populated.

So how did you go about designing the player's method of interacting with the game?

Our goal was to keep it as simple as possible. Point-and-click appealed to me because I always saw *Last Express* as a game that would appeal to a more mainstream audience of adults. People who don't usually play computer games and aren't particularly handy with a joystick aren't going to sit still to learn a large number of keys and what they all do. Pointing and clicking is something that adults in our society know how to do, so the challenge was to construct a game where you wouldn't have to know how to do anything beyond how to pick up a mouse and move it over the screen. The cursor changes as you pass over different regions to show you what you can do: you can turn left, you can talk to a different character. The specifics of how that works evolved as we tested it. During the development we worked out problems like: "Do 'up' and 'forward' need to be different-shaped cursors?" We decided yes they do. "Do 'look up' and 'stand up' need to be different?" We decided no, they can both be the up arrow. But the basic idea that it would be hot-spot based, point-and-click was very much a part of the original design.

So how much film did you shoot for *Last Express*? It seems like there is a monstrous amount of footage in there.

The whole project, because of its size, was a huge logistical challenge. The film shoot was actually only three weeks long. Which is not very much, when you consider that an ordinary feature film shoot takes at least four weeks, shooting an average of three screenplay pages a day. Whereas for three weeks, we shot about fifteen screenplay pages a day. We had a few tricks that allowed

The Last Express

us to move that fast: the fact that it was all blue-screen, the fact that we were shooting silent and had recorded the sound previously, and the fact that we were under-cranking, shooting seven and a half frames per second in some scenes, five frames per second in others. With the goal being to select key-frames and then reanimate them, as you see in the finished game. All that let us shoot a lot of material.

But in terms of keeping track of it … Just to give an example, the first phase of the shoot was in the train corridor. We laid out a fifty-foot track representing the corridor, with yellow lines on the blue-painted floor with a blue-painted cyc-wall behind it. And for three days we marched all thirty characters on the train up and down that corridor. The key moment, when a character walks toward the camera, is the moment of eye contact — friendly or unfriendly — the nuance of that glance being one of the things that brings you into the game as Cath, makes you feel that you're not just a phantom presence on the train but that people are reacting to you, even as they pass you in the corridor. For the first three days we just filmed corridor walks, and we had it basically down to a science. The camera was locked down for three days; it didn't move. If the camera moved, then we would have footage that didn't line up.

After three days in the corridor we moved to the restaurant, and again we had to do that in a very unusual way. Instead of shooting one scene at a time and covering each scene with a variety of camera setups, as we would in a film, instead we shot one camera setup at a time. From each camera setup we would shoot all the different scenes or actions that could possibly be seen from that angle in the course of the entire story. We would lock down the camera in each position, say, the "seated at the table looking straight ahead" view. We'd set up the other tables, and film every piece of action that could be seen from that view — August Schmidt walks in, sits down, orders dinner, the waiter brings him the food, he eats it, puts down his napkin, gets up, and walks away. Then with the camera set up from a different dining room angle, we'd have the same actors repeat the same actions. To make the shoot as efficient as possible was a bit of a jigsaw puzzle, figuring out which actors to bring in on which days and when to let them go, and is it more economical to move the camera one extra time so that we can send a bunch of actors home early, or should we leave the camera where it is and pay the actors for the whole day. That times nineteen days was a logistically very complicated film shoot. With a lot of the action being filmed from multiple angles, since in the game, you never know what angle the player's going to see it from.

And once it was all shot, it must have been a tremendous challenge to keep it all straight.

We did the editing on an Avid; without that I don't know what we would have done. We dumped it all onto huge hard drives on this Macintosh-based non-linear editing system, and selected the frames we wanted. We pushed that Avid system to its limits. At one point our film editor had to call tech support because the system was slowing down so much. When he told them how many effects he had, they were startled, and couldn't believe it was still functioning. We had more frame dissolves in just one of our scenes than they had anticipated anyone would ever have in a normal feature film. We were picking still frames and dissolving from one to another, so that every frame in the game was a special effect.

The official number is that we had forty thousand frames of animation in the game. In comparison to an animated feature film, however, that number is misleadingly low. In a typical dialog scene we're dissolving between still frames on the average of once every second or once every two seconds, whereas a conventional film runs twenty-four frames per second. So to get the equivalent in terms of how much action we really covered, you need to multiply forty thousand by twenty-four. Also, a lot of frames are reusable. You've got one hundred fifty frames of the character walking up the corridor toward camera, then one hundred fifty frames walking away from camera. Using just those three hundred frames, the train conductor character, say, might spend ten hours walking over the course of the game. When you walk into the dining room, you see six tables, and each table can have its own action going on independently. If you play the game from start to finish five times, the sixth time you might see two characters in the room together, whereas before they were always in the room separately. Just because the action unfolds a little differently. So the number of combinations of that footage is pretty much unlimited.

So what made you come up with the effect of dissolving between frames every one or two seconds used in *Last Express*? Why didn't you use the more traditional, full-motion style throughout the game?

From our point of view, full motion is basically an expensive special effect. It looks great, as in the corridors, as in the fights. But if we had decided to use that for the entire game, I think we would have ended up with something that was visually very flashy but not very deep. We're limited both by the amount of frames that can be kept in RAM and by the number of CDs. But ultimately, you're limited by the processor's ability. When you walk into the restaurant and it's full of people, with a number of different animations happening on the screen at the same time, as well as multiple tracks of audio streaming from the CD, that's possible only because each character is only animating every few seconds.

But there's also an aesthetic disadvantage to full motion. Say the technological limitations could be overcome, and we had a thirty-second loop of a character eating dinner. Sooner or later you realize the character is repeating. So you say, "Why is it that when he

The Last Express

takes a sip from his wine glass and then takes a bite of steak, the steak keeps getting replenished every time he eats it?" That's not helpful to the game, to have the player's attention distracted by following those little full-motion bits. When it gets down to it, we decided that what's important for the game is that the player believe the character is there, having dinner for an hour and fifteen minutes. And any time during that hour you can talk to him. The fact is that dissolving between still frames gives just as good an impressionistic sense of "dining" as the full motion would, and in some ways better, because you don't have that glitch when the film loops. So, with this convention, once the player accepts it, it opens up the world and gives you the ability to tell this huge story that goes on for three days and three nights with thirty characters doing all kinds of things. It would have been a drastically smaller story had we stuck to full motion.

I noticed in the credits that for almost all the characters you have one actor doing the physical acting — what the player sees on the screen — and another doing the voice. Why did you decide to use different actors for the visual and audio aspects of the game?

Casting was a tremendous challenge with a cast where you've only got two Americans, and everybody else is French, Russian, Austrian, Serbian, Arabic… The Orient Express was a truly multilingual train. We made the decision to have the characters not just speak English with a foreign accent, as when they're talking to the American hero, but to also speak their native language, subtitled, whenever they would normally do so. When the two French conductors are chatting with one another off-duty, they'd naturally be speaking French. So casting American actors who can do a fake German or French accent just wasn't acceptable to us. We needed native speakers for each language. I think we were very lucky to get such a good cast both for the faces and for the voices. But to ask for the perfect face, the perfect voice, and the perfect nationality to be united in one person for each role would have been too much to ask — especially in San Francisco, on our budget! There again, the fact that we weren't doing full-motion lip-synching gave us the flexibility we needed in casting.

Tatiana is a case in point. We used three casting agencies and auditioned hundreds of actors in both L.A. and San Francisco, looking for the face and voice of a sixteen-year-old Russian princess. The actress who ended up doing the voice is Russian and lives in L.A., the one we filmed is American and lives in San Francisco. To find one actor who was that good for both, we would have certainly needed to go out of state, if not to Russia!

By the way, we recorded the voices first and then created animated visuals to match, so the voice actors were free to create their own performance, as they would with a radio play or doing a Disney cartoon. It gives you a more natural voice performance than overdubbing. I think when you force actors to lip-synch to previously filmed action, you lose something in the performance.

Reality seems to have been a dominant goal in your design of the game, whether it's the native speakers for the voice acting or it's the authentically modeled train cars. Why did you go to such great lengths to make the game as real as possible?

It's a matter of respect for the player. Whether it's a history world or a fantasy world, I think that players respond to the amount of detail and consistency that the creators of the game put into it. And even if the player doesn't pay enough attention to the conductors to figure out that one of them is close to retirement and the other one is a young married guy, or that they have opposite political views, even so, whenever you pass them in the corridor and overhear a little bit of one of their conversations, you get the subliminal feeling that you're hearing a real conversation between two real people. If we hadn't bothered, then whenever you walked by, you'd hear something artificial and think, "You know, that sounds like something they just staged for my benefit." The fact that what you see in the game is just the tip of the iceberg, and that all the characters have their own history, and their own reality under the surface, you feel the mass of that, and the weight of it, though you don't actually see anything more than the tip.

Do you think computer games in general should strive for greater realism?

Well, realism is a bit of a loaded term. I don't mean to imply that games should be more realistic in terms of representing our world. Even something like *Super Mario Bros.*, which is completely a fantasy setting, has its own consistency. If a character can jump off a ledge and float to the bottom in one situation, you shouldn't have another situation where he jumps off and he gets crushed. As long as the creators actually took the time to think, "What are the rules for gravity in this world, and under what circumstances can you get hurt?" As long as the game plays by its own rules, players will accept it. In *Last Express*, we chose a real historical moment, and we were very conscious about trying to represent faithfully what was going on in the world at that time, and to respect that reality when drawing the constraints of our fictional world.

You use a very unique technique in *Last Express* where, though the actors were filmed, in the end they look like very well-crafted cartoons. Why did you decide to do it that way?

To begin with, I like the cartoon look aesthetically. I think the look of cartoon people against a 3D rendered background is very attractive. Films like *Snow White and the Seven Dwarfs* had technical reasons why they had to be flat — they were painted on cels — but they bring out the character nicely, and I think it's a look that has good connotations for those of us who as kids wanted to step inside the cartoon and become one of the characters.

The Last Express

I think for computer games there's another advantage to having the characters be cartoons, as opposed to live, filmed people. The experience of the computer game player depends on being able to put yourself into a fantasy world, suspend disbelief, and believe that what you're doing actually has an effect on these fictional characters. If you're watching a filmed live actor, intellectually you know that this is someone who was filmed on a sound stage, in a costume, with lights and cameras, and whatever he's saying and doing on the screen is what he did on the set. You know you're watching a cut-scene. Whereas with a cartoon, they're not real to begin with, so if you can believe that a cartoon character can walk and talk, why shouldn't he also be able to change his behavior in response to your actions as the player — for instance, run away when he sees you coming?

So it adds to the suspension of disbelief?

Or, at least, it doesn't break it, whereas filmed action would. And I think that's part of the reason why video cut-scenes haven't been successful in computer games at large. It's just not a good fit.

Finally, of course, there's one last reason why the cartoon style works in *Last Express*, which is a historical one. Most of the images we have, culturally, from 1914 come to us through drawings of the time: newspaper drawings, magazine advertisements, poster art by artists like Alphonse Mucha and Toulouse-Lautrec, which were in an Art Nouveau style which was really the forerunner of the modern comic book. So I think when we see someone in 1914 dressed as a cartoon, it feels right in a certain way, whereas if we saw a 1914 person as a 3D polygonal model, it wouldn't have that same resonance.

So do you think a game with a more modern setting could use the same cartoon-character approach to the visuals?

Well, I like the look a lot, and it could work in a lot of different situations. I don't think it needs to be a historical setting. But it was just one more reason why, for *Last Express*, it was too perfect to resist.

So since the characters ended up looking like cartoons, why didn't you just draw them from the very start, instead of filming actors and then making them look like drawings?

One reason was that, to get the high quality of animation and cel-type expression that you have in a Disney film, you need to spend as much money as Disney spends. As expensive as this game was by computer game standards, it's a tiny fraction of the budget you would spend on an animated feature. We wanted to assure consistency that the same character would look like the same character, whether they were seen from up close or far away, angry or happy, and from different, very difficult-to-draw angles. And to achieve that for forty thousand animated frames, there's just no way you're going to be able to do that on the budget we had.

The goal of our automated rotoscope was to take a black-and-white filmed frame and to turn that into something resembling a pen-and-ink line drawing, where an artist could pull up that frame and colorize it in less than two minutes. We got to the point where we had it set up like an assembly line. And not only that, but you could have two different artists working on the same character, and because the digitization and the rotoscoping were done automatically, it would yield very similar results. Anna looks like Anna, regardless of who colored her for that sequence.

We didn't want it to look like a processed film image, and we didn't want it to look exactly like a cartoon. If you see a character walking toward you down the corridor and you're not quite sure whether you're looking at a drawing or a processed filmed image, then we pretty much achieved our goal. And I think we did. Occasionally we have someone ask, "Did you draw all this by hand?" If they can't tell it was filmed, then it worked.

I thought one of the most innovative design elements in the game is the save-game system you used. Players never actually save their game, but *Last Express* automatically remembers everything they do, and they can "rewind" to any point in their game they want, if they want to try something a different way. How did you come up with this system?

I'm glad you asked. I'm very proud of the save-game system. The funny thing is that some people, including some reviewers, just didn't get it. We still occasionally get a review where they say, "It's too bad you can't save your game." Our goal, of course, was an extension of the design philosophy that went into the point-and-click system; we wanted it to be very simple, very transparent, and intuitive. To have to think about the fact that you're on a computer, and you have to save a file, and what are you going to name the file, and how does this compare to your previous saved game file — to me that breaks the experience. The idea was that you'd just sit down and play, and when you stopped playing, you could just quit and go to dinner, or use the computer for something else, or whatever. And when you go back to playing, it should automatically put you back to where you left off. And if you make a mistake, you should be able to rewind, like rewinding a videotape, go back to the point where you think you went wrong, and begin playing from there. And I think it works. The six different colored eggs were inspired by, I guess, *Monopoly* where you can choose which piece you want: the hat, or the car… The idea was that if you have a family of six, everybody will have their own egg, and when someone wants to play they can just switch to their own egg and pick it up where they left it off. People who complain that you can only have six saved games, or that you have to use colors instead of filenames, are fixated on the conventional save-game file system; they've missed the point. An egg file isn't a saved game; it's essentially a videotape containing not just your latest save point, but also all the points along the way that you didn't stop and save. You can usually rewind to within three to five real-time minutes of the desired point.

Music also seems to have been effectively used in *Last Express*. It shifts depending on what's going on in the game, as opposed to music in most adventure games that just plays in the background, never changing. How did you approach the game's musical aspect?

We knew that music would be very important to the texture of the game, and finding the right composer was very important. And we found him: Elia Cmiral, a very talented film composer from Czechoslovakia, who, by the way, is not a computer game player, had never scored a computer game, and I think even to this day has never played a computer game. We approached it as a story, as situations, and once he understood that there were mutually contradictory situations possible in the same story — that in one outcome Cath gets stabbed and killed and in another outcome he gets past that and goes on with the story — he had no problem scoring the different variations. (Elia has since achieved success as a Hollywood composer with scores for *Ronin, Stigmata*, and other films.)

Actually, although the cliché is that the composer always wants to add more music and turn down the sound effects so the music can be louder, Elia is very disciplined about the role of music. For scenes where I thought he would put a big dramatic chord or at least a little bit of underlining, he'd say, "No, that's corny, it plays better without it." So he was really reducing the number of situations, saving the music for places where it could really add something. We don't have any wallpaper music in *Last Express*; there's no point at which music is just repeating in the background, waiting for you to do something. The real music of *Last Express* is the noise of the train. You become very attuned to subtle shifts in the ambience: a door opens, the train noise gets louder, or you hear a door close somewhere, or you hear a rumble of thunder in the distance, or the train slows down as it arrives at a station. All of that almost comes to the foreground in the sound track, so that when the music does appear it's really noticeable. And in the dramatic scenes, the cut-scenes, we scored those as you would in a film, using music, I hope subtly, to bring out the different characters and situations. The fact that Anna, the leading lady, is a violinist, gave Elia a major instrumental motif for the score. There's a few hours of gameplay on the second day where Anna is practicing in her compartment, and if you walk through the train you hear her playing Bach partitas, tuning up, playing scales, and so forth. Her character's main theme is a violin theme as well, and appears in different guises in different situations as the story develops.

It's a game you really wouldn't want to play with the sound off.

Certainly it would lose a lot without the sound. In *Last Express* the sound is more than just the dialog. Without the shift in ambient noise, the music, the sound effects operating as clues, the feeling of hearing a conversation so far away you can't quite make out the words and then getting closer to it, and then the effect of hearing conversations in foreign languages that you can't understand no matter how close you get, all of that's really integral to the experience of *The Last Express*. It's funny because people tend to focus on the graphics. But one of the more technically innovative things we did was on the sound track. Most people aren't aware of it, but we actually have six tracks of sound being simultaneously streamed off the CD and mixed on the fly. For example, you can have the train ambient noise, the sound effect of a door opening, two people talking, thunder rolling in the distance, and a bit of music trailing off from the last cut-scene, and all of that going at the same time. It really creates a very rich sonic tapestry.

Again differing from many other adventure games, *Last Express* offers a fairly non-linear experience for the player, where there seem to be multiple ways to get through to the end. Do you think non-linearity in adventure games is important?

It's crucial; otherwise it's not a game. There are a couple of game models which I wanted to steer away from, one of which is where you have to do a certain thing to get to the next cut-scene or the story doesn't progress. Another is the kind of branching-tree, "Choose Your Own Adventure" style, where there's ten ways the story can end, and if you try all ten options you get to all ten of

The Last Express

them. One of the puzzle sequences that I think worked best in *Last Express* is one of the first ones, where you encounter Tyler's body and you have to figure out what to do to get rid of it. There are several equally valid solutions, and each one has its own drawbacks, ripple effects down the line. For example, if you hide the body in the bed, you risk that when the conductor comes to make the bed he will discover the body there, so you have to deal with that somehow. You can avoid that problem by throwing the body out the window, but if you do that, then the body is discovered by the police. And they board the train at the next stop and you have to figure out how to hide from the police when they're going compartment to compartment checking passports. Either way, your actions have consequences on the people around you. As another example, if you throw the body out the window, you may overhear François, the little boy, saying to his mom, "Hey, I saw a man being thrown out the window." And she'll say to him, "Shut up, you little brat, don't tell lies!"

I hadn't even noticed that.

The game is full of little things like that.

So is that why you don't tend to like other adventure games, because they're too set in "primrose path" style?

Some adventure games have great moments, but in terms of the overall experience it's rare that a game consistently keeps that high a level. In *Last Express* too, there are parts of the game that don't quite live up to the expectations set up by that first disposing-of-the-body puzzle. Defusing the bomb is one I wasn't so happy with. You just have to grit your teeth and follow the steps; there's no way around it. It's not a particularly clever puzzle. But again, the main concern was that the story would work overall, and that the overall experience would be satisfying.

I've heard many adventure game designers say that to effectively tell a story, you really need to limit the player's options and force them on a specific path. Do you agree with this notion?

It's true, of course; it's just a matter of *how* you limit what the player does. The too-obvious-to-mention limit in *Last Express* is that you can't get off the train. Any time you get off the train, the game ends. The only way to win is to stay on the train all the way to Constantinople. So in that sense, yeah, it's the ultimate linear story. You're on a train, you can't get off. But given that, within the train you should be able to move around as freely as possible. There are some doors that we just had to close because they would have changed the story too much and they wouldn't have let us get to the ending we wanted to get to. What if you take the gun and go through the train and kill everyone? We decided you just can't do that. So there's definitely a trade-off. The more wacky, off-the-wall options you give the player, the more that limits the complexity and the power of the story you've set out to tell. Whereas if you want to keep a very ambitious, central narrative that's itself large in scope, then you have to start closing doors around that, to make sure the player stays in the game.

Every game approaches this challenge in a different way. With *Last Express*, the train motif gave us the metaphor that we needed to keep it on track. I think once people get the idea that they're on the train, time is ticking, and they have to do certain things before certain stops, and they have to get to Constantinople or else they haven't really made it to the end of the line; once they get that, the story works. It's a matter of finding a balance for what works for each particular story. What's right for one game might not be right for another. I wouldn't even begin to know how to use the *Last Express* engine to do a game that wasn't set on a train.

***Last Express* seems to have not sold well because of the lack of an adventure game market. Yet adventure games used to be very popular. I'm wondering if you had any idea what happened to all of the adventure game players.**

That's a good question, and I have to say that I was caught by surprise when I woke up to find the adventure game market was dead, because I'd never really thought that much in terms of genres. Even doing *Last Express*, the fact that *Prince of Persia* was an action game while *Last Express* was an adventure game, I just wasn't thinking about it that way, right or wrong. As a game player, I'm not a big adventure game player myself, for a lot of reasons. Usually the graphics weren't very good, the story lines were kind of arbitrary and contrived, the characters and the plot just didn't stand up in terms of the kind of story that I would want to see in a movie or a novel.

So with *Last Express* I wanted to do a game that would have what I saw as the qualities that were missing from most of the adventure games that were out there. So as a player, I guess I have to assume my share of the guilt for not supporting the adventure game market. I think I underestimated the degree to which the games market had been stratified by the different genres. You had people out there who saw themselves as action game players, as strategy game players, as role-playing game players, or as adventure game players. I never shopped for games that way, but I guess over a period of a few years there in the early '90s, even computer game publications started to stratify games according to genre. So did publishers, so did shops, and I guess I didn't see that coming.

So you don't have any ideas about why the adventure game market dried up?

Well, I can only look at my own experience as a player. I enjoyed playing adventure games back in the Scott Adams days, and then I kind of got bored with them. I think adventure game makers need to stop asking, "Where did the market go?" I think the question is, "Why do people no longer find these games fun to play?" Maybe it's something about the games themselves.

Your first two games, *Karateka* and *Prince of Persia*, were both solo efforts, where you did all of the designing, writing, programming, and even drew the art. How do you compare working with a large team on *Last Express* to working by yourself?

It's a lot more exciting and rewarding than working alone, because you have the chance to work collaboratively with a large team of talented people who are really dedicated and who excel in their own specialties. It was one of the most thrilling experiences of my professional life. The downside, of course, is that you spend all your time worrying about where the next payroll is going to come from. One thing that was really nice about the old days was that the cost of developing a game was negligible. Once you'd paid the two thousand dollars for the computer and you've got five blank floppy disks, it was basically paid for. Whereas with a large project there's a lot of pressure to meet budgets and schedules.

Computer games seem to be one of the only art forms that have shifted from being predominantly solo endeavors to being more collaborative efforts, at least for commercial titles. How do you think that affects the final games?

It's interesting. What I'm doing right now, writing film screenplays, reminds me more of programming than any other activity I've done in a long time. Like programming, writing screenplays is basically a matter of closing the door behind yourself in a room with a computer and nothing else. You're trying to create something from scratch. If you write a screenplay that gets

Karateka

made into a movie, at that point, like a modern computer game, you've got the whole circus, with highly specialized, skilled people, and it's a creative collaboration between hundreds or more, all of whom bring their own area of expertise. A big-budget movie, for all the daily chaos of production, lives or dies on the strength of the script that was written, often, years before. A modern game is a collaborative effort in the same way, on a very tight budget, with money being spent daily, usually with a publisher who's banking on being able to ship it by a certain date. There again, what makes it work or not is the strength of the concept, the initial vision, which usually predates the whole production. There's just no time to change your mind on the fly during production about what the game should be.

But that tends to limit what kind of game designer can be successful, doesn't it? One who needs to make radical changes throughout the project to find the ideal gameplay would have been more successful in 1982 than now. Now he wouldn't be working at all.

He just wouldn't be working on a big-budget, multimillion-dollar production. A game like *Tetris* I think is well within the means of anyone to dream up and program, and if it takes them a year to find just the perfect combination of rules that's going to make it endlessly addictive, that's fine, it's not that expensive. But you can't take on a project with the latest 3D engine and forty artists at your beck and call and think that halfway through you're going to get to say, "Oh, now I realize what this game really needs, I wish I'd thought of it a year ago."

We're at a pretty tough time in the industry. I'm not sure it makes much sense economically to be a developer. I think it kind of makes sense to be a publisher, but even then there's only room for a few. This is a scary time because the number of hits is small, but the size of those hits is bigger than ever. If you're a publisher with a *Myst* or a *Tomb Raider* that sells two or three million units, that's great; your other ten titles can be flops and you still survive. But if you're a small developer with only one title in production, as Smoking Car was, you absolutely need to hit the jackpot. Only a handful of titles each year sell upward of half a million units, and that's the category you need to aspire to in order to justify the kind of budgets we're talking about.

And to make a game with *Last Express*'s production values you really need a large budget?

I think on *Last Express* we stretched the budget quite far for what we actually got up there on the screen. We saved a lot of money; we got people to work for less than their usual salaries or to defer salaries, we didn't spend a lot of money on the film shoot, we used a non-union cast and a non-union crew, and we didn't have any big names. So we pretty much saved money everywhere we could think of. And yet, just because of the nature of the project, the scale of the game, the number of people that were involved, and how long it took, it ended up costing a lot.

If you don't mind telling, just how much did the game cost?

About five million.

And the development took four years; was that your original intention?

It took two years longer than planned.

What made it take so much longer than you thought?

Tool development was one. To develop our own rotoscoping technology, we had to do a lot of tests — different types of costumes, makeup, processing — to get it looking the way we wanted. That was one. And the 3D modeling; that model was huge, the train interior and exterior, and the number of rendered images was tremendous. 3D modeling and rendering, animation, and tool development were the areas that burst their boundaries. The film shoot itself actually came in on schedule and on budget; that was the easy part.

So, looking back, do you wish you had managed to get the project done in a shorter amount of time, on a smaller budget? Or are you satisfied that that's just how long was necessary?

Well, personally I took a bit of a bath on *Last Express*, financially. So in that sense, it probably wasn't a smart move. And I feel bad about our investors who also hoped the game would sell half a million units, and were disappointed. It's kind of like having purchased an extremely expensive lottery ticket.

On the other hand, I'm proud of the game, I'm glad we did it, and I don't think we could have done it much cheaper than we did. I'm happy with the finished game. Of course, the ideal would have been to design a smaller game. If at the beginning, we'd looked at things and said, "OK, this is going to take four years and cost five million dollars," there wouldn't have been a publisher in the world that would have touched it. I wouldn't have touched it myself! For better or worse, there's a certain amount of willful self-delusion that most of us in the software industry indulge in just to get ourselves out of bed in the morning. Even games that take two years to develop often start out with the producer and the marketing department telling each other that it can be done in a year and be out by Christmas. The more technically ambitious the project, the less you know what you're getting into.

The film industry, by contrast, is relatively good at budgeting and scheduling shoots and doing them in just as long as they're supposed to take. The trade-off there is that they're not often trying things that are really new. When they do, like using a new technology for the first time, or filming on location in a war-torn country, or filming out at sea, they often experience the same kind of budget and schedule overages that are common in computer games. On *Last Express*, the whole production hinged on our development of this new rotoscoping process, so to a certain extent, at the beginning when we said, "Yeah, we'll develop it and it will take x months and cost this much," we were basically operating on blind faith, going forward assuming that we could resolve whatever problems there were and that it would work — which it did, eventually. It's very hard to make accurate time and cost projections when you are doing something for the first time. On *Last Express* we were doing maybe ten things that had never been done before, all at the same time. That was probably unwise.

Overall, unrealistic planning is not a good thing for developers; it doesn't really help us. One of my regrets about this project was that we were under so much financial strain from day to day that I was spending half my time worrying about the game and half my time worrying about raising money. That's the situation I put us in by undertaking such an ambitious project.

Last Express **is the first of your personal projects where you didn't do any of the programming. Do you miss it at all?**

One great thing about programming is that, when you're really on a roll, you can lock yourself in a room and have the satisfaction of making progress every day; it's just you and the machine. The times when I would miss that the most was usually when I'd just spent two days in back-to-back meetings. Why did these meetings have to happen and why did I have to be in them? On *Last Express*, we had four programmers working on the project, and although I often envied their lot, I had my hands more than full with the game design, script, artists and animators, casting and directing the actors on the voice recording and film shoot, working with the composer, sound designer, and editor, to list a few things that I actually enjoyed doing. At various points I did offer my services to the programmers, but since my last area of code expertise was in 6502 Assembly Language [on the Apple II] they decided they didn't really need me.

Last Express **is an extremely unique game in both setting and design. In contrast, most of the rest of the new games coming out seem to be set in either fantasy or science fiction settings, and are all based on last year's big hit. How do you feel about the industry's trend toward "me too" games?**

With the occasional magnificent exception, I think you're right about the majority of games. I don't know if the "me too" problem is primarily in terms of setting. I guess I feel it more in terms of genres. You can take *Doom*, and change the textures so that it's an express train in 1914, but I don't think that's really what the industry needs. What's more interesting to me is experimenting with game design itself, how the game is constructed, what the player is actually doing, trying to create a new form that works. That kind of experimentation was a lot easier to do when the publisher's stock price wasn't riding on the success or failure of the

The Last Express

experiment. It's definitely easier to get backing for something that's a sequel or variation on a proven formula. The harder it is to describe or explain something new, the fewer people or companies you'll find who are willing to risk money on it. I think it's unfortunate, but I don't know what to do about it. It's pretty much an inevitable result of the cycle; when we go to the computer store as a shopper and look for the next game, let's be honest, what are we looking for? We're more inclined to look at things that are heavily promoted, that we've read about in magazines. So titles that come out with little fanfare are going to have a harder time reaching the bigger market. So in a sense, as a public, we're getting what we asked for. But as a game designer, yeah, I do miss it.

My friends who make films for a living always used to say: "Oh boy, I really envy you making computer games. There you've got the chance to do something really original. While down here in Hollywood all they want are retreads of last year's sequel." It's kind of interesting how the game industry now has the same set of problems that filmmakers have been complaining about for years. Maybe even worse. Along with bigger production values, bigger markets, and more glitzy award ceremonies, we've achieved a kind of genre paralysis, and it's become more difficult to break new ground.

So you just feel frustrated more than anything.

I guess resigned. I think every new art form goes through stages of its evolution. With computer games we've lived through the exciting early years, and now we're in the growing pains years. This definitely doesn't mean that innovation stops. Even in filmmaking, which is a hundred years old, every couple of years a film does come out that, whether because of societal changes or technological changes, could not have been made a few years earlier, and is a valuable step forward. It's just that you have to weed out hundreds of clones and mediocre films to find those few gems. I think we're in the same place with computer games. Every year, out of hundreds of new games, there's a couple that push the envelope in a new and interesting way. The best we can

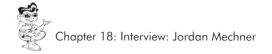

do is just keep trying to do that, and quit griping about the glorious bygone early years, 'cause they're over!

So how involved were you with the *Prince of Persia 3D* project?

My involvement was limited to giving them the go-ahead at the beginning and offering occasional advice and creative consultation along the way. It was a Broderbund project. Andrew Pedersen, the producer, initiated it. It was his baby. He brought the team together and worked hard on it for two years. So I can't take credit for that one.

It's very difficult to take a 2D game and make it work in 3D instead, with full freedom of movement for the player.

That's the problem, really. When you convert *Prince of Persia* to 3D over-the-shoulder, one problem is how do you keep the controls simple. And the other is how does the player know what kind of environment he's in. Because you only see what's right in front of you. A crude example is you're running toward the edge of a chasm. With a side view you can look at it and see if it's a three-space jump or a four-space jump and are you going to clear it or not. If it's too far, you know there's not even any point in trying. Whereas in a 3D over-the-shoulder game, you don't quite know how far it is until you try. And even then, when you fall you wonder, "Was I not quite at the edge? Or did I not jump in quite the right direction?" So it makes it a different kind of game. You gain in terms of visceral immediacy and, of course, the richness of the environment, but I think you lose something in terms of a clean strategy.

So you don't think that making every game 3D is necessarily the correct approach?

Well, you have to distinguish the real-time 3D graphics technology from a particular interface. I think there's a lot that can be done with real-time 3D graphics engines. *Doom*, the first-person shooter, was obviously the first prototype and that was the trend for a couple of years. And then *Tomb Raider* and *Super Mario* did the following camera. *Prince 3D* falls into that category. So I think the challenge is in finding new ways to present the action cinematically that will be as much fun as the old games but still have all the visual excitement of the new 3D games. I think there's plenty of ground yet to cover. *Prince 3D* had a few intriguing moments in it that I'd like to see pushed much further to invent the next big thing in 3D action games.

I read that you enjoyed *Tomb Raider* quite a bit. That seemed to be an attempt to put *Prince of Persia* into a 3D environment in order to produce something new and exciting.

I think the key word there is new. Yes, I was really excited by *Tomb Raider* as a player, because it was something that hadn't been seen before. But I think now that that's been done, we can more clearly see the pros and the cons of that type of game. If you want to do *Tomb Raider* today, you need to find a way to go beyond what they did in '96. You can't just do the same thing over and over.

So did you come up with any good solutions to 3D-space navigation in *Prince of Persia 3D?*

For me, *Prince of Persia 3D* is a bit on the complex side, in terms of the number of weapons and the number of moves. It's not the kind of game that I would design for myself. But they were aiming at a particular audience. I think the core audience as they saw it were people who were a lot more hard-core gamers than I was with the first *Prince of Persia.*

How did *Prince of Persia: The Sands of Time* **come about and how did you get involved with the project?**

In 2001 Ubisoft approached me with the idea of bringing back *Prince of Persia* and doing a new game for consoles. I went up to Montreal to meet Yannis Mallat who was the producer of the project and the small team that he'd assembled.

Had they already started development?

It was actually kind of interesting the way they started. They showed me some AVIs that they had done in the couple of weeks before. These were really quick AVIs. They didn't focus on the look of the world or any graphic kind of bells and whistles. They were very crude, and had an animated character running up a wall, jumping onto a ladder.

Prince of Persia: The Sands of Time

Just very quick little demos of the kind of gameplay they had in mind. The great innovation that was already apparent was here was a guy who could run on walls. So they'd really taken the dynamic of *Prince of Persia 1*, which was a 2D side-scroller, and brought it vertically into a third dimension. Which was something I hadn't seen done in any *Tomb Raider* style action-adventure game. It was just a brilliant idea that opened up a whole world of possibilities as to how this game could capture the excitement of the old-time side-scrollers in a modern real-time 3D game. So based on that we made the deal for Ubisoft to go ahead and start this project. My involvement increased. I had originally thought I would just be a consultant on the project, but I came on board to write the story and the screenplay, and once I'd done that I ended up directing the actors in the voice recording, and finally joined the project full time as a game designer. I was commuting between L.A. and Montreal and my trips kept getting longer and more frequent until for the final stage of the project I moved up to Montreal with my wife and kids. That was the last four months, the summer of 2003.

So you were sucked back into game development against your will?

That's a good choice of words. [laughter] The other word I would use is seduced. It was just such a fun project and the team was so talented and working so hard and the potential was so clearly there from the beginning. They wanted to do something really extraordinary. Ubisoft Montreal was not yet on the map then the way they are now, following *Splinter Cell* and *Sands of Time*. At the time this team had not yet done those types of high-profile games but they were certainly capable of it. They just had to prove it to the world. It was a very refreshing atmosphere; working with them was a real pleasure.

It's interesting that *Sands of Time* is so radically different from the prior 3D incarnation of the game, *Prince of Persia 3D*.

That was one of the first things that I talked about with Ubisoft when they proposed doing a new *Prince of Persia* game. Neither of us wanted to do another *Prince of Persia 3D*. So we kind of mutually reassured each other that that wasn't what we had in mind. The problem with *Prince of Persia 3D* from the moment it was proposed and on through the early stages, the obvious question to ask was, "Isn't this just *Tomb Raider* with baggy pants and a turban?" And ultimately I think in the end it really was *Tomb Raider* with baggy pants and a turban. That wasn't enough. So for *Sands of Time*, Ubisoft and I basically said let's not even look at *Prince of Persia 3D*. Let's look at the original titles — why were they fun, what aspects of that make us think that a remake now is worth doing? What are the aspects that we want to try to capture from the original? In what ways is this going to be a totally new and different game? *Sands of Time*, in many ways, was like doing an original title. It had been so long since *Prince 1* and *2*, ten years, the expectations of what a video game should be are so different now. There was no possibility of literally sticking to the rules of gameplay or the character or the story or anything like that. We needed a new character, new story, new gameplay, new rules.

    Prince of Persia ultimately represented a style of game, a kind of feeling that you get playing it. One of the main inspirations for *Prince 1*, back in 1986 when I started to program it on the Apple II, had been the first ten minutes of *Raiders of the Lost Ark*. The idea of doing a game that would have that kind of running, jumping, seat-of-your-pants improvising these acrobatic responses to a dangerous environment. And then of course the story being a swashbuckling adventure movie in the spirit of *Raiders*, and

Prince of Persia: The Sands of Time

before that the films of Errol Flynn and Douglas Fairbanks in the '30s. So all of that was also an inspiration for *Sands of Time*. But when you get down to the details of what can the game character do and how do you control it, we didn't feel compelled to follow the rules that had been set up in the ten-year-old 2D side-scroller. And I think that was all to the good.

To take one example, potions: you find a potion, you drink it, it restores your strength. That was fine in *Prince 1*, but wouldn't work in the new game. Because why would you have useful magic elixirs sitting around in a dungeon, waiting for someone to find them and drink them? Why wouldn't they have been drunk already by a thirsty guard or prisoner? In a 1989 2D side-scroller, you can assume a certain suspension of disbelief. But when you have a realistic environment that's lavishly rendered with all the painterly beauty and lighting effects and so on that the PS2 or Xbox are capable of, it just doesn't make sense. Ultimately we went with the concept that water itself is the substance that revives you. Water is a natural feature of Islamic and Persian palaces and gardens. You've got fountains and waterfalls. That was a way to take a feature of the environment and make it useful and important for the gameplay. So any place you find water in the game, even if you're standing in a pool, if you drink, it restores your strength. That's one example. If you've played *Prince 1* and *Sands of Time*, you can see that when you get right down to it, nearly every game feature is different. It's just the overall feeling, the spirit, that has been preserved.

The dagger is a really nice element in the game, because it is really important both to the gameplay and the story. Did that start out as a gameplay mechanic or a story device?

Rewinding actually started out as a gameplay wish from creative director Patrice Desilets. When you die and have to restart, you kind of break the spell of the player's involvement in the game. Patrice thought rewinding would be a nice, organic way to allow the player to continue to play uninterrupted, without dying so often. That then gave rise to an engineering challenge, which was "Can this be done on the PS2, on a console system that doesn't have a hard drive?" The engineers worked on that for a while and ended up proving that it could be done. So it was a gameplay idea that gave rise to an engineering innovation that then led to the story question of "How do we justify the player having this ability?" and to the concept of the dagger and the Sands of Time.

The Sands of Time serve a number of functions in the story. First of all, they're the substance that enables you to turn back time. As the player, you have to find ways to collect the sand, and then as you turn back time you use it up. Second, the way that you collect the sand is by killing these sand creatures that are possessed by the sand. They're like undead monsters in the sense that you can hit them as many times as you want with your sword, but the only way to get rid of them for good is to use the dagger to retrieve the sands that possess them, then they disintegrate. So the sand gives you an incentive and a reason to want to fight these enemies. All the other powers of time — being able to freeze your enemies, move at hyper-speed, the sand vortex that when you enter it gives you a glimpse of what's to come — came out of trying to take the central idea and weave it through as many aspects of the game as possible, while keeping the story as clean and simple as possible.

The storytelling in *Sands of Time* is very elegant, but the plot is actually quite simple. Do you think that more games should strive for streamlined plots? Or was that just something that *Prince of Persia* specifically called for?

It's a good thing for a game to be as simple as it can be. But depending on the type of game, it calls for a different kind of simplicity. The complexity in *Sands of Time* should come out of the acrobatics, the nuts and bolts of how do you get through this room. Do you grab on to the pillar and then jump on to the platform, or do you run on the wall and swing on the bar? Those are the kinds of issues that should absorb the player. So the story shouldn't be distracting them with things that have nothing to do with the gameplay. The cut-scenes in *Sands of Time* are relatively brief and tend to contain the same kind of action that's in the game. In the game you're doing acrobatic action and fighting monsters. So that's mostly what you're doing in the cut-scenes as well, with the occasional brief shouted line of dialog. The conversations that you have with the female sidekick character, Farah, are very much in the midst of this action, this relationship that's being developed very quickly under fire and under pressure. We're not cutting away to another place to have big dialog scenes between characters that we've never met before. The two biggest cut-scenes in the game are the one that launches the story, when the prince actually uses the dagger to open the hourglass to release the Sands of Time, effectively opening Pandora's box, and then one at the end that resolves it. The premise of the story has a dark element, in that the hero himself causes the catastrophe that makes it necessary to play the game. So all of that dovetails very nicely.

Though you kept the story in *Sands of Time* fairly simple for a modern action-adventure, in terms of the previous *Prince of Persias* or *Karateka* it is quite a bit more complex. For example, the prince never spoke before, and the cut-scenes were much shorter and more infrequent.

Prince 1 and *Karateka* were like silent movies. Silent movies didn't have dialog; they had title cards. Nowadays, with the level of sound and graphics that we're accustomed to, we expect that characters will talk, unless there's a story reason why they can't talk, as in a game like *Ico* where they don't share a common language. But here you've got a king, a prince, and a princess; you're not going to get away without defining their characters and their personalities to a certain extent. So it's really more a matter of creating a story and dialog, both in the cut-scenes and in the game action itself, that will develop the relationships among the characters and advance the story while entertaining the player.

Also in contrast to the previous *Prince of Persia* games, which as you mentioned earlier prided themselves on having fairly simple controls, this new one is really quite complex, with all of the different moves the prince can pull off with his multiple weapons, and so forth. Was this done to bring the gameplay up to modern expectations?

That's de rigueur for the genre. It's not a handheld game that you play on your cell phone, it's not a point-and-click game like *Last Express*; this is a console action game, and your audience is going to be people who like to pick up a controller and play.

However, within that, I think we did a pretty good job of keeping the controls simple and consistent. We didn't have the kind of semi-arbitrary memorized combinations where you have to hit X-X-Triangle-Circle. Each of the four action buttons does a fairly simple, understandable thing, and from that is generated quite a lot of richness as to what the player can actually do. And that comes from

Prince of Persia: The Sands of Time

having the controls be context-sensitive. So that, for example, pressing X if you're clinging to a pillar will cause you to eject from that pillar, whereas if you press X when you're standing on the ground, it will make you roll or it will make you jump, depending on the situation. In *Sands of Time*, it's the same principle as in *Prince 1*: our goal was to get the player to the point where he doesn't have to think about what button is he going to press, but just develop that instinct of reaching for a certain button in certain types of situations and have the richness flow out of that.

Prince of Persia: The Sands of Time **seems to be pushing forward and innovating the storytelling/gameplay blend that's very popular these days. How do you see that evolving in the coming years?**

Certainly story is becoming more appreciated as an element of games. But games are not about story. A movie is about the story, a game is about the gameplay. A good story can enrich a game, it can add to the pleasure, in much the same way that a good musical score can add to the enjoyment of a movie. But game designers can sometimes fall into the trap of developing a really complex story and thinking that somehow makes the game more complex or more interesting. Most action/adventure games with complex stories suffer from a clunky alternation between gameplay and cut-scenes. My personal preference to enhance the story aspect of action games is to bring the story into the gameplay. If an interaction can happen while you're playing rather than while you're sitting back and watching a cut-scene, then that's the best place for it. *Sands of Time* does that to a degree in the relationship between the prince and Farah. As they're fighting off monsters they shout to each other, they call warnings to each other, and occasionally if the prince is hurt after a fight, Farah will express concern. There's a lot of natural opportunities for humor, whereas humor in a cut-scene can seem kind of forced. The times that we do stop the game for a cut-scene between the prince and Farah are actually pretty few and brief, and those scenes focus on significant plot twists that flow out of the gameplay and then right back into it with changed stakes.

Do you hope to one day get rid of the cut-scenes entirely?

Oh absolutely. The more we can create a seamless experience where the story unfolds through the gameplay, the more convincing that world becomes. When you bring the story out of the cut-scenes and into the gameplay, the gameplay then becomes more cinematic. In *Sands of Time*, the camera is not just glued behind the prince's head, follow- ing him around.

Prince of Persia: The Sands of Time

Sometimes you enter a room and the camera takes a cinematic approach, showing you the environment, emphasizing certain features, directing your attention to certain clues. During gameplay, the camera will cut from one angle to another for a dramatic introduction of enemies, to show the prince unsheathe his sword to fight, to show what Farah's doing. As the game camera becomes smarter and freer, that allows you to do things in the game that previously you could only have done in cut-scenes.

Do you think you will ever manage to work on another game other than a new *Prince of Persia*?

Much as I enjoyed working on *Sands of Time*, I don't foresee repeating that level of personal involvement in a *Prince of Persia* game. This was a special situation because it was really essential both for Ubisoft and myself to get the series off to the strongest start possible. It was such a long gap between *Prince 2* and *Sands of Time* — ten years — that it didn't feel like doing a sequel, it felt like an original title. Now that *Sands* is done, there's a lot of great talent at Ubisoft Montreal and they are very good at building on their franchises and taking them in new directions. I'm excited to see what Ubisoft will do with *Prince* but for my next game, I'm most interested in exploring original ideas and new directions.

That's not to say I'm done with *Prince of Persia* because my current project is writing the screenplay for the *Prince of Persia* movie, which Jerry Bruckheimer is producing for Disney. John August and I are executive producers on the project.

Do you find that your game designs change much over the course of a project?

With *Karateka* and *Prince of Persia* I had the luxury of letting the game evolve over time, since it was just me in a room with a computer, with no budget and no corporate bottom line. I thought *Prince of Persia* would take a year and it ended up taking three, and that was OK — that was what it was. *Last Express* was different because it was such a large project. With the machine that we constructed with hundreds of people and net-worked computers, every day was expensive, so changing the design in midstream was not an option. There I spent a lot more time at the beginning trying to work out the game in detail. You just have to pray that the original design is solid and doesn't have severe flaws that will reveal themselves down the line.

But your earlier games did change significantly over the course of their development?

Oh yeah. One example: *Prince of Persia* was originally not supposed to have combat. One of my bright ideas there was an answer to what I saw as the clichéd vio-lence of computer games. I wanted the player to be an unarmed innocent in a hostile world full of spikes and traps. There would be lots of gory violence directed against the player,

Prince of Persia

which it would be your job to avoid, but you would never actually dish it out. That was also a way of dealing with the fact that I didn't think there was enough computer mem-ory to have another character running around on the screen at the same time. Luckily, I had stalwart friends who kept pushing me to add combat. When your friends tell you your game is boring, you'd better listen.

Shadow Man, the character, was a serendipitous accident because I thought, "There's no way to add another character in there, we don't have the memory for it." Only if the character looked exactly like the Prince, if he used the same animation frames. I can't remember who suggested it, but by shifting the character over by one bit and then exclusive ORing with himself you got a black shape with a shimmery white outline. So I tried that, and when I saw Shadow Man running around the screen I said, "Cool, there's a new character." So that suggested the whole plot device of the mirror and jumping through the mirror and having an evil alter ego who would follow you around and try to thwart you by closing a gate that you wanted to be open or by dropping things on your head. And then there was the resolution, where you fight Shadow Man at the end, but you can't kill him, since he's yourself, and if you kill him you die. So you have to find a way to solve that. Call it Jungian or what you will, it was a way to take advantage of the fact that we didn't have that much memory.

So later on you must have found some more memory so you could put in the other characters.

A lot of the time that goes into programming a game like *Prince of Persia* on a computer like the Apple II is taking what you've done already and redoing it to make it smaller and faster. Eventually the stuff that was in there just got more efficient and left enough room to come up with a limited set of character shapes for the guards. If you notice, there's a lot that the guards can't do. They can't run and jump and chase you. All they can do is fight.

Your games have all been very visually appealing. How did you balance the games' visual appearance with the requirements of the gameplay?

I think along with what we already talked about with the simplicity of the controls and consistency of the interface, visuals are another component where it's often tempting to compromise. You think, "Well, we could put a menu bar across here, we could put a number in the upper right-hand corner of the screen representing how many potions you've drunk," or something. The easy solution is always to do something that as a side effect is going to make the game look ugly. So I took as one of the ground rules going in that the overall screen layout had to be pleasing, had to be strong and simple. So that somebody who was not playing the game but who walked into the room and saw someone else playing it would be struck by a pleasing composition and could stop to watch for a minute, thinking, "This looks good, this looks as if I'm watching a movie." It really forces you as a designer to struggle to find the best solution for things like inventory. You can't take the first solution that suggests itself, you have to try to solve it within the constraint that you set yourself.

So what made you decide to stop working in games and pursue screenwriting full time?

I've always sort of alternated games and film projects. I think there's a lot of value to recharging your creative batteries in a different medium. *Karateka* took a lot of inspiration from my film studies at Yale, especially silent films. *Prince of Persia* would not have been as rich if I hadn't spent those couple of years after *Karateka* thinking and breathing film, writing a screenplay. The same with *Last Express*. That project came on the heels of doing a short documentary film in Cuba called *Waiting for Dark*. And *Sands of Time* came after my longest break from games, several years during which I wrote screenplays and directed another documentary, *Chavez Ravine*. Right now, the challenge of writing the *Prince of Persia* movie and getting a good film made is my top priority. After that, I don't know whether my immediate next project will be a film, a video game, or something else. To me a compelling project is one that I have to talk myself *out* of pursuing, rather than talk myself into it.

Technology is evolving pretty fast. A video game now is so different from what a video game was ten years ago, who's to say what we'll be doing in ten years?

So it's not that you prefer working in a more linear form. It's more of an alternate pursuit for you.

It's a different form, but a lot of the challenges are surprisingly similar. With a computer game, although it's a non-linear means of telling a story, you still have the fascinating mystery of what is it about a particular world or a particular set of characters that makes that game thrilling and gripping. What makes people say, "I want to play this game, I want to be Mario," and then look at another game that might be technically just as good and say, "I have no interest in being this character in this world." Same with a film. There's some mysterious chemistry between an audience and a storyteller that causes the audience to decide, even based just on the trailer, whether or not they want to live this particular story.

The two art forms are not all that dissimilar when it comes to sitting down and wrestling with a set of elements and trying to get them into some kind of finite shape. The challenges of taking an established genre and breaking new ground with it somehow, of making it surprising and suspenseful, of economically using the elements at your disposal, are very similar whether it's a game or a film. The hardest thing with *Karateka* and *Prince of Persia* on the Apple II was coming back to it day after day, looking at something that had taken me a week to program and saying, "You know what? I got it working, but now I have to throw it out and find something different." Same with screenwriting. You have to be willing to throw away your own work repeatedly over the course of a long project in order to arrive at that finite set of elements that works just right.

I've heard a lot of people say that film was the dominant art form of the 20th century, and now games are going to dominate the 21st century. As someone who's worked in both games and film, I wondered if you wanted to comment on what you think of the future of the two mediums.

I don't know. I sort of scratch my head about that type of statement. Is film more dominant an art form than music? What does that really mean? I think film and video games are very different art forms. We're going through an interesting period right now where video games are more like movies, and movies, or at least a certain type of summer blockbuster movie, are more like video games than they have been at any time in the past. There's a great interest in Hollywood and the video game industry of creating these kind of cross-marketed properties so that you can have the hit movie and the hit video game and the hit theme park ride all come out at the same time. But that doesn't mean that every single film that's made has to be a summer popcorn movie. It also doesn't mean that every video game that's made has to be this sort of spectacular, story-driven, film-friendly thing. The extreme example of a game that has no movie potential is something like *Tetris*. It succeeds purely as a game. The gap between *Tetris* and Krzysztof Kieslowski's *Blue* is pretty huge. [laughter] So there's plenty of healthy room for innovation in both fields, and that's not going to change any time soon.

Jordan Mechner Gameography

Karateka, 1984
Prince of Persia, 1989
Prince of Persia 2, 1993
The Last Express, 1997
Prince of Persia 3D, 1999 (Consultant)
Prince of Persia: The Sands of Time, 2003

This interview originally appeared in a different form in *Inside Mac Games* magazine, www.imgmagazine.com. Used with permission.

Chapter 19:
The Design Document

"It wasn't until *Ultima IV: Quest of the Avatar*, that *Ultimas* really started having compelling, purposeful stories, and it was the first game in the series to have a social commentary subtext. Not only did I want to build worlds that were large, epic, and meaningful, I also wanted to add a subtext to each game which might not necessarily be obvious in the actions your characters took in the game, but one which ultimately would give the game a more lasting meaning. So in *Ultima IV* you had to prove yourself to be a good person, one who could be an example to the people of Britannia. The game acted like a 'Big Brother,' requiring gamers to behave in a 'heroic' fashion in order to win the game. I thought that design was pretty cool, since gamers were accustomed to pretending to be the hero yet they would beat up all the townsfolk in order to become powerful enough to beat up the character who was supposed to be the big bad guy, even though he generally didn't do anything bad in the game."

— Richard Garriott

For some years, while I was still an aspiring professional designer, I wanted someone to tell me what the official format for a design document was. I knew that Hollywood screenplays had a very precise format, and I figured there must be something comparably rigorous for design documents. What sort of information is it supposed to include? How should it be laid out? What format should it use? Only recently, after numerous years as a professional, did I figure out the big secret, and it is one that I am happy to pass on to you in this book. Yes, here my years of experience in the gaming industry will impart on you this precious information.

There is no format! Everyone who writes a game design document just makes up their own format! Have you ever heard of anything so incredible? Whenever I have asked people what format I should be using for a particular document, they invariably answer, "Well, you know, the standard format." No one really knows what this mythical "standard" format is, yet all refer to it. In the end, as long as it communicates the nature of the game effectively and in sufficient detail, whatever you hand over to the people who will review your document will be regarded as the "standard" format. There is definitely a certain type and quantity of information that belongs in a design document and which must be included for it to be useful, but there is no standardized form you must use in documenting that data.

Certainly within some companies, especially large ones, there may be an agreed-upon format that all of the in-house designers must use for their documents. Your design document will end up standing out if it diverges too much from other design documents in the industry. It makes sense for you to get your hands on every official design document you can, just as you might seek out practice exams before taking major standardized tests. Optimally, you will be able to obtain some documents that were used for games that were actually published. Or, at least, you will want to review documents written by designers who have completed and shipped games. This is hard to do, since gaming companies are fanatical about protecting their intellectual property and do not want to reveal how chaotic their internal development may be, but see what you can find. The *Atomic Sam* and *The Suffering* design documents included at the end of this book are good ones with which to start.

A design document is all about communicating a vision for a game, for mapping out as much information as possible about how that game will function, what players will experience, and how players will interact with the game-world. Organizing and structuring all of this information into appropriate sections is one of the key challenges in writing a good design document. Again, many companies may prefer their documents in a format different from what I describe here, and you should certainly organize your data in the form desired by the people for whom you are writing. If the development team is familiar with navigating design documents written in a specific format, you should mold your data to fit that format. Remember, the design document is not the end result of your efforts; the game is. As such, the format of the design document is relatively unimportant. As long as the format allows for the effective communication of the pertinent information, the design document will be a success.

The Writing Style

Before we delve into which sections your design document should contain and what areas it should cover, it is worth discussing the style you should employ when writing your document. The design document is meant to be a reference tool and, as such, you want to make it as easy for people to search and refer to as possible. A big part of this will be maintaining a good Table of Contents, as we will discuss in a moment. In writing the text of your document, you will want to break it up with lots of titles, headings, subheadings, and so forth. This will make it easier for readers to skim over the document and zoom in on the information they are seeking. Breaking your information into lists, either numbered or bulleted, wherever possible will further allow readers to easily realize what different attributes a given part of the game will need to include. Some find it more difficult to write in a bullet-point style, as it requires you to constantly shift indentations around and bold-face titles instead of just including all your ideas in a single narrative paragraph. You may find it easiest to write out your document first, and then go back and format it properly. That way you get all the content down, and when you go back to edit the document, you can simultaneously properly format it. Other designers actually prefer writing in a bullet-point style from the start to keep their ideas straight. Though writing in a bullet-point style may involve more hassle for you, the end result is a more useful document for the members of your team. Furthermore, the managers and executives will appreciate it, since it makes the document that much easier to skim.

Some designers use special writing tools for composing their document. These might be applications better suited to writing text with lots of headings, subheadings, bulleted lists, and so forth. These various applications may allow for the autoformatting and indenting of text, which could save you a lot of the time you would spend in a regular word processor dragging around indentation markers and tab stops. That said, I have never used such a tool, nor have I ever worked with someone who did. The primary problem with these tools is that once your document is done, you will need to pass it around electronically for everyone to read. Chances are slim everyone will have this unique formatting tool. Instead they will have a regular word processor. The document will be read by everyone from the other members of your development team to the people in management to the executives at your publisher. You cannot expect all of these people to have installed whatever eclectic design document authoring tool you have chosen. If the tool you use provides an exporter to a standard word processor file format such as Rich Text Format (.rtf), that will usually solve this problem, but make sure the exporter actually exports a document that matches the one you have composed. Still, I have always been quite content using standard word processors for my own needs, and have not felt the need for a more capable tool.

Though there is a great temptation to do whatever is necessary to "bulk up" your document in order to make it seem more thorough and complete, you want to avoid repeating information as much as possible. This is challenging as you talk about an element of gameplay that directly relies on another system you discussed ten pages back. Instead of redescribing the system, refer your reader to the system's original definition. This is important since, as you find yourself updating the document over the course of the project's development, you will need to change data in only one place instead of several. Often, if the same gameplay mechanism is described in detail in more than one place, when it comes time to make a change, only one of the descriptions will get updated. This leaves the other description out of date, thus resulting in an internally inconsistent document. Nothing is more frustrating to the reader than to find contradictory information in the design document. Inconsistent information in a specification can also throw up a red flag for producers, who will begin to question your competency to develop a game when you cannot seem to keep your facts straight.

Many people like to read design documents on their computer, as it allows them to search for words and navigate the document more easily than with a large heap of paper on their desk. For these people, it makes sense to include hyperlinks wherever appropriate. Most modern word processors make it easy to create links from one part of your document to another, allowing the reader to quickly navigate to another relevant section. This can be quite helpful as you try to avoid repeating any more of your design than is absolutely necessary. Instead of repeating, include a hyperlink to the pertinent location so that the reader can jump there if she needs to remember how a specific system functions. A Wiki hypertext system can be great for allowing you to easily link from one part of a document to another, or, more often, to break your big document into smaller chunks that can all be interlinked easily. Wiki also allows you to easily link to other content that does not belong in the design document, such as the technical design document for a given feature or the art bible that shows what a particular character looks like.

As you write your document, you want to write as well as you possibly can, but keep in mind that the design document is supposed to be a reference document for the creation of an entertaining game, not an entertaining document in and of itself. You want your writing to communicate the information necessary in as concise and succinct a manner possible. Do not spend a lot of time worrying about making the document stimulating reading. No one is looking for excitement when reading the bulk of a design document; they are looking for information. I usually try to make the Introduction and Story Overview the most readable sections of the document, where someone could actually sit down and read through those sections and be interested while doing so. But for the rest of the document, you will be successful if you simply manage to include all of the information necessary. Spending a lot of time dressing it up with fancy verbiage will do nothing to improve your game. Similarly, though you should try to write as correctly as possible, do not spend too much time worrying about editing the document for grammatical mistakes. If the members of your team — your document's audience — are able to read it and get the information they need, they will be happy. They really will not care if you used a gerund correctly or not. That said, if your document is so dry or badly written that no one can stand reading it, people will be less likely to turn to it for the information they need. Furthermore, if you are writing your design document as a really large pitch document that you hope will convince people to fund your project, you may need to be a little more refined and sales-oriented with your writing, while still keeping the document useful and relevant for the development team.

As you write your document, it will be awfully tempting to compare elements of your design to other games, certainly ones the readers are likely to have played. Though in Chapter 5 I discouraged you from using such comparisons in your focus, in the design document comparisons can actually be useful, but with a caveat: you must fully explain your system, even if it is "just like the mechanic found in *Super Mario 64*." A comparison to a popular game can provide the reader with a starting point to understanding a complex game system you are describing. If she can remember that game, she will instantly have some idea of what you are talking about. Of course, to prevent any confusion, you must still include a thorough description of that aspect of your design. Comparisons are rarely useful enough to replace a thorough explanation of how a system is supposed to work. Therefore, do not rely on a comparison as a crutch to save you the trouble of documenting some gameplay. Nonetheless, having started with the comparison, your readers will have a better chance of understanding exactly what you are driving at when you go on to fully describe and document the system.

Though comparisons to existing games, such as the oft-cited *Super Mario 64*, may be appropriate in the design document, the designer should be careful to fully explain what she means by the comparison.

The Sections

The game design documents I write typically break down into the following major sections. Within each of these, there will be further subdivisions, and not every game may require that all of these sections be used.

- Table of Contents
- Introduction/Overview
- Game Mechanics
- Artificial Intelligence
- Game Elements
- Story Overview
- Game Progression
- System Menus

Table of Contents

The reader may laugh to think that I list this as an important part of the document. Of course a document over fifty pages in length and containing multiple sections will have a table of contents — why even mention it? What bears emphasis, however, is the nature of the Table of Contents section. Since creating an index is a time-consuming task for a large body of text such as a design document, it is unlikely you will have time to make one. In the absence of an index, the Table of Contents ends up as the tool people use to navigate your document. When a member of the development team needs to find a specific piece of information in your document, she will be inclined to look first in the Table of Contents to try to find where that information is most likely to be. So the more detailed and inclusive your Table of Contents, the more likely she will be able to quickly find the information she needs.

No simple novel-style table of contents will do in the design document — in other words, no listing of only eight separate sections with the reader left to navigate the pages within the sections on her own. The Table of Contents must include subsections, sub-subsections, and perhaps even sub-sub-subsections. We have already discussed how you will need to use bolded headings throughout your document to make it easy to navigate. In addition, any commercial word processor will allow you to turn these headings into entries in a table of contents. These entries will then automatically update for you as those headings move around within the document. Most word processors even allow someone reading the document on her computer to click on an entry in the table of contents and be taken directly to the appropriate part of the document. Making a detailed Table of Contents for your design document is crucial to making it useful.

Introduction/Overview or Executive Summary

It is a good idea to have a single-page overview of your game's design at the beginning of your document. This summary is not very useful to developers actively toiling away on the project, who, as you may remember, are the target audience for the document. However, for new team members who come on board the project, a summary will be a good starting point for understanding the game. Indeed, for anyone reading the document for the first time, be they a producer, an executive, or a marketer, getting an idea of the game's "big picture" through a one-page summary can be quite helpful. Even if whoever reads the Introduction is not going to have time to read the rest of the document, this one-page summary should allow them to understand the essence of the gameplay.

The Introduction should limit itself to a single page. Longer than that and the Introduction stops being an effective summary. Any information that does not fit on a single page is simply not part of the game's core design. If you find yourself going over the limit, figure out what is least important among the data you have in the summary and cut it. Repeat this process until the summary fits on a single page. Think of the summary like your resume: longer than a page and you may lose your reader. Write a gripping first paragraph that sums up the entire game, with the following paragraphs filling in the structure outlined in the opening.

Before writing the design document, you should have worked on defining your game's focus, as I explored in Chapter 5, "Focus." That focus is an excellent starting point for your summary. Recall that the focus is a summing up of your game's most compelling points in a single paragraph. Start with your focus as the opening paragraph of your overview, and then use the following paragraphs to go into more detail about each compelling part of your game.

One of the body paragraphs of your overview should sum up the game's story, if any. In this paragraph, focus on the adventures players will experience during gameplay, while not dwelling so much on the back-story or history of the game-world. Follow the game through to the story's conclusion, mentioning the different types of worlds players will navigate and characters they will encounter. Always keep in mind that this is just a summary, so it does not need to go into that much depth. Just touch on the high points of your story and move on to the next paragraph.

The other body paragraphs of your Introduction should discuss different aspects of your gameplay, using the key parts as outlined in your focus. What features of the gameplay are most central to the game and will be most instrumental in making gamers want to play your work for hours and hours? Of course, you should not focus on features that all games have ("Project X includes the ability to save the player's game at any time!") but rather on features that will make your game stand out, the parts that define your game as a unique and compelling experience.

The conclusion should then come in and sum up the entire overview, with a special emphasis on why this game will be so compelling to the user, what this game does that no other game has. The reader should finish the page on an up note, enthusiastic about the project. Think of this page summary as rallying the troops, psyching up the team, and getting people excited about the project without forcing them to read over the entire document.

Game Mechanics

The Game Mechanics section is the most important part of your document. When looking at a design document for the first time, this is the section that I look at first to determine what the gameplay really is for the game. Indeed, the Game Mechanics section could also be called the "gameplay" section, since it describes what players are allowed to do in the game and how the game is played. By describing what sort of actions players can perform, the Game Mechanics section defines the game itself. Because of this, the Game Mechanics section is one of the hardest to write in the design document. Describing gameplay is an extremely challenging proposition, and as a result many bad game design documents skip this section entirely, preferring instead to focus on story, visuals, or menuing systems, all of which are easier topics to write about. The old saying goes, "Writing about music is like dancing about architecture." Writing about gameplay is just as challenging and imperfect, yet it must be done for your design document to be useful to the team who will create your game.

Except for necessary references to the player character, you will want to avoid detailing any specific game-world objects or characters in the Game Mechanics section. Save those descriptions for the relevant content sections later in the document. For instance, you will want to describe the possible effects of the different weapons players might pick up and how players will control those weapons, but you will want to save the actual list of the different weapons found in the game-world until later in the document. The specific weapons represent instances of the functionality you describe in the Game Mechanics section. You can think of it in the following fashion: many different games could be made from what you lay out in the Game Mechanics section. For instance, the design documents for the *Thief* games follow a nearly identical Game Mechanics description. It is only the weapons, items, levels, and enemies that change from *Thief* to *Thief II*. The core game remains the same, and it is the core game you are documenting in the Game Mechanics section.

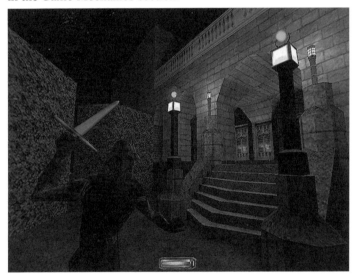

Sequels are often able to use a Game Mechanics section in their design documents that is identical or extremely similar to the original game. Pictured here: *Thief II*.

It makes sense to introduce the players' different capabilities in the same order someone playing the game for the first time would experience them. For instance, start out simple. What are the most basic moves players can do? Say you are working on a game where players control a game-world surrogate (be it a human, a spaceship, an airplane, a robot, or whatever your imagination may have concocted). You should probably start with how that character moves forward and backward, turns left and right, and so forth. After you introduce the simpler moves, introduce more complex ones such as jumping, crouching, rolling, and so on, as appropriate. If your game is more of an RTS game or *Diablo*-style RPG, it may be that players move their surrogate(s) using point-and-click, and you will want to describe precisely how that works. How good does the player character pathfinding need to be? What does the game do when the surrogate cannot reach the place players clicked? Do you have separate buttons to select a character and then to move it, or is it more of a one-button system?

As you describe the character's movements, you will want to list the physical commands users need to perform to pull off those movements. For instance, "To move forward, players will need to press and hold the Forward Button. If players just tap the Forward Button, the player character will only move a tiny amount." It is probably a good idea to name the different keys or buttons players have as their controls instead of referring to them specifically; use "Forward Button" instead of "Up arrow" or "Blue X button." This keeps your description of the players' controls more platform-independent and allows you to change which keys do what later, without making you change a lot of instances of "the Up arrow" in your design document. A programmer who is implementing your control system does not care so much what the literal key assignment for a command is, but she needs to know how many different commands users will have and what game-world actions are associated with which commands.

Once you describe how players command their game-world surrogate, the next logical step is to describe the surrogate's movement model. Does it follow a realistic physics model or something more simplistic? Does it ramp up to full speed slowly or does it achieve terminal velocity immediately? Does it move more slowly up inclines than on flat surfaces? Is its responsiveness quick and tight like *Quake* or slow and precise like *Tomb Raider?* How does it react when it bumps into an object — slide off, turn, or just stop? These are the sorts of details you will need to consider and describe in depth.

It may be that moving game pieces or player surrogates around is not the key operation in your game. Think of what players starting a game would do first, and describe that. If you were describing *Railroad Tycoon*, for instance, you would want to talk about how players lay down track and the rules governing that. If you were writing the design document for *Lemmings*, you might want to describe how players can change a regular lemming into a special lemming, such as a blocker or a digger. If you were describing *SimCity,* you would want to explain how players zone an area.

RPGs such as *Diablo II* often start the game with the player creating her character. Of course this will need to be fully described in the design document.

If your game starts out with players needing to create their character, as they might in an RPG such as *Diablo*, you will want to describe that process, summarizing the significance of each statistic players must choose. What does "strength" or "dexterity" represent? Later on in the Game Mechanics section, when you are describing an action that is affected by a particular statistic, you will be able to refer the reader back to that particular statistic's original definition.

Having started with the basics, you can proceed to the players' more complex actions, trying to logically structure the document so that each subsequent action builds on the previous one as much as possible. You want your different game mechanics to flow one into the next so the reader can see the structure of the game building. And, of course, you want to avoid referring to mechanisms you have not yet defined or detailed.

Certainly the topics you will cover will vary widely depending on what type of game you are creating. If your game involves combat, you will need to go over that in detail, explaining how the players use different weapons and what the possible effects of those weapons are on the game-world. If the player's surrogate is able to pick up and manipulate objects, you will want to explain fully how they are picked up, how they are accessed, how inventory management works, and so forth.

The Game Mechanics section is also a proper place to lay out what sort of puzzles players might encounter in the game-world. Indeed, if your game is a puzzle game, this will take up a large portion of the mechanics section. You will want to describe how puzzles function and how players are able to manipulate them, and give direction as to how the puzzles will be created, without actually listing specific puzzles. As with the descriptions of specific weapons, save lists of puzzles for the content sections later in the document. For instance, say you were describing puzzles in the original *Prince of Persia*. You would want to explain that puzzles can involve hitting pressure plates, hidden knock-away ceilings, falling floor segments, gates that can be raised and lowered by the pressure plates, spikes that spring out from the floors and walls, special potions, certain types of magical effects, and whatever other components the game-world allows. You will not actually list any specific configurations of these components that will be found in the levels. Save that for the level-specific sections later in the document, or for the level designers to figure out on their own. Here you should list the palette of objects and behaviors from which the puzzles can be created.

Describing the variety of puzzle components found in a game such as *Prince of Persia* is appropriate in the Game Mechanics section.

If the game in question involves players switching into different modes in order to accomplish different tasks, each of these modes should be described in detail. For instance, in the original *Drakan: Order of the Flame*, players maneuver the player-surrogate, Rynn, through the world using forward and backward keys, while the mouse turns the character. However, when players press the inventory key, the game goes into inventory mode. From this mode players no longer control Rynn's movements, but instead are presented with a mouse cursor with which Rynn's inventory can be manipulated using standard drag-and-drop functionality. In the design document for *Drakan*, the designer would want to clearly describe how the controls shift from one mode to the next and how the game-world is manipulated in each.

Some sections of the design document will be dependent on the technology the game will be using, whether 2D or 3D, indoor or outdoor, real-time or pre-rendered. Though one tries to separate the technological aspects of the game into the technical design document and keep them out of the design document as much as possible, what is being created is still a computer game, and as such it is inherently tied to the technology it will use. Writing a design document without having any sense of what sort of technology the game will have access to is usually impossible and at the very best impractical. You do not need to know how many polygons per second the engine will be able to handle, or whether it will support NURBS or not. However, you do need to have some base understanding of the tools that will be available to the designer. Designing a control or combat system that works in a 3D world and one that works in a 2D one are completely distinct and different tasks. You want to play to the strengths of the technology the game will use while dodging the weaknesses.

For example, the Game Mechanics section will need to describe what players see while they are playing the game. This includes how the players see the world, what sort of camera view will be used, and how players will be able to affect that camera's position. In order to write about this, you need to know what the camera will be capable of doing, which is entirely dependent on the game's engine. It may be that the engine will only support a first-person view, only a side view, or any number of other limitations. Nonetheless, how players see the world is such a central part of the game's design that you must discuss it in the Game Mechanics section.

The GUI is extremely important to games such as *Alpha Centauri*, and will need to be thoroughly described in the design document.

The in-game graphical user interface (GUI) is of critical importance to your game, and therefore it should be described in detail in the Game Mechanics section. You should describe any data that is overlaid on the depiction of the game-world, such as, for an action game, the players' health or other statistics needed during gameplay. The GUI section should also cover any other GUIs that are part of gameplay, such as what players see when their surrogate becomes involved in a conversation or when managing inventory. Describing the graphical interface is even more important for games like *Alpha Centauri* or *The Sims*, which include many different GUIs and in which players constantly use the GUI to play the game. The descriptions of these GUIs can either all be included in one part of the Game Mechanics section, or can be detailed during the description of the system to which they are relevant. Remember that you want your design document to be as reader-friendly as possible. If the art director is looking for the different GUIs that need to be created and they are scattered throughout the Game Mechanics section, some may be missed. On the other hand, a programmer might prefer to find the GUI for a particular system included with the description of that system. You need to decide which approach is in the best interest of your document and the project. In the Game Mechanics section, you want to describe only the GUIs that are used in the game and are therefore relevant to gameplay. Any of the front-end GUIs used when players are starting a new game or loading an old one are not really part of the gameplay. As such, the front-end GUIs should be separated into the System Menus section, which I discuss later in this chapter.

It is easy to assume a lot when writing a Game Mechanics section, but a good designer will avoid assuming anything. For instance, a designer may be working on a first-person shooter in the *Quake* mold. She may make the assumption that when players run over an object, their character will automatically pick it up. The designer has played so many first-person shooters that it is totally obvious to her that this is how she wants it to work. But if she fails to write it down in the document, the programming team may assume it will function some other way, copying their own favorite game. Do not assume that the same gameplay components that are obvious to you will be obvious to whoever is reading your document. Spell everything out explicitly so there is no room for confusion.

You can almost think of the Game Mechanics section as an extremely detailed first pass on the manual. You are describing in intense detail how players will accomplish every different action in the game-world — what commands players will use and what the results of those commands will be. If you are writing your game design document as a journalist might write a news story, in the Game Mechanics section you should be concerned with the "what" and "how" — what players do in your game and how they do it. Later in the document, you will get to the "where," "when," and "why."

Artificial Intelligence

If the Game Mechanics section describes how players can interact with the game-world, then the Artificial Intelligence section documents how the world will react to the players' actions. How will the opponents that players face in the game-world behave? What will they do in which situations? This section may also describe how the game-world behaves when players are not doing anything. For instance, it could discuss ambient behaviors such as how townspeople go about their daily business.

In games such as *Doom II*, the player mechanics and the behavior of the AI agents are discrete enough to be described in separate sections of the design document.

Some design document authors may prefer to include the Artificial Intelligence section in the Game Mechanics section, but I prefer to keep them separate if possible. Whether or not to include the Artificial Intelligence section within the Game Mechanics section depends on the nature of your game. For some games such as *Tetris*, the AI is so negligible that it does not warrant its own section. For a game such as *Lemmings*, where player controls and the AI are tightly intertwined, it makes perfect sense for the author of the design document to discuss them in the same section. But for a game such as *Doom*, where the players' manipulation of their game-world surrogate, the Space Marine, is relatively distinct from the behavior of the enemies he fights, it makes sense to split up the information into two sections. Such separation makes the programmer's navigation of the document easier, since the process of working on the players' movement and the creatures they will battle are customarily separate coding tasks.

In the AI section you will want to do your best to fully describe how you expect the game to behave for players. If you are working on a game in which the players move their character around in a game-world where it encounters other characters, you will want to describe how those characters react. Do they ignore players until they initiate a conversation or are they attracted to the players? Can they pathfind around the area in an apparently intelligent manner or are they walking on predefined paths? Some NPCs may initiate combat with players; when and why do they decide to do this? Is it based on seeing the character? Hearing it? Are they activated by level-designer specified triggers? Perhaps all three actions initiate combat in different situations. How smart are the characters? Are they able to hide around corners, sniping at players from safe locations? Do they flee when wounded? There are a number of questions you should answer in the AI section, enough to give the AI programmer an idea of what she needs to implement. The more questions you answer, the more likely the programmers will create behaviors in the game that match your expectations and vision.

Designing an AI for a strategy game can be a significantly more involved process. Suppose you are working on an RTS game like *WarCraft* or a turn-based strategy title such as *Civilization*. What sorts of strategies will the enemy use to overwhelm the players' units? How will the units work together? If applicable, when will the computer player decide to build more units, and how many will it make? Will the AI pick up on and defend against different attack types performed by the players, such as flanking maneuvers? Is the enemy AI supposed to be a real match for players or is balance achieved because the computer simply has more powerful equipment? If necessary, you can provide a walk-through of a single game experience and how the enemy AI would behave at different junctures of that game.

Describing the collaborative tactics the AI will use is very important in the design document for strategy games such as *WarCraft II*.

Working on the Artificial Intelligence section is a good place to enlist the help of programmers on your team. Find out what sorts of AI they have experience working with, and explore how that might be applicable to your project. Find out what is difficult to accomplish and what is easy. It is often hard for a designer (especially if she is a non-programmer) to comprehend that getting an AI agent to flee when wounded is a trivial task, while getting it to pathfind up some stairs and jump over a ledge can be extremely difficult. Instead of going for pie-in-the-sky notions of what you would like the AI in your game to be capable of, work only with real, accomplishable goals. Remember that a programmer who reads a design document filled with descriptions of implausible AI that is in no way grounded in reality is likely to become irritated at the document, and it will be a challenge for that document to be taken seriously in the future. Having a programmer work with you on the game's AI documentation will help make that section of your document that much stronger, as well as assuring that the AI programmer really understands what is expected of the agents in the game.

In working on your Artificial Intelligence section, try to follow the same rules you did when writing the Game Mechanics section. Do not refer to specific NPCs in the game, but rather to general behaviors that different agents may exhibit. You will get to the specific NPCs and what set of behaviors they will use in the Game Elements section later in the document. Again, try not to assume anything. Put in as much detail as you can about how the agents in your game will behave, even if it seems obvious to you.

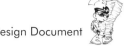

Game Elements: Characters, Items, and Objects/Mechanisms

If you think of the level designers on your team as painters, then the game elements are the colors they have on their palette. These elements are the different parts of your game that will be brought together in the levels to create a compelling experience for players. The designers will be able to take these elements and, by combining them in unique and interesting ways, create a variety of levels that will keep players interested for hours. Of course, not every game has levels, but nearly every game has game elements. Whether these elements are the various types of foes players fight in *Robotron: 2084,* the different sorts of special buildings that can be created in *SimCity*, or the different blocks in *Tetris*, they need to be listed and detailed in the Game Elements section.

Now that you have spent a good many pages focusing on the more general game mechanics and artificial intelligence capabilities of your game, it is time to move on to specific content. Remember that you kept the Game Mechanics and AI sections general enough that one could make many different games using them. These sections may even remain relatively unchanged for a sequel, should your game have one. But the enemies, NPCs, objects, items, and mechanisms players will encounter in the game-world will probably be unique to this game. This content is usually closely tied to the story, which you will delve into later in the Story Overview and Game Progression sections of your document. It is actually a toss-up if you want to list your characters, items, and objects before or after the story sections. It is up to you to determine what makes the most sense for your particular document and game.

I customarily use three classifications of game elements: characters, items, and objects/mechanisms. You may wish to create a separate section in your design document for each of the classes, or you can make each class a different subsection in one all-inclusive Game Elements section.

- Characters: The characters class includes all the enemies players will battle, all the personalities they might meet and potentially have conversations with, and all the different types of AI agents in the game. Think of the character grouping as containing all of the active, non-player-controlled elements in the game.

- Items: The items class includes any entity that players can pick up and use or manipulate in some fashion. Certainly any weapons players might use would be listed here, as well as any items that might make their way into the players' inventory, such as notes, keys, or health elixirs.

- Objects/Mechanisms: The third group contains what I call objects or mechanisms. These elements are entities that appear in the game, that are not AI driven, and that players cannot pick up but can operate in some way. This would include doors, switches, puzzle elements, or other objects that can be manipulated through the course of the game.

Again, depending on the type of game you are working on, you may not need to use all three classifications. A shooter like *Half-Life* would have all three: the aliens players fight would be among the characters, the weapons they find would be listed under items, and the different game-world mechanisms players encounter, such as the redirectable laser beams, would fall under the third classification. An RTS game like *StarCraft*, however, might instead have a units listing (which is essentially a combination of characters and items) detailing all of the different units that the players or their adversaries can control, along with an objects/mechanisms list that details any objects players interact with, such as doorways or teleporters. If the RTS being designed is one in which units could pick up objects, however, you might want to create a third classification after all. An RPG such as *Diablo* might add fourth and fifth groupings for listing the players' skills and spells respectively, since these are game elements that do not really fall into any of the three classifications I have discussed. Try to separate your game-world elements, whatever they may be, into the most logical groupings possible. Depending on the nature of your game, it is not unreasonable to have only one class or as many as ten; compelling games can be created in either case.

The design document for *Diablo II* might contain separate Game Elements sections for describing the player's spells and skills.

Within each class, try to list the objects in the most logical order possible and group different subclasses of objects together. For instance, if you are working on an RPG, you might want to list all of your potions in one spot, all of your bladed melee weapons in another section, and all of your ranged weaponry in another. An RTS might want to separate its units into offensive, defensive, and construction, or perhaps static and mobile. Again, take a look at the kind of game you are making, and try to divine the method of representation that best suits the data you are presenting and that makes it easily navigated and understood by readers. The Game Elements section should provide information for both the art and programming teams. The art team will need to make sure art assets get created for all of the elements you describe. The programming team will want to read the Game Elements section in combination with the Game Mechanics and AI sections to get a full understanding of what the game will be expected to do. Keep the artists, other designers, and programmers all in mind as you work on cataloging the game's characters, items, mechanisms, and whatever other classifications your game may demand.

In listing and describing these game elements, you want to avoid assigning actual statistics to any of them. This level of detail about the items or enemies is simply not something you can predict before you have a functioning game in which you can test the behavior of the AI or weapons and balance them properly. Statistics that you come up with in preproduction, where you have no real chance of play-balancing or trying them out, are a waste of your time as well as that of anyone who might have to read them over.

Instead, try to write descriptions of the game elements in question and their relation to the other elements. How do they compare in difficulty to each other? What traits does a particular AI agent have? Is this one more or less likely to run away in combat? Which AI capabilities will this element use and to what intended effect? How do the entity and its various effects appear to the player? How big is it compared to other objects? Include enough information for a programmer to understand what code will be required for the entity and sufficient description that an artist will be able to make a concept sketch. You want to provide as much useful detail as possible without overdoing it. Readers, whether artists, programmers, or other designers, will know when you are just documenting for documenting's sake, in which case your document stops being practical and useful. Do not waste their time by making them read reams of fluff to get the information they need.

Story Overview

Though not strictly necessary for a design document, I think having a brief Story Overview can be quite helpful in a design document, assuming your game has a story at all. Properly written, the overview provides all of the document's readers with an easy-to-read narrative of what transpires in the game. Much like the design document's overview, the Story Overview is a quick way for everyone on the team to understand the story's "big picture." To achieve this, you must keep the overview to an easily readable length while trying to include all of the major story points. A couple of pages should be sufficient, though this may vary depending on the complexity of the game's story; a shooter might only require one page, while an RPG might take a few more.

Certainly you do not need to include all of the game's sub-quests or describe every conversation players will engage in or every character players will meet. Try to make the Story Overview as compelling and readable as possible, so people will want to read it. While the Game Mechanics section may be difficult to read with its bullet-point lists and attention to detail, your Story Overview should be a pleasure to read. Indeed, if it is not a pleasure, try to figure out why not. Is it because your story is not that compelling? Do you need to refine and improve it in order to make it more interesting?

Game Progression

Depending on the nature of the game, the Game Progression section may well turn out to be the longest in the design document. This is where the game designer breaks the game down into the events players experience, and how they change and progress over time. This section will provide a guide for both the art team and the level designers as to what types of environments they will need to create for the game. The level designers take this section as a guideline for what each level is supposed to include and then fill in all the details as they build out each level, bringing all of the components of the game together.

For many types of games, including RPGs, RTS games, first-person shooters, action/adventures, and mission-based flight simulators, the Game Progression breakdown will be best done by level. For each level, you should describe in detail what challenges players will face, what story (if any) transpires on them, and the visual aesthetics of the levels. Figure out and describe what the major challenges will be on a given level: fighting with a horde of enemies at location A, meeting and talking to a specific character at location B, and solving a gameplay puzzle at location C. You certainly do not need to break down the level to the point where every single conflict is listed in minute detail. As with the character statistics, this is something that you will only be able to do when you are actually working with the level, when you are able to try the conflict a certain way and test it out. Explain how the appearance of the level will communicate the game's story, if applicable. What objects and items must be in what locations for the story to progress properly? Also discuss which elements from the game's "palette" will be available on this level. Which types of enemies will players expect to encounter and what types of items will they find along the way?

More than anything, try to put into words how the level should affect players, not just in terms of how difficult the level will be, but what sort of gameplay experience players will have. How do you want players to feel when they are playing the level, and how should those feelings fluctuate over the course of the level? Should players feel constant conflict and challenge, or is this level more slow-paced and centered on exploration? Is the story at a climax in this level, resulting in increased tension, or is the level more slow-paced, focusing on filling in the game's back-story? As you write your Game Progression, always keep in mind how players should feel when playing a given level, and try to communicate that emotional state in your writing.

Of course, not every game has levels, and so your Game Progression may not break down so easily into self-contained units. But most games have stages of some kind. Try to determine what the stages of your game are, and break down your Game Progression into these stages. For example, the original arcade game *Centipede* has a series of waves players play through. In that game, once players kill all the segments of the centipede, they progress to the next wave. The waves are cyclic, with each subsequent wave throwing in a different centipede, either in terms of its length or speed.

Free-form strategy games such as the *SimCity* series will not require a Game Progression section, since what happens during the game is entirely determined by the player's choices and the game mechanics. Pictured here: *SimCity 2000*.

Also, from each wave to the next, the conditions under which certain enemies appear change. For instance, the flea never comes out in waves in which there is a twelve-segment centipede on the play-field. If one were to write a Game Progression for *Centipede* (which would not need to be very long at all), one would want to break it down by waves, clearly delineating how the game changes from wave to wave.

Some games may not need a Game Progression section at all. For instance, a design document for a strategy game like *Civilization* or a software toy like *SimCity* could describe all of the relevant gameplay in the Game Mechanics, AI, and Game Elements sections. Since the levels in these games are randomly generated anyway, there is not much use in having a Game Progression section. However, if the game in question is to include certain scenarios that do start on predefined levels in specific configurations (as the *SimCity* games do), a Game Progression section would be the ideal place to describe these different scenarios and how they will challenge the player.

System Menus

The System Menus section is where you should detail the main menu and whatever other options screens players will be presented with at various points outside of the game itself. These menus do not actually impact the gameplay in any significant way, and as a result should be separated into their own unique section. You should include descriptions of how players will save their game and how they will load it later. Describe what type of interface players will have with these menus: will they use mouse-pointer-based point-and-click, or will they use the Enter and arrow keys, or both? Try to be as complete as you think is necessary to ensure that the system menus are intuitive enough to allow players to enjoy playing the game itself. Producers love to see that you have fully described the flow of these menus, so it may be important that you include a System Menus section, though, in my opinion, such a section is not truly required for a complete design document. It might even make sense to make the System Menus section into its own separate document, since they are so divorced from the gameplay proper.

One Man's Opinion

In the preceding pages, I have presented the format I like to use for game design documents. Let me repeat that it is by no means the industry standard format. Many great design documents have used formats wildly different from mine, both in terms of structure and in terms of how much detail they provided. But if you present a document structured as I have explained, you will not be laughed at or thought a fool. As I have stated previously, what is most important is that you communicate your vision for the game to the people reading your document. You are free to present your design information in whatever form makes the most sense to you while providing for maximum clarity and utility for your data.

Part of the reason why the design document format can vary so much from project to project is that games are not yet (nor do I think they ever will be) a standardized art form, as plays, movies, or symphonies are. Just as a writer's style guide for a cookbook and a romance novel would be extremely different, one can hardly expect the design document for a first-person shooter such as *Halo* to be of the same form as one for a strategy game like *Rise of Nations*. What the games accomplish and the experiences they provide are too radically different from each other, and hence their design documents must be different as well. Sure, within gaming there are certain genres or types of gameplay, and the design document format for a given genre, such as a first-person shooter, can be standardized. But even then, as the form of the shooter changes, as it implements new gameplay styles and mechanics, the structure of the document will need to adapt to these changes in order to communicate them effectively.

The design document for a first-person shooter, such as *Halo*, would be extremely different from one used for a strategy game.

Inauspicious Design Documents

As I previously recommended, it may be useful to try to get your hands on some professional game design documents in order to give you an idea of what the industry expects in such specifications. However, you must be careful. It is likely that the document you obtain will not be any good. Many of the documents that have been used for published games and that were written by experienced professionals are truly terrible. By way of example, and in order to best teach you what to avoid, I will explore a few of the different types of horrible design documents, and why they fail so miserably at what they are supposed to accomplish.

The Wafer-Thin or Ellipsis Special Document

These thin little volumes, certainly none longer than thirty pages, startle and amaze the experienced game designer with their total and complete lack of any useful content whatsoever. They use meaningless descriptions like "gameplay will be fun" and "responsiveness will be sharp." In these documents, many comparisons to other games are made: "This plays like *Super Mario 64*" or "The game has a control scheme similar to *Quake*." While such comparisons can be slightly useful, as I have discussed, the writer of the Wafer-Thin Document almost always fails to explain the control scheme of *Super Mario 64* or *Quake* in any detail, let alone the scheme to be used by the game in question.

Often these documents spend a lot of time, maybe half their pages, talking about back-story. Usually this back-story is very weak and poorly developed and is only tangentially related to the game being developed. The Wafer-Thin Document also spends a lot of time talking about how the menus will work. Not the in-game menus, but the system menus where users select what type of game they want to play, set their options, and so forth. Many mock-ups are made and options are carefully listed. What exactly the options will affect in the game is seldom described in any detail, since the game itself is barely defined. Figuring out the menu system is something best pursued once the game is working, when the designer knows what sort of options might be important and what different gameplay choices players will have; it is certainly far from the most difficult part of game design, nor the most important system to nail down first.

Wafer-Thin Documents are often constructed by managers who like to think they are game designers. The reason these can also be called Ellipsis Special Documents is that they are often littered with ellipses. For example, the worlds players will encounter in the game will be described in the following manner: *"Jungle World* is a very hot and sticky place where the Garguflax Monkeys swing around and torment the player…" And that will be all the document provides in way of description for the world, ending at an ellipsis, as if to say "insert game design here." It is unclear whether the writers of these documents plan to come back and fill in at the ellipsis later or that perhaps they do not deem it worthy of their valuable time to actually explain how their game works. They just assume someone somewhere will fill it in and make them look good.

Another example of the content found in Ellipsis Special Documents might be: "Players will be given an option of many cool weapons. For example, the Gargantuan Kaboom does twice the damage of the players' other weapons and has a special effect. The Barboon Harpoon will allow users to kill enemies at a distance with a nice camera effect. Other weapons will be just as fun and cool…" Here the writer of the Ellipsis Special fails to describe the weapons the game will have to any useful level of detail, and then, having listed two weapons, decides to leave the rest up to the imagination of the reader. Of course, readers are very usefully told that the other weapons will be "fun and cool." The writers of the Ellipsis Special mistakenly think that is all the description necessary to develop a game.

The only upside to the Wafer-Thin or Ellipsis Special Document is that it allows whoever gets to implement the design to pretty much take over the project and turn it into her own. I say this is an advantage, since usually the ideas the manager included in the Wafer-Thin Document are beyond ridiculous and do not make for viable gameplay. But one must be wary. Problems arise when the manager shows up six months later and complains: "But that's not what I wrote!"

The Back-Story Tome

Unlike writers of Ellipsis Special Documents, the designer who writes the Back-Story Tome spends a lot of time working on her document. These books (it is hard to call them merely documents) usually stretch into the hundreds of pages — 300-, 400-, even 500-page documents are not out of the question. There's a lot of information in there.

The first mistake these documents make is usually a poor table of contents and the lack of an index. In a design document, well-ordered information and a good table of contents can replace an index, but the absence of both is a huge error. The problems are compounded when the document is as long as *War and Peace*. The primary reason for the existence of game design documents is to allow team members to quickly look up information about a section of the game they are working on. If a programmer wants to know how the AI for a particular enemy is going to work, she needs to find that information quickly and easily. If she cannot find it, she may just make something up. Similarly, when an artist wants an idea of the textures that will be needed for a given area in the game, she wants to be able to find where that area is described as quickly as possible. Design documents are not read like novels. No one starts at the beginning and comes out at the end. Primarily, design documents are reference materials, and if team members cannot easily retrieve the data they are seeking, they are liable to give up.

However, once one starts hunting through one of these Back-Story Tomes, one is startled to find that, indeed, there is no information about the gameplay in there. It is all back-story. And at 500 pages, it is far more back-story than most computer games will ever use. The history of all the characters in the game, the friends of those characters, and all the relevant parents and siblings are all described in minute detail. It may be very interesting stuff (though usually it is a disorganized mess), but in the end the reader is left with very little idea of how the game is supposed to function. These documents are often the sign of the frustrated novelist or a writer from a non-interactive medium who does not truly understand game development. A lot of games make story-telling one of their central concerns, and a story bible can be quite useful to game creation. In such a case, it makes sense to discuss the game's story in the design document to some extent. But first and foremost, a design document is supposed to contain the game's design, which is very different from a game's story. Remember, your most important consideration when writing a design document must be, "what can the player do?" Though these tomes are very significant in terms of weight and will probably impress the venture capitalists, the programmer who has to work with such a document as her only guidance is going to end up designing the game herself.

The Overkill Document

Some designers think they can describe every last aspect of a game in the design document. It is certainly true that many design documents lack the necessary detail to be useful, as we found in the Ellipsis Special Document discussed above, but at the same time, going to an excessive level of detail can be a waste of the designer's time as well as that of the person who has to sift through all of that excess information. Furthermore, excessive documentation can lead to the illusion that the designer has created a complete, thorough document, when in fact she has gone into far too much detail about certain subjects while skipping other areas that need to be addressed.

For example, suppose that the game being documented has a number of characters that perform certain actions in the game-world. Say the game has townspeople, and they need to walk around, sit down and stand up, talk to each other, and sleep. The document should describe these behaviors in the AI section. A truly thorough document might break this down into separate animations: stand from sitting, sit from standing, idle sitting, idle standing, walk, converse with hand gestures, and so on. Probably this is not necessary, since good animators and artists will be able to break this down better than a designer can. But some designers may go overboard and actually sketch or list the individual animation frames. This is absurd. There is no way to know in the design document stage how many animation frames will be required for a given animation. This sort of decision can only be made and adjusted during the game's production. Not to mention that listing animation frames is insulting to the animator who will only feel demoralized by this degree of micro-management. Furthermore, the design document should stick to gameplay design, and not veer into the territory of the art bible or other art documentation.

Another example might be what I call "balancing data." These are the actual statistics for the weapons, items, and characters found in the game. The design document should probably list what different attributes weapons and characters will have. For instance, a weapon might have a range, accuracy, number of shots, and rate of fire. Furthermore, the design document might want to describe the qualities of a given weapon: "The Double Barreled Shotgun has a short range and a low accuracy, but does a large amount of damage in a large area." However, actually listing the values for a weapon's attributes is not very useful in the design document. Saying "Shotgun Accuracy: 2" does not really serve any purpose since the number "2" does not have any context and therefore no meaning. These values are best determined when the game is actually functioning, when a designer can balance the weapons as they will be used by the players and thus the designer can experiment with different settings to achieve the desired effects. Creating large tables full of data before this information is actually testable is by and large a waste of time. Filling in a chart quickly may be a way to convey some raw ideas that were hard to describe through words alone, but at best such a table is a first pass that will no doubt change many times before the game ships.

As with animation minutia and precise balancing data, source code also does not belong in the document. Designers who start writing out algorithms in their design documents are going too far. It does not matter if the designer is also a programmer. There should be no code, not even pseudocode, in the design document. Including code will only serve to bloat the document and distract from omitted information that needs to be covered. Some simple if-then-else type logical explanations may be useful and are completely appropriate. Such examples may help communicate all the contingencies to the person actually writing the code, and if nothing else force the designer writing the document to consider all the possible cases and outcomes that the game will need to support. But by the time the examples start looking like compilable C++ code, you know your document is overdoing it.

If there is any useful information in the Overkill Document, it is so hidden in the river of useless data that team members will be too intimidated to look for it. The author thinks that she can preplan everything, and that she is far more talented than any member of her team. While such excessive attention to detail can be impressive to those who do not really know what they are doing, a design document that goes too far will only infuriate the team that has to work with it.

The Pie-in-the-Sky Document

These design documents often have noble intentions with grand ideas for truly magnificent gameplay. Sadly, the writers of them typically lack any technical grasp of what the computer is capable of or what a team of twenty people is likely to accomplish in a year and a half. As a result, these overly ambitious documents put forth fancy ideas with no basis in reality or feasibility and end up frustrating and infuriating the teams assigned to "make them happen."

Pie-in-the-Sky Documents include ideas such as "a fully modeled replica of Manhattan will be the players' primary game-world, complete with AI agents representing all of the city's seven million inhabitants in real-time." The authors of Pie-in-the-Sky Documents do not want to be bothered with messy details such as the reality that no existing computer system can simulate seven million humans in any sort of reasonable time frame (let alone real-time). Another feature suggested might be "a natural language parser will be included that allows users to type in full, complex English sentences, which the characters will respond to with their own dynamically generated dialog." The guilty designer does not want to hear that research institutions have been working for decades on natural language processors that still have trouble with short, simple sentences. When confronted with a Pie-in-the-Sky Document that you must work with, the first thing to do is call a reality check meeting involving key programmers and artists as well as the management who want this document implemented. With them all in the same room, some simple and quick calculations on a piece of paper or white board will often reveal how fundamentally impractical the game proposed is, and if the management still refuses to accept the reality of the situation, it might be time to start looking for a new job. Pie-in-the-Sky Documents are often combined with Ellipsis Specials to create truly wretched design documents, where the guilty designer outlines a completely impractical project without bothering to go into much detail about it.

The Fossilized Document

Any of the above flawed design documents can also be a Fossilized Document. Indeed, a design document that does not necessarily suffer from any of the above problems and was once a fine reference tool will become a Fossilized Document over the course of a project if the designer is not diligent in her efforts to keep the document up to date. I know of no original game project whose design has not changed significantly during the course of its development, and when the design changes but the design document does not, that document starts to become fossilized.

Suppose a programmer on the development team looks something up in the Fossilized Document and the information she finds is out of date. She may start implementing the old, long-since-modified functionality. At some point, a designer or producer who is aware of the changes that have taken place in the design will notice that the programmer is creating a system that is no longer appropriate, and will chastise the programmer for doing so. This creates frustration for both parties, not to mention wasting the programmer's time. Furthermore, whenever the programmer needs to know something about the design in the future, she will not trust the design document, and instead will go hunt down a designer or producer to find out how a given system is supposed to function. Of course, this defeats the purpose of the document, as the designer must stop whatever she is working on to explain the system to the programmer. This new system may be described correctly in the document, but the programmer is not going to get burned again by using the Fossilized Document. When the designer fails to update the document when design changes occur, the entire document becomes useless. No one can trust it, and as a result no one will bother to read it.

Wiki systems can be great for more easily keeping a document or collection of documents up to date. With Wiki, any member of the team can update a section of the document through their web browser, and full version control and history is supported to prevent the accidental loss of data. So, for example, the programmer who is implementing a particular feature can slightly modify the text of the design document to match how the feature actually ended up working, to add more information, or to link to the newly created technical design document for that particular feature. On a large enough project, keeping the design document completely up to date can be a full-time job.

A Matter of Weight

It is often joked that design documents are not read, they are weighed. This is not surprising given the heft of many design documents and the lack of desire among team members to read them. Shockingly, this statement is often true. I once heard an ex-producer from a major gaming publisher talk about her experience with design documents and the project approval process. She said that the "decision-makers" would bring a scale to their "green-light" meetings. When it came down to two similar projects that were both relatively worthy of funding, they would take the design document for each project and place it on the scale. Whichever one weighed more would get accepted, the other rejected. Much as it pains me to tell you, if you are in the commercial gaming business and groveling for dollars at publishers, you need to make your document hefty. You need it to be impressive to pick up and flip through. Many will never read it at all. Others will read only the Overview and Table of Contents at the beginning. But everyone will pick it up and remark on its weight.

Of course, many of these super-thick documents contain a lot of information of negligible value toward the actual development of the project. They may be stellar examples of one of the failed types of documents I discussed earlier, such as a Back-Story Tome or an Overkill Document. It is your challenge as the game designer to make the document as practical as possible by providing only useful information in the document, while making it hefty enough to impress the suits. One might want to include a large number of flowcharts or concept sketches or choose to use a bigger font, all while not being too obvious. Indeed, a great game (though a simplistic one) can have a perfect design document only ten pages long. One wonders how many great, simple games have been cast aside by publishers who were unimpressed with the mass of their design documents.

Thankfully, over the last few years many publishers and developers seem to be wising up to the unwieldiness of massive design documents. Design consultant Mark Cerny has been preaching the concept of starting development with only a simple "macro" design document of perhaps ten pages in length that can be expanded on as needed over the course of development. As I have discussed, others are starting to use Wiki as a means of organizing and interlinking a lot of design information contained in many smaller documents. And fewer and fewer publishers are funding development based on a phone book-like design document alone, with prototypes and high-level, graphical pitch documents becoming increasingly important. The days of padding out the design document just for the sake of it seem to be thankfully drawing to a close.

Getting It Read

Once your design document is written, one of your biggest challenges may be getting anyone on the development team to read it. Often, many programmers, artists, or even other designers will not want to put the time into a careful reading of your document. Others may have been burned by bad design documents in the past and will jump to the conclusion that yours is of similarly poor quality. Keeping your document up to date, including only useful information, providing a detailed table of contents, and limiting yourself to practical, accomplishable gameplay elements will help. Including numerous short, high-level summaries before each section of the document can also help team members get high-level information for aspects of the game they don't need to know so much about. At the same time, such summaries can give readers a big-picture vision before they dive into the gritty details of the document. If your team members sample your document and find it to be of superior quality, they are more likely to return to it for reference when they are actually implementing a given system or working on a particular piece of art. As with any written document, you need to earn the trust of your readers if you hope to keep them reading.

Another key method of getting your design document read is to make it easily available to anyone who wants to read it. Keep it in the same source-control system that your team uses for asset management. You want your team members to be able to get the latest version of the design document as easily as they get the latest build of the game. Since you will be constantly revising and updating your document to keep it up to date with the project (and to prevent it from becoming a Fossilized Document), source control will be a valuable tool for keeping track of the previous revisions. Not to beat a dead horse, but a Wiki system run over a company intranet can also be great for distributing the document to the team, with developers at any time being able to easily read the very latest version of the document through their web browsers.

When you check in the latest version of the document, send your team an e-mail telling them that it is available and explaining what has changed. That way, people can easily skim over the changes. If one of the changes is relevant to their work, then they can get the latest version of the document off the network and read over the relevant updates. Updating your document does not do any good if no one knows you have updated it or if people are still reading old revisions. It is probably a good idea to use a version number with your document, such as 1.3 or 2.7. Include this version number, along with the date, in a header on every page. Often people will print out a design document and not realize how old or fossilized it is. If they can quickly compare a date and a version number, they will know which version of the document they have and whether they need to get a new one.

Documentation Is Only the Beginning

Some designers or aspiring designers seem to think that a thorough design document is, by itself, enough to build a game. Indeed, some companies have had designers write design documents, only to then have those designers move on to write other design documents while a separate team actually executes their design. At its best, a design document is a rough outline, more the suggestion of a game than anything else, and without being involved in a game's creation until it goes gold master, one cannot truly be considered to have designed the game. A designer who takes any pride in her work will want to be there throughout the project, ready to change the design as necessary to make it the most compelling game possible and updating the document as the design is changed and revised (and rest assured it will be continuously changed and revised). A committed game designer will want to be there to balance the weapons, the AI, the controls, and certainly the levels. She will want to make sure the game follows the focus through and that the initial vision is realized.

If a designer writes a design document and then passes it on to others to actually build, the people who do the actual creation will change the design to match their own interests and artistic drives. The design document will be a springboard for their own acts of creation, not the original designer's. The design document is an integral part of the game's creation, perhaps, but a design document is not all that is required. To claim any sort of meaningful authorship on the project, a designer needs to be involved for the duration. In a way, writing the design document is the easy part of computer game design. Actually taking the document and creating a compelling gaming experience is much, much harder.

Chapter 20:
Game Analysis: The Sims

Designed by Will Wright
Released in 2000

Based on its concept alone, *The Sims* is not a game that many people would identify as one they would want to play. Indeed, a focus group conducted early in the
project's development was so unfavorable that the game's designer, Will
Wright, had trouble getting any staff on the project. And why would it be fun? "Control a
collection of characters at home in a simulated suburbia." To hear that description of the
game, it seems disturbingly too much like real, mundane, suburban life to possibly be
entertaining. Indeed, all that is simulated in the game is home life — no going "out" to

concerts or roller rinks for these "sims." But to hear someone talk about *The Sims* is to instantly become intrigued. "Well, I was trying to get my sim to flirt with this woman, but her husband became upset and decked my character!" So what is it that makes this game so brilliant and so fiendishly entertaining?

To summarize, players start playing *The Sims* by first creating the characters they want to control by assigning quantities to different attributes: Neat, Outgoing, Active, Playful, and Nice. Players can then place these characters in a home, either pre-built or one they construct themselves. From there, it is the players' responsibility to make sure the house has all of the objects the sims will need to live: a bed, a toilet, a kitchen, a phone, objects for entertainment, and so forth. The Needs indicators help communicate what the sim requires to achieve happiness, including listings for Hunger, Energy, Comfort, Fun, and Social. Players also must see to it that their sim finds a way to bring in money to pay for all the nifty stuff players purchase, a goal accomplished by looking at the job listings in the newspaper. In addition, the game has an elaborate social component, where other sims can be invited over, talked to, entertained, flirted with, and befriended. The game provides such an amazing breadth of areas for players to explore, one is amazed that all of them are also quite deep in their functionality.

Abdicating Authorship

The Sims is a very good example of what Doug Church at a Game Developers Conference lecture described as "abdicating authorship" in computer games. That is, instead of the game designer coming up with the game's story ahead of time, as is the case in 95 percent of adventure, role-playing, and action games made today, the authorship of the game's story is abdicated to the players. Players can then take the story in whatever direction they want, no matter how prurient, dull, or hackneyed it may be. Indeed, at first players may not even think of the experience as being a story, just as they may not think of their own life as a story. Yet it still is a story. In *The Sims*, the storytelling becomes more of a collaborative effort between players, who direct the action, and the

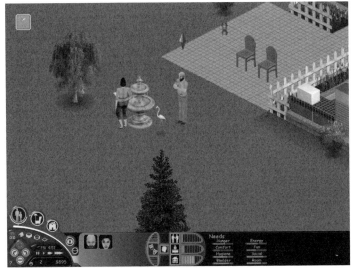

The Sims provides a framework upon which players can author their own stories.

game designer, who provides the framework, tools, and space with which the players can work. Since players are intimately involved in the creation of the story, that story becomes theirs, and as a result players becomes that much more involved in the game. Instead of having their strings pulled by the game designer as has happened in so many other games, it is the players who are now pulling the strings. The feeling of empowerment is tremendous indeed.

It is widely agreed that *The Sims* is a software toy and not technically a game, even though it is frequently called a game and discussed in the same breath as other titles that definitely are games. Indeed, *The Sims* is a toy because it does not present a definite goal to players, though it may insinuate or imply one. There is no "winning" or "losing" *The Sims* beyond what players define those terms to mean. Perhaps players will think they have lost when their sim dies as the result of a cooking fire. Or maybe players will think they have won when their sim manages to build the largest, most extravagant house in the neighborhood and has reached the apex of her chosen career path. However, these victory/loss conditions are ones that players are suggesting into the game, not ones that the game demands. This abdicates authorship to players more than a goal-oriented game ever could. For instance, every time someone plays a racing game such as *San Francisco Rush*, the ending of the game is predetermined; once players or one of their opponents cross the finish line on the track, the game ends. Thus the end of the "story" that *Rush* is telling is predetermined. Players may be able to author how well their own car does in that race and what sort of tactics it uses to try to win, but how the story ends is a known, unchangeable quantity. Even a game like *Civilization*, which gives players a great deal of freedom as to how they will play their game, still constrains players by saying the game is over when the year 2000 rolls around, when a civilization wins the space race, or when one achieves military dominance. By setting up victory conditions, the game designer is authoring how the game will end. Since *The Sims* and other software toys do not dictate how the game must end, players are left to decide when enough is enough. The familiar subject matter of *The Sims* certainly helps players to define their own goals while playing; since they understand the world of *The Sims*, players have some idea what success in that world might mean, and thereby can make up their own goals easily. Some players, perhaps primarily the hard-core gaming aficionados, see this lack of winning and losing as a detriment to the game, but for many players it would seem to make the playing experience all the more compelling.

Familiar Subject Matter

Of course, *The Sims* is not the original software toy, nor is it even Will Wright's first. His first success with the software toy genre came with *SimCity*. It too simulated a sophisticated system and allowed players to truly control their city's destiny. Though *SimCity* is an excellent, entertaining title, *The Sims* is more compelling still. A lot of this has to do with the fact that players of *The Sims* are controlling humans instead of a city. In other words, it follows Chris Crawford's insistence that games should focus on "people not things." In general, most players will find people to be much more interesting than things, and players will be able to form an emotional bond with a simulated person much easier than with a simulated city. After playing *The Sims* for a while, players will feel sad when their sim's amorous advances are rebuffed or when their house burns to the ground. Though certainly not as smart or interesting as actual humans, the simulated people in *The Sims* are close enough to being plausible that players will want to believe in their sims' virtual existences and will fill in the simulation's deficiencies for themselves.

Furthermore, almost all the players who play *The Sims* will have an intimate knowledge of the subject being simulated before they start playing. They will feel that they are something of an expert on this "suburban life" subject and think they will be able to play the game better as a result. For instance, players know by instinct that they should set up a bathroom with a shower, a toilet, and a sink. If the job were to simulate an alien life-form's daily life on another planet, players would have much less of an idea how to proceed and would need to figure out the life-form's culture before they could expect to succeed at the game. Because players already know so much about the subject matter of *The Sims*, they are that much more drawn into the game. From the moment they start up the game, players feel good because they are putting their real-world knowledge to use in creating these simulated lives. When Will Wright made *SimEarth*, he created a game involving systems that players knew very little about, and this may explain why so many people found the game to be quite difficult. For *SimCity*, players had a better sense of what was going on; while they may not have been experts on urban planning and dynamics, players at least thought they knew how a city should be laid out and were familiar with problems such as traffic, pollution, and crime. With *The Sims*, most players know infinitely more about the topic than they do about city planning. Hence, the game is that much more compelling to play. Its very familiarity draws players in like nothing else can.

Of course, simulating a subject many of the players will be familiar with can be a challenge as well; if the designer gets it wrong, players will know instantly. In the alien-life simulator, who is to say what is accurate since the world and creatures are made up to begin with? This grants the designer more artistic license for how the world is constructed. However, in a reality simulation like *The Sims*, if the designer makes the wrong choice about what will provoke a sim to do what action, players will see the error

Though the subject matter of *The Sims* may seem pedestrian, the game is so fascinating because it provides players with a safe world in which to experiment.

and their suspension of disbelief will be shattered instantly. Working with a subject that players are intimate with may serve to draw them in, but if it is not done correctly it may drive them away as well.

Safe Experimentation

On first inspection, one might not think that what *The Sims* simulates is actually all that interesting. Indeed, for the suburbanites who are likely to own a computer to play the game and have the disposable income to purchase it, how different is the game-world of *The Sims* from real life? It would seem that the escapist and wish-fulfillment qualities many games possess are totally lacking in *The Sims*. Furthermore, *The Sims* does not even present "life with all the dull bits cut out." The players' sims still have to engage in the more mundane aspects of modern life, such as going to the bathroom, going to work, paying bills, and taking out the trash. Is this fun? Strangely, it is, since these more tedious chores lend an air of "realism" to the proceedings, which makes the players' successes or failures all the more meaningful.

What *The Sims* really provides to players is an environment for safe experimentation. While prudence may prevent players from pursuing a career as a criminal or professional athlete in real life, the game will allow players to take their sims in that direction with little risk to the players. While building a house is a major undertaking involving great financial risk for the purchaser, in *The Sims,* players can build lavish houses, spend money on frivolous trinkets for their sims, throw wild hot tub parties, or pursue homosexual relationships just to get a sense of what life might be like if they lived it differently. If these experimental lifestyles turn out to not work as well as the players had hoped, the only loss is for their sims, an effect considerably less serious than real-world bankruptcy or social ostracism. Indeed, if players avoid saving their game after a catastrophic event or decision, the loss is easily undone entirely. The life players control in *The Sims* may be one quite close to their own, but the ability to try new things without fear of serious repercussions makes the experience compelling and exciting.

Depth and Focus

A big part of what makes *The Sims* work is the range of choices players are presented with for what they can do with their sims. Abdicating authorship is all well and good, but if the designer fails to provide players enough meaningful choices, players will find themselves only able to author a very narrow range of stories. Indeed, it is the designer's responsibility in creating a software toy to design that toy with a broad enough range of possibilities that the appeal of playing with it is not quickly exhausted. And Wright did that expertly with *The Sims*, leaving players with a constant feeling that there is so much more to do and see in the game-world, that one could never hope to do it all.

Players can concentrate on building their house, starting either with some of the pre-built houses or constructing one from the ground up. A robust set of house-construction and landscaping tools allows players to create a very large variety of houses, with probably no two built-from-scratch houses ever being the same, even with millions of people playing the game. Once a house is built or purchased, players can concentrate on filling it up with all manner of interesting possessions, which have a variety of effects on the inhabitants of the house. Of course, players get to construct the inhabitants as well, picking from a large range of personalities, body types, ages, ethnicities, and even hairstyles, with the option to make children or adults as well as males or females. Once the sims move into the house, players are able to determine what they eat, what they study, what career they pursue, how they have their fun, and with whom they socialize. Whether it be house building, property acquisition and placement, character creation, or life control, any one of these components includes far more choices than most games provide. When all of these different systems are combined, the range of choices available to players increases exponentially, creating a game with truly unprecedented depth.

Of course, what the sims cannot do in the game is significant as well. The sims cannot leave their homes except to go to work, and when they do players cannot follow them. Being able to go to other places would be nice, but consider how much more complex the game would need to be to simulate the rest of the world. A massive amount of additional work would have been required, and had that sensible limitation not been made early on in the title's development it might never have been completed. By focusing on the home life, the game is able to "get it right" in a way it could not have had the game-world of *The Sims* been larger. In short, what would have been gained in breadth would have been lost in depth. If a designer spends all her time adding an unreasonable range of possibilities to the game, it is likely that any one of the features the game includes will be far shallower than if the designer knows how to focus her efforts.

The Sims also expertly captures the "just one more thing" style of gameplay. This type of gameplay is perhaps best exemplified by *Civilization*, where players are constantly looking forward to the next technology to be discovered, the next unit to be built, or the next discovery of new territory. Similarly in *The Sims*, players may be working on having their sims meet new people, trying to advance their careers, hoping to put an addition on the house, and thinking of someday having them raise a child, all at the same time. Because of these constant aspirations, there is never a good place to stop playing the game; there is constantly something on the horizon to look forward to. Hence the game is fabulously addictive, with captivated players devoting hour upon hour, day after day, and week after week of their lives to the game.

Interface

The best a game's interface can hope to do is to not ruin the players' experience. The interface's job is to communicate to players the state of the world and to receive input from players as to what they want to change in that game-world. The act of using this input/output interface is not meant to be fun in and of itself; it is the players' interaction with the world that should be the compelling experience. But since the interface determines how players interact with the world, if that interface is not up to the task then at best players will become frustrated and at worst players will be unable to perform the actions they want.

The Sims' user interface is a beautiful example of how to do an interface correctly. It provides players with a staggering amount of information about the game-world, while allowing players to easily and intuitively make whatever changes they want. Unlike many modern action games, the tutorial primarily provides players with information about how to play the game, not how to manipulate the interface. The interface is so simple and intuitive that players pick it up with very little difficulty, no doubt the result of rigorous playtesting. Indeed Wright has stated that ten versions of the interface were thrown out before they arrived at the version with which they shipped. The fact that help is embedded throughout the interface is key, allowing players to click on any text item for an explanation of how it is important and why it is relevant.

The Sims has an extremely intuitive interface that includes multiple ways for the player to accomplish the same action.

A big part of the success of *The Sims'* input/output scheme is its similarity to systems players are likely to understand before they ever start playing the game. For instance, the buttons that determine the game's simulation speed look like those one would find on a tape player, something with which almost all players will be familiar. A large amount of the interface is reminiscent of Microsoft Windows, with the pointing and clicking players do mirroring that OS wherever appropriate. Item manipulation is reminiscent of Windows as well; players can use drag and drop to place objects, or simply click and click. The standard Windows "X" appears in the upper right-hand corner of dialog boxes to indicate that they can be closed, and the regular OK/Cancel button combinations are used wherever appropriate. While the functionality mirrors Windows in many ways, it is important to note that the appearance of the interface does not look exactly like Windows. All of the buttons are nicely drawn in a friendly art style that is a far cry from Windows' cold, utilitarian sterility. If the game used the actual dialog box art that Windows provides, players would instantly be reminded of working with the file picker or some other Windows interface, not an experience they are likely to remember fondly, certainly not as a "fun" activity. However, by putting a new visual style on the behavior of Windows, the interface is intuitive and familiar to players without actually reminding them of file management.

Another example of this is the "head" menu used throughout the game. When players want to have a sim perform an action on a particular object, players simply click on the object in question. From there a floating head of their current sim appears, with a range of different actions the sim can perform surrounding it in a circle. Players then simply move the mouse over to the action they want and click on it. While moving the pointer around, the sim's head actually tracks the cursor, watching it wherever it goes. This menu functions identically to a pop-up menu in Windows, but with several distinct advantages. The first is that it does not look like a pop-up menu, and thereby players do not associate it with boring Windows functionality. Second, the menu only lists the options that are available for the current object at that time. A normal pop-up menu would list all of the objects possible, with currently unavailable options grayed out. Third, by having the sim's head in the center, the menu brings players closer to the core of what they are doing: directing the sim to perform a certain action. The directive they are giving to their beloved sim is more intimate than it would have been through a more sterile, bland, and standard pop-up menu.

Controlled Versus Autonomous Behavior

In *The Sims*, players are able to direct their sims to perform certain actions: take out the trash, call up a friend, take a shower, and so forth. The sims will also, however, function on their own without the players' direction. The sims contain enough internal logic to tend to their most pressing needs, whether it is to eat, to go to the bathroom, to play a pinball game, or to read today's paper. As players make additions to the house or purchase further possessions, the sims will walk over to new objects and either applaud or complain about them, their reaction dependent on how much they like each particular object. This communicates to the players whether the sim is generally going to be happy with the new possession or if the sim would rather it were not there. Since the way the house is set up is a big component of the sim's total happiness, this provides crucial information to players about how to best set up the house.

The sims have some intelligence of their own, which frees up the player from having to worry about every last detail of their lives.

The autonomous behavior of the sims also allows players to set up the house and then sit back and watch how the sims live in it. This makes the game more like *SimCity*, in which players could only set up the framework of the city — its streets, its zones, its key buildings — and then see how the inhabitants of the city live in it. Players of *The Sims* can build a pleasant house that they think would be good to live in, then sit back, and watch the sims inhabit it, using their default behavior. This provides yet another avenue for interesting gameplay.

The sims generally do not have the foresight of players, however, and as a result will perform better, be more productive, and be happier if players smartly direct their every move. For instance, the sims will not try to improve their career-boosting skills of their own volition, such as improving their creativity by learning how to paint. So it is often in the players' best interest to override the sims' internal choices for what action to perform next, if they want the sim to attain her full potential. This keeps the player feeling smart, or at least smarter than the computer. However, the autonomous behavior avoids players having to micro-manage every little decision. Sure, being able to tell the sims exactly what to do is a key part of the game, but if players are controlling a number of sims at once, planning something for every one of them to do at a given moment can be quite a task. The sims' internal behavior helps to off-load this responsibility from players when the players do not want to worry about it.

A Lesson to Be Learned

The Sims is perhaps the most original commercial game design released in recent years. The game does not take as a starting point any other published game, but instead seems to have emerged entirely from Will Wright's brain. To look at the game is to marvel at its creativity and innovation. There is so much that is done right in *The Sims*, an entire book could be devoted to an analysis of its design. The game is truly like a computerized dollhouse, providing us the ability to play-act real human scenarios in order to better understand them. The description of the dollhouse found in the game is quite illuminating:

Will Lloyd Wright Doll House

This marvel of doll house design is meant for everyone, allowing children as well as adults to act out fantasies of controlling little families. This incredible replica comes complete with amazingly realistic furniture and decorative items. Don't be surprised if hours upon hours are spent enjoying this little world.

What is perhaps most interesting and compelling about *The Sims* is the potential it has to teach us about our own lives. What is the relationship we have with the possessions we own? How does the space we live in affect our lives? How does jealousy start in a relationship?

Of course, no one would argue that *The Sims* is a completely accurate simulation of human motivations and activities, but does it need to be completely accurate to cause us to think about our lives in new and interesting ways? As we move our sims around and watch them interact, we may disagree with how the simulation models their behavior. But in that disagreement, we think about what we really would expect them to do, with that reflection shedding new light on the relationships we maintain in our real lives. This, it seems, is the potential of computer games — not to allow us to escape from real life or to even replace it, but to open up new areas of thought, to be able to see the world through a different set of eyes and come back to our own lives equipped with that priceless information.

Chapter 21:
Designing Design Tools

"Man is a tool-using animal . . . Without tools he is nothing, with tools he is all."
— Thomas Carlyle

An integral part of developing a good game is creating compelling content for that game. In order to create superior content, the design team will need to be equipped with well-designed, robust game creation tools. Therefore, one can conclude that designing a good game is about designing good game creation tools.

Other than the development environments the programmers use to compile the game's code and the graphics packages the artists use to make the game's art, the most commonly used game creation tool is the level editor. What distinguishes this tool from the others I mentioned is that it is typically built specifically for a project or, at least, for the engine the team is using to power the game. It is the responsibility of the development team to make this level editor as powerful as it can be in order to facilitate the job of the level designers and allow them to make the best game-world possible.

The simple levels found in early games such as *Defender* did not require a sophisticated level editor to be created.

Of course, not every game has levels. Many of the classic arcade games from the early 1980s such as *Missile Command* or *Space Invaders* do not have levels as we think of them now. And the games that did, such as *Defender* or *Tempest*, certainly did not require sophisticated level editors to create their game-worlds. Sports titles have levels that are quite simple and mostly require the construction of visually pleasing stadiums to surround the gameplay. Games like *Civilization* and *SimCity* auto-generate the basis of a level using randomness combined with specific internal rules that will ensure the map will be fun to play. They then allow the players and AI to build the rest themselves, during the game. I discuss the nature of levels in games in more detail in Chapter 23, "Level Design." Many modern games employ sophisticated levels, levels that have a tremendous impact on the shape and form of the gameplay that takes place on them. These games demand that their development team create an editor with which the level designers can build the game-world.

Surprisingly, many development teams fail to invest enough programming time in making their tools as strong as possible. Often teams have no idea what is standard in other tools used in the industry. Frequently, not enough time is invested in preplanning and thoroughly designing how a level editor will work. As a result of all of these factors, it is often many months before the level design tools are reasonable to use. Frequently a programmer is stuck with implementing or improving the level editor as "extra" work on an already full schedule, and is forced to use the trusty "code like hell" method of implementation to get it done in time. Often, key timesaving features are not added until midway through a project, by which time the game's designers are already hopelessly behind in their own work. Up-front investment in the tools and their continued support throughout the project is certainly a lot of work, but in the end it is time well spent.

Desired Functionality

So what sort of functionality should a level editor include? Many might suggest an important part of any level editor is having hot keys hooked up to all the important functionality. Others would recommend plenty of configurable settings that allow different designers to turn on and off the features they prefer, when they need to use them. It goes without saying that a level editor should be stable enough that a designer can use it for a number of hours without it locking up. But these suggestions are all obvious; they are the bare minimum that an editor should do to be useful. What sorts of features should be included to allow an editor to truly shine, to empower designers to do the best work possible?

Visualizing the Level

The most important objective for a world creation tool must be to allow the designer to see the world he is creating while simultaneously enabling him to make modifications to it. This is often called What You See Is What You Get (WYSIWYG) in the domain of word processors and desktop publishing packages, but is not something that level editors are universally good at. I will call such a WYSIWYG view the "player's view" since it represents what players will see when they play the game. The world the designer is crafting should be seen in this player's view window using the same rendering engine the game itself will employ, whether this means 2D or 3D, sprites or models, software driven or hardware accelerated. This seems to be the most important feature of any level editor. How can a designer hope to create a good looking world if he must first tweak the world's settings in the editor and then run a separate application to see how it looks in the game?

The designer should be easily able to move the camera in this player's view so that he can quickly maneuver it to whatever section of the map he needs to see in order to work on the level. This movement is probably best accomplished with a simple "flight" mode in which the designer can control the camera's position using simple movement and turning keys. In this mode the camera should move without colliding with geometry or other game-world objects. Though one may also want to provide a mode for the player's view where the designer can maneuver through the game-world as players will in the final game, the editor should always allow the designer to move around the level unconstrained. In order to finely edit a level, the designer must be able to look closely at whatever he wants without having to worry that a tree blocks his way.

Every difference that exists in what the designer sees in the editor and what will show up in the game will make the levels look that much worse. Suppose only the unlit view is available in the editor, while the game itself has fancy lighting that creates pronounced shadows. This will create frustration for the designer, since he will not be able to easily tell how the level will appear in the game. Sure, the level looks great when playing, but while in the editor he has to guess what the lighting will be like and how the changes he makes will affect the final level. A limitation like this would be especially unacceptable if the gameplay relied more on lighting and shadows.

Of course, the world as it will appear in the game is not always the best view from which to edit that world. For this reason, level editors often need to include an "editing view" in addition to the player's view. The editing view is often top-down, but may also consist of a rotatable wire-frame view or multiple views. The last option is particularly useful for the editing of 3D game-worlds. For instance, the popular *Quake* engine editing tool Worldcraft, which was used to create all the levels in *Half-Life*, provides the designer with the popular "tri-view" setup, with which the designer can see top-down (along the Y axis), from one side (along the X axis), and from another side (along the Z axis) simultaneously in three separate windows. The three side views appear in addition to a 3D "player's view" window. Having multiple views is of particular importance for editing complex, overlapping 3D architecture, such as one finds in *Quake* levels. In contrast to the player's view window, which exists in order to show the designer exactly what the level will look like in the game, the editing view's purpose is to allow the designer to easily modify and shape what he sees in the player's view window. Of course, the editor should allow editing views and a player's view to be all up on the screen simultaneously, and the changes made in one window should be instantly reflected in all the views. Also, just because I refer to one view as the "player's view" and one as the "editing view" does not mean users shouldn't be able to edit all the game content in all the views.

The view provided in the Zoner level editor for *Odyssey* was perfectly suited to editing a 2D world.

In some cases there may not be a need for separate editor and player views. For instance, in a 2D world such as was found in my first game, *Odyssey: The Legend of Nemesis,* the player's view of the world may be perfectly suited to editing the levels. While I worked on the many levels for that game, not once did I wish for another view of the game-world. Similarly, in *StarCraft*, the representation of the world as it appears in the game is sufficiently clear to allow the designer to make modifications to it directly. For this reason, the *StarCraft* Campaign Editor provides only a player's view window for the designer to edit in. However, for the *StarCraft* editor, it might have been beneficial to provide a separate editing view. Because of the isometric view the game uses, a view which can sometimes be confusing to look at, a strictly top-down view in which the designer could edit his level could have been quite useful in the placing and manipulating of units and other game elements. The *StarCraft* Campaign Editor does include a top-down "mini-map" of the level being created, but the designer cannot actually change the level using that view, nor is the mini-map large enough to allow for easy editing.

The Big Picture

I have argued that it is important for a game's level editor to allow the designer to see the level exactly as he will see it in the final game, but the player's view window does not always need to represent exactly what players will see. It can be quite useful if the level editor can also show the designer various extra information about the level that will assist in that level's creation. For instance, suppose that the game being developed involves various monsters maneuvering the level on predetermined paths. Being able to see exactly where these paths go is key to understanding how the level functions and to making sure the paths are set up properly.

In many level editors, this sort of level functionality information is communicated in the editing view but not in the player's view, but it makes sense to display this data in both places. Certainly the player's view window should not always be filled up with this sort of level functionality information, but the ability to turn on and off the rendering of different data can be quite useful in setting up the level's behaviors. This is especially true for 3D games. Returning to the path example, why should the designer have to extrapolate in his head from the 2D top-down or side editing view exactly where a path will end up in the 3D view? Instead, the editor should just draw it for him, so there is no guesswork.

When working on *Centipede 3D*, a programmer was adding code that would prevent players from traveling up slopes that were too steep. In order to debug this new slope-restriction code, he added functionality to the level editor that allowed it to toggle on and off lines that separated the different triangles that made up the landscape. These lines would change color depending on whether or not a given edge could be crossed by players. The triangles themselves were marked with a red X if they were too steep for players to rest on. The programmer added this functionality primarily to aid in his debugging of the slope-restriction code, never realizing what a boon it would be to the level designers. Now the designers could see exactly where players could and could not travel on the level. An even better side effect was the rendering of the triangle boundaries, which created a sort of wire-frame view of the landscape, functionality that had not previously been available in the editor. This then vastly simplified the editing of geometry, for now the designers could see exactly which triangles created which slopes and then modify the level accordingly. The addition of the wire-frame view and the slope-restriction markers led directly to better, more refined geometry in the final game. And the beauty of this functionality was that it could be turned on and off in the editor, so if the designer wanted to see how the level looked he could turn it off, and if he wanted to see how it functioned he could turn it on.

As with paths, it may also be useful if the designer can turn on and off the rendering of objects such as triggers and other normally invisible objects. Similarly, it can be enormously helpful to display the bounding information for the objects in the world (which often does not exactly match the visual composition of the object's sprite or model), so the designer can easily observe how the bounding information will impact the ability of players and NPCs to navigate the game-world. Marking off where players can and cannot go can be quite useful as well. And again, each part of this functionality data should be easily toggled on or off via hot key, menu, or button, so that the designer has the choice of seeing exactly the data he needs for the problem he is working on. And the data should absolutely be rendered in the player's view window in addition to the editing view, so that the designer can see exactly how the trigger, path, slope restriction, or other object is placed in the game-world, without having to guess from a top-down view. By using a visually authentic view of the game-world that can also display game behavior data, the designer is able to work on a level's aesthetic qualities just as well as its gameplay attributes.

Jumping into the Game

For games where players are manipulating a character through a world, it is important for the designer to be easily able to know how the level "feels" to navigate. To this end, in addition to having the player's view of the world represent what players will see in the game, it can be quite useful to allow the designer to actually maneuver in this view as he would in the actual game. With this sort of addition, the designer is able to test whether players will be able to make a certain jump, how it will feel to navigate a particular "S" curve, and whether or not the players' character moves smoothly up a set of stairs. In addition to this "gameplay" mode, the level editor should retain the unconstrained "flight" mode I mentioned previously.

Bungie's Forge level editor for the *Marathon* engine included a "visual mode" where the designer could actually maneuver through his level exactly as a player would in the game.

The Vulcan editor for Bungie's *Marathon* engine was particularly well suited to allowing the designer to test the "feel" of the level while constructing it. The *Marathon* technology was similar but a bit better than *Doom*'s, and was licensed for use in a number of other games, including my game *Damage Incorporated*. Vulcan was subsequently revised, renamed Forge, and released with the final game in the series, *Marathon Infinity*. Vulcan/Forge allowed for a "visual mode," which functioned as a player's view window. In visual mode the designer could navigate the world just as players would in the final game. The shortcoming of this was that the designer was unable to edit the world, aside from texture and lighting placement, while in this view. This was no doubt due to the speed of processors available when the editor was created, and the comparatively small size of affordable monitors at the time. Today, it would definitely be expected that this view could be opened simultaneously with other views, allowing users to switch back and forth from it trivially with a mouse click or hot key press. Similarly, designers would expect to be able to edit more than just the lighting and texturing in this view. Nonetheless, the visual mode in Vulcan was quite useful, and the switch from editing mode to gameplay mode was fast enough to allow the designer to make a change, see how it felt, and then switch back to make more changes as necessary.

Of course, one might conclude that the next logical step is to allow the designer to actually play the game in the player's view. In this way the designer can see how well different mechanisms function, and what sort of a challenge different adversaries will present. However, this opens the programmer up to a large amount of implementation difficulties. In order for game-world objects to function as they do in the game, many objects will move from the position they start out in when players begin the level. For instance, an aggressive troll might run toward the player character and attack. Do these moving objects then actually move in the level editor as well? And what happens if the designer saves the level in this new state? Surely that is a bad idea, since all of the locations in which the entities have been carefully placed will be changed. What a designer wants is to be able to quickly test a level at any given location, and once he is done playtesting have the level revert to its "unplayed" state. This may best be accomplished by allowing the designer to quickly enter a "test mode" and then exit it just as quickly, instantly returning him to level editor functionality. The quicker this transition the better, for the faster and easier it is, the more likely the designer will want to go back and forth to test and retest the playability of his level. If the designer has to wait a minute or longer to playtest, he will not be able to try as many different changes to the level before he gets behind schedule. For this reason, it makes sense to have a programmer focus on smoothing out and speeding up this transition as much as possible.

Any seasoned game designer will tell you that whether a game succeeds or fails is largely dependent on how well it is playtested and balanced. Even the most brilliant initial game design can be completely destroyed if the implemented game is not playtested thoroughly. I do not mean just for bugs, but for gameplay — for how the game feels to play and for how it captivates players. Playtesting is an iterative process that involves trying a type of gameplay, then modifying it, then trying it again, and repeating this loop until the game is fun. It can be very hard, then, to properly iterate through playtesting if the level editor does not facilitate the modification of the game's levels, and then easily allow the designer to try out what has been changed. The easier it is for designers to jump into the game, try something, jump back out of the game, make a content change, and then jump back in again, the more likely they are to repeat the playtesting cycle again and again until the game is as perfect as possible. If the level editor does not facilitate such testing, designers are likely to become frustrated or simply not have the time they need to sufficiently balance the game.

Editing the World

The best development tools for a game are composed of a delicate mix of off-the-shelf programs and proprietary editors. A good team will know just how much of each to use so that they are neither wasting the time of their programmers by having them develop overly sophisticated tools when a good commercial package is better suited, nor unreasonably restraining the efforts of their designers by not allowing them to refine the game's content from within a custom level editor. Though no team should be forced to develop a game without a level editor, it is equally foolhardy to force the team to do all of the game's content creation from within proprietary tools.

It is important that the level editor actually allow the designer to modify all gameplay-critical aspects of a level. This would seem to me to be an obvious prerequisite for an editor, but I have heard so many stories of teams working with 3D Studio MAX and "entity editors" that it bears mentioning. Often teams think they can get away with using an off-the-shelf tool such as MAX to create all of their world geometry, and then create a level editor only for importing the meshes from MAX and positioning the items, NPCs, and other game-world entities. Though this is workable given enough time and tenacity, it will not lead to as good levels as will a fully featured editor. As the designer is placing creatures in the map, he needs to be able to simultaneously change the geometry to fit the placement of that creature. If a designer must exit the editor and then run a 3D modeling application (which are seldom known for their speed), modify the geometry in that program, and then re-import the level into the proprietary editor before he can test out his modifications, he will certainly be discouraged from making too many "tweaks" to the geometry. As a direct result, the geometry will not look as good or play as well in the final game. Not allowing a designer to edit the level's gameplay-critical architecture in the editor itself is tantamount to tying one arm behind his back. It is my experience that designers work best with both hands free.

When I started working on *Centipede 3D*, the level editor we had was really more of a game entity manipulator than a proper level editor. The geometry for a given level was derived from a grayscale, square height-map, with those used in *Centipede 3D* all consisting of 32 x 32 pixels. Each pixel therein represented a height value on the landscape. These height-maps, which could be created in Photoshop or any other pixel-pushing tool, were a good way to create an initial version of a level's geometry. Unfortunately, in the version of the editor used at the start of the project, the height-maps could only be modified in a paint program; they could not be edited in the editor itself. This was a shame, since looking at a top-down 2D representation of a 3D level is not exactly the best way to get an idea of how the level will end up looking. As a result, the levels that were created early in the project were simple and a bit flat. It was not that the level designers were not working hard to make the levels attractive, merely that there was only so much that could be accomplished with the tools provided.

However, midway through the project, functionality was added to the tool to allow the designer to edit the height-maps while in the level editor. The height-maps could still be created in Photoshop and brought into the game, and this remained the best way to make a first pass on the level's architecture. After that first pass, however, the geometry was easily manipulated in the level editor, where the designer was able to see the level in 3D while modifying the height-map. As a result, the designers were able to tweak the geometry until it was perfect. The change in the quality of the levels was dramatic. As always, time did not allow for us to go back and redo the earlier levels. Since the levels were made in the order they appeared in the game, anyone playing *Centipede 3D* will be able to tell at what point the level designers were given the new and improved tool. It was not that the designers could not create levels with the previous incarnation of the editor, it was just that level editing was so much more difficult that the levels failed to look as good as the designers wanted.

There is a lot to be said for being able to create fancy level geometry in a fully featured 3D package, and even level editors with sophisticated geometry editing capabilities would benefit from the ability to import externally created architecture. The key to creating quality game art assets, whether they are 2D sprites or 3D models, is being able to import from commercial packages. I do not know that anyone was ever forced to create 2D sprite artwork for a game using only an in-house tool. Yet, it seems that many unfortunate artists have only been allowed to model characters or other objects using proprietary modeling tools. I have discussed how important it is to allow the level designers to manipulate a level's architecture in the editor. But certainly forcing game designers or artists to model every game-world element in the level editor is a big mistake. Artists should be able to create game-world objects such as trees, weapons, or trash cans in their favorite modeling package and import them into the game. Simply put, there is no way a game's programming team is going to be able to code up an art editing package with all the power, robustness, and stability of a Photoshop, 3D Studio MAX, Maya, Softimage, or any of a number of other popular off-the-shelf products. Without the many features found in these packages, artists will simply be unable to create the best quality art possible. Furthermore, most artists are already familiar with one or more of these packages, and so when they come on to the project they will be that much closer to being "up to speed."

At the same time, the team will need to be able to manipulate this art using proprietary tools. Having an in-house editor with which to set up animations, nodes on a skeleton, collision data, or other information is essential to making the art function properly within the game. Teams who attempt to avoid setting up any sort of art editing software will frustrate their artists, designers, or whoever gets stuck with configuring the art and its animations to work in the game. A proprietary art manipulation tool that does exactly what the game engine needs it to do is a key ingredient in a bearable game development experience.

Scripting Languages and Object Behaviors

It seems to have become the norm for games to use a system where designers can set up and balance the enemy, weapon, and other game behaviors exactly as they need them, without involving a programmer. Many games now include scripting languages which, though relatively simple, allow for complex entity creation without requiring the game engine itself to be recompiled. These scripting languages provide many benefits to game development. Probably most important is that they encourage the creation of more unique behaviors in the game, whether these are reusable in-game entities such as NPCs or unique events for a specific level such as NPCs carrying on a particular conversation while the player watches in *Half-Life*.

One great benefit of a properly designed scripting system is that it is completely portable to other systems. This means that when the game is ported from the PC to the Dreamcast, for instance, all of the enemy behaviors that have been scripted and debugged on the PC will be equally functional on the Dreamcast, provided the script interpreter and its associated functions are properly ported as well. In that vein, a robust scripting language is also more stable to work with than programming in C. The scripting language gives the script's author less opportunity to thoroughly crash the game, and when a script does something illegal, the game can spit out a properly informative message instead of just locking up. Often scripting languages are not as complex as actual C programming, and thereby allow designers with some programming savvy to take on the creation of unique world behaviors, thus freeing up harder-to-find programmers for more complex tasks. In most systems, scripts can also be loaded on demand, which means only the scripts that a particular section of the game uses will need to be resident in memory, thus freeing up more code overhead. An added bonus of a game having a scripting language is that it allows for complex user modification of that game. A well-designed and appropriately powerful scripting system will empower motivated players to make their own "mods" for the game for distribution to friends.

Scripting languages have their downside as well. First is the time involved in implementing a scripting system. If the language is to be actually useful to the game as described above, it will need to be very stable and provide its user with a lot of power, which is certainly non-trivial to implement. Debugging a problematic script can also be quite a lot of trouble, since no game developer is going to have the time to implement a symbolic debugger as nice as the one that comes with Visual Studio or CodeWarrior. Most of the time, the scripts are compiled at run time, and as a result can be significantly slower than C/C++ code. Again, no matter what the developer does in terms of optimizing performance of the scripts, he will not be able to match the compiling power of the C++ compilers made by Watcom, Microsoft, or Metrowerks. And finally, though one of the big advantages to scripting languages is supposed to be that they can be used by non-programmers, it often turns out that, if the scripting language is actually powerful enough to create AI for an NPC, it is going to be so complex that it requires a programmer to use it effectively. And if a programmer's time is being tied up in the creation of scripts, why stop him from just doing his coding work in C?

Of course, one of the main advantages of scripts is that they greatly simplify the balancing of gameplay. Instead of a programmer tweaking a number in the code and then waiting for the game to recompile, a designer can adjust a value in a script and just run the game. But what if one wants to achieve this benefit of scripts without having to implement a scripting system? What if, instead, the designers were able to adjust behavior parameters in the level editor itself? This is the approach taken by Surreal Software's Riot Engine. In Surreal's Level Editor, designers are given access to all the settings or "behavior variables" for a given AI, weapon, or other game-world entity. The behaviors themselves are coded in C++, with the programmers leaving "hooks" to all the crucial settings that determine how the game-world object will behave, such as how fast it moves, what its detect radius is, what it does when it is destroyed, and so forth. This provides much of the game-balancing benefit of scripting languages by empowering the designers to endlessly tweak the game while still taking advantage of the speed of a powerful C++ compiler and debugger. This functionality makes the

Surreal Software's Riot Engine Level Editor allows the designer to tweak all sorts of settings for different game-world entities.

level editor not just a tool for modifying the game's levels, but turns it into more of a gameplay editor, where the designer is able to change much of the game's content on the fly. Of course, you don't always need a fancy editor to pull off easily tweakable variables; many games have allowed designers to modify gameplay values via text files that can be edited in any text editor and that are then read in by the game at run time. Of course maintaining a number of text files can be less user friendly than an editor specifically designed for modifying this type of data. But at the same time, if you don't have enough time to invest in your tools, editing text files may be preferable to data that is only modifiable in an especially clunky or broken editor.

"Scripted events" in levels are another thing that game scripting languages do well. Each level in the game can have a unique script that sets up and triggers various unique behaviors on that level. Having complex, unique behaviors has recently become a much bigger concern of game developers. An early and influential example was Valve's excellent use of scripted events integrated into the more dynamic gameplay proper in *Half-Life*. Of course, there is a key difference between "scripted events" and the "scripting language" one uses to set them up. *Half-Life* had great scripted events, but apparently a difficult-to-use method for setting them up. Creating a solid and simple scripting system is the best way to ensure that the designers will make use of it. Instead of involving a separately compiled, text-based scripting language, level editors can include the ability to empower designers to easily set up complex game events. Surreal Software's STOMP editor, used in the *Drakan* games as well as *The Suffering*, though not the most bug-free piece of software ever written, allows designers and animators to set up complex scripted sequences relatively easily in the editor and view them in real-time 3D as they are built. The sequences, which can be used both as cut-scenes and in-game scripted events, can be easily edited in real-time using an interface reminiscent of Adobe Premiere. *StarCraft*'s Campaign Editor is an especially good example of a more gameplay-oriented scripting system with a well-conceived and user-friendly interface. Its "Triggers" editor allows designers to use a very familiar point-and-click interface to set up complex scripted events. Pop-up menus provide lists of all the commands available, and then further pop-ups show the designer all of the different parameters that can be passed to those commands. The whole system is easily comprehensible to someone looking at it for the first time, with commands written in plain English. Thus, the Campaign Editor allows unique events to occur in *StarCraft* levels without involving the overhead of a full-blown scripting language.

The *StarCraft* Campaign Editor allows for easy scripting using triggers and a simple point-and-click interface.

Us Versus Them

Unfortunate as it may be, the development of the tools for a project often comes down to a battle between the programmers and the designers. Game programmers are often loath to work on tools for a variety of reasons. First, many of the programmers who wanted to get into gaming did so because they did not want to program databases, spreadsheets, or 3D modeling packages. They wanted to make games, and tools often seem too much like "real programming." There's also a perception that getting one's code in the game is more important than getting it in the tools. If the title is a big hit, the game will be played by millions of people. The tools for a given project, however, will be used by perhaps ten or twenty people. When a programmer's friends ask him what he worked on while he was at that wacky game company, most programmers do not want to have to answer, "I worked on the tools." There is a certain lack of glamour there.

Further complicating matters is the perception that a programmer's time is more valuable than a designer's. So if a designer has to spend five times as long making a level because a programmer does not have the time to make the level editor better, well, that's OK. The level still gets made, right?

As I have stated previously, game developers should not be asking themselves the question, "Do the tools allow for the game's content to be created?" Instead, they should ask, "Do the tools allow for the game's content to be made well?" If a designer is constantly fighting with the level creation tools, he is not going to be able to invest time into truly refining the level. In fact, he may be so irritated at perceived programmer laziness that he throws his hands up in disgust and does not work on the level as much as he might otherwise. A good level designer will be inspired by a good tool set to do the best work he can, because he can see direct results. The example I used before about the level design tool and the resultant quality of the levels in *Centipede 3D* is a good lesson for game developers. With the creation of a superior level editing tool, level quality will improve dramatically.

A tools programmer should be able to take pride in having worked on a really good tool that facilitates the designer's work. The programmer responsible for a well-conceived and well-implemented level editor that greatly facilitates the creation of beautiful levels should feel that he played a vital role in the creation of those levels. For without the features of the level editor, the designer would not have been able to create the landscapes or structures he did. The designer must always make it a point to remember the programmer who made possible the creation of such levels and be suitably appreciative of his efforts.

Blizzard's *WarCraft III* World Editor automatically sets up transitions between different types of landscape textures, thereby saving designers a lot of work.

At one point I added a texturing feature to the Riot Engine Level Editor. At the time, the Riot Engine employed tiling textures for its landscape, with transition textures available for when a grass texture meets a rock texture, for example. I added the functionality that allowed the editor to automatically place the proper transitions between two different texture types. Interestingly, this was a feature included in the level editor for my first published game of five years prior, *Odyssey: The Legend of Nemesis*. Indeed, this auto-transitioning functionality is found in many 2D terrain level editors, such as Blizzard's *StarCraft* Campaign Editor or *WarCraft III* World Editor. Before I added the feature, the level designers at Surreal had to pick by hand the transition texture that was needed. Certainly the auto-transitioning feature was not absolutely necessary for the creation of levels. All of the levels for the game *Drakan* had been made without the use of the auto-transitioning tool, and certainly they were very beautiful levels with transitions in all the right places. The key difference is that those transitions took a lot of designer time to set up. Once I added the auto-transitioning tool the designers were delighted, since now a large and tedious part of their jobs had been all but eliminated. One even said, "Richard could take off the next month and we could keep paying him." He was appreciative of the feature I had added and was thoughtful enough to communicate his thanks to me. With praise like that, tools programmers are much more likely to keep adding nifty features to the editor.

The Best of Intentions

However, one must be careful. Sometimes when programmers are tasked with adding functionality to the editor, they may end up adding features that no one really needs. It is difficult for a programmer who, most of the time, does not make the game's levels and therefore does not spend a lot of time working with the level editor, to properly understand what that editor is lacking. Indeed, what a programmer may see as a cool feature can turn out to be functionality no designer will ever want to use. When a programmer goes to a lot of trouble to implement a feature for the editor and then the designers fail to use it, resentment tends to grow in the programmer. Then when a designer comes to the programmer requesting a more practical and necessary feature be added to the editor, the programmer is likely to ignore him, thinking, "He never used the vertex-warping tool that I worked so hard on, so why should I work on this model-aligner for him? Forget it."

Anyone who has worked in the industry knows that, in a lot of ways, designers and programmers think differently. For this reason, it is very important for the designers and programmers to be in constant communication about what features the editor needs and how they can best be implemented. When developing an in-house tool set, the programmer has the tremendous advantage of having his user base down the hall. He does not have to guess what they want from the program; instead he can go ask them. Similarly, the designers have the advantage of being able to go to the editor's developer and make suggestions on how the tool should function. With a good flow of information between the parties involved, the tools cannot help but improve.

One possible technique for facilitating the creation of a good tool is to assign one programmer to be primarily responsible for the maintenance and improvement of the level editor, instead of passing editor tasks off to "whoever has time." This one programmer can then become quite familiar with the workings of the tool and can take pride in what a good application it is. If one programmer does most of the editor work, the designers will know which programmer they can turn to with their suggestions for improvements to the tool. That programmer will get a better sense of what the designers like and do not like. Of course, if the programmer assigned to working on the tool really wishes he was working on lighting effects or AI, the tool is going to suffer as a result. Finding a programmer who really wants to work on the tool is important if this strategy is to succeed.

Another useful tactic is to actually have a programmer make a complete, simple level using the tool. That way, the programmer can easily spot areas for improvement in the editor, and can finally understand what the designers have been complaining about for so many weeks. If the level is of sufficient quality and fits the needs of the project, you may even want to consider shipping this programmer-created level with the game. But even if you don't, the understanding the programmer gains through using the editor as it is really used will be invaluable. Without actually having to sit down and fully use the application they are creating, the programmer is likely to conclude that the designers are overemphasizing the problems with the editor (known in industry parlance as "whining"). But by actually having to use the tool he is working on, a programmer is likely to easily identify editor shortcomings that can be easily fixed through a few hours of coding. Designers frequently fail to understand the complexity of different programming tasks, and as a result make requests for nearly impossible features in the level editor, while thinking easily remedied problems are unfixable. Perhaps the best solution of all is to have a designer who is also a programmer, and thereby spends a lot of time working with the editor. This designer/programmer is directly motivated toward improving the tool he must work with every day, and is likely to do whatever he can to make it the best tool possible. Ten years ago I am sure this was not that uncommon, but for full-scale projects in development today it is fairly rare. Programming a level editor and designing levels have each become tasks that fully consume an individual developer's time, and unfortunately the days of the designer/programmer seem to be mostly a thing of the past.

A Game Editor for All Seasons

A level editor does not actually need to be bug free. Bug-free software is the stuff one buys in stores, if one is lucky. Really great in-house tools can have plenty of bugs in them. What is important is that these tools be buggy in predictable ways. The bugs should occur in patterns that the designers can learn how to predict and teach themselves to avoid. Once a designer becomes adept at the tools he will know what not to do and will be able to easily work around the trouble spots. Proprietary level editor tools are one place in software development where the old joke "Doctor, it hurts when I do this!" "Then don't do that!" really rings true.

Of course, if the tools used on a project are good enough, marketing may catch on and can come up with the bright idea, "Hey, we can release the tools with the game!" Indeed, shipping a game with its level editor and having users create add-on levels for your title can help to keep interest alive in a game long after it has been released. Hard-core fans will love to make "mods" for the game to circulate among their friends or the general public. For the tools to be released, they really will need to be relatively bug free, or at least much more stable than when they were only being used in-house. The possibility of releasing the level editor to the fans should function as an incentive to encourage the programming team to create the best tools possible. Of course, some publishers still fail to see the logic of having the fan community build add-ons and refuse to release the tools used for the game's creation. The argument they often give is that if users can build more levels themselves, who will want to buy the sequel? Of course, id Software, the company that popularized releasing level editors to the public, continues to do quite well financially, suggesting that protectionist thinking in terms of level editors is somewhat foolish.

In the end, it all comes down to what should be recognized as an axiom in the gaming industry: a game can only be as good as the tools used in its creation. A well-conceived level design tool can make the difference between a great game and a mediocre one. One can think of the ideal level editor as a place where the designer has total control of the game-world: of its architecture (where players can go), of its aesthetic appearance (lighting, texturing, and sounds), and of its gameplay (NPC, item, and other entity placement, movement, and behavior). Of course, the best level editor in the world is not going to make up for a subpar engine, a fundamentally flawed game design, or a demoralized development team. But those are topics for another chapter.

Chapter 22:

Interview: Will Wright

It is hard to measure the impact Will Wright's game *SimCity* has had on the industry. At the time of its release in 1989, the game was so radically different from any other piece of interactive computer entertainment that for many years the project had trouble finding a publisher. Now the game's influence can be seen in the countless "builder" games released every year. Sid Meier readily admits that *SimCity* was one of his primary inspirations in making *Civilization*. Astonishingly, Wright managed to surpass *SimCity* with his grand triumph, *The Sims*. Again Wright came totally out of left field with a game that he had to fight to get made. While the majority of games released in the last ten years take only evolutionary baby steps of improvement, with *The Sims* Wright created something truly revolutionary that was the most original game design seen in years. Talking with Wright is an experience in itself, as one is instantly made keenly aware of why he has developed such brilliant and innovative games.

How did you first become interested in game development?

I got totally into computers shortly after I bought an Apple II around 1980. I just got infatuated with games. As a kid I spent a lot of time building models, and I bought some of the very early games, such as the very first version of *Flight Simulator* with the wire-frame graphics. You had to write your own machine language patch to get it to run — that was funny. But just the idea that you could build your own little micro-world inside the computer intrigued me. So I saw it as a kind of modeling tool. At some point I just got so into these things that I decided I would try to make one myself, and that was right around the time the Commodore 64 was first coming out. So I bought one of those, figuring that it would be better to start on a new machine where everybody was on a level playing field, because other people had learned the Apple II years before I decided to do this. So I bought a Commodore as soon as it came out and just dove into it, and learned it as quickly as I could. And that's what I did my first game on.

So how did you come up with the design for *Raid Over Bungeling Bay?*

Back then just about all the games were arcade games, you know. I had always loved helicopters, so I wanted to do a little helicopter game. And then I was looking at the Commodore. It was driven probably more by the technology than the game design side. I found that the Commodore had this really cool trick where you could redefine a character set, make it look like graphics, and then smoothly scroll it around the screen. So you could give the impression that you were scrolling over this huge bitmap, when in fact all you were doing is moving ASCII characters around on the screen. And when I saw that feature, I thought that would be really cool looking, because I knew the Apple couldn't begin to move that much in the way of graphics around the screen that smoothly. So I designed the game around that feature in a way.

I understand the game was much more popular in Japan than it was in the States.

I think that was right when piracy was probably at its peak. We sold around 30,000 copies in the U.S., which was average for a game like that. But then everybody I've talked to who had a Commodore back then had played it. Whereas the same game on the Nintendo in Japan sold about 750,000 copies. It was a cartridge system, so there was no piracy.

Do you still look back on the game positively?

Oh yeah. I look back on it with fond memories. It was a learning experience. It was one of those times where you realize that the last ten percent, getting the game out the door, that's the really hard part. And unless you plan for that last ten percent, it's just a killer. So I learned a lot of lessons from it. And back then programming wasn't nearly as elaborate as it is now. Every game was written by one person and that game was about eight thousand lines of machine language. So you could totally control the memory and totally control the machine. It was a good learning vehicle. It's kind of a shame that the programmers who learn to program nowadays are coming at it from a totally different point of view.

You mean because they're using higher level programming languages?

Oh yeah. Which isn't necessarily bad, I guess. But you still have the old hacks like myself. There were eight bytes of memory free on that machine when I finished that game, and I felt bad that I didn't use those last eight. And there are a lot of tricks you do when you're running out of memory, because the memory was the ultimate concern. There were some cool little tricks for that.

I read that the level editing tool for *Bungeling Bay* **was your inspiration for** *SimCity*.

It was a character set that actually described a bunch of islands with little roads and cities on them. And so there was such a big area that I developed my own little character editing program to draw this scene that I could scroll around really smoothly, like a paint program. I found that I was having so much more fun with the paint program than I was with the game that after I finished the game I kept playing with the paint program. And it eventually evolved into *SimCity*.

So you wouldn't cite any other games that inspired *SimCity?*

I'd say the biggest inspiration, if there had to be one, was the work of Jay Forester, who is considered the father of system dynamics, and one of the very first people to use a computer for simulation. So when I started getting the idea for *SimCity*, I started going to the library and reading. He did a lot of his work back in the '50s, working with very primitive computers and very primitive models, but yet he was the

SimCity

first person to try to simulate a city. And he did it with like twenty variables: one was population, one was production, one was birth rate, stuff like that. Very simple models.

System dynamics is a way to look at a system and divide it into, basically, stocks and flows. Stocks are quantities, like population, and flows are rates, like the death rate, the birth rate, immigration. You can model almost anything just using those two features. That was how he started system dynamics and that was the approach he took to his modeling. I uncovered his stuff when I started working on *SimCity* and started teaching myself modeling techniques. I also came across the more recent stuff with cellular automata, and *SimCity* is really a hybrid of those two approaches. Because his approach was not spatial at all, whereas the cellular automata gives you a lot of really interesting spatial tools for propagation, network flow, proximity, and so forth. So the fact that pollution starts here, spreads over here, and slowly gets less and less, and you can actually simulate propagation waves through these spatial structures. So *SimCity* in some sense is like a big three-dimensional cellular automata, with each layer being some feature of the landscape like crime or pollution or land value. But the layers can interact on the third dimension. So the layers of crime and pollution can impact the land value layer.

What made you think that such scholarly techniques could lead to something that people would find fun?

At that point I wasn't trying to build something that people would play for entertainment value. It's more like I was just having fun doing this on my own. At the same time I was reading about urban dynamics, just on the theoretical side. And having this little guinea pig city on my computer while I was reading about the subject made the subject so much more interesting. So I could read a theory and then try to figure out how to formalize it, code it, put it in the model, and see what the results of it were.

At what point did you start to think it might be something that other people could have fun with?

After about six months or so I started attaching some graphics to it. It was fairly abstract to begin with. And then I started thinking, you know, this might be an interesting game. I had actually done my first game with Broderbund Software, and I showed it to some people there and they thought it was pretty cool. They agreed to pick it up, and we had a contract for it and everything. And I worked on it for about a year to the point where it was where I wanted it to be. And they kept thinking it wasn't finished. They kept saying, "When is it going to be a game? When is it going to have a win/lose situation?" It was very unusual for its time, and this was about five years before it was actually released. This was around 1985, and we didn't actually release it until '89.

They didn't think it was enough of a game to fit in with their other products?

They just didn't see how they could possibly sell it. And I just left it there, and they left it there, and that was that.

So were you pretty discouraged?

I always thought it was a cool little thing I did; I never really thought it would be a mainstream thing. But I thought it would be worthwhile getting it on the market. So later I met my eventual partner, Jeff Braun, and I showed it to him. And he thought it was really cool. He really, really was into it. He, in fact, thought there was probably a big market for something like that. At that point, the two of us decided to start a company ourselves, and that's when we started Maxis.

So it had sat around, unpublished, for a number of years?

Yeah, for a couple of years. About the time we decided to start Maxis, the Macintosh had just come out, and the Amiga was coming out, and we decided we would rewrite the game for those computers. So we hired a couple of programmers, and I recoded the simulator in C. It had all been in assembly before. We had these other programmers helping on the graphical front ends on the Mac and on the Amiga, and those were actually the first versions that were released. We actually did go back and release the Commodore version about a month after we released those.

So originally *SimCity* didn't have a mouse-based, point-and-click interface?

No, actually it did. The Lisa had come out while I was doing it on the Commodore, and I actually had implemented a cursor-based system with icons. The interface was on a Commodore, but it still had that iconic, paint-program kind of feel. It looked like MacPaint in a way. So, in fact, it did have a similar graphic front end but at a much lower resolution.

SimCity

Did the design change much from what you had originally done?

It got more elaborate, more layers were added, and there was higher resolution on the map, but it had the same basic structure for the simulation and the same basic sets of tools. But, for instance, there were only roads, there weren't roads and highways. The map was 80 by 90, instead of 128 by 128. Of course, the graphics were much lower resolution; they were about four pixels square for a tile, instead of the eventual sixteen. But the core of the model and the tuning of the model didn't actually change that much. And it actually didn't change all that much for *SimCity 2000* or *3000*.

So Maxis finally got it out to the market by self publishing it?

It's actually kind of interesting. After we had redone it on the Mac and the Amiga, we knew we could afford to produce it in the boxes and all that, but we had to have a distributor. And in fact we came back to Broderbund and showed it to them, and when they saw the Mac and Amiga versions they were much more impressed. Plus it was years later, at which point the market was getting into much more interesting games. At that point they offered to become our distributor, and so we had an affiliate publishing relationship with Broderbund. We were incurring most of the financial risk because we were the ones paying for the boxes and all that, so they weren't really risking that much on it. The people at Broderbund were really nice people and I hold no grudges against them at all. They helped us a lot in getting Maxis off the ground. And the Carlstons, the people who started Broderbund, were my role models for business people. They were just really nice people to deal with.

Did you come up with the term "software toy"?

I think I did, because I was giving a talk at the Game Developers Conference, way back, and I decided that would be the name of my talk. It was "Software Toys: The Intersection of Creativity, Empathy, and ... " something. Some high-falutin' sounding talk.

How would you distinguish between a software toy and a game?

Toys can be used to build games. You can play games with toys. But you can also engage in more freeform play with toys. It doesn't have to be a goal-directed activity. I think of toys as being more open-ended than games. We can use a ball to play a game such as basketball, or we can just toss the ball back and forth, or I can experiment with the ball, bouncing it off of different things. So, I would think of toys as a broader category. Also, toys can be combined. I can strap Barbie to my R.C. car and drive her around, thus making up a new activity by combining toys. Games tend to be isolated universes where there's a rule set, and once you leave that universe the rule set is meaningless. Another way to think about it, and this is a more recent version of the same idea, is that I tend to think of the games we do in more of a hobby kind of way, whereas most games are thought about more in terms of a movie or cinematic form. Movies have a beginning and an end, there's a climax, there's one particular story line, and a lot of games are built more on that model.

Our games are more like a hobby, which you approach in a different way. Like with a model train set, some people get totally into the scenery and the details on the cliffs and the hills. Other people get into the little village in the middle. Other people get into the switching on the tracks. And sometimes these will play off of each other when a community builds around a hobby. You'll have certain people in the community who are very into certain aspects of the hobby and they have expertise which they can teach to other people. And you have subspecializations within the community. People can create things and trade them, or they can just share ideas. I tend to think of hobbies as being a bit more community based than the cinematic model. That's more of a shared experience, it's a kind of cultural currency: "Oh, did you see that movie last night? What did you think?"

But with a software toy like *SimCity*, only one person is really playing it at any one time.

The community I'm referring to now more than ever is the online community. I can go online and I can start trading strategies with people, or I can upload my city or my family or my stories, or I can make skins for *The Sims*. And if someone gets really good at it they can have a standing in the community: "Oh, he makes the best skins." So there's this whole community on the web that develops around the game, with people creating things and sharing things.

Which is more possible now than when *SimCity* originally came out.

Back when *SimCity* came out, it was really just a few sporadic message boards on some of the online services like CompuServe or later AOL. It was mostly just chat discussions and things like that. There wasn't really a forum where people could meet. It wasn't really a very involving online community. But even before we had our first web site, people were already uploading their cities to AOL and trading them. There were big sections with hundreds of cities trading. CompuServe was the first place where large collections of cities started to appear, not too long after the game came out.

The biggest complaint I've seen about *SimCity***, and I've seen this mostly from other game developers, is that since it is not a game and there aren't any goals, it doesn't hold the player's attention very well.**

I think it attracts a different kind of player. In fact, some people play it very goal directed. What it really does is it forces you to determine the goals. So when you start *SimCity*, one of the most interesting things that happens is that you have to decide "What do I want to make? Do I want to make the biggest possible city, or the city with the happiest residents, or the most parks, or the lowest crime?" Every time you have to idealize in your head, "What does the ideal city mean to me?" It requires a bit more motivated player. What that buys you in a sense is more replayability because we're not enforcing any strict goal on you. We could have said, "Get your city to 10,000 people in ten years or you lose." And you would always have to play it that way. And there would be strategies to get there, and people would figure out the strategies, and that would be that. By leaving it more open-ended, people can play the game a lot of different ways. And that's where it's become more like a toy.

Simulations in general give you a much wider game-space to explore. There are probably no two cities in *SimCity* that are identical and created by different people. Whereas, if you look at a game like *Zelda*, I'm sure there are tens of thousands of saved *Zelda* games that are identical. Computationally you can look at this as the phase-space of the system, or how many variables does it take to describe a current state of

SimCity

the system. Another way of looking at that is it's how much creative exploration the player is allowed. How unique is your game from my game? In some sense that implies a certain level of creativity available to you. In some situations that can also be interpreted as how many different ways there are to solve a given problem. So if we start with the same exact city that has a lot of traffic, there are a huge variety of ways that we can attack that problem successfully. In a lot of games there's a locked door and until you find that key you're not going to be able to unlock that door.

So it provides the player with a lot more variety.

There's a lot more variety, but also, because every player can take a unique approach, they can be more creative. And the more creativity the player can realize in a game, the more empathy they tend to feel with that game. Especially you see that in *The Sims*. If

they spend all this time building up a family and running their lives for months, people really start to empathize with those characters because they have invested so much time in the creation of them. And the characters, in that sense, are a reflection not only of themselves, but it's a reflection of their current understanding of the game. Same with *SimCity*. You can look at somebody's city in *SimCity* at any time, and the design of the city is a reflection of what they understand about the model. From their understanding that was the best way to build a road network at that point.

But once they come to understand the game better...
It changes, exactly. You can go back to an old city and say, "Oh, right, that's when I thought highways really worked well, before I learned that they didn't." So in some sense it reflects your mental model of the game.

But if you play *Zelda* a second time...
Your mental model doesn't really evolve that much. You learn the surprises, but your model of the underlying mechanisms isn't really all that different once you've played the game through.

I'm a bit curious about the disaster feature in *SimCity*. It seems strange that players would want to spend a lot of time building something up and then just destroy it with a tidal wave or a fire.
Yeah, I always thought that was kind of curious myself.

You must have anticipated it, though, since you put it in the game from the very beginning.
No, actually, it wasn't in the original Commodore version. I later added it, though. When I first started showing the Commodore version, the only thing that was in there was a bulldozer, basically to erase mistakes. So if you accidentally built a road or a building in the wrong place you could erase it with the bulldozer. What I found was that, invariably, in the first five minutes people would discover the bulldozer, and they would blow up a building with it by accident. And then they would laugh. And then they would go and attack the city with the bulldozer. And they'd blow up all the buildings, and they'd be laughing their heads off. And it really intrigued me, because it was like someone coming across an ant pile and poking it with a stick to see what happens. And they would get that out of their system in ten minutes, and then they would realize that the hard part wasn't destroying it, but building it back up. And so people would have a great time destroying the city with a bulldozer, and then they would discover, "Wow, the power's out. Wow, there's a fire starting." And that's when they would start the rebuilding process, and that's what would really hook them. Because they would realize that the destruction was so easy in this game, it was the creation that was the hard part. And this is back when all of the games were about destruction. After seeing that happen with so many people, I finally decided, "Well, I might as well really let them get it out of their systems, I'll add some disasters to the game." And that's what gave me the idea for the disaster menu.

Plus you had the disasters randomly occur.

Yeah, that seemed obvious after I had the disaster menu, that they should randomly happen, but I didn't originally have that.

***SimEarth* seems to be a logical extension of *SimCity*. How did you come up with the idea for that game?**

It was more my interest in certain subjects that drove me to it. I was very interested in certain theories, most notably the Gaia hypothesis, and also general environmental issues that a lot of times are counterintuitive. I thought it would be interesting to have a model of a global ecosystem. I learned a lot from *SimEarth*. Actually, I was very proud of the simulation of *SimEarth*, and pretty disappointed in the game design.

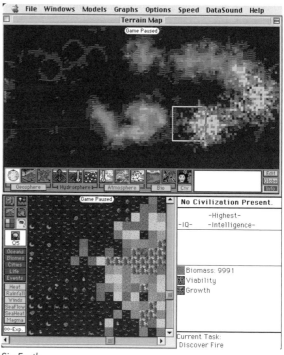

SimEarth

How do you mean?

It wasn't a terribly fun game. It's actually a very nice model, and we did a lot of research of the current climatic models, and I have still never seen anyone do an integrated model with an integrated lithosphere, hydrosphere, and atmosphere together like that. And we were getting some effects in the model that were real effects, that really show up, that even some of the more elaborate models that NCAR [National Center for Atmospheric Research] makes weren't capturing. But as far as the game goes, I started realizing that you can roughly look at all of our *Sim* games and divide them into one of two categories: the economic ones and the biological ones. And, in general, the economic ones have always done better.

Which ones would you include in that group?

SimCity, *SimTower*, *SimCity 2000*, *The Sims*, and *SimFarm*, though that's a bit of both. The biologicals would be *SimAnt*, *SimEarth*, and *SimLife*, roughly.

Why do you think the economic ones have been more successful?

I think it has a lot to do with how much control you have over the systems. The biological systems tend to be very soft, squishy things that you can do something to, and then it kind of reacts and adapts. It's not really clear what you did to it, because it'll then evolve around you. Whereas in the economic ones you have much better credit assignment. When something goes wrong, you can say, "Oh, it's because I forgot to do this. I should have bought one of those." I think people can reason through their failures and assign credit to the failures more easily with the economic models. Plus the idea that you have money and you make money this way and you spend money on that all seems very natural to people, whereas when you get into the complex things like diversity, food webs, and things like that, people just don't have an instinct for it.

And nothing's more frustrating than playing and not understanding why you're losing...

Right, exactly. And so in *SimEarth* people would be playing and all of a sudden their planet would freeze up and they'd have no clue why it happened. And I, as the simulation engineer, couldn't tell them either!

One thing I like about *SimEarth* was how it could play tones that would communicate information about the state of your planet.

I always wanted to do more with that, but I never really got around to it. There's been some interesting work on data auralization. Instead of visualization, you can take complex data and map it to sound, because there are certain sound ranges that we're incredibly good at discriminating. There was actually some work done at the Santa Fe Research Institute in those areas. One of the things that they did that was remarkable was taking seismograph data, from earthquakes and whatnot, and mapping it into sound waves, using pretty much the same waveform just mapped to a different frequency. And they did the same thing with underground nuclear tests. From the seismograph, if you look at the waveforms, they're

SimEarth

pretty much identical. It's really hard to tell any difference at all between the nuclear test and the earthquake. But when you map it to sound, there's a very definite tinniness to the nuclear test, which you can instantly recognize. And it's interesting that, no matter how they mapped the waves visually, they couldn't find a way to discriminate between them. But as soon as they mapped it to sound it was obvious.

So you thought you could better communicate to the player the condition of their planet through sound?

Well, it was just kind of a stupid little experiment in that direction. At some point I'd like to sit down and do it right. The one that I thought worked pretty well was where it would map your atmosphere into tones ongoingly, starting at the North Pole and going to the South Pole. And if you left that in the background with the volume down, it was pretty useful, because you could tell changes from that much sooner than you could actually see them reflected on the visual graphs. And so, as a kind of threshold alarm, I thought that worked pretty well. Because you could actually be doing that subconsciously. After a while, you start getting used to this little tune, and then all of a sudden when the tune changes, it comes to the foreground of your mind. And it can be doing that while you're doing other things, so you don't have to be sitting there staring at the display all the time. I always thought that was pretty cool.

SimEarth is a pretty serious game compared to many of your other titles. Why did you opt for that approach?

I didn't want to do too much anthropomorphizing in the game. One of the precepts of the game is that humans just happened to be the evolved intelligence on this planet. It could have just as easily been trichordates or something else. So I was really trying to avoid a human-centered approach to the game. And, really, the focus of the game was supposed to be on the planet. I'm trying to put myself back in my mind-set back when I worked on that, it was so long ago. I mean, it's one of those things that once you get into the subject you're just fascinated by it. I'm still to this day just blown away by continental drift and things like that, stuff that most people think sounds pretty boring. So it's kind of hard to express the passion I had for that subject. _SimAnt_ was the exact same way. Still, I think ants are just the coolest thing around, and I don't think I clearly communicated that with the game.

SimAnt does seem to be a lot wackier than _SimEarth_ or even _SimCity_.

It's hard to take ants too seriously. Also, _SimAnt_ really surprised me. It's the first time I did a game that appealed to a totally different demographic than I was expecting. _SimAnt_ was actually a big hit with ten- to thirteen-year-olds. Parents would buy it, and the kids would play it, and the kids just loved it. Still to this day a lot of people tell me, "I loved _SimAnt_; it was my favorite game." And it did

SimAnt

very well. It's just that I was expecting it to be more older people that would appreciate how amazingly interesting ants are as an example of distributed intelligence. In some sense, I was trying to use a wacky approach to show how intrinsically interesting ants are as an information processing system. But in fact, I ended up appealing to twelve-year-olds who just loved playing with ants.

An ant simulator seems to be a pretty strange premise for a game. Why did you choose to do it?

I'd have to go into why I love ants. *SimAnt* always seemed obvious to me. I was always wondering why no one had ever done a computerized ant farm, and I kept expecting someone to do it for years but they never did. The time just seemed right. Most of my games have been influenced heavily by things that I have read. So, *SimEarth* was kind of inspired by James Lovelock and the Gaia hypothesis. *SimAnt* was definitely inspired by the work of Edward Wilson, who is kind of like *the* myrmecologist. He's written a lot of books. He actually wrote a Pulitzer Prize-winning book the year that *SimAnt* came out called *The Ants*, which was just an amazing resource. We used a lot of his books heavily in building the model for *SimAnt*. In fact, we probably couldn't have engineered the model without his work, as we probably could not have done *SimEarth* without James Lovelock's work.

Did you encounter any resistance to doing as unique and strange a game as *SimAnt?*

No, not at all. I think I met more resistance on *SimEarth* because everybody was expecting *SimCity 2* and I really didn't want to do *SimCity 2*, I wanted to do something different.

SimAnt **seems to be a lot more of a game than** *SimCity* **or** *SimEarth*.

I think probably *SimAnt* was my slight overreaction to *SimEarth*. When *SimEarth* came out I realized at the end that, God, this is like sitting in the cockpit of a 747 in a nosedive. That's what it feels like to most players. So I wanted *SimAnt* to go in the opposite direction: something non-intimidating, something lighthearted, something fun, something where it was really clear what went wrong. Though I never could quite tell how successful it was, one of the things I really wanted to do with *SimAnt* was to have the idea that you have this light, easy to get into game, but you get more and more serious about it. That's why we had this little online database about ants, the little encyclopedia. And the idea was to get people interested enough, just through the game, that they would actually start reading this little encyclopedia and a lot of it would pertain to the gameplay. So you could actually learn new strategies for the game while at the same absorbing all this cool information about ants.

The game reminds me of a very strange wargame.

It's kind of like an RTS game. In *SimAnt* we did some wacky things. *SimAnt* in some sense was very experimental. There were some weird things in there, like the mystery button. On the interface, there's one button that has this big question mark, and it's the mystery button. Every time you press that button something very strange happens, and usually it's different. There are thirty different things that can happen, and they're totally weird things. Like, all your ants die. Or your ants double. Or a giant rainstorm starts. Or you switch sides. Totally non-linear, random things happen when you click that button.

SimAnt

Kind of like the disasters from *SimCity* taken to an extreme...

It's almost meta-level disasters. Things that would all of a sudden erase your game or give you twice the number of your opponents. Like the disasters in *SimCity*, what a lot of people would do is they would play and play and play for hours and when they were ready to stop, just before they would quit they would burn the city down just for the hell of it. In *SimAnt* people would play the game for a while and then, just before they quit, they would hit the mystery button to see what it did today.

Your next project was *SimCity 2000*. How did that come about?

Well, actually, before I did that, I had spent about six months working on the very first incarnation of *The Sims*. I had actually done a little prototype and some coding. At that point Fred Haslam was working on *SimCity 2000*. He was the guy who I ended up doing it with and who had done *SimEarth* with me. *SimCity 2000* wasn't going nearly as fast as everybody liked, and they didn't like the graphics and all this stuff, so I got dragged

SimCity 2000

into it. At this point, the company was really depending on *SimCity 2000* being a best-seller and all that, so I basically dropped everything I was doing on *The Sims* and dove in with Fred. And, in fact, I took the code shell I had written for *The Sims*, and we actually ended up using it for *SimCity 2000*. In fact, if you go back and look at the source code for *SimCity 2000*, to this day the draw routines say DrawHouse and DrawYard, because it was the original code shell for *The Sims*. So then I got into that, and Fred and I, basically we started from scratch. Fred and I work together really well, and we did it in almost record time, for that complexity of a game. We did it in about twelve months flat.

So the idea was to improve on what had worked well in the original *SimCity?*

Roughly. Also, at that point, we had hundreds and hundreds of fan letters saying, "Oh, you should do *SimCity* again and add this and add that and add the other." And I read through all those letters. And there were a few things that were very common. And so we added the really common and obvious suggestions: altitude, mountains, a water system, more road types, that type of thing. Beyond that it was all of the things I wished I could have done in *SimCity* that, now that computers were faster and graphics were better, we could do.

So, compared to *SimAnt,* **it seems a lot less wacky. Was that because you were working with the company's prize franchise?**

It was wacky enough I think, in its own way. It had the expected *SimCity* wackiness, plus a lot of things that were not in the original *SimCity*. We had a lot of hidden things in *SimCity 2000* that people didn't realize for a long time that helped its longevity. There was the Loch Ness Monster in there. It would only appear every two or three months that you played the game, and it would only appear for about four seconds. And so there were a lot of rumors about it. Two months after the game had shipped, people started saying they had seen this monster in the water, and most people didn't believe them because it was so infrequent. And it was almost a year after we shipped the game that someone actually managed to take a screenshot of it. And then you had Captain Hero. Only under certain weird conditions you would get this superhero that would fly around and fight your disasters for you. So we had a lot of stuff like that hidden in the game. The original *SimCity* didn't really have that level of depth.

Did you feel constrained since you were just doing a sequel?

Not really. At that point I was more in project management mode. I had a pretty clear idea of what the design would be, since we were basically just doing a sequel, which is always easier. It was more just making sure the engineering was good and the performance was decent. It was a pretty tight piece of code. The original *SimCity 2000* ran in 1.3 megs on a Mac. So, for what it was, it was actually pretty tight to work in that little memory.

Was *SimCopter* **your next project?**

That came quite a bit afterward, since I was actually working on *The Sims* in the background while I was working on *SimCopter*. So, at that point I had a programmer dedicated to *The Sims*. In fact, in *SimCopter*, the behavior of the people that walked around were actually using a very early form of Edith, which was the programming language we developed for *The Sims*. A lot of people at Maxis decided we really wanted to try something where you were doing a 3D game inside of *SimCity*. So that was the original premise for *SimCopter*. They asked me: "Can you design a game where you're doing something in 3D in *SimCity*? Whatever it is, driving around, flying around, whatever." So *SimCopter* was the design I came up with. It was the first 3D game I ever did, and actually the first 3D game a lot of our team ever did as well. So we

SimCopter

were definitely going up a learning curve a couple of years behind a lot of other people. The biggest problem with *SimCopter* I don't think was in the game design, it was in the graphics. They were really substandard for when it came out.

Did you like the way it turned out? Or did you not care so much since you were more interested in working on *The Sims*?

Well, I was actually concentrating on *SimCopter*. We didn't have a big enough team on it, we basically had four people doing it. And to do a 3D product at that point in time, that was just not enough at all. So I felt like I was really resource constrained on the product, plus we had this hard schedule that we absolutely had to make. For various reasons we could not miss Christmas, which meant we really couldn't aim too high. Had we had another six to eight months to work on it, graphically I think it would have turned out much, much better. The gameplay and tuning I'm still pretty happy with. It could have used a few more missions. But there was something really neat about having a city that you'd built in *SimCity* over many hours, and then all of a sudden being in it in 3D and seeing the people and the cars and flying around it. There was a real eerie quality to that. It worked well.

Now, you weren't involved at all with *SimCity 3000*. **Were you just burned out on the whole idea of doing another city simulator?**

Yeah, that's pretty much it. You hit the nail on the head with that. It was a running joke around Maxis that whenever the *SimCity* team would come to ask me for advice I would go running. They finally gave up. You know, the day they shipped *SimCity 3000* was one of the happiest days of my life. They proved that we have a team within Maxis that knows how to build *SimCity* without my involvement. And before, when *2000* came around, there was just nobody else to turn to. I had to work on it or it just wasn't going to happen. Whereas now we have the expertise in-house to do *SimCity*, a really great, talented team. The franchise is in good hands from my point of view.

So you were pleased to not have to be involved with that.

That's an understatement. Just doing one sequel for me was excruciating. Once I got into it, I had fun with *SimCity 2000*. But there are just so many games that haven't been done at all that I'd like to do, as opposed to going back and redoing games I've already done. Probably my favorite part of designing a game is the research and learning a new subject, and just totally diving into it. And, I've spent a lot of time reading about urban dynamics and city planning. I still love the subject, but I'm kind of burned out on the research in that area. There are so many other subjects I'd love to dive into and learn right now.

I do have one question about *SimCity 3000*. When I originally saw a prototype for the game it was fully 3D. But when it shipped it was back to the classic iso-metric viewpoint. Why did that change so radically?

SimCity 3000

Well, for a number of reasons, and it was a pretty hard decision to make. In retrospect, I'm convinced it was the right decision. Part of it had to do with user interface. A lot of people who play *SimCity*, who tend to be a much broader group, a lot of the more casual gamers, have a hard time moving around and controlling a 3D camera. And when you put on top of that the idea of editing a system and then give them a three-dimensional camera, it takes what used to be a very simple, Lego-like thing, and turns it into an AutoCAD. "What am I looking at? Oh, I see, I'm facing the building two inches away." It becomes that kind of experience. So that was part of it. The other part was the technology. Without going with really severe restrictions on what you could build, we just couldn't have a decent frame rate and have the level of detail that we could have in an isometric viewpoint. We're getting to the point today where it's pretty much feasible. But you deal with real RAM limitations of texture memory and real polygonal limitations. At the time that we were working on it, there weren't enough people out there with 3D hardware to require that. So we would have had to have a software solution that was acceptable. There were a lot of reasons, but I'd say the two primary ones were performance and user interface.

So you actually started *The Sims* right after you finished *SimAnt*.

A long time ago, yeah. I also had a couple of projects that I started and then killed along the way.

Anything of interest?

Well, I had project Z. For a while there I had project X, Y, and Z. X was what we were calling *The Sims* for the longest time. Y was *SimCopter*. For Z, I wanted to do a simulation of the Hindenburg. And I really researched that and really enjoyed it. This was a really odd idea. But it was a combination of *Myst* and a flight simulator, if you can imagine that. It was going to be a very elaborately rendered, beautifully, meticulously drawn virtual Hindenburg that you could walk through and explore, every little nook and cranny. But it would also be completely functional, so every valve that you would turn would have the real effect, and every switch that you would flip would do what the real switch did. And you would find yourself all of a sudden, on the Hindenburg, over the Atlantic, heading to Lakehurst. You would be the only one aboard, you'd be on this ghost ship. Basically, history would keep repeating itself, and if you didn't do the right thing you would always blow up when you got to Lakehurst. And so it was going to be kind of a mystery game. And we were going to take the top ten or twenty theories for why the Hindenburg blew up, there are quite a few of them actually. And every time you started a new game it would pick one of those at random. So every time you played the game it wouldn't be the same reason why it blew up. So there'd be a totally different set of things you'd have to do to prevent it. In fact, you could also go up to the control cabin and pilot the thing, you could fly it around to different areas. You'd actually have to learn how to fly a zeppelin from scratch, which for one person is quite difficult.

That's really quite different from any of your other games.

Yeah. You know what really killed that project the most, the reason why I really gave up on it? It seems like a really minor reason, but it was the fact that the Hindenburg had a swastika on its tail. And even if we took the swastika off, a lot of people have this association in their mind of the Hindenburg as a Nazi symbol. Which is unfortunate, because the guy who designed and built the Hindenburg was one of the fiercest opponents of the Nazis, and he actually had to sign this pact with the devil to get the thing built. And so the Nazis actually paid for its final construction. So, anyway, that was one of my failed game designs.

So did *The Sims* stay pretty much the same throughout its development?

It definitely went through a focus change, from architecture to more about the people, but not a major one. In fact, I uncovered a tape, just before we finished *The Sims*, which I had forgotten I had. It was a tape of one of the very first focus groups we did back in '93. And on the focus group tape, the moderator describes the concept that I had written down of *The Sims*, and it's remarkably close to what we ended up shipping.

Did the focus group like the idea?

No, actually, this was probably the most negative focus group experience I have ever seen. It was actually quite remarkable. They universally hated it.

Was that why you couldn't get staff for the project at first?

Yeah, that was part of it, that certainly didn't help. It wasn't my idea to have the focus group in the first place. Our marketing people said, "Hey, let's have a focus group and make sure about this." Of course, when everybody in the focus group said, "There's no way I'd buy that," that made it a little more difficult for me to sell the idea.

So how did you finally get a chance to make it?

I convinced everybody to at least give me one programmer to work on it in the background. It was a guy named Jamie Doornbos, who was the eventual lead programmer. A really bright, young guy out of Stanford, a good science student. He was the one that was developing the behavior model with me in the background. We were trying to figure out how we could simulate an open-ended system where the behaviors were expandable and they had the level of intelligence that we would require for the game, so that they could basically live out their whole home life and we could simulate it reasonably. So Jamie and I probably spent a year and a half just working on the behavior model, as a little research project. At some point it just started really working out, and really looking pretty good. And that's the point at which I started getting more people on the team. And even then, I had to fight and kick and struggle for every person I got.

After your success with *SimCity*, it's surprising that no one trusted you.

But in fact, it's funny, because just recently I started on a couple of other back-burner type things. The last one I did, I started telling people this idea, and everybody said, "That's great, that's great, go do it, here's a programmer." And in a sense it was disappointing. It's much more satisfying when everybody says, "That sucks, no way that will work out" and then you go disprove them, rather than if everybody says, "Oh, that'll be great" and then if it doesn't turn out to be great... So in some sense I miss the struggle.

What was your original inspiration for *The Sims?*

I think the original inspiration for *The Sims* came from a book called *A Pattern Language* written by a Berkeley architecture professor named Christopher Alexander. It's a very interesting book, it's kind of controversial in the architecture world. It's almost like the Western version of feng shui. He's got two hundred fifty-six design rules, and each one looks at some aspect of human behavior and then derives a design rule that you can use. And the very first rules are where cities should be placed on a countryside. As you move up the rules, to rule ten or fifteen, it starts talking about the design of cities and neighborhoods, and circulation systems within cities. And then you move

The Sims

up to the higher rules and it's about how to design a neighborhood block and where you should put the schools and play-centers. And then it moves in closer, and it's about how you should place your house in the yard, and how you do private and public areas in the house. And as you move up to the highest level, it's about where you should put your flower planters on the windowsill and how to place a park bench. So the rules go through all these different scales, but they're all based on aspects of human behavior. And they try to extrapolate. The fact that we like to have private spaces, and a lot of our activities at home we consider private activities, and other ones are public activities. And so the design of the house should reflect that. There should be some pretty clearly private areas in the house and more clearly public areas. So, that's the way he looks at an aspect of human behavior and then extrapolates a design rule from it. And then he gives examples of how you might implement that design rule. So basically he's coming up with one proposal for a grammar of design. And a lot of people have odds with the particular grammar he came up with, but I always thought his attempt was very noble.

So you thought you could come up with a simulation that would simulate his rules.

It wasn't even his rules I was after. What I was after was trying to get this linkage between human behavior and design. If you look at most architecture magazines nowadays they're about what textures are in this year, what colors, what fabrics, or what decorating styles. They have very little to do with human behavior. Architecture used to be about how you design spaces to facilitate human actions, tasks, and activities. He wrote an earlier book called *Notes on the Synthesis of Form* which drove home the point a little more clearly. He actually did a lot of third-world design, where he would go in and study these tribes or cultures, fairly primitive people, and look at their activities. Which activities did they do together and what groups of people collaborated on these activities. And from this he was actually able to extrapolate some design rules for their culture. How their houses should be laid out and how their towns and villages should be arranged. And I just thought that was a very refreshing approach to architecture, getting back to the functional reasons for and requirements of architecture as opposed to the aesthetic and "architecture as modern art" sort of approach. If you look at a lot of these modern architecture books you see these houses in there that I would not want to live in. They're really cool looking, and they look really pretty, especially when they're empty and they're so stark. But I couldn't imagine living in them. There's this big disconnect.

So originally it had to do more with building your house?

It had more to do with enabling behavior and interaction through design. And in some sense it still retains that. Just with not quite the same amount of focus.

When I played the game, I got much more wrapped up in the interpersonal interactions.

Yeah, I think that's where the focus really changed. We didn't realize how engaging the social part of the game would be. The original concept was that you were trying to keep this family happy at home. The idea that you would have these visitors that you would develop these long-term relationships with was definitely a later concept.

So that just grew organically out of other aspects of the game?

It had a lot to do with the success of our behavioral model, which was working better than we thought it would. Or, at least, people's interpretation of our behavioral model. Which is to say we were fooling them better than we thought we would.

So you're saying that people perceive the behavioral model as more impressive than it actually is?

In fact, that became also a big focus of the design. There was another book that became very influential later in the design, a book called *Understanding Comics* by Scott McCloud. And he makes some very good points that are very applicable to game design. One of the ones that we used the most is the idea that the activity is a collaboration, in this case between the game designer and the player. And also that the level of

The Sims

abstraction that you present to the player gives them a very significant clue as to how much of this they should be modeling in their head versus on the computer. So, in fact, when somebody's playing *The Sims* and interpreting the experience, they may not realize it but they're doing a lot of the modeling in their head, not on the computer. The computer will sit there and it will pop up this gibberish conversation. Most people will actually sit there and roughly interpret what they're saying. They'll say, "Oh, I see, he's upset because she didn't take the trash out." And they'll be simulating in their heads the other side of the model to a greater level of detail than the computer ever could. People can't help but look at a sequence of events and overlay some kind of narrative on it.

We noticed that a while back, so we really decided to make use of that. And so when we designed their conversations and the iconic language and even their gestures, we tried to leave them open to interpretation so that the players can come in and have fairly creative interpretations of what they're seeing on the screen. And then later we were watching people play the game in early playtest sessions and some of the narratives they were creating were so entertaining and funny that that's what gave us the idea to put in the scrapbook feature. With that, they can actually record their particular narrative of what is going on and then share it.

Did you think *The Sims* was going to be such a big success?

I always thought *The Sims* seemed to have much more potential than *SimCity* ever did. I was never that confident about *SimCity*. And I'm not sure why I was that confident about *The Sims*, but just because it hit so close to home with human nature, I always suspected that people would like playing with people, as close as they could possibly get. And most games don't let you get that close to people, or if they do it's in a very scripted, linear format. It's not in an open-ended format.

Usually it's more in a *Zelda* sort of way, where you can talk to this character but they always say the same thing.

Exactly, and instantly the model breaks in your head and you say, "Oh, it's just a robot and it's repeating the same thing over and over." And if we could keep it open-ended, and we didn't try to get too close to the people and left the interpretation in there, people could reasonably believe that these were little creatures with desires and relationships and all these things.

Among all the praise, I've seen a lot of little complaints about the game. Like there aren't any weekends, or you can never play with your sims outside of the home environment. Do you often hear such complaints about your games?

That happens a lot. It's happened probably more with *The Sims* than any other title I've worked on, probably because more people consider themselves an expert on the subject than they do on ants or planet thermodynamics. It's hard to look at *SimEarth* and say, "Well, I really don't think ocean currents have that much of a thermal transfer rate with the atmosphere." But anybody can look at *The Sims* and say, "Well, I don't think we would slap her for that." We're more experts in that field, so that's kind of natural. The other thing though, is that, judging by the things that they feel that they're missing, people don't realize how much of it is actually clicking and working. Because there were so many hundreds of things that had to work before they were complaining about weekends. For weekends to be the big concern, that implies that a lot of the other stuff that we were sweating over is actually working.

Was deciding what to include and what to leave out a function of how much time you had to complete the game?

That was certainly a big part of it, although whenever we hit one of those situations we tried to leave the game open-ended so that we could expand it in that direction with a download. We haven't fully demonstrated how much we can expand the game with downloaded objects. Also, it's easy for people to say that they want weekends, but they're not thinking through all of the ramifications of it, which we did. And most people, when I sit and explain why we don't have weekends, all of a sudden they realize why not and say, "Oh, you're right, I guess I don't want weekends."

So how did you decide what limits to put on the simulation?

That very much was a resource issue. We could have put in the nightclub and the work and all that and added another year to the game's development. At which point it would have been past its best time. Another thing is, we could have done all that on a similar schedule, but done everything a lot worse. I figured I would much rather do the house really well than do everything poorly. Which I think is what would have happened, realistically, knowing how projects go.

So your advice to game designers is to focus their designs?

You also really have to understand what the core of the fun is going to be in the game. And if you're adding this stuff just so you can put more bullet points on the back of the box, but it's not actually making the game more fun, it's totally wasted effort. There's an old Japanese saying that I love, and it's about gardening: "Your garden is not complete until there's nothing else you can remove."

So you think that adage applies to game design?

Oh, very much. If you look at the amount of stuff we took out of this game, it would probably surprise you. Like the needs, for instance. You know, we have the eight needs. At some point it was twelve, and then it was ten, and then it was eventually eight. We were actually much more concerned with simplifying the game than we were with expanding it. And our interface. Our interface went through eleven iterations — total, complete redesigns of the interface. And each one ended up dropping a button here, a button there, or we found ways to combine functionality. I really thought that *The Sims*, if it was accessible, would appeal to a very wide audience, but it had to be incredibly accessible, through the interface. It couldn't be your standard strategy game interface, or we would turn off most of our customer base. So we went way out of our way to do that interface. Most people don't even realize how elegant parts of it are. I mean, parts of it are still fairly clumsy, but there are some things that we really sweated over, that are minor, minor details, but ended up making a huge difference. A lot of it is minor things that add up, like the pie menus. You can either click, drag, and release an object, or you can click, release, move over, and click again. So we're basically mirroring the Windows functionality that most people are used to.

Having the 3D head come up and respond, look in the direction you move the mouse. The fact that every single bit of text in the interface has embedded help. A lot of people don't realize this, but you can roll over any word down in that interface, and it will actually highlight as you roll over it, and if you click it comes up with a pretty elaborate explanation of what it is. So we did a lot of embedded help. And things like that just add up. There's no one thing that really makes it work. We probably ran a hundred playtesters through this thing in the last year of development. And these were things where one of the other designers or I would sit down and watch them play it for an hour and write notes about all the mistakes they made and misconceptions they had. So we did a lot of playtesting on the interface. If it turns out that five people made the same conceptual mistake that you rotate by doing this, or they were trying to drag an object by doing that, then we would try to figure out a way to solve that without breaking it for all the other people.

You've always had the iconic interface for your games, but yet each interface is quite a bit different than the one before it. Why is that?

The Sims

It's really hard to just do an interface out of context. You really have to take a look at what the game needs, and how you're going to interact with things in the game. That's going to determine a lot of your interface. You also have to take a look at the environment you're living in, which is to say, what are the other applications and the other games doing? There were things that we did in *The Sims* to maintain consistency with *SimCity 3000*. Like the right button scrolling, where you right-click and drag, and the edge scrolling — we tried to mirror *SimCity* there. And in general you just learn. I think that each interface I've worked on for a game has been better than the last one. Also, as games reach a wider and wider audience of more casual people, that puts even more requirements on that interface. It just has to be that much easier if you're going to capture these people. It used to be hard-core computer people playing these games, and they would put up with anything. Now it's people who are much more casual, and if they find the interface frustrating in two minutes, they're going to put the game down.

In general, I'd say the PC designers, myself included, are still catching up to the console developers. This is something the console people learned a long time ago on the Nintendo and Sega because they were dealing with a casual, wide audience, younger kids for the most part. So they've had much more accessible, simple, and understandable interfaces long before we have on the computer side.

For *The Sims* you have a hybrid world with 3D characters walking around in an isometric world. Was that for the same reasons as in *SimCity 3000*?

Yeah, since the editing and building of the house and all that, if we had a full 3D camera and all that I don't think there's any way we would have made it as easy as it is now. Also we would have had some real graphic load issues. We could not have gotten the detail we had on the objects if they were geometry.

Was there ever pressure to make the game 3D since so many other games were 3D?

About three years ago it seemed like everything was going to 3D, and if you weren't 3D you were just dead. At some point that kind of hysteria passed and people started looking at the top-selling games and realizing, hey, you still had *Age of Empires*, *SimCity*, and all these very good selling games that were not 3D. In fact, if you look at the top-selling games, a minority of them are 3D. So now the idea that consumers would accept a non-3D game is a given. There isn't this idea that it has to be 3D whether it makes sense or not.

I very much enjoyed the way the characters talk in *The Sims*. Was that a disk-space limitation, or did you go with the gibberish speak in order to leave it open to interpretation to the player?

Even if we had had five CDs worth of recorded voice, that stuff would have gotten really repetitive. And my biggest concern was that it didn't get repetitive and that you didn't hear the same string over and over and over. In fact, we recorded hundreds and hundreds of voice strings, each one with different emotional nuances. And we decided that the voice was entirely for the emotional content: you could tell if the person was flirtatious, upset, laid back, or tired by the tone of the voice and the cadence. But the way it works out is, because you don't get the semantics, because you're not hearing the words, you naturally sit there and imagine the words fairly fluidly. But the emotional context you get very easily. You know: "Wow, she sounds pissed."

So, yeah, I'm actually really happy with the way that worked out. You hear them talking over and over and over, but it's very hard to hear the exact repeats. Because in fact you are hearing a lot of the waveforms repeat eventually. But we actually designed that language so it was very hard to detect. And that was a long slow process, figuring out how to do that. Originally, we were planning to use a real language, but a really obscure one that people didn't understand. And we did a lot of tests with Navajo and Estonian. And they were still too recognizable. Even though you wouldn't understand the language, you would still recognize that, "Oh, that was the thing I just heard." A lot of it had to do with the number of hard consonants in an utterance, and also the cadence and rate at which it was going. It was a long process to get that figured out.

It seems remarkably progressive for a game to include the homosexual possibilities that *The Sims* does. Why did you choose to allow that?

One of the things we knew that a lot of people were going to do with this game was model their real family. And the last thing I wanted to go in and do was say, "Oh, we're not going to recognize your family." So we wanted to give people a reasonably, fairly open-ended way to construct whatever family they came from or could imagine or wanted to play with. But we were dealing with an ethical and moral

The Sims

minefield that we had to thread very carefully. And there were a lot of things that we left out of the game on purpose. And there were a lot of things that we really wanted to have in the game at various levels, and homosexuality was one of the things that we really wanted to have in the game, in some way.

What sort of things did you leave out on purpose?

There were a couple of things that became somewhat issues and we did slight modifications. One of them was the domestic violence issue. When the characters get upset, they can slap each other. I don't know if you've noticed, but there are two types of slap. There's one slap where they rear their arm back and then *whack* and it's as if they're breaking their jaw. And there's another one that's kind of an insulting British Army slap. Whenever you have people of the same gender slapping, they use the really hard slap, like a man slapping another man or a woman slapping another woman. But whenever you have a man slapping a woman or a woman slapping a man, they use the polite slap. Because before, when we had the strong-arm slap, and you had a husband slapping his wife, it rubbed a lot of people the wrong way, just from the domestic violence point of view. And that was one of those things where we were right on the edge and being very careful, but not losing the feature.

So it retains the emotional content without being too violent.

Right, and it doesn't make people think about serious domestic abuse. And, in fact, it was funny, because we also have an attack interaction. If they really don't like each other they can actually get in a fistfight. But because we did the fistfight like a cartoon fistfight — there's this big cloud and you see arms and legs poking out — no one had any problem with that. Even if it was a man and woman, it was always so cartoonish that it was never an issue compared to the slap. There were certain places that we just didn't want to go with the game at all. For example, pedophilia. And in general they don't kill each other. The sims will not directly kill each other, though objects can kill them and various disasters can kill them. So, yeah, there were certain things we decided we would leave out, certain things we wanted to get in, and others that we had to be very careful how we treated.

With the inclusion of homosexuality, were there ever any concerns that senators who up until then had been concerned with violence would now be outraged by *The Sims*?

Actually, there was and it's very surprising to me that it hasn't materialized in the least. Not at all. There has just been no reaction to that, and it just really surprised me. I thought primarily if it came it would come from the Christian conservatives or some other group like that. Maybe they just don't play these games, maybe they could care less, I don't know. Yeah, but we've had absolutely no problems with that at all. We've had a couple of people on the bulletin boards, probably fourteen-year-old kids complaining, but you can tell their age by their spelling.

It seems like there were a lot of moral decisions you made in designing the game. For instance, the gameplay seems to be geared toward improving your

career so you can get more stuff. It seems pretty materialistic.

Yeah, that was actually the intent. That's what most people interpret when they see the game, and even when they play it for a while they think it's very materialistic. It's only the people that play it a long time that start realizing the downside. Just about every object has some built-in failure state or maintenance requirement. If you keep buying stuff, it will eventually go bad or die or need to be cleaned or whatever. So in some sense it's like you're filling up your house with all these potential timebombs. And so at some point you end up spending so much time fixing these things and doing this, that, and the other, that these objects you originally bought to save you time end up sucking up all your time. And this is pretty long into the gameplay that you start realizing this. But it was very definitely engineered that way. So in some sense it's the people who first start playing the game who say, "God, I can't believe how materialistic this game is." But then it's the hard-core players that say, "God, I'm not going to buy that much crap next time I play."

I guess it's open-ended enough that players can try to concentrate on the social aspects instead of object acquisition.

In some sense the social side has the same dynamic, where you make these friends, but the friendships decay over time. And your friends, once they decay to a certain point, will actually call you up and say, "Hey, you better invite me over, I haven't seen you in a while." So once you make about twenty friends, you'll start noticing that every day they're clamoring to come over, and that they're sucking up your time in a different way.

What can you tell me about the scripting language Edith?

Well, that was the thing that Jamie and I were working on for the longest time. It's a programming scripting language, it's visual, and we actually developed our own editor and debugger, all integrated with the game. So, in fact, you run this from within the game and you can program and debug and step through objects while you're playing.

So you can use it to add new objects to the world?

In fact, almost all the behavior in the game is in these objects, including the social interactions of the people, and it's all programmed in this language. The primitives of this language all sit atop C level code routines. The C level code routines are things like routing primitives, variable peeks and pokes, and things like that. But the language itself is very clean, and there are about thirty or forty primitives that it's all built out of. The main thing, though, is that it's all machine-independent tokenized code that travels with the object. Which means that you can drop a new object into the game and instantly the people know when to use it, when it's appropriate to use it, and how to use it. And the animations, sound effects, code, and everything is all contained within the object that you download.

So you created the language to make it easy to add new objects.

Yeah, that was the original specification of the language. We wanted to have a language we could write all the behavior in that was totally expandable, at the object level. That way the behavior of the people within the house is totally a function of the stuff in their house and we could always add new things, even Trojan Horse things, into the house.

Such as the guinea pig object.

Yeah, the guinea pig object is an example. Actually, in the design we were thinking that they should get sick, and we had planned to do sickness, but we just ran out of time. But then we realized, "Hey, we could just make that a download." Of course, nobody's going to download sickness, so we hid it in the guinea pig. It's funny, because some of the early reviews of the game said, "It's got all this stuff, but it doesn't have sickness. I don't know why." Of course, those are probably the same people that complained when we gave it to them. The reason we're releasing this language is that eventually I want the users to start making these things.

And you made it simple enough so that you wouldn't have to be a hard-core programmer to use it?

You'd have to know how to program, but you wouldn't have to be a hard-core programmer at all. I mean, this is a much simpler language than Visual Basic.

Doesn't it bother you that, with a tool like that, the game is never completely "done"?

Yeah, I think, again, if you go back to the hobby model, hobbies are never done. They're just a continually growing thing. And they grow pretty much as a function of the amount of people involved in it and how committed they are. And the more powerful tools they have, the stronger the hobby itself becomes, and it infects more people.

I also read a quote from you where you said: "The real long-term attraction of _The Sims_ is as a storytelling platform." Now, when most game developers talk about stories in games, they're talking about them in that _Zelda_ sense. To those people, something like _The Sims_ doesn't have any story at all.

There's a big distinction between _Zelda_ and _The Sims_. You're creating the story in _The Sims_; in _Zelda_ you're uncovering the story. In some sense, the stories are just one aspect of player involvement. There are actually all these different levels. Some casual people will just play the game a few hours and have a good time and put it down. Other people will play it longer, and get into designing really cool

The Sims

houses, and maybe even uploading them on the web site for people to see. Other people that get into the game even deeper will not only build interesting families and cool houses, but will use that to tell a story and upload it to share it with other people. And the even more hard-core people will start editing custom skins or wallpapers for the game and start sharing them. And then pretty soon they'll be able to create their own objects, custom objects, and put them on the web to share. So there are these different levels of player involvement. And each level higher is a much smaller number of people. But in some sense they're feeding the people beneath them. We have something like ten thousand homes on our web site that people have uploaded, but those ten thousand homes have been viewed over one hundred thousand times.

So it's like a pyramid scheme.

Exactly. There are like thirty people out there making really good skins for the game. But there are probably thirty thousand that are downloading them and using them. So, for your really hard-core, talented fans, if you give them the tools and the ability to create content for the other ninety-nine percent, they will. And it will just benefit both sides. It gives them an audience to build these things for, and gives the audience cool stuff for the game that might eventually draw them in deeper. It'll increase the likelihood that these casual people eventually become those hard-core people.

So someday everyone on the planet has to be playing *The Sims*.

Right, so this is kind of like the zombie scheme, where the zombies go around, and then they start eating brains and turning the other people into zombies...At some point when it's five zombies against the world it doesn't look too good, but once you get a critical mass of zombies and they start converting other people into zombies fast enough...

On *The Sims* **you are listed as just a game designer, while in the past you had served as both a programmer and a designer. Did you do any programming on the project?**

I did quite a bit of programming in the Edith code. I didn't touch the C code in *The Sims*. It's probably the first project that I didn't do any of the C coding in. I did a lot of programming of the social interactions and stuff in Edith, but for the most part, even then, it was more a question of me going in and tweaking and tuning the algorithms the way I wanted. We had a really good team on *The Sims*, a really great team of engineers. So I didn't feel any need at all to go into the code.

It's not something you miss?

Oh, I kind of missed it. I enjoyed going into Edith and hacking stuff. But there was just so much to be done on the design side that I didn't have the time to waste programming. Not to say that programming is a waste of time, but I was never a great programmer. I was always persistent, and I could always make cool stuff out of computer code just because I was persistent. I mean, I know great programmers, and I'm not one.

So you didn't have any trouble communicating your vision for the design to the engineering team?

There were problems, but not for any lack of foresight or intelligence. Just because it was a complex thing. In fact, I didn't know what we were building for a long time myself; a lot of it was experimental. But yeah, in terms of the programming staff, I could always sit down and explain the dynamics I was looking for and be very confident of getting them.

You also made the transition from doing everything yourself on *SimCity* to working on a large team for *The Sims*. How big was the team?

It depends on what you count as the team. You know, there were probably sixty people who worked on it at some point, but what I would consider the team grew to about thirty.

So that's a pretty big shift from working in a small group. And the management required for that big team is quite significant.

It is, and it has a huge amount to do with the quality of the people involved. And Electronic Arts also, they came in with a totally different orientation. Before they came in, I had about four or five people working on *The Sims*. And it was actually a very good little group and it was working out great, but I just couldn't get any more resources. When Electronic Arts came in, they came in and said, "What do you need?" And that was the point at which we just started really building the team up. But Electronic Arts also has a very strong concept of production and what producers do. They have like ten levels of producers, and they put a very heavy load on the producers. So it's one of those things where if you get the right people in those slots, this stuff works pretty well; you can actually manage a pretty large team efficiently. If you get the wrong people in those slots, it's a total disaster, absolutely unmitigated disaster. At that point hiring practices become important, and how do you interview and make sure you get the right people, and how do you quickly find out if you don't have the right person. So it's a model that works with the right components and the right people, but if you get the wrong people, you've blown it.

We basically got the right people. At the same time, in our situation at Maxis, Electronic Arts brought in this one guy to run the studio, to replace most of our old management. His name was Luc Barthelet. And Luc and I hit it off from day one. We get along great. Luc is not your typical manager in any possible sense. I mean, he's very technically literate. So for *SimCity 3000*, they were having problems with the traffic model, and he came in and wrote the traffic code.

Really?

Yeah, the C level code. So it's unusual that you can have somebody running a studio that can also write some of the trickiest code in one of your simulations. And Luc's that kind of guy. There's really an art to management, and what Luc is great at is knowing exactly at what level you need to be concentrating on any given day. And so there was this point when it was crucial that we got this one feature in *SimCity 3000*. It was going to have a big impact on the success of the product, and that was the day he pulled out his compiler and started working on the traffic code. In most of the cases, it was, "How does the German distributor feel about this product?" and he'd be on the phone to the German distributor. You really have to pick your battles. And if you pick the right battles, you'll only have to win five percent of them. So anyway, there's this certain business savvy that certain people that Electronic Arts brought in had in abundance, that I was very impressed to learn from.

How did *The Sims Online* come about, and what were the initial design goals?

EA wanted to explore the online space. We had kind of a hit with *The Sims* and we wanted to leverage the franchise into the online space; that was how the project came about. Early design goals were to make an online game that was extremely approachable that felt very different, kinda more in line with *The Sims* world, and where primarily the players were constructing the world they were then playing in. Also, we

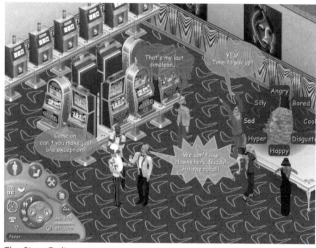

The Sims Online

wanted to put more emphasis on the social connections between the players, almost as an alternate topology that the players were playing within.

What was the process you went through adapting such a distinctly single-player game to be multi-player?

A lot of it was weird tactical issues. The first, most apparent thing when anybody played *The Sims Online* was the fact that they couldn't speed up time. We had to have one timeline for everybody, obviously. How we were going to let the players customize the environment was kind of an ongoing discussion. We had all wanted to have players be able to bring in custom content. It turned out to be extraordinarily hard to achieve for a number of reasons.

Why was that?

It had to do with bandwidth issues and validating the content, making sure it was robust enough that it didn't crash somebody's application. For us it was the first big online game we'd ever built. And in fact, if you looked underneath the hood of this thing it's ten fairly elaborate pieces of software running on different platforms that all have to be synchronized for the thing to work. It proved to be a very, very high friction environment for design. On the other hand, we had a lot of assets for *The Sims* expansion packs that we were getting pretty much at half-price, because they were being developed anyway, the art assets and everything. We reprogrammed most of them, to some degree. But still we had this large content pool that was a big leg up, that we weren't developing just for the online game.

Within *The Sims Online* we were trying to have different metagames the players could pursue based around different lot categories. So we were trying to make different viable economic paths, for someone building a romance household or an entertainment house or a skill house or a work house. Then we were also looking at different nested social groups that we wanted to have in the game. First there's you, and then you might have a close group of friends that you connect with through the friendship web, then you might have some longer term playmates that you bring into a household and become roommates and that's a larger social group, and then above that we had the neighborhood where different households could form associations together. To this day they're still kind of working on the next level, which would be levels above the neighborhood, the clubs, eventually evolving into a form of governance.

How did you design the game such that those social webs would work well and not just be a big mess of people?

Well, the design changed a fair amount, but initially we wanted to have a pretty tight linkage between who was in your social web and who you actually spent time playing with. We wanted people to formally acknowledge who their friends were, in a Friendster kind of a way, and then have that visible to other players. So I can find friends of my friend or see if we had somebody in common that we both knew. And so that became a major component of the game, people declaring friendships or enemies and then having this structure appear, the friendship web that you could peruse, basically a social network graph. In that we rolled in certain reward structures so that if you had beyond a certain number of friends, you would start earning more social interactions for your avatar. For a lot of people that became the primary game. Other people, there was a whole other game based around the graphical topology, or the houses that people were building. And that was more of an economic game, where players would earn money, then spend it on their house to build a cool place that they would hopefully attract other people to. And so it became kind of this game of who can build the coolest house that everybody wants to spend their time at. Kind of a capitalist, economic model. So players were competing to entertain the other players. And that was the basic dynamic we were going for; we wanted to reward players for entertaining each other rather than killing each other.

You mentioned before how you are unable to adjust time in *The Sims Online*. That's a fairly critical feature in the original version of *The Sims*.

Yeah, when you're going from the offline *Sims* to the online *Sims* the first thing you notice is you keep trying to speed up time and there's no button for it. Because you spend so much time in the offline *Sims* with time zipping by, getting to the interesting parts.

Was that a problem you tried to solve?

There were things we did, but we couldn't get around the central fact that everybody was on the same timeline. For instance, whenever you tell a sim to go somewhere in *The Sims Online*, they pretty much run everywhere to minimize the routing time. We experimented a lot with transportation time and cost between lots, and we ended up doing that in a slight way, but for the most part we found that just wasn't fun

The Sims Online

— having a lot that's further away takes longer to get to. So there wasn't a lot of topology to the world in that sense. Although we started adding a little bit of topology to it, in terms of your motives will be drained as you were moving between lots, and the further you went the more your motives were drained, so the more you'd have to recharge at that lot. So we wanted to have some feeling of locality. But aside from that, a lot of your interactions got sped up, so that when you sleep in *The Sims Online* it happens about five or six times faster than *The Sims* offline. So those interactions that you were basically just using to fill your motives, your bars, where it wasn't an interesting activity but more of just a maintenance thing, we sped those up relative to the offline *Sims*. So we did a lot of adjustments to try and alleviate the time issue.

In the end did you feel it sufficiently solved the problem?

For the most part, yes. Once we adjusted that stuff, at that point it didn't feel like a big deal. The trick was, don't put the player in a situation where they're sitting there waiting for something to complete and they don't have anything to do. We have other things that do take longer to happen, but you're actually making decisions or there's a mini-game involved.

Did you spend a lot of time trying to make the game like the offline *Sims*? Or did you just view *The Sims Online* as a separate game?

It was pretty apparent to us really early on that it was a totally different game. It looked a lot like *The Sims*. That was the weird part is people look at it and say, "Oh, that's *The Sims*." And then they play it and realize it's an entirely different game. First of all you're controlling just one person, you don't have that God-like control, there's no cheating allowed, you can't speed up time, the other people are real people doing God knows what. The original concept was that we were going to build something that would not be as elaborate and would be a peer-to-peer experience. And due to some business decisions it was decided we should be building an online persistent world with a monthly subscription. So about six or eight months into the project we dropped everything and went in a totally different direction to support that. Originally we were basically designing a game that did not have a secure economy, that was based more around the idea of custom content flowing around, and was probably even closer to an IM [Instant Messenger] graphical chat room.

I've heard the game called the world's most expensive chat room.

Actually that was one of our design goals, even with the persistent one. We were aiming really for a very casual crowd of people that were totally different than played online games. And so at the very basic level, we decided that if nothing else it had to be the ultimate graphic chat room. We were actually looking at two targets. We were looking at the AOL customers and *The Sims* players. At the time when we started this project there was this pretty tight relationship between AOL and EA, which isn't such a big deal now, but at the time it was considered a pretty major aspect of the project. In hindsight looking at it, I think that the game needed to be a lot more exciting and have more obvious goal structures in it. I think also that the online subscription cost really killed us because if you look at our player base and how many of them don't even have credit cards. They're not hard-core players at all.

These are the players of *The Sims* offline?

Yes, right. Even the AOL customers, a lot of them.

Don't AOL customers need to have credit cards to subscribe?

Well their parents do, that's the thing. A lot of the people who are actually spending time on AOL are actually twelve- and thirteen-year-old kids. Their parents get AOL for them. I, as a hard-core gamer, am really reluctant to pay ten dollars a month to subscribe to a game like that. To get a casual player like that who has bought maybe one or two games in their life to do that... In talking to people it turned out to be a just huge barrier to entry to playing the game.

Would you do the game significantly different if you were designing it now?

Yeah, I would change the game design significantly and I would look for an entirely different business model. Until we could find a different business model I don't think I'd even bother trying it.

Did you make a lot of adjustments to the game after it went live?

Yeah, we were doing it quite a bit. A fair amount of it was just tuning level things; retuning objects that were in the world, reward structures, and so forth. Other parts were actually reengineering the reward structure or the activities. We spent a lot of time on the boards, before and after release, where we would post our early designs on the boards and get feedback from the players, way before the feature was actually implemented. And we would make modifications to the feature based on that early feedback. We had three areas of the boards. One that was just blue sky ideas that we were thinking of. Next we had one for things that were in design and we were actually posting our design documents for players to read. And then the last one was "This is about to be deployed." So we had three levels of designs that were flowing through where the players had pretty high visibility and knew what was coming. And they felt like they had pretty good interaction with the design team. On the other hand, if you look at the interaction, about half or more of the features we describe on the board, invariably half

The Sims Online

the players would say, "Oh, we love it," and the other half of the players would say, "Oh, we hate it." It's not like it was always really clear feedback as to what was good or bad. Because we had players in the game doing totally different things with totally different motivational structures. So, you just can't please everybody all the time.

So how did you decide what to add?

Some of the things we pretty much felt like they were fundamental things that we had to push through design, even if the players were half and half for and against. At that point we just had to go with our own gut feeling, our own design sense. I think part of it is it's good just in general to give players the ability to have feedback. If they know that you're listening to them, that's half the battle right there. The players are seeing that it's an even split, so if you fall on one side or the other they're not going to really blame you. But if ninety percent of the players say that sucks and you go ahead and do it, that's when they'll nail you.

How did playtesting proceed on *The Sims Online*?

It was a little tricky because our really early tests were just in-house tests with thirty or forty people playing, and we didn't have nearly the critical mass we needed to validate a lot of the features. So it wasn't until we actually got into beta testing that we got a real sense of the way players were going to behave. We also had different types of players flowing through the game at different points in time. In the beta test we had a very different kind of player than we had five months after launch. And they valued the features entirely differently.

How so?

The early people were more socializers, the later people were more goal seekers, in general. Also, the players got more casual over time, basically, just in terms of how game savvy they were. I think it felt like it got younger over time. We were collecting a lot of metrics on the players that we would study every day. And we would study the trends on these metrics, in terms of which objects they're buying, what they're doing, what social interactions they're choosing, how many friends do they have, and all these things, looking for patterns. It was amazing how sometimes just one little thing that was unbalanced would radically change the play pattern of everybody. And these were mostly economic balance issues, some of them involving exploits. Somebody would find an exploit based around one of the job objects in the game, and all of a sudden the next week everybody would be using that job object and nobody would be using any of the other ones. We actually probably found a lot of our exploits and bugs quicker through the metrics than we did through players reporting it or testers finding it.

So did the change in your audience over time make the game hard to balance?

It felt like we were always trying to balance against a moving target. Sometimes we'd try to lead the target, but I'd say it was always a fairly chaotic process. We could usually look at the metrics and say, OK, that's out of balance, and then we'd have two or three different possibilities for bringing it into balance. And as we started balancing that thing out, all of a sudden something else would kind of go wacky, and we'd look at that. And of course it's all interrelated too. There were some social trends too that were longer-term things, fads that happened in the world, that nobody foresaw at all and that started affecting things.

What would be an example of that?

There's a map in the game where you can see thumbnails of the houses as you scroll across this map. The thumbnails are about 50 pixels across or so. At some point, somebody decided to decorate their roof, and they did it in a way where they used different colors on the roof tiles, and when you made the thumbnail of it, it ended up as this nice little picture. Somebody did Madonna or Michael Jackson or something. So somebody did that one day, and then everybody said that's cool, and then within two weeks there were ten of these in the world, and two weeks later every other roof was decorated with some image. It was just one of those things that nobody had really foreseen, and it took one player to figure this out. Somebody wrote a program that would actually scan an image and then automatically configure a roof in the game. But things like that were happening all the time.

Did you like to see those sort of emergent behaviors?

Oh yeah, that was really what we wanted to encourage as much as possible. Especially ones like that, that weren't affecting other people. There are other ones that were more problematic, like there was this whole mafia organization that started in the game, which became a big deal. It became probably the largest point of conflict in the entire game. It was pretty organized; they actually had capos and this whole hierarchy reporting structure, and there were hundreds of players involved in it. And they saw themselves as the guardians of the game. They actually would go out and grief players that they thought weren't playing it right or that were trying to ruin the game. So they were basically vigilantes. But then other people thought they were just picking on people for no apparent reason. And so there was this other group pissed off by the mafia that was opposing them. That became this big power struggle in the game. We had these friendship webs, and as one of the things on this friendship web we were rating who the most popular person was in the game by how many incoming friends they had. And there was one woman who very rapidly went to the top of that list and she was the one that actually founded the mafia. Because she had this incredible social network already in place, and she leveraged that to become the head of the mafia. She became very notorious. Some people loved her and thought she was helping the world; other people thought she was the worst griefer in the whole game.

Was that something you felt you needed to put a stop to?

We had certain specific terms of service, so if somebody violated this terms of service and somebody else reported it, then we had an obligation to go in and deal with it. These mafia people were very, very good about just skirting the edge of that, and so they almost never did anything that was over the boundaries of the terms of service. In other words, you're allowed to go in and make somebody an enemy. That's just part of the game design. Basically, you get the rewards for having lots of friends, and you lose those rewards if you have more enemies. So, one of their tactics was they would decide that there was a person that was doing something bad or had slighted them or had scammed a newbie or whatever they didn't like. Then they would put out the word through the mafia network, and then fifty of them would descend on that person and all declare him an enemy, which would remove all of the social things that he had earned. That was the way that they were griefing. So it was actually within the game rules.

But we were following this quite a bit, and it was really interesting the social turmoil that this caused in the game. In some sense it was good; I think the game really needed more of that. Because what it caused people to do was polarize, and get together and talk about this, and what are they going to do. Basically having a common enemy on either side caused people to bond together more strongly. A few weeks after this had happened, something interesting happened. It wasn't really clear if somebody was in the mafia or not — you couldn't really look at somebody and tell, and frequently they wouldn't let you know. And this wave of McCarthyism swept the world, with people accusing somebody of being in the mafia: "No I'm not!" "Yes he is!" Things would be whispered about various people. It was just kind of interesting how all these human social behaviors manifested in this little microcosm.

I guess that's one way to know when you've succeeded, when you've created a system that allows those sorts of behaviors to happen.

At least you've enabled a certain amount of human nature to flow into it.

Previously you mentioned using metrics to assess the state of the game before making adjustments. Did you find you could trust metrics more than the feedback from players?

I think they were both valuable. The metrics would give you no insight into intention or motivation. They just say that more people are doing this today than tomorrow, and you have no idea why. Then we would actually go and talk to people or look at message boards and try to uncover the actual motivations behind the behaviors. Also, a lot of

The Sims Online

people would say they hated an idea, but then you put it in the game and all of a sudden… Games are so emergent sometimes that even if you tell the players what you're about to do, they can't really imagine the actual result of it in the game. So, sometimes you have to discount what the players are telling you, if it happens to be something that feels like it's going to be a very non-linear, non-intuitive kind of dynamic. But you still know that you have a PR issue, that you have to sell the players on the value of the feature.

Are you working on *The Sims 2* currently?

Not really, no. I'm working on something else right now.

It's curious to me how you could make a sequel to a game as good as *The Sims* without just making the game more complicated but not necessarily better.

Yeah, that's kind of a sticky point. Any player will look at a game and say, "Oh, that would be so much cooler if they added this, that, and the other." And, really, you get to a great game not by adding a bunch of stuff but by figuring out what to take out. And that's the really hard part. On the other hand, the technology has progressed, probably the players are a little more advanced. You obviously want to do something different with it. It is a struggle with a high-profile sequel like that because with the first *Sims* we were this little game and the fact that we succeeded was all upside. With something like *The Sims 2*, it kinda feels like all they can do is fail. There's all these expectations heaped upon the project. But I think you have to figure out what the core of the original game was that people enjoyed and which parts of the original game were irrelevant or tangential to the success. And those are the areas that you have opportunities to go in and expand, modify, rethink. And of course technology has progressed, but there are a lot of considerations that go into it.

Are you glad to be working on something other than *The Sims*?

The very first prototype I made of *The Sims* was in '93, so it's been over ten years. Actually I worked on *SimCity* about ten years, from the very first version of *SimCity* to the last one I worked on, which was *SimCity 2000*, and ten years is about my limit on anything. [laughter] And so since *The Sims Online,* I've kind of gone on, and I'm in a totally different space right now, which is really fun. What I enjoy is finding other maxima in the game design space, and occasionally I'll find a nice maxima like *SimCity* or *The Sims*. And then of course the company wants to keep exploring that maxima, doing a lot of things, basically build a franchise. But at some point I just have to walk away and go look for another maxima.

Were there guiding principles that people had to follow when designing and developing the Sim family of games?

Well, we basically always saw them as being for the most part non-violent, although we have broken that rule on occasion. But for the most part we've considered that one of our distinguishing features. A lot of our employees who work for us really want to work for Maxis because Maxis is known for their non-violent games. I don't want to sound like I'm making some moralistic statement, because I love *Doom* and *Quake* and those things myself. Some of my favorite games are wargames. I play wargames heavily. I just think that there are so many people making those games that we don't need to, and they're doing a good job of it too. So I'd rather be making games that nobody's making. But from the public's point of view, we do have this reputation for tending toward the more non-violent, more educational, more socially relevant games.

Do you ever feel constrained by making Maxis-style simulation games? Do you ever want to make *Raid Over Bungeling Bay II*?

In some sense *SimCopter* was almost *Raid Over Bungeling Bay II*. There were a lot of Easter eggs hidden in *SimCopter*. In fact, you could get an Apache and lay waste to the city. In fact, if you had the Apache and you came across a nuclear power plant, you could blow up the entire city. Even in *The Sims*, a couple of times, I tried to get away from the political correctness here and there. So there are a lot of things we

SimCopter

did in *The Sims* that aren't terribly politically correct, that didn't even make sense, you know, more of the wacky side. We didn't try to let the Maxis thing constrain us, but the domestic violence thing was probably a good example. You'll see a lot of games where there's a much higher level of violence, much higher than a man slapping a woman. But we were sensitive to how people would be interpreting this, knowing that families would be playing it.

Your games always seem to have this strong educational component. I was wondering, how do you balance that with making the game entertaining?

I was never concerned with education until the game was fun. Any educational value a program might have is totally wasted if people won't play it. Probably the one game which I learned that the most from was *SimEarth*. *SimEarth* was potentially the most educational game I ever made, but yet it wasn't fun. A surprising number of people bought it; I'm still surprised by the sales figures. I think most of them played it for two hours and then put it away. So I really think the fun has to come first. And the educational side, it's not something that you tack on, it's got to be fundamental to the design. In *The Sims*, it was all about learning to extrapolate design from behavior. That's a fairly deep lesson, it's not just a fact that I'm going to teach you. It's more like a way of looking at things. If the entire design is true to that, it might be educational at some deep level even though you might play the game for hours and not think of it as educational even once. One of the main things that *SimCity* teaches — it's not explicit but it's there — is the shape of chaos. The fact that the best-laid plans can always go wrong, and that the system is more complex than you think it is. Building a road to solve traffic doesn't always solve traffic; it frequently breeds traffic. Those types of lessons are hard to explain in other media. But when you've experienced them through a process like *SimCity*, you really get the lesson much deeper. It's experience rather than exposition.

Do you ever have to compromise realism to make the game fun?

Oh, all the time. There's also a frequent thing that we did in our games where we would decide to match expectation and not reality. In fact, nuclear power plants don't blow up. They just don't. But when everybody saw it, they said, "Oh, a nuclear power plant, can I make it blow up?" It's just what they thought of. So there are a lot of things we do just because people expect them to happen that way for fun, even though it's not realistic.

With the open-ended nature of your games, do you have to spend a lot of time in playtesting them?

We do, but it's invaluable time. You spend that time, or else you go spend months building the wrong thing and solving the wrong problems. We just had what we call "kleenex" testing on one little component of *The Sims* multi-player that we're working on. We have this one data display that's convoluted and twisted. And the programmer just got it implemented a few days ago, so we scheduled five people to come in today. We call them kleenex playtesters because we use them once and then they never come back, just because we want people who have never seen it before, with totally no preconceptions about it. We don't even tell them what it is, we just say, "Look at that, play with it," and have them describe to us what they're seeing and what that represents. We got some very consistent feedback from all five people today where we understood that three of the variables we were communicating they all understood, the other three they had no clue about. So for the last tester, we turned off the last three variables that everybody was having trouble with and it was perfect. We do this at every stage of the project now. It's not just at the end when we have the whole thing working, we do this with little components, even the art prototypes. And this was a lesson that was really driven home to me by the late Dani Berry. She's the one who did *M.U.L.E.* and all those things. She was drilling this into me years ago, that playtesting is probably the most undervalued thing that any game designer can use, and you really have to do it. And I started taking her advice and she was right. It's just invaluable.

Whether it's *SimCity* **or** *The Sims*, **you seem to have a knack for coming up with unique and very original game designs around complex topics. I'm curious about how you go about coming up with new design ideas.**

I think every designer has a totally different technique. So I think if you ask every game designer out there how they design a game you're going to get totally different answers. I guess a lot of times my own internal process is fairly opaque even to me. I'll try a lot of different ways to look at a subject and not get stuck into one viewpoint or one approach. And for me the value is in a set of diverse approaches that I execute in parallel. Each approach is one way of looking at games or entertainment or whatever; some might be very analytical approaches, other ones might be very emotional or kinesthetic approaches. And, usually, and this is the opaque part, something in my head is actually telling me, "Oh, I'm getting better traction on this approach." Or "What about this one? This is a really weird way to think about it." So a lot of times I try to imagine what's the strangest way for me to approach a subject or a challenge, just on the assumption that'll take me down a different path than most people will go down to get there. They might end up in the same spot, but if I take a totally different approach to the problem I'm likely to uncover some maxima that other people are not seeing. Every year I try to give a talk at the Game Developers Conference to talk about design and process and all of that, and I'm never quite satisfied, because I still feel like my internal process is fairly unknown to me. That's the only reason I really give talks, I don't really enjoy talking at all. I'm not really a social person, I'm a pretty introverted guy, actually. But I find that when I have to prepare talks, in fact I'm having to dig into my own experience and self-reflect on my own thought process. So I actually find it more valuable to myself than probably the people who actually hear the talks, because it forces me to become consciously aware, at least to some degree, of my internal process.

In *Understanding Comics*, **Scott McCloud talks about the two types of creative people: those who enjoy examining their process and those who don't want to for fear it will break.**

I'm not worried about breaking it, it's just that it's buried down in there pretty damn deep, and it takes a lot of digging for me to get to it.

For both *SimCity* **and** *The Sims*, **you had trouble convincing anybody that they would be popular. Do you think there are many games out there with the same problem that never see the light of day? What do you recommend someone with a wacky game idea should do?**

Oh, I'm sure they're all over the place. It's kind of depressing to think about it, how many wonderful masterpieces there are out there. For me, it's just that I am a very, very persistent guy. I think if you're really, really persistent, if you really want something, you can make it happen. It might take years. With *SimCity* it was like five years to actually get the first version out. With *The Sims* it was like seven. Aside from that, based on my track record, I don't know if I'm the one to be offering advice there. Whenever

something unusual comes out like *The Sims*, I like to think that all of a sudden people say, "Hey, that was really off-the-wall, and it sold great!" Maybe that might help to green-light some other off-the-wall projects at other companies that were having problems getting approved. But I think realistically they're more likely to say, "Oh, we want a game just like *The Sims*." Unfortunately, that's probably the lesson they're going to carry from it.

The Sims

Will Wright Gameography

Raid Over Bungeling Bay, 1984
SimCity, 1989
SimEarth, 1990
SimAnt, 1992
SimCity 2000, 1994
SimCopter, 1997
The Sims, 2000
The Sims Online, 2002

Chapter 23:
Level Design

"My policy always rises from the instinctive part of human beings. For example, did the inventor create the telescope because he wanted to make something that would enable people to see far and beyond? No, I think it was more simple. The inventor must have just had a strong desire to see far away. I start with the hypothesis that people make products because their desire and instincts make them want them. Human desires and instincts lie at the core of game design. There are now new devices coming out, but whatever new form of technology appears, we will always design by what humans instinctively desire."

— Tetsuya Mizuguchi

As computer games have grown in size and scope, the tasks that in the past were performed by one person are now performed by multiple people. This division of labor is necessary for the timely completion of the sophisticated and massive games the publishers demand and the marketplace has come to expect. One of the unique roles created through this division of labor was that of the level designer. Once the core gameplay for a game is established, it is the level designer's job to create the game-world in which that gameplay takes place, to build spaces that are fun for players to play in.

The number of level designers required for a project is directly proportional to the complexity of the levels to be used in that project. For a 3D game with extremely detailed architecture that all must be built by the level designer, it is not unreasonable to have two levels per designer, perhaps only one. Sometimes the game's primary designer also serves as a level designer, sometimes she draws up plans for the levels for the level designers to build, and sometimes she merely oversees the team of level designers working on the project. For a simpler 2D game, it is not out of the question for the game's lead designer to craft all of the game's levels. Even with a very detailed and complex 3D game, it is not out of the question for the lead designer to first build the prototype level to which all subsequent levels are compared.

Level design is where all the different components of a game come together. In some ways creating a level is like putting together a jigsaw puzzle; to build the levels, the level designer must make use of the game's engine, art, and core gameplay. Often level design is where a game's problems become most apparent. If the engine is not up to snuff, the levels will start behaving erratically in certain situations, or the frame rate will not be able to support the planned effects. If the art is made to the wrong scale or has rendering problems of any kind, these difficulties come out as the level designer starts placing the art in the world. If the title's gameplay is not able to support a wide enough variety of levels to fill out an entire game, or, even worse, if the gameplay just is not any fun, this problem will become apparent during the level design process. It is the level designer's responsibility to bring these problems to the attention of the team, and to see that the difficulties are resolved properly. Often this can result in the level designer being one of the least liked team members, since she must always be pestering people to fix problems, but if she instead tries to ignore the problems she encounters, the game will be worse as a result. The job of the level designer is one that comes with great responsibility.

With all the different aspects of the game's content to worry about, the level designer's job is certainly not an easy one. Beyond making sure all of the game's components are up to snuff, if the level designer's own work is not of the highest quality, then the game is likely to fail miserably. If the levels do not bring out the best aspects of the engine, the art, and the gameplay, it does not matter how good those component parts may be. Without good levels to pull it all together, the game will fail to live up to its potential.

Levels in Different Games

The definition of a "level" varies greatly from game to game. It most commonly refers to the game-world of side-scrollers, first-person shooters, adventures, flight simulators, and role-playing games. These games tend to have distinct areas that are referred to as "levels." These areas may be constrained by geographical area (lava world versus ice world), by the amount of content that can be kept in memory at once, or by the amount of gameplay that "feels right" before players are granted a short reprieve preceding the beginning of the next level. Though many classic arcade games such as *Centipede* or *Space Invaders* took place entirely on one level, others such as *Pac-Man* or *Joust* offered simple variations on the game-world and game challenges to prolong their gameplay. Thus, the different mazes in *Pac-Man* constitute its levels. In

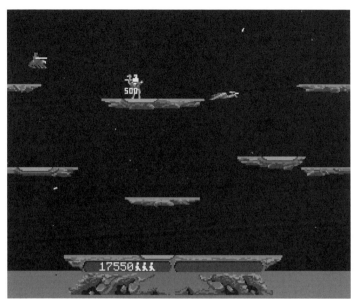

Joust made simple changes to its game-world to produce different levels.

a campaign- based strategy game such as *StarCraft,* the levels or scenarios are defined by maps accompanied by objectives players must accomplish, such as defend the Terrans against the Protoss forces in this amount of time. In a racing game, a level would be one of the tracks available in the game. In a sports game, say baseball, the levels would be the different stadiums featured in the game. Here the difference between the various levels is completely aesthetic, since in terms of play mechanics, a baseball game played in Wrigley Field is only subtly different from one played in Yankee Stadium.

Games such as *Civilization* and *SimCity* do have levels, but one key difference from the games described above is that the entirety of a player's game takes place on a single level. The base level is also often randomly generated following carefully designed rules, and from there it is largely the user's responsibility to construct the level as she plays. This is why these titles are often referred to as "builder" games. For these titles, the authorship of the level is almost entirely abdicated to the players.

This chapter deals primarily with games that use pre-built levels that have a major impact on the gameplay. Though sports titles and "builder" games may have levels, their construction is left up to the artists and players respectively, and therefore is not generally of concern to designers. For games like *Doom, Tomb Raider, Super Mario 64, Maniac Mansion, Pac-Man, StarCraft*, and *Fallout*, however, the design of the levels has everything to do with gameplay and therefore the designer must be intimately involved with their creation.

Level Separation

How a game is broken down into its component levels has a huge impact on the flow of the game. Players often play a game a level at a time. If a parent announces dinner while a child is playing a game, that child is likely to beg to be allowed to "just finish this level." In console games, frequently players can only save their game between levels,

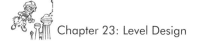

which places further importance on the end of a level as the completion of a unit of gameplay. A level can function like an act in a play, a chapter in a book, or a movement in a symphony. It gives the audience a chance to see a discrete unit within a larger work, to understand what portion of the work has been completed and how much awaits ahead. Carefully orchestrated levels are set up such that they have a series of tension and release moments to create an emotional curve for the player to experience. When players finally see that the level has ended, they know that they have accomplished a significant amount of gameplay and should feel proud of themselves.

Technical limitations often dictate where the end of a level must occur. Only so many textures, sounds, and level data can fit in memory at once, and when those resources are used up, the gameplay has to stop long enough for different world data to be loaded in. New technologies present the opportunity for more seamless environments. Even on the technically limited PlayStation, the developer Insomniac was able to avoid loading screens entirely in *Spyro the Dragon*, instead just having Spyro fly into the air for a second (while the necessary data is swapped in) and then having him fly back to earth in the new level. To casual players watching *Spyro*, the break is much less jarring than seeing a "loading" screen come up. The *Spyro the Dragon* levels still have to be divided into sections between these non-loading screens, however, meaning that the gameplay in those levels is still limited to a certain amount of space. A good designer, of course, can take the memory constraints and use them properly to create levels that are fun and challenging to play while also fitting in the space available. Again, the designer must take the limitations of the hardware and embrace them.

Half-Life is another interesting example of level division. Here the team at Valve wanted to create a more seamless experience for players, but were still using the limited *Quake* technology. *Quake* had featured thirty or so levels, each of which took a significant amount of time to load. In *Quake* the levels existed in separate universes from each other; never would a monster chase players from one level to another, never would players return to a previous level. The programmers at Valve came up with a system where, if the levels were small enough, they could be loaded in less than five seconds. They also made modifications so that monsters could track players across the boundaries between maps. The level designers at Valve were able to make their levels very small, much smaller than a standard *Quake* level, but then created a great quantity of them. The areas between two levels contain identical architecture, such that players can run across the border between two of these levels and, aside from the brief loading message, not even know they had crossed a level boundary. The result is a much more seamless experience for players. Evidently the team still felt the need for story arcs in the game, since text "chapter titles" appear briefly on the screen at key points during the game. Indeed, these titles work quite nicely as mini-rewards for the players, letting them know they have accomplished a good chunk of gameplay, much like used to be conveyed by a long level load. But since the programming and design teams were able to create a near-seamless level loading system, the design team was able to separate the game into these storytelling units wherever it felt best, instead of where the technology dictated. The ideal for an immersive game like *Half-Life*, of course, would be to eliminate these load times entirely.

Since *Half-Life* was released, some games have managed to pull off a completely continuous world, including *Jak & Daxter* and *Dungeon Siege*. These games only managed this feat after the investment of a large amount of development time, though the payoff seems to have been worth it.

Level Order

The order in which the levels occur is also important to the overall flow of the game. Perhaps big shoot-out levels should be alternated with more strategic or puzzle-oriented levels. If a game places all of its strategic levels early in the game and then crowds the end with more action-oriented episodes, the game will seem to change midway through, upsetting the balance players have come to expect. At the very least, the designer should know how the order of the levels will affect the flow of gameplay, and should be aware of how moving different levels around will affect it. For example, if a game has thirty levels and six boss monsters, one logical way to place these adversaries in the game would be at the end of the fifth, tenth, fifteenth, twentieth, twenty-fifth, and thirtieth levels. The bosses certainly do not have to be on those precise levels, and each can be shifted slightly forward or backward in the level order without causing any serious problems. If the bosses were placed one each on the last six levels of the game, this would be obviously unbalanced. It would seem strange to players that after twenty-four levels of no-boss-monster gameplay, suddenly they have to fight one every level.

The way the game is broken up into its different levels and the order in which those levels must occur differs from game to game. For a game like *Unreal*, as with the *Doom* and *Quake* series before it, the designers were only instructed to make some cool levels, with little concern for story (since none of these games really had one) or which events should happen before which other events. Some thought was put into at what point certain adversaries would first appear in the game, and hence the earlier levels were more restricted in which creatures they could use. Similarly, of course, the earlier levels had to be easier and the later ones had to be harder. But for the most part, the level designers just tried to make the coolest levels possible, almost working in a vacuum from the other designers. Certainly they would see each other's work and this might inspire them to make their own levels better, but none of the levels really had to match up thematically with the levels that came before or after it, and the lack of a story meant that this did not adversely affect the game.

In games such as *Indiana Jones and the Infernal Machine*, *Knights of the Old Republic*, or *The Suffering*, however, the story plays a much larger role. In order for the story to work, the levels need to support it. Hence, for a more story-centric game, a great deal of preplanning is done by the game's design and story teams as to which story events need to happen in which levels. In what sorts of environments should those levels take place? What types of adversaries will players fight there? The order in which the levels appear in the game cannot be changed as easily as in *Doom*, since that would radically change the story as well. In order for the entire game to flow and escalate in difficulty appropriately, the type of gameplay found in each level must be planned ahead of time. The levels do not need to be planned down to minute detail, however, as this is best left to the level designer, who can place the individual encounters, objects, or minor puzzles as they best fit the level. A mini design document explaining what the level has to accomplish in order to function within the game's story will allow the level designer to know exactly what she must include in the level; from there she can fill in the details.

In a game like *The Suffering*, the story and levels are so tightly interwoven that the levels cannot be reordered and still make any sense.

The Components of a Level

Once the levels a game needs have been decided on, possibly with some idea of how those levels must support the story, the next task is to actually create those levels. Regardless of its location in the game as a whole, the goal of every level is to provide an engaging gameplay experience for players. When working on the levels for a game, it is important to constantly keep in mind the focus of the game. What is this game trying to accomplish? How important are the different aspects of the game? What will the level need to do to support the type of gameplay this game has? In addition, depending on the amount of preproduction design done on the levels, one may need to consider how this level may play differently than others. Is it a "thinking" level after an action-intensive one? Is this level more about exploration and discovery than building up the strength of the player character or characters? In *The Suffering*, we made a conscious decision to make some areas stand out in terms of tone and gameplay, such as the asylum level. Since that level was located in the middle of the game, by the time they reached it players had become used to a steady stream of combat and were ready for something a little slower and more puzzle oriented.

Before level design begins, the design team should convene and break down the different gameplay components of the game, since each member must completely understand how the gameplay functions. For specific levels, this may mean the lead designer makes a rough 2D map of the area and then lets the level designer finish it off, or it may mean that the level designer draws up the map and runs it by the lead. Regardless, each level designer must understand how her level will use that gameplay before she starts building anything. In some games it is easy to make major changes to the layout of a level, such as in a tile-based game like *StarCraft*. If problems arise with the level, it can be easily reworked. For a game using the latest incarnation of the *Unreal* engine, however, once a level is built and the art department has polished its aesthetics, it is very labor-intensive to radically alter it. Producers will be reluctant to invest another month of architecture construction time to rework a level because it is not playing well. Therefore understanding ahead of time the gameplay of the game and the level in question is important. One perhaps simplistic but still useful way to break down the components of a level's gameplay is in terms of action, exploration, puzzle solving, storytelling, and aesthetics.

A level for the latest revision of the sophisticated *Unreal* engine requires significantly more work than one for a simpler 2D game. As a result, making changes to an *Unreal* level is significantly more time consuming. Pictured here: *Unreal Tournament 2004*.

Action

Action is the most obvious component of the levels for many games, and indeed for many titles the action element is the only justification for the level's existence. Of course there are some games that eschew the action component entirely, such as many adventure or puzzle games, but nearly all other games contain some action components, whether it consists of blasting demons in a shooter like *Doom*, incapacitating walking mushrooms in *Super Mario 64*, slaying mutants in *Fallout*, stealth-killing a guard in *Metal Gear Solid*, or speeding by the opponents' cars in *Need for Speed: Underground*.

Whatever your game's action component is, the level designer's job is to understand how much action the level contains and at what pacing this action component should be presented to players. What percentage of your level should be action filled and exciting? How many battles will players fight? Is the combat fast and furious or are there "breaks" or intermissions between major conflicts? Should the players' adrenaline be pumping during the entire level because of a constant fear of death? Of course, the amount of action is entirely dependent on what type of game you are making, but regardless, you need to have a clear idea of what amount of conflict players will encounter.

For a game with a lot of action, how that action will play out must be kept in mind while constructing the levels. The level designer must consider how the enemy AI functions and what types of maps will lead to the most interesting conflicts. What geometry will give players lots of locations in which to duck and cover while dodging enemy fire? How can the levels be best set up to encourage players to figure out her own strategy for defeating the opposition? Knowing what sort of action your game will have and how that action best plays out is critical to designing levels that bring out the best in the action gameplay.

Exploration

What will players be doing when not in the heat of battle? Exploration is a major part of many action/adventure titles such as *Tomb Raider* or *Super Mario Bros*. Instead of just providing a bridge between different action set pieces, if properly designed the exploration can actually be a lot of fun for players. It is often hard for the design team to see this after slaving away on a map for months. How much fun is exploring architecture with which you are already painfully familiar? Always try to keep in mind that for players experiencing a map for the first time, the thrill of exploring a new virtual world can be quite stimulating. It may be important to constantly be showing your level to first-time viewers or playtesters, and getting their feedback on whether they enjoy exploring the level or not.

The designer must keep in mind how players will explore the level to know how best to lay it out. What cool piece of art or architecture will players see around the next corner? How excited or awe-inspired will players be on finding new areas? Making exciting exploration a part of your game goes beyond creating exciting architecture for players. It is also determined by how the level flows, and what players will have to do to reach an exciting new area. Being dropped right into the middle of some nice architecture is much less satisfying than having to navigate a large area of the map to finally make it to an exploration payoff.

Part of making the exploration aspect of a game work is determining the flow of a level. Will players need to explore several offshoots from a main, critical path, or will they generally only have one way to proceed? Will the path players must take to complete the level be obvious at first, or will they need to experiment and look around quite a bit before they find it? Games that are very action-oriented will tend to put players on

As far back as *Super Mario Bros.* on the Nintendo Entertainment System, Miyamoto's games have included exploration as a key gameplay component.

a path that leads directly to the next conflict. Games that encourage players to poke around may make the path less obvious.

I once saw someone criticize Shigeru Miyamoto's games as being all about exploration, and therefore not very good games. The observation that exploration is the focus of the later *Mario* was a correct one. The mistake was in asserting that this is not a fun part of gameplay, as millions of *Mario* fans will refute. The challenge lies in making exploration entertaining and rewarding for players, something Miyamoto's games do expertly.

Puzzle Solving

Sometimes progressing in a level involves more than just finding a path to the next area while killing the adversaries that stand in your way. Instead it may involve figuring out what needs to be accomplished in order to open a certain door or clear a large obstacle out of the way. Some of the simplest examples of this are the "switch flipping" puzzles found in many older first-person shooters. In these games (often for no particular reason) players need to navigate through a large section of the map in order to flip a switch. This action opens a door somewhere else that leads players to another area where another switch is in need of flipping. And so it goes. This switch may instead be a key or any other object that opens a door or may be disguised as some type of device that blocks the players' progress. For example, *Call of Duty* disguised switch flipping as placing explosives on anti-aircraft guns. This is the simplest form of a puzzle in an action/exploration game. Here the focus is mostly on players exploring until they find the puzzle, with the solution to the puzzle itself then being trivial. In the case of the switch, once it is found all players need to do is flip it.

Some would say that all puzzles are keys in the end, but this misses an important point and opportunity for more compelling gameplay. More sophisticated variants on the switch/door combination can be situations that require players to actually figure something out in order to progress. Perhaps a laser beam needs to be refracted around a series of corners in order for players to move on. In order to refract it correctly, players will need to move several reflective plates. Players must understand the simple physics of the situation that govern how the beam will behave when reflected in different ways. In *The Suffering*, early on players come to a puzzle where they need to block a gate that keeps swinging shut with a large stone statue. Players need to experiment in the environment and with the game mechanics in order to solve this puzzle. With challenges of this sort, the focus here shifts from just finding the puzzle to finding it and then figuring out how to manipulate it correctly. The player's gaming experience is enhanced by this puzzle instead of it merely delaying the end of her game. Determining how much emphasis your level will have on puzzle solving is important to keep in mind, especially within the context of the game as a whole. A sure way to frustrate players is to suddenly throw a bunch of arbitrary puzzles at them after the entire game up to that point has been more action-oriented.

Storytelling

In a historical game such as *Gettysburg!*, the gameplay is very much tied to a particular story from history.

Setting is a big part of storytelling, and levels are a vital component of establishing the setting for a game. Therefore, levels are an integral part of telling a game's story. If the story is more than something tacked onto an already completed game, it only makes sense for the game's levels and the story to work in synergy. Depending on the type of storytelling that the game employs, it may be necessary for players to meet and converse with characters in the levels, such as in *Half-Life* or in almost any RPG. Setting up the levels to support the appearance of these characters becomes very important. In some games it is obvious that the levels were designed from the very start with the story in mind. For instance, in *Myth: The Fallen Lords*, the players' goals for a certain level are directly tied to the progression of the story. Similarly in *The Suffering*, we mapped the whole story out and then tried to figure out what interesting level environments would work within the narrative. In a historical wargame such as *Gettysburg!*, the battles players fight have to be tied to the story, since it could hardly be a historical simulation otherwise. Indeed, any game that hopes to tell a story really needs to make sure its levels support that story; players will notice when the levels were just built willy-nilly and are only barely connected to the game's plot.

Knowing the story goals for a given level prior to constructing that level is crucial to communicating the story effectively. The story should still be loose enough to allow the level designer to be creative in making the best level possible. There are still concerns about gameplay — about balancing the right amount of strategy, action, puzzles, and exploration — and since it is nearly impossible to balance these components before the level actually exists, the level designer should not be tied down by an overly restrictive story. Indeed, it may turn out that the story needs to change in order to accommodate the gameplay needs of the level, but having an idea of what story needs to be told on a particular level is essential to designing that level so it fits properly into the overall narrative.

Aesthetics

How a level looks and sounds are probably the driving factors behind many level designers' work. And it's easy to see why: surface aesthetics are always commented on first by management, the press, or even players. I certainly would not dispute that a level's appearance is crucial to its overall success. At the same time, however, the aesthetic component becomes a problem when how the level looks becomes the designer's primary concern, a situation that usually has a detrimental effect on how the level plays. Suppose a level designer spends a lot of time creating a massive, gorgeous cathedral for a level, and the appearance of that cathedral is constantly at the forefront of her mind. What if it turns out that the cathedral is hard for players to navigate, the AI agents easily get confused when trying to pathfind though it, and the whole structure is a bit more than the engine can handle, resulting in the level running slowly? If the cathedral looks great and its construction sucked up a lot of man-hours, who will want to cut it? It may translate into some fabulous screenshots on the back of the box; too bad it will not be any fun to play.

A big part of the level designer's job is to balance appearance with the other requirements of a given level, as I have listed above. There is always an achievable middle ground where the level looks good, plays well, renders quickly, and suits the needs of the game's story. Level designers spend a lot of their time learning the "tricks" of a given engine or level editor. What can they do that will use the fewest polygons while still looking good? Often the solutions they come up with are not necessarily "real" but rather "faked." Of course the whole purpose of creating levels for a virtual world is creating "fake" content, so a level designer need not worry if an effect is achieved by "faking" something. If players cannot tell it is faked, if they cannot see behind the magic curtain, that is all that matters. One of the principles behind all special effects is to create something that looks like something it is not. The level designer's job is to make players see something that looks like something it is not, giving the level what *Unreal* level designer Cliff Bleszinski would call "schlack" and that others call "chrome": a shiny and fancy coating over an otherwise uninteresting level. Shiny and pretty is not necessarily a bad thing, it just should not be used to substitute for quality gameplay.

The visual side of a level can have a big impact on the other concerns of a game's level, as I have listed before. For instance, in order to make a level playable, the textures on a level should be laid out in such a way that players are able to see where they should or should not be able to go. Instead of wondering if a particular slope is too steep for their game-world surrogate to climb up, a different texture can serve as a visual cue to the players as to which slopes are passable and which are not. Lighting can be used to conceal secret areas, or a big puzzle in the level may be figuring out how to turn the lights on. If certain special areas are supposed to be rewards for diligent exploration, making those special areas look impressive is essential to maintaining the players' interest in the level.

A lot of time can be spent on the aesthetics of a level. The amount of time is directly proportional to the complexity of the engine and level editor being used as well as the desired visual effect of the level. In fact, it may be the case that all of the gameplay and story elements of the level can be set up first and then the visual appearance can be tweaked for weeks to come. Lighting can be endlessly adjusted, textures can be shifted or switched for other textures, and polygon faces can be adjusted to better represent the visual effect the team is trying to achieve. Indeed, level design work has become so labor intensive that many design teams have started passing off the aesthetic pass to the art team, a technique used in the development of both *Halo* and *Half-Life 2*. Regardless of who is doing the aesthetic work, the level designer must be fully aware of the effects changes in the level's appearance will have on the gameplay.

Balancing It All

Because a good level must balance action, exploration, puzzle solving, storytelling, and aesthetics, the work of the level designer is a bit of a balancing act. Even if the level may look better a certain way, how does that impact the story being told? Do the story requirements for the level mean that it cannot have much in the way of combat? How important is combat to the game, and can the level survive without it? Is the quantity of puzzle elements in the level preventing players from being able to enjoy exploring it? The action, exploration, puzzle solving, storytelling, and aesthetic qualities of a game level all have interdependencies, which the level designer must be constantly aware of and be constantly maintaining. The price of good level design is eternal vigilance.

Level Flow

For different types of games, what a level is expected to accomplish changes significantly. Consider action/exploration games such as *Super Mario 64*, *Tomb Raider*, or *Doom*. Though the gameplay in these three games is significantly different, the functions the levels serve in each are remarkably similar. In all these games, players customarily play through the level from a distinct beginning point to a separate end point. A big part of playing the level is exploring the spaces it contains, and as a result, once players have played through the level, it is significantly less fun to play a second time. Furthermore, any encounters players might have with characters or adversaries in these levels are carefully predetermined and set up by the level designer. Every time players play such a level, they will have roughly the same gameplay experience as the last time they played it. The flow of the level is more or less linear, with perhaps only a few choices of how to get from point A to point B.

RPGs offer roughly the same flow pattern as the action/exploration games discussed above, but with a bit more non-linearity. The designer usually intends for players to navigate to a particular location in a particular way. RPGs may tend to be a bit more non-linear than action/adventure games, usually allowing players to choose the order in which different actions can be performed. Often "hub" style gameplay allows players to branch off on different adventures while returning to a central location, such as a town. Players may also stay in the town to hone their skills for as long as they like. In the end, though, RPGs offer similar level flow as action/adventure titles.

In a level from a strategy game such as *WarCraft* or *Civilization*, however, the action is less canned and the level flow is less clearly defined. *WarCraft* and *Civilization* may be as different from each other as *Super Mario 64* and *Doom*, but the way they use their levels is the same. Exploration is not such a central part of the enjoyment of these strategy games, and the battles may take place on any part of the map. Different locations may provide specific strategic advantages when used correctly, but battles can start in one location and move to another, or certain sections of the map may go completely unexplored and unexploited by the players and their opponents. The gameplay on such a map is often significantly less predictable than on an action/exploration game's map. The level's flow is more nebulous.

The flow of a level of a real-time strategy game like *WarCraft* is less defined than in an action/exploration game: combat encounters can take place all over the map.

Of course, there is at least one distinguishing characteristic that makes the level flow in *Civilization* significantly different from that of *WarCraft*. In *Civilization*, any one game consists of play on only one level. That is, players start a game of *Civilization* on one level and play on that level until they win or lose, while in *WarCraft* players encounter a series of scenarios on a series of levels. *Civilization* presents a much more continuous gameplay experience for players, which may in turn make it that much more addictive. Whereas a game like *WarCraft* presents players with an easy stopping point — the end of a level — a game like *Civilization* has no such breaks. Both types of games may include levels with unpredictable flows, where different players can play the levels significantly differently, but since players in *Civilization* spend all of their time on one map, the overall feel of the game is radically different. Of course, the fact that *Civilization* is turn-based while *WarCraft* is real-time significantly changes the flow of the games as well, but that is a change in gameplay rather than a change in level design and usage.

Returning to our action/exploration games, if we were to take a multi-player death-match level from a game like *Quake*, we would see that the level's flow is much closer to that of a strategy game. That is, exploring the level is less important and combat can take place in completely unpredictable ways all over the map. Indeed, many players of multi-player death-match games will find a map they like and stick to it, at least for a while. Players will need to have explored the map thoroughly before they actually have a chance of winning a death-match on that map, certainly when playing with more experienced players. Exploration and memorization of the map may be an integral part of the metagame in that such exploration leads to the players' victory in future games, but the exploration is only a means to an end, not an end in and of itself, unlike in a single-player game where exploration is a big part of the fun.

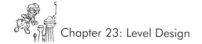

"Sandbox" style games like *Grand Theft Auto*, *The Getaway*, or *True Crime* are interesting in how they combine elements from RPG, strategy, and death-match level flows. In them, players need to go to different locations to get missions from people, often covering ground they have traveled previously to get there, much like in an RPG. And like a strategy game, the action and combat sequences can flow all over the map depending on where the battle happens to go. Finally, like a death-match map, players will only start excelling in the game once they have memorized the city streets and are thereby able to get to locations more quickly.

With the exception of racing games, sports games typically provide a very non-linear flow to their gameplay. The flow of a basketball game's levels more closely resembles a death-match or strategy game's levels than an action/exploration game's maps. Action takes place all over the level or court, with the players' movement flowing back and forth across the level, covering the same ground but in unique and unpredictable ways. Exploring the level is relatively unimportant, as the shape of the level is completely simple and typically the entire court or a very large chunk of it is on screen at once.

In a racing game, players move from a distinct start location to a distinct end location. This movement is quite similar to an exploration-oriented action game such as *Doom*, with the key differences that typically the race's start and end locations are the same (the track loops) and usually the race-path is repeated multiple times before the level is over. Though there is a good deal of non-linearity in terms of the gameplay and how players race against their opponents, the level flow is even more linear than in an action/adventure title. Modern racing games such as *Project Gotham Racing* or *Cruisin' World* incorporate some of the exploration elements of action/exploration games by making the levels look visually stunning and varied, making the first time players round a corner an aesthetically thrilling experience. Older racing games (such as the venerable *Pole Position*) relied more on the challenge of navigating the track to entertain players rather than the thrill of racing through new, fantastic locations. Many more modern racing games also include alternate paths or shortcuts that players can take for varied gameplay results. The *SSX* games, which are racing games despite not involving cars, are particularly good at providing a wide variety of secret paths for players to explore. The flow is still in the same general direction, but some branching allows players to concentrate on more than just how tightly they can take a given corner.

From my discussion of these gaming genres and the way that gameplay flows on their respective levels, one could divide the games into roughly two groups: those with more linear levels (action/adventure, role-playing, and racing games) and those with more non-linear, unpredictable gameplay experiences (strategy, sports, and multi-player death-match games). Of course, that is not to say that the two do not overlap. For instance, specific *StarCraft* levels do everything to encourage players to play them in a specific path, especially the small-team indoor levels. Similarly, many *Super Mario 64* maps allow for multiple viable paths players can use to play them through. If the designer is creative enough in her efforts, the distinction between the two types of levels can be blurred, which can often lead to more varied and interesting gameplay.

Elements of Good Levels

As you design a level, there are a seemingly infinite number of details you must keep in mind. You must be concerned that you balance the elements of action, exploration, puzzle solving, storytelling, and aesthetic appeal. You must work with the artists and programmers to achieve the effects you want. For 3D levels, you must make sure the whole level is optimized so that it can run on the target system. And in the worst of situations you have to deal with unruly level design tools that seem to thwart your every attempt to make something cool.

Often a level designer will come up with rules of thumb to follow while making a level, even if she does not write them down. Every designer will have her own list of "dos" and "don'ts" that she keeps in the back of her mind, and this list can change significantly from project to project. Some games will have their own "design rules" established ahead of time and which the designers can then follow, but there are also rules that can apply to any project. Here I present a partial list of my own rules, which I use to attempt to make a level that is stimulating to play.

Players Cannot Get Stuck

This should be obvious but is a frequent newbie designer mistake. Players should never become hopelessly stuck when playing your level. There should be no pits that can be fallen into but not climbed out of, no objects which, when moved incorrectly, permanently block the players' progress, and no doors that fail to open if players approach them a certain way. Though this goal may seem perfectly obvious, it will actually consume a large amount of your time as a level designer. Consider a puzzle where players have a certain amount of dynamite, and that dynamite needs to be used to blow a hole in a wall so players can progress in the level. What if players use up all their dynamite blowing up the wrong things? Without any more dynamite, the players are now completely stuck. Similarly, suppose players need to talk to a particular NPC to get a particular object. What if, instead of talking to that character, players kill him? Either the game must end nearly instantly, or there must be some alternate way to progress through the game. Designing your level in such a way that, whatever players do, they can still finish the level, takes a lot of thinking and planning. As a level designer, you must always be asking yourself, "But what if players try it this way?"

Sub-Goals

As the players play a level, they should have understandable sub-goals. Instead of playing through the whole level just trying to get to the exit or accomplish some large goal, players should be able to recognize that there are various tasks they can accomplish that contribute to the final goal. A very simple example of this would be the different keys in *Doom*. Players know that once they get the blue key they are that much closer to finishing the level. In an arcade racing game like *San Francisco Rush*, instead of having just one finish line per track, most games have multiple "checkpoints" along the track at which players are given a time bonus and informed of how well they are doing. In an RPG, players may be working to defeat an evil force that is tormenting the land, but along the way they are able to go on various sub-quests for villagers who need their

In racing games such as the *San Francisco Rush* series, players are given sub-goals through checkpoints, which award more time. Pictured here: *San Francisco Rush: The Rock — Alcatraz Edition*.

help. These various sub-quests lead players toward the larger goal, and provide players with positive feedback that they are, in fact, playing the game well. Platformers like *Ratchet & Clank* are particularly good at leading players through the levels with their many pickups, with the acquisition of each basically being a tiny sub-goal. A sub-goal is useless if players do not understand what they have accomplished. Therefore, it is also important to provide players with some sort of reward for achieving the goal, whether it is audiovisual bells and whistles, a new weapon, bonus points, or more time on the racing clock. If the designer does not provide enough sub-goals on a particular level or if those sub-goals are so transparent that the players do not realize they have achieved them, players may become confused as to what they are supposed to be doing and whether they are getting any closer to succeeding.

Landmarks

The more complex your level, the more players are likely to get confused navigating it. Unless confusion is your goal, which it usually should not be, it is a good idea to set up memorable landmarks in your level to ease the players' exploration. A landmark is any unique object in your level that players will recognize the second time they see it, whether it is a particularly ornately decorated room, a large statue, or a steaming pool of lava. In terms of exploration, then, when players return to this landmark, they will know that they are returning to a location they have previously visited, and will thereby begin to understand the layout of the level. Landmarks do not necessarily need to be big red signs labeled "Checkpoint A," but can instead be worked into the story and setting of the level itself. For example, *Grand Theft Auto III* made the very large Liberty City much easier to learn to navigate by including lots of large and unique buildings as part of the map. Each of these landmarks, in addition to how they helped the player learn the level, supported the game fiction perfectly.

Critical Path

Even though I am a big proponent of non-linear gameplay, I am also a big fan of a nice critical path in a level. A critical path gives players a sense of a direction they can use in order to complete the level. This direction may be a physical direction, such as "head north" or "head for the rainbow," or it can be a more ambiguous goal, such as finding a creature and defeating it or retrieving an important object. Always giving players a primary goal to accomplish is crucial to making your level playable. Players should have a goal and, as I discussed, sub-goals that work toward achieving that primary goal. Players should always be aware of the goal and the related sub-goals, and should always have a sense of what they can do to progress in the level. Separate optional side-goals may be less obvious or hidden, but nothing frustrates players more than having no idea what they are supposed to do. Having a clearly established critical path is a good way to help prevent players from becoming confused.

Limited Backtracking

If your game relies on exploration for a large part of its gameplay value, it is probably a bad idea to make players backtrack through large sections of the level that they have already explored in order to continue in the game. That is not to say that your level cannot have branching paths for players to explore. It merely means that each branch should loop back to the main path without players needing to backtrack along the same path. If your game is more of a role-playing or adventure game where creating the illusion of reality is important, the necessity of backtracking may be more acceptable. *Grand Theft Auto III* is certainly an example of a realistic setting resulting in a need for backtracking, though the game ameliorates the situation by making driving around the city fun no matter how many times you do it. Certainly in an RTS, sports, or death-match game, players will be covering the same ground over and over again, but the appeal of a basketball game or *WarCraft* is not so tied to exploration as *Super Mario 64*, which does a very good job of eliminating the need for backtracking entirely.

Success the First Time

If most players are able to beat your level the first time they play it, you have probably made a level that is too easy. Nonetheless, the possibility should exist that players could make it all the way through your level on the first try. I do not mean, however, that players could make all of the right choices just by happenstance. Instead, you should provide enough data to the players that they have a reasonable chance of avoiding all the obstacles put in their path if they are observant and quick-witted enough. Whenever players fail in your level, they should feel that they had a fair chance of avoiding that failure if they had only been more observant or had thought more before they acted. Nothing frustrates players more than realizing that the only way to make it through the level is by trial and error combined with blind luck. Of course, your level can still be hard. Your clues as to what to do can be quite subtle, the monsters to be defeated can be really strong, or the choices to be made can be truly challenging, but if players do everything perfectly, they should be able to get through your level the first time they play it.

Navigable Areas Clearly Marked

Players should have a clear idea of where they will be able to go in the level simply by looking at the environment. Slopes that players will slide on should appear to be significantly steeper than the slopes that can be walked on. Textures may be used to differentiate between areas players can navigate and those they cannot. It can be very frustrating to players when an area that appeared to be unnavigable turns out to be the only way out of a particular area. Another example might be a room with ten doors in it. Players try three of these doors, and they are all locked. At this point, players will probably conclude that the doors are there only for show and will stop trying any of the other doors. No information, whether visual or through a verbal clue, is given to players to indicate that the other doors might be openable when the first three they tried were not. If it turns out that the only way out of this room is through the sole unlocked door, I would suggest that this area has been poorly designed. The only way out of such a room is through tedious trial and error. The fun in a game may involve trying to get to certain areas or the thrill of running around in those areas, but there is little fun to be found in determining which areas the designer arbitrarily decided could be navigated and which could not.

Choices

This may seem obvious, but choices are something level designers can often forget to keep in mind as they are building their levels. Good levels give players choices of how to accomplish goals, just as good gameplay gives players lots of choices for how they will play the game. Choices do not necessarily mean multiple paths through a level, though that may be a good idea as well. In a first-person shooter, choices could mean giving players different options for how to take out all of the enemies in a room — plenty of different places to hide, different locations that the enemies can be shot from, and so forth. Such a setup creates a variety of different strategies that will successfully defeat the horde of advancing demons. Choices could also mean bonus objects that are challenging for players to get, such as a rocket launcher in the middle of a pool of lava — players have the choice to risk going for it or not. In a strategy game, interesting choices mean different places where battles may play out or different places players can choose to rally their troops or gather resources. In adventure games, the genre most notorious for not giving players enough options, choices mean multiple solutions to the game's puzzles, different characters to talk to, and plenty of different ways to move through the game. Indeed if a designer is going to add choices to her levels, it is important that she make sure she is adding interesting choices. The decision to go left or right around a pillar is a choice, but if both lead to the same place and produce basically the same experience the choice is not terribly interesting. If one side of the pillar is on fire while the other side has an intimidating thug guarding it, the choice is more interesting. Players become frustrated when they feel that they are locked into just one way of playing the game, especially if that one way is not the way they would like to play it.

A Personal List

Certainly the list I have provided above is far from complete. As you work as a level designer, it makes sense to establish your own list of design goals to keep in mind while creating your level. As you work on levels that are received well by your peers or players, try to analyze the levels to see what you did well. Then try to abstract these accomplishments into a list of goals to keep in mind as you work on subsequent levels. This list does not necessarily need to be formally written down; just keeping a mental checklist may be sufficient. The options I listed here may be a start for your own list, or you may find yourself coming up with a completely different set of goals. Every designer approaches level design in her own way.

The Process

The process of constructing a level can vary greatly from designer to designer. What works for one person may not work for another. Each team is likely to have its own process and method for building an environment. That said, I have found the following progression of steps to be one that works well for me. I may not always follow the steps precisely, but generally speaking, this progression produces more consistent and efficient results than just cranking out a level without any plan of what to do first or how to proceed.

Step 1. *Preliminary*

Before starting development on an action/exploration game such as those found in the *Tomb Raider* series, it is important to have a clearly defined set of moves for the player.

Before starting to design a level for the game, ask yourself if the gameplay is in a close-to-final state. Do you have a solid foundation to build upon? Are your game mechanics nailed down? Is the game going to change so much that the level you design will no longer be fun to play? Or worse, will the level no longer be playable? For instance, suppose you are developing a third-person action/adventure such as *Tomb Raider*. Before you start making a level for the game, you need to determine how final the movement of the main character is. Will more moves for the character be added? Will the game's hero someday be able to do a double forward flip that will radically change the distance she will be able to jump? Often when you begin working on a level the game itself is far from complete, and some changes will probably be made to the main character's movement. But if the team is aware that radical changes to the player movement model will be made, having level designers start working on levels is a big mistake.

On one project I worked on, we started working on the levels before the ability for the main character to jump had even been added to the game. As a result, once it was added, we went back and had to modify the levels to include areas that would use this jumping ability. Unfortunately, after the jumping had been in the game for a while, it became clear that the jumping was not that much fun, and that we would have to go back to the levels and remove a lot of the jumps we had put in. The end result was not nearly as clean as if we had known from the very beginning how the jumping would work. The problem here was that production had started on the levels before the game mechanics were sufficiently hammered out, implemented, and their fun level ascertained. As I discussed in Chapter 15, "Getting the Gameplay Working," you will probably need to have one level in progress while you work on implementing the gameplay, so you can test out different behaviors as they are added. But working on more than that one particular level is a waste of time that may be detrimental to the project in the long run. Furthermore, it may make sense to scrap the test level once the gameplay is firmly established, since that preliminary level usually turns out to be far from the best work you are capable of.

Step 2. *Conceptual and Sketched Outline*

Before beginning work on a level, I think it is very important to understand what that level is going to need to do from a gameplay and story perspective. What sort of challenges will players face here, and what sorts of environments best facilitate those challenges? How exciting and nerve-racking is the gameplay in this level? Where will players need to be rewarded? What story elements need to be conveyed through the level? At all times, but especially during the planning stage, you must keep in mind the game's focus and how your level will work to support that focus.

Once the designer has some grasp of what the level is supposed to accomplish, a pencil and paper sketch of the level's general layout is a very good idea. This avoids the perils of "designing yourself into a corner." Say you are designing a building in a military compound for a fully 3D first-person shooter. In your compound you need to include a room with a large generator. When you start making the architecture for the building, you first lay out all the halls, then start working on some of the cooler rooms before you finally get to the generator room. Then, whoops, it turns out you failed to leave as much space as necessary for the generator. The room is now too small to be easily navigable. Unfortunately, the only way to make it big enough involves ripping up a lot of the halls you had made already. At this point, some designers would just move the generator room to a less-logical or less-optimal location rather than having to redo a lot of geometry they already spent time building. Of course, a level sketch might not always prevent this problem, but if done correctly it might point out to the designer how small the generator room was at a time when making it bigger only involves using the eraser on her pencil. Changes to a sketch are much easier to make than changes to a fully constructed level. A sketch may also be valuable as something that you can show to your team leader, who may want to look it over to make sure you are on the right track with the rest of the team and the game as a whole.

Step 3. *Base Architecture/Block Out*

As game engines become more sophisticated, the amount of time required to build a level increases dramatically. For example, a professional level using the *Quake III Arena* engine will easily take weeks to complete.

Once you are happy with your sketch, the actual construction of the level can begin. This construction stage varies in time and scope depending on the complexity of the level being created. For instance, a 2D, tile-based engine will allow for much quicker construction of a level than a 3D engine. Similarly, the complexity of the 3D engine being used will radically alter how much time is required to build out the level. An excellent map made with the *Doom* engine can be pounded out in a day or two. A level of similar quality made with the much more sophisticated *Quake III* engine can easily take weeks of hard work.

At this point, keep in mind that you are just creating the base layout for your level. You are not adding niceties such as lighting or texturing, nor are you concentrating on making the geometry as pretty as possible. On this first pass you want to get the level to the point where players can navigate through it and all of the locations are accessible. At this point it makes sense to use temporary textures and primitive forms of geometry. Instead of putting a real chair in the game, just place an appropriately scaled box. This allows you to get a sense for whether the level's layout feels right without wasting any more time than necessary.

Step 4. *Refine Architecture Until It Is Fun*

At this point you need to repeat step three until your level starts feeling good and navigating it starts to be fun. For instance, if you are working on a first-person shooter, you should experiment with navigating your character around the 3D world, and see if the corners are fun to swing around, if the jumps are of just about the right difficulty, and if the areas come out at the size you had wanted them to. Take a look at the level as a whole and see if it makes sense and flows as you hoped it would. Once you actually spend time looking at and navigating the level as players would, instead of just fiddling with it in the level editor, you stand a better chance of determining if your level is working out. If the level is not working out as you want, now is the time to make changes until it does.

Step 5. *Base Gameplay*

Now that your level feels right in terms of player navigation, it is time to start implementing the gameplay your level will use. Certainly you had the gameplay in mind through all of the steps of this process and you planned it out thoroughly before you even started building, but now is the time to see if it will actually work out as you had hoped. The best designers can come up with ideas and sketches for levels that successfully translate into fun levels in the end. Others start with a sketch, build some architecture, and when it comes time to add the gameplay, find they need to make some significant modifications to what they have already built. With experience comes the ability to predict whether abstract ideas will turn out to be any fun or not. Before you become experienced, however, the process involves a great deal of trial and error.

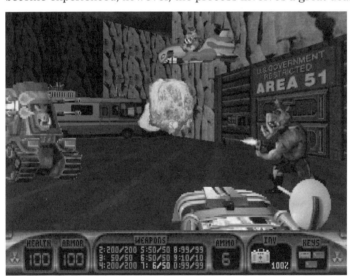

Setting up the gameplay in a level from a game like *Duke Nukem 3D* consists of placing monsters and weapons, and configuring puzzles.

A level's gameplay consists of whatever actions players are allowed to perform in that level. In a first-person shooter such as *Duke Nukem 3D*, this means placing the monsters players will shoot and the items players will pick up. In a role-playing or adventure game, this is expanded to include whatever puzzles players will need to solve, the characters with which players may talk, and the quests on which these NPCs send players. In a real-time strategy game, the designer will need to figure out starting unit placement and quantities for players and her opponents, as well as whatever reinforcements may appear later in the level. In a way, sports and racing titles have an easier time with this step, since their gameplay is the same from level to level and therefore does not need much setup for a particular stadium or track.

Step 6. *Refine Gameplay Until It Is Fun*

Of course, the gameplay is what makes or breaks the game, so it is absolutely essential that the designer repeat step five until the level is fun to play. Sometimes, refining the gameplay may take you all the way back to step number three. It may turn out that the area you thought would play well just is not suited to the capabilities of the AI. Or that the creature you thought would be able to spring out at players from a fissure in a cliff does not really have enough space to hide. You may need to change the layout of your level to compensate for the problems you discover once you start implementing the gameplay.

For some designers, modifying existing level architecture to suit the gameplay can be quite a painful process. For instance, suppose a designer builds some architecture she is happy with from an aesthetic standpoint. If the gameplay then does not work in that space, the designer may be reluctant to go back and rework that geometry and may instead settle for substandard gameplay. Of course, this is the wrong choice to make. As painful as it may be, in order to get the best gameplay you may need to throw out some of your work. This is why I suggested only making base architecture without refining it too much; that way making radical changes to the level will not mean that too much work was wasted. In the end, gameplay must always trump all other considerations, whether aesthetics, story, or technology. If it's not fun in the end, nothing else matters. Therefore it is only logical that you must first get the level fun before you spend a lot of time on other aspects of the level.

This is the step where your level really comes together and you start to get a sense of whether it is a success. Now you can take this space you created and really start to play in it. If you do not start enjoying yourself at this point, you may need to take a look at your level and ask yourself why it is not fun to play. In the worst case, you may realize that the level will never be fun, and as a result you need to start fresh. Ideally, however, this stage can be truly revelatory, as all of the work you put into the level starts to come together and pay off.

Step 7. *Refine Aesthetics*

Now that the level is playing well, you have an opportunity to make it look good as well. You may recall that in steps three and four we just set up base architecture, enough to allow players to navigate and to give you a feel for the level. Now is the time to texture your level as needed, apply lighting effects, add decorative objects, and really flesh out your level from a visual standpoint. Depending on your development process, this may be the point at which you hand the level off to an artist. Many teams spend the bulk of their time working on aesthetics for their levels, and certainly you should put in the time to make the level look as good as possible. But, as I have emphasized, it is crucial that you put off finessing the level until you are confident that the level plays well and that it accomplishes its gameplay objectives. Otherwise, you may waste your time making areas look nice that end up being scrapped. As you are finessing the level aesthetically, you must always remember not to break any of the gameplay you have already set up.

Step 8. *Playtesting*

Now that all the parts of your level are in place, it is time to show it to some other people, let them play it, and get some feedback. Playtesting is a crucial part of game design, and level design is no different. These test subjects may include other members of your team, but should also include people less intimately involved with your project. A lot can be said for a fresh pair of eyes looking at your game and your level and giving you feedback on whether the gameplay accomplished what you had hoped.

Playtesting a level can be as easy as giving a level to someone, asking her to play it, and having her tell you what she thinks. Another useful method, especially for level testing, is to actually be there with the tester when she tries to play your level and observe how she plays it. Does she get stuck in locations you had not thought of? Does she have trouble finding her way around? Do the gameplay situations provide her with enough challenge? Watching other people play your level can be extremely educational and informative as to whether the level flows and plays well.

In the worst case, playtesting may reveal that your level is not as fun to play as you had thought, and that major reworking will be necessary to make it fun. As a designer you must not be resistant when someone tells you your level is hard to navigate, confusing, or simply no fun. Certainly, get a second and third and fourth opinion on it, but when you start hearing the same complaints from a number of different people, you need to realize that there may be some truth to their comments and your level may need some serious reworking. Many designers who have invested a lot of time and energy in a level find it very difficult to then take criticism of their work. There is no denying that hearing someone tear apart a month's worth of work can be disheartening, but this is the purpose of playtesting. You need to take your testers' comments to heart, recognize the problems with your level, and start working on the level again. Thorough playtesting can often be the difference between a merely good level and a truly great one.

Process Variations

Of course, the process for level design I outline above is not the only way to make a level. Like the "dos" and "don'ts" of level design I described earlier, each level designer needs to find the method that works best for herself and her team. Many good designers use a method not entirely different from what I have outlined above, but with variations that better suit their own style of designing.

One potentially useful variation is to incorporate steps three through six. Instead of laying out the entire level, you can start with a particular room or area. Then, before moving on to set up the rest of the level, try to set up gameplay in just that area. Once you are happy with how well that section plays, move on to setting up the rest of the level, adding gameplay to the areas as you create them. This way, if an area has to be enlarged to make the gameplay work properly, less work is wasted since the areas around may not have been built yet. As I mentioned before, it is important to be careful to not design yourself into a corner. You do not want to spend a lot of time working on the gameplay for a specific area only to have to remove it later since the rest of the level no longer fits in the space available. If you are going to set up gameplay for particular areas before the entire level is built, it makes the most sense to build the architecture for an entire, discrete play-space, such as a specific building or structure. Then you can make the gameplay work in that entire area before moving on to the next.

Another useful idea is to incorporate playtesting earlier in the process, perhaps after step six. Once you have your level playable, have some people whose opinions you trust try playing the level. The aesthetics may not be fully refined yet, and you should certainly explain this to them as they play, but if you are able to get feedback at this early stage, you may be able to make important changes before you have spent a lot of time refining the aesthetics of the level. A possible drawback to testing the level this early is that others may not be able to understand that visually the level is not yet complete. As a result they may get hung up on criticizing the appearance of your level instead of providing feedback about the gameplay. Be sure to communicate what type of feedback you are looking for at this stage and hope that the playtesters can see beyond the lack of fancy lighting effects. Testing at this early stage does not replace testing after the level is more final, but it may prevent some unpleasant surprises and can make the final testing go more smoothly.

Who Does Level Design?

Throughout this chapter, I have spoken as if you are responsible for all aspects of your level. Many development studios do still operate on the "one designer, one level" method of level design. This has many advantages, of course, since it helps to keep the levels focused. That one designer is constantly aware of what her level requires in terms of gameplay, art, and programming, and can keep that level on track. When it comes time to set up the level's lighting, for instance, the designer will remember that she thought that gameplay in one part of the level would play best in the dark with disorienting flashing light. Having one person working on one level from start to finish helps to ensure the level has a consistency of vision that can lead to great gameplay.

But the "one designer, one level" technique is not the only method that may work, and many developers have adopted more of a "team" approach to level design. If your team has one designer who is particularly good at making pretty architecture but is less skilled at getting the AI agents to work, it may make sense to have a different designer set up the gameplay on that designer's levels. Artists may be better trained and suited to making a level look especially pretty. One designer or an artist may be particularly good at lighting effects, while another may be adept at the scripted sequences. You may want the sound designer to set up your sound effects, since she will be better at correctly placing the audio effects she created. The price of having a level that is of high quality will almost inevitably involve a greater degree of specialization of your team members. Of course, as with any task that is divided among several people, you need to make sure that they are all "on the same page" in terms of what that level is trying to accomplish. For instance, the architecture designer may have built a canyon that she thought would be ideal for an ambush, but when the designer who sets up the gameplay comes along, she may not notice that particular canyon and might set up encounters in less optimal locations. Communication between the different people working on a particular level is essential, just as it is between the programming, art, and design teams.

As I stated previously, as games become more complex, it becomes necessary to divide tasks that used to be accomplished by one person between multiple people. As games continue to become more complicated, designers will specialize more and more, and having multiple people working on a single level will become increasingly common. Keeping the game focused on such a project will be quite a challenge, which emphasizes the importance of project leaders and lead level designers. However, as people specialize in a particular area of level design, the possibility exists that they can become better at their specific area of expertise as a result, raising the bar in terms of final quality. Furthermore, if one person sets up the AI and gameplay for all of the levels in the game, those levels as a whole may achieve a greater gameplay consistency than if each level designer was setting up her own gameplay. If managed correctly, these highly specialized level designers and artists can lead to better levels in the final game.

Collaboration

As games have grown in complexity, the number of level designers required for a particular game has increased. Whereas one designer used to be able to truly control every last facet of a game's design, now a lead designer must find level designers she can trust to build levels that will make a significant contribution to the game's design. Though a lead designer may be able to look over the shoulder of these level designers and do her best to direct the efforts, in the end she has delegated a large part of the gameplay's creation to these invaluable members of her team. This can have both a good side, as more voices in the game's design may make the game a more robust experience, and a bad side, as the clarity of artistic vision becomes diluted by so many different people working on the project. Such are the perils of most all modern commercial game development.

Chapter 24:
Game Analysis: Grand Theft Auto III

Designed by Chris Rothwell, Craig Filshie, William Mills, and James Worrall
Released in 2001

In terms of game design, *Grand Theft Auto III* is a shining example of the triumph of systems-based design. The title features a game-world in which emergent behaviors and a wide breadth of player choices combine to create an amazing gameplay experience where players feel truly empowered to play however they want. If sales can be extrapolated to popularity, then *Grand Theft Auto III* and its sequel *Grand Theft Auto: Vice City* have each captivated more players than any other game of the PlayStation 2 console generation. Anyone who has played these games can tell you the reason why: the games brilliantly combine uniquely fun core mechanics with giving players enough freedom in the environment that the game becomes an entertaining experience players will enjoy much longer than almost any other action game.

In terms of production, *Grand Theft Auto III* is an example of a sequel done right, and how sequels can take advantage of advancing technology to push their game design to new places. Many game sequels incorporate more advanced rendering technology and graphics merely out of a desire to improve the visuals of a game, and unfortunately these enhancements often end up getting in the way of the original game's play mechanics. *Grand Theft Auto III*, by contrast, used technology to radically alter the play experience and make the new game a lot more playable than its predecessors. By changing the camera view from the top-down found in *Grand Theft Auto* and *Grand Theft Auto 2* to the familiar racing game chase cam, *Grand Theft Auto III* made the driving experience a lot more intuitive and a lot more fun. While driving in the earlier games was often frustrating since players could only see so far ahead of their vehicle in a top-down view, with a chase camera players could clearly see the streets they were hurtling down. The further addition of some relatively simple physics to the driving model made the core mechanics fundamentally enjoyable in a way that had been missing in the previous games.

Believable Game-World

From the very beginning of the series, the *Grand Theft Auto* games' biggest hook has been their realistic setting with which anyone who has driven a car in a city can immediately connect. Even with the particularly cartoonish graphics and top-down view of the first *Grand Theft Auto*, the idea of driving around a city, hurtling like a madman over sidewalks or down alleyways, potentially running over pedestrians that get in your way, smashing your car up in the process, and then stealing any car you might find, proved uniquely compelling. Anyone who has ever been irritated waiting for slow pedestrians to get across a crosswalk has probably wondered "What if I just ran them over?" Everyone has fantasized about avoiding a traffic jam by popping the car up on to the sidewalk like in an action movie. Anyone who has seen a fancy vehicle pull up next to them at a stoplight understands the desire to just ditch your own car and take this better one. These are all taboo activities that many people fantasize about on a daily basis. Surely, they would never do them in real life, but in the safe context of a game-world where the worst consequence is having to start your game over, who wouldn't want to try it out? And since the first two *Grand Theft Auto* games were hits in their own right, we can conclude that many players were willing to overlook the clunky driving mechanics so that they could engage in these taboo activities.

Grand Theft Auto III is a model of how to truly evolve your game with a sequel. It retains the exciting city-driving hook of the first games while fixing its viewpoint and control issues, thereby making the game a lot more compelling to a lot more people. Indeed, many of the design concepts found in the third game are also present in the first, whether it's the ringing telephones giving players their missions, the feel of a living city with other cars and pedestrians all going about their lives in a believable way, the "rampage" mini-games, or the satirical nature of the game-fiction including the highly amusing car radio.

Though in the film and literary world sequels are often looked down upon as a crass way to cash in on a previous success, in gaming one needs to consider sequels a bit differently. Games in general keep being played much longer than their linear media counterparts; think about how many people still consider chess, *Monopoly*, or *Scrabble* to be their favorite board games and continue to play them year after year. With a single-player story-based game, the game may be primarily fun because of its mechanics, yet those mechanics are made meaningful and interesting because of the specific content of the game (whether the location, the selection of usable objects, or the missions and storyline). Players may still enjoy the mechanics once they have worn out all the content. Much as the tabletop RPG *Dungeons & Dragons* spawned endless scenario packs one could play while using the same core rules, when players really love a computer game they want to keep exploring its mechanics but with new and interesting content. On the PC side this can often be accomplished with a mission pack. However, due to the technical limitations of consoles, developers are often required to release an entire new game just to provide more content for players to experience (such as *Grand Theft Auto: Vice City*, which kept basically the same mechanics as its predecessor). At the same time, a sequel gives designers the opportunity to polish and refine their game mechanics, fixing what was glaringly broken and adding the features they regretted cutting due to time constraints the first time around.

Finally, with gaming technology advancing as quickly as it does, games are able to look radically better within the space of only a few years. In particular, with each generation of console hardware, players want to have new versions of their favorite games that fully exploit the new technological capabilities of their new systems. Sometimes the advance in technology is so significant that developers are able to rethink their game and take it to a new level, as was the case with *Grand Theft Auto III*. When a game's fundamental experience can be improved as much as it was in that game, one can hardly say that game sequels are purely exploitation.

A Living City

Grand Theft Auto III is one of the few action-oriented games to present players with a game-world that truly feels like it is alive. Unlike so many other games that have claimed to be set in the real-world, *GTA3* made that world believable, blending in exactly enough reality to allow players to suspend their disbelief. First and foremost, the landscape of *GTA3* allows players to navigate the city in any way they want. Players can drive down any street or alley, over any bridge, through any park, up any set of stairs that is wide enough, and even use ramps to make jumps over obstacles. There is very little sense of being artificially constrained as is so often experienced in most games, thus avoiding the sensation of, "The designers did not want me to go there so there's an invisible wall blocking my way." In *GTA3*, players are confined by a limited number of tall walls and fencing but more by the water that surrounds the island on which the game is set. This consistency of world navigation is made possible by a car physics simulation, which includes enough responsiveness to make the driving seem quasi-believable (at least in an action movie sense), yet keeps the driving fun and fairly forgiving. Similarly, though the cars are able to sustain much more damage than is realistic, if you treat a car badly enough, it will eventually explode, hopefully without you inside it.

Within the city, the game also presents a very believable traffic simulation, with cars waiting for traffic lights, staying on the right side of the road, honking at each other, and some cars weaving in and out between others. Similarly, the pedestrian simulation seems just as authentic, with citizens going about their own lives in the city instead of appearing to have been placed there strictly for the players' benefit. In sharp contrast to most games, *GTA3* creates the sense that this world does not revolve around the player at all; the player character is just one guy in a city full of shady characters. At the same time, both the traffic and pedestrian simulation will react to the players' actions in a believable way. If players run up and punch one of these random civilians, he will fight back while the other citizens flee in terror. Any police who happen be around will run up to try to stop the fight. If players stop their car in the middle of street, traffic will stop and the drivers will honk. All of this contributes to the feeling of a believable world. Though the game-world is far from "real," the world is recognizable and these various systems create a consistent space in which players will enjoy playing. In a way sadly few games do, *Grand Theft Auto III* fosters the spirit of play in players, encouraging them to try out that crazy jump, see if they can find some way inside that fence to a tantalizing power-up, or daring them to try to outrun an entire SWAT team. David Jones, Creative Director at DMA Design when the first two *Grand Theft Auto* games were developed, has stated that the first goal of the games was to build a believable city environment in which gamers could have fun just playing around. Turning the game into a crime and car-jacking game came later, after the city simulation was already enjoyable by itself.

Despite *Grand Theft Auto III*'s impressive world simulation, it is equally interesting what the game-world does not attempt to do. The pedestrians and traffic on the street are intelligent enough to support the illusion of reality, but at the same time are not exactly brilliant. For instance, the pedestrians sometimes appear to be walking around the world like zombies and can easily get hung up on a car left parked in the middle of a sidewalk. Furthermore, these civilians do not make much of an effort to get out of the way of a car heading straight for them. A more advanced simulation of these pedestrians could probably have fixed these problems, but might have made them more computationally expensive and meant fewer of these NPCs could be walking down the street at any one time. Clearly the designers came to the conclusion that having enough NPCs to make the world look truly alive was more important than making each one of them super smart. So too with the art: if one looks at the graphics, no one piece of it is particularly breathtaking. But taken together, the graphics become impressive because of the sheer size of the city and the amount of variety contained in it. In order to make the world so large and to allow players to see so far at any one time, the game's art is all fairly low polygon. Indeed, the developers seem to have embraced a cartoonish art style more compatible with their limited graphical horsepower, probably because they understood their limitations at the start of development and decided to embrace these restrictions instead of fighting them. But players forgive the somewhat low-rent appearance of the game because of its incredible depth as a gameplay experience. In

Grand Theft Auto III, players are never able to go inside buildings during gameplay, with all interior interaction happening exclusively during cut-scenes. Lots of games have certainly allowed players to go inside interior spaces, and this limitation is one of the most obvious omissions in *GTA3*. Part of the problem inherent in developing a game based in a quasi-realistic world is that players will crave more and more realism as they play and may become frustrated when they reach the borders of the simulation. Yet one can understand why *GTA3*'s designers made that choice: given all the other systems and content they needed to create, being able to also go inside structures would have been a whole new headache and they would almost certainly not have had enough time to implement them at a high quality level. Indeed, *Grand Theft Auto: Vice City* included interior spaces but failed to implement them particularly well, making the interior sections some of the weakest and most frustrating parts of the games. In *GTA3*, deciding not to let the players go inside was a wise choice, and once most players became familiar with this restriction they understood the boundaries of the simulation space and forgot about their desire to go inside.

Despite how much players are allowed to do in the game, it is interesting to note just how few actions players can actually perform. The whole game is based around moving through the environment, either in a car or on foot. Each mode is different, with foot travel accomplished by pressing the left stick in the direction you want your character to go, while driving involves steering the car with the left stick while accelerating, decelerating, or using the hand break with various buttons. Players are able to perform attacks in either mode, on foot using either brawling or guns, in a vehicle through ramming into targets (other vehicles or humans), or through shooting out the window "drive-by" style. The interface for attacking is kept fairly simple, particularly when in vehicle mode. When on foot with projectile weapons, auto-targeting is employed, though the interface for this is one of the weakest parts of the game. Beyond world-navigation and attacking, players are also able to pick up simple objects by running over them; on foot these are items like money or weaponry, while in a car one can stop the vehicle next to passengers to let them get in, if they are amenable. Each mode adds a few more custom options: on foot, you can sprint and jump, while in the car you can switch the radio station, honk the horn, or access custom vehicle features, such as playing the game in taxi, ambulance, or fire engine mode.

For a game with such a wide range of player expressive potential, the above mechanics are actually quite limited. *Grand Theft Auto III* comes across as positively simplistic compared even to standard modern first-person shooters, almost all of which include features such as crouching, strafing and backing up, alternate weapon firing, a complex inventory, and so on. Indeed, in terms of the sheer numbers of buttons players need to use, *Grand Theft Auto III* is quite a bit more simple than most modern action-adventures. It may not achieve what Brian Moriarty has referred to as the "desperately simple" interfaces of mass-market breakthroughs like *Myst* or *Tetris*, but the game does more to accommodate non-enthusiast users than most of its contemporaries. The game provides its depth through players combining these mechanics and improvising within the game-space.

Actions and Consequences

In many ways, *Grand Theft Auto III*'s systems-based design centers the game on actions and their consequences. For instance, players are given the freedom to drive recklessly in the city and run over whatever pedestrians happen to be in their way. But if there happens to be a police officer nearby who witnesses the wanton slaughter, players will suddenly become wanted by the police for their crime (which is represented on the players' wanted meter) and will need to avoid the pursuing law enforcement until their wanted level decreases. Similarly, players are able to steal any car they want in the game, but if a police officer witnesses the theft, the players' wanted level will increase. Stealing a police cruiser is also possible, but the police become especially mad when players do so and will pursue them even more doggedly. Outside of just the police reacting to crimes, if players shoot a member of a gang, the other members of the gang are liable to come after them with guns blazing. Players are allowed to drive their car as recklessly as they want, careening into the sides of buildings or making insane jumps. But every time players hit something the car takes damage and, after it has sustained enough hits, will eventually blow up. Thus players are forced to make interesting and sometimes difficult choices: they can cut corners to get somewhere more quickly, damaging their ride along the way, but if they damage it too much they will find themselves without any kind of transportation. If they play it safe, their travel time will be longer and they may fail the mission. Similarly, the police make players think twice about the choices they make. Players may need a car right now to get through a mission, but there's a police officer watching. Can they outrun the cops? Or do they have time to run around the corner and try to steal a vehicle when out of sight?

Grand Theft Auto III's level design is another key component of the game that gives players meaningful choices. Though there are many mini-games and other diversions players can participate in to refine their skills or earn extra cash, the core of the game sends players on a variety of different missions. The missions are quite well set up to provide players with a good variety of goals to accomplish, all of which exploit the game's same core mechanics but reuse them in interesting ways. Players will have missions where they need to assassinate a particular enemy, steal a specific car, pick up a person or a package and drop them/it off at a second location, and so on. The missions are set up to make sure players explore all the different parts of the city, frequently crossing the whole island to accomplish a specific mission. From a level flow perspective, what's most interesting is how players can take any route they like through the city to get somewhere. Furthermore, in some missions the target of the job may move around the city space freely and unpredictably. A battle that starts outside of a specific restaurant may lead to a chase through the city that plays out differently each time the user experiences it. Some missions are timed, meaning players will need to make careful choices about what route they take or how long they let a battle play out. This makes the flow of the map in *Grand Theft Auto III* more like a strategy or sports game, where a battle can naturally and dynamically flow around the environment. There is no critical path to the map. *GTA3*'s Liberty City is so large, navigating it can be quite daunting at first, with players spending a good amount of time getting lost before they figure out their way around. This experience is much like moving to a new city and needing to learn the lay of the land. Fortunately, every inch of Liberty City is completely unique and there are plenty of distinctive landmarks for players to use to get their bearings. An innovative and useful HUD map shows players the nearby streets and smoothly zooms in and out based on the player's current velocity, making navigating the unfamiliar city much easier. And since the game's core mechanics and light physics implementation make driving a vehicle so enjoyable, players are more than willing to put in the time it takes to learn their way around since they can have such fun doing so.

More than any other action adventure title, *Grand Theft Auto III* is a game that causes players to tell each other tales of the amazing chase sequence they had with the police or all the improvisation they used to pull off a mission. Personally, I remember one mission where I had to kill a rival mob boss who ended up chasing me in his armored Mafia Sentinel vehicle. Our showdown had raged across various parts of the city, and my car had sustained so much damage that it was on fire and I had to abandon it. My enemy was still on my tail, and without a vehicle I was a sitting duck. I remember we were fighting near a gas station when I ditched the car, and a thug was barreling at me when I jumped over a low wall that he then smashed into. Suddenly his car had sustained more damage than I'd managed to inflict by ramming him with my now-dead vehicle. He wasn't out of commission yet though, and he drove around the wall to try to run me over again, but this time I ducked behind a gas pump, which he proceeded to ram into. I managed to pull off a number of these matador-like maneuvers until his car finally exploded from all the damage it sustained, and I passed the mission. It was definitely an "I couldn't do that again if I tried" moment. I had passed the mission, the goal of which was completely predetermined, but the way in which I accomplished it involved a method I had come up with on the fly. I had pulled it off in a way the game's designers were unlikely to have anticipated. As a result of my involvement in the authorship of the scenario, it is one of the most memorable experiences I have ever had in a video game. These are the type of scenarios that well-implemented systems-based game design makes possible.

Storytelling

Amidst all the emergent gameplay and interesting choices, *Grand Theft Auto III* also manages to tell a compelling story. The bulk of this storytelling happens in cut-scenes, but it is interesting to note how short and to the point they are. The opening of the game manages to convey a lot of information — the player character's involvement in a bank robbery, the girlfriend who betrayed him and leaves him for dead, the trial that sends him to jail, the main character's subsequent involvement in a prison transport break that leaves him a fugitive from the law — all in approximately two minutes. The cut-scenes that come at the start of each mission are even shorter and to the point. The fact that the game is exceedingly well written and has top-notch voice acting certainly helps to make the reliance on cut-scenes more forgivable.

But the game tells its story through more than just the cut-scenes, with the believability of Liberty City perfectly supporting the game-fiction. Players are sent on missions to various neighborhoods that show the diverse types of life that exist in the city, with the types of cars driving around and the pedestrians walking the sidewalks matching the flavor of the neighborhoods appropriately, all contributing to a remarkably consistent world. The radio stations players can tune into while driving any of the vehicles also contribute to this fictional space, with each station playing into the satirical themes of the game and its biting take on American culture. And again, the writing on the radio is some of the best satire you are likely to find in any medium.

Though the missions and cut-scenes that make up the main story arc are completely pre-scripted and cannot change based on the players' actions, the designers made a number of decisions that allow players to still feel like the story is their own. First of all, though the objectives themselves do not change, the order in which players attempt many of the missions is left to their own discretion. Furthermore, players can play through the game's main story arc without even going on all the missions, meaning each user will likely play a different subsection of the content that is available. Also, in *Grand Theft Auto III* the designers deliberately kept the main character mute so players could feel more immersed in the game, avoiding the distancing effect of having a main character that talks. Since players are already making choices in the game-world that define the personality of their character, keeping him from speaking allowed this personality to be dominant in the players' minds, instead of something the designers established for them. Interestingly, *Vice City* added speech for the main character, though this was not particularly praised by users or the press.

Of course, one could hardly discuss *Grand Theft Auto III* without bringing up the controversy its release created in the mainstream media. What seems to have upset people the most was the players' ability to have the choice of running over innocent pedestrians and, specifically, paying to sleep with a prostitute and then killing her to get their money back. Such complaints seem to come from critics who do not fully understand the nature of an interactive world. In such a world, players have the choice to play as they want. Would it be better if pedestrians magically jumped out of the way of players' cars? What lesson would that impart to players? Indeed, many players of the game will go out of their way to avoid pointless killing. I have discussed the game with plenty of players who deliberately avoid killing innocents as they move through the world; they simply see it as something they don't want to do and it becomes part of their role-playing experience. In the end, creating a world where players are able to make meaningful choices means making a world where they may make some very bad choices indeed. The people who complain about a game that allows for the making of such poor choices are the same people who would prefer to censor what people can read and see in other media as well. If one believes in free speech for novels and films, one must also allow players the freedom to act as they want inside a simulated game-space.

I have seen a few members of the development community complain about all the awards that the game received. Surely a game that pushes violence and taboo subject matter as far as *Grand Theft Auto III* does should not be rewarded? Certainly, it should not be rewarded based on that alone, nor should it be rewarded based on its tremendous popular success. However, the fact of the matter is that *Grand Theft Auto III*, through its systems-based design and emergent gameplay, pushes games toward their tremendous potential more than most other games of recent memory. And based on that, the game truly deserves all of the accolades it has received.

Chapter 25:
Playtesting

"The common denominator, I would guess, is passion. Everyone says, 'Well, why aren't games better — why aren't there more really good games?' And I think that the answer is that what this industry doesn't do, amazingly, is play the games it makes. We create a game, we ask the teams to work all the hours God sends, and we don't give them time to play the game. That's really what makes the difference — sitting down and playing for hours and hours and hours."

— Peter Molyneux

Playtesting can be one of the most exhilarating parts of the game development cycle. It is then that you take the project you have been working on for months or years, during which time only the development team has played the game, and show it to people outside the team. And, if all goes well, you can watch as they are entertained by your work, want to play it more, compliment you on what you have done, and have suggestions for how you might make it better. Playtesting is not just a minor stepping-stone to getting the game shipped to the duplicators or uploaded to the

Internet. Instead, playtesting is a key time during which you can transform your game from average to excellent, from something that shows promise to a game that is truly great. Few games ever came out of the developer's hands in absolutely perfect shape. Ideally, it is the playtesting cycle that gives your game the extra push to be the best it possibly can.

It is worth clarifying what exactly I mean when I say playtesting. This is not the same as debugging. Debugging is a more programming-oriented task in which all of the inherently broken aspects of the game are tracked down and fixed. This can be anything from the improper implementation of some game mechanics to graphical snafus to problems that actually crash the game. Certainly these bugs must be eliminated, but this is more a matter of concern for the programming team.

Playtesting is the design equivalent of bug fixing, though it is considerably less cut and dried. When playtesters look at a game, they try to see if the game is any fun and try to find faults in the game mechanics. This can be anything from a unit in an RTS game that is too powerful and allows players who acquire it early to totally dominate the game, to the illogical nature of how one enemy AI agent attacks players, to an unintuitive and difficult-to-use control system. It is in the playtesting stage that the game mechanics are tested and refined. Unfortunately, some game developers focus entirely on fixing bugs and too little on determining if the game is actually any fun to play. As a result there may be nothing actually wrong with the game, and it may be completely stable on all the systems it is supposed to run on. Too bad that no one wants to play the game because it is not any fun. All players would rather have a game that plays really well and crashes occasionally than one that runs flawlessly but is not worth the time it takes to play it. At least the former game is fun some of the time, while the latter game is boring all of the time.

Finding the Right Testers

Finding the right testers is perhaps one of a game designer's biggest challenges in playtesting his game. Not just anyone will be able to playtest a game effectively. Almost any player can tell you whether he likes your game or not, but a surprisingly small number will be able to explain why they do not like it and what you might do to improve it. Of course, getting feedback from someone's general impression of the game can be useful: "that was fun" or "that was tedious" or "that was too hard" are all pieces of information you will be able to apply to your work in order to make your game better. Truly useful advice, however, comes in a more constructive form: "When I was fighting the twelfth clown on level three, I thought he was too hard to defeat. I had no idea what I was supposed to do to kill him, or whether the attacks I was attempting were having any effect at all. I thought maybe I was supposed to roll the boulder at him, but I could not figure out how to do so." In this example, the playtester has provided the designer with very specific information about the problem and a detailed explanation of why he thought it was not much fun to play. Playtesters who can do that sort of analysis consistently are extremely rare, making a talented playtester a truly priceless asset for your team.

A key part of working with testers effectively is knowing them well enough to know how seriously to take their opinions and what biases they may have. Different testers will have different motivations, which will necessarily color the opinions they give you. This is why picking a random person off the street to test your game can sometimes be ineffective, since you have no past experience with him and hence do not know whether you can trust his opinion or not. When you do have experience with a particular tester, you will be able to know if that person has any shortcomings. For example, some testers can be best described as "whiners" who complain about every-thing, even things that do not need fixing. Other testers may be shy, only saying, "Maybe you should look at the power of the Elephant Rider unit," when what they truly mean is, "Obviously, the Elephant Rider completely throws off the game." Try your best to understand the personalities of the testers you will be working with; it is key to effectively using the feedback they give you. And in the end, regardless of the testers' tendencies, if a number of them bring up a similar issue, then something probably is wrong, even if they are diagnosing the problem incorrectly. Similarly, if you have enough random people off the street tell you something is amiss with your game, it is probably worth investigating.

Who Should Test

There are various types of playtesters a project may have, and it is a good idea to have some from each group working on your project. No one type of tester can provide all of the feedback you need for your project. Indeed, it makes sense for there to be a good number of testers, since having a broad range of opinions can be essential to getting beyond individual bias and understanding if your game plays well or not. While argu-ments can be made for keeping the size of your team small, especially in terms of designers and programmers, with playtesters more truly are merrier.

The first type of playtester is a member of the development team. These are cer-tainly not the only testers you should have, and some would not technically consider these people playtesters. However, throughout the project, it is important to have your team members playing your game. This serves multiple purposes. First, it keeps them enthused about the project. Assuming development is going well, they see to what end their art, sound, code, or level construction is being used. Second, as they see their work in action, they are better able to understand how it might be improved. And third, they can provide you feedback about how the game is working and what you might do to improve it. Toward the end of the project, in particular, as all of the art, most of the code, and the levels are completed, the members of the development team will be able to pro-vide essential feedback about sections of the game that might need some last-minute improvements. Of course, members of the development team are very close to the pro-ject, and as a result may be far from objective in their comments about it. Furthermore, since they have been playing the game for so long, they will have trouble seeing it with a fresh set of eyes and their opinions will be skewed accordingly. Also, since they have contributed to the project, they may tend to like or dislike their own work for personal reasons. Similarly, they may like or dislike the ideas of other members of the team not because of the merits of the ideas themselves but rather because of their opinions of that person. Despite these drawbacks, getting playtesting feedback from the members of your team is essential.

The second type of playtester to have is the traditional playtester. This is someone who starts playtesting your game around the stage it enters "alpha" and is actually fully playable, and continues until the project ships. Often these playtesters spend half of their time tracking down bugs in the code, but they also provide vital feedback about how the game is playing, whether it is too easy or too difficult, if the controls are intuitive or obtuse, and so forth. On fully funded projects, these testers are typically paid employees who spend a full workweek playtesting your game and providing bug reports. Typically these testers love computer games and play a lot of them, both as part of their job and in their off time. Therefore, their opinions of how the gameplay needs to change are understandably skewed to the perspective of the hard-core gamer. Also, since these testers work on the project for such a long time, they can become used to certain inherent problems with the game, and may stop complaining about those shortcomings.

Many first-impression testers were used to refine and perfect the interface in *The Sims*.

The third class of playtesters are first-impression testers. Will Wright, in his interview in Chapter 22, refers to these people as "kleenex testers" since at Maxis they are used once and then never used again. Wright used them extensively to test the GUI for *The Sims*. These are people who are neither on the development team nor testing the game full time. Instead, these testers play the game for a short period of time and provide their gut reaction as to how well the game plays. This may be for a few hours or a few days. These first-impression testers are useful because they see the game as first-time players would. They can provide essential feedback about unintuitive controls, unclear presentation of information, or unfairly difficult portions of the game. It is essential when observing these first-impression testers that the developers say nothing to coach them or influence how they play. Furthermore, the important point about first-impression testers is that you must keep bringing in new ones, since a human can only truly have a first impression of a game once; after that they are "tainted" by their knowledge of how the game works. Especially toward the end of the project, when the development team is extremely familiar with the game and the traditional playtesters have played it for a thousand hours or more, first-impression testers can be essential to making sure the game is not too hard to learn to play.

The fourth type of playtesters includes game designers or developers not actually working on your project. These are people whom you know and trust and whose opinions you respect. They may not be able to test your project full time as traditional testers can, but the feedback they provide can be extremely useful. Fellow game designers who are not working on your project will be able to play your game and provide insight about its strengths and weaknesses in ways that other testers cannot. These testers understand game design in a way that allows them to analyze how your project may come up short and how it might be improved. Many experienced game designers will use these testers particularly early in the process, when they are still trying to get a sense of whether their new game design is truly compelling or not. These game designers turned testers will be better able to overlook the game's obvious shortcomings at this early stage, such as bugs or incomplete features, and can look beyond to see if the game shows the promise of becoming a good game in the future. Steve Meretzky, in Chapter 10, mentions how useful the "Imp Lunches" were. At these lunches, the Infocom implementers would gather to discuss their different game design ideas. When a new Infocom title first became playable, other implementers would be the first to start testing the game, while there was still time to make any fundamental changes necessary. Of course, fellow game designers will typically be too busy to spend a lot of time playing your game and giving you feedback. Whatever feedback these fellow designers give you can be extremely helpful, both in helping you pinpoint problem areas you had not anticipated, as well as reassuring you that your design is on the right course, if it actually is. If you are not fortunate enough to have developer friends with enough free time to assess your game, there are numerous design consultants in the industry who, for a fee, are available to review your work and provide valuable feedback.

The fifth class of testers that I find to be of particular value are non-gamers. All of the types of testers I have discussed thus far have, for the most part, been pretty big fans of games. They will have an especially high tolerance for the things that games traditionally do badly, such as having overly complex controls or simply being too hard to play. Having some people who are not big enthusiasts can provide fabulous feedback, pointing out fundamental problems that hard-core gamers will overlook and forgive. These testers can be literally anyone: the guy who comes to fix the coffee machine, a neighbor, a team member's parent, or literally someone right off the street. As long as they will be honest about what they think of your game, anyone's opinion can be valuable here. Combining the third group, first-impression testers, with non-gamer testers can be particularly useful in determining if an interface is too confusing or the game is too unforgiving. These testers will seldom be able to provide constructive feedback on how you might improve your game, but they will be able to point out fundamental problems in a way that other testers cannot.

Who Should Not Test

There are a number of people or groups of people whom you typically cannot trust as playtesters. These are people whose opinions are colored by their own personal motivations, or who may be unwilling to provide truly objective opinions. Though you may be forced to hear the feedback of these people, it is important to understand the motivations behind their comments so that you can apply their advice appropriately.

The first of these inappropriate testers is your boss. A key part of the game designer's relationship with a playtester is being able to get the playtester's feedback and then apply it as the designer sees fit, not as the playtester dictates. Playtesters often do not understand the game well enough to provide the best solution for a problem they encounter, and if your boss is the person who has found the problem it is likely he will try to impose a solution on you, even if it is not the best one for the situation. Some bosses may be wise enough to understand that, as the game's designer, you know how best to fix an issue. They show you the problems, and don't care how you fix it. Nonetheless, getting advice from someone who is signing your paycheck cannot be the same as advice from someone who is in a less dominant position.

The second class of people ill suited to testing your game includes anyone from the marketing department. Marketing people have too many conflicting agendas when looking at your game and are unlikely to tell you what they actually think of it. Instead, they will attempt to figure out what the "target demographic" wants. As I have mentioned repeatedly in this book, it is extremely hard to anticipate what an audience other than yourself will like or dislike, yet this is what marketing people attempt to do. You do not want their second-guessing, which when it comes to gameplay is wrong as often as it is right, to muddle up your game. Furthermore, the opinions of these people are likely to be colored by whatever is "hot" in the industry right now, often falling into the "game of the week" syndrome. All this does not mean their feedback does not have value, merely that you need to understand how it is affected by their own agenda. Regardless, you should not consider feedback from them the same way you consider the rest of your playtesting data.

A third group of people who should not test your game consists of those who are too close to you personally, be they your close friends from way back, your family, or your significant other. When these people look at your game, though they may claim they are being objective, their true agenda is often to strengthen their relationship with you. As a result they will be hesitant to criticize your game too harshly. Some friends may understand that the best way they can strengthen their friendship with you is to tell you the truth, but many will sugarcoat their opinions out of misguided kindness. It is true that many authors use their spouses as their first and most effective line of criticism, and if you can develop a relationship that is that honest it can be a wonderful thing. But the fact remains that many relationships are not that honest, and you should not deceive yourself that their feedback is completely objective.

The fourth type of people that you do not want to have testing your game is idiots. Idiots tend to say idiotic things and have idiotic opinions, and as a result will not be of much help to you. It is best to notice and isolate idiots as soon as possible and, if you must work with them, learn to ignore everything they say. Of course, I am exaggerating; idiots certainly do not dominate testing teams. But every so often you will come across a tester whom you are better off ignoring completely.

The fifth group is testers who think that they are designing your game for you. These testers may have some useful suggestions, but mostly will try to get you to change aspects of your game not because they are wrong but simply because they would have done it differently. A truly good tester will recognize that you are the driving artistic force behind the project and that the game will reflect your individual preferences. They will suggest ways to strengthen the game, instead of ways to simply change it.

A sixth group to be wary of is extremely hard-core fans, particularly those who are fanatical about your game's genre or, in the case of a sequel, the previous version of the game. These testers will tend to see every difference in your game from other games in the same genre as being a serious design flaw and will, as a result, stifle whatever creativity you may try to incorporate in your new game. Appealing to the established fans of your franchise can be quite important for sequels; yet following every bit of their advice may result in a game that is not sufficiently different from its predecessors.

When to Test

When is the right time to start playtesting your game? As I have discussed earlier in this chapter, playtesting can be a key part of your game's development cycle from as soon as you get your game playable until it is finally released. That said, there are specific times when particular types of testing are best applied, and other times when certain types of testing may be ineffective or even pointless. Knowing when to use each type of tester is key to not wasting their time.

Of course, your development team should be playing the game as much as possible through all the phases of its development. As I have mentioned, this is essential to keep them interested in the project and to enable them to do the best work possible. Assuming the game is not falling apart, a developer who knows exactly how he is contributing to the project and how that project is turning out will be better informed and motivated to do his best work possible.

Early playtesting is best done by people experienced in game development, whom you know very well, and whose opinions you hold in high regard. Early playtesting requires that the tester overlook many problems: the game crashes frequently, all of the art is place-holder, sections of the game are obviously incomplete, there is only one level to play, and so forth. Many people, when given such a game, will be unable to look beyond these extreme shortcomings. For instance, traditional testers, even if you tell them to ignore the large sections of the game that are missing, will most likely start pointing out the completely obvious bugs that need fixing. However, a fairly experienced QA lead will understand the development process better and can start providing valuable feedback fairly early in the project. Additionally, a friend who is also a game designer will be able to look at the work and see beyond its current shortcomings, seeing instead if the game shows promise. These designers have seen their own projects in the state yours is currently in, and understand why not everything works yet. These experienced professionals will be able to recognize and explain fundamental problems your game design contains better than anyone else.

It makes good sense to establish a small group of people whose opinions you trust and whom you can show your game to at various stages of development. These may be fellow game designers, as discussed above, or friends who understand the game development process and will be able to provide you with useful feedback. Over the course of the project, you may want to keep showing your game to this trusted group, so they can see how the game is progressing and give you their opinions on whether they like where the game is going and if they think that direction is the best one possible. Since these testers will work with you over the course of the project, they will have a better understanding of the game and why it has developed as it has. And as I mentioned before, if you are unable to call in favors with friends who have this much experience, you may want to consider hiring a design consultant to come in periodically over the course of the project and critique your work.

As you are implementing the GUI and the controls, it will make sense to bring in some first-impression testers to experiment with these new controls. Set up a simple test level, area, or situation where players can attempt to use the controls and GUI, and see how well these testers fare. This makes sense since the most important aspect of interface and control design is that these systems are as intuitive as possible, and the best way to determine that is by having some first-time players try them out. It should not take very long to determine if your I/O systems are intuitive, since if players do not figure them out immediately, you will know your game needs work.

As the game becomes more complete, when a majority of the features are complete and a large section of the game is playable, it makes sense to bring in the traditional testers to go over the work. This period is typically called "alpha," though this definition varies from company to company. When they first start testing, the traditional testers will find a seemingly endless number of bugs in the code, as they try all manner of actions that the development team had never anticipated, but you should encourage them to look beyond the bugs and give you feedback about the gameplay itself if they can. Of course, getting feedback at this early stage is much better than in "beta" when, if the project is on a tight schedule, the focus will be less on refining the game and more on getting it out the door. At some point, you stop being able to make fundamental changes to the gameplay for fear it will break the game in some major way. As a result, you will need to make large-scale alterations while there is still plenty of time to track down all the bugs they may cause. Even with simple game balancing, without time to fully test the repercussions of a change, you stop being able to change anything for fear it will throw something else off. This is why starting gameplay testing early enough that you can still fix the problems is so essential.

On projects with tight deadlines and "must ship by Christmas" edicts, management sometimes likes to think that they can speed up development by bringing in testers early, sometimes long before the game has even reached alpha. This way, they erroneously think, once the game finally gets to beta it will already have had most of its bugs removed and can be shipped immediately. Of course, what they fail to understand is that, before a game is "feature complete," it is likely to change fundamentally from a code point of view. As that code changes in major ways, old bugs are eliminated completely while new ones are introduced. If the testers point out bugs in old code and the programmers have to spend time fixing them, this is essentially wasted time since those bugs would have been eliminated completely later when chunks of the code were rewritten, and you are still left with the new bugs that the restructuring of the code will bring about. That said, it may make sense to bring on a small group of very experienced testers earlier who can do targeted testing of specific systems the development team thinks are ready for testing.

To some extent, the same holds true for gameplay. When large parts of the game are missing, having testers report problems like "Levels 10, 12, and 17 have no enemies to fight and are therefore not much fun to play" is far from useful. Forcing designers to go through these meaningless bugs will waste far more time than it may save. It makes the most sense to bring in the traditional testers only when the game is in a state that is truly appropriate for testing. In the end, bringing them in too early will only delay the game's progress.

How to Test

How you have your playtesters work on your game is as important as who you have testing and when you have them do it. Game designers will often ruin the effectiveness of their playtesters by making a number of fundamental errors in how they interact with them. These are all problems that can be easily avoided, as long as the designer is conscious of the way he deals with his testers and what he does and does not tell them.

The most important part of interacting with playtesters is to actually spend most of your time watching them play instead of telling them how to play. Let them play the game their own way and see how they fare. The temptation to correct playtesters' actions is great and can be hard to resist. By the time the traditional playtesters start on the game, the designer has already played the game so much that he is intimately familiar with what the players are "supposed" to do in a given situation and how the game is "supposed" to be played in general. When watching over the shoulder of a playtester for the first time, the temptation is to say, "Go over there next," or "You want to use the strafe buttons for that," or "Why don't you try to get the power-foozle?" Watching someone stumble while playing a game the designer is intimately familiar with can quickly turn him into a teacher.

But the point of the playtesting is to see how players will actually play the game without the game's designer coaching his every move. Certainly, the designer cannot fit in the box the game comes in or even be downloaded over the Internet. A certain amount of stumbling about and learning the controls is to be expected, and the best way to playtest is to let the testers do this initial exploration on their own. And if the players truly do get stuck or if they never seem to be able to master the controls, the designer needs to ask himself what is causing these problems. Is the game too hard or too confusing? How can it be made simpler so that players have a fair chance of understanding it and learning how to play? These are the lessons a designer is supposed to take away from playtesting, but they are lessons the designer is never going to learn if he corrects the tester's playing at every step. Beyond that, when I sit in on a playtesting session, if the testers do not know any better, I try to pretend I am not on the development team to avoid having them color their opinions to be nice to me. Indeed, most gameplay focus tests are conducted using a one-way mirror, since people will behave differently when they think they are alone than if they have someone standing over their shoulders taking notes, regardless of how quiet that person is or who he claims to be.

While watching the testers play, the designer should try to observe the way in which they try to play the game. Players may not try the approach or solution the designer had thought of to a particular situation. The designer must then ask, does the game support what the tester is trying to do, and if not, could it and should it? The testing period, if started early enough, is a time when the designer can add a breadth of content to the game that will allow the game to truly be accepting of multiple playing styles. Up until this point, the people playing the game have been limited to the development team and the preliminary testers that may have been brought in. Now that there is a broader range of people playing the game, the designer will likely observe a broader range of playing styles than he had anticipated. The testing period is when the designer can make the game accepting of these playing styles, allowing players to truly play the game their own way on their own terms.

Of course, the designer cannot be present for all of the playtesting the game will undergo, not if the game is going to be thoroughly tested and released in a reasonable time frame. Often you will need to rely on what the testers report to you about their playing experiences. Though not as useful as watching the testers play firsthand, this information can nonetheless be quite helpful. When you do get this feedback, it is crucial to truly listen to what the testers tell you. This may seem obvious, but it is surprising how many designers prefer to ignore the feedback they get on their game. Often most of a game's testing, particularly that done by traditional testers, takes place late in the development process, after a good deal of work has gone into the project. At this point the designer is probably fairly confident that the game is working as he wants it to work. Therefore, it can be difficult for the designer to hear testers contradict this, perhaps pointing out fundamental problems in the game that the designer has overlooked for months of development.

The designer's first defense is often to claim that the testers do not know what they are talking about. Excuses can range from the tester being a fool to the tester not being the target audience for the game to the tester just complaining for the sake of it. Granted, often testers do make suggestions for changes to the gameplay that are best avoided, and if only one tester out of ten suggests that a certain piece of gameplay needs to be changed it may be because of that tester's personal preference. But when the designer hears the same complaint from a number of different testers, he needs to realize that there probably is something wrong with the game that needs to be addressed. The testers may not even be complaining about the right aspect of the game or suggesting an appropriate fix, but the fact that something is ruining their experience warrants investigation. The designer must avoid dismissing the complaints of testers and honestly look at each complaint to see if it has any merit. It is amazing the number of designers who will resist any and all suggestions the testers make. Often, these same designers come to regret their obstinacy later when the game is finally released, only to have players and members of the press complain about the same issues the testers had complained about earlier. Of course, once the game is released, it is too late to do anything radical about the problems.

Guided and Unguided Testing

One can divide the kind of testing being done on the project into two distinct classes: guided and unguided. Guided testing customarily happens earlier in the project, when the game is not yet completely functional. In that period, the designer knows what portions of the game are clearly incomplete, but wants to get some feedback on a section of the game he thinks is working fairly well. Then the designer may direct the testers to try a particular level or section of gameplay. Directed testing may also occur later in the project, when the entire game is functioning but a particular section has just been changed or reworked. At this point the designer may need feedback on just that section, to see if the changes fix an existing problem or break the game in some major way. A designer may also direct his testers to try crazy and illogical ways of playing the game, to see if the game breaks under those circumstances. What may seem like a foolish way to play the game to you or even the tester may well be a style many players will try to use when playing the final product. More experienced testers know to keep trying every play style they can imagine when testing the game.

It is essential to allow and encourage your testers to do unguided testing as well. Give them the game, tell them to start playing it, observe what they do, and listen to their feedback. Many designers make the mistake of using only guided testing, usually having the testers test only the system on which they are currently working. When the testers bring up complaints about some other portion of the game, the designer will complain that he is not interested in working on that now, or that the problematic part of the game is already "done." Directed testing has its place, but if it is all the designer ever does, then he is likely to miss larger problems in the game that he may not have even realized were problematic. Undirected testing gives the designer feedback about the game holistically, something that is essential to resolving all of its problems.

Of course, even when you do direct your testers to test only a certain section of your game, often they will not be able to resist pointing out the other problems they see along the way. It takes an extremely disciplined tester to truly test only the system that the designer requests. Getting feedback on parts of the game that you are not currently working on may be frustrating but can be useful in the long run. When testers give you off-topic suggestions about how to improve the game, even if you do not want to address those issues immediately, be careful to take note of them to come back to later. Nothing is more frustrating than recognizing a problem in the game after it has shipped, only to realize that one of your testers had told you about the problem in plenty of time to fix it.

Balancing

The only time you can properly balance a game is when most of the game is done. Balancing your game ahead of time, before all of the gameplay is working and all the levels, if any, are made, can only be considered to be preliminary balancing. Preliminary balancing can be very valuable, however, and you will want to do it just to get your game fun as early as possible, with the full knowledge that you will need to adjust it later. That said, you cannot truly get a sense for how the entire game needs to function and how the difficulty must escalate over the course of the entire game until the game's content is complete. You can view your game as a collection of different systems that make up one large system. For a level-based game, each level can be considered to be a system in itself. Then, within each level, each combat encounter or puzzle can be considered to be a system. In order for the game to be balanced, all of these systems must be in place, since changing one system impacts how the other systems must be set up in order to achieve the overall balance you are seeking. At the same time, if you wait for all the systems to be final and some are running behind, you may well run out of time to get the game as balanced as you want. For example, on *The Suffering*, too many aspects of the levels were not completed until quite late in development, and as a result balancing was put off until it was too late to do it to the quality level we would have liked. Starting balancing a little earlier, before every last element of the game is in place, may be necessary to make sure you do not run out of time.

Balancing in *The Suffering* took place very late in development.

The time at which the game is largely complete and true balancing becomes possible usually coincides with the time when the game is in full-on testing. This works out for the best, since balancing and testing are closely intertwined activities. Balancing often involves changing some settings in the game and then playing it to see if those changes create the amount of challenge you are interested in. For each pass on the balancing, both you and the playtesters should try to play the game. Then the testers can give you feedback about just how effective your efforts to balance the game have been and, combined with your own analysis of the game's condition, you can make more changes and iterate through the process again. People who can successfully balance a game by themselves, without the input of other playtesters, are rare. Often designers who attempt to balance a game by themselves succeed in balancing the game only for themselves, usually resulting in the game being too hard.

The best way to balance the game is to break down different systems into groups of numbers that can be easily adjusted and tweaked. For instance, suppose you were making a melee combat action game of some sort. If the players use a baseball bat in the game, that bat will have a number of different attributes associated with it, such as how much damage it does, how fast it attacks, how many times it can be used before it breaks, how much it costs to buy, how many hands are required to hold it, and so forth. Similarly, one can also break down enemy, player, and other system attributes into collections of numbers that can then be adjusted to vary the usefulness or challenge of that object. It is these values that you will continually adjust and massage in order to achieve the balance you are seeking. This of course assumes that at a basic level your game is already fun, with a sufficient variety of challenging encounters. If you wait until too late to get the game fun at a basic level, it may become too risky to make the changes necessary.

As you are balancing, you must be keenly aware of how the different values you change affect each other. You may change one weapon in order to make one combat situation a lot of fun but end up making another location in the game actually unbeatable. The more complex your game, the more impact the changes you make may have on systems you might overlook. As you are balancing you must fully consider every part of the game that your changes are affecting and make sure you do not break the game. The only way to be truly sure you have not thrown off the entire game is by testing it thoroughly. As a result, making significant changes close to your ship date is a nerve-racking experience. What if the changes you make break something that no one catches before the game is sent to the duplicator?

Of course, the method for balancing I have described above necessitates that the data that affects the behavior of the game's different entities be accessible and modifiable by the designer. This means that the code needs to be written in such a way that makes changing this information easy. This last point may seem obvious, but I have seen many engines in which changing information such as weapon statistics was far from easy to outright impossible. From the very beginning of the game's development, the programmers must keep in mind how the designers will go about balancing the game at the end of the project. If, instead, they bury a collection of "magic numbers" in the code, the game will become "locked" in a particular state, making balancing it impossible. Though balancing can only take place once the game is largely complete, the programming team must start preparing for that balancing from the very beginning of the project or effective balancing will be impossible. If the designer is to have any chance of balancing the game well, this balancing information must be broken out of the code through configuration files, level editing tools, or other designer-accessible formats.

Your Game Is Too Hard

When I wrote the first edition of this book, I included the following paragraph:

> While balancing your game you should keep one rule of thumb in mind at all times: your game is too hard. Regardless of the type of game you are making or how talented your development team may be, by the time your game nears completion and enters testing it will be too hard.

Having just completed *The Suffering*, however, I can now say that this is not always the case. Following the "your game is too hard" rule of thumb, we managed to make *The Suffering* too easy, at least according to the press and many of the fans. This was in part because we did not allocate enough time to balancing the game, as I mentioned earlier. Nevertheless, I still think the above paragraph holds a lot of truth, since most of the time games are too hard when they enter the balancing phase.

Games usually turn out too hard because, up to the point at which testing starts, only the development team has been playing the game consistently. The development team has been working on the project anywhere from nine to eighteen months and during that time they have honed their gameplaying skills and have become quite good at the game, probably better than 90 percent of the players who will ever play the game. In order to keep the gameplay interesting for themselves, the development team has made the game somewhat challenging for themselves to play, which in turn means it will be too hard for 90 percent of the players out there.

The first comment testers will often make is, "This game is too hard." As I discussed above, your first reaction will be to ignore this complaint, to chalk it up to their incompetence or inexperience with the game. "They'll get better," you may say. And, unfortunately, that is true. If the game spends three months in testing, the testers will be just as good at the game as the rest of the development team. Then they too will probably stop thinking that the game is hard. It is entirely likely that the game will ship with the development team, including the testers, having no clue just how difficult it is.

As a designer you must be very careful to maintain an honest sense of how hard your game is, and during the balancing phase you must concentrate on making the game something that first-time players will have a reasonable chance of succeeding at when they first start playing. Always remember what the first impression of the testers was, and ask yourself if you have addressed the problems they immediately identified. If necessary, you should bring in new first-impression testers to see if the game is still too difficult.

Unfortunately, sometimes you may not always be able to make your game easier through balancing alone. You may have created a game design that, on a fundamental level, is hard to play. If you truly want your game to be something first-time players have an easy time getting into, you need to concentrate on this from the very beginning of your game design. My project *Centipede 3D* is a good example of how a game can become far more difficult than the development team ever anticipated. Attempts were made to balance the game to make it easier, but the gameplay was intrinsically designed to match that of the original arcade game. As a direct result, *Centipede 3D* did everything it could to make the players' game short and fast paced. Unfortunately, players of home games want their games to last a little longer than what they get for 25 cents at the arcade. As hard as the game was in its shipping version, it is chilling to think that before it went into the balancing phase the game was easily ten times as hard.

The *Marathon* games were tested for difficulty by forcing the development team to play through the game on the hardest difficulty setting using only the weakest weapon, the fist. Pictured here: *Marathon 2*.

When designer Jason Jones was balancing the *Marathon* games, he had an interesting technique for making sure the game was not too hard. If he and other members of the development team could play through the entire game on its hardest setting using only the game's "fist" weapon, he figured that the game would be reasonably challenging for other players. Of course, other players get weapons far more powerful and easy to use than the fist, and they do not have to play it on the hardest difficulty setting. Jones handicapped himself in order to see how hard the game would be to normal players. Using techniques like this is wise. If the designer can win the game with both arms tied behind his back, other players will probably have a fair chance of playing it through with both arms at their disposal.

In the end, balancing your game is often more of a "gut feeling" than anything else. Some developers, such as Microsoft, have tried to develop more objective tests to determine how well balanced a game is, accumulating player metrics about the average time players spent in a level, number of times they failed a challenge before passing it, how much ammo they used up, and so forth. Though this data can be quite valuable, it can never fully replace design instinct. Though you may almost always assume that your game is too hard, there are few other rules you can follow to balance your game. You need to be able to see your game holistically, to understand how players who have much less experience with the title than you will play it, and to realize what will challenge them without being unfair or even cruel. Knowing how to balance a game is a skill that comes with experience, both from playing other games and from designing your own. In order to become truly skilled at balancing, you must do both as much as possible.

The Artistic Vision

I have mentioned at various points throughout this book the evil that is known as the focus group. It is important to understand the distinction between playtesters and focus groups. Focus groups, particularly those gathered early in a game's development, are customarily groups of "off the street" people who are given a one- or two-hour presentation, often on a series of different games. Many times they are not allowed to play the games, as often the games have not even been developed yet. They hear about game concepts and, based on the descriptions, are asked whether they would be interested in buying such a game or not. Playtesters, on the other hand, are people whom members of the development team know or whom they at least have a chance to get to know. Knowing a person is crucial to understanding how seriously you should take their opinion. Furthermore, playtesters get to play the games in question, while early focus group members often do not. As a result of these key differences, focus groups tend to be antithetical to the creation of original, creative games and encourage the development of safe, less innovative games. As Mark Cerny has put it, a focus group can tell you primarily "what was cool fifteen minutes ago." One can only imagine how the focus group for games like *Pac-Man*, *Tetris*, or *Civilization* would react. We know from the interview with Will Wright in Chapter 22 that the focus group for *The Sims* went so poorly that the game was nearly canceled. It should be telling that focus groups are run by the marketing department, while playtesting is handled by the development team. One group's primary interest lies in making money for the company in the simplest way possible, while the second, it is hoped, is interested in producing compelling and stimulating games. Of course, the two motives need not necessarily be at odds, but when one aims primarily for the former instead of the latter, one is likely to end up with neither. Focus groups can also be conducted later in development, when the group can actually play a section of the game. These tests can be much more useful and informative, particularly when trying to get the opinions of people who do not play many games. Since these are "off the street" people, however, it will be difficult to gauge each person's individual opinion. As a result, for the focus test data to be statistically valid, you will need a fairly large number of participants.

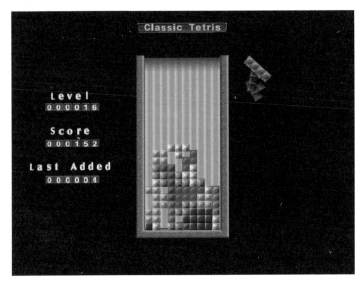

When released, *Tetris* was an extremely unique game. Chances are, an early focus group for the game would have gone terribly. Pictured here: classic mode in *The Next Tetris*.

As you are testing, it is important to remember that you cannot please everyone. Given a large enough testing team, there are bound to be people who dislike portions of your game, or even who dislike the entire game. If you start trying to make every single person on the testing team happy, you often end up making the game less fun for other people. While you may have started with a game that a bunch of people liked a great deal and a few people thought was dull, if you start trying to please everyone you may end up with a game that everyone thinks is OK, but which no one is truly enthusiastic about. Given the choice, I always prefer to give a certain group of people an experience they truly love than try to give everyone something they like only marginally.

Playtesting should also not mean game design by committee. You do not have to take every suggestion that your development team presents and implement it. Some of these ideas may be perfectly reasonable but you may feel that they just do not fit with your game. That is a totally acceptable response to have. In the end, it may be that every single playtester you have tells you that some part of the game must change, but if you feel, in your gut, as an artist, that you do not want to change that portion of the game, then leave it as it is. In the end you must be the final arbiter of what happens in the game. A committee, whether it consists of executives, testers, or even members of the development team, can never have the unity of vision and certainty of purpose that can be maintained by a single person. This makes game development a significantly more risky proposition for the game designer, since if the game fails he will be the one largely to blame. At the same time, if it succeeds people will recognize his impressive achievement. In the end, being an artist and doing quality work is all about taking risks.

Chapter 26:
Interview: Doug Church

In an industry increasingly intent on delivering a more cinematic, highly orchestrated, and largely scripted experience to gamers, some developers have continued to buck the trend. These mavericks insist that it is not the game designer alone who should create a game experience, but instead the designer and player in collaboration. By creating games where players make meaningful and complex choices, these designers endeavor to emphasize the interactivity that, among all art forms, only games can provide. It is interesting to note that most of these developers are somehow tied to the history of Boston-based developer Looking Glass Studios, which in the 1990s created a string of uniquely compelling games that were far ahead of their time. One of the original small band of designer/programmers there at the start of Looking Glass, Doug Church was one of the primary design visionaries of the studio. In particular, his three games *Ultima Underworld*, *System Shock*, and *Thief* all pushed the boundaries of what an immersive and systems-based game could be, all while blending in innovative storytelling techniques. Church is that rare designer who has fully abdicated the authorship of the gameplay experience to his players, counting on their creativity to complete the equation that leads to a truly compelling interactive experience.

What was your driving motivation to get into game development?

I worked on some little games in college with some friends, and so I was sort of interested in gaming then. I fell in with some friends and started writing some online games on the side, nothing too sophisticated, but it was fun to do little three- to four-person creative projects. My first gig wasn't games, though, it was network simulations. But then when I heard that a friend of a friend was starting a games group, I thought, "Well sure, that sounds like more fun." I don't know, driving motivation might be a little strong, but I was definitely into it. And I definitely had been looking for opportunities to do games.

What about game development attracted you to it?

I had always played games. The whole idea of being in an interactive experience is really compelling and the idea to author that and let people try things was always something that seemed cool. I've always enjoyed reading fiction, and games just seemed like a natural step in some ways. Different in other ways too.

What were the origins of the *Ultima Underworld* project?

Paul Neurath and Ned Lerner had gone to Wesleyan together, and afterward they did a game called *Deep Space* for Sir Tech. Then Paul went off and did *Space Rogue* for Origin and Ned went off and did an early *Chuck Yeager* for EA, and then he did *Car & Driver*. *Space Rogue* had already been half RPG but with a very, very low polygon count

Ultima Underworld: The Stygian Abyss

3D flight engine. And so in that same vein he had this idea of doing a dungeon simulator. And so he assembled a little team of four of us in May of 1990, and using some of the assembly code from *Car & Driver*, some of Paul's old math code, plus a bunch of code we hacked together, we wrote a demo in May, which he then took to CES in June of 1990 to show to Origin. And he said to them, "Hey look, we'll do a 3D dungeon simulator; it'll be great." And they basically said, "Sure, whatever, tell us when it's done."

So then we kind of worked on it for a year, getting the basic tech going, and then pitched them a couple story concepts. And then the one that one of the other guys and I wrote caught enough that they were comfortable with it as an *Ultima*, and so we then just went ahead and built that, basically. We only went to Texas twice on that project, once at the ten-month point and once at the sixteen-month point. Warren [Spector] was the third producer on the project, but he was the one who stuck to it. He came in about halfway through the project, and then in the final quarter he started coming up to Boston a lot.

Origin wasn't overly protective of the *Ultima* franchise?

Well, the first story that was written, that I didn't write but one of the other guys wrote, was a little too traditional fantasy and not enough *Ultima* elements, and they said, "Well, this doesn't feel very *Ultima*. Try again." I was a huge *Ultima* fan, and Dan Schmidt, who was the other guy who wrote the story to *Underworld*, was maybe not as big an *Ultima* fan as I was, but still a pretty big fan. So we didn't approach it as what story did we want to write but instead what was a cool *Ultima* story we could tell. We certainly thought it was fun and interesting, but we were very conscious of how do we write an *Ultima* story here. We certainly didn't write the best or most amazing *Ultima* story ever written — we wrote it in about two days or whatever — but we were definitely thinking "There should be the eight virtues, and it's an *Ultima* story." And they were basically "Well, seems pretty *Ultima*, go for it."

***Ultima Underworld* seems to have been pretty ambitious in how it blended genres, combining simulation-style technology with an RPG. How did that come about?**

You've got to give Paul a lot of credit there first off, simply because he had the initial idea. And if you look back at *Space Rogue*, that was a 2D tile map *Ultima*-style RPG, but then you'd get in your ship and fly around in 3D and shoot pirates or not and shoot cops or not. It was a very early, fairly open-ended story RPG with a space flight 3D element. Which was definitely a very hybrid genre, because the space stuff was pretty glitzy, where there were wormholes where you had to follow these 3D rings through space, and there were battles and trading, and yet there was also this little story-based walk-around the tile map, talk to people, and so on game. So I think it came pretty naturally to Paul.

Of the original guys that were hired, there were a couple of people who had a tiny bit of game experience. One of them we got rid of fairly early because he wasn't appropriate for what we were doing, and then the other two guys we got were friends of mine from school who I recruited. So three of the four of us building the tech and all of

Ultima Underworld II: Labyrinth of Worlds

us doing the design, none of us had any game experience and we were all twenty. In college in the late '80s the consoles weren't nearly as big a deal. I had actually played *Space Rogue* because one of my friends had a Mac, but the clusters were all Unix boxes so I ran

X-Trek and *Net Hack* and things, but I hadn't played a PC game in five years or some-thing. So we just said, "Let's do a really cool dungeon game in 3D, let's go." It's interesting, because a lot of people talk about how we were doing such a *Dungeon Mas-ter* game, but as far as I know none of us had ever played *Dungeon Master*. It was a very much "Hey, let's go for it." We didn't have any idea that we were doing anything that wasn't just obvious in some sense, because we had no context and the last time any of us had played a game was back when we were fourteen. We played games in college, but they were very different; you're playing networked *X-Trek* or something, it doesn't feel like a home computer game. For *Underworld* we wrote four movement systems and we wrote three combat systems, because we'd just write something: "Oh, this seems cool, let's go for it." We'd get it half done, and we'd say, "Eh? That's not working." Which is nice in a lot of ways; it let us do a lot of things we probably wouldn't have done other-wise. But it also meant that we worked a lot. All the time, basically, for a long time. We spent a lot of time and a lot of energy to make it work.

Given all that, it is pretty impressive it turned out as well as it did.

It was kind of amazing it ever got done. I remember my first thought when I saw it in a store was, "Don't they know we're not professionals? We never got a license to do this! If people buy that, they'll realize..." It's pretty weird to see your thing shrink-wrapped. It's just very odd, you get that moment of, "Wait a second, I guess I just go do what I want to do with my life."

It's interesting. Paul was very day to day at the beginning of the project. Later he got more involved in running Looking Glass, which was Blue Sky at the time, starting up new projects and dealing with business stuff and money and all that. But I have to say he was a huge help at the beginning, just giving us a grounding framework that was very open. He was very good at painting a picture of where to go. He brought this idea of games as this awesome, creative, open thing and you can do all these amazing things, and what do we want to do? And I'm not sure it would work right now with an eighty-person for $12 million or whatever we do games for these days, but for three, four people in a tiny rented office space in New Hampshire, most of us twenty years old and not particularly being paid piles of money, it was awesome.

Paul set a very good example by finding the right staff. And a bunch of us had been at school together, so we had that "You're in college, and you're an engineer, and you go figure things out." Which, once again, often leads to a lot of thrashing and hard work and trying and retrying. It's sort of like we were always a preproduction team, because at our largest we were five. I knew every line of code, I knew every level, I wrote conver-sations, I wrote a bunch of the editor. You could hold the whole game in your head and that let you iterate and improvise in a way that's a lot harder now. So I think Paul set a really good agenda of "You're a programmer/designer, you've got to care about creativ-ity, you've got to get it done, you've got to know your computer, you've got to be smart, you've got to write fast code...." And for the final part of the game when Warren got really involved, not only was he great creatively to help us put finishing touches on it and clean it up and make it real, but he also knew how to finish projects and keep us motivated and on track. He had that ability to say, "Guys guys guys, you're focused in totally the wrong place." Working on *Underworld II* and *System Shock* with him, when I was project leading more full time, it was nice to have Warren there to say, "Hey

Warren, here's what I'm thinking, I'm trying to do this, this, and this…" in our weekly phone call, or once a month when he would come down to Boston. His ability to say, "Yeah, Doug, I hear all that stuff you're saying, but fifty percent of it you shouldn't even care about now. And twenty-five percent of it will be fine however you go; just pick something. The other twenty-five percent is pretty scary; we're going to need to figure that out. And you know there's this other twenty-five percent you're not even talking about and I don't know why. To me that's the scary stuff." He had that ability to help me and the rest of the guys reset, from the big-picture view of someone who has done it before and was really creative, but who also understood getting games done. It was a huge, huge win.

So we got really lucky, between Paul and Warren as our two experienced vets. The other programmer who wasn't from the school gang was an ex-Infocom guy who had done a ton of tools programming, and he just said, "Hey guys, come in to work and do the work, and get it done." So we had a decent balance early on to learn from, so that we didn't just get obsessed and be college kids flailing forever and trying to be super creative. But we also had enough pushing us that we didn't just try to get the code written as fast as possible and call it done. So we got pretty lucky in the people we had around us to learn from, look up to, and get ideas from.

Was there ever a worry from Origin that the *Underworld* gameplay was too much of a departure from the previous *Ultimas*?

I would say for the first year they didn't really think it was ever going to get done. They didn't pay any attention at all, frankly. We had two producers, one of whom quit without anyone there telling us. We called the switchboard after two months and asked, "Hey, we haven't heard from our producer in a while." "Oh, he doesn't work here anymore." "Awesome. I'm

Ultima Underworld II: Labyrinth of Worlds

sure that's good news for our project." And then the next producer didn't really get it either. I think we were very lucky to find Warren who was like "My God, first-person 3D immersive play simulation indoors! This is totally new and amazing!" Warren really believed in it. I think we had the advantage that our inventory panel looked very much like an *Ultima* inventory, and on some level things were just simpler then. There were fewer products and you collected swords and your points went up and you had some skills and, you know, rock and roll! That's somewhat glib, obviously; it was something we worked on for twenty hours a day for two years. Paul had done a couple of games with them, they were busy doing their games, and they thought the demo looked cool, and "Oh, you can move around and it's textured!" The first demo they saw had no lighting or anything; it was just a very simple wall texture, something that we did in three and a half weeks or something, so it was not exactly the most advanced piece of software ever written. I think they basically thought it was never going to work, it would never be fast enough, or it would never come together. And then, by the time Warren picked it up and got excited about it, we had the play experience already there. You could move around, you could fight, you could swing your weapon, and your stats moved around and that kind of thing. We pitched a couple of stories and they bought into it. And so they said, "OK, Warren, why don't you take care of it?"

We had a huge advantage in that even though we were trying to make a hybrid game and we were trying to figure out what a dungeon simulator was, we had all the *Ultima*-ness of it to fall back on. Sure, we were inventing how to move and how to swing your sword and all that stuff, but at the end of the day it was an *Ultima*. You talk, you get, you drop, you combine reagents, you use runes. We made up that spell system with the tiles because that worked better, but even there we used the *Ultima* runes. I was a huge *Ultima* fan. The first time I got to meet Richard, which was a year into the project, it was awesome. It was like, wow, it's Richard Garriott, rock and roll! I was so excited when I got my *Ultima VII* beta copy because we were working on an *Ultima* at the same time. We just really thought *Ultimas* were cool on some level, and it was cool to be working on it. I think they could tell that: "OK, these guys are trying to do the right thing." And the second story we brought was very *Ultima*, and they were like "OK, these guys want to do an *Ultima*." Once Warren got involved they obviously felt that Warren could help make sure things stayed on track, and it was pretty casual. There's a reason it's called "UW," because it wasn't *Ultima* at first, it was just *Underworld*. We did a lot of work on our own assuming that that was what it was going to be but knowing we had to prove our mechanics. And then hey, there it was…

It seems like *Ultima Underworld* was very much designed around the technology, instead of the other way around. How did the game design process work?

We'd all played *Wizardry I*. It's not like we had nothing in mind. I had played tons of *Bard's Tale 1* when I was in junior high school, and we'd played the early, early dungeon games. And we were obviously incredibly conscious of the technology. When you're sitting there timing all your assembler loops and trying to figure stuff out, there you are, right? And it's not like it was fast enough even with all our attempts to make it fast. Game making is a lot different when your programmers are your designers and you have one artist. It's just a very different thing. You're conscious of everything. You run the game, and you hit the hotkey to switch into editor mode and then you attach the trap and oh, the trap doesn't really have the parameter you want. So you exit, change the code, change the parameter, go back in, change the trap, go back into the game, hey that worked, and so on. Because who are you going to talk to about it? Obviously, the three of us who did most of the programming on the second half talked all the time, but even so, we all built levels, we all wrote conversations, we all worked on the editor, we all worked on the game. It's a very different thing. Back then, one person could easily have the whole game in their head. All disciplines, all elements, all content. Maybe not easily, that's probably a little glib, but they can do it. And then five years later you probably couldn't have the whole game in your head but you probably could have a whole discipline in your head, or the story, or how it's structured. And nowadays, if you're a project leader your job is to get the eight or ten managers all seeing vaguely the same thing. Because what you have to do is get those eighty people to all act like they're seeing the same thing. That's hard, because the fact that humans communicate at all is sort of magical, as far as I can tell. And when you're talking about creative collaboration, creative collaboration's really, really hard. I really do think as a project leader these days your job is to Vulcan mind meld your team.

How did *System Shock* originate? Did you have more of a formalized plan than with *Ultima Underworld*?

Probably a *little*. *Underworld II* was initially going to ship in February, but then we all tried to pull it in for Christmas. So inevitably we signed off on December 30th with everyone working overtime over Christmas, in that classic, genius game development way. So we shipped that in January, and I actually went down to Origin in Texas for a couple of weeks for that,

System Shock

while the guys were still up in Boston. And finally the final two guys in Boston and I would get on the phone and make sure I had all the new code and modem it back and forth and all that kind of excitement we had back then, reading hex checksums of all the files over the phone to make sure we were building the same thing. There's nothing like, three in the morning, reading off two hundred sets of hex numbers. Awesome, totally awesome. *Underworld* was at zero bugs for a week and a half, *Underworld II* actually was at close to zero bugs for a while but there was actually one bug in it that we failed to catch, so we were all embarrassed by that. Back then, your final couple of weeks there really were almost no bugs, you were trying to be at zero bugs for several weeks in a row with no new bugs found. So you had a fair amount of time, and you'd try to play your game to break it, but really, with your own game, there's only so many hours you can spend a day playing it before you completely burn out. So we started talking then about doing an immersive simulation game but taking it out of the fantasy space. We talked a little bit about going modern versus going sci-fi, but the only problem with going modern is it will just beg so many questions: why can't I pick up the phone, why can't I get on the train, and so on. So we did a bunch of talking, and we probably did three or four high-level designs for sci-fi games.

Do you mean you and Warren?

Mostly Warren and I, but Paul Neurath back in Boston along with Austin Grossman who was one of the writer/designer guys on *Underworld II*. So we all bounced some ideas around, and I think Paul came down for a couple of days, and then Paul and I came back up to Boston, and Paul, Austin, and I bounced some ideas around and came up with a couple of little meta-settings. The abandoned spaceship or the abandoned moon base kind of things. And frankly the most important thing that came out of all of that was Austin, Warren, Paul, and I wrote up a bunch of minutes of gameplay. Just sort of "Here's what a minute of playing this game is going to feel like." You know, "You hear the sound of a security camera swiveling, and then the beep of it acquiring you as a target, so you duck behind the crate and then you hear the door open so you throw a grenade and run out of the way…" We had a couple of little docs like that which Austin and I took and revised. And in a lot of ways those became the game design. Obviously we put real story around it and all that kind of thing. So that was pretty important for *Shock*.

We kind of wanted to do something different with it. *Underworld* was designed by a screenshot that Doug Wike had done with Paul before Paul even hired any programmers. Doug was the artist who had worked on Paul's older games and had worked at Origin. Doug was the main artist on *Underworld*. A guy named Carol Angell also did a bunch of work in the second half of the project, but Doug was there at the beginning, and he did this screenshot, which was a screen layout and a little twenty-frame animation of an orc walking down the hall at you and you swinging your sword. On some level, whenever we had a design question on *Underworld*, we would just pick up that screenshot and go, "Well, I guess there's a little 'lips' icon over there, I guess that's how you talk. OK, better write some code." And obviously we had to make a lot of actual design decisions about combat and game mechanics and spells and all that, but you could still come back to that screenshot about how the game was supposed to feel. And so for *Shock* the minute of gameplay served a very similar purpose.

On *Underworld* we had stats and inventory and talking and movement, and in *Shock* we really wanted to unify that. I felt that *Underworld* was sort of three different games you played in parallel. There was the stats-based game with the experience points, the inventory collecting and management game, the 3D moving around game, and there was the talking game, the conversation branch game. And much as the world was very low-fi, it was still way more hi-fi than any of the actual characters were. Branching conversation trees do not represent human interaction very well. Even worse than moving a mouse around represents walking. So for *Shock* we really wanted to get rid of some of that, and that's why *Shock* has the full-screen mode with the HUD. Everything was an overlay; the auto-map was an overlay, the inventory was an overlay, and so on.

One of the reasons we wanted all the audio for the voice-overs was because the whole idea of killing everyone on the station and then making all the people only accessible through their data logs was that you could keep playing the game. You wouldn't have to stop to have a conversation or stop to read or stop to choose, you'd just be moving around and, if you wanted to, you could listen to a log from the person there and they'd be describing a scene that had happened in this very room you were in. We felt that *Underworld* did a good job of exploring. You explored spaces, and people really remembered the spaces, they talked about them, they'd been there. They'd say, "There was that room where there was that fight between the trolls and the knights and there was all that blood and that's where I did this thing." They had a very visual memory of their exploration, and they had a very clear sense of exploring the inventories and what you could do and pick up. So we wanted to make the plot and the story development of

System Shock be an exploration as well, and that's why it's all in the logs and the data, so then it's very tied into your movement through the spaces and to the world. The floppy disk version had only text and no voice-over and should never have been released. I fought against that and lost. The voice version is just so much better because you never have to take your eyes off the world: "Here I am and moving around and hearing all this creepy stuff."

So it doesn't interrupt your play experience.

Exactly. It just felt much more integrated. I think in *Shock* we did do a good job of integrating everything into one piece a little better. The tone of the whole game was a little more consistent, a little more scary and alone, and the systems were much simpler. There were no stats any more. In *Underworld*, there was all this dice rolling going on off-screen basically, and I've always felt it was kind of silly. Dice were

System Shock

invented as a way to simulate swinging your sword to see if you hit or miss. So everyone builds computer games where you move around in 3D and swing your sword and hit or miss, and then if you hit you roll some dice to simulate swinging a sword to decide if you hit or miss. How is anyone supposed to understand unless you print the numbers? Which is why I think most of the games that really try to be hard-core RPGs actually print out "You rolled a 17!" In *Warhammer* when you get a five percent increase and the next time you roll your attack you make it by three percent, you're all excited because you know that five percent increase is why you hit. In a computer game you have absolutely no idea. And so we really wanted to get rid of all that super-opaque, "I have no idea what's going on" stuff. We wanted to make it so you can watch and play and it's all happening. So that was really the driving force for *Shock*. And, as I said, those minutes of gameplay describing this tense experience, with the computer looking for you with security systems and cyborgs. Everything's gone horribly wrong and you're trying to figure it out. Those two or three little documents were the things we referred back to.

It's interesting you used the game minute technique, since that lays out just one way events can take place in a given location. With a game that tries to be as non-linear and player-choice oriented as *System Shock*, how do you make sure the game minutes don't lead to a very linear experience?

I think you have two things you can do. One is, you do a couple of them, to illustrate some different possibilities, not necessarily for the same room. Actually on the project I'm working on now one of the things we're doing is taking a specific scenario and we're doing two or three walk-throughs of it, specifically for that reason. But, even back then, I think the main thing we would do is write it so you would have your character check out the other options in some sense. Your minute of gameplay says, "She thought of running for the door, but realized it would be a hard fight. Instead..." And you hint at the systems and you hint at the sorts of things that matter. And then you count on setting up a development culture that's all about "What else could I do?" not "Let's go implement this." But I think it's a good point. We're a non-linear medium — at least I think the best examples of us are usually non-linear — and yet much as I'm sure hypertext is the most wonderful thing ever, it really isn't the solution. A linear medium isn't the solution really either, and so what do you do to express gameplay in a systems-based world? The reason it's interesting is because it is a simulation and it is open ended, but it's hard to write down that simulation in a doc file. So a lot of it is expressing possibilities and what the player decided to do and making it very clear that they had choices. And a lot of it is doing different examples to express different types of things. But yeah, it's easy to do it wrong, like so many things.

It seems like you designed *System Shock* around how you could tell a story better than in *Ultima Underworld*. Was improving your storytelling one of your primary goals?

I think we obviously always cared about story — we were definitely interested in fantasy/sci-fi possibilities. On some level I think we stumbled into a nice villain, in the fact that the villain could speak to you from anywhere and set these ambushes up and actually affect your game. One thing that worked really well that we didn't understand at the beginning but that we learned to somewhat take advantage of by the end was that having the computer and the station be the enemy meant that on some level you could interact with your nemesis fairly regularly and fairly often in non-final ways. You had a recurring, consistent, palpable enemy, who mattered to you because

System Shock

she could lock doors or sabotage you. And that helped the story a lot. The voice-over was nice, especially when you actually had audio as opposed to text, for the logs, because you could put in Foley and all that stuff, and I think that's a huge part of what makes the game work. I don't think the floppy version works nearly as well, because rather than just reading the text you're hearing the explosions in the background and the desperation in someone's voice. There's a lot of text in that game — it's not short on story. But even so, it's not like every room you go into you're in this endless conversation you have to walk back and forth through. We were forced to tell this story and boil it down into bite-sized chunks. And there are some that are too long; we didn't catch all of them. But the bite-sized chunks meant that we had to make them a little more digestible. And that's not why we did logs, we didn't do logs to say "Hey, let's have all these little bite-size pieces of story so you don't get overwhelmed but you feel like you're really putting the mystery together and it all ties together and we can have great Foley to make it seem more emotional and blah blah blah." But at the end of the day that's kind of what it did. And that was a huge help. I don't think the story itself is so awesome or spectacularly outrageous. I mean, it's fine, but I don't think if you wrote the novel it would fly off the shelves.

It's the way it was told.

I think the bite-sized chunks plus the Foley and ambience plus the continual pervasive enemy. Even when you weren't interacting with Shodan, you'd see a security camera you had to take out. All those little actions become part of the story in some sense. And the fact that you're exploring the story as opposed to having the story force fed to you, I think was a huge help as well. The fact that it's not "You have to talk to me now." Instead you pick up this log but maybe you don't read it right away or maybe you want to think back on something so you can go back and bring the log up again and explore it. It's all smoke and mirrors, but I think it makes the player feel more central. And I think that makes people take more possession of it and feel that it's theirs more.

It seems like *System Shock* went out of its way to blend different game genres together even more than *Ultima Underworld*. Was that intentional?

In all honesty I don't think any of us really thought about that stuff very much, which has been something that has always gotten us in trouble. But I think on some level, it was "Hey, let's make this game." Obviously, for us, we said, "Hey, *Underworld* was fun but all that conversation stuff was kind of a pain and those stats seemed to be distracting you and all that number and detail stuff. Can't we streamline this a little bit? Can't we make it a little more action and a little more immediate?" And that was pretty much it. I don't think we were specifically thinking, "Hey, let's do an action-RPG" or whatever. I think it was more an evolution of *Underworld* more than anything else.

Since the first *Underworld*, *Wolfenstein 3D* had come out and had become a huge hit with a much more simple, action-oriented experience. Did you guys deliberately try to avoid the visceral shooter gameplay they had staked out?

No, I think we were just doing our own thing, frankly. We knew the id guys and obviously their stuff was awesome — we all were fans in the sense that we thought it was cool. But by the time *Wolf* had come out we were pretty much done with *Underworld* so it wasn't like we were looking at them to get ideas, per se. They were kinda doing their thing and we were kinda doing our thing. I don't know if they respected our stuff or liked it; we certainly respected and liked their stuff. But we weren't like, "more of that!" We certainly talked about how it was better and faster and cleaner than *Underworld*, far more than we talked about any other game that was out. That was probably one of our weaknesses at the time, that we were pretty introverted, and pretty much doing our own thing in almost everything we were doing. We were doing *Terra Nova*, which was obviously a weird hybrid game. And we were doing *Flight Unlimited*, which in some sense was a weird hybrid game; non-shooting yet non-big commercial flight simulator. We were kinda just doing our own stuff.

So you tried to avoid comparing yourself to whatever else was going on in gaming?

It's not that we didn't play and like other games. We did. And we certainly thought about what we did and didn't like about them, and we certainly talked about games a lot. But I don't remember being in meetings and people saying, "Make it more like this other thing." We were kinda just doing the game we thought we should do. And, for good or for bad, that was pretty much in reference to the games we had done already. And obviously we were seeing all the Origin stuff that was in development, and we were sort of influenced by that RPG/story aesthetic that Chris [Roberts], Richard, and Warren had been building up down there.

System Shock, **like** *Ultima Underworld* **before it, was a pretty non-linear game experience. Was that one of your primary design goals?**

System Shock

I think on both *Underworld* and *Shock*, we didn't want to build games where you clear out every square on this level and then you go on to the next level. *Underworld* had lots of things that would cut you off and you had to come back to later, or at least you should come back to later. For example, now that you've reached level seven, you're going to have to go back to areas that you couldn't get to before. Both games had their four or five major checkpoints, but we'd always believed that player choice was pretty central to what made it fun for people. And that player-centric stuff was what you remember. You remember the clever little thing you did more than you remember some cut-scene. To us, giving players the ability, even if they don't think of it as such, to go their own way is where they're going to be more likely to do something they remember and care about. In *Shock* we certainly tried to build some systems like upgrades or the security cameras where you had a fair amount of freedom in which order you did it and how you did it, where it wasn't just "Go do this sequence of four things." It was "Well, there are going to be twelve cameras here and you gotta take out eight of them. Figure it out." We gave you that option of "Well, that one seems like a mess" or "I don't want to fight that guy. OK, maybe I can find another way…"

I think that was our philosophy of design. We were very state-based as opposed to event-based. We didn't do a very good job on those early games, but we tried to do as many things state-based as we could. Those cameras are a good example. It wasn't a matter of saying, "If you've destroyed these eight cameras in this order, then do this." It was much more a case of "When we are in this state, the following thing happens." And that way you give the player ability to get into that state however they want. Obviously back then, with our incredibly remedial physics and so on, there was a limited amount of that we could do, and obviously as we get worlds where you can do more stuff and more interactions that becomes more powerful. But even back then we were thinking about it that way, as much as we could at least.

System Shock seemed to be one of the earliest games of its type to use physics, even in a pretty primitive form.

I think we saw that in *Underworld*, where we had this incredibly remedial physics but people still had fun throwing things and bouncing the superball around and trying to hit targets with things. And we said, "Hey, let's do more of that because worlds have physics." On some level it's still just a dungeon simulator, and we're still just trying to evolve that idea. I really do think *System Shock* is just the somewhat obvious evolution of *Underworld*. We rewrote it all for 32 bit with Watcom, as opposed to the old 16-bit stuff, and that gave us some more power and some more possibilities. But philosophically it was a refinement and a focusing of the previous thing.

It always seemed to me like a pretty significant step forward.

I think we certainly were attempting to refine and focus. This was the stuff we thought we'd done OK on, which was primarily this idea of exploration, and how much players liked doing their own thing and remembered spaces and places and stories that we told. Some of the best stuff I think in *Underworld* was where there was no dialog. The story was all told through what was on screen. A lot of people at the time remembered the troll/knight battle. There was this room where we set up a bunch of debris and decals and objects to make it look like there had been this big fight: skulls, broken swords, and stuff were left all over the place. And you could talk to testers or people at trade shows who had played the game or whatever, and they'd say, "Man, there was that big fight!" And they'd tell you about the fight between the trolls and the knights even though we never said anything about it, because they'd seen it. So we really thought that the exploration and the visual context was really important to people. So in *Shock* we really tried to focus on that, to do what we could to come up with other ways to let people explore, and not do so much where we tried to tell them or force them. I thought it worked pretty well. There's obviously stuff one would change in retrospect, like with anything one ever does, but I think we did a decent job of focusing. There's still a lot more focusing to do.

I always thought the idea of having the separate cyberspace mode in *System Shock* **was pretty interesting. What were the motivations behind adding that?**

We thought it just fit from a conceptual standpoint: you're a hacker, shouldn't you hack something? We thought it would be fun to throw in a different movement mode that was more free-form, more action. In retrospect we probably should have either cut it or spent more time on it. There is some fun stuff in it, but it's not as polished as it should be. But even so it was nice because it at least reinforced the idea that you were the hacker,

System Shock

in a totally random, arcade-y, broken sort of way. But at least it suggested that you're something other than a guy with a gun. Like I said, we were pretty intro-focused then. We were looking at ourselves and said, "Oh, of course we should have cyberspace. We're a cyberpunk game, we gotta have cyberspace. Well, what can we do without too much time? What if we do this crazy thing?" Off we went…

Though the Looking Glass games did pretty well commercially, they never were massive hits like the id games that came out around the same time, despite using similarly impressive technology. Was the company ever distressed by this?

I don't know about distressed… In general, I think we were doing things which were technically more aggressive. I certainly don't mean to say in any sense we were technically better because it's hard to imagine how one would write an engine that was more efficient or powerful than one of Carmack's engines. And John's an incredibly bright and amazingly talented guy. But if you look at *Wolfenstein*, it was walls, no lighting, no floors and ceilings, no look up and down, all flat, period, while *Underworld* had slopes, and lighting, and floor and ceiling textures, and jumping, and little physics stuff, and so on. Now, does that make it a better game? Of course not. It has nothing to do with whether the game is good or not. I think we were trying to do a little more than the machines probably were ready to do or even that we were ready for. I think we were pretty good programmers, but who knows, maybe someone else could have done it a lot faster than we did. The fact that in general most people got to it a couple of years later when the machines could actually do it was probably them being a little smarter about the market, and us being a little dippier. But, A, we were trying to do a little more than we could handle and reach a larger audience, and B, we were into these games that were a little more complicated and required a little more investment. That's just a different thing. Even if we'd been using literally identical technology I think it's easier to express what was going on in *Wolfenstein* or *Doom*. It's easier to say, "Hey, here's what you're doing: you've got this gun and you have to keep yourself alive with all these crazy things coming after you. Go for it. It's really spooky, it's really fast, it looks great." Awesome. They did a great job. We were a nichier product, we just were.

So selling more copies wasn't too much of a concern?

There was some discussion about it: "Wow, gosh, it'd sure be nice if we were making more money and selling more copies so we can do crazy games of the type we want as opposed to having to worry about how we're going to sell more." Hey, I'd love it if the public was more into what I like to do and a little less into slightly more straightforward

Ultima Underworld II: Labyrinth of Worlds

things. But I totally get that they're into straightforward things. I don't have any divine right to have someone hand me millions of dollars to make a game of whatever I want to do. If the market wanted a bunch more *Underworlds*, they would have bought them. At some fundamental level, everyone has a wallet, and they vote with it.

Was there ever talk of making your games play more like the id games to make them sell better?

id was doing a great job at doing that game. And more power to them. I think you want to do things that connect with the market and you want to do things that people like and you want to do things that get seen. But you also want to do things you actually believe in and that you personally want to do. Hey, if you're going to work twenty hours a day and not get paid much money, you might as well do something you like. And, I love *Mario 64*, and lord knows I'm probably not talented enough to build it. But even if I was I wouldn't do it because I love the game and I love playing it, but I have no interest in building it. And we were building the games we were interested in; we had that luxury. We didn't have spectacular success and a huge win, but we had enough success that we got to do some more. And at some level, at least for me, sure I'd love to have huge, huge success and be able to take five years and do ten indie games and do whatever the hell I want. But if I get to do another game that I find interesting, that's pretty hard to complain about. People certainly discussed it, it's not like we weren't aware of it. And every so often someone would come in and say, "Why don't we just do *Doom* with this?" But as a team I think we were pretty into the stuff we were doing.

The *Flight Unlimited* project seemed to be a pretty big departure from what Looking Glass had been doing up to that point.

When *Shock* finished, *Flight* and *Terra Nova* were in development. Most of the *Shock* team ended up on *Flight* for a little while to help it ship and then they moved on to *Terra Nova* and whatever else was going on at the time. Looking Glass was going through this period of trying to do a lot of things at once and sort of overreaching itself and being a little overambitious and a little cocky. The company was trying to establish itself as a publisher at a time when that was very, very hard to do. All the other mid-sized publishers were mostly going out of business or getting bought, while we were trying to branch into new genres and do more things and start up an affiliate label and self-publish *Flight* and all this other craziness. No one in the management chain of the company really paid any attention to *System Shock* because *Flight* was going to be the first self-published product, and fair enough. From a company standpoint, *Flight* was the product that had to be the hit, because it was the self-published title. Ned and Paul had merged to become Blue Sky Research, which became Looking Glass, and Ned had obviously been into flight simulators, having worked on *Chuck Yeager*. And Seamus [Blackley] obviously was into the whole flight simulator thing. The company's focus was the attempt to self-publish and get out of the treadmill of waiting for advances and get a chance to get some solidity behind things so one can make forward-looking decisions instead of just focusing on the short term. Obviously it did not work, but it's easy to criticize in retrospect, in that hindsight way. I think there was plenty of clarity up front on some of the mistakes, but some of the mistakes were quite honest and quite reasonable. You look at them and say, "Well, yeah, I can see why they did that."

How did the *Thief* project originate?

We had a bunch of high-concept ideas about game design which, in practice, very few of actually happened in the final game. We had a lot of thoughts about having different factions. As I discussed, we felt that character and conversation were something that was hard, to put it mildly. So we had conceived of factions of people in the

Thief

world being a better foil for the player because you can interact with a group in a slightly more iconic and abstract way than you can interact with an individual. Because someone can come and say, "I speak for these people and we think you're a bad guy" or whatever. And they can do that in a way that's a little less personal and direct and therefore has a little less requirement on the AI and conversation engine. It was this idea of having factions who you could ally with or oppose yourself with or do things for or not.

The other big idea was that these same factions would help you in off-screen ways, because we didn't want to have actual teammates. We didn't want to write AI that you would have to pay attention to and worry about whether they leapt the chasm when you leapt the chasm and all that kind of mess you get when you put a second character in an actually interactive environment as opposed to a big fat plane where you just fight. So, the initial ideas were along those lines, where we set up a couple of game worlds where there were a lot of different factions and you were primarily interacting with them and they had lots of opportunities to help. You'd see the evidence of their help, such as an arrow would come shooting in from off screen or something, but we weren't going to have to actually do all the AI work required to do real allies. So we had a couple of designs along those lines. Also, most of the designs we were trying to do were a little more interesting, a little less standard.

You mean in terms of the game fiction?

In terms of fiction and structure. We had a post-Cold War zombies proposal called *Better Red than Undead* in which you were fighting off zombies in a communist Cold War era and running around and having different groups — communist spies and communist government and Western government and all these different spy groups. Meanwhile, the zombies were trying to take everyone over so you had to pick which groups you were going to ally with and go against while everyone had this common enemy of the zombies. But of course no one gets along so you had to play this delicate game of getting everyone on your side or enough people on your side to get the job done.

And then we had this reverse-Arthurian fiction where you were Mordred and your advisor was Morgan le Fey, who was sort of a good person. Lancelot was this evil jerk and Merlin was a time-traveling marketing guy from the future. All the Knights of the Round Table wore jerseys with logos and numbers, and the Holy Grail was this fake thing that they didn't think existed but they were using it as a way to continue to oppress the masses and take all their money and treat them poorly. The excuse was that they needed all the money to go find the Holy Grail and they'd just sit around and have parties. So you as the Black Knight had to break into Camelot. And Guinevere was this butch lesbian who would help you by betraying Lancelot because she really hated him and all that sort of thing. Actually our marketing department wasn't really into that one. Not too surprising, I suppose. But we had a bunch of random ideas we were playing around with and we did storyboards and initial setup and stuff.

But they were all still immersive simulation, first-person games?

Yeah, yeah. Once again, in *Better Red* there were all these spy groups and in *Dark Camelot* there were all these different groups of outcasts you could work with to try to get into Camelot and mess things up. But as we started worked on some of the *Dark*

Camelot stuff, A, we were having infinite challenges trying to convince anyone it was marketable, and B, the missions that we had the best definition on and the best detail on were all the breaking into Camelot, meeting up with someone, getting a clue, stealing something, whatever. As we did more work in that direction, and those continued to be the missions that we could explain best to other people, it just started going that way. With the faction thing we never got whatever we needed to actually make time to make a prototype. The thing about that is it requires a lot of play mechanics until it starts working, whereas the basic stealth model was something you could kind of get the basic idea of by having the guard looking the other way and you going past pretty quickly. So Paul had been pushing for a while that the thief side of it was the really interesting part and why not you just do a thief game. And as things got more chaotic and more stuff was going on and we were having more issues with how to market the stuff, we just kept focusing in on the thief part. We went through a bunch of different phases of reorganizing the project structure and a bunch of us got sucked on to doing some other project work on *Flight* and stuff, and there was all this chaos. We said, "OK, well, we've got to get this going and really focus and make a plan." So we put Greg [LoPiccolo] in charge of the project and we agreed we were going to call it *Thief* and we were going to focus much more. That's when we went from lots of playing around and exploring to "Let's make this thief game."

It seems like at the time there were not a lot of other stealth games.

Not that we knew of, at least. Right before we shipped, *Tenchu* came out in Japan, and I think it came out in the States shortly thereafter. So we certainly looked at *Tenchu* when it came out, but by that point our game was mostly done other than tuning, and they were much more an action-y arcade game. They were a lot more about killing people in cool ninja ways. *Tenchu* was a cool game, but it was a different focus than our game.

It's interesting to me that you considered *Thief* the more bankable game concept, even though its game mechanics were in a lot of ways totally new and original.

I think it was more that we believed in it. I mean, Eidos never really believed in it and until the end told us to put more monsters in the levels and have more fighting and exploring and less stealth and I'm not sure there was ever a point they got it. I mean, the trailers Eidos did for *Thief* were all scenes with people shooting fire arrows at people charging them. So you can derive from that how well they understood or believed in the idea.

Yet they still funded it...

Certainly. If they hadn't done that, we wouldn't have done the game. So very thankful for that. I'm not sure we ever got to a point where they said, "Oh yeah, this is gonna work." I think they at least had "OK, we're selling this anti-hero cynical thief guy, maybe we can do that," in a way that selling reverse Camelot or whatever was just not appealing to anyone.

How did you convince people internally that *Thief* was promising?

We got some very early prototypes that were super, super-rough and only tiny bits of that code were used in the shipping game. But that was just guys on patrol, noticing you or not, and you ducking out of the way. And we did do a bunch of mission write-ups for the *Dark Camelot* stuff, not that we used them in the real game, but we thought, yeah, that would be kinda cool. You'd sneak in and do this and this guy would do

Thief

this, and in the end you could make this happen. I think we had a critical mass of cool little elements. That said, it wasn't until right when we shipped that it all came together into something that worked at all in a way that players might actually want to play as opposed to intellectually "this could work" way. We had a habit by that point of pulling games that were lots of different elements together so that you had to connect the dots in your mind until near the end, which isn't exactly how the industry likes to work these days.

Would it have been better to be more cohesive earlier?

Well, certainly it would have been great to be more cohesive earlier, though I'm not sure what we would have had to sacrifice to do that. Obviously, these days in the industry we try to get a lot more working early on, but I think that means it's harder to take as many risks. More to the point, it's much harder to do games that require a lot of systems. And in a way that's good because super-overcomplicated games rarely work. But if you do it right I think you can have a lot of systems that work together in a very elegant and transparent way, but that's the kind of thing that's very hard to show right now because you're told, "All right, well, before we do any real development, we need a prototype that works," and that means you're only going to be able to do a few new things at a time built upon whatever you did last. I think that makes it very hard to do something as simple as *Thief*, which is an incredibly focused game, but it still requires light and shadows that work, and shadow detection that works, and AI that can understand shadows, and a speech system so that the AIs can communicate to you about the shadows. It's not rocket science, but it's a lot of stuff. Like I said, we hacked together some stuff at the beginning to give us an idea that, OK, this could probably work, but I'm not sure it would have ever convinced a publisher it was going to work; obviously it generally didn't convince Eidos. It convinced them enough to fund it, and hey that's great, but I'm not sure that would be true any more. I think the stuff we used back then would be hard to use as proof now. And maybe that means you should have a year of pre-production with a small team where you write tons of stuff, but most publishers aren't thinking that way at the moment. It's more, take an engine, add a couple of features, and then you're safe and can go forward. And that's certainly more stable. I think you want a lot of that, but you certainly don't want all your products to be like that.

Aside from the publisher side of it, with a truly innovative game, how do you convince the development team the game is going to work and how do you keep them on track with the vision?

Yeah, that's a super hard one. Part of it is you've got to get a team that's comfortable with the degree of ambiguity. There are some people who are comfortable in that environment and others who aren't. And it's not good or bad in either case; it's just how people are. But I think that's a huge part of it right there, whether you get people who say, "OK, that sounds kind of interesting. I'm not sure I get it, but I think I get it pretty well so I'll go off and start trying to figure it out." Or whether you get people who say, "I'm just not seeing that, and I'll have a hard time building it or doing work toward it until I really understand it." So I think the attitude of the people you have is a huge piece of it, and I think that's where minutes of gameplay and storyboards and trying to describe the experience is so important; ways to communicate what you're trying to build before you've built it. For *Thief* we had a huge advantage because at the end of the day we could say, well, is it making the character more thief-y? Hmm, that looks like it makes him stronger and brawnier, probably don't need that. Hmm, that looks like it makes him cooler and stealthier, let's do that. Not all games that try to innovate have such an easy focus, but I think that was a crucial part of *Thief.* You could always go "Is the thing I'm typing going to make him stealthier?"

Did you use game minutes on the project?

Yeah, we definitely did some of that on *Thief.* Not as much, I think, because we did a couple at the beginning and then it was pretty clear that, OK, we want this idea of guards trying to find you but not if you're hidden in the shadows and not if you're sneaking up behind people and conking them on the head. Once again, the idea of *Thief* is a lot more transparent than the idea of *System Shock*. The name *System Shock* doesn't tell

Thief

you what the gameplay is like, whereas *Thief* does. Now that certainly leaves you with a lot of detail to work out and a lot of role-playing where, now if I shot the rope arrow at the ceiling and climbed up, what's the guard going to have to do to react and that kind of thing. There was less of a need to set an overall high-concept direction on *Thief* because the high concept was so clear. And so *Thief* was a lot more about mechanics and systems and tuning and what parameters you need to tune, and how will you make it so the guard can detect you and not look stupid but not detect you so well that you never win, and so forth. Whereas on the other games it was more about setting the high-concept goals, not just the low-level goals.

For a game like *Thief*, how do you balance the pure systems side of the game with specific scripting?

The goal is certainly to minimize the scripting in something like *Thief*, because not only does the scripting take forever, but it also means that you're likely to have situations where the AI reacts differently in different places, which is the death knell for a game like that because the player can't plan or understand and then nothing is repeatable and then the player is driven insane. So in *Thief* there were some places that had heavy scripting, but they had more to do with playing out story events: "When this happens you're going to have to make these four AIs go over here because story-wise this event happens." So there's some of that scripting but not a lot. We spent a while where we had some fairly sophisticated scripting systems, but it was fairly complicated and really no one but the programmers ever used it. And then Tom Leonard, who was our main AI guy, took the key elements of the scripting stuff you wanted to do with the AIs and built this pseudo-script interface which was this Mad Lib-like Windows dialog where you could say, "Oh, on these sort of messages or these sort of events, do these sort of things and go to this object or figure out what's on the other side of this link and go over there or try to grab that thing." And as soon as Tom did that, designers were doing a lot more improvisation and a lot more "Oh, I want this specific AI when this alarm goes off to go over here and then say this thing." So they would script a lot of the reacting to major events. That said, the minute-to-minute play was almost all systems-based, where the lead designers would go and decide how the vision cone works and how sensitive the guy was and how likely he was to fight or run for help or whatever. The designers would place some waypoints and say, "Well, you should go to the kitchen, and then you should go to the upstairs hall, and then stand around the staircase for a couple of minutes and then go back to the kitchen" or whatever. But all the actual moving and detecting and turning and all the detail of the AI and when they detected you and what they do when they did was all pretty much sense systems and generic code.

Did you need to enforce a rule with the design team about how much or how little to script?

I think everyone got it pretty well. Most of the time the scripting was just for the story stuff as I said. I think everyone got the idea that it was going to be systems-y just because it was clear that so much of the game was going to depend on you getting a visceral sense of how the AI behaved so that you could then elude them. And everyone knew that meant they had to be pretty repeatable and systems-based. And so for the designers it was a lot more about building spaces where you had good lines of sight where you could see the AI's path. A lot of that game comes down to how do you get closure moments and how do you get scope.

What do you mean by closure moments?

In most games you're killing everyone, so you get nice moments of closure when you win each battle, whereas in *Thief* you're going past people. Which means all those encounters are open-ended. It's like all the sentences start but they don't end. So a lot of time was spent on how do you get closure from these encounters that didn't really have closure. And a lot of that had to do with building spaces where the player can really see what's going on. If it gets too claustrophobic, the player doesn't really have any idea. In a lot of the early levels the AIs were on these incredibly interesting and complex paths which looked great on the overhead map but when you were playing the game it felt like it might as well be random. Because you'd just have no idea what was going on: a guy would show up and then he'd be gone and then he'd show up some other place and you'd forget to hide a body but you'd have no idea if someone was going to find it. Because the player only had a very local sense of what was going on, we had to change the scope of the AI behaviors to be very local as well. Otherwise it just felt like randomness. And so a lot of the designers' challenge came down to how do you build these spaces that can run in the engine fast enough, which certainly had a whole set of constraints about size and so forth, but at the same time big enough with clear enough line of sight or clear enough iconography. You had to be able to say, "Oh, this is that main hallway and it looks just like that other main hallway so I bet the guard's on this rotating patrol through this hallway. OK, I get it. I better go hide the body off the hallway." Ways for the designers to make it possible for the player to make rational plans, given that the player couldn't bring up a radar or switch to the God's eye view and go, "Oh, I see." How to keep that first-person immersion of "Here I am, what's going to happen" without making it so opaque that you might as well flail around randomly and hope you win.

As with your previous games, was having fairly non-linear environments one of your primary design goals?

Yeah, definitely. There's no question that we were always about maximizing the player choice as much as possible and I think that in *Underworld* in particular we had a lot of watching people do things we hadn't expected or be clever in ways we hadn't expected. Or just watching where a couple of systems would come together in interesting ways. You know, "I'm

Thief

being chased by a guy and I run into a locked door and now I have to pick the lock but the guy's behind me trying to shoot me and I finally get through the locked door just as I'm about to die but, oh my god, there are enemies in here so I jump in the water and try to swim away but..." Just these little sequences that were not scripted or planned out in any way, they were just players in the space improvising. And so in *Thief*, though obviously it was a much more focused game, we wanted to keep that sense of do whatever you want to do and do it however you want to do it so you can kill people or not, you can try to evade them or take them out, you can use your gear to sneak around or you can go straight in the front. We very consciously wanted to maximize the players' ability to do it their own way.

It's interesting that the systems approach to game design is more rare in the industry. Among its supporters, such as yourself, it seems so clearly the right way to go, yet so few games actually use it.

I think you can point to some examples in the industry. *GTA* is very systems-based in some ways, so I think there are a couple of examples of people doing systems-based work.

But they're still definitely in the minority.

Oh, I agree. I think there's a couple of things. One, I think it's just generally harder to do, which makes it a risk. I also think it's easy in systems-based games to get distracted by the big things and just build something that's confusing or obscure. And certainly our games, I'm proud of them all, but I think there are times we overdid things, in some sense. And also, I think one of the problems with systems-based gaming in general is it's easy to get games that feel very flat. It's very hard to moderate the emotional curve of a systems-based game. We did not do that nearly as well as we should have partially because I think we weren't looking at it that way enough.

What do you mean by moderate the emotional curve?

You know the beauty of a systems-based game is the player can take it as they want. The beauty of a purely scripted, *Medal of Honor*-style roller coaster is that you're guaranteed players are going to have this intense experience and then they're going to have a little bit of rest and then something really cool is going to happen visually and then there's going to be a challenge. You can build more tension and an emotional arc. In the stupidest sense, you can build more of a random reinforcement schedule for the player that gets them hooked and makes them feel that they're getting this tense entertainment experience. And I think in systems-based games it's easy to end up with a lot of systems that are kind of interesting but a little cold or a little flat. It's easy to end up playing a game that doesn't have that many highs or lows.

When you get the memorable moment in a systems-based game it's usually much more powerful, because it's something that you did on your own. I think players really do remember things that they did more than they remember things that we write. I think when you talk to players about their game experience, the things they remember are mostly the clever thing they did or the cool way they approached a problem or the amazing thing that they didn't think was going to work but that they pulled out at the last second. They don't tell you about "Oh, in the thirty-seventh cut-scene, the guy on the right was really cool because he had spiky hair and a cool shirt on. He was my fave." Even the plot twists; they have that emotional moment of "Oh wow, I never would have guessed," and then they forget about it because it's passive. And gaming's an active media.

Thief

I think moving forward for the people who care about systems-based work, we've got to figure out how to get some of the emotional pacing and strong emotional reactions and so on that a scripted game has while keeping the player freedom and player choice that a pure systems-based game has. There's a lot from the scripted and more pre-constructed experiences that the systems people needs to think about and understand how you do. That said, personally I find the systems stuff more interesting because I do think it's more about the player and if you want to write novels or movies, why do them in a game? There certainly is an appeal to playing through the movie experience. Even just having a combat system that lets you turn the pages of the book is kind of interesting and does make you invest a little more and certainly brings something that either one by itself does not. *Tekken* by itself or a book by itself are different experiences than a book where you have to play *Tekken* every so often to turn the page, which is what a lot of story/fighting scripted games are. There's nothing wrong with those games, I think they're fine, I like some of them. I just think that in gaming we can do more than that.

So you think emotional pacing is the key to why pure systems-based games haven't been as commercially successful as more scripted games?

I don't know if that's the only key, but I think that's certainly part of it. I think for us in particular we've always built games that were a little harder to get into or we didn't do a good job on selling players on the fantasy and why they wanted it. We haven't done a great job on our ramp-up at the beginning of getting the players involved in an elegant way in terms of telling them why they want it and in terms of telling them how to do it. It's one of those things: how do you show something where the interest is "Hey, after you play it for a while you start developing your own style" and all of that? When you have two or three minutes of someone's time before they're like "Yeah, whatever."

And I think a big challenge for the games industry is that some of the coolest games are games that take a while to get into. I think the people who are making those games have to think about what to do to make them more accessible so that we don't end up with only games that are fun in the first second. It would be great if every game were fun right away and could clearly distinguish itself from the rest of the market right away. In practice I think we are going to make games that are easy to get into and I think almost everything will get to the point where people can just pick it up and play it and have fun. The question then is how you distinguish which has more depth and if that is the depth that you as a player are interested in. And that's where at the moment as an industry we have no real way of communicating any of that. If it was five dollars a game, who would care? You'd just pick it up because it sounded interesting and you'd see if you like it. But at fifty dollars a pop, we have a bit of the McDonald's syndrome where people say, "I'll go to McDonald's because I know what it tastes like even though maybe it's not the best food in town, but I don't have to risk seeing if that sub place on the corner is any good." We get some of that in our industry, where it's "Well, that sounds interesting, but I don't know. I'll just go buy that game I know about already where I know exactly what it is and I won't be disappointed." The answer is changing. Fifteen years ago something like *Underworld* sold pretty well but it was selling to a very different market than the console market. People were going into that with expectations about role-playing and how much time they were going to have to invest to get a handle on it. Whereas now there are still some games like that but in general most people are thinking more about entertainment and a little less about a challenging mechanic.

I've always thought it was pretty impressive that Looking Glass had such a good success rate with some pretty innovative titles.

It's kind of weird. The thing about Looking Glass is that Paul and Ned had obviously done a few games each before, but in a lot of ways the bulk of the company over the years was always new to games. A lot of people were just out of school, even on the design and programming side of it, and there were a lot of people who had an interest in gameplay and game mechanics and hadn't been at a lot of companies. We didn't have much context I guess; we hadn't worked other places. There wasn't anything to compare it to, so it wasn't "Hmm, how are we doing and how are those other guys doing?" It was more "Well, gotta make some more games, let's go!"

The fact that you were all so green makes your success even more surprising.

Sort of, except the advantage there is that you have a lot of people who believe they are going to work really hard and make it work. As opposed to "Oh, I already know how to do it, we're just going to do it the same way" or "Oh, that will never work, we don't have time" or "Oh, it should have sold better so now I'm disappointed." Instead it was just "Let's go!" Which is nice. Projects were smaller, budgets were smaller, which makes it much easier. I'm not sure how you get that vibe on a hundred-person team.

Were you sad to see Looking Glass finally go under?

Obviously, yes, in some sense. It had a pretty good run. I left five or six months before Looking Glass went away, and I had a degree of frustration with how things had gone over the last couple of years. And some of the changes, some of them were inevitable I think given the scale the company had grown to. And some of them were probably not inevitable, but hey, they happened, so be it. At some level I had personally been like "OK, well, that's over." I obviously wished those guys the best and would have liked them to stay around and continue to do cool things. Certainly when I left I didn't think the company sucked or wasn't cool. I know a lot of people there who I really liked and there were some really good games being worked on. But for me, on some level I had already said this is a cool company but a very different one, and I think ten years is enough and there's enough things that frustrate me that I don't want to be here at the moment. But even so, yeah, obviously Looking Glass was a cool group and a lot of us put a lot of time and energy and a large part of our lives into it and it's sad when that doesn't work out. So there's some part of me that says, oh that sucks, that's not fair, but it's the real world and it had a pretty good run.

The next thing you worked on was *Deus Ex*. What was your involvement with that?

I did very, very little, a tiny, tiny amount. Obviously Warren and I talk all the time so I'd seen design docs whenever I was down visiting and I would play the game and give them some feedback. But I was only down there for a couple of months, near the end, where I tried to do a little bit of work in making the AI a little more forgiving. I tried to point out some of the lessons of *Thief*. I'd say, "Hey, I don't think you guys should do

Deus Ex

the same thing we did, but guys on sniper towers fifty meters away shooting you in the back that you've never seen? Reality yes, fun no." I did a little bit of that, I did some miscellaneous code cleanup, debugging, tried to help out with a couple of the systems a little bit in terms of a few things that hadn't come together or things that were really broken in terms of performance. Obviously the game had some performance problems when it shipped, but we did a little bit of work on that. Mostly I was just down there hanging out and talking with Warren and reporting a ton of bugs and fixing a little bit here and there and trying to improve some things and debug some things. But mostly it was just "I'll go hang out with Warren for a couple months and help out with whatever he's working on."

It seemed that, to some extent, *Deus Ex* popularized a lot of the concepts you had pioneered with *System Shock* years earlier. How did you think it developed those ideas?

Looking Glass had gone on the focus focus focus track. Get something really deep even if it's narrow, whereas *DX* was exactly the opposite. It was incredibly broad but incredibly shallow. Tons of scripting, tons of special cases, attempt to do conversation and inventory and other things. And I think the cool side of that is it gave people a lot more epic scale and a lot more possibilities and people who were willing to buy in, there was a lot there. There was a lot to invest in and care about. And fictionally I think they set it in a good timeline that people could get into pretty easily. Starting it out at a destroyed Statue of Liberty was a nice way to set a tone early and connect it to the real world yet give yourself enough freedom to do interesting things. I think they provided a pretty accessible game-space, and they provided enough systems stuff that you could play around but not so much that it was distracting. Personally, I thought maybe it was a little too easy to find yourself poking behind the curtain, a little too easy to go "Oh, wait, that wasn't real, I can't really do that." They react to that in this one case but in these other ten cases they're not going to. But I think that's fairly inevitable given the type of game they did. I don't think it's because they did a bad game, I think it's because they took on an incredibly ambitious, hard problem. But I think *DX* was a pretty cool achievement, definitely. I personally feel that in the long run you're more likely to get to where we want to be ten, twenty years from now by doing a *Thief* where you make something incredibly focused and small but it works. Then you keep growing and growing and adding to it, until you get the breadth you need but you keep the depth the whole way. Whereas obviously the *Deus Ex* approach is to get all the breadth right away with none of the depth but then go back and start adding the depth. Is either "right?" Whatever, who knows. It's just a different approach, and in practice I'm sure twenty years from now is going to look different than any of us expect anyway.

So the next thing you worked on was *Frequency*. What was your involvement with that?

Greg LoPiccolo was the project leader on *Thief* and had done the music for *System Shock* and had been audio director at Looking Glass for a while after that. Greg left to go to Harmonix. And Dan Schmidt had done the music on *Underworld II* and was project leader on *Terra Nova* and so on and so forth. Dan was on *Thief* for three or four months but then decided he'd rather be at Harmonix. Dan's double major had been computer science and music and he was a singer/songwriter so Harmonix was a perfect fit for him, and so obviously he was missed at Looking Glass but we all understood why he had gone there. After I'd left LG and done some work on *DX* and was back in Cambridge, obviously Looking Glass wasn't around any more at that point and that was right when the Harmonix guys were beginning to talk to Sony about moving *Frequency* over to PS2. So I said, "Hey, I've always wanted to write some PS2 code in order to understand the system, so I'll come in and write a little demo of what your game might look like on the PS2 if you'll let me play with your dev kits." And they were all busy doing their PC stuff to hit some milestones and get some stuff working, so I just came in for a month playing around with writing a bunch of PS2 examples, getting up to speed on it, and thinking what would we have to do and so on. And then when they got the deal and decided to go ahead and make it a PS2 game, they asked me, "Hey, if you want to stay around and write some code and sit in on design meetings and talk about games, that'd be great." Which is awesome. I really like the guys there, they're some of my favorite people in the industry, I think they do really, really interesting stuff. I think they have a pretty strong vision for what they want to accomplish, which is great and which is really different from what other people are doing. And I've always liked music and music games, so, hey, good time.

I mostly wrote code; I did some graphics work for a while and then I actually wrote all the sound code for *Freq*, all the low-level IOP sound engine, and then I went to a bunch of design meetings. Obviously the game was fairly well along before I got there, so certainly in no way at all was I one of the main designers on that game. I was a coder who helped out and then sat in on some meetings. I certainly, as I always do, talked a lot about design and suggested things and this, that, and the other, but I was more just a guy hanging out and helping and suggesting some stuff and trying some stuff. I mean, Alex and Greg had a pretty clear idea, "Hey, we want this to be about trying to emulate the experience of live performance," with the whole multi-track thing. They had a pretty strong vision for where they were going. The rest of us just did a lot of "How do we make that real, and when it doesn't work, what do we do to fix it?" and "Oh maybe we need to try this other mechanic" and that sort of thing.

Working on *Frequency* must have been a pretty big departure from all of your reality and simulation-based games. Was that a nice change of pace?

Yeah, I'm not sure I'd want to do it for fifteen years or whatever but it was certainly very interesting to work on essentially an arcade game. To work on something where a game lasts for three minutes and you have a score. One of the biggest differences there was on almost everything else I've worked on you can work on how you make it easier on the player. Do you make the AIs easier? Do you make the player do more damage? Here you are on *Freq* and you think, "Hmm, the player has no rhythm. What do we do about that?" And there's only so much you can do. You can make the windows bigger and you can slow the song down, but at some point either they can hit the notes in sequence or they cannot hit the notes in sequence. So that was interesting, it was definitely very different.

Almost all the games you have worked on have been first-person perspective games. Was that a deliberate design choice for you? Do you think first-person is clearly the best perspective to use?

I think for *Underworld* it was because we were doing a dungeon simulator and it was "OK, well, we're going to take a flight simulator and put it in a dungeon." Hey, guess what, first-person. Going back to the talk about fidelity and how good a conversation system is, five, ten years ago third-person characters looked pretty bad. Maybe a Mario looks awesome because he's iconic, but doing an up close video of a human is not something that the PlayStation 1 or the early PC was very good at. I think that's changing now. I think if you look at *Splinter Cell*, *Thief 3*, and *Prince of Persia: The Sands of Time*, I think the characters look pretty good. I think we still haven't quite mastered the animation as well as we should, so there's still times where the fact that you're third-person forces things to either look bad or to not allow you to do a move you want to do. And that's still when I personally get the most frustrated with third-person games: I know the only reason I can't do that is because the game doesn't have an animation for it. And I still think in a lot of ways first-person has a lot of very compelling advantages.

Personally I think we're now at the point where graphics and technology mean we can do third-person to a fidelity that makes it worthwhile and really robust, even in realistic games. We've always been able to do it for platformers or non-realistic games. But I think in realistic games we're getting to the point where the fidelity of the third-person experience is strong enough that it's

Thief: Deadly Shadows

OK. *Thief 3* does a seamless first-third transition whenever you want dynamic. and I think it works pretty well. I think they made that decision a little late in the development process, so I think the third-person stuff's a little dodgier than maybe it should be; if they'd known at the beginning they were going to do that I'm sure it would look a little better. But even as it is, I think, given the timeline they had, they did a pretty good job of doing a third-person. So I think it's more about whether it lets the player have the experience they want. In something like *Thief*, in a way it's better because it's that whole fantasy of sneaking around and being in the shadows, which is almost enhanced by being in third-person because you can see all the shadows on yourself. In a weird way you're almost a little more disconnected from your character in first-person in *Thief* because you're always trying to understand how well hidden you are, which actually kind of hurts the experience, despite the fact that you're first-person and therefore a little more immersed because you're right there. So I think it's game by game and technology by technology. I certainly don't think that first-person should go away and I certainly don't think that first-person is only relevant for shooters, though obviously that's where you mostly see it at the moment. But I certainly think the fidelity and increased quality of third-person means that third-person's a lot easier to integrate into a realistic, systems-based modern game than it was five or ten years ago.

It's interesting to hear you say that, since Warren always seemed to be making the choice of doing first-person from a game design and immersion perspective, whereas you were more concerned with the aesthetic consequences.

Well, I think we were saying that first-person lets us do a lot more right now. So we do increase the immersion, but simply because it works better, because if I go to third-person and look at these third-person games I feel like this kind of weird robot. And in first-person it's very natural to look around and interact with things, I don't have to have some weird arm that's trying to motion blend and looks horrible, all that kind of stuff. And as I said I still think that's somewhat true, depending on your game design and whether you can support third or not. But I think if you look at something like *Thief* where the player only does a limited number of things with the environment and you can do that fairly robustly in third-person, I think in that case you can immerse almost as well if not better in different ways. I personally still think that first-person is pretty exciting and pretty compelling in a way that other modes often aren't. But I don't think it's the only way to get a player fully involved. It's just always hard when you're looking at a character to be the character at the same time. Are you puppeteering or are you the character? And I think that's a weird thing. That's not yet at the point where we understand it so well that we have an answer.

Despite all your first-person games, you've always deliberately stayed away from making a shooter, which many seem to find to be the most obvious thing to do with that particular viewpoint. What are your motivations for avoiding it?

I don't dislike them. Personally it's just not all that interesting to me. I don't really play FPSs very much, I mean I do, every couple of years I play something. I played *Call of Duty* last year, I'm sure I'll play *Halo 2* and *Half-Life 2* this year, assuming they come out. It's not that I dislike them, it's just that they're not what gets me most excited as a creator. It just feels to me that there's a lot of interesting stuff to do that isn't that. In some sense, shooters have ultimate player choice, because they're all about systems-based damage dealing and damage avoiding. They're incredibly choice based. But on the other hand, that choice is incredibly limited. A role-playing game where I get to decide whether I'm the guy who kills people with axes or the guy who kills people with fireballs, that is a choice, but it's just not that compelling to me. So I guess for me I always feel that I've always tried to think about what can we let the player do that's cool and different and more about their own choices. And it just seems like FPSs are a slightly limited palette for that.

I've seen you discuss the concept of game developers abdicating authorship to the player. What exactly do you mean by that?

It's basically the same player stuff, in that we're the media where the player can be on stage, and the consumer of the media can be the one that's at the center of the experience. It's not like in a painting you don't bring yourself to the painting, but that's a slightly different experience than being the person moving around. And so when you think about the unique DNA of gaming and the unique things that we can do that other media can't, that idea of empowering the player and making the player the center of the experience is really pretty compelling to me. As I said, when players remember things, a lot of the stuff they remember is the stuff they did, not the stuff they read about. You talk to Miyamoto and he talks about "Hey, I started with the controller." And a lot of designers talk about verbs and the interactions and what are we going to let the player do. It's not that you're not authoring an experience — you're very clearly authoring an experience — but you're authoring a set of systems which generate an experience with the player. My hope would be that fifteen or twenty years from now that idea of player-centric mechanics is going to be in more of our games. I hope more of our stuff will be clearly a game that wants to be a game and is empowering the player to show off, and less games that are cool because they've got someone from a movie or the cut-scenes are great or the explosions are extra-special. Not that those things aren't great; hopefully we'll have all that stuff too, but hopefully we'll also have a player that's a little more involved.

Despite your goal to make your games offer players choices, they're almost all focused on physical conflict and players killing something or avoiding getting killed themselves. And certainly the rest of the industry is even more focused on killing and not getting killed. How long to you think until games offer players really more meaningful verbs to work with?

Yeah, I think we're still a ways off though we're making slow, slow progress. Right now the issues are just at some level those are the interactions that are easiest to explain to people and easiest to implement. Those are the emotions that are easiest to be definite about. People don't necessarily want gray or detail, and as I said, the closure moment of killing someone or knocking them off the cliff is pretty clear: "Yup, I got my score, OK great, next." Whereas when it's more about negotiating a truce or whatever, it suddenly gets a lot more vague, and I think that's why games are like they are. Twenty years ago, the question was whether the pixel was on or not. Hey, you have one bit, that bit is alive or dead. It doesn't seem like we've made as much progress as we should have in the last twenty-plus years.

Are you fairly pessimistic about the state of the industry?

Oh yeah, definitely. I find the industry incredibly frustrating, but yet incredibly compelling as well. There's good and bad.

For the last couple of years you've been fairly involved with the Indie Game Jam, where a bunch of programmer/designer types get together in a central location and crank out a bunch of unique games in three days, without really any regard for commercial viability. Do you see more hope for innovation in game design coming from something independent like that?

It's a couple of things. Part of it is just, hey, it's fun. On one hand those things are cool and do make a statement, but on the other hand it shouldn't be overlooked that part of their value is just a bunch of people getting together and having some fun. There's no real law against that. That said, there's only so much interesting risky stuff one can do in the industry, mysteriously, despite the fact that games now cost five or ten million dollars or more. That seems to constrain us more than it helps us at times. And I think as an industry we've got to learn how to deal with that. I don't literally think that we're going to do Indie Game Jams and then some year it's suddenly going to revolutionize the industry, and Bing Gordon will go to an EA stock announcement and talk about how, using the model of the Indie Game Jam, EA has restructured North American development. That seems somewhat unlikely. I don't think those things are there to say, "Here's exactly what the result was," but I do think hopefully they at least get individuals in the industry thinking "Oh yeah, that's cool," or "That's really crazy," or "Boy, you really could stay up all night for a couple of days in a row and write some crazy little demo." It can remind people about all the stuff that's left to go explore and all the ways you can play around and do little things. Even if they're not shipping commercial products, they can still remind us of why games are cool and remind us of all the things there are still to figure out.

The gaming press is sort of horrifying and marginally relevant at best anyway, but I think if you honestly rated games they'd all get a .05 or something. That's not true; there are certainly games that do a pretty good job at giving you a pretty cool experience that is relevant. *NBA Street* is a fine little street basketball game or whatever. But when you start talking about realistic games or games with characters, I think you right away notice, "Well, if that's a 9.6, then what are we going to be doing for the next 100 years?" Because I think there's a lot more than .4 left to go. So it's just good to keep an eye on the big picture occasionally and all the craziness that's out there to explore that isn't a street racing game, a thug-based shooting game, or whatever.

In general, you seem to balance your time working on games with being active in the game development community. What's your motivation for that?

I think games are really interesting and I certainly have a lot of opinions about them and some degree of frustration that we haven't done as much as we maybe should have or could have. And I think that as a community we're obviously a much bigger community than we were ten or fifteen years ago but it's still a fairly small group of people, big-picture wise. So I think we have a responsibility to try to understand our media and do interesting stuff. On some level we're clearly a commercial media, fair enough, and at the end of the day either we stay in business or we don't, so that's clearly top concern and I don't see anything wrong with that. But I don't think that's the be-all and end-all. I don't think there's any reason not to also think about what the industry will look like in five or ten years or think about where we could push and try to innovate or think about what's possible. So that we can all keep our eyes on what's out there and stay excited and stay involved. It just seems like the right thing to do.

Doug Church Gameography
Ultima Underworld: The Stygian Abyss, 1992
Ultima Underworld II: Labyrinth of Worlds, 1993
System Shock, 1994
Flight Unlimited, 1995 (Consultant)
Thief, 1998
Deus Ex, 2001 (Consultant)
Frequency, 2001 (Consultant)

Conclusion

As I stated in the introduction, this book is not a definitive guide to computer game design. No book can be. But it has attempted to inform the reader of what I know about game design, in addition to sharing the thoughts of seven of game design's most accomplished masters. Of course, none of the information in this book will amount to much if the reader is not prepared to use it to the right ends. As with any art form, computer games demand that their authors have a personal investment in their creations if the games are to be truly worthwhile. I feel that computer games have a great power to affect their audience, and a game designer has a tremendous responsibility to use that power wisely.

Art

The game development industry seems to be constantly involving itself with discussions of whether computer games qualify as an art form. Some other discussions center around whether computer games will ever be "legitimate" art. Such arguments are completely fruitless. We cannot make the public see us as legitimate merely by tooting our own horn and bragging of our accomplishments. Some people still fail to see film or jazz music or comic books as "legitimate" art and those forms have a body of work which, due in part to their age, dwarfs what computer games have produced. The question must be asked, "Would you do anything differently if computer games were or were not art?" Surely the best way to convince the public that we are legitimate is to act like it by producing works as compelling as those found in any other media.

Of course computer games are art. Could anything be more obvious? This is especially true if one uses the definition of art that I am most fond of, from Scott McCloud's magnificent book *Understanding Comics*: "Art, as I see it, is any human activity which doesn't grow out of either of our species' two basic instincts: survival and reproduction." It would appear that many game developers who constantly scream "games are art" have a certain insecurity complex and feel the need to justify working in games to their family or friends, to the public as a whole, or even to themselves. Such insecurities seldom lead to an artist working at her full capacity, since she is constantly going out of her way to prove herself. This seldom leads to great work; more often it leads to pretentious trash. When asked if he agreed with critics who said his films qualified as art, Alfred Hitchcock replied, "Oh, I'm very glad when they do, but it's not like taking page one of a script and then saying, 'I will now start a work of art.' It's ridiculous — you can't do it." Quality games are most likely produced when those developing them have no motives other than creating the most compelling experience for players.

532

The Medium

So often, we in the game development community are envious of other media. In part, this may be game designers wishing for the respect that other media command in society, the "legitimacy" that I spoke of earlier. Others may secretly, subconsciously, or even openly wish they were working on something other than games. A game designer may say, "I want my game to have a similar effect on the audience as the movie *The Godfather*!" or "I want people to enjoy playing this game the same way they enjoy listening to The Jimi Hendrix Experience's *Electric Ladyland*!" But this is the wrong approach to take. The strength of our medium lies in what it does differently from other media and the emotions it can evoke in the audience that no other art form can. If we endlessly try to ape other media we will forever be stuck with second-class, derivative works. Surely Jimi Hendrix did not try to emulate a movie he had seen when he recorded *Electric Ladyland*. Similarly, Francis Ford Coppola knew he would have to radically alter Mario Puzo's book *The Godfather* in order to make a good movie out of it. Indeed, Coppola's mastery of film allowed him to create a movie significantly better than the book upon which it is based. Both have nearly the same story, characters, and even dialog, yet Coppola's telling of the story cinematically outdid Puzo's literary telling in nearly every way. Though the effect a game has on a player may be different than a book has on a reader, a film has on a viewer, or a song has on a listener, it is not necessarily a worse effect, merely a different one. Computer games have strengths of their own that we must master if we are to produce the best work possible. Surely our medium presents challenges for those who choose to work with it, challenges not to be found in other art forms, challenges we have a duty to face if we hope to be more than charlatans and conmen.

In his book *Understanding Media*, Marshall McLuhan is famous for saying, "...the medium is the message. This is merely to say that the personal and social consequences of any medium — that is, of any extension of ourselves — results from the new scale that is introduced into our affairs by each extension of ourselves, or by any new technology." McLuhan argues that while people concern themselves with the content of television shows or plays or music, a medium's true message comes not from the content but from the medium itself. Now, I certainly do not claim to be a McLuhan scholar, yet I cannot help postulating what the nature of our medium of computer games is, a medium that did not exist when McLuhan wrote those words. The inherently interactive nature of computer games creates a mass medium that encourages players to be active participants in art in ways other media cannot. I cannot help but conclude that the fundamental message of our medium is one of participation and empowerment.

Game designers make a product that either facilitates the interaction between others, in the case of multi-player games, or sets up an interaction between a single person and the computer, for solo games. In the latter case, it is somewhat incorrect to say that the true interaction takes place between the person and computer, since the computer is nothing more than a medium for the interaction; the interaction actually takes place between the player and the game's creator. When I spent weeks of my early life alone in the dark computer room in the back of my parents' house playing *The Bard's Tale* and *The Bard's Tale II*, I never thought of myself as being alone. In a way I was there with Michael Cranford, the games' creator, playing in the world he had made, exploring the piece of himself he had put into the game. This medium seemed so powerful I knew immediately that I wanted to work with it to create my own games, so I could put a part of myself in games for players to experience.

The Motive

I have talked at length in this book about why players play games, but perhaps the most important question you as a game developer should ask is why you make them. Film director Krzysztof Kieslowski said that no artist has a chance of understanding her work if she does not understand herself and her own life, and what events have brought her to where she is. As you embark on your life as a game designer, questioning your own motivations in your work is vital to effectively using your medium.

The first question a designer should ask herself is how she came to work in computer games. Was it happenstance? Did a friend in the business happen to know of a position that was open? Was she aimlessly searching the classifieds only to find an ad about game development to which she responded, "Hey, that might be fun"? Did she see game development as something cool to do, much hipper than the jobs of her sorry friends who have to shuffle papers for a living? Did she really want to work in some other field, such as film or television, and when that career did not work out as planned she found that she could earn a living in the gaming business in order to pay the bills until something better came along? Or did gaming just turn out to be the profession which, given her skill set, would pay the most money?

As the reader might guess, none of the above are among the best motivations for working in games. There are people who come to gaming with more pure motivations, people who pursue it because it is what they want to do more than anything else. Of course, a designer might come into the world of game development with the wrong motivations only to find a passion for creating games stirred inside herself. Regardless of why she started working in games, what is essential is that now that she is developing games, she wants to truly make the best games possible.

I am continually surprised and disappointed by the number of people working in games for all the wrong reasons: because it is cool, because it pays well, because they do not have anything better to do. Game development may be more fun, stylish, and potentially profitable than many other professions, but these are side benefits that cannot distract from the true goal a designer must have: to make compelling interactive experiences. When other motives become a designer's primary guiding directives, her work is hopelessly compromised in a way that will hinder it from achieving its full potential.

The most likely person to make really brilliant games is a game designer with a dream. A dream that involves advancing the art of games beyond the more puerile and trivial concerns it may be seen wallowing in from time to time. A dream that involves a game-world so compelling players lose track of their regular lives as they play it. A dream that involves creating a work that captivates and involves players in the art as no other media can. A dream of computer games that enrich their players' lives for the better. Do you have such a dream?

Appendix A:

Sample Design Document: Atomic Sam

The following design document is for a simple console character-action game called *Atomic Sam*. The game itself is far from revolutionary and, from a design standpoint, part of its appeal is its simple nature. It is part of a project I was previously involved with that was never developed into a finished game. Despite this, the reader can consider the document to be "authentic," since it is written in the exact style and format I have used in design documents for projects that have made it all the way through production.

As a result of its simplicity, the design document for *Atomic Sam* is not very large. I have written documents five times the length of this one for other projects, and even those documents were not as big as others in the industry. Parts of this document were deliberately kept short, since it was not intended to be a complete design document, but rather to give its reader an idea of what *Atomic Sam* would be without fully detailing every part of the game. In particular, certain sections have deliberately been kept short. For instance, the listing of enemy robots is much smaller than it would be if the document actually described all of the enemies in the game. Similarly, a full version of this design document would include descriptions of more projectiles for Sam to throw, more devices and contraptions for him to manipulate, and more of the characters he would meet in the game-world. The game might even be expanded to include more areas than just the five described here.

In fact, more detail could be used throughout the document. The way this document is written assumes that the author is going to be involved throughout the development process, guiding the design in the correct direction. If this document were for a project that the author did not expect to be actively working on, it would make sense to add more detail throughout in order to be completely clear about the direction the project should take.

For example, the section about level design could be significantly more detailed. Indeed, readers may find it interesting to compare the level of detail in this document with *The Suffering* design document included in Appendix B, as that document is significantly more detailed in its level flow. However, if one has a team of level designers who understand the gameplay and can be trusted with the responsibilities of designing a fun level, the descriptions contained in the *Atomic Sam* document could be a sufficient starting point for level design. From this document, the level designers are given a great deal of freedom in terms of how to build their levels, a system that works well if the level designers are up to the challenge. Certainly, if you will be designing many of the levels yourself, you do not need to plan everything out in minute detail in advance. Many successful games have been made this way, including a number of the projects I have worked on. For instance, *Centipede 3D* had only a general notion of the AI, mushroom types, and power-ups designed before the level construction process began, and it was a system that ended up working quite well.

Of course, before writing a design document, the designer should have a good idea of the focus of the gameplay, as I have discussed elsewhere in this book. Here, for example, is the focus statement I had in mind when I started working on the design document for *Atomic Sam*.

Atomic Sam: Focus

> Atomic Sam *is a non-violent, fast-paced action game whose gameplay centers on defeating various villainous robots in creative and inventive ways, using a variety of projectiles and environmental devices. The story is one of a young boy separated from his parents for the first time who learns about the world through mentors, friends, and new experiences.* Atomic Sam *takes place in a unique "retro-future" with whimsical, nonsensical devices providing a unique backdrop to the unfolding of the story and action.*

Armed with the direction provided by the focus, the game design grew organically from there into the design you will read below. As I have stated before, there is no set-in-stone format for design documents. It is the designer's responsibility to present the design in as much detail as is necessary, in a manner that clearly communicates the design to all the members of the team.

Atomic Sam

Design Document
Version 2.0

This document and Atomic Sam are ™ and © 2000 Richard Rouse III,
all rights reserved.
Atomic Sam character designed by Richard Rouse III and Steve Ogden

Table of Contents

I. Overview

Atomic Sam is an action game with a strong storytelling component. In it the player controls Sam, a young boy separated from his parents, who must battle his way through hostile environments and defeat the robots that try to prevent him from finding out what happened to his mother and father. The game is one of quick reactions and clever planning in a whimsical futuristic world, a setting that will appeal not only to children but to game players of all ages who enjoy fast-action gameplay. The game is suitable for any modern console system.

The player's main task in *Atomic Sam* will be to navigate young Sam through the various environments of the game while defeating the robots he encounters. Though the game is centered around this combat, it is a non-violent game from start to finish, with Sam incapacitating but not destroying the robots that try to stop him. Whenever Sam is defeated, he is always stunned or trapped, never actually killed. The whimsical and optimistic nature of *Atomic Sam* requires that the game not play up any sort of gore-factor and that violence be kept to an absolute minimum.

The game will reward the player's creativity by setting up situations where the player can use environmental objects to defeat the robots that come after him. Rube Goldberg-esque contraptions will be everywhere, providing whimsical ways for Sam to incapacitate the many mechanized adversaries he will face. Figuring out what to do in different situations will be just as important as quick reactions and manual dexterity.

Atomic Sam is easy to pick up and play with simple, intuitive controls. An in-game tutorial section at the beginning of the game will provide an easy way for new, inexperienced players to learn how to play the game. In each of the middle three sections of the game, Sam will be accompanied by special friends who will help him defeat the enemies he faces. All the while, these friends will tell Sam interesting stories about this world of the future.

The setting of *Atomic Sam* is in the Earth of the future, but not exactly the future as we imagine it now. This is the future as foretold in the first half of the twentieth century, a world where all of the optimistic predictions about how technology would change our lives have come true. Atomic energy has created a pleasant, trouble-free world, with robots answering to humans' every beck and call and mankind the happiest it has ever been. Yet, key advances from the latter half of the twentieth century are notably absent in this world. For instance, jet-propelled airplanes have not been popularized, and as a result citizens travel on giant propeller craft and zeppelins from one mammoth metropolis to another. Similarly, no one has ever heard of a compact disc, microwave, personal computer, or video game.

The game's story starts with Sam returning from school only to find his parents strangely missing. Setting out to find them at their office using the rocket-pack they gave him, Sam finds himself attacked by menacing robots along the way. Finding that his parents are not at their office either, Sam meets up with the mysterious Electric Priestess. She sends Sam to look for his parents in the underwater city of Benthos, the robot city called Harmony, and all the way to the Moon colony named New Boston. On the way, Sam gathers evidence and discovers that Max Zeffir, one of the world's richest men and also his parents' boss, had them kidnapped when they learned something they shouldn't have. Sam then goes to confront Zeffir in his giant propeller-driven and atomic-powered airship the Ikairus. Finally, Sam defeats Zeffir and is happily reunited with his parents.

Because of its whimsical nature and youthful protagonist, the most obvious appeal of *Atomic Sam* might appear to be to a young demographic. Parents will certainly be pleased that the game has the player capturing enemies rather than killing them, and that when the player loses in a particular situation, Sam is always incapacitated in some non-lethal manner. But due to its sharp, frantic gameplay, assortment of unique environments, and inventive adversaries, the game will also appeal to young adults. And with *Atomic Sam*'s retro-futuristic look and emphasis on story line, the game will also appeal to older players, those who may well remember how differently we thought of the future fifty years ago.

II. Game Mechanics

Overview

Atomic Sam is a third-person, floating camera 3D action game in the tradition of *Super Mario 64* or *Spyro the Dragon*. *Atomic Sam* is different, however, in that the gameplay focuses less on exploration but instead on the player battling his way through the levels, avoiding the robots and other adversaries that try to block his progress. That being the case, the game mechanics are designed in such a way as to allow the player intuitive and extensive control of his game-world character while enabling the player to appreciate the interesting and compelling game-world in which he is placed.

Camera

In the game, the player will control the character Atomic Sam. At all times, Sam appears in the center of the screen, with a "floating" camera above and behind the character, in an "over the shoulder" type of view. The camera will be at such a distance that the player has a reasonable view of Sam and his current environment. The camera will be "smart" enough to avoid penetrating objects in the world and will always give the player a clear view of Sam. If necessary, in tight situations, the camera will zoom up closer to Sam. If Sam is too large on the screen and prevents the player from viewing the world adequately, Sam will appear translucent to the player, thus giving the player a clear view of the world. This translucency is apparent only to the player, and has no effect on the game-world or how the enemies react to Sam.

The camera will try to stay behind Sam as much as possible while providing a smooth visual experience for the player. If Sam turns around in a hurry, the camera will slowly catch up with his new direction instead of suddenly jerking into the new position. If the player changes Sam's direction for only a brief period of time before returning to the original position, the camera's orientation will not change at all. This allows the player to make minor adjustments to Sam's positions without having the camera swinging around wildly.

In-Game GUI

The majority of the player's screen will be taken up by a view of the game-world with the player's character, Atomic Sam, near the center of that screen. A few other elements will be overlaid on top of this view in order to provide the player with information about Sam's status and goings on in the game-world.

- **Current Projectile + Count:** In the lower left corner will be displayed an iconic representation of Sam's currently readied projectile. Next to this will be a series of "chits" or "ticks" representing how many of that projectile Sam has in his inventory. More information about the projectiles used in the game can be found in the Projectiles description below and the Game Elements section.

- **Selecting the Current Projectile:** When the player presses and holds the Next Projectile button, the player will see a horizontal display of the projectiles in Sam's inventory along the top of the screen. The player can then scroll through this list and select the object he wants Sam to ready. The weapons will be represented as icons. Once the player releases the Next Projectile button, this display will disappear.

- **Flight Time:** Sam's rocket-pack has a limited amount of flight time. This will be represented by a horizontal bar next to an iconic picture of Sam's rocket-pack in the lower right corner of the screen. The bar will appear full when Sam's rocket-pack is fully charged and will slowly go down the longer Sam stays airborne. For more information about the rocket-pack and its functionality, see the Flying Movement section below.

- **Current Dialog:** Different people will talk to Sam during gameplay; the friends Sam has accompanying him on his adventures, the Electric Priestess via the radio she gave him, and other characters Sam encounters may all say things to Sam. All of this dialog will be prerecorded and played back to the player. In addition, however, in the upper left-hand corner of the screen a 2D cartoon representation of the character will appear with the text appearing next to it. This will be important for players playing with the sound off or who did not manage to hear the dialog as it was spoken. This GUI element will disappear a reasonable period of time after it appears, allowing enough time for the player to read the text. When the game is in a non-interactive cut-scene, however, the dialog will appear at the middle of the bottom of the screen, as it would in a subtitled movie.

Replaying and Saving

The player has no "lives" in *Atomic Sam*. When Sam is incapacitated by one of the robots or another adversary (always in a relatively non-violent way), the player is able to go back to the last checkpoint and play that section again as many times as he wants until he passes it. Checkpoints are scattered throughout the levels, and the game automatically and transparently remembers when the player has reached such a checkpoint. The checkpoints will be carefully placed so as to enhance the challenge of the game without making it frustrating for the player.

During the gameplay, the player will be able to save at any time. However, when the saved game is restored, it will only start the player back at the beginning of whatever level the game was saved on, instead of at the exact location (or checkpoint) where Sam was on that particular level. This encourages players to finish a given level before they stop playing the game.

Control Summary

The player will use a number of different controls to maneuver Atomic Sam and to navigate him through the game-world. These controls are discussed in detail below. First, however, is a summary of the different commands, which will give the reader an overview of Sam's capabilities. The controls are designed with modern console controllers in mind, and can be easily adapted for whichever system *Atomic Sam* is developed.

- **Up, Down, Left, Right (Analog Controller):** The player will use this control to maneuver Sam along the horizontal plane in the game-world. Utilizing its analog nature, if the player presses the control a little bit Sam will move slowly, while if he presses it all the way in a given direction Sam will move quickly in that direction.
- **Fly Up, Fly Down (Left and Right Back Triggers):** The player will use these controls to propel Sam vertically in the game-world.
- **Throw (Right-Pad Down Button):** This throws one of Sam's currently readied projectiles.
- **Next Projectile (Right-Pad Right Button):** The player uses this button to scroll through Sam's inventory of projectiles.
- **Action (Right-Pad Up Button):** The player uses this control to perform miscellaneous actions in the game-world, such as flipping a switch, talking to a character, or picking up a large object.
- **Look (Right-Pad Left Button):** The player uses this button to activate the camera-look functionality.

General Movement

While Sam is on the ground or in the air, the player can move Sam forward, backward, left, and right in the game-world. The player will control Sam's movement in these directions using the analog controller on the game-pad. Control is always relative to the camera's view of the world. Therefore, pressing forward or up on the controller will move Sam away from the camera while pressing backward will move Sam toward it. Similarly, pressing left or right will cause Sam to move in the corresponding direction in the game-world relative to the camera.

Moving in a Direction

When Sam starts moving in a direction, he will at first maintain his current facing before turning to move in the new direction. For instance, if Sam is facing away from the camera and the player presses to the left, Sam will start side-stepping or side-flying in that direction. Only after the player holds that direction for a short period of time (approximately one second) will Sam then turn his whole body to face the new direction of movement. The same applies for moving backward from the current facing: at first Sam moves backward, and then after a second he will spin around 180 degrees and keep moving in this direction. This will allow Sam to reposition in small amounts in any direction without actually changing his facing.

Variable Movement Speed

Use of the console system's analog controller for movement in these directions will allow Sam to move either slowly or quickly in a given direction. If the player pushes the analog controller fully in a given direction, Sam will move in that direction at high speed. If the player presses it only a small amount in that direction, Sam will move much slower. This will give the player precise control over Sam's position in the world.

Flying Movement

Key to Sam's navigation of the game-world is the rocket-pack he wears on his back. The player has Fly Up and Fly Down buttons to control this rocket-pack, which allow Sam to move vertically in the game-world. Once in the air, Sam will hover at a given altitude if neither button is pressed.

Moving Up and Down

Sam will not move up and down at a constant speed. When the player presses up, at first Sam will move slowly, gaining speed the longer the player holds down the Fly Up button. This speed will eventually (after about a second of upward movement) reach a terminal velocity after which Sam will not gain any more speed. The downward movement functions in much the same way.

Stopping

When the player stops flying either up or down or in a given direction, Sam will not stop immediately, but instead will "coast" to a stop. Sam's animation when stopping will show him quickly shifting his weight to change the direction the rocket-pack faces. This means the player will have to practice flying Sam in order to get him to stop precisely where she wants.

Flight Speed

Sam's pack is not an extremely fast device, providing a maximum speed approximately 1.5 times Sam's speed when he is jogging on the ground. Whenever the player maneuvers Sam to the ground Sam will return to a walking/jogging animation and will move at the slower speed associated with being on the ground.

Directional Flying

Sam can, of course, move forward, backward, left, or right while also moving vertically. The player can accomplish this simply by pressing the analog control in a direction while also pressing the Fly Up or Fly Down buttons. Sam will appear to pitch in the appropriate direction to correspond with his overall movement.

Burst Speed

The Fly Up and Fly Down buttons will both move Sam at the same maximum speed, but tapping either button twice quickly will result in a "burst" of speed in that direction, moving approximately 1.5 times faster than the regular maximum speed for a short period. But moving at this high speed will also use up more of the rocket-pack's charge. This can be helpful for quickly dodging enemy attacks.

Limited Flight Time

The rocket-pack has a limited amount of flight time, though fortunately it can recharge simply through not being used. The rocket-pack's charge is used up whenever Sam is not standing on the ground, whether he is flying up, flying down, or just hovering. The amount of charge remaining in the rocket-pack will be represented by a small bar drawn on top of the game-world view in the lower right-hand corner of the screen, so the player will always be able to know when Sam's flight time is about to expire. The rocket-pack's charge will be decreased different amounts depending on how Sam is using his pack. The ratios of usage will be approximately as follows:

Usage	Charge Depletion
Flying Up	4
Flying Down	2
Hovering	1
Burst Up	6
Burst Down	6
On Ground	−3

Landing

Since the rocket-pack's charge is limited, the player must land Sam periodically in order to allow the pack to recharge. The player lands Sam simply by maneuvering him close to the ground or any flat surface he can stand on. Because Sam has a limited flight range, the player will have to plan Sam's movements accordingly in order to get Sam from one location to another. This will allow for puzzle elements in the levels where the player has to figure out how to navigate Sam to an area, given Sam's limited flying abilities. The "as the crow flies" route will often not be the route that Sam must take to reach a far-off platform.

Falling to the Ground

Having the rocket-pack run out of charge while Sam is in midair will not result in his death. Sam's outfit includes specially made shock-absorbing boots with extra thick soles, which will allow Sam to land safely when falling from any height. But when his rocket-pack's charge runs out, Sam will plummet at a great speed, providing a very disorienting experience for the player when Sam falls from a great height.

Limited Altitude

The rocket-pack will also only be able to attain certain altitudes. If the player tries to fly Sam too high, the rocket-pack will start to sputter, indicating that Sam cannot fly any higher. Because of this limitation, the levels can have open skies without allowing the player to actually fly out of the levels.

Rocket-Pack Upgrades

Throughout the game, Sam will periodically find rocket-pack upgrades. These will either be attachments Sam can add on to his pack, or Sam may find game characters that will be able to tinker with Sam's pack in order to improve it. These changes will provide a variety of enhancements to Sam's flying ability.

- **Longer Flight Time:** Sam can fly longer without having to land. This means Sam may have to acquire certain upgrades in order to reach certain locations.
- **Faster Burst Speed:** Sam can fly faster using the pack's "burst" functionality.
- **Faster Overall Speed:** The pack's maximum speed and acceleration are increased, allowing Sam to move vertically faster.
- **Improved Maneuverability:** The pack is better able to "stop on a dime." Instead of coasting to a stop, Sam can now stop as soon as the player lets go of the control stick.

Surfaces

Generally Sam can walk or land on any flat surface, whether it is the sidewalk or ground or a platform high in the air. Sam will be unable to land on surfaces that are significantly rounded or sloped. If Sam tries to walk up or land on a curved or sloped surface he will instead slide down the surface, stopping only when he reaches flat terrain.

There will be certain substances Sam will not be able to land or walk on. These include water, tar covered areas, or electrically charged floors. If the player navigates Sam onto such a surface while on foot, Sam will start an animation indicating the peril of the surface. For instance, if Sam comes up to an electrically charged floor, he will play an animation of starting to be shocked by the floor. If the player does not shift the direction of the controller to direct Sam out of the surface, Sam will quickly become incapacitated. Similarly, if the player tries to land Sam on such a surface while the rocket-pack still has charge remaining, Sam will start to be shocked, playing an animation early enough to indicate that the surface is perilous and to provide the player a chance to navigate him out of harm's way.

If the player runs out of charge while over such a surface, Sam will fall onto the surface and be incapacitated without any chance for the player to save him. Of course, whenever Sam becomes incapacitated, the player will have to start playing again from the last auto-save checkpoint. In order to succeed in the game, the player will need to avoid both navigating Sam onto such surfaces and letting the rocket-pack's charge run out while Sam is over such surfaces.

Picking Up Objects

Whenever Sam flies close to an object he can pick up, he will automatically pick it up if there is enough room in his inventory. The objects Sam can pick up include projectiles, rocket-pack enhancements, and the Electric Piranha. Sam will play an animation and a sound will be played to indicate that Sam has picked up the object.

Sam can also pick up certain larger objects but cannot add them to his inventory. Sam may need to move these objects for puzzles or may want to drop them on enemies to incapacitate them. The player can have Sam pick up these objects by pressing and holding the Action key while Sam is near them, and then can drop the object by releasing the Action key.

Throwing Projectiles

Key to dealing with the robotic adversaries Atomic Sam will face throughout the game are the different objects that Sam can find and throw. Though Sam will never find or use any sort of a gun, he will obtain different objects that can be hurled at enemies in order to incapacitate them.

Inventory

Sam will have a simple inventory that can hold up to fifty of each type of projectile. This is where projectiles Sam picks up will be automatically stored. The inventory is simple to use since the player cannot make room for another type of projectile by carrying fewer of another type of projectile. Sam can only remove items from his inventory by throwing them.

Picking Up Projectiles

In addition to starting the game with a small number of projectiles, Sam will find more projectiles throughout the game. Usually when Sam finds a projectile, he will find a group of them; for instance, ten Water Balloons or twenty Goo-Balls. Sam will automatically pick up these projectiles by maneuvering close to them. If Sam throws and misses with his projectiles, he may be able to retrieve them by going to where they landed, ideally after that particular encounter with enemies is over. In this way, players who are not very accurate at controlling Sam's throwing will get to retrieve their projectiles so they can try throwing them later.

Readying Projectiles

When a projectile is readied, the player will see Sam holding whatever his current projectile is, and an icon and counter in the lower right corner of the screen will reveal how many shots are left of that particular projectile. The readied projectile is the projectile that Sam is prepared to throw as soon as the player presses the Throw button.

The player will be able to select the "readied" projectile with the Next Projectile button. If the player quickly presses and releases this button, Sam will switch to the next available projectile in his inventory, if any. If the player presses and holds the Next Projectile button, the player will see a horizontal display of all the types of projectiles currently in Sam's inventory at the top of the screen, with the currently selected weapon appearing in the center. The player can then use the left and right directional controller to select previous and next projectiles, respectively, with the list of projectiles sliding left or right accordingly. The list will "wrap around" such that the player will be able to get to any projectile by pressing right or left repeatedly. Whatever projectile is in the center of the screen when the player releases the Next Projectile button will be Sam's new readied projectile.

Once selected, the player will see Sam holding whatever the current projectile is. If the player then does not throw the projectile or select a new readied one, after five seconds Sam will appear to put the projectile away. This is so that, visually, Sam does not appear to travel everywhere ready to throw a projectile. However, even if Sam does not appear to have a projectile ready, hitting the Throw key will instantly throw the readied projectile, just as quickly as if Sam had his arm out ready to throw.

Throwing the Projectile

The player will be able to throw Sam's current projectile by using the Throw button. The projectile will travel approximately in the direction the player is facing, though Sam will not have to be "dead on" in order to hit a target; the game will auto-target his shots at the closest adversary within the general direction Sam is facing. The current target will be labeled with a cross-hair so that the player always knows what target Sam will attack. It will be important to balance this auto-aiming so that it does not result in the projectile hitting targets the player did not want to hit, or in making the game too easy.

Throwing Speed and Distance

Releasing the Throw button will cause Sam to throw a projectile. A simple toss can be accomplished by a simple press and release of the Throw button by the player. However, if the player holds down the Throw button, Sam will be able to throw the projectiles faster and farther. This will be represented by Sam's arm starting to spin while the player holds down the Throw button, moving in a motion like a softball pitcher's windup, except continuing in a circle. Eventually, once Sam's projectile is going to leave his hand traveling at the maximum speed, Sam's arm will appear as a cartoon-style blur because it is revolving so fast. Though the auto-targeting will line up the player's shot with an adversary, if the player does not throw the projectile with enough force it may fall short of hitting this target. Part of the game's challenge for the player will be making sure the projectile is thrown hard enough to reach its intended target.

Projectile Capabilities

All of the projectiles in the game will be able to disable different types of enemies. For instance, the Goo-Ball projectile will cause enemies who are walking on the ground or on the walls to stick to the surface they are on, rendering them immobile. The Goo-Ball will be useless against flying adversaries. Another projectile, the Water Balloon, will be best used against non-waterproof robots, causing their wiring to short-circuit. Heavily armored robots or human adversaries will be invulnerable to the Water Balloon. The player will have to pick carefully the correct projectile to use in a given situation. A more detailed description of the capabilities of the projectiles can be found in the Game Elements section.

Electric Piranha

In addition to the projectiles and improved rocket-packs Sam will find in the game-world, the player will also find a special object that works in a passive way to protect the player against attacks. The Electric Piranha is a metallic green fish-shaped mechanism which, when found and picked up by Sam, will float or "swim" around him as if in orbit. This Piranha will be able to block incoming projectile attacks from adversaries by throwing itself in their path and "eating" the projectile. If the enemies attempt melee attacks while Sam has an Electric Piranha around him, the enemies themselves will be incapacitated when the Piranha sinks its teeth into the attacker. A Piranha explodes when it successfully defends Sam from an attack. Sam will be able to collect up to four of these Electric Piranha at any one time, and they will be key for his surviving particularly hairy situations.

Actions

The player will have a special Action button that will cause Sam to perform different actions in the game. The Action key will provide a variety of different actions, and the game will automatically determine what the correct action is for Sam in a given situation, if any.

Flipping Switches and Pressing Buttons

If Sam is near a button or a switch and the player hits the Action key, that button will be pressed or that switch will be thrown. The switch may do something as simple as opening a door or raising a platform, or it may perform a more complex action such as activating a crane or turning on a steam vent.

Pushing and Manipulating

Certain objects can be pushed by Sam, and pressing the Action key will allow him to do so. These may include crates, barrels, and balls of various kinds that may need to be pushed for a variety of reasons, including the blocking and unblocking of passageways.

Picking Up, Carrying, and Dropping

Sam will be able to pick up certain large objects using the Action key. This is different from the projectiles Sam will automatically pick up since he will not add these objects to his inventory, and while Sam holds one of these objects, he will be unable to throw any projectiles until he puts it down. When near such an object, the player can have Sam try to pick it up by pressing and holding the Action key. Once Sam has the object in his hands, he can carry it around with him, only dropping it once the player releases the Action button. While Sam is holding an object, particularly a heavy one, his movement may be slowed significantly. The player will want Sam to carry objects in order to aid in defeating adversaries. For instance, Sam could pick up a large anvil, fly with it up into the air, and then strategically drop it on a troublesome robot.

Talking

Some of the non-adversarial characters in *Atomic Sam* will be willing to talk to our hero, if only for a sentence or two. If the player wants Sam to talk to a character, he should press the Action key when near that character. These characters can fill in some of the back-story of the world of *Atomic Sam* while making the levels seem inhabited and interesting. Included among these characters will be "information robots," inventions of Sam's age that provide helpful advice to humans. Beyond just obtaining information, Sam will also want to talk to the characters that will be able to provide him with rocket-pack upgrades.

Reading

The player may see different informational signs or posters displayed on walls. In order to quickly zoom in and read these signs, the player can hit the Action key. These signs may include maps, which will help the player navigate the levels, or "tourist information," which describes the history of the area that Sam is in.

Interactive Combat Environments

In addition to throwing his projectiles at his enemies, Sam will also be able to defeat them by using parts of the level against them. The player can use the Action key to activate different events that will help incapacitate the various adversaries Sam is battling. The levels in *Atomic Sam* will be full of these contraptions, some of which may take on a Rube Goldberg-like level of complexity. Spotting and using these different setups correctly will be a major component of defeating the different robotic adversaries throughout the game. Indeed, the player will be unable to defeat certain adversaries without using these devices. In a way, these contraptions are "combat puzzles" in that the player must solve them in real-time in order to figure out the best way to defeat Sam's enemies.

These contraptions will be designed and set up by the level designer in order to best suit the level in which they are going to be used. Some key devices may be repeated throughout a level, perhaps in different configurations. Some of the devices will be usable only once, while others can be used repeatedly. The use of devices that operate multiple times gives the player a better chance of figuring out how to use the device through trial and error. When creating these contraptions and environments, the level designer will need to set them up in such a way that the player has a fair chance of figuring out what they do and how to use them correctly. A few examples of potential devices include:

- **Steam Vent:** A switch next to a hot steam vent may cause steam to shoot out, stunning or melting whatever is in its path. If the player waits until the precise moment when an adversary is in the path of the steam jet to flip the switch, the adversary will be disabled by the steam.
- **Fan:** A switch next to a large fan will be able to turn that fan on for a moment. This can be useful since it may blow whatever is in its path in a certain direction. For instance, if a steam vent is in operation across from a fan, a well-timed blast of the fan could force a creature into the steam vent.
- **Oil Drum and Lever:** Sam may come across a board laid across a steel box, creating a simple lever. A large, empty oil drum could then be placed on the lower end of the lever. If the player hits the Action key while Sam is near the higher end of the lever, this will cause Sam to press down on the lever, thereby causing the oil drum to flip through the air and possibly capture an enemy or two in the process.

If any of these devices are used incorrectly, they may backfire and end up hurting Sam. For instance, if Sam hits the steam vent switch when he is in the path of the steam, his rocket-pack may melt in the heat, sending him hurtling to the ground. Of course, a big part of using these contraptions effectively will be getting the enemy in the right place, and luring the robots and other adversaries into these traps will provide an interesting challenge for the player.

Looking

The player will have a Look button he can press. This functions similarly to Look buttons in other games such as *Super Mario 64*. While the player holds down the Look button, the camera will zoom in to be inside of Atomic Sam's head, and the player's forward/up, backward/down, left, and right controls will now pitch and turn the camera in those directions while Sam stays in one place. This will allow the player to get a clear view of Sam's surrounding environment, without Sam getting in the way of the visuals. This will be useful for examining puzzles and combat contraptions. As soon as the player releases the Look button, the camera will return to its normal gameplay mode.

Friends

Atomic Sam will not have to battle his way through all the game's levels alone. In each of the three intermediary game sections — Benthos, Harmony, and New Boston — Sam will meet game characters that will help him battle the robots and other adversaries he encounters. In Benthos, Sam meets Xeraphina the flying girl, in Harmony he hooks up with Scrap the robot, and in New Boston he is helped by Dulo the Moonie. (For more information about these particular characters, consult the Game Progression section of this document.)

These friends will not be as good at defeating the robots as Sam, but they will be helpful in taking out some of the enemies, warning Sam about impending attacks, hinting at solutions to puzzles, pointing out items that Sam can pick up, indicating hidden areas, or showing the best direction to go next. The friends will talk to Sam frequently as they make their way through the levels, providing back-story, useful information, and amusing chitchat. These friends will never actually die or become captured during regular gameplay; they will always be able to fend off the enemy attacks directed against themselves. For more information about the AI for these friends, consult the Artificial Intelligence section of this document.

Speaking

A big part of making *Atomic Sam* an appealing and memorable character for the player will be the lines of dialog he speaks throughout the game. These won't occur just during cut-scenes, but also during actual gameplay. Not controlled by the player but added in order to color the gaming experience, Sam will have a variety of generic utterances he speaks as he defeats various adversaries. These will fit both his age and the optimistic retro-futuristic setting of the game. Some of these slogans will include: "You can't stop the future!", "Atomic is the answer!", "Infernal machine!", and "You're outdated technology!" Sam may provide useful, informative comments when he's running out of projectiles or his rocket-pack is close to being out of energy. Sam will also have lines of dialog specific to special events in the game, such as when he first walks on the Moon's surface or when he first encounters a particular boss monster. By keeping Sam talking during the actual gameplay, the player will grow fond of the character and will be even more concerned for his welfare in the game-world.

Cut-Scenes

Brief cut-scenes will be used in the game to help convey the story line to the player. The game's 3D engine will be used for these cut-scenes, so there will be a consistent visual appearance between the interactive gameplay and the non-interactive cut-scenes. The cut-scenes will include talking between Sam and different characters such as the Electric Priestess, the different friends Sam has accompanying him, or other characters he finds in the different areas to which he travels. For particularly short conversations consisting of only a few lines, conversations may happen during gameplay without the use of a cut-scene.

Cut-scenes may take place between or during levels. Between levels they will explain upcoming environments and challenges, usually through information provided by the Electric Priestess. Cut-scenes that briefly interrupt the gameplay mid-level will include short, conversational exchanges between Sam and the characters he encounters. These mid-level cut-scenes will be visually seamless with the gameplay environment; their primary difference will be the change in camera angles. When Sam first travels to a new area, the player will see Sam traveling by blimp, auto-gyro, monorail, or other means of transport to the different locations in the game. On the whole, the cut-scenes will be as short as possible in order to get the player back into the gameplay quickly.

Storytelling

An important part of *Atomic Sam* is the story, and various devices will be used to convey that story. One, of course, is the aforementioned cut-scenes. These will convey all of the key information the player needs to be successful in the game. However, since they are non-interactive, they will be strictly kept to a short length so that the player can quickly get back to the gameplay. In order to convey more story, more sections of the story will be revealed through devices used during the actual gameplay.

Environments

Of course, the environments (levels) themselves will provide a key storytelling component by conveying a sense of setting. Special care must be taken to make sure the levels fit with the world of *Atomic Sam* and do not conflict with any story components.

Friends

The friends Sam meets and who accompany him in the various worlds will share the information they have with Sam while they are flying around with him. The characters may explain the history of a particular environment or some interesting data about the world of the future. Sam, after all, is a young child and still has much to learn about life. Of course, these friends will only talk to Sam during non-combat situations, when the player is focusing on exploration instead of defeating threatening robots. All of the speech that the friends speak will appear on the screen via the in-game GUI, as discussed earlier in this document.

Radio

After they first meet, the Electric Priestess gives Sam a small radio, which he can wear clipped to his ear. The player will hear information broadcast to Sam via this radio as he explores the levels. As with the friends, the Priestess may explain to Sam about the culture of the areas he is navigating and the nature of the adversaries he is facing. All of the dialog that the player hears over the radio will appear on the screen via the in-game GUI, as discussed earlier in this document.

Signs

As discussed earlier in the Actions section, Sam will also find static information displays that he will be able to read. These signs are yet another way to communicate the story of the world of *Atomic Sam*.

Levels

Atomic Sam is different from other console third-person action/adventures in that the gameplay focuses less on exploration and more on Sam's battling his way through the levels, avoiding the robots and other adversaries that try to block his progress. Certainly the levels will be interestingly designed and appealing to look at, but the player's motivation for continuing in a level will be more to confront the next interesting challenge than to merely uncover more of the level. Overall, the gameplay in the levels will be frantic and harried, and the player's split-second decisions and manual dexterity will be key to Sam eventually finding his parents. Sam will generally fight robots in two ways. The first way will be multiple robots at once, with all of the robots being of lesser power. The second way will be fighting a single, much more powerful or "boss" enemy. Usually the battles with the boss enemies will involve figuring out a particular method necessary to defeat the enemy, and will involve a bit more thinking than the battles with multiple adversaries at once. The method through which the player will maneuver Sam and the ways he will interact with his environment have been discussed earlier in this document.

That said, not all of the game will be frantic and combat-oriented. Between the battles with robots there will be calm, "safe" moments in the levels where the player can rest and regain his bearings. It will be in these calmer sections that the auto-save checkpoints (described later) will be included. This will allow the player to restart her game in a relatively safe area. Some of these "safe" sections may also require simple puzzle solving in order for the player to progress in the game.

Critical Path

All of the levels in *Atomic Sam* will have a definite "critical path" to them, a particular route the player is encouraged to travel in order to complete that level and move on to the next one. Though there may be bonus or secret areas off to the side, the critical path will remain strong throughout the levels. For each of the different sections of the game — Gargantuopolis, Benthos, Harmony, New Boston, and the Ikairus — the player will have to complete the levels within that section in a specified order; this will help to communicate the story line effectively, to build tension appropriately, and to ramp up difficulty over the course of a series of levels.

Training Level

The very beginning of the game will also provide a special "training" opportunity for players who want it. When Sam first returns to his apartment and finds his parents missing, he will decide to don his rocket-pack to go after them. The rocket-pack came with a helpful Instructobot—a pint-sized robot that speaks in robotic tones and instructs Sam how to use his rocket-pack. In fact, the Instructobot will encourage the player to experiment with the rocket-pack to get the hang of controlling it. In the safe environment of his house, the player will be able to experiment with Sam's different maneuvers before venturing into the more hazardous outside world.

The Electric Priestess' Home

The most "calm" section of the game is the Electric Priestess' bubble home. A mini-level where there is no combat, the bubble home acts as a "hub" between the worlds of Benthos, Harmony, and New Boston. In the Electric Priestess' home, the player will talk to the Electric Priestess and will be able to choose one of the different sections of the game to progress to next without any threat of harm. For more information about the Electric Priestess and the different worlds found in the game, consult the Game Progression section later in this document.

World Order

The player will get some choice in the order he experiences the game's different main areas or "worlds." After completing the Gargantuopolis levels at the beginning of the game, the Electric Priestess will present Sam with a choice of which area he will travel to next: Benthos, Harmony, or New Boston. Each of these areas will be fairly equivalent in difficulty, though due to the different challenges present in each area, different players may find one of the three harder or easier than the others. As such, the player can choose the one he finds easiest first. (In the middle of a given section, the player will have the ability to instantly revert the game to the Electric Priestess' bubble home, from which the player can choose a different section, if the one he was playing proves to be too challenging or he simply grows tired of it.) For more on the flow of the game, consult the Game Progression section of this document.

III. Artificial Intelligence

Since *Atomic Sam* is based around interesting combat scenarios, the primary function of the game's AI is to support these conflicts, providing the player with a compelling challenge. The AI will also be essential for imbuing the friends Atomic Sam encounters with some semblance of life, making them seem like more than just automatons.

Enemy AI

Many of the adversaries Sam faces will be robots. As such, the AI for these adversaries can be quite simple-minded while still being believable. Indeed, the simple-mindedness of some of his opponents will allow Sam to set traps for them using the interactive environments found in the levels. Not all robots will be simpletons, however. As the game progresses and the levels ramp up in difficulty, the robots will become more and more intelligent and thereby more and more challenging. Still later in the game, the player will fight human adversaries such as the Merciless Mercenaries. These human opponents will need to appear as intelligent in their combat decisions as a real-world human might be.

Player Detection

Different AI agents will have differing abilities to detect and track the player, which will in turn affect how much of a challenge they present to the player. Some robots will only be able to see in a very narrow cone in front of them, while others will have full 360-degree vision. Also, the distance of detection can vary from adversary to adversary; some can only see Sam when he is close to them, others can see him before Sam can see them. Some of the robots may have "super-vision," which allows them to see through walls and to always find Sam, regardless of how he may be hiding.

Some robots will also have very short memories. If Sam manages to run behind these robots, fully out of their field of vision, they may forget entirely about Sam and will return to an idle state. Other robots, once locked on to Sam's position, will never lose him. The player will need to figure out how well an adversary can detect Sam and use that to his advantage.

Motion

All adversaries will move in believable ways, employing a simple physics system to give the appearance that Sam's world is a realistic one. However, the feel of Sam's gameplay is one of a console action game, and hence does not need to rely too heavily on truly "authentic" motion systems. Indeed, the retro-future setting of Atomic Sam with its fantastic, implausible flying machines suggests a world that does not adhere to the laws of physics too closely.

Flying

Many of the adversaries Sam fights will be airborne, and it will be important to convey a sense of believable flight for these creatures. The type of flight motion involved will vary significantly depending on what type of flying equipment that enemy uses. An enemy kept aloft by a blimp will only be able to make slow turns and will not be able to move up or down very quickly. A creature with wings and propellers will be able to make turns, but will need to be able to bank to do so. Sam is the only character in the game who will have a rocket-pack, and this pack grants him a significant amount of maneuverability, something which will prove to be a great advantage over many of the adversaries he will face. Again, the flight model used by these creatures does not need to be truly authentic, but must be believable enough that the player gets a sense that the enemies Sam is fighting are truly flying.

Pathfinding

Detecting Sam is only the first part of the challenge for the robots. Once they have found Sam, the simpler robots may be too stupid to actually reach him. Pathfinding ability will vary significantly from the dumbest robot to the smartest. The dumbest robots will use a "beeline" technique and will be unable to maneuver around objects that get in their way. Somewhat smarter robots will be able to navigate around objects that they run into, but can still get hung up on corners. The smartest robots and the humans will always be able to navigate to the player, including opening doors and pushing obstacles out of the way as necessary. The player will need to exploit the deficiencies in the robots' pathfinding in order to succeed in the game.

Taking Damage

Many of the robots and other adversaries Sam faces will be incapacitated by a single hit from one of Sam's projectiles. Other, larger robots may take multiple hits before they are actually incapacitated. For instance, an electrical robot with heavy shielding may be able to survive three hits from water balloons before finally short-circuiting. Of course, different projectiles will have different effectiveness on different enemies, and some robots or enemies may be completely immune to certain attacks. See the Projectiles section under Game Elements for more information about the projectiles.

Combat Attacks

The AI agents in *Atomic Sam* will have a variety of attacks they can use to try to incapacitate young Sam. Many of the enemies will have multiple attacks to choose from in a given situation; for instance, an NPC may have a melee, close-range attack, and several projectile, long-range attacks. The NPCs will be able to pick which attack is most effective, or, when several attacks may be equally effective, will pick one at random or cycle through them in series.

Evading

The projectiles thrown by Sam travel at a slow speed, and as a result some of the smarter enemies will be able to dodge out of the way of incoming attacks. Of course, the AI agents will not be so good at dodging that the player never has a chance of hitting them, but just enough to provide an interesting challenge for the player.

Special Actions

To keep the challenges fresh and interesting to the player, there will be a variety of special behaviors that only the more advanced robots and human adversaries use. These will appear later in the game, and will force the player to adapt to them in order to succeed.

Taking Hostages

The battles the player fights with his enemies will often take place in inhabited communities, with non-hostile characters walking around to provide color. Some of the smarter AI agents will know to grab some of these NPCs and hold them as hostages. Sam will now need to avoid hitting these hostages with his projectiles. If the player flies Sam up close to these hostages and presses the Action key, he will be able to snatch them away and fly them to safety.

Internal Repair Arms

As some of the robots take damage from Sam's projectile attacks, the more sophisticated robots will be able to repair themselves. A common way for this to work is that a special "repair arm" can spring from a compartment on the robot. This arm can then bend around the robot's body to weld broken parts back together. The effect is more cartoonish than realistic, but conveys the sense that the robot is repairing itself. Some robots may first retreat to a relatively safe location, such as around a corner or far from Sam. Other robots will be able to multi-task by having the repair arm work on them while continuing to fight Sam.

Collaboration

Some of the enemies, in particular the Merciless Mercenaries, will know how to work together. Many of the robots will be singular in their purpose (attack Sam) and will know nothing of the other robots that may simultaneously attack Sam. But the significantly more intelligent Mercenaries will know that working collaboratively will be much more effective in defeating Sam. For instance, while one Mercenary keeps Sam busy with attacks from the front, others may swing around to the flank and attack Sam from there. Of course, having the enemies work together will allow the enemies to provide a much greater challenge for the player.

Trash Talking

While Sam fights these adversaries, he will hear them making derogatory comments about him, suggesting he can never win against their superior numbers: "Admit defeat, human!", "Your success is statistically unlikely," and "Steel is stronger than flesh! Relent!" Not all of the robots are able to speak English, and some may utter beeps and squawks as their means of communication. Others may be so cruel as to taunt Sam that he will never see his parents again.

Falling into Traps

A big part of the game mechanics in *Atomic Sam* is the player using the environment to his advantage by triggering various traps and contraptions that will help to defeat the robots Sam faces. The AI will actually facilitate the player using the traps effectively, in part through the robots' lack of intelligence. In addition, designers will be able to set up these adversaries to have a tendency to maneuver into areas where the player will be able to incapacitate them if she is clever. For instance, if there is an empty oil drum set on a lever that the player can activate, the robots will have a tendency to fly by the potential trajectory of that oil drum.

Non-Combatant Agents

The various areas Sam travels to are places where the people of Sam's world live and work. As such, the areas will not only be inhabited by the enemies sent to capture Sam, but also by normal citizens. These citizens will not be very smart, and their inclusion in the levels is not in order to create the impression of a "real" environment. These citizens are mostly there for color, while also creating targets that Sam must be careful not to accidentally hit with his projectiles.

Fleeing

Often, at the first sign of trouble, these citizens will run away, trying to find cover away from the battles between Sam and the robots. Of course, the mere existence of flying robots or a boy with a rocket-pack will not be anything too exciting to the jaded people of the future; it is only when the fighting starts that the citizens will realize the dangerous situation they are in. The level designers will be able to set up paths for these citizens to walk along and positions they will try to flee to for safety.

Talking To and Helping Sam

Of course, certain citizens will be willing to talk to Sam, and may share information about the area Sam is currently navigating. Others may even be willing to give Sam objects, or to make improvements to Sam's rocket-pack. Citizens who will be able to help Sam will have a tendency to wave to Sam as he flies by, differentiating them from the citizens who are merely there to add color and variety to the game environment.

Friends

One of the most complicated pieces of AI that will be needed for *Atomic Sam* is that which will control the friends he meets throughout the game. These agents need to be able to follow along with Sam and provide him with help in key locations without ever getting lost or stuck. Making a teammate AI that can support the player without seeming stupid or canned will be quite a challenge, but will have a significant payoff in terms of gameplay.

Invincible

The friends that follow Sam through the levels will not be able to be killed or captured by the robots and other hostile creatures found in the levels. First, the enemy creatures will have a tendency to attack Sam instead of the friends, since indeed it is Sam that they have been sent to subdue. Second, the friend AI agents will be able to defend against any attack that does happen to come their way. Similarly, if Sam should happen to throw a projectile at a friend, the friend will easily be able to bat it out of the way, saying something to the effect of "You've got to be careful with those things!" The logistics in terms of the friend AI being defeated and what this does to the gameplay is simply too complex to deal with. It may be useful, however, for the friends to be temporarily stunned, only to return to full helpfulness within a few seconds.

Following Sam

The most important task these friend AI agents must be able to perform is to follow the player around the levels. This means the friends will have to be able to flawlessly follow the player through the potentially complex 3D environments that make up the *Atomic Sam* game-world. If the player ever turns around to find that a friend got stuck a distance back on some sort of structure, the gaming experience will be ruined.

The NPC will not necessarily be right on top of Sam at all times. Indeed, the flying friends will be able to fly in and out of frame, giving the player the sense that they are always nearby without actually being on the screen constantly. Sometimes the friends will be just in front of Sam, sometimes just behind him, but always close by.

Guarding Sam's Back

These friends will play a crucial role in the gameplay by pointing out enemies that may be attacking Sam from a given direction that Sam has not seen: "Watch out, Sam, it's coming up behind you!" In some cases, the AI agents will be able to use their own attacks or projectiles to help defeat an enemy before it gets too close to Sam, though in any given situation the agents will be far less successful than Sam. It is important that the player will still have to fight robots on his own and will not be able to just sit back and let the friends take care of everything for him.

Providing Advice

Similarly, the friends in *Atomic Sam* will be able to provide the player with advice about different enemies as they arrive: "That one looks like trouble!" or "I don't think water balloons will work on that one!" In certain situations in the levels, the friends will be able to point out secret areas or show Sam a cache of projectiles he might otherwise have overlooked. The player will be able to navigate Sam close to a given friend and then press the Action key, to which the friend will always provide an answer. Sometimes the answers will not be useful: "I'm glad I met you, Sam" or "You really showed that last robot!" Other times, having Sam talk to the friend will provoke them to provide a hint: "Take the fork to the left; that will get us there faster" or "The best way to take care of these climbing robots is to throw something sticky at them. Do you have anything like that?"

Storytelling

In addition to the snippets of advice the friends can provide, they will also be key in communicating elements of the story to the player. When Sam reaches a certain part of a level, friends may start talking about the history of the area or about their own past. This provides additional story content to the game in a non cut-scene format, since Sam is still navigating the world while hearing about the story. The friends will be smart enough to only talk in "safe" situations when Sam is not actively being threatened by an enemy.

IV. Game Elements

Items

Sam's Projectiles

As Sam flies through the levels, he will be able to pick up a variety of different projectiles he can use in defeating his enemies. Different projectiles will work better or worse against different specific adversaries in different situations, and as such the player will have to constantly be selecting the most effective projectile for any given moment. The different projectiles are as follows:

- **Goo-Balls:** Greenish balls of a sticky substance, which make ground-based or wall-crawling monsters stick to their surface. Depending on the strength of the creature, it may end up stuck there just briefly or forever.
- **Water Balloons:** Able to disable robots with exposed wiring by causing them to short-circuit. Robots with protective coverings may require multiple hits to short-circuit.
- **Magneto-Mass:** A powerful magnet attached to a heavy weight, which will stick to metallic flying robots and drag them down to the ground.

- **Spring-Cage:** A small black cube with six rods sticking out of it. On impact with a target the Spring-Cage will expand to surround the target, entrapping it in a strong cage. Works best against small flying adversaries; larger enemies will be able to smash out of the cage.

- **EM Disrupter:** A small sphere that, when thrown, will fly a distance and then activate, rendering all electrical equipment within a certain radius of the Disrupter immobile. Flying robots will plummet to the ground, robots that cling to the walls will fall off, and ground robots will grind to a halt. The EM Disrupter does not work on humans or atomic-powered robots. The player will have to be careful when using the EM Disrupter while he has the Electric Piranha (as described in the Game Mechanics section), as the device will also cause Sam's Piranha to cease functioning and clatter to the ground below.

- **Bubble Wand:** Similar to the bubble wands/rings used by children to blow soap bubbles, this wand produces much stronger bubbles that will envelop a target and prevent it from escaping, at least for a few minutes. One of the more effective of Sam's "throwable" objects in the game, the Bubble Wand won't work on enemies with sharp objects, spikes, or propellers on them.

- **Atomic Bola:** One of the most powerful projectiles in the game, this looks like a traditional bola: two black spheres connected by wire. But these bolas are powered, and when the bola starts to wrap around a target the engines in the bola-balls activate, causing the bola to wrap around the target many times, very tightly. The Atomic Bola will not work on any flying adversaries that have any sort of propellers or rotor blades on them.

Rocket Enhancements

The player will be able to get various improvements to Sam's rocket-pack throughout the game, either through having an NPC tinker with the pack and make an improvement, or through an add-on that Sam can find and simply install himself. These enhancements provide a range of improvements to Sam's abilities.

- **Burst-Master:** The Burst-Master is a simple modification to the pack that will cause it to have much faster speed when the player uses the pack's speed burst functionality.

- **Speedifier:** The Speedifier will cause the overall speed of the rocket-pack to improve, such that Sam can navigate the world at a higher speed than he could before getting the enhancement.

- **Gyromatic:** The Gyromatic will grant Sam much more stable flight using the rocket-pack, allowing him to stop and start much quicker, instead of having to coast to a stop. The Gyromatic is a simple "snap-on" attachment to the pack that Sam can easily install himself.

- **Atomic Compressor:** A simple box with a dial on it that can attach to the side of the pack, this device will provide Sam with a longer flight time. The device works using a unique method to "compress" the atomic energy the pack constantly generates, thereby allowing the pack to store more of it at any one time.

Miscellaneous

Atomic Sam will also include other miscellaneous devices that Sam is able to pick up. These devices have a variety of functionalities that will improve Sam's abilities to navigate and survive the levels.

- **Electric Piranha:** Throughout the levels Sam will find numerous Electric Piranha — small devices that will "swim" through the air around Sam and deflect attacks for him. The full functionality of the Electric Piranha is described in the Game Mechanics section.

- **The Spidersonic:** The Spidersonic kit allows Sam to stick to any vertical surface as a spider would. Using this kit, Sam can grab onto the side of a building and stop flying, allowing his pack time to recharge before he flies on to the next location.

- **Moon Suit:** Found in New Boston, this handy Moon Suit will allow Sam to travel outside of the Moon colony and survive on the surface of the Moon. Fortunately, Sam's rocket-pack and utility belt can both be placed outside the suit so that Sam will be able to continue to fly and throw projectiles, though both will be affected differently by the Moon's gravity.

Characters

Sam will encounter a variety of characters in *Atomic Sam*. These include both friends and allies as well as enemies and, eventually, the man who kidnapped his parents.

Atomic Sam

The player controls Atomic Sam, a ten-year-old with a rocket-pack who uses his wits and dexterity to evade countless robotic and human adversaries throughout the game, not to mention navigating tricky areas, all in order to find his parents. Sam is about three feet tall and wears brown jodhpurs with a red aviator's jacket, the latter with gold trim. He also has a brown leather belt with various pouches on it. The large, clunky, "moon boot" type boots that Sam wears are silver in color. On his back is mounted the atomic-powered rocket-pack he uses to fly. It is a fairly small, compact device that is several inches narrower than the width of his shoulders, and several inches shorter than the distance from his belt to his neck. Sam has short black hair and wears a pair of 1930s-style aviator goggles. Sam's abilities are covered throughout this document. Sam's personality is what would be expected of a ten-year-old boy of the bright future: optimistic and smart. At the same time, Sam is without his parents for the first time in his life, and is somewhat frightened of the world he must now explore on his own.

Friends

- **Xeraphina:** In Benthos, Sam will meet a twelve-year-old girl named Xeraphina. A daughter of artists, Xeraphina has grown up entirely in Benthos, and has never seen the surface, a place she dearly longs to go. Xeraphina is able to glide around the city using a unique set of wings her parents invented, and will help Sam in his battles against his robotic adversaries. Xeraphina wears a tight-fitting light green outfit, with semi-translucent green shawls flowing around her body as she flies through the air. Her wings are made of a less translucent crystalline substance, are a darker jade green color, and are a good eight feet from tip to tip. Attached at her shoulder blades, they are a rigid construction, but flap slightly when she flies. She has a very friendly smile and wears her long brown hair in a bun behind her head, with a small paintbrush stuck through it to keep it in place.

- **Scrap:** In Harmony, Sam will meet Scrap, a shiny-new, recently constructed robot no more than a few weeks old. Scrap is a very friendly fellow who enjoys using his high-pitched voice to tell jokes whenever he can; puns are his specialty. In many ways, Scrap behaves like a robotic version of a ten-year-old, and dreads the day that he will be sent off to his work assignment, though he does not yet know what it is. Scrap is happy being a robot, but just wishes he would never have to "grow up," and dreams of a life traveling the world. Scrap is about Sam's size and is humanoid in form, except that he has four arms and a particularly small head. Scrap can use his pogo-stick-like legs to jump great distances, helping Sam to defeat his robotic adversaries in whatever way he can.

- **Dulo:** Dulo is Sam's parents' assistant. His general appearance as a Torso Moonie is described fully in the Moonie description below. In particular, Dulo wears special purple bracelets that he likes very much, which will help to make him stand out from the other Moonies, who all pretty much look the same, at least within the Torso or Bi-Header groups. Dulo is able to hop around and help Sam in defeating the robotic adversaries; his long tentacles are well suited to grabbing the robots out of the air and smashing them on the Moon's surface.

Other Characters

- **Electric Priestess:** The Electric Priestess is the mysterious woman who helps Sam to find out what happened to his parents and provides him with much useful information about the world. By the end of the story, the player learns that the Priestess is actually Max Zeffir's sister and was also one of his chief researchers.

She lost her leg in a zeppelin accident due to Zeffir's lax safety standards. The Electric Priestess continues to love her brother, while despising the money-hoarding madman that he has become. The Priestess dresses in a long jade-green dress with a large black hat that partially obscures her face. She has only one leg remaining, the other having been replaced by a clunky, robotic prosthesis.

- **Ike:** In Harmony Sam meets Ike, an old robot assistant his parents had some years ago of whom they grew very fond. Unlike many owners, when Ike got old Sam's parents released him from his work for them instead of just shutting him off, and allowed him to return to Harmony to live out his time with other robots. Ike is quite smart, though his memory is failing, as is explained in the Game Progression section. Ike does not say much, but once his memory is activated he will speak with great love and respect for Sam's parents. Ike looks a bit older in design than many of the other robots Sam will find, with a boxy, clunky shape and a larger frame than many newer robots, such as Scrap. He is also quite slow moving because of his age. Ike moves around on tank treads, and was designed with only one arm, a long, five-jointed limb connected to his torso in the middle of his chest.

- **Tool:** Tool is the "robot doctor" whom Sam will need to locate in Harmony in order to save Ike. Tool is a huge robot who looks like he would be very violent and destructive. Instead he is very kind and caring, in a "gentle giant" sort of way. Tool is mute, and speaks only through a text display in the middle of his chest. Tool floats through the air a short distance above the ground using an anti-gravity unit he wears around his waist. When "operating" on robots, Tool does not use the massive arms and fists that are attached to his upper torso. Instead, a small compartment springs open in his chest from which small, spindly robotic arms pop out to do precision work.

- **Moonies:** "Moonies," as Earthlings call them, average about four feet in height and hop around on the lower half of their bodies (they have no legs). For arms they have two tentacles, one on either side, which are quite long and strong, yet prehensile enough to use a human pen to write. Though the Moonies are asexual, there are two different physical varieties of the creatures; one with two heads that sit atop their bodies as humanoid heads do (which Earthlings call "Bi-Headers"), and another that has no head at all, but instead has its eyes and mouth located on its torso (which Earthlings call "Torsos"). The Moonies also have white bumps on their bodies that can glow when necessary, allowing them to maneuver through dark areas. This lighting is necessary for them to navigate on the Dark Side of the Moon, where they have lived for all their recorded history.

Enemies

Arctic Immobilizer Blimp   The Arctic Immobilizer Blimp (AIB) is an easy to middle difficulty robotic adversary that Sam will have to disable or evade. Shaped like a cylinder, made of shiny, silvery metal, and suspended from a miniature zeppelin, the AIB floats through the air at a relatively slow speed, being propelled forward by a small rear propeller. Two metal claws extend from either side of the tube, and the AIB will wiggle these claws menacingly at Sam. The front end of the cylinder has four metal spikes that close over the front opening. The AIB will be able to move up and down (again, at slow velocity) in order to line up with Sam and attempt to attack him, but its slow speed will prevent the AIB from giving chase if Sam successfully evades it and flies away. Since the AIB flies, if Sam uses the Goo-Balls on it they will have no effect. One of the best projectiles for defeating the AIB will be the Magneto-Mass, which will quickly bring the enemy to the ground.

The enemy has two attacks, one a melee attack and the other a mid-range attack.

- **Claw Attack:** If in close range, the AIB will be able to slice at Sam with its two claws, possibly cutting off his rocket-pack. Sam will need to avoid getting in close range of the AIB in order to avoid this fate.

- **Freeze Mist Attack:** For the AIB's second attack, the four metal spikes that cover the front of the tube will fan outward, revealing a small nozzle. From this nozzle will come a liquid spray, which will freeze whatever it contacts. The spray generates a cloud of mist in front of the AIB, and if Sam comes in contact with this cloud before it dissipates he will be frozen solid in a block of ice and plummet to the ground.

Arachnaught The Arachnaught is a fairly easy to defeat robotic enemy. The Arachnaught looks approximately like a four-legged spider, with each leg being a three-jointed appendage with a spiked end. The legs all come together at a fairly small main body, which contains a curved vision-sensor that gives the creature a good range of sight. The Arachnaught cannot fly at all, but instead can climb up the sides of buildings just as easily as walking on the ground. The Arachnaught moves quite quickly, in a scurrying fashion. Since it crawls on surfaces, the Arachnaught will be impervious to Sam's projectiles that work on flying adversaries, while being particularly susceptible to the Goo-Ball projectiles.

The Arachnaught has three attacks: melee, projectile, and a short-range "tractor beam" effect.

- **Claw Attack:** The Arachnaught will be able to attack with its sharp legs, devices that will easily allow it to slice off Sam's rocket-pack, thereby incapacitating him.

- **Sticky Web Balls:** The Arachnaught can shoot large, slow-moving globs of a uniquely sticky substance. If Sam is on the ground when hit by this substance, he will be stuck to the ground and immobilized. If Sam is in the air, he will be temporarily unable to throw any projectiles, as he attempts to struggle out of the sticky substance. If Sam runs into any surfaces with the web ball still on him, he will stick to that surface and become incapacitated.

- **Web Strand:** The Arachnaught's most fiendish weapon may well be its web strand attack. Using this, the Arachnaught can shoot a long strand of webbing toward Sam and, if it hits, can then pull Sam back toward itself. Then, once Sam is close, the Arachnaught can use its claws to rip Sam's pack off, thereby putting him out of commission. Sam will have to fly in the exact opposite direction of the web strand, only breaking free after five seconds of resistance.

Merciless Mercenary   Though many of Sam's adversaries in the game will be various robotic constructions, Sam will encounter human foes on Max Zeffir's flying fortress, the Ikairus. Dubbed the Merciless Mercenaries (MMs), these humans are highly trained and will be quite difficult for Sam to evade or incapacitate. Dressed in black uniforms with red trim and fierce-looking steel helmets, the MMs are able to fly by an anti-gravity belt fastened around their waist. The belt allows them to float in the air, and in order to actually propel themselves, the MMs need to perform a "swimming" type motion. Many of Sam's projectiles will be useless against the MMs; the only effective weapon will be the Atomic Bola, which will wrap around the MMs' legs and prevent them from "swimming" any farther. The MMs are one of the more mobile adversaries Sam will encounter. For this enemy, running away will be hard since the MMs will be able to track Sam and move almost as fast as he does.

The MMs have a total of three attacks: one melee and two ranged.

- **Tri-Power Trident Melee:** The MMs carry gold-colored, metal tridents called Tri-Power Tridents, which have two functionalities. The first is as a simple melee attack, used if Sam gets too close. The sharp ends of the Tri-Power Trident will easily be able to rip Sam's rocket-pack right off.

- **Tri-Power Trident Ranged Attack:** The second attack of the Tri-Power Trident is to shoot a large, slow-moving mass of light blue, sparking energy into the air. This travels toward Sam, tracking him, but it alone will not hurt him. When it gets close enough to Sam, it stops moving and explodes into six miniature energy balls. These small balls hurtle at great speed in random directions outward from the main ball, and if they come into contact with Sam burst into a perfect energy sphere with Sam trapped inside. Unable to break out of the sphere, Sam is now immobile.

- **ElectroNet:** Finally, the Mercenaries have an ElectroNet, which they will throw with their other arm (the one that does not have the Tri-Power Trident in it). This net, similar to Sam's Atomic Bola, has heavy black balls at its ends that propel it in the direction thrown. Of course, if the net manages to wrap around Sam, he is incapacitated.

Visionary   At the end of Harmony city — the town that is the hub of robot manufacturing — Atomic Sam will face a fierce boss enemy. In appearance the Visionary is a giant eyeball-like mechanism, with two metal structures on each side, both of which have helicopter blades on them. These blades keep the Visionary aloft, giving it great maneuverability. The Visionary can travel up and down at speeds much faster than Atomic Sam can manage with his rocket-pack, though it is a bit slower at turning than Sam.

From the bottom of the eyeball emerge three steel tentacles, each with a different mechanism on its end. Each of these devices is the basis for one of the Visionary's three attacks.

- **Electric Blades:** One tentacle features three rotating blades that all point in the same direction like a claw. These blades continually rotate menacingly. Their real power, however, is to shoot an electric shock wave that can stun Sam into unconsciousness. The blades spin up to a high-speed whirlwind and then unleash the blast from their center. This ranged "beam style" attack will be tricky for the player to avoid; once the player sees the Visionary's blades start spinning at high speed, she must be careful to move Sam out of the path of whichever direction the blades are pointing.

- **Magnet:** One tentacle has a giant, U-shaped magnet on the end of it. The Visionary can turn on this magnet, attracting the metal in Sam's rocket-pack and sucking the player toward the robot. Sam will have to use all his dexterity to avoid getting too close to the enemy, where the robot will be able to rip Sam's rocket-pack off using the tentacle arm with the blade attachment.

- **Smog:** The third tentacle has a giant funnel on its end. From this funnel the Visionary can shoot a thick, black cloud of gas, which will cause Sam to have an uncontrollable (and game-ending) coughing fit should he be so unfortunate as to fly into it. This smog cloud will hang in the air for some time after the Visionary shoots it, and the player will have to be careful not to fly into that cloud until it dissipates.

As with all the boss monsters in the game, most of Sam's regular projectiles will not be very effective against the Visionary. They may slow down the robot for a short time, but they will not permanently defeat it. The player will need to use the setup of the level itself in order to incapacitate the Visionary. This makes defeating the boss less a matter of dexterity, repetition, and perseverance, and more about understanding the puzzle, which, once figured out, is not that hard to repeat. Since the player is battling the Visionary at the end of the Harmony levels, the battle will take place in a robot factory. The Visionary emerges from a storage crate riveted to the ceiling at the top of the play area where Sam will battle the robot. Scattered about the area are various appropriate pieces of equipment used in a robot factory, as well as four high-powered fans. Sam will be able to turn on these fans by using his "action" ability near them. He will also be able to use his Action button to rotate the fans and change the direction they are blowing. By activating and blowing all of the fans upward beneath the storage crate, Sam can create a windy vortex which will be able to push the Visionary — since it is kept aloft by helicopter blades — back up into the case. Sam will then, by using a switch near the crate, be able to close the crate and trap the robot inside, hence defeating the creature.

Max Zeffir   Zeffir is the founder and owner of Zeffir Zoom, and is widely considered to be the richest man on the planet. Zeffir started acquiring his fortune with his zipper company, Zeffir Zippers, and then moved on to virtually every other industry he possibly could. His companies include the aircraft manufacturer Zeffir Zeppelins, the clothing line Zeffir Zest, and the Zeffir Zeitgeist news network.

Max Zeffir is also the employer of Sam's parents and, as it turns out, the one who kidnapped them in order to keep them quiet. Sam will finally have a showdown with Zeffir in the end-game, where Zeffir will turn out to be quite a formidable opponent himself.

When the player finally meets Zeffir he will be wearing a 1920s-style "railroad baron" black pinstripe suit with an extra large top hat. Zeffir sports a stringy black mustache and a mischievous grin. Zeffir will battle Sam on his Negativity Platform, so named because it negates the effects of gravity. A circular disk that floats on the air and is much more maneuverable than Sam's rocket-pack, the platform features waist-high handrails, which he holds on to while the platform flies around.

Zeffir's combat will consist of two methods of attacking the player:

- **Robots:** Zeffir will battle the player by summoning robots to fight Sam. These will be all manner of robots that Sam has been fighting throughout the game, and they will emerge from various compartments throughout the large, domed room in which Sam and Zeffir battle. Sam will have to defeat these robots as he normally would in the rest of the game. Zeffir will bring out a maximum of three robotic adversaries at a time.

- **Tuning Fork:** Zeffir will also hold a six-foot-long tuning-fork-like device in his hand. When Zeffir strikes this bar on the rails of the Negativity Platform, it creates a sonic blast, which he can aim at Sam. If the blast hits Sam, he will be temporarily stunned and have to stop flying and raise his hands up to cover his ears. This will make Sam particularly susceptible to robot attacks, since he will be unable to move or throw projectiles.

The player will be able to defeat Zeffir using a variety of different tactics, which can be used in different combinations.

- **Brute Force:** Once hit with a lot of projectiles of the right sort, Zeffir will finally be defeated. Only some of Sam's projectiles will work, however; the Magneto-Mass and Spring-Cage will be ineffective against Zeffir, while the others will slowly wear him down. It will take a lot of hits, however, and Zeffir will do his best to bring out more robots and to blast Sam with his Tuning Fork at the same time. As a result this is the most difficult of the ways to defeat Zeffir, but it is also the most obvious.

- **Disable Negaposts:** Zeffir's Negativity Platform is actually held aloft by four Negaposts, which are on the ground in four opposite corners of the room. As Zeffir moves about on the Platform these posts glow. Sam will be able to take out one of the posts by hitting it with three water balloons. When the post goes out of commission, Zeffir temporarily loses control of his craft, only to regain it quickly. Sam will need to incapacitate all four posts before the Negativity Platform will actually stop working and clatter to the ground of the room, where Zeffir will surrender.

- **Get Zeffir's Ear Protection:** The player will notice that Zeffir is wearing a bulky pair of "ear protectors," large devices that look like headphones but which serve to block out the dangerous sound of the Tuning Fork. If the player is clever enough, he will realize that if he hits the Negativity Platform hard enough the ear protectors will be knocked off of Zeffir. They cannot be knocked off simply by pelting Zeffir with projectiles, however. The player will need to cause Zeffir to steer the Negativity Platform into a larger swinging girder that hangs from the top of the domed room. If Sam is simultaneously pushing the girder while Zeffir is flying toward it, the impact will knock the ear protectors right off. If the player then flies Sam down to where the ear protectors fell, Sam will put them on. Now Sam is immune from Zeffir's blasts and will have a much easier time defeating him, using either brute force or by disabling the Negaposts, as described above.

V. Story Overview

Atomic Sam is the story of a young boy, separated from his parents for the first time, who must rise to the challenge of discovering what has happened to them. Though *Atomic Sam*'s focus is as an action/adventure game, the humorous and touching story sets the game apart from many other console action games.

The setting of *Atomic Sam* is the Earth of the future, but not exactly the future as we imagine it now. This is the future as foretold in the first half of the twentieth century by magazines like *Popular Science* and *The Electrical Experimenter,* as well as by futurists like Norman Bel Geddes and Buckminster Fuller. Certain innovations that we see as obvious today never came to pass, such as jet airplane travel; instead, people still travel aboard giant propeller craft and zeppelins. Similarly, the personal computer and certainly the Internet are unheard of, while super-intelligent and always helpful robots are ubiquitous. Man has even colonized the Moon and found the extraterrestrial life that lives there, the "Moonies." It is in this whimsical and fun future that the story of *Atomic Sam* takes place.

One day, young Sam returns from school to his parents' apartment only to discover them mysteriously missing. Sam's parents are both scientists at Zeffir Zoom, a transportation company, but they always make it a point to be home when Sam returns from school. Distraught, Sam decides to go looking for his parents. He dons a red jacket and puts on the atomic rocket-pack they gave him for his birthday, and renames himself Atomic Sam, gaining courage through his new alter ego.

Sam travels through the city of Gargantuopolis toward his parents' office, but along the way is attacked by robots who try to block his progress. Sam finally reaches their office, only to find them missing from there as well, with only a mysterious note remaining. A friendly robot soon arrives, however, and escorts Sam to a towering building right next door. Sam travels up to the top floor and meets a strange woman who calls herself the Electric Priestess. She tells Sam that, though she does not know what has happened to his parents, she will help him find them. She offers Sam transportation to three locations where Sam may try to discover their fate.

Sam will travel to Benthos, the city beneath the sea. There he will meet Xeraphina, the flying girl, who will help Sam locate his parents' private office. Next is Harmony, the robot city, where Sam will try to look for Ike, the robot who was his parents' loyal assistant for years. Along the way Sam meets Scrap, a plucky young robot who strangely doesn't want to "grow up" and go to work. Finally, Sam travels to New Boston, the Moon colony, searching for another friend of his parents, Dulo the Moonie. At each of these locations, Sam is attacked by merciless robots out to defeat him and stop his inquiries. After having fully explored each of these areas, Sam finds a piece of a wax cylinder which, when all of its pieces are assembled, can be played back to reveal what happened to his parents.

The cylinder contains a warning message from Sam's parents: they think they have stumbled on a safety problem with the monorail system being developed by Max Zeffir, their employer. Unfortunately, Zeffir does not want to fix the problem because of its prohibitive cost and, as a result, has kidnapped Sam's parents to keep them quiet. The Electric Priestess will now be able to lend Sam an auto-gyro to take him to the Ikairus, Zeffir's massive airship. There Sam will battle still more robots before confronting and defeating Max Zeffir. Then, finally, Sam is reunited with his parents.

VI. Game Progression

Setting

Atomic Sam takes place on an Earth of the future, at an indefinite time, perhaps in the twenty-first century. This is not the future as our culture of the turn of the twenty-first century envisions it now, but instead as people optimistically foresaw it in 1920s, 1930s, and 1940s America. Instead of jet planes transporting passengers across continents, the world of *Atomic Sam* is filled with zeppelins and "giant wing" propeller craft. In *Atomic Sam*, nuclear energy has not turned out to be a disappointment as it has in the second half of the twentieth century. Instead, it has fulfilled its tremendous promise of cheap, clean energy, and has been refined to the point where it can be used safely in a child's toy or in zeppelins.

This is a future that has conquered poverty through technology, a future in which the skyscrapers stretch to unprecedented heights, and there is enough room for all to live happily. Private planes and auto-gyros (a plane/helicopter hybrid) are not uncommon, and many land on the roofs of the towering skyscrapers. Rail travel is a very important part of this future, and high-speed monorails provide quicker travel between cities than slower zeppelins.

Intelligent robots are everywhere, and people can purchase robots either to be workers in their factories or butlers in their homes. Instead of running people out of work, however, these robots have increased everyone's leisure time, while in turn enhancing everyone's prosperity. This is not the bleak, troubling future found in so much science fiction of the last two decades, but an optimistic world where technology has set the human race free to be happy.

The advance in robots did create some interesting problems, however. Robots are now basically as smart as the smartest humans, with intelligences so developed that they have emotions and desires of their own. Certainly many robots are more physically strong and resilient than humans. Yet the robots have not risen up to conquer the humans, as many science fiction works might foresee. (All of the aggressive robots that Sam faces in the game are following the orders of a villainous human.) Instead, these robots are still obligated to follow the laws humans make, for reasons that are never fully explained. Indeed, robots have no rights and are treated very much as property by the humans, not unlike African slaves were treated in the first hundred years of United States history. For instance, if part of a robot breaks, it may be cheaper to replace the whole robot than to fix it. If this is the case, it is the prerogative of the owner of the robot to permanently shut it off if he so chooses, and few humans would question that decision as being the right one. *Atomic Sam* does include some hints of a robot "underground," which tends to the old robots in the most humane ways possible, as is explored in the Harmony section of the game.

In this future Earthlings have managed to reach the Moon and have set up a Moon colony there called New Boston. This colony consists of a number of domed structures, which provide a breathable atmosphere and Earth-like gravity. Moon walks are allowed for the residents, using space suits, of course, with many Moon residents finding such excursions to be a fun way to take a break from dome life.

When humans did finally reach the Moon, they were surprised to find a race of extraterrestrials there. These creatures had lived unnoticed on the Dark Side of the Moon for many centuries, only in the last thirty years revealing themselves to humans as the Moon colony was built. In addition to their generally strange appearance, the Moonies come in two varieties: the "Bi-Headers" and the "Torsos." The Bi-Headers have two heads on top of their bodies, while the Torsos have none, instead having a mouth and eyes on the front of their torsos. The Moonies do not breathe and are much denser creatures than humans, and as a result can survive in either Earth or Moon atmosphere. The Moonies, though not technologically advanced, are just as intelligent as humans, and on making contact with Earthlings are quick to learn English. The Moonies and humans now live cooperatively on the Moon, helping each other in many different ways.

On first contact, the reaction of humans to the Moonies was one of shock and disbelief. Over time, however, humans came to realize that Moonies did not pose a threat and became quite friendly with them, in particular with the Bi-Headers. It seems that since the Bi-Headers looked a bit more humanoid than the Torsos, humans found them more acceptable. As a result, only the Bi-Headers are allowed in New Boston, while the Torsos must stay outside on the Moon surface. Humans found the Moonies to be great collaborators on scientific projects, using their unique way of thinking to help advance technology. However, though both sets of Moonies are equally intelligent, only the Bi-Headers are allowed to work with humans in an academic capacity.

Though we now see many of the technological advances described above as either impossible, impractical, or undesirable, this is the world of *Atomic Sam*, where the illogical nature of the environment is part of its charm. On the other hand, while this future contains many advances we see as impossible today, it also doesn't include a lot of the advances we take for granted today. For example, in this future people have no idea what a personal computer is, and in turn, computer games surely don't exist. Though television exists, it is still on a tiny television screen and is vastly inferior to a movie theater experience. While in some ways the world of the twenty-first century in *Atomic Sam* is more technologically advanced than 1990s America, in other key ways it is certainly less advanced, giving it a unique "primitive future" look.

Introduction

The player controls the game's namesake, Atomic Sam. A normal though precocious boy ten years of age, Sam returns from school one day to find his apartment home ransacked and his parents mysteriously missing. Donning the atomic-powered rocket-pack given to him by his parents for his birthday, Sam renames himself Atomic Sam and vows to venture through Gargantuopolis to find his parents.

Gargantuopolis

Following this brief introductory cut-scene, the player gains control of Sam inside his parents' apartment. Here the player will be able to follow the instructions given to him by the Instructobot that came with his rocket-pack. These instructions will teach the player how to effectively control Sam. The player will also be able to skip by that section and proceed out into the city, trying to get to his parents' office deep in the city.

Gargantuopolis is a mammoth city of the future, with towering buildings creating something of a sense of claustrophobia, and Sam's rocket-pack is unable to fly him over their tops. Traveling through the city, Sam is attacked by a great variety of robots that try to prevent him from discovering what has happened to his parents. Where these robots came from and why they are trying to subdue Sam remains a mystery at this point in the game.

Sam's parents are atomic scientists at Zeffir Zoom — a company that works at harnessing atomic energy for increasingly fast modes of transportation. Upon reaching his parents' office at Zeffir Zoom's main research complex, a cut-scene will take over, showing Sam finding a hastily written note left by his parents proclaiming, "Someone has to check on Sam!" Along with the note is a fragment of a wax cylinder used for voice recording. Since the cylinder is incomplete, Sam is unable to play it back at this point.

The Electric Priestess' Bubble Home

Distraught at having failed to find anything out about his parents' disappearance, Sam is suddenly approached by a friendly robot who quickly leads him to a nearby building. Here Sam takes the elevator to the top floor, where he meets a mysterious woman who calls herself the Electric Priestess. Quite a mysterious figure, the Electric Priestess lives alone in a sphere-like "bubble home" dwelling atop a high skyscraper. The ceiling of this bubble home is entirely glass, providing a breathtaking view of the surrounding city. In the home are numerous large steel doors, which lead to various forms of transportation at the Priestess' disposal.

The Priestess explains to Sam that she knows of his parents' disappearance, and offers to help him. At this point in the story, why the Electric Priestess is helping Sam is still unclear, but she seems quite concerned for his well-being. On hearing of Sam's concern about his parents she offers to help by guiding him to the other fragments of the wax cylinder. She offers Sam transportation to three different locations where she believes he may find more information about his parents and other fragments of the cylinder. She also gives Sam a miniature radio, which he can hook on to his ear and which will allow him to stay in contact with her.

The player will now regain control and have a choice of navigating Sam through any of three doors that will lead to transportation to the middle three sections of the game: Benthos, Harmony, and New Boston. The player can play these areas in whichever order she chooses, though she must complete all of them before proceeding to the final area, the Ikairus. The Priestess will be happy to provide Sam with some background information about any of the areas before he goes there. Once the player selects one of the doorways, a brief cut-scene of Sam being transported there will follow, and then the player will regain control in the new area.

Benthos

First is Benthos, the city beneath the sea. The Electric Priestess sends Sam on her private, robot-operated auto-gyro to the undersea monorail that leads to Benthos. Benthos' population is made up primarily of two classes of people: undersea researchers and visual artists. The latter group mostly relocated to Benthos because of the solitary, remote lifestyle it provides. Benthos is a domed city, into which oxygen is pumped via ducts that float on the ocean's surface many miles above. Because of the low height of the dome, Benthos consists of smaller buildings than the mega-skyscrapers found in the surface cities. Scattered throughout the city are many sculptures that have been created by the artists who live there; the work is of amorphous, abstract, yet streamlined forms, many resembling "space age" versions of Picasso's sculpture work.

The Priestess informed Sam that his parents kept a private lab in Benthos, and Sam will set out across the city to look for it. As in Gargantuopolis, Sam will be waylaid by numerous mechanized adversaries who try to prevent him from reaching his parents' lab. Combat in Benthos will have less to do with flying to great heights as it did in Gargantuopolis, since the dome prevents anyone from flying too high. Flight will still be the key to fast maneuvering and effectively battling the robotic creatures Sam must defeat at every turn. In Benthos, Sam soon meets the flying girl Xeraphina, who will help him find his parents and tells him about Benthos.

Finally, Sam will make it to his parents' lab, a small office full of his parents' equipment and with a number of pictures of Sam on the walls. Once Sam reaches the office a cut-scene takes over to show Sam discovering another fragment of the important wax cylinder his parents made before they disappeared. With it in hand, Sam will get back on the monorail and make his way back to the Electric Priestess' home, where he can proceed to the next area.

Harmony

From the Priestess' home, one of the doors will lead Sam to her private zeppelin that will take the player to Harmony. A good distance from Gargantuopolis, Harmony is a special "planned" community that includes both large green parks and industrial, metropolitan areas. Harmony is the city where most of the country's robots are built, and here the robot inhabitants greatly outnumber the humans. In Harmony, Sam will need to learn to differentiate between friendly robot natives and the more vicious adversaries who continue to try to stop his quest for his parents.

In Harmony, Sam will meet Scrap, a super-friendly robot who befriends Sam and helps him battle the robots who would block his process. Sam also hopes to find Ike, the old robot assistant of his parents. The Electric Priestess explains that Ike went to Harmony to retire among his own kind, and Scrap helps lead Sam to the senior robot.

However, on finding Ike, it turns out that the aged robot's memory has been damaged, leaving him with only two state-sanctioned options: be turned off forever or have a new head attached. Opting for the latter, Ike is soon to have a replacement head put on, a common procedure. But Scrap is afraid Ike will lose his memory of Sam's parents, since memories are often lost in the head-replacement procedures. Scrap suggests they try to find an "underground robot doctor," a fellow robot who works in secret to repair old robots, thereby saving their minds and memories from the junk pile.

Sam and Scrap will need to travel across more of Harmony to locate this robot doctor, and then lead him back to Ike. They eventually find one who is willing, a massive robot named Tool who agrees to do the necessary work. Of course, while traveling through Harmony, the player will still have to face ill-intentioned robots at every turn.

Once Tool is brought to Ike, a cut-scene takes over as Tool performs the procedure to restore the old robot's memory. Tool is successful, and Ike now remembers the wax cylinder fragment Sam's parents sent to him and will pass it on to Sam. With another piece of the puzzle in hand, Sam can board the Priestess' zeppelin and return to her bubble home.

New Boston

Finally Sam will be able to travel to New Boston, the Moon colony. Sent there on the Electric Priestess' private rocket, Sam will encounter the friendly extraterrestrials known by Earthlings as "Moonies."

On some of their research projects, Sam's parents had worked with one of the Torso Moonies, a fellow by the name of Dulo. It is this Moonie Sam must find, since the Electric Priestess suspects that he has another piece of the wax cylinder. New Boston itself is another domed city — like Benthos — and its inhabitants are able to live much as they do on Earth. Earth-like gravity is maintained inside the dome, and a device called an Atmospherator generates breathable air for all the inhabitants. Some Bi-Header Moonies live inside New Boston, assisting with research projects.

When Sam inquires about Dulo, he will be told that Dulo, as a Torso Moonie, is not allowed inside the Moon colony, so Sam will have to acquire a space suit and go out onto the Moon's surface to find him. Shortly after going out onto the surface, Sam will meet Dulo. Dulo explains that, as a Torso Moonie, he was not able to work with humans. Sam's parents, however, noticed that Dulo had some special talents in their field of research, and as a result were willing to leave New Boston and travel to Dulo's home on the Moon's surface.

Dulo says that, yes, he too has a piece of the wax cylinder, but has stored it in his home, a good distance from the dome. Sam will go with Dulo to get the cylinder. Of course, throughout New Boston as well as on the surface of the Moon, more robotic adversaries will try to stop Atomic Sam from achieving his goals. Like Xeraphina and Scrap, Dulo will work with Sam in defeating the adversaries they encounter on the surface, helping to incapacitate the robotic nuisances. Once Sam reaches Dulo's home he will be able to get the fragment of the wax cylinder from him. Sam must then fight his way back to New Boston and return to Earth from there.

Return to the Electric Priestess' Bubble Home

After Sam has completed each of the three areas, he will have collected all of the fragments of the cylinder he thinks he needs and will return to the Electric Priestess' bubble home. In a cut-scene, the Electric Priestess says that she is most impressed with Sam's work in recovering all the fragments of the cylinder. Unfortunately, when Sam tries to put it together, he finds that one piece is still missing. The Priestess then reveals that she has the final piece, with which Sam can fully assemble the complete cylinder.

Fortunately, the Priestess has a machine with which to play back the cylinder. On the cylinder Sam's parents explain the work they had been researching, and how it led them into conflict with Max Zeffir, the owner of their company, Zeffir Zoom, and the man who has abducted them. Sam hears his parents explaining that in their work for Zeffir Zoom they discovered a dangerous flaw in one of Zeffir's new monorail systems, something that would mean huge losses for the company in order to successfully redesign. Unfortunately, they relate, Max Zeffir himself became aware of the problem but refused to have it fixed, and needed to silence them so the monorail system could go ahead without delay.

With the cylinder's playback complete, the Electric Priestess reveals that, in fact, she is Zeffir's sister. She was the original head scientist for Zeffir Zeppelins, and lost her leg many years ago in a zeppelin accident, which she blames on Zeffir's cost-cutting. She suspected all along that Zeffir was behind Sam's parents' disappearance, but felt she must have proof before she could reveal her suspicions to Sam. In fact, she explains, she has been a friend of Sam's parents for some time, and when they started to fear that they would be caught by Max Zeffir, they broke up the evidence, in the form of the wax cylinder, and scattered the pieces, putting one in their apartment, one in their office in Benthos, and mailing the remaining pieces to Ike, Dulo, and the Electric Priestess herself. The Priestess now concludes with certainty that it has been Zeffir sending robot minions to try to stop Sam from discovering the truth about his parents.

The Ikairus

His parents, the Electric Priestess reveals, are most likely being held captive aboard Zeffir's atomic-powered flying fortress the Ikairus. A constantly airborne, mammoth craft — its atomic power allowing it to fly indefinitely — the flying fortress is Zeffir's pride and joy, and is also where he resides. Kept aloft by some eighty propeller engines, the craft looks like a gigantic flying wing, and is large enough for other aircraft to land on.

The Priestess again lends Sam her private auto-gyro, which flies him to the Ikairus. On board the flying fortress Sam will have to battle still more robots in addition to the very challenging Merciless Mercenaries. The battles on the Ikairus take place in much more small and confined spaces, representing the corridors of the ship, and the player will need to adjust his fighting style accordingly. Finally, Sam will be able to confront the quite insane Zeffir. Zeffir not only has Sam's parents held captive, but he has also captured Xeraphina, Scrap, and Dulo. While Sam and Zeffir battle, Zeffir brags of what he will do to Sam's friends once he has defeated Sam. Finally managing to subdue Zeffir, Sam will at last be reunited with his parents, who are quite glad they gave him the atomic rocket-pack for his birthday.

VII. Bibliography

The following books were key points of inspiration for the setting and world of *Atomic Sam*. Those working on the game will find researching these books to be quite useful in getting a feel for what a "retro-futuristic" setting is all about.

Corn, Joseph J. and Brian Horrigan. *Yesterday's Tomorrows*. Baltimore: The Johns Hopkins University Press, 1984.

A great historical treatment of the various visions of the future from the past century, including many invaluable photos and documents.

Moore, Alan and Chris Sprouse. *Tom Strong*. La Jolla, CA: America's Best Comics, 1999.

Moore and Sprouse's brilliant comic book *Tom Strong* is set in the "clean and friendly" world of the twenty-first century, following the adventures of "science hero" Tom Strong.

Motter, Dean and Michael Lark. *Terminal City*. New York: DC Comics, 1996.

Motter and Lark's future as seen in *Terminal City* is a bit bleaker and darker than *Tom Strong*, but with the same sort of retarded technological development. Both *Tom Strong* and *Terminal City* include brilliant visual design and amazing environments, perfect for a video game such as *Atomic Sam*.

Appendix B:

Sample Design Document: The Suffering

U nlike the previous appendix, in this section I have included the design document for a published game that shipped in early 2004: *The Suffering*. Developed at Surreal Software and published by Midway, the game endeavored to explore the horror genre but apply a significantly more action-oriented experience to it. I was lead designer and writer on the project, meaning it was my responsibility to create and maintain the design document. The document has been included here in an unedited and unpolished form, "warts and all" as it were. This is exactly the version of the document used during development. As I stated in Chapter 19, "The Design Document," it is not actually that important that your design document be written with flowery verbiage or perfect grammar, as long as it conveys the information you need to get across.

For space reasons, this document was edited down from its original form, which was just about twice as long as what you see here. Most of what has been removed are the specifics of various game-world entities (weapons and NPCs) as well as a lot of the Gameflow section, which described specific environments on a room-by-room basis. These details were all specific to *The Suffering*, and are repeated in other examples you will find still in the document. I have tried to maintain the overall structure of the document, however, leaving in all the major section headings. Whenever you see "[…]" you will know that something was cut from the document at a particular location in order to allow it to fit in this book.

It is interesting to notice what information is not included in the document that probably should have been. The main area in which *The Suffering* innovated was through in-game storytelling techniques, and, strangely, many of these unique techniques are not covered in this document. Our morality/reputation system was also one of our biggest points of differentiation, but the mechanics of how it works are not discussed in this document. Also, we amped up the horror components of the game quite a bit midway through development, though those changes never made it into the document either. Finally, we did a lot of work on enhancing the behavior of the creatures, but none of that data was added to this document. For each of these changes and refinements to the game, new documents were drawn up, but they were never incorporated into this main design document. As I have discussed, one problem with a big design document like this is that it can be unwieldy to find information in. Thus, for these later changes to the game, it was easier to isolate the new information in a smaller document to which people could easily refer. Further complicating matters are some sections of the document that were added not because they were well thought-out or even especially needed, but because someone not on the development team requested them, to make the document seem more complete. For example, the section on vibration is not particularly detailed and the final vibration implementation is significantly different.

Indeed, if I were to create this document all over again, I would try to write a significantly more condensed document that would convey information more simply and in less space, while also hyperlinking to separate, more detail-oriented documents. A number of sections of this document could easily be broken out into separate documents. For example, it would be good to have most of the back-story and character descriptions in a separate story bible. Having a number of separate documents would probably work best over a Wiki-type web-based system that everyone on the team could easily access and update. Also, the biggest problem with this document is how "fossilized" it is. There are many sections that are out of date, such as references to the game's old targeting system that was scrapped midway through development. In part, the reason so many other documents were made instead of updating this one is because, after a given point, the programming team knew not to trust the design document for the definitive word on any given feature.

Since it was so out of date, fans of *The Suffering* will find many differences between this document and the final game, some of which may prove amusing. In addition to all of the changes from earlier in the project that never made it into the document, readers will notice that this document is dated July 7, 2003, a full eight months before we finally shipped. Of course, during this time many changes were made to the game. Some of the more interesting differences include:

- The game was originally called *Unspeakable*, but this was changed halfway through development, and I saw no need to update the document for this cosmetic change, except in the title page of the document.
- The "Quest Items" were cut from the game completely, and the puzzles that used them were redesigned.
- Dozak was renamed Xombium.
- The Cartwheeler creature was renamed the Slayer, and the creature that was originally called the Slayer was renamed the Marksman.
- On the art side, the "Stun Stick" was conceptualized, modeled, and textured, but its functionality was never implemented because there was some concern whether it would be a fun weapon to use and we ran out of development time.

- The introductory "Level 0" was added very late in development and is not in this document at all. It was subsequently cut from the game and re-added as a bonus, unlockable feature. A different introductory section to the game is described in this document. This introduction was never attempted because it was decided it was too high risk and labor intensive for what it accomplished.

- Of all the sections of the document, the gameflow changed the most. Of the gameflow included here, the basement is much shorter and simpler than what is included in the shipped game. The basement was an example of unanticipated level-bloat that occurred during development. That said, it is generally agreed the final basement level turned out quite well and is one of the spookiest spaces in the game.

Despite all the changes, it is interesting how much the final game matches a lot of the mechanics, story, and general goals set out in this document. Fairly early on in development I made a focus statement for the game, and the final game follows it to a remarkable degree.

> Unspeakable *is designed to at once frighten and horrify the player, while being a fast-paced, action-oriented game. The controls will be tight and responsive, with an emphasis on allowing the player to easily navigate the 3D environments while defeating a large number of opponents. The player's character will be strong and dexterous to the point of being superhuman; the character will be able to overcome overwhelming opposition with primarily projectile weapons. The horrific creatures the player battles will take the form of perversions of the human form, creatures that "should not be" and which are upsetting to look at in both appearance and movement. The setting, with the exception of the monsters, is fairly realistic for a computer game, and the game touches on portions of human history that will inevitably be unsettling and disturbing to the player.*

In the end, despite everything that did change in the game but not in the document, it was still an essential tool for developing *The Suffering*. Though I would write it differently in the future, many games in the past have certainly done far worse.

Surreal Software
Game Design Document

The Suffering
Revision 1.51
7/7/03

Table of Contents

Section I: Introduction

Unspeakable captures the disturbing and frightening nature of the horror genre in a compelling third-person action/adventure game. By alternating periods of tense and cautious exploration with frenetic and stylized combat sequences, the game seeks to create a uniquely tense and visceral gameplay experience. Though the player is well stocked with weapons and ammo, the strength and quantity of the enemies he must face creates a feeling of nearly insurmountable odds. In the dark world of *Unspeakable*, creatures jump out of shadows, fall out of trees, and erupt out of the ground, attacking the player in the most frightening ways possible.

Unspeakable features a continuous game universe, where the gameplay is unbroken by cut-scenes or other distractions, causing the player to feel constantly threatened and unsafe. Storytelling is kept to a minimum and is conveyed through in-game events and voice-over dialog that the player "hears" through various devices (a voice crackling out of a disconnected speaker, voices echoing out of a quarry, the twisted speech of the creatures themselves). The continuous game-world will be key to making *Unspeakable* a thoroughly terrifying game to play.

The player controls the prisoner Torque, a hardened inmate in his late 20s, sentenced to die for a murder he may or may not have actually committed. Torque is around 6' 2" with black scruffy hair and a darkish skin tone, though he is of unspecified ethnic origin. He has the hardened, muscular physical frame of a long-time prisoner, and he wears a dirty, torn prison outfit. Torque has kept himself safe in prison by exuding a "don't mess with me" tough attitude, something he communicates through his wiry build and his aggressive body language. Underneath this tough exterior hides a man who is not quite psychologically balanced, who fears far more than he would ever admit to. As a side effect of his mental instability, Torque has flashbacks to the events from his past, throbbing images that depict the events that led up to the crime for which he was imprisoned. Torque is also subject to blackouts, during which he becomes extremely violent and the player sees him transformed into a massive monster who is a ferocious melee combatant.

The setting of *Unspeakable* is Carnate, an unspecified, dark and foggy island off the mid-Atlantic coast of the United States. Though the date is not specified, it seems to be around present day. The island is home to a decrepit, decaying federal prison, Abbott State Penitentiary, with architecture that makes it appear to have been built in the late 1940s. This is where the antisocial prisoners that are considered beyond rehabilitation are transferred. Scattered around the island are numerous other abandoned structures of various ages, including a quarry, a long abandoned asylum, a crashed slave ship, a lighthouse, and the small cluster of houses where the prison workers lived.

At its core, *Unspeakable* is the story of Torque's quest to confront his own demons and the events that happened to land him jail. In the grand horror tradition, the details of the world of *Unspeakable* are kept vague and largely unexplained, allowing the player's imagination to fill in the gaps, forming mental images far more frightening than what can be portrayed on a TV screen. The story of *Unspeakable* starts with Torque being transferred to the island prison. From his cell, the player overhears the prison being overrun by bizarre creatures, the screams of the guards and other prisoners echoing through the halls. Freed from his cell in the ensuing chaos, Torque precariously makes his way through the island, fighting off hordes of creatures everywhere he goes, desperately trying to find a way to the mainland. Torque meets a few other humans on the island who have not been killed by the creatures, and they each have their own, incorrect theories as to why the island has been overrun. The player is left not knowing what to believe. At the end of the game, the player must face his monstrous alter ego and, having defeated him, a flashback of Torque's crime is finally revealed, with the nature of the crime determined by the way the player played the game.

Unspeakable merges the highly popular horror setting with proven third-person action gameplay and a unique story and locale to create a gameplay experience distinct from anything currently available. The player will not just control Torque but actually become him, battling his way through a world gone awry while coming to grips with his past and conquering his own personal demons.

Section II: Game Mechanics

Saving

In *Unspeakable*, the player will be able to save their game at any time. The player will be able to have as many save-games as they can fit on the current memory card. The player will then be able to load these games at will from either the main menu or the in-game pause screen, and doing so will restore the player's position and status in the game-world to exactly its state when he saved that game.

Checkpoint Saving

The game will create automatic saves for the player at certain points in the game. These checkpoint saves will be placed at the end of major gameplay challenges, to give players who never explicitly save their game a fair chance at playing through the game without feeling like they needlessly repeat sections that they can easily get by. Checkpoint saving will be completely transparent to the player and will allow the player to play through without ever having to explicitly save his game. There will be an option on the main menu to automatically save the player's game to the memory card at checkpoints without any confirmation from the player being required.

Continue

The main menu will feature a "Continue" option, which will always appear when there is a save-game available to load. When selected, this will automatically allow the player to load up the last save-game that was made for *Unspeakable*. This way, if the player shuts off their console and returns to it later to play some more, all they need to do is select "Continue" and they'll be right back in the game without having to choose a save slot.

Auto-Loading

When the player dies, he will be able to load his most recent save-game (be it a regular save or a checkpoint save) by pressing any button when dead. With the combination of the auto-loading functionality and the checkpoint saving, novice players will be able to play through the whole game without having to ever explicitly load or save a game.

Difficulty Levels

Unspeakable will feature four difficulty levels: Demented (Easy), Disturbed (Medium), Schizophrenic (Difficult), and Stark Raving Mad (Impossible). These difficulty levels will have a dramatic effect on the difficulty of the gameplay. On the Easy setting, even non-gamers will be able to play all the way through the game with only minor challenge. At the Impossible setting, even the most hard-core players (such as members of the development team) will have a hard time making it through the game. The difficulty level will affect vitality, accuracy, and damage-inflicting abilities of the enemies, but at the easiest level there will be fewer creatures for the player to engage with, with fewer enemies in each battle. Ammo and health pack placement will also be varied. Furthermore, the difficulty of the puzzles will also be made easier or harder depending on the difficulty level, with more hints provided at the Easy difficulty, and more challenging solutions necessary at the Impossible setting.

In-Game Help

Unspeakable will not feature a tutorial level. Instead the player will be introduced to the game's mechanics through the gameplay itself. As the player plays and comes to new areas that require him to perform new actions, help text will appear on the screen explaining how different mechanics work. For instance, when the player picks up a weapon for the first time, the text might say "Press SQUARE to Attack." Once the player picks up a second weapon, the help text might explain how the inventory system works. Once the player's Insanity Meter fills up for the first time, and the player is in Aimed Weapon Mode, the help text would say "Press TRIANGLE while holding down R1 to enter Insanity Mode." After the text has been on the screen long enough for the player to read it, or the player successfully accomplishes the action he is being instructed about, the text will fade away. Help text can be turned off by a setting in the options screen, so that the player will not need to see again it if they replay the game.

In-Game HUD

There will be a number of in-game heads up displays (HUDs), which will appear as needed to communicate information to the player about the state of the game-world. Typically, these HUDs will only show up when that information will be useful to the player. For instance, the health meter will only show up when the player has recently lost health or when in Aimed Weapon Mode. In this way, the screen will not be cluttered up by HUD graphics when they are not needed, helping the player achieve a greater sense of immersion in the game-world. HUD elements will "slide" onto the screen when they are needed, similar to games such as *Jak & Daxter*.

Some items will appear in certain situations, regardless of what mode the player is in.

- *Flashlight Charge*: This small indicator will show up on the screen when the player's Flashlight is on. A bar will indicate charge remaining on the Flashlight, and will turn to a different color once the Flashlight starts losing strength. A small number will be displayed next to the Flashlight, indicating how many batteries the player has.

- *Recently Equipped Weapon*: When the player changes his currently equipped primary or thrown weapon, a large view of the object will show up on the screen for three seconds after the weapon switch, along with the name of that weapon. This will help make clear to the player what their new weapon selection is.
- *Recently Picked Up Items*: When the player picks up an object, a view of that item will be displayed on the screen along with the item's name. This will help communicate to the player what item they just obtained.

Combat HUD

When the player enters Aimed Weapon Mode, a number of components of the combat HUD will be brought onto the screen. Since the player will always be able to enter Aimed Weapon Mode without penalty, this information will be available to the player whenever he wants it.

- *Health*: The player's health will be displayed graphically as part of a bar that will disappear as the player loses health, leaving an empty bar behind it. In addition to being on the screen in Aimed Weapon Mode, this bar will be brought onto the screen whenever the player is actively losing health, and will stay on the screen for five seconds thereafter. When the player loses or gains health, this bar will flash, and will slowly slide to indicate the decrease in health.
- *Insanity Meter*: The Insanity Meter will communicate how many Insanity Points the player has at any one time, communicating how many more the player will need to go into Insanity Mode. As the player gains Insanity Points, the meter will flash and will slowly fill up. As the player remains in Insanity Mode, the meter will lightly pulse as the points in it decrease.
- *Current Weapon Ammo*: The ammunition for the current weapon is displayed graphically by bullets for projectile weapons or a gasoline bar for the flamethrower. The quantity that the player has of the current thrown weapon is also displayed. When the player is on a mounted weapon, the ammunition for that weapon is displayed in a similar fashion.
- *Reticle*: When in Examine Mode or when on a mounted weapon, a reticle will show up in the middle of the screen, indicating where the player will shoot when he presses the Attack button.

Inventory HUD

When the player presses and holds the Inventory button, the player's current weapons will be displayed on the screen, sorted by type. The player is then able to navigate through these weapons, which will scroll around the screen. The functionality of this is described in the Inventory section of this document.

Map HUD

The player will find maps for various areas in the game, which can be pulled up and examined at any time. An arrow will be drawn on the map indicating the player's location and current facing. Also in the map view HUD, the player will see the current quest items that he is carrying, lined up along the bottom of the screen. For more information on the functionality of the map, consult the Maps section of this document.

Camera

Unspeakable uses three primary types of camera that follow the main character through the game-world and allow the player to view the contents of the game-world. One is used when the player is moving around the world without his weapons aimed, the second is for when the Target button is held down and the player is in Aimed Weapon Mode, and the third is for when the player is in First-Person/Examine Mode.

Movement

The player views their character in the game-world from a third-person, over-the-shoulder view, much like that found in games such as *Syphon Filter* or *Drakan*. The camera will stay behind the player so that the player has a view that matches what Torque sees. Furthermore, the player will be able to intuitively turn Torque and have the camera rotate with him, allowing the player to look at and target enemies in whatever area of the game-world he wants. The player can turn and pitch his character with the right analog stick, which lets them see the area surrounding his character, while simultaneously changing the character's facing. When the player releases the right stick to its center position, the camera will remove the pitching, returning to a vertically centered view, an effect called "lookspring." When the player character is not moving, the camera finds a position slightly off to the side of the player character, so that it isn't "locked" on to his back and provides alternate views of the character. When the character is moving, the camera will stay more immediately behind Torque, to allow the player to intuitively navigate the game-world.

Aimed Weapon

When the player is in Aimed Weapon Mode, Torque is pointing his gun forward, either at a general area in front of him (if there is no target available) or at an auto-picked target. With no target, the camera will maintain its orientation in the world, moving but not rotating along with Torque. When there is a target, the camera will also not change its orientation, unless the current target is going to go off the screen, either because Torque's movements would force the target off the screen or because the target's own movement would do the same. When the target is going off the screen, the camera will rotate itself to keep Torque in the center of its view while also keeping the target on the screen. The player's ability to pitch will also be limited by the necessity of keeping the current target on the screen. The desired functionality of the camera here matches that found in the *Syphon Filter* series.

First-Person/Examine Mode

The player is able to go into a first-person view of the game-world, which represents seeing through Torque's eyes. Torque is invisible to the player while in this mode. The left analog stick allows the player to pitch the view up and down and turn left and right, looking around the game-world. The right stick allows the player to strafe left and right at a slower-than-normal speed, allowing the player to shift the view horizontally slightly. This mode will also be used when the player uses mounted weapons.

Player Movement

Unspeakable features a free-roaming three-dimensional environment. The game controls will allow the player to navigate their character intuitively and explore *Unspeakable*'s game-world easily. All navigation in *Unspeakable* will be "tight," like that found in games such as *Syphon Filter* or *Drakan*. This means that when the player presses the control stick to the left, Torque will turn left immediately. There will be next to no delay or lag between the player pressing a given action button and their character performing that action.

Basic Movement

The player navigates their character through the game-world using intuitive controls for moving forward or backward and turning left and right. The left analog stick on the controller will control moving forward and backward, and turning left and right. The left directional-pad will duplicate these controls. The amount the player pushes forward or backward will determine how fast the player character moves in that direction, from a medium speed walk to a fast run. Similarly, the player character will turn at different speeds depending on how much the stick is pushed in a given direction. As described in the Camera section above, the right analog stick will be used for pitching up (if the controller is pushed down) or pitching down (if the controller is pushed up). The degree of pitch will be determined by the amount the analog stick is pushed in a given direction. In one of the alternate control schemes, the player will be able to use the left stick to move Torque forward and backward and strafe left and right, while the right stick will be used for turning and pitching.

The player will be able to use the commands for moving, strafing, and turning in combination to make their character perform logical actions:

- **Move + Turn:** The character turns while moving, moving along a parabola.
- **Move + Strafe:** The character moves diagonally, moving along a line.
- **Turn + Strafe (Same Direction):** The player moves in a circle facing outward.
- **Turn + Strafe (Different Directions):** The player moves in a circle facing inward. Known as "circle-strafing."

Aimed Weapon Movement

If the player presses and holds the Target button, Torque will raise his arms up to ready his weapons for firing. Torque will automatically rotate his body and pitch his arms up and down to point at the best target relative to his current position. (Auto-targeting is described in detail below.) While in Aimed Weapon Mode Torque moves at a "fast walk" and at a constant speed. When the player is in Aimed Weapon Mode the camera will stay at the same rotation it was at when he pressed the Target button, and Torque will now move relative to that camera's position. Thus, if the player presses forward, Torque moves away from the camera, pressing back causes him to move toward it, and pressing left or right moves him left or right. The player is unable to turn Torque while in Aimed Weapon Mode.

When in Aimed Weapon Mode, Torque will play one of five directional animations, which correspond to the following directions: forward, right, left, back right, and back left. Simultaneously, Torque will rotate his upper body to keep his aim dead on the enemy he has targeted, or, if there is no target acquired, Torque will keep his upper body oriented in the direction he was facing when the player entered Aimed Weapon Mode. This will give Torque a dynamic look while he is moving in Aimed Weapon Mode, as he shifts from foot to foot to keep moving in the desired direction. This is similar to the animation system used in *Devil May Cry*.

While Torque is in Aimed Weapon Mode, if he has a target acquired, the camera will rotate to keep that target on screen, as described above in the Camera section. Because of the camera-relative controls used in Aimed Weapon Mode, this will have the side effect of making Torque rotate around the character he has targeted, if the player keeps pressing the same direction on the control pad. If the player simultaneously rotates the stick to compensate for the rotation of the camera, the player will easily be able to make Torque continue to run in a straight line despite the camera's rotation. This is similar to the effect found in *Syphon Filter*.

Water

Since the game is set on an island, obviously there will be water found in the world of *Unspeakable*. However, Torque is unable to swim. The player character will be able to wade into water up to their chests and will be prevented from walking into water above his head. Torque will die if he stays in too-deep water too long. The difference between safe and dangerous water will be clearly indicated in the levels, so that the player will intuitively understand which water systems they can safely enter and which they cannot.

The player's reactions to different water depths will be as follows:

- **Calf-Deep:** The player will move through this water without slowing down or changing animation at all.

- **Knee-Deep:** The player's motion will be slowed to his walk speed, preventing him from moving quickly through deep water.

- **Above Chest:** The player will be slowed down exactly as in knee-deep water, except he will now be unable to enter Aimed Weapon Mode and will be unable to fire his weapons. If the player is in Aimed Weapon Mode when he enters this type of water, he will be forced out of that mode.

- **Above Head:** The player will be stopped from walking into water that is above his head; he will simply not be able to move in that direction. If the player falls into water that is deeper than the distance to his head, he will immediately drown.

Jumping

At almost any time in the game, the player will be able to make Torque jump by pressing the Jump button. Jumps can be performed while the player is in the middle of other common actions, such as moving, targeting, or shooting. This will allow Torque to jump over gaps in the terrain as well as to get out of the way of enemies. The height to which Torque jumps and, as a side effect, the distance he travels, will be determined by how strongly the player presses the analog Jump button. The type of jump movement Torque will do will be affected by which direction he is moving, if any, as well as whether he is in Aimed Weapon Mode.

Normal Movement

- *Not Moving*: Torque will jump straight up in the air.
- *Moving Forward*: Torque will do a running jump forward, covering a significant amount of terrain. Torque will land on his feet and will be able to keep running seamlessly.
- *Moving Backward*: Torque will vault himself backward, landing on his feet, though it will disrupt his movement backward somewhat.
- *Strafing Left/Right*: Torque will do an evasive dive/roll to the appropriate side.

Aimed Weapon Mode

Torque will be able to fire his weapon while in the middle of jumping. If he does so, Torque will appear to "hang" in the air slightly, frozen in a jumping pose but not falling to the ground as quickly as if he had not fired. This will allow the player to get a number of shots off while jumping. This is the same jumping/firing functionality as is found in *Devil May Cry*.

- *Not Moving*: Torque will jump straight up in the air. Player is able to fire his weapon while in the air.
- *Moving Forward*: Torque will jump forward. If the player presses Attack while Torque is jumping forward, he will fire his weapon.
- *Moving Backward*: Torque will jump backward, more elegantly than the normal jump backward. As with jumping forward, Torque will be able to fire while jumping backward.
- *Strafing Left/Right*: Torque will do a quick evasive dive/roll to the appropriate side. Torque will not be able to fire while doing the dive roll. The roll will be extremely quick, however, so Torque will only be blocked from firing for a short time.

Clambering

Torque will be able to jump up onto high ledges and platforms by using his clambering behavior. This action will consist of a single animation in which Torque jumps up to the height required and throws his legs up and on to it, immediately standing up and becoming ready to start moving again. There will be minimum and maximum heights to which Torque can clamber, with the minimum height being the maximum height Torque can jump onto normally, and the maximum height being approximately a foot taller than his own height. When the player presses the Jump button when next to a surface Torque can clamber onto, the game will automatically have Torque do the clamber motion instead of the regular jump animation.

Ladders

When the player is climbing on a ladder he is considered to be in "ladder mode." The player enters ladder mode by walking up to a ladder and pressing the Use button. Once on a ladder, the player character can climb up or down for an arbitrary amount of time, limited only by the height of these objects. The player will get off a ladder automatically once he reaches the top or bottom of the structure. The player cannot turn, strafe, shoot, or perform any other actions that involve the character's hands while in ladder mode. However, the player will be able to pitch the camera up and down and look left and right while on the ladder by using the right stick. In ladder mode, some of the player's movement control buttons will perform different actions:

- **Move Forward Button:** The Move Forward button will cause the player to move up the object.
- **Move Backward:** This button will move the player character down the object.
- **Jump or Use Button:** These buttons will cause the player to immediately jump off/dismount the ladder at their current location.

Ladders will be found in the game-world rotated at arbitrary angles, though there will always be enough space left at their top to allow the player to appropriately play the dismount animation.

Immobilization

Player can become immobilized by certain monsters' attacks. Typically, the monster will grab the player tightly and continually damage him until the player breaks free. For example, the Mainliner immobilizes the player by jumping onto his back and wrapping his limbs around him, while the Nooseman grabs the player with his strong arms while hanging from the ceiling. (For more information on the way the creatures immobilize the player, see the NPCs section later in the document.) While immobilized, the player is still able to turn and pitch the camera, but cannot move forward, backward, strafe, or jump. The player must hit the Attack or Jump button repeatedly while immobilized in order to break free, throwing the monster off of himself.

First-Person/Examine Mode

At any time when he is on the ground and not immobilized, the player can enter a first-person state called Examine Mode by pressing and holding the First Person button. The camera will change to be a first-person view as described in the Camera section above. The player is able to look around the environment using the left stick to pitch up and down and turn right and left, while the right stick will allow the player to strafe slowly to the left and right.

In this mode the player will be able to see their current weapon at the bottom of the screen pointing away toward a reticle, which is drawn in the center of the screen. The player will be able to attack with any of his weapons in this view, though he will not be able to do so with the benefit of target-locking, instead needing to aim to hit targets. The player will be able to use this mode to take aimed shots at targets which may not be auto-targetable, such as puzzle elements, explosive barrels, or light sources. The player's accuracy with his weapon increases when in First-Person Mode. For some characters, the player will be able to extra damage to his targets by shooting them in particular areas, such as the heads of human characters.

The player will not be able to jump or use any objects, or enter Insanity Mode while in First-Person Mode. However, he will be able to throw grenades, switch weapons via his inventory, activate the map, and turn on and off the Flashlight.

Aimed Weapon Mode

As described above, while the player holds down the Target button Torque will be put into Aimed Weapon Mode. This affects Torque's movement and the behavior of the camera in the manner described above. While in Aimed Weapon Mode, Torque is not able to "use" any items, and if the player presses the Use button while in Aimed Weapon Mode he will enter Insanity Mode. Torque will also not Object Look while in Aimed Weapon Mode, instead looking at his current target, though the player will still pick up objects as normal. The player will only leave Aimed Weapon Mode a full second after the player releases the Target button, meaning that if the player releases the button and then quickly presses it again, Torque will seamlessly stay in Aimed Weapon Mode.

Auto-Targeting

When the player presses the Target button to enter Aimed Weapon Mode, the player will find the "best" target for Torque to try to shoot at. This will be determined by a combination of factors including how close the target is and how close it is to the center of the screen. Torque will only auto-target hostile targets, and will only target enemies within a maximum range. If the current target or Torque moves, causing the distance of the target to be out of the maximum range, the target lock will be broken. If the player releases the Target button and then quickly presses it again, the game will try to find the next best target on the screen after the one that was targeted before. This process of cycling through targets will continue through all of the targets on the screen, only returning to the first (best) target once all of the other threats on the screen have been targeted. This functions similarly to the targeting system used in *Syphon Filter*. It may be necessary for there to be a visible "target reticle" used to indicate to the player which enemy is currently targeted; this can be better determined once the game is functional than predicted at this time.

Attacking

The player can at any time press the Attack button, which will cause the player to attack using whatever weapon he currently has equipped. When the player is in Insanity Mode, the player is unarmed and will perform a variety of melee attacks. When the player is completely unarmed, as he is at the very beginning of the game, and when he is not in Insanity Mode, pressing the Attack button will have no effect. The player also has a Throw button, which will cause the player to throw the current type of lobbed weapon. Often the player will not have a thrown weapon available, and at that time the Throw button will have no effect.

The type of attack the player does when the button is pressed will differ depending on the type of weapon the player currently has equipped. For instance, the player will slash with a melee weapon, while he will shoot a projectile weapon. The effect of pressing and holding the Attack button will also differ depending on the weapon: the player will fire a pistol only once per Attack button press, while pressing and holding the Attack button will empty the clip of the machine gun. Furthermore, melee weapons will use the analog fidelity of the Attack button to determine which type of attack to do. The description of how the mechanics work for each specific type of weapon in the game can be found with the listing of each weapon in the Resources section of this document.

Melee Weapons

With the melee weapons, the player will be able to attack repeatedly without the weapon ever running out of ammo or breaking. Melee weapons each have a variety of attacks for the player to perform with them, which is varied based on how many times the player presses the button and how heavily they press the analog button. Melee weapons will vary their effectiveness and the effectiveness of their different attacks by a number of factors.

- *Damage:* Different weapons and attacks will have the potential to do more or less damage to the object they hit.
- *Ready Time:* Different weapons take different amounts of time to draw the weapon from the player's inventory.
- *Speed:* Certain attacks will be quicker for the player to perform than others. Typically this will be inversely proportional to how much they do.
- *Motion:* The visual appearance of the attacks the player does will be unique for each type of melee weapon.
- *Range:* The player will have a slightly bigger swing with some weapons than with others, and as a result will be able to hit enemies at a greater distance with different weapons and different attacks.
- *Stunning:* Heavier attacks with heavier weapons will be more likely to knock back or stun an enemy than other attacks.

Consult the Resources section of this document to see how these different weapon attributes apply to the different weapons in the game.

Projectile Weapons

When using a projectile weapon the player will automatically fire at what he currently has auto-targeted. If the player does not have the Target button held down when he presses fire, Torque will immediately be placed into Aimed Weapon Mode and will stay in that mode for several seconds after the firing is completed. When forced into Aimed Weapon Mode in this manner, the game will also auto-target an enemy for the attack to be aimed at, in the same manner as if the player had been pressing and holding the Target button.

Projectile weapons will vary their effectiveness in a number of key ways:

- *Damage:* Different weapons will do different amounts of damage to the targets they hit.
- *Secondary Damage Effect:* In addition to doing damage to what they hit, some projectile weapons will have a secondary damage effect such as catching something on fire.
- *Ready Time:* Like melee weapons, different weapons will take a different amount of time for Torque to get ready.
- *Single Shot or Continuous Fire:* Some weapons will be able to fire a continuous or near-continuous stream of projectiles while the player holds down the Fire button, while others will just fire a single shot.

- *Rate of Fire:* Single-shot and continuous-fire weapons will all vary their rate of fire — the maximum speed at which they can fire projectiles.

- *Number of Shots Fired:* Some weapons will be able to fire more than one shot at a single time.

- *Accuracy/Range:* Weapons will vary their accuracy by firing each bullet within a random angle (cone) from their "dead-on" trajectory. This will mean that the player can unload a weapon into an enemy and see the projectiles hit randomly around that creature and, if at a great enough distance, the player may actually miss the target even though he may be target-locked on to it. By varying the accuracy of the projectiles, the weapons also vary the range at which they are effective at hitting targets.

- *Stunning:* Different weapons will have different stopping power. This affects how much a given projectile will slow the approach of an adversary: some will have no effect, some will slow the creature down, and some will actually knock the creature over.

- *Type of Ammunition:* Each weapon will use a unique type of ammunition that the player must collect.

- *Maximum Loaded Ammunition:* Weapons will also vary how many shots they hold at once. This translates into how many shots the weapon can fire before the player must reload.

- *Reload Time:* Weapons will fire a number of shots in a "clip" (their Maximum Loaded Ammunition size) before the player must reload them. This will be quite quick for most weapons, but will still be a break in the player's firing.

Each type of projectile weapon uses a type of ammunition unique to it. The player must have some of the appropriate type of ammunition in his inventory for the player to fire a weapon. When the player finds a weapon it comes with a certain amount of ammunition loaded in it, and the player can supplement this by finding more ammunition in the game-world or by finding additional instances of that type of weapon (with the player able to remove the ammunition from that weapon on picking it up). Each time the player shoots a given weapon, the amount of ammunition the player has for that weapon decreases by one, and the rates of fire for the different weapons will cause the player to be able to more quickly use up the ammunition for different weapons. The amount of ammunition available for the current weapon is displayed in the in-game HUD. This HUD is visible only when the player is in Aimed Weapon Mode. Since the player is automatically placed into Aimed Weapon Mode after attacking, the player will always see the amount of ammunition he has when it is being depleted. The player will also be able to see how much ammunition they have for all of their weapons in the weapon inventory, as described in the Weapon section of this document.

In *Unspeakable*, ammunition will be provided such that the player will run out of ammunition for certain weapons in certain situations. If the player is particularly wasteful of the ammunition, it is possible he will run out of the ammunition for all his projectile weapons. The ammunition will be distributed through the game-world in such a way that this is unlikely to happen for all the projectile weapons, with typically the player having an overabundance of at least one type of projectile ammunition, reminiscent of the ammunition distribution in games like *Half-Life* and *Max Payne*.

Weapons have a certain maximum amount of ammunition they can hold at once, and when this runs out the player will automatically reload the weapon with the other appropriate ammunition he has in his possession. However, reloading will not start while the player is holding down the Attack button. While the player continues to hold down the Attack button while firing an empty, continuous-fire gun, the gun will play a clicking "empty" sound. This means for continuous-fire weapons (such as the machine gun), where the player may have been holding down the Fire button to empty the weapon's clip, they will have to first release that button and then press it for the weapon to reload and the player to be able to continue firing. When a particular weapon runs out of ammunition, the game will automatically switch Torque to using the next loaded weapon. Since the player finds the Shiv first in the game and the melee weapons have no ammunition, the player will always have a weapon to use.

Double pistols present a unique situation for the ammunition system, since both pistols use the same type of ammunition and the player can switch back and forth between single and double pistol. To make this as simple as possible, when the player switches from single to double pistol, the game will automatically reallocate the pistol ammunition the player has between the multiple weapons, so if the player has only six shots left, three will be placed in each pistol. If the player then switches from double pistol back to single pistol, the ammunition he has will all be placed into that one weapon.

Thrown Weapons

Thrown (grenade-style) weapons are grouped together and the player can attack with these weapons by pressing the Throw button. These weapons provide the player with an alternate attack to go along with their primary melee/projectile weapon. The system is designed such that the player can be firing their main weapon, then quickly lob a thrown weapon, and then immediately return to using their melee/projectile weapon.

The player's current grenade shows up attached to the back right of Torque's belt so the player can easily know what thrown weapon they have ready to throw. The player can select their current thrown weapon using the inventory system described below.

When a thrown weapon is available and the player presses the Throw button, Torque will continue to hold his primary weapon in his left hand. Using his now free right hand, Torque will immediately grab the current throwable weapon off his belt and throw it. The thrown weapon is automatically thrown at the current target; if no target is available the weapon is thrown in the direction the player is facing. The thrown weapon will arc through the air using realistic-looking, gravity-based movement. If the player is not in Aimed Weapon Mode when he presses the Throw button, just like when using a melee/projectile weapon, the player will temporarily be forced into Aimed Weapon Mode.

While the weapon is being thrown, Torque will be unable to do his melee/projectile attack, and pressing the Attack button will have no effect. While throwing, the player's motion will be undisrupted, and he will be able to keep moving in all directions while throwing. Once the weapon is thrown, Torque will re-ready his current melee/projectile weapon.

Thrown weapons will be differentiated by a number of variables:

- *Damage and Radius:* When they explode, thrown weapons do damage over a radius on impact.
- *Secondary Damage Effect:* Certain thrown weapons may cause a secondary damage effect on objects that they damage, such as catching them on fire.
- *Stunning:* Like projectile weapons, thrown weapons have a certain ability to stun the targets they damage.
- *Time to Detonate:* Some thrown weapons detonate on hitting an object, whereas others will bounce off objects and only explode after a certain amount of time has passed. Some weapons will never detonate on their own, and will require the player to press the Throw button again when he wants to detonate them.
- *Throw Speed:* This is the time it takes for the weapon to be thrown, the time before the player can return to attacking with his primary weapon.
- *Accuracy:* Some thrown weapons will be more accurate than others at actually hitting their target. Like projectile weapons, they will have a small amount of potential range which, when farther from the target, will cause them to fall short or go past their target.

Mounted Weapons

The player will be able to "mount" certain stationary weapons found in the game. This will be accomplished by walking up to the weapon and pressing the Use button. At this time, the player will be forced into First-Person/Examine Mode, with the mounted weapon showing up on the bottom of the screen and pointing toward its target in the distance. An on-screen reticle will be drawn to show where the weapon will hit. The ammo available for this weapon will be shown in the ammo display portion of the in-game HUD. Once in First-Person Mode, the player will be able to aim the weapon and press the Attack button to fire at targets without the assistance of auto-targeting. The player will be able to dismount from the weapon by pressing the Use button again.

The variables that determine the behavior of the mounted weapon will be the same as the variables for the projectile weapons except that mounted weapons are not reloadable and do not need the player to have ammo for them. The mounted weapons will have ammunition with them when the player finds them, and that will be all the ammunition they will ever be able to fire for that particular weapon. Once the ammunition is out for a mounted weapon, the weapon will be unfirable though the player may still "Use" the weapon. Attempting to fire an empty mounted weapon will produce a "clicking" empty sound.

Certain mounted weapons will not have any ammunition but will produce a different effect from the player moving them around. An example of this is the high-power spotlights found in the prison, which shine their light around as the player moves them. Pressing the Attack button will have no effect on these non-firing mounted weapons.

Insanity Mode

As the player attacks and kills creatures, he gains points on his "Insanity Meter," which is a component of the in-game HUD. Once this Insanity Meter is completely full, the player will be able to enter Insanity Mode by pressing the Use button while in Aimed Weapon Mode. In Insanity Mode, the player transforms into a giant, somewhat horrific creature that looks to be an extremely formidable combatant, with one hand composed of a giant spike and the other featuring a massive clawed hand. As this creature the player will only be able to perform brawling attacks, but these attacks will be extremely damaging and effective against the enemies he encounters. The player can leave Insanity Mode at any time by pressing the Use button again. As the player spends time in Insanity Mode, the points in the Insanity Meter will decrease, and if the points reach zero the player will transform out of the mode but fall over on the ground in a fetal position, babbling gibberish to himself, and the game ends. Thus, to continue the game, the player must leave Insanity Mode before his time runs out. When the player returns to his Torque form, if he has killed any creatures at all while in Insanity Mode, Torque will appear to be covered with blood. This effect is described in detail in the Blood Effects section later in this document.

The Insanity Mode represents Torque's blackouts when he sees himself turning into the creature, which is the subconscious representation of his dark side. Though the player and Torque both see the creature when in this form, in actuality Torque does not really transform into a creature at all but instead is being fueled by an adrenaline rush, which sends him into a psychotic rage during which he attacks creatures with his bare hands. The true nature of the Insanity Mode will be hinted at in various points in the game's story. In addition, a few effects will hint at the true nature of Torque's blackouts. Whenever the player passes a mirror in Insanity Mode he will see himself as Torque in that mirror. Periodically while Torque is in Insanity Mode he will flash for one or two frames to appear as Torque, subliminally indicating that Torque hasn't really transformed at all.

Due to the creature's large size, the player will sometimes find Torque to be in locations where it is too small for the creature to stand. In these locations, when the player tries to enter Insanity Mode, Torque will start to morph into the creature, but will then fail to change, reverting immediately back to Torque. Similarly, if the player tries to enter these small locations while already in Insanity Mode, the player will be blocked from doing so, and will have to leave Insanity Mode to enter them. Also, the player will be entirely unable to use objects while in this mode, first of all since it makes little sense for the player to do so, but second of all because pressing the Use button while in Insanity Mode will cause the player to exit Insanity Mode. While in Insanity Mode, the "item look" behavior will be disabled, though the creature will still be able to pick up objects (such as health, ammo, and new weapons), though obviously the player will not be able to use the weapons until he exits Insanity Mode.

The player will not be invulnerable to damage while in Insanity Mode, though he will lose health at a much slower rate than Torque would. It will be entirely possible that Torque can die while in Insanity Mode, at which time he will visually immediately revert to Torque and fall over dead.

Insanity Meter and Points

The Insanity Meter shows up on the screen whenever the player is Aimed Weapon Mode, and since the player is forced into Aimed Weapon Mode whenever he attacks, the meter will always be on screen when he is gaining points in it. Whenever the player accomplishes a kill, which increases the meter, the meter will flash and will fill up to its new level instead of just switching to that level. This way the player will see when they gain more points for certain moves than for others.

The "cooler" the player looks while pulling off a move the more points he receives, similar to the way points are accumulated in fighting games like *Soul Calibur* or sports-trick games like *SSX*. How "cool" a move is is determined by a number of factors, which can be combined to further increase the number of Insanity Points the player receives. The Insanity Meter has a base 100 points in it, and points will be added as follows.

- *Single Kill*: Varies from creature to creature. The most common creatures will only be a few points, while more rare and dangerous enemies will be worth significantly more points. Killing friendly human characters will give the player more Insanity Points, though this will make the game harder in other ways, as well as contributing to the player getting one of the game's more negative endings.

- *Jumping Kill*: If the player kills a creature while jumping, he receives 1.5 times the normal Insanity Points.

- *Melee Kill*: For killing a creature with a melee attack, the player gains 2 times the Insanity Points.

- *Double Kill*: If two creatures are killed in quick succession, the player gains 2 times the Insanity Points.

- *Triple Kill*: For the third creature killed in quick succession, the player gains 3 times the Insanity Points.

- *More than Triple*: For each monster after the third, the player will also receive 3 times the Insanity Points for that creature.

- *Explosives Object Kill*: By shooting explosives (such as a large crate of dynamite) near a creature in order to kill it, the player gains 1.5 times the points.

The above multipliers for the amount of points granted will be cumulative, meaning that if the player combines these methods, he will get still more points. For instance, killing two creatures each worth 5 points, and shooting both while in the air will net the player $5 * 1.5 = 7.5$ points for the first, and $5 * 1.5 * 2.0 = 15$ points for the second, 20 points in all. For three creatures that are standing in front of some explosives, and for shooting the explosives while in the air, the player will net $5 * 1.5 * 1.5 + 5 * 1.5 * 1.5 * 2 + 5 * 1.5 * 1.5 * 3 = 67.5$ points. The player gains no Insanity Points for killing creatures while in Insanity Mode. Once the Insanity Meter is full with 100 points, it will not gain any additional points, making it to the player's advantage to go into Insanity Mode as soon as it is full so as not to "waste" points.

Movement

Though a larger creature than Torque, the Insanity Mode creature is a bit faster at navigating the world than Torque. He is able to move exactly like Torque for both normal movement and the slower, camera-relative Aimed Weapon movement, when the player has the Target button depressed. The creature is also able to move forward and backward at different speeds depending on how much the player presses the analog stick forward or backward. In this larger form, the player cannot jump, and pressing the Jump button will produce a particular attack, as described below. The larger form of Torque will also prevent him from moving into certain areas, such as doorways, since the player is now simply too large to fit through them.

Melee Attacks

While in Insanity Mode, the player will be limited to performing melee attacks, but these attacks will be extremely effective and damaging to their targets. Using these attacks effectively, the player will be able to take out a relatively large number of creatures while in Insanity Mode.

- *Large Swipe Right*: Player taps Attack button for this action.
- *Large Swipe Left*: Follows up large swipe right. Player taps Attack twice to get the right and left swipes in succession. Does the same damage as the large swipe right.
- *Large Swipe with Both Arms*: Follows up large swipe left. Player taps Attack three times for this series of attacks. Does damage to anything in a half-circle in front of the player. Does more damage than the other large swipes.
- *Impale Attack*: Player heavy presses the Attack button for this attack. The creature does a large uppercut motion with his left arm, which does more damage than the other attacks. Certain characters will actually be impaled on the monster's spike, but only when it is the fatal/final blow to them. Thus the creature will be dead, but will be seen to be fully impaled on the spike, and the creature will then throw it off the spike. The creatures will play custom animations specifically for this situation. This will only happen for specific NPCs who have it enabled and for whom it makes sense, such as the Cartwheeler.
- *Shockwave Attack*: Player activates this attack by pressing the Jump button. Player jumps in the air a short distance at the start of this attack, and when landing brings its hand and spike together to smash the ground. Anything that is in the path of the two-arm smash takes a significant amount of damage, while the landing on the ground creates a large shockwave that causes all enemies within a certain radius to fall over, stunned.
- *Charge*: When in Insanity Mode, the player can do some damage to NPCs by charging at them, similar to a football player. This is accomplished by pressing the Throw button while in Insanity Mode. In addition to doing damage, the creature will be seen to knock NPCs over and out of the way with this move, causing them to do their heavy hit reaction.

Effects

As discussed above, Insanity Mode represents what happens to Torque when he thinks he is blacked out, and only has hazy memories of what happened while he "lost control." To communicate this to the player, a filter will be used over the world that will both tint the game-world a different, somewhat reddish color, as well as warp the screen and make it appear blurry. The motions of the Insanity Mode creature himself will also be blurred, which will add particular dramatic emphasis to his attacks. Since the player will be unable to use his Flashlight in Insanity Mode, the creature will appear to radiate light all around it. This implies less that the creature is giving off light, but more that the creature has superior night vision than a human.

Player Health

The player starts the game with 100 points of health. This number will be decreased by taking damage from various sources in the game.

- *Melee Attacks*: The player will be attacked by creatures throughout the course of the game, almost all of whom will have melee attacks in which some part of their body, a sharp blade for instance, comes in contact with the player, causing him damage.
- *Projectiles*: The player will sustain damage from being hit by various projectiles.
- *Explosions*: Various objects in the game will explode and cause radius-based damage to the player.
- *Collapsing and Falling Objects*: In *Unspeakable*, ceilings and other objects will fall from above and wound the player. Typically, these objects will do a sufficiently large amount of damage that they will kill the player immediately.
- *Falling*: The player is able to fall off of objects a certain distance without taking damage. After a certain point, the player will take damage relative to how far he has fallen. Falling from a great enough height will kill the player immediately.
- *Drowning*: If the player falls into water that is too deep, he will drown and will die immediately.

Once the player's health reaches 0, the player will be dead. The player will lose control of the game and a death animation will be played. At this point a text message will come up, prompting the player to press a button to load from the last saved game, whether that game is an automatic checkpoint save or a player-initiated save. (See the Saving section of this document for more information on saving.)

Healing

The player will automatically regain health up to 20 points (20%). This health will slowly increase, taking a full 30 seconds for the player to go from 1 health back up to 20. While the player's health is lower than 20 points, Torque will appear to limp and will not be able to run at full speed.

The player can regain health above the 20-point mark by collecting bottles of anti-psychotic pills. As he picks these up, they are automatically applied to his health, though the player's health will never increase beyond the 100-point mark. The player will not pick up the bottles of pills when his health is already at full.

Stunning

If the player takes too much damage at any one time, he will become stunned and will be unable to move. Torque will not actually fall over, but may drop to one knee. This will be particularly likely to happen when the player takes falling damage.

HUD

The player's current health is represented by a meter, which appears as part of the game's in-game HUD. The health meter shows up only when the player is in Aimed Weapon Mode (along with the rest of the in-game HUD). Or, if the player takes damage, the health meter will appear on the screen immediately. As the player loses health, in addition to the meter going down, it will also pulsate to alert the player to his losing health.

Inventory

Unspeakable will feature a simple inventory similar to that found in games like *Syphon Filter* and *Max Payne*. The space that the items take up is not a concern and the player is only limited in the amount of ammo he can carry, though even this is a fairly large amount. This allows the game to maintain a fast and furious action component without bogging the game down, while allowing for a variety of weapons to deepen the gameplay. This system allows the player to never have to worry about managing inventory and to easily switch from one weapon to the next without ever disrupting the action. Once picked up, items can be used up and removed from the inventory, but the player cannot drop them.

The player character will be able to carry one type of each weapon, though he will be able to carry two pistols at once to allow for double-pistol combat. The player will be able to carry a finite amount of each type of ammunition for a given weapon. If the player attempts to pick up a weapon that he already possesses, the player will instead take the ammunition, if any, from that weapon.

Selecting the Equipped Weapon

The player will be able to switch from the current weapon he has equipped to the next type of weapon in his inventory by tapping the Inventory button. For the purposes of the inventory, the game's weapons are divided into the following groups:

- *Melee*: Including the Shiv, Fire Axe, and Stun Stick.
- *Pistol*: Including single- and double-pistol options.
- *Shotgun*: Including only the shotgun.
- *Machine Gun*: Including only the machine gun.
- *Flamethrower*: Including only the flamethrower.
- *Thrown Weapons*: Including the TNT Stick, the Concussion Grenade, the Molotov Cocktail, and the Shrapnel Grenade.

When simply tapping the button, the player switches to the last used weapon of each type above, not including the thrown weapons. In this way, the player will cycle through all of their available weapon types in five presses of the button. The system will skip weapons that do not have any ammunition, preventing the player from equipping them.

Instead of just tapping the Inventory button, the player will be able to press and hold the Inventory button to bring up a visual display of the available weapons. The weapon groups listed above will be displayed horizontally across the screen, with columns of each type of weapon. While holding down the Inventory button, the player will be able to navigate these weapons by pressing left, right, up, and down on the direction pad or with the left stick, stopping on the weapon he wants to use next. The player can scroll left and right to select another weapon type, or up and down to select a weapon within a group. The player will also be able to choose single or double pistols using this interface, both showing up under the pistol type. This system functions much like the one found in *Metal Gear Solid 2*. Weapons that have no ammo will still be displayed in the menu but will be grayed out, and if the player navigates onto such a weapon, the selection will go past it onto the next weapon. Each weapon will also have a number displayed next to it, indicating how much ammunition the weapon has.

Selecting Grenades

With the Inventory button held down, the display will also show the current thrown weapons the player has in a single column. The player will be able to select the current thrown weapon from this list. Selecting a thrown weapon in this view will leave the player's current melee/projectile weapon the same as it was before the Inventory screen was entered.

Equipping a Weapon

Once the player has selected a new current weapon, either by tapping the Inventory button or holding it and navigating his weapons, the player will immediately switch to that new weapon. In order to speed up this transition, whatever weapon the player previously had equipped will simply disappear out of his hands and he will play the "unsheathe" animation for the new weapon. When the weapon switches, the newly selected weapon will be drawn in a close-up view on the right side of the screen to communicate to the player what his new current weapon is. This display will stay up for a number of seconds. The ammo HUD art will also change to the appropriate one for the new weapon, if the ammo HUD is currently on the screen.

When the player selects a new thrown weapon type, Torque does not play any animation, though the type of thrown weapon shown attached to his belt will immediately change to indicate the new selection.

If the player tries to equip a new weapon while targeted, the target is broken. If the Target button is still pressed after weapon switch, the player reacquires a target. While in Insanity Mode, pressing the Inventory button will have no effect.

Item Interaction

As the player navigates Torque through the world, the player will be able to pick up certain objects. Objects that can be picked up are referred to as items. Items may be of a few basic types:

- *Weapons*: The player finds a variety of weapons that can be used to fight the monsters he encounters. The use of weapons is discussed in depth in the Attacking section of this document, as well as the Inventory section.

- *Ammunition*: Ammunition is necessary for many of the weapons the player finds, with different types of ammunition useful for different weapons. Ammunition will be found in various quantities for each particular type of ammunition. Like weapons, ammunition is discussed in the Attacking and Inventory sections of this document.

- *Flashlight & Batteries*: Flashlights and the batteries they require are discussed in depth in the Flashlight section of this document.

- *Health*: The player finds bottles of pills, which instantly increase his current health up to the player's maximum health. Health items are discussed more in the Health section of this document.

- *Maps*: The player will find multiple maps for different locations in the game. Maps are discussed in the Maps section of this document.
- *Quest Items*: Including keys, mechanical components, and other objects the player will need to collect in order to progress in the game.

The list of the specific items found in *Unspeakable* is discussed in the Resources section of this document.

Item Placement

Items may be pre-placed in the game-world, sitting on the floor, on tables, or wherever else is appropriate. Items may also be found inside of lockers or other storage devices, with the player able to get to these items by opening them or destroying them. NPCs may also drop items on death. Items will be rendered realistically in the world, though the objects will be noticeable enough that the player will realize he can pick them up. The player's ability to notice game-world objects will be assisted by Torque turning his head to look at items as he walks past them, a technique referred to as "item-look." In the case of multiple items, Torque will look at the item that is closest to his current position. Torque will not look at items that he cannot currently pick up (such as a weapon he already has and doesn't need the ammunition from, or a health item when his health is full). Torque will also not item-look at items while in Aimed Weapon Mode, Insanity Mode, or First-Person/Examine Mode.

Item Pick Up

The player can pick up items simply by walking near them. The player will not necessarily need to collide with an item to pick it up. Standing next a table, for instance, the player will automatically pick up useful objects that are on top of the table if they are within a reasonable reach of the player. No animation will be played for picking up objects; it will simply immediately occur. A realistic sound will play to indicate an object has been picked up. Also, on picking up an item, the in-game HUD will display the name of that item and a close-up view of the object, so that the player will know he has picked something up.

Picking up some objects will result in an immediate effect, such as the map becoming available to look at or the player's health increasing. Other objects, such as the flashlight, batteries, ammunition, and weapons, will automatically be stored in the player's inventory, and will not automatically trigger anything to happen when they are picked up.

The player will be prevented from picking up certain items if he has no need for them at the time he comes close to them. For instance, the player will be unable to pick up health objects if his health is already at maximum. Similarly, the player will not pick up ammunition if Torque already has the maximum amount of that type of ammo. The player will also not pick up weapons that he already possesses, though he will convert weapons into ammunition where possible. In the cases where Torque does not need such an item when he comes across it, the player will often be able to return to that location later when he does need it.

In some cases, the player will need to collect multiple parts of a certain object. Once the player collects all the necessary parts, the component items will disappear from the player's inventory and will be replaced by another object.

Unknown: Should some items be randomized: ammo quantities/amounts, weapon placement, puzzle part placement, health pack placement (can be overridden, of course).

Flashlight

Early in the game the player finds a flashlight, which he will use extensively to illuminate his way through the game-world. The player is able to toggle the Flashlight on and off pressing the Flashlight button. It will be to the player's advantage to turn the Flashlight off when he doesn't need it because the Flashlight continually uses up the charge of its battery. As the Flashlight loses its charge, its range gets shorter and it becomes dimmer in both brightness and color. Eventually, the light is quite dim, though it never goes out completely. If the player finds additional batteries or already has them in his inventory, they are inserted into the Flashlight as soon as it starts going dim.

The Flashlight automatically shines in the direction the camera is facing, creating a spotlight on the surfaces ahead of the player. This means that as the player pitches the camera up and down, the light automatically moves with it. This is also true in Examine Mode and when using a mounted weapon. In each, the light shines directly at where the camera is pointing. Visually, the Flashlight appears clipped on to Torque's shirt, so the light emanates from a chest height. It is necessary for the Flashlight to be clipped on to the player's shirt to free up his hands for using weapons. The light is not in any way blocked by Torque or any of his weapons.

Because of their aversion to the light, the player will be able to frighten away some monsters by shining a light at them. This will not make the player invulnerable to their attack, but it will make his life significantly easier. Of course, once the light gets dimmer as its battery life is nearing its end, the Flashlight will be a far less effective tool for scaring away creatures.

The Flashlight can be triggered to be broken in certain situations, according to the needs of the gameflow. In these situations the player will completely lose the ability to use the Flashlight and it will disappear from his inventory. The player will only regain the ability to use his Flashlight when he finds another one.

When the Flashlight is in use, a small Flashlight charge bar will show up as part of the in-game HUD. The bar will indicate how much charge is left and will change color once the Flashlight starts becoming dimmer. The HUD element will also show a number that will communicate how many spare batteries the player has for the Flashlight.

Map

Unspeakable will include a map system that will help the player navigate the environments in the game. As the player navigates the game-world, he will come across map items that Torque will pick up. Maps may be for the area the player is currently in, for an upcoming area they will need to explore, or potentially for a location they have already been to, with such maps revealing hidden areas he might have missed. There will be no maps available for some areas of the game. The player will also find an overview map, which provides a view of the entire island of Carnate.

The player will be able to pull up the map at any time by pressing the Map button. Once in Map Mode, the game is paused, and the game-world is no longer visible. Map

Mode will fill the screen with a photo-realistic 2D image of a map for the current area. In Map Mode the player will have the following options:

- *Zoom In, Zoom Out*: There will be two levels of zoom for any map. The farthest view presents the entire map on one screen. The closest view presents a detailed section of the map.
- *Scroll Left, Right, Up, Down*: When zoomed in, the player will be able to scroll around to different sections of the map.
- *Select Previous, Next Map*: Though the map will bring up the relevant map for the player's current location, the player will have the option to look at any of the maps that Torque has found, including the overview of the island.

The map view will include an arrow, which is drawn over the map and represents the player's current location and points in the direction that Torque was facing when the player entered Map Mode. Pressing the Map button again will exit Map Mode, while pressing the Pause button will take the player to the in-game pause menu, just like during regular gameplay.

Also in the map view, the player will see a display of the current quest items he is carrying, starting in the lower left-hand corner of the screen and stretching horizontally. The items are represented iconically, with a short text description underneath them, such as "Factory Keys." There will not be an excess of quest items at one time, so this listing will never become too large or need to wrap around.

Using Objects

The player will be able to accomplish a number of actions by pressing the Use button. When the Use button is pressed, the game will check for nearby usable objects, and will compare if the player is within 45 degrees (approximately; actual angles being specified as the object requires) of facing them. The game will then pick the closest of the nearby usable objects, and the player will use that one. For most usable objects, Torque will quickly transition into a position relative to that object, and will then play an animation specific to the using of that object. Some objects, however, will not require Torque to be repositioned and will not play any animation. There are a number of different potential actions that can be accomplished by pressing the Use button, as described below.

Open and Unlock Doors

When the player comes up to a door that is closed, pressing the Use button will open that door. Once a door is open, the player can close it by pressing the Use button again while near it. Some doors can only be opened by explosives, by being attacked by the Fire Axe, or through other damage-causing effects. For some of these doors, explosives will blow off a padlock or other locking device which, once gone, will allow the door to open and close normally. Other doors are entirely unopenable but can be destroyed by explosives. These doors will allow Torque to use them, but Torque will play a "failed to open" animation and speak a line such as "It won't budge."

Some doors may be locked and will fail to open when the player tries to open it, indicating that the player will need to open it elsewhere (using a switch, for example), wait for it to be opened by some other event, or try to find a key for that door. If the player has a key for the locked door he is trying to open, the game will automatically use that key to open the door. Once the player uses a key in a door to unlock it, that door will remain unlocked for the remainder of the game. Often when unlocking a door, that will be the only use of that key, and the key will be automatically removed from the player's inventory as the door is opened. For cases where a key opens a series of doors, the key will only be removed from the player's inventory once the final door is opened. Some doors that the player has opened will automatically re-close at some point after the player has passed through them.

Open Chests/Lockers

This works exactly the same as opening doors except that the player does not actually walk through/into them once opened. Some chests will be locked and will require keys to open, while others can only be opened via explosives that blow off their locking mechanisms. Often the player will find useful items inside the opened chests.

Flip Switches

Switches are used to activate events in the game-world, such as setting off explosives, activating a machine, or opening a gate. Switches come in three basic types:

- *One-Time Switch*: The one-time switch can be flipped once and will never be able to be used again.
- *Reset Switch*: A reset switch will return to its original state after being activated. It differs from the one-time switch in that it can be used multiple times, reactivating a particular event.
- *Toggle Switch*: The toggle switch alternates between two positions, on and off, and, like the reset switch, can be used repeatedly.

Mount Ladders

The player will be able to mount and dismount ladders by pressing the Use button when near them. Consult the Player Movement section of this document for more information on movement on ladders.

Mount Weapons

The player will be able to mount mounted weaponry by pressing the Use button. Consult the Attacking section of this document for more information on mounted weaponry.

Use Quest Items

In some situations the player will need to collect specific items in order to progress in the game. Once the player has collected these items, he will need to go to a particular location where he can use them. When in this location, when the player presses the Use button, the game will automatically determine what items can be used at this location and use them, removing them from his inventory at the same time.

Enter Insanity Mode

When the player presses the Use button while in Aimed Weapon Mode, if the player has sufficient points on his Insanity Meter, the player will enter Insanity Mode. See the section on Insanity Mode for more information.

Security Monitors

Players will find various TV screens in the game that will be hooked up to security cameras at remote locations. When viewed in the game-world, the screens will have actual real-time renderings of the areas the security cameras are looking at, with "monitor" filters applied over them. If the player presses the Use button when near such a security monitor, the player's view will be shifted to a first-person view of looking directly into the security camera. While in this Security Camera Mode, none of the player's ordinary commands will have any effect, except the player can press Use again to exit the Security Camera Mode. Some tables will have multiple or "banks" of security monitors for the player to use. Security monitors and cameras are fragile devices, and if either is shot or blown up, the hookup will stop working.

The security cameras themselves can be either fixed in their orientation, or may rotate/pan side-to-side in their view of the world. Of course this will translate into the player's view of the world when looking at the camera. The player will never have control over the rotation or panning of the camera.

Pushable Objects

The player will encounter objects in the game-world that he can move around. When the player comes up to one of these objects, the player can press Use to "engage" it and enter Push/Pull Mode. The player can press the Use button again to exit this mode.

While in Push/Pull Mode, the player will move as if in Aimed Weapon Mode: he will be able to move forward, backward, and strafe, but he will not be able to turn. For every move the player makes, the pushable object will move along with him. If the pushable object is blocked, the player will be unable to move at all. The pushable object will move along a rectilinear grid, with the player having to push the object fully from one grid location to another and being unable to move the object along a diagonal. This movement system is like the one found in *Ico*.

Pushable objects can be used for a variety of gameplay scenarios, such as pushing an object out of the way of a passageway, providing a step-up onto a passageway, pushing an object to block something else, or other puzzle-oriented uses.

Destroying Objects

The game-world in *Unspeakable* will be littered with objects that can be destroyed during gameplay. Some objects will be destroyed by predetermined events, while some will be destroyed dynamically depending on the gameplay situation. For instance, if the player throws a TNT stick at a particular office the desk, chairs, and security monitors may all be destroyed. The player will be required to blow up certain objects, such as wooden doors that won't open, in order to progress through the game or just to access secret areas.

Objects that can be destroyed will be assigned a health value that indicates how much damage they can sustain before being destroyed. Certain objects will be invulnerable to certain types of damage. For instance, some objects may only be blown up by TNT sticks, while others can only be damaged by fire, with each taking no damage at all from bullets.

When destroyed, some objects will reveal one or more items inside them, such as a weapon, ammunition, or health. This will be done in as plausible a way as possible: for instance, blowing up a footlocker will cause its contents to be left behind.

Unknown: Should the player be able to blow up ammunition. That is, if you shoot a box of TNT sticks before picking it up, will it go off, destroying the ammunition in the process.

Exploding Objects

When some objects blow up, they will cause explosions or other effects themselves. For instance, if the player shoots a gas can, it will explode and cause damage to all of the objects within a certain distance around the player, while also setting them on fire. Such explosions may of course cause chain reactions, setting off other objects that explode and so forth.

Glass

The player will be able to destroy some glass windows, but some glass will be impervious to damage. Breakable glass will sustain a number of projectile shots, each creating a hole in the glass, before the entire window finally shatters to the ground. Walking on broken glass will cause Torque to leave bloody footprints behind him as if he had walked through a puddle of blood. See the Fluid Effects section for more information on footsteps.

Effects

A number of effects will be central to creating the believable and frightening game-world of *Unspeakable*. The effects that are relevant to game mechanics are described below.

Lighting

Lighting will be a huge part of creating a frightening environment in *Unspeakable*, where seeing a creature half in darkness will be far more frightening than seeing it in full light.

Lighting will also be used to influence the movement of creatures in the levels. A number of the creatures have an aversion to the light, and will do their best to avoid it. Thus, by turning all the lights on in a particular area, the player will potentially be able to prevent certain creatures from attacking him.

The player will be able to turn on and off many light sources via light switches, which will be used in a realistic and logical way (light switches placed next to doors), while simultaneously supporting fun gameplay (the lights will be broken in rooms where that leads to more compelling combat). Some lights will be set up on a timer, where a number of lights will stay on for a certain amount of time before their circuit breaker shorts and the player must go reset it. Lights will also be susceptible to being shot out or destroyed in explosions. Since generally more light is better for the player, the player will need to be careful where he shoots and what he blows up in order to avoid destroying the lights.

Of course the player's Flashlight is a major source of light in the game, and the player will need to use it effectively to survive. Consult the Flashlight section of this document for more information. The player will also find high-powered spotlights, which he can mount and use as a more effective flashlight. Consult the Mounted

Weapons section of this document for more information.

Fire

Objects and characters in *Unspeakable* can be set on fire by a variety of sources. They may be already on fire when the player finds them, they may be ignited by the player's weapons (such as the Molotov Cocktail or flamethrower), they may be set off by explosions (such as a gas can exploding), by the creatures themselves (such as the Inferna), or as part of scripted events. Any object that is on fire may set other objects on fire, so that if a chair is on fire and an NPC moves too close to it, that NPC will be set on fire as well, or vice versa.

Fire will burn for a specified amount of time (depending on the intensity of the fire), and then go out, though some fires will be set to burn continuously. As fires burn, they will inflict damage on the object that they are attached to, unless that object is resistant to fire damage. Damage will be specified on a per-second basis.

In some special cases, NPCs will spawn out of large fires. So if the player creates a large blaze with his own weapons or through shooting some explosives, in certain areas the player will now have to contend with additional creatures spawning out of those fires. The creatures that spawn out of fire will be impervious to damage from the fire while spawning.

For certain NPC enemies, once that creature is set on fire, its movement will become more chaotic while taking burning damage, though it will continue to attack and pursue the player. For friendly human NPCs, once set on fire they will go into a frantic version of their fleeing behavior. All NPC characters once set on fire will have custom screaming sounds to communicate that they are taking damage by the second.

Fluid

Unspeakable will include dripping water, blood, and other fluids to create atmosphere in the game. Fluids will also be able to create pools, which will have a variety of important effects on the game mechanics. Pools may be flammable (such as gasoline), so if the player shoots or brings fire next to them they will ignite. When the player walks through pools he will leave fluid-appropriate footprints behind him for a small number of steps, with the footsteps themselves fading away over time. Pools will also be capable of spawning certain enemy NPCs. Pools can be created dynamically, either appearing after a rainstorm or from the blood of a killed creature.

Streams of fluid will also be used aesthetically. However, if a thick enough stream of water is poured onto a fire, the fluid will extinguish that fire.

Unspeakable will also include bodies of water, such as the ocean that surrounds the island and the rainwater that fills up the quarries. Creatures will tend to either stay out of this water completely or completely ignore it, depending on their behavior. The player's interaction with water is described in more detail in the Player Movement section.

Weather

Over the course of the game, the weather effects will vary from a clear night, to light rain, to a ferocious downpour. As it rains, the rain may collect in pools of water on the ground, as described above. The rain will be accompanied by lightning bolts and other storm appropriate effects.

Blood & Amputation

Blood and gore effects will be a central part of achieving a "gross out" horror feeling in some portions of the game. When creatures are shot they will spurt geysers of blood, which may in turn lead to the creation of pools as described above.

Certain creatures will be set up to potentially lose certain limbs or their head. This will be done in a "canned" way such that the same creatures will always have the likelihood of losing the exact same limbs in the same way. Once a limb is shot off, the limb itself will turn into "chunks" that will fly off and then fade away. Some creatures will start bleeding to death after they have lost a limb, though they will continue functioning for a short amount of time. Other creatures will continue functioning as normal once they have lost a limb.

As Torque kills creatures, he gets bloodier and bloodier. Torque will get bloodier if he kills a creature with a melee attack or with a close-range projectile attack than if he kills creatures from a distance. If the player is already bloody when he gets some more blood on him, Torque will become even more bloody. Torque will become the most bloody from killing creatures while in Insanity Mode, with the red color literally covering his body. There will be four stages of "bloody" Torque. The blood on Torque will then fade away over time, eventually returning Torque to his original, relatively clean state. Torque will tend to frighten away certain friendly NPCs if he comes up to them while extremely bloody.

Projectiles

Of course projectiles will be a core element of the game, and their mechanics are covered in detail in the Attacking section found earlier in this document. There will also be a number of aesthetic effects associated with projectiles.

Projectiles will be able to leave tracers behind them. This will be especially useful for bullets, which will, except for the tracers, be invisible to the player. The tracers on the bullet streaks indicate motion and will be reminiscent of those found in the game *Oni*.

When projectiles hit surfaces, they will generate impact effects appropriate to the material they hit: wood will splinter, stone will chip, metal will spark, and so forth. Projectiles will also leave behind bullet holes and pockmarks. The pockmarks and impact effects will vary both by the type of material hit as well as the type of projectile fired (a shotgun pellet leaves behind a different mark than a pistol bullet).

Flashbacks

Over the course of the game, Torque will have flashbacks to the events surrounding the crime that landed him in jail, a crime his conscious mind has blocked out. Each flashback will portray a bit more of Torque's back-story. The player's actions in the game will determine the form of the player's final flashback, which reveals the nature of his crime. If the player helps the NPCs he finds, it will turn out Torque was framed for his crime, while if the player kills every human he comes across, it will turn out that Torque savagely killed his wife and children.

The appearance of the flashbacks will disorient the player and will come suddenly and without warning. The flashbacks before the last one will be short, lasting only a few seconds. The flashbacks will be pre-rendered, using still paintings that pan and zoom across the screen, with the use of some point animation or blur effects as necessary. The flashbacks are brought on because of events or locations that remind Torque of the crime in some way.

Game-World Events

Many of the events that happen in the *Unspeakable* game-world will help to shock and startle the player and are central to some of the game puzzles as well as communicating portions of the story. However, the player will not lose control of the game during these scenes, helping to keep the player immersed in the game-world instead of breaking him out of it through a completely canned "cut-scene." The effect will be extremely reminiscent of how *Half-Life* effectively used in-game scripted events to tell its story.

Events can be triggered in a variety of ways, such as a player reaching a certain location or flipping a switch. Other events will only be triggered to occur when the player looks at a certain location, thus making it more likely the player will see the event take place.

Some events may be set up behind glass doors and behind walls in ways that the player cannot interfere with them. Other scenes will take place at a far enough distance that the player cannot get close enough to interact or interfere with the scene. The participants in these scenes will be set to an invulnerable state so the player, if he manages to shoot them at a distance, will not disrupt the scenes. Other scenes may be interrupted or aborted entirely based on the player action. For instance, if the player kills a friendly NPC before he has a chance to perform a scripted event, the scene will never happen. Similarly, if the player kills a participant of such an event while the event is transpiring, the event will be immediately aborted, with still-living participants returning to their normal AI behavior. For instance, if a scene involves a prisoner being killed by a monster and the player kills the prisoner while that is happening, the prisoner will die and the monster will start attacking the player.

Vibration

Controller vibration will be used extensively yet not excessively in *Unspeakable*, with unique vibration types set up to create different effects. Typically, vibrations will be varied by pattern and intensity, with the intensity being controlled from within the code (for instance, playing the same vibration pattern but at different strengths based on the amount of damage sustained).

Damage

When the player takes damage of any kind, the controller will vibrate. The type of vibration will differ based on the amount and type of damage the player is sustaining. The basic vibration types are: fire, explosive, projectile, melee, electrical, and gas. While battling The Black One at the end of the game, when the player sustains damage as a result of attacking the creature when it is in the same state as the player (Insanity Mode, for instance), there will be a unique damage vibration.

Insanity Mode

While the player is in Insanity Mode, the controller will continuously vibrate lightly to indicate the player's unstable state.

Attacking

When the player attacks with a certain weapon, the controller will play a vibration for that attack. When melee weapons connect with their target, another, heavier vibration will be played. The types of vibrations the different weapons will use can be found in the Resources section of this document.

Landing

Whenever the player lands from a fall, a landing vibration will be played, with the vibration varying depending on the height of the fall.

Environment

Certain places in the environment will trigger the controller to vibrate. For instance, being next to a large generator while it is on will cause a light rumbling. This will be set up as the levels are created.

Controls Overview

References in the Game Mechanics section of this document have been made to various buttons but not their configuration, since that may differ from platform to platform. This section lists the actual button mappings for the game.

PlayStation 2 Default:

Directional Pad & Left Stick: Player moves forward/backward and rotates.
Right Stick: Player pitches and rotates.
X: Jump (pressure sensitive for height of jump)/Escape Immobilization
SQUARE: Attack (pressure sensitive for type of attack)/Escape Immobilization
TRIANGLE: Use/Insanity Mode (while in Aimed Weapon Mode)
CIRCLE: Throw Grenade

L1: First Person (modifier)
R1: Target (modifier)
L2: Flashlight on/off
R2: Next Weapon/Inventory (modifier)

SELECT: Map
START: Pause Game Menu

PlayStation 2 Alternate Controls 1: Dual Analog

Direction Pad & Left Stick: Player moves forward/backward and strafes left/right.
Right Stick: Player pitches and rotates.

X: First-Person Mode
SQUARE: Flashlight on/off
TRIANGLE: Use
CIRCLE: Inventory

L1: Jump
R1: Attack
L2: Target
R2: Throw

SELECT: Map
START: Pause Game Menu

Section III: Resources

Melee Weapons

Shiv

A shiv is any sharp weapon crafted by a prisoner to serve as a weapon within the prison. The Shiv found in *Unspeakable* is made out of metal support for a bed, with one end sharpened and the other end wrapped in cloth for a makeshift grip.

The player is able to do three types of attacks with the Shiv. The first is accomplished by lightly tapping the Attack button, and produces a slash attack. If the player taps the button up to three times, he will do three different attacks, creating a "combo," with the final attack being more powerful than the first two. The second attack is accomplished by heavily pressing the analog Attack button, and this produces a lunge/thrust motion. This second attack does more damage and stuns the target for longer, but takes longer to pull off. The third attack is a jumping attack, performed when the player hits Attack while jumping with the Shiv readied.

The Shiv is an effective melee weapon, with a skilled player able to inflict more damage with the lunge attack at close range than with a pistol at a far range. The Shiv also has an advantage over the pistols in terms of stopping power and stunning.

Fire Axe

[…]

Stun Stick

This weapon is typically used by prison guards as a means to subdue targets without actually causing any permanent damage to them. The Stun Stick looks a bit more stylized than real-world devices, but is still believable. While the weapon is in use, electricity will arc over the length of the weapon.

Attacking with the Stun Stick involves a simple lunging motion. As soon as a target is touched by the stick, it will become immediately immobilized in its current position/pose for a certain period of time. Immobilized creatures will appear to twitch. If the player keeps the Attack button pressed, the Stun Stick will remain extended and will continue to stun the target, with the total time the target will be immobilized directly proportional to the amount of time the Attack button is held. While a target is being stunned, electricity arcs over its body. Though the Stun Stick is battery powered, it never runs out of charge.

The Stun Stick is effective for temporarily blocking creatures that have gotten too close to be dealt with any other way, and will need to be used in conjunction with other weapons. For instance, the player could stun a creature and then switch to the Shiv to get in a number of damaging melee attacks before it becomes mobile again. The player could also stun a creature and then reposition to a more distant location from which to use his projectile weapons.

Projectile Weapons

Pistol

This Pistol is an extremely large revolver-style handgun. On reload, the revolver's chamber rotates outward from the body of the gun, allowing all the spent shells to be ejected simultaneously. The Pistol is fired in an arm-extended pose. For the purposes of *Unspeakable*, the reloading of the Pistol will be unrealistically fast, allowing the player to fire his six shots with only a slight pause before being able to continue firing. The player is also able to use two Pistols simultaneously, resulting in a slightly reduced accuracy but with a double rate of fire. Even with two Pistols, the player can still only target a single enemy at a time.

The Pistol will fire a single shot for each press of the Attack button, meaning the player will have to repeatedly press the button in order to keep firing. The Pistol is the most accurate and thereby has the longest effective range of any of the game's projectile weapons, except for the Mounted Machine Gun. The Pistol has extremely light stopping power and no stunning capabilities.

The Pistol is the core weapon in *Unspeakable*, and will likely be the weapon the player uses the most. The Pistol also has the most available ammunition.

Shotgun

Unspeakable features a pump shotgun with a shortened barrel and a small grip, of the type that might see use in a prison or in other aspects of police work. The Shotgun is fired from a lowered position, with both hands holding the weapon mid-torso. After each shot is fired the player will automatically re-cock the weapon, forcing a noticeable pause between each shot. When the weapon is out of shots, the player will very quickly be seen shoving more cartridges into the weapon, which will result in the longest reload time of any of the projectile weapons.

When the Attack button is pressed, the Shotgun will fire a number of shots simultaneously, with each shot's direction randomized such that it creates a "spread" pattern on whatever it hits. Similarly to the Pistol, the player will have to repress the button to fire a second group of shots. Because of its multiple shots fired, the Shotgun has extremely effective stopping and stunning capabilities.

The Shotgun will be a more effective weapon against enemies who are in close range to the player, especially with its stopping power. However, because of its inaccuracy, players will be wasting their bullets if trying to hit distant targets.

Machine Gun

[…]

Flame Thrower

[…]

Thrown Weapons

TNT Stick

The TNT Stick is typical of the type routinely used in mining and other construction projects. A stick of a processed compound of gunpowder and nitroglycerine is packed into a cardboard tube. The explosive is fairly stable and will not tend to explode from being jostled but will explode when shot or set on fire. The stick has a long piece of detonation cord trailing out of its end, which can be lit, with the stick exploding once the wick burns down. The wick will visibly burn down as this time passes.

The TNT Stick appears unlit on the player's belt. When the player presses the Throw button, the player grabs the stick and it becomes instantly lit and then thrown. The TNT Stick will not explode until five seconds after the player presses the Throw button, and the TNT will be seen to bounce off of whatever it hits until that time. On explosion the TNT Stick does a significant amount of damage in a radius around itself, with a large amount of stopping and stunning power to the targets it hits. The TNT Stick will also be effective at blowing objects up as well as blasting down unopenable doors and revealing otherwise inaccessible locations. Due to water-resistant detonation cord, the TNT Stick will still go off if thrown in water. The TNT Stick has a medium effective range when thrown.

The TNT Stick is the most common thrown weapon in the game and when used correctly will be quite effective at taking out groups of enemies. The player will also find it helpful for puzzles and uncovering hidden locations.

Molotov Cocktail

The Molotov Cocktail is a classic "homemade" weapon. It is constructed of a glass liquor bottle filled with gasoline with a rag hanging out the end. Just before throwing, the rag is lit. Then, on impact, the bottle shatters and the flame ignites the fluid inside, creating a large and persistent flame in the process. In *Unspeakable*, the Molotov Cocktails appear unlit on the player's belt, and when thrown the rag becomes immediately lit without the player's animation needing to actually light it. If the player shoots or otherwise damages an unexploded Molotov Cocktail, it will immediately detonate.

On impact, the Molotov Cocktail catches whatever it hits on fire, with the fire persisting for fifteen or more seconds. The Cocktail also splashes fluid that creates sub-fires around the point of impact, with these fires being weaker than the primary flame. The fires it creates are of medium damage. The Molotov Cocktail has no effect when it lands in water, since its wick is immediately extinguished. The Molotov Cocktail has low stopping power or no stunning effect, and is most accurate at short ranges.

The Molotov Cocktail is an effective and visually spectacular weapon that will be best used against creatures who are especially vulnerable to fire damage.

Concussion Grenade

[…]

Shrapnel Grenade

[…]

Mounted Weaponry
Mounted Machine Gun

This is a military-style, belt-fed, tripod-mounted heavy machine gun, which appears to be of World War II vintage, such as the Browning M2. This machine gun is too heavy to be picked up and carried around, but the player will be able to use it in a stationary manner through Mounted Weapon Mode. The player holds the Mounted Machine Gun by two grips at its back, though the player will not see this since he can only use the weapon while in a First-Person Mode (see the Mounted Weapon Mode description in the Game Mechanics section of this document for more information).

The Mounted Machine Gun functions identically to the regular Machine Gun when the Attack button is pressed. Pressing and holding Attack will generate a continuous stream of fire, while tapping it will produce short bursts. The Mounted Machine Gun features an even faster rate of fire than the regular Machine Gun, and does significantly more damage. The Mounted Machine Gun also features extremely high stopping power and hitting an enemy enough times will knock it over. Since it is mounted on a tripod, it is also effective at extremely long ranges. The Mounted Machine Gun comes with a certain amount of ammunition when the player finds it, and once empty the gun cannot be reloaded and will become useless. When fired, the Machine Gun creates a heavy buzzing/stuttering sensation in the controller's vibration.

Spotlight
[...]

Miscellaneous Objects
Ammunition

The player is able to get ammunition for each of his projectile weapons by picking up additional weapons, with Torque automatically removing the ammunition from these found weapons if he already has that weapon. In addition, the player will sometimes find just ammunition. Ammunition is unique to each type of projectile weapon, and cannot be shared between weapons.

- **Box of Pistol Speed-Loaders**: .44-caliber ammunition for the revolver. Comes in a box of four six-bullet "Speed-Loaders" that can be used to insert all six shots into the gun. Total is 24 bullets per box.
- **Machine Gun Clip**: A "barrel" style clip for use with the Tommy Gun. .45-caliber.
- **Box of Shotgun Shells**: A simple box of 30 shotgun shells.
- **Can of Gasoline**: Looks like a standard red metal gasoline can, becomes one of the components of the homemade Flamethrower.

Health

Health objects in *Unspeakable* are instantly used when they are picked up, with the player not picking them up if he is at full health. Health comes in the form of antidepression prescription medication that Torque can consume, of the brand name "Dozak."

- **Small Bottle of Dozak**: Looks like a small bottle of pills one purchases at a pharmacy, with the prescription and medication instructions written on its side. Restores 20% of the player's health.
- **Large Jar of Dozak**: Looks like a large glass jar of the type a pharmacist would use to fill prescriptions, with a large label on its side. Restores 50% of the player's health.

Flashlight and Batteries

The Flashlight is a special-case item and will be the player's most-used item throughout the game, since it allows him to navigate the dark world of *Unspeakable*. The player will always be able to turn the Flashlight on and off by pressing the Flashlight button. Turning the Flashlight off when it is not needed is necessary since the player will have a limited amount of battery life. Picking up the Flashlight and its batteries is similar to the player's mechanic for picking up weapons and their ammo: for every Flashlight the player finds after the first one, the player will be able to remove the batteries from it and store them for later use.

- **Flashlight**: Is a military-style "clip-on" flashlight that Torque will attach to his shirt. Has a silver, ribbed look popular in flashlights from the 1950s.
- **Batteries**: Appears as a D-cell sort of battery, though it will be unrealistically large to make it clearly visible to the player.

Maps

The player will find maps throughout the game that will help guide him through the environments. Maps may cover a specific area of the game or, at one point, the player finds a map that provides an overview of the entire island. Maps appear in the world as folded-up "roadmap" style maps, though they are not colorful beyond pure functionality. The maps the player can find include:

- **Carnate Island Map**: Provides an overview of the entire island.
- **Death House Map**: Has a separate map for each floor of the building, but not including the basement.
- **Prison Map**: Provides an overview of the entire prison, but is not especially detailed and does not include the basement.
- **Asylum Map**: Has a separate map for each floor.
- **Clem's Map**: Provides a map of the Woods, the Beach, and the basement of the prison, with Clem having marked numerous locations.
- **World War II Fort Map**: An old layout of the Fort as it existed when it was operational during the war.
- **Town and Docks Map**: Does not include the cave entrance the player must find in order to return to the Lighthouse.

Quest Items

There are various items that the player will find throughout the game which he will need to pick up in order to solve puzzles in order to progress in the game. These items will typically stay in the player's inventory until they are successfully used, at which point they will be removed from the inventory and cannot be picked up again.

- **Corrections' Officer Keys**: Found near death row, allows access to a locked door.
- **Dallas' Keys**: An oversized ring of a number of keys. Dallas has these keys, and he will use them to grant access to the cellblock.
- **Radio Parts**: Found in the Asylum, these parts are needed to get the Radio in the prison operational again.
- **Sliding Lever Handle**: A long metal bar, which the player will need to find to operate a sliding wall puzzle in the basement of the prison.
- **Jack Handle**: Used for the jack puzzle in the woods.
- **Generator Parts**: Found in the town, the player will need to collect a certain quantity of these (out of a larger maximum number that can be found) in order to get the generator in the Lighthouse functional again.

Section IV: NPCs

The monstrous creatures the player fights in *Unspeakable* are all undead creatures that have been brought back to life by The Black One, the central villain of the game and the architect of the chaos that takes place. All of the creatures the player must fight correspond to a specific method of execution that has been used on the island at some point in its storied history. For some creatures the connection will be extremely obvious (such as for the Nooseman, the hanged enemy), while others will be more subtle (such as the Cartwheeler, who was beheaded). The theme for each of the creatures exists for the player to find if he is interested and thinks about it, while it will not be overdone or thrown in the player's face.

The NPCs have varied means of attack and ways of moving through the game-world, which will serve to prevent visual and gameplay monotony, while also allowing creatures to be used in interesting combinations to create different gameplay situations for the player to cope with.

Since all of the enemy NPCs are derived from humans (though their actual appearance will be twisted into horrific form), the creatures will all be able to "speak" to the player as he battles them. Depending on how twisted the creatures are, these voices may be more or less intelligible, and the very manner of their speech will be frightening to hear.

NPC Base Mechanics

The creatures Torque battles throughout the game are of course a major component of the gameplay in *Unspeakable*. The mechanics for these creatures are discussed in a per-creature fashion below. NPCs share some base mechanics common to all of them, as described here.

Health

Almost all NPCs take damage at one time or another, though some will be invulnerable or sometimes invulnerable to damage. Vulnerable NPCs take damage similar to the player, from melee weapons, projectiles, explosions, or effects (such as fire). NPCs are unable to regain their lost health, however, and will die permanently once their health reaches zero.

NPCs employ a resistances system, such that certain types of damage will be more or less effective on different NPCs. For instance, the Slayers are partially resistant to damage from projectiles, while taking extra damage from melee attacks. The Infernas are invulnerable while they are moving, but once they have completely burned down to a pile of cinders, their cinders are invulnerable to fire-based attacks. They are extremely vulnerable to explosive or melee attacks and take normal damage from projectile attacks.

Taking Damage

Monsters can be slowed down in their movement by certain weapons, while other weapons will actually knock them over and/or stun them. The stunning depends on the creature, the amount of damage sustained, and the origin of the damage. For instance, the Festers are relatively immune to being slowed or knocked down, while Cartwheelers are easily pushed back. Furthermore, being shot by a shotgun will be much more likely to knock a creature over than being shot by a pistol bullet.

There are eight possible reactions for an NPC to have when he takes damage:

1) No reaction.

2) Hit reaction animation played, monster speed is unaffected. Hit reactions will vary from NPC to NPC based on types of hit reaction (for example, light, medium, heavy), which will be based on the amount of damage sustained. There will be a minimum of damage that must be sustained to trigger any hit reaction.

3) Hit reaction played, monster is slowed down.

4) Monster plays a "knocked back" animation and is actually pushed backward by the weapon.

5) Monster is actually knocked down/stunned by the weapon, then can get up after the duration of the stun.

6) Monster is killed by the damage and plays an appropriate death animation.

7) Monster is killed by the damage and sent flying through the air by the damage sustained. This occurs if the damage comes from a position below the NPC.

8) Monster is killed by the damage and the damage is so great that the creature "gibs" (parts of his body sent flying in various directions).

Reaction to Light

In general NPCs tend to stay out of the brighter areas, though some are far more averse to it than others. For instance, the Cartwheeler doesn't mind light that much, the Mainliner will always flee to a dark area when illuminated, and a Burrower has no reaction to light and dark. Extremely bright lights, such as the prison spotlights, will cause all NPCs to flee from their path.

Standard Enemies

Cartwheeler

The Cartwheeler is a creature that was executed by being beheaded. He is relatively humanoid in appearance, but on all four of his limbs his hands/feet have been removed, and long swords have replaced them. The Cartwheeler is able to walk and stand upright by balancing on these blades, as the Movement section below describes. The Cartwheeler's head is somewhat crooked on his torso, and stitching is visible around the circumference of the neck, as if the head had been sewn back on after being severed. Stitching is visible on other parts of his body, such as on his shirtless chest. His head is covered by a bizarre and horrific mask.

Movement

The Cartwheeler has a variety of methods of navigating his environment, including moving on the floor, on the ceiling, and jumping through the air. When using all four of its limbs to move, the Cartwheeler is able to travel extremely fast, either on the ground or on the ceiling. On the ceiling the creature crawls with its head looking at the floor and its limbs bent back behind it, moving with a spider-like motion. On the ground, the Cartwheeler moves on all fours reminiscent of a monkey. On the ground, the Cartwheeler can also move by walking on its two legs like a normal human, though he moves much slower in this fashion than when using all four limbs. The general motion of the Cartwheeler has a start/stop feel, with the creature moving extremely fast for a second and then slowing down to a crawl, which will make its motion erratic and unpredictable, but also a bit disturbing.

The Cartwheeler is able to switch from moving on the floor to moving on the ceiling by leaping in the air while simultaneously moving its limbs in order to stick its blades into the ceiling. Conversely, the Cartwheeler can easily drop off of the ceiling and onto the floor. Cartwheelers will decide to switch from being on the floor to being on the ceiling and vice versa when it is to their advantage during combat or simply to efficiently navigate the game-world. Cartwheelers can be flagged to stay only on the floor or on the ceiling in certain specific situations.

The Cartwheeler is quite skilled at jumping, which it uses to move from the floor to the ceiling as described above. The Cartwheeler can also jump in order to cover large distances in a short amount of time, or to lunge at the player in order to attack him. This is described in detail below. Cartwheelers can also spawn into areas by jumping and landing from great heights, such as off of rooftops or, in one case, out of the sky itself. In such cases the Cartwheeler will use a special "heavy landing" animation.

When moving on any surface, the Cartwheeler's blades stick a few inches into that surface. This will provide a visual explanation for why the creature is able to stay attached to the ceiling. Though the Cartwheeler has a human body with normal joints, these joints are able to bend in "wrong" directions as if extremely double jointed. This allows the Cartwheeler to pull off the various moves it needs to in order to navigate the environment, while simultaneously making the creature's movement disturbing to watch.

Melee Attacks

The Cartwheeler has a number of specific melee attacks, which it will pick from based on whether it is on the floor or ceiling and depending on the range of its target. Each of the Cartwheeler's four blades is capable of doing damage to the player on contact, and some attacks will allow the creature to hit with multiple blades at once.

- **Ground Slash Right, Left, Both:** While on the ground and standing on its legs, the Cartwheeler can slash at its target with its right or left arms individually, or swipe with both blades at once. The Cartwheeler can perform this attack while moving.

- **Ceiling Slash Right, Left**: While on the ceiling the Cartwheeler can swipe downward with either of its arms, slashing at a target when in range. The Cartwheeler can perform this attack while moving.

- **Ceiling Swing Slash Front, Back**: While on the ceiling, the Cartwheeler can pull both its legs out of the ceiling while staying attached to the ceiling with its arms and swing toward its target, potentially striking it with both blades. Similarly, it can leave its legs attached to the ceiling and swing down with its arms. After completing one of these attacks, the Cartwheeler will immediately swing back up to the ceiling, once again attaching itself with all four of its limbs. The Cartwheeler must be stationary in order to perform this attack.

- **Leaping Attack:** The Cartwheeler leaps through the air toward the top of its target, with all four of its blades facing forward. The Cartwheeler can significantly damage the target with all four of its weapons using this attack.

Ranged Attacks

The Cartwheeler has no projectile attack, though its ability to leap through the air and do a melee attack achieves a similar effect (see above).

Behavior

The Cartwheeler and Mainliner are natural enemies of each other and will attack each other on sight. The Cartwheeler prefers to ally itself with the Burrower.

In some areas on specific NPCs, the Cartwheeler can do an "impaling" attack where it runs its blades deep into a creature, killing it instantly. Performing this move will not be part of its regular behavior, and will be considered scripted.

Cartwheelers tend to favor the darkness and will try to avoid the player's Flashlight beam or other sources of intense light. Despite their fear of the light, Cartwheelers are still quite effective when in an illuminated environment.

Mainliner

The Mainliner was killed by lethal injection, though the form of its body is far more twisted and horrific than such a manner of execution would imply. The creature resembles a human torso with its two legs amputated right below the knee, one arm missing its hand, and the other arm longer than the first, bony, and multi-jointed. The second, longer hand clutches a massive hypodermic needle. In its back are jabbed thirty or more hypodermic needles, which wiggle a bit as it moves. Its head is bald, though two syringes have been jabbed completely through the back of its skull (where the plunger ends still stick out) and exit the skull where the Mainliner's eyes once were. Except for the syringes, the creature is reminiscent of some of the more disturbing carnival characters in the movie *Freaks*.

Movement

Because of his deformity, the Mainliner is not able to stand upright, but instead crawls along the ground using its two leg stumps to wiggle forward, while jabbing its hypodermic needle into the ground to assist in pulling itself along, all leading to a very distinctive movement sound. Despite this awkward method of locomotion, the Mainliner is able to cover quite a bit of ground, though it does not move quite as quickly as the player. To compensate for that, the Mainliner is able to jump great distances in the blink of an eye, which is a key component of its deadly melee attack.

The Mainliner may appear normally in levels, but can also spawn out of sufficiently large puddles of fluid on the ground. That fluid can be water, blood, gasoline, or any other liquid.

Melee Attack

For its melee attacks, the Mainliner is able to leap onto the player from a significant distance. From there, it can perform one of two attacks:

- **Grab**: If it finds itself positioned correctly relative to the player, in midair the Mainliner will attempt to grab. It then wraps its legs around the player's torso just below Torque's arms, holding tight with its vise-like grip, putting the player into the immobilized state. Once attached, the Mainliner starts moving the arm that holds the syringe toward the player's neck, raising it high over his head, preparing to jab in its deadly chemicals. To prevent the Mainliner from actually sticking the needle into him, the player must press the Jump button repeatedly, forcing the creature's arm away from Torque as the player taps the button. Once the arm is fully pushed back for a certain amount of time the creature detaches itself from the player and jumps off of him. If the Mainliner is successful in jabbing the player (which causes a large though not necessarily fatal amount of damage), the creature leaves the needle stuck in the player's neck and jumps off of him, simultaneously grabbing a new needle from among those stored on its back.

- **Slash**: If the Mainliner cannot align itself for the Grab attack, it will simply slash at the player with its needle arm. This will cause significantly less damage than the Grab attack, but will be much easier for the creature to pull off.

Ranged Attack

The Mainliner can also hurl the hypodermic needle it holds toward the player, using it as a projectile weapon. The needles are medium range, slow-moving projectiles and do much less damage than the Mainliner's melee attack. On impact, the syringes inflict damage and stick into objects, including the player's flesh. Once the Mainliner has hurled its syringe at the player, it immediately grabs a new one from the collection off its back, though the number of syringes back there does not actually decrease, and the Mainliner has an unlimited amount of ammunition.

Behavior

The Mainliner is a bitter enemy of the Cartwheeler, but is the frequent companion of the Fester.

Mainliners are most effective in darker areas, and will tend to spring out of the shadows toward the player, or simply do their ranged attacks. Mainliners are afraid of the light and will try to navigate to the shadows when possible, and will tend to flee from the player's Flashlight beam. Mainliners do make a distinctive sound as they drag themselves along the ground, and sporadically make a dripping/sucking sound reminiscent of a hypodermic needle being depressed. Their projectile will also have a distinctive "whooshing" when it is hurled.

Nooseman

[…]

Burrower

[…]

Fester

[…]

Slayer

[…]

Inferna

[…]

Boss Enemies

Killjoy

Killjoy is a twisted doctor/psychiatrist dressed in garb historically appropriate for a surgeon from the year 1900. He is seen wearing a bloodied apron and clutching a bizarre medical device in his right hand. Killjoy looks the most human of all the enemies found in the game, though still twisted and disturbing. Killjoy was an adherent to radical techniques that could be used to "cure" patient insanity, the lobotomy being the least grisly of his methods. Killjoy was a hideous creature while living and he has barely been altered in appearance for his post-death form. In the game, Killjoy appears as if projected from sepia-tone film, a proto-hologram kept alive on dirty, worn, and deteriorated film stock, his image appearing crackled and dusty as old prints of films do when shown in a theater.

Movement

Though Killjoy appears to look like a normal human, he is no longer able to move normally. All of Killjoy's movements are performed backward and with a unique twitching motion. This also fits with Killjoy's ability to resurrect the dead, in fact turning back time for those he resuscitates. Killjoy is quite fast in his movements and will be able to easily get away from the player in most situations. Generally Killjoy tries to stay far away from the player, preferring to have the creatures he resurrects attack the player.

Melee and Ranged Attacks

Killjoy has no attacks of any kind. He is able to damage the player only through the creatures that he reincarnates and sends to attack Torque.

Behavior

The player encounters and battles Killjoy in the Asylum as the game's first boss encounter. Early in the game, the player gets a glimpse of Killjoy in the prison death house as he administers a lethal injection to a man strapped to a gurney, but the player is unable to fight him at that time.

Killjoy is invulnerable to damage directly from the player. Though he is unable to attack the player himself, he is able to indefinitely resurrect fallen creatures so they can attack Torque for him. When the player fights Killjoy in the Asylum, the combat area will include a number of Cartwheelers. These creatures provide the true threat to the player's health, and he will need to concentrate on keeping them at bay. As the player kills them, however, Killjoy will run up to them (if they are not too close to the player) and return them to the living by performing a quick operation on them. During this battle, Killjoy hangs back behind the other creatures.

Killjoy is not exactly mentally stable himself, having delusions of his own grandeur and fame, as the statue of himself he had erected on the Asylum's lawn will testify. During his life Killjoy was fixated on film stars and fame, and bought projection equipment to film the treatment of his patients. Killjoy became delusional, believing that his filmed "performances" were beloved by audiences of millions when in fact no one at all watched them. When the player encounters Killjoy in the game, he is still extremely narcissistic and obsessed with his own status as a superstar.

Horace

[…]

Hermes

[…]

The Black One

[…]

Friendly Characters

Humans

Humans are important characters in the *Unspeakable* game-world and will be key to communicating the story. Humans have a realistic, believable appearance, which contrasts with the stylized creatures the player must kill. Humans come in two forms — guards and prisoners — but both manifest the same behavior.

- **Guards**: Guards tend to look tough and physically imposing, though not excessively muscular. Guards appear in the game with multiple flesh tones and with slightly different texture sets for their clothing. They can also be visually differentiated by their attachments (hat, etc.).

- **Prisoners**: Prisoners appear in appropriate prison uniforms, and are a bit larger in size and stature than the guards, but are also not too large. Like the guards, texture variations provide them with a variety of flesh tones and slightly different clothing.

Movement

The human characters move through the game-world as the player will expect a human to. They are able to go anywhere Torque does, including up stairs and ladders, though they will not be able to jump. Human characters are able to move slightly faster than Torque and thus will be able to follow behind him without getting left behind. Conversely, they will be able to slow down their speed in order to lead Torque somewhere without leaving him behind.

Melee Attacks
Human characters have no melee attacks.

Ranged Attacks
Humans will be able to use different weapons, depending on what they are equipped with in the level. The humans will be able to fire single pistols, shotguns, or machine guns. These weapons will behave similarly to how they do for the player. Some guards will have no weapons at all and will thus be unable to attack and will flee when in a combat situation.

Behavior
When killed, human characters will drop their weapons. The player will be able to pick up these dropped weapons to use them or, if they already have that type of weapon, to get additional ammunition.

Humans are naturally the enemies of all the monstrous creatures found in the world, and all the monstrous creatures will attack the humans when given the opportunity. As a result, human characters will fight alongside the player, in some situations meaning the difference between life and death. If the player attacks a human character, the human will now consider the player as hostile as well, and as a result will either retaliate against him (if he's armed), or will flee from him (see below). Some humans will be set to be hostile to the player from the onset, such as crazed prisoners or guards who assume the player (as a prisoner himself) will attack them.

If a human character has no weapon and is in a dangerous situation (where it's threatened by either monsters or if the player attacks them) the NPC will flee. Fleeing will consist of the NPC trying to find a designated "flee" location, which is farthest away from the threats it is facing. Once the NPC has nowhere else to flee to, it will cower there. Some "crazed" humans will flee from the player even if he has not actually attacked them.

Human characters will be able to talk to the player. This will involve them speaking lines of dialog to the player without the player responding. Humans can be set up to approach the player and speak to him in certain situations, while other humans will speak when the player approaches them and presses the Use button. All human characters who are not hostile to the player will have some response when the player presses the Use button near them.

In certain situations, humans will lead the player to predetermined locations in the levels. In other situations, the humans will need the player to lead them out of a dangerous situation to somewhere safer. Some humans will be used to help the player out by opening locked doors, suggesting the solution to a particular puzzle, or by warning the player of a dangerous creature right around the corner. Some humans may request the player to help them in other ways, such as bringing another human or object to them or fixing a certain device (such as a generator). Humans may reward the player by giving him an object.

Section V: Story

Game Progression Overview

As the game begins, it is night, and Torque is brought by boat to Carnate Island and Abbott State Penitentiary, where he will eventually be executed for the murder of his ex-wife and two children. Torque's boat ties up at the docks on the east side of the island, and he is then moved to a short, black school bus that transports him up to the prison. The bus passes numerous landmarks during the journey, including the town, the lighthouse, and the World War II fort. In the prison, Torque undergoes the standard admittance procedure and is then escorted to his cell by two guards who discuss his crime between them along the way. Once they reach his cell, one looks at his watch and mentions how, if his watch is right, the prison has just now finally executed Willie Wiggins after ten years on the row. The guard drops off a box containing Torque's personal effects, including an artist's sketchpad.

Locked inside his cell, Torque has a minute to look around. Looking at the artist's pad, he sees a few drawings falling out of it, one of them a version of what the player will later become introduced to as Torque's monstrous form, the image of his "dark side" that he came up with as a child.

Suddenly, chaos erupts outside his cell and Torque hears people screaming and other bizarre noises as the entire building shakes as if an earthquake is happening. Soon a creature rips off the door of his cell, and Torque is able to move about the death house structure. Initially, Torque's primary goal is to keep himself alive as he navigates his way through the building, including its various execution chambers and abandoned basement. Torque acquires weapons as he goes that makes staying alive possible.

Leaving the death house, the player meets Dallas, a prisoner who befriends Torque and wants to help him. Dallas presents the first of many bogus theories Torque will hear about why the monsters have come to Carnate: there were government scientists experimenting on prisoners and those experiments have gone horribly awry. Dallas leads the player through the several areas of the prison, and eventually the player is able to open a gate, which allows Dallas to make a break for freedom and safety.

The player proceeds cautiously through the prison, navigating his way through a cellblock, and eventually making his way into a guard tower. From the top of the guard tower the player is able to see the island's lighthouse to the east, shining its light through the fog accompanied by the intermittent wail of its foghorn. In the guard tower Torque meets Luther, a large guard who has mentally snapped, and is now afraid of everything he encounters. Using a spotlight to scare creatures away from Luther, the guard leads Torque into the communications building so they can call for help. Unfortunately the radio has been damaged and needs parts to be fixed. Luther explains that the guards use the abandoned asylum on the far west side of the island as a place to relax away from the prison and away from their families, who live in the small town on the east side of the island. In the asylum they have another radio that should have the parts this radio needs. If Torque can go there and return with the parts, they can get the radio working and summon help to the island.

Luther suggests that the best way to get to the asylum is to leave the prison through the graveyard entrance. Following his instructions, Torque successfully makes it out of the prison and to the graveyard. Needing to navigate through the graveyard, where the player will expect to find creatures to battle but instead hears only disembodied voices, the player progresses to an abandoned quarry. Used for prisoners sentenced to hard labor in the years following World War II, the quarry has been abandoned for decades. Torque must navigate through the quarry to reach a path that winds up the hill to the asylum.

The asylum has been abandoned for nearly a hundred years and looks it: ceilings are collapsed, the tile floor is rotting, the paint is peeling off the walls, and the player is only able to access a small section of the building. Once inside, Torque is quickly locked in the building by the projected form of the long-dead head of the asylum, Doctor Killjoy. The player soon meets Sergei, a guard who was in the asylum hanging out with some fellow guards when the monsters started appearing. All of his fellow guards are now dead, and the player will find their bodies horribly mutilated around the facility, as if they have undergone postmortem operations and experiments. Sergei is clearly intoxicated and is decidedly calm about everything, explaining that he's ready to let whatever happens happen. Sergei does tell the player where the radio is located in the building so that Torque can get the parts he needs. He also explains about the circuit breaker in the basement that the player can use to turn on the lights in the building, and adds that he'll be thankful if the player can turn it on so he can listen to his record player again. He's certainly not going to risk his life to go turn it on himself, though.

As the player navigates the asylum, Killjoy repeatedly appears in a strange "projected" form, taunting the player from afar. Once the player has recovered the parts he needs from the radio, the player is lured into a final confrontation with Killjoy, who speaks to Torque and claims that he knows about the player's "condition" (the blackouts), and suggests he can possibly cure him. Once the player smashes all of Killjoy's projectors, he is defeated, and the player is finally able to leave the asylum. It is impossible to return to the prison through the quarry, so Torque has to go back via the beach.

On the way to the beach, the player travels through a large expanse of woods. Along the way, he may discover the somewhat hidden location where the island's natives were massacred 500 years ago. In the woods the player will meet Clem, an intelligent and well-read prisoner who had been planning an escape for months and who complains that the appearance of the creatures has ruined everything. Clem knows of a way the player can get back into the prison, through the escape tunnel he dug, which terminates on the beach. Clem has planned a way of getting himself off of the island via a raft he constructed out of various pieces of junk from the prison. But Clem cannot go down to the beach and use it because of the horrific monsters that are lurking there. If the player will help him, Clem will gladly show the player the location of the escape tunnel as well as some other secrets.

On the beach the player finds the wreckage of the slave ship that crashed on the island in the 18th century. An old rickety set of stairs used to lead up off the beach to the prison, but they collapsed in the earthquake. From the beach the player can once again see the lighthouse on the eastern side of the island, but now its light has gone out. Clem shows the player the escape tunnel, which will get him into the prison's abandoned basement. The player will need to defend Clem while he gets his raft ready to go, and if the player is successful, he will watch Clem float out to sea.

Navigating through the narrow escape tunnel dug by Clem while fleeing from a swarm of rats, the player comes up in the abandoned basement of the prison. There he discovers that some of the corpses of executed prisoners have been preserved in strange glass cases. The player finally emerges from the basement back in the death house, arriving in the electric chair room. Suddenly the player is trapped inside and must fight the bizarre boss creature, Horace. Defeating him by shutting off his power, a fire erupts in the death house, and the player is forced to flee to the second story and death row, where he must return to his original cell.

In his cell, Torque finds a stack of bodies, one for each of the innocent humans he has killed in the game up to this point. Also on the wall is a crayon drawing of the Dark Side creature Torque becomes when he blacks out. The drawing is labeled, "T, age 5" and has the word "Bad Man" scrawled under it. Also in the cell is a medical report signed by Doctor Killjoy that diagnoses Torque's "condition," explaining, in obtuse medical jargon, what happens to Torque when he blacks out.

Avoiding the fire, Torque makes his way back out of the death house, and can now return to the guard tower containing Luther and the radio. On returning to the room where he left him, however, Torque finds that Luther has been killed while defending the radio from a Cartwheeler. The player is still able to use the parts he got from the asylum to get the radio to work and make contact with the outside world. A Coast Guard ship responds, saying they can't reach the island because their computers are down and, with the lighthouse out, it is too foggy for them to navigate into the harbor. If Torque can get the lighthouse working again, however, they will be able to attempt it.

Navigating his way out of the prison, Torque must set a large bus rolling down an incline to smash through the main prison gate. Once open, Torque can head toward the lighthouse, following the road that leads to the drawbridge to the eastern side of Carnate. Swarming with enemies, the player must battle them and then jump across the partially open drawbridge without falling into the chasm below.

On the east side, the player travels for a bit before he comes up to a World War II fort, which has been abandoned for many years but is still structurally intact. Here the player may find the wreckage of a crashed Nazi plane and the location where a paranoid colonel executed all of his German-American troops during the war. The player comes across a machine gun nest with a large number of dead creatures surrounding it, indicating that someone has recently used the gun to defend themselves. As the player explores the fort, a human suddenly shows himself, screaming for help: Jimmy, a young prisoner who has used his wits and a good amount of luck to survive the monsters' onslaught. But Jimmy has sustained a serious head wound and blood is covering his eyes, preventing him from being able to see. Jimmy says he knows there is an infirmary in the basement, and if the player can get him down there, he'll be able to bandage himself up. The player will be able to lead Jimmy down to the basement where he will patch himself up. With Jimmy able to see again, the young prisoner helps Torque get to the natural cave system, which leads to the lighthouse.

The cave system leads the player into the basement of the lighthouse, where the player will be forced to battle strange gaseous creature Hermes, defeating him by turning on a fan, which blows his gaseous form into an old coal furnace that the player must then quickly shut and ignite. With Hermes defeated the player can progress up into the lighthouse itself. Here the player will see that the generator that powers it has been damaged by the monsters and that it will need new spark plugs to become functional again.

Traveling to the makeshift town where the guards' families lived, the player at first finds it oddly devoid of creatures, instead seeing a swarm of little girls come running out and asking him strange questions. Suddenly these girls burst into flame and reveal themselves to be the dangerous Inferna creatures. Subsequently the player meets Ernesto, a guard from the prison who, immediately after the monsters arrived, ran to the town to check on his wife and child, only to find them dead. Now he is angry, feels his life is no longer worth living, and, armed with a machine gun, will help the player battle whatever creatures they find. On the south edge of the town the player finds the site where witch trials were conducted in the late 18th century, with the resulting "witches" being burned alive.

While battling the neverending waves of Infernas that populate the town, the player will find the spark plugs he needs scattered in various places, such as in a car, in a lawn mower, and in the small general store that served the town, with Ernesto pointing out places the player might look for them. With enough spark plugs, the player attempts to return to the lighthouse, but finds he cannot go the way he came since an avalanche has mysteriously collapsed on the road. Ernesto indicates that the only other way back to the lighthouse is through a hidden cave system, which leads into the sizable basement of the lighthouse.

Once back in the lighthouse, Torque is able to use the spark plugs in the generator, move it into position, and get the lighthouse turned on again. He must then crank up the lighthouse mirror and align its bulb before the Coast Guard informs him via a radio that they are sending a ship in and that Torque should head down to the docks to meet them.

On the docks, the player hears a number of strange voices, saying things like "Torque, you're one of us," "We brought you here to meet us," and "Join us." These voices represent the collective evil presence of the island, a force which has been causing horrific acts to take place here for hundreds of years. As Torque hears the voices coming from all sides, The Black One shows up and the player must battle him.

With The Black One defeated, the player's final flashback is shown to him, revealing the nature of his crime, which changes depending on how the player treated the friendly NPCs he encountered throughout the game. During the flashback, the player hears more of the voices who, in the "good" ending, say that Torque is not who they thought at all, while in the "bad" ending they point out "We told you you were one of us...." With the flashback concluded, for the good and middle endings, a Coast Guard skiff arrives and Torque gets on it to leave the island. For the bad ending, Torque is seen transforming into a huge version of his beast form, and then walking back onto the island to live among the other monsters.

Flashbacks

At five distinct points in the game, the player will have a flashback to the events surrounding the crime that landed him on death row. These flashbacks will be as jarring to the player as they are to Torque, suddenly ripping him out of the gameplay as he slowly remembers the details of this traumatic event. The first four will be generalized to all of the multiple versions of the crime and will all be quite short (three seconds at most), while the fifth and final flashback, which he sees at the end of the game, is significantly longer (though still fast paced) and shows what Torque actually did and reveals whether he is innocent or guilty. All flashbacks take place through a first-person view, representing what Torque sees.

- First Flashback: The player sees a closeup Malcolm drowned in a tub of water, floating slowly beneath the surface. His lips are blue and his eyes are wide open in disbelief.

- Second Flashback: The player sees Cory dead on the sidewalk outside Torque's fourth-story apartment in Baltimore, obviously having been killed from the fall. Cory's limbs are bent in obviously incorrect ways and his body has been slightly smashed on the sidewalk, a pool of blood having formed around the body.

- Third Flashback: The player sees a closeup of Carmen's face, her eyes wide open in a death stare, her expression one of shock, a copious amount of thick blood pouring out of her skull through her braided hair.

- Fourth Flashback: We see through Torque's eyes and he opens the door to his apartment, speaking, "Carmen, are you here?"

- Fifth: Torque's crime is revealed when the player sees one of three flashbacks, depending on his actions in the game.

  - *Positive*: Torque walks into his apartment, looking for his ex-wife and children. He first finds Carmen in the bedroom, dead on the floor. We hear him exclaim, "Carmen, oh my god!" He turns and questions, "Boys, where are you?" In the bathroom he sees Malcolm drowned in the bathtub, and we hear him scream, "No! Cory, where are you?" Now in Cory's bedroom, we see the window is open with the curtains being blown in by the wind outside. Looking out through the window we see Cory dead on the sidewalk below. Torque speaks, "Who did this? Who? Why?" Suddenly Torque hears a sound behind him and turns around to see two darkly dressed males run out the door of his apartment. He chases after them to the stairs that lead up to his apartment, but they are gone.

  - *Neutral*: We see Carmen arguing with Torque in Torque's bedroom: "I have the money now, I want the boys up in New York with me." We hear Torque shout back: "You're just trying to take my boys from me!" "Where were you for those three years, Torque?" "How many times can I tell you that…." Then we see Torque's fist swing out and hit Carmen on the jaw, sending her flying to the ground. On the way down she hits her head on the bed frame, creating a large gash in her skull. She falls, dead, on the ground. We hear Torque speaking: "Carmen? Carmen? What have I done?" The camera turns to look at the door of the room where Cory is standing, anger visible in his eyes and his stance. He turns to run out of the room, and the camera follows him. First we see him run into the bathroom and drown his brother, Malcolm, in the tub. Then we follow as Cory runs into his own bedroom, opens the window, steps up onto the windowsill, and throw himself out onto the pavement below. We hear Torque screaming and weeping: "Cory! Malcolm! What have I done?"

- *Negative*: We follow from Torque's point of view as he enters his apartment. Carmen is there in his bedroom, smiling at him. Torque gets close to her and then savagely starts pummeling her with his fists. She falls to the ground and he smashes her skull against the frame of the bed. Soon we see that she is not moving and is apparently dead. We hear Torque breathing heavily over her dead body for a second. Then, keeping with Torque's POV, we go into the bathroom and Malcolm looks at him from the tub, saying: "Daddy, what's happening?" Torque takes his hand and shoves his son's head under the water. Bubbles flow out of his mouth as his body writhes and, shortly, Malcolm is dead. Now Cory is in the bathroom, asking, "What's going on, what's happening?" Torque grabs Cory under his arm and carries him into the child's bedroom where he opens the window with his free hand and hurls him out to the pavement below. We see Torque breathing heavily for a few seconds, looking out the window at his dead son.

Back-story

The following sections provide reasonably detailed accounts of the back-stories of some of the elements in the game. These are included here to give the places and people a history so that they will be consistently and compellingly portrayed in the game, though the specific details of these accounts will never be fully revealed to the player.

Carnate's History

Situated several miles off the mid-Atlantic coast, Carnate is an island that has been a home to evil for centuries. People who have come to the island have found themselves committing acts of brutality and cruelty beyond what they would have done elsewhere. The precise nature of this evil is never explained in the game.

In 1681, a small agrarian community of puritanical settlers is living on the island. In this small village, a nine-year-old girl decides to seek revenge against her strict parents and others who have upset her by proclaiming them witches. She enlists two friends as part of the scheme, which ends up leading to the burning alive of 11 "witches" as the town becomes hysterical over the satanic forces in their midst. Fearing being caught, the girls flee to the woods and, as the concluding act of their pact together, fling themselves off a cliff into the ocean.

In 1732, a slave ship sailing from Africa ran aground on the northern end of the island. Few were injured in the crash. However, the slave traders were frightened to let the slaves out of the holds, since they might join together and revolt against the traders. Instead the slave traders left the slaves trapped in the ship, where they slowly starved to death and were eaten alive by the rats. The slave traders themselves were never able to make it off the island alive.

[…]

Torque's History

Torque is an extremely tough and "street smart" individual who, when in the company of strangers, puts up an outward facade of extreme confidence, strength, and intimidation. Torque developed this persona over the course of his life as a protective shield against the harsh world he grew up in. When around the people he is friendly with, however, Torque reveals his softer side, and can be quite affectionate, gentle, and loving. Torque primarily reveals this side of himself when with his children, wife, and some of his close friends.

When Torque was two years old he was abandoned and ended up a ward of the state. As a result he has no memory of his real parents and was raised in a group home in inner-city Philadelphia. Life in the group home was far from pleasant and certainly not a loving environment, and Torque felt very much alone in the world and soon learned that he would have to be responsible for bettering his own life, because no one else would help him. Torque always had a fierce temper and was a bit prone to violent outbursts. At a young age he drew a picture of a monstrous creature that, though he did not realize it, represented his dark side. Torque would continue to have visions of this creature throughout his life.

[…]

Friendly NPCs

Over the course of the game, Torque meets six NPCs who will help him, either by pointing out solutions to puzzles or by actually joining him in combat against the monsters. These NPCs will speak more dialog than the other NPCs, and will stay alive for a good amount of time, if not for the rest of the game, assuming the player doesn't kill them himself. As with the Back-story section above, not all of the information about these NPCs will necessarily be communicated to the player. Suggested lines of dialog contained in this section are intended as a guide, and are not necessarily representative of the final dialog to be used in the game.

Dallas

Dallas is an African-American prisoner from one of the rougher neighborhoods of Baltimore. He exudes bravado and confidence, and takes pride in the neighborhood he grew up in and the friends he keeps. While putting up the front of being extremely tough around men, Dallas is a great lover of women, being tender and caring around females, always eager to please them. While on the outside, Dallas slept with as many of them as would have him, with his good looks and charming personality making him quite a success as a ladies man. In Abbott, however, Dallas had to find another outlet for his sexual energies, and ended up in a consensual sexual relationship with a large Caucasian male inmate, Byron. Coming across Byron's corpse will upset Dallas significantly, though he is quickly able to compose himself. Though obviously intelligent, Dallas did not receive much of an education and betrays this in his speech. Dallas also presents the first bogus theory about where the monstrous creatures come from, suggesting that the government has been conducting medical experiments on prisoners and that they have now gone awry: "I heard the government's been conducting experiments on us inmates, next phase of MK-Ultra if you can believe that shit."

Dallas actually was friends with Torque from a previous stint the two of them did back at the Eastern Correctional Institution in Maryland. Dallas knows what an intimidating and forceful person Torque can be, yet respects him for his inner strength and integrity. Once Dallas finds Torque, he immediately realizes that Torque is the one man who can help him stay alive with all of the monsters around. The player's goal is to keep Dallas alive as long as possible, which is not an easy feat since Dallas is completely unarmed and thereby incapable of defending himself. He is familiar with many areas of the prison and will be able to warn the player of impending threats, thus rewarding the player for keeping him alive.

Luther

Luther is a large guard with a heavily muscle-bound physique who is extremely tough and physically intimidating. A dark-skinned African-American originally from Northeast Washington, D.C., Luther has an extremely deep voice, though he speaks quietly and with a slight stutter. Luther has a theory about what is happening on the island but is fairly vague about it. Torque will hear him mutter various biblical references and speak of the "end times."

When the player comes across Luther in the prison's guard tower, Luther has been severely traumatized by witnessing the appearance of the horrific monsters that have caused so much carnage around the prison. Luther is in a state of shock and is deathly afraid of everything he encounters, including the player. The player will have to chase after Luther and then try to talk to him for him to calm down. Once calm, Luther can be set off again by anything, such as the appearance of another monster or even the player firing his weapon, causing him to run screaming in terror once more. Once calm, however, Luther is extremely cogent and leads them to the radio room, explaining to Torque that in order to get the radio working, he must collect parts from the asylum. Unfortunately, when the player returns to the radio room significantly later, he finds that Luther has been hideously slaughtered by a Cartwheeler creature. The player finds Luther dead with a Cartwheeler's blades sticking through him, though the Cartwheeler has apparently been killed by a fire axe that Luther had obtained, which is buried in its body. It appears that Luther finally stopped being afraid of the monsters and, in his final action, defended the radio from the Cartwheeler's attempt to destroy it.

Sergei

[…]

Clem

[…]

Jimmy

[…]

Ernesto

[…]

Section VI: Gameflow

This section describes the major areas, events, items, and characters the player finds as he progresses through the game. The final game will no doubt include additional items (such as health), encounters, small side-rooms, and other details that are not mentioned here. These will be added as needed for balancing as the level is developed. Note that each weapon is specifically mentioned when it is first introduced to the player. After that point, these weapons will be liberally sprinkled through the game as dictated by the needs of the game balance.

Prison

Intro: During the introduction the player does not have control of Torque's movement, but is able to use the game's controls to look around at the environment he is led through. As the game begins, it is night, and the player sees Torque brought by a **Small Boat** to **Carnate Island** and **Abbott State Penitentiary**. Torque's boat ties up at the **Docks** on the east side of the island, and he is then moved to a short, black **Transfer Bus** that transports him up to the prison. The bus passes numerous landmarks during the journey, including the **Town**, the **Lighthouse**, and the **World War II Fort**. Finally inside the prison, Torque is taken into the **Admissions Building** where he undergoes the standard admittance procedure and is then escorted to his cell on **Death Row** by two **Guards** who discuss his crime between them along the way. Once they reach his **Cell**, one looks at his watch and mentions how, if his watch is right, the prison has just now finally executed Willie Wiggins after ten years on the row. The guard drops off a box containing Torque's personal effects. This introductory sequence takes approximately a minute of game-time, though in reality it would take much longer. This is achieved through fade-outs that cut the player from one key section of the introduction to the next.

Area: Death House, Top Floor

DH1. After the intro finishes, the player starts the game in **Torque's Cell**. Torque's Cell is a small, tight area containing a bed, a toilet, and a small table. There is no window. The door is shut and has a small barred window through which the player can look to see the **Death Row Hallway** outside. Torque overhears inmate chatter outside his cell. Torque will be confined to his cell long enough for the player to become familiar with the controls.

DH2. Chaos ensues outside **Torque's Cell**. Torque hears explosions, screaming, earthquake-like rumbling, as the **Monsters** start appearing and killing everything in sight. The entire building shakes, indicating that a massive earthquake is taking place, but that shaking eventually subsides.

DH3. Door of **Torque's Cell** is ripped off by a fast-moving **Cartwheeler** that the player sees only as a blur.

DH4. Torque leaves his **Cell** and is in the **Death Row Hallway**. **Death Row** consists of the hallway and six cells in a single block, with a barred door at the end, behind which is a hallway. The **Guard Station** adjacent to the hallway includes a window that looks in on the Death Row Hallway as well as the hallway just outside Death Row. The player sees the door of the cell adjacent to his slam shut, the implication being the **Cartwheeler** that ripped his door off is now in that cell. The player sees a **Scared Prisoner** grab onto the bars and scream for his life before he is ripped off the cell door by the Cartwheeler from the darkness behind him. The player hears the screams of the Scared Prisoner suddenly come to a stop as he is apparently killed in the darkness.

DH5. The **Flashlight Guard** in the **Guard Station** walks out from the station to the hall outside **Death Row**. He shines his **Flashlight** toward the player and says, "Prisoner! Back to your cell while we sort this out!" Suddenly he is jerked up into the ceiling, blood drips down, and his Flashlight clatters to the ground below, leaving only the **Batteries** for Torque to pick up (once he leaves the Death Row cellblock).

DH6. Investigating the rest of **Death Row** after seeing the guard killed, Torque sees one **Other Cell** with its door open. Torque goes into the Other Cell and in it finds a dead inmate with a look of terror frozen on his face, a **Shiv** stuck straight into his chest. Walking close to the body, Torque gets the Shiv.

DH7. From within this **Other Cell**, Torque hears a door-being-ripped-off sound and, leaving the Other Cell, sees the gate to **Death Row** has been removed. Foreboding and frightening sounds come from the darkness of the hallway.

DH8. Leaving the **Death Row** area, Torque ventures into the dark and frightening hallway (picking up the **Batteries** along the way), expecting to see the **Creature** that killed the **Flashlight Guard**. However, there is no Creature there any more. The player finds a **Map** of the **Death House** in the **Guard Station**.

DH9. To the left the hallway leads to a door that is locked and a **Miscellaneous Room** that contains a **Large Window** that the player can go into to find some **Revolver Ammo**. Here the player finds a number of dead guards. The player can look out of the Large Window and see the **Courtyard** below, watching an altercation between **Prisoners** and **Guards**. Soon indistinct **Creatures** rush into the fight and the Prisoners and Guards unite to try to fight them off, but are slaughtered in the process.

DH10. A dimly lit hallway stretches in the opposite direction of the dead end. As the player moves down this hallway, an **Escaping Prisoner** emerges and runs up to him, saying, "We gotta get out of here, follow me!" He then turns and runs down a hallway that has an **Open Door** to the outside and an **Exterior Set of Stairs**. Light streams in from the wide open door. The Escaping Prisoner gets ahead of the player and says, "Hurry up!" right before the whole building rumbles and the **Ceiling** caves in on him, crushing him and blocking the exit.

DH11. Turning around from the dead end with the collapsed ceiling, the player moves toward a completely darkened hallway, out of which a **Winded Prisoner** runs, panting, leaning over on his knees. "Thank God I made it to the light," he wheezes. As the player gets close to him, a **Cartwheeler**, apparently clinging to the ceiling, swings out of the darkness, impales him with his blades, and yanks the prisoner up toward the ceiling. The Winded Prisoner's decapitated head then falls back to the ground. The Winded Prisoner drops a key to the ground, which the player can use to open a nearby control room.

DH12. The player is then forced to open the gate the Winded Prisoner was killed behind using a control switch in the nearby control room. He then heads into the dark area where the Cartwheeler was, expecting to be killed.

DH13. As the player rounds a corner and the hall continues, he spots the **Cartwheeler** up ahead on the ceiling that drops down in front of him, blocking his way. Suddenly the player hears gunfire as the Cartwheeler is shot down and killed by an **Armed Guard** farther down the hall.

DH14. The **Armed Guard** calls to the player and the player approaches him. The Armed Guard tells the player they need to work together, and tells him to go get a **Flashlight** from the **Equipment Room** just down the hall.

DH15. In the **Equipment Room**, the player finds a **Flashlight** that is fully charged. A mysterious **PA speaker** in the room talks to the player in a nefarious voice, urging him, "You can't trust him, kill him before he puts you back in your cell."

DH16. Leaving the **Equipment Room** with the **Flashlight**, the **Armed Guard** tells the player that they need to head down the **Stairs** toward the exit. The Armed Guard leads the prisoner downstairs.

Area: Death House, First Floor

DH17. The **Stairs** lead down to the first floor, where it is pitch black, though the player can now use his **Flashlight** to shine the way. At the bottom, a **Cartwheeler** appears, but the player can use his Flashlight to frighten him away, potentially wounding it with his **Shiv**. After a moment a **Second Cartwheeler** appears.

DH18. While the player is fighting, the **Armed Guard** is also attacking the **Cartwheelers**. He apologizes for putting the player at risk like that. At the room at the bottom of the Stairs, there are two passageways: one to the abandoned **Electric Chair Room** and one to a hallway that leads to the **Electric Chair Control Room,** which looks in on the chair. The Armed Guard tells the player to look in the executioner's room while he checks out the execution chamber.

DH19. Suddenly, the **Armed Guard** hears a sound coming from the **Electric Chair Room**, and he runs off to investigate it. Once the guard has entered the room, suddenly a burst of lightning fills the room, and the Armed Guard is killed and disappears.

DH20. The player can now go to the **Electric Chair Room** to find that all that is left of the **Armed Guard** is a pile of ash, though the player can now pick up his **Revolver**.

DH21. If the player decides to kill the **Armed Guard** at the top of the **Stairs**, the Armed Guard will fight back with his **Revolver**. If the player successfully kills him, however, he will get his Revolver, but will have to fight the **Cartwheelers** at the bottom of the Stairs by himself. Step 19 will be skipped entirely.

DH22. Continuing down the hallway that leads to the **Executioner's Control Room**, the player comes to a **Large Foyer**. Locked double doors lead to the outside. A hallway leads to the Gas Chamber and Electric Chair Observation rooms, but has been collapsed by the earthquake. Another hallway leads north, but is blocked by a **Double Lock Down Gate**. A **Lock Down Gate Control Room** is also off the north end of the Large Foyer, which has a locked door on it. Four **Cartwheelers** drop out of the ceiling (though not necessarily all at once) and provide the player with his first experience at gun combat. If the player didn't pick up the gun, this battle is going to be difficult to survive.

DH23. With all the **Cartwheelers** killed, a final one rips through the door to the **Lock Down Gate Control Room** and hurtles into the room. Defeating the **Cartwheeler**, the player is then able to go into the Lock Down Gate Control Room.

DH24. In the **Lock Down Gate Control Room**, the player can operate a **Lock Down Switch**, which operates the **Double Lock Down Gate** that blocks progress out of the **Large Foyer**. However, it only opens the first gate, closing the second. Re-flipping the switch inverts the positions of the doors. In order to get through the gate, the player must first make the first gate open, and then push a **Statue** from the **Large Foyer** to the gate. Then, while the first gate is open, if the player pushes the Statue under the gate, and then re-flips the switch, both of the gates will be opened and the player can proceed down the hall.

DH25. Straight ahead, the hall passes the **Gas Chamber Control Room** and then leads to another hall that forks off to the east. If the player passes that hall and continues, he comes upon the **Lethal Injection Control Room**. In that room the player finds some **Revolver Ammo** and **Batteries** for the Flashlight. The player can also look in on the **Lethal Injection Room**, though he cannot access it at this time. If the player continues down the hall past the Lethal Injection Room, he finds that the hallway has collapsed and he cannot progress. Along this section, the player fights a number of additional **Cartwheelers**.

DH26. The player must go back to the hallway that veered off to the east. Traveling down that hallway, the player comes to the door to the **Lethal Injection Room**, which is locked, as well as the door to the **Gas Chamber Room**, also locked.

DH27. The player must go back to where he passed the **Gas Chamber Control Room**. There the player will be able to see into the **Gas Chamber Room**, which is barren except for the **Gas Chamber** itself. Strapped into the chair inside the **Gas Chamber** is a **Gas Chamber Victim**, who turns to look at the player and is crying out for help, though his cries are inaudible. In the room is the **Gas Chamber Switch**, which the player can flip if he wants to. If he does, the **Gas Chamber** fills with gas and the **Gas Chamber Victim** is seen to be struggling and screaming as he dies.

DH28. Also in the **Gas Chamber Control Room**, the player will find a **Door Switch**, which opens the previously locked door to the **Gas Chamber Room**. Now the player can travel down to the Gas Chamber Room door and enter.

DH29. Entering the **Gas Chamber Room**, the door suddenly slams shut behind the player and the player cannot re-open it.

DH30. If, in DH27, the player killed the **Gas Chamber Victim** in the **Gas Chamber**, the Gas Chamber Victim is slumped over in the chair, dead, and the door to the **Gas Chamber** immediately springs open and gas starts billowing out.

DH31. If, in DH27, the player did not kill the **Gas Chamber Victim**, the man is still in the **Gas Chamber**, screaming (almost inaudibly) for the player to let him out. However, the player is unable to open the door to the Gas Chamber. Looking into the **Gas Chamber Control Room** through the glass wall that separates the two, the player sees a shadowy, indistinct human figure who flips the **Gas Chamber Switch** that fills up the **Gas Chamber** with the deadly gas. The **Gas Chamber Victim** inside is killed in the same manner as if the player had flipped the switch.

Once the **Gas Chamber Victim** is dead, the door to the Gas Chamber springs open, just as in DH27.

DH32. The gas flowing out of the **Gas Chamber** causes continuous damage to the player if he lets it reach his mouth, and so the player must avoid it by running to the other side of the **Gas Chamber Room**. Here there is a glass wall that looks into the **Gas Chamber Observation Room**.

DH33. Now, with the player up against the glass wall that joins the **Gas Chamber Room** to the **Gas Chamber Observation Room**, the player sees a **Cartwheeler** in the Observation Room. The **Cartwheeler** bashes up against the glass several times before finally breaking through, allowing the player to escape the gas from the **Gas Chamber** by fleeing into the **Gas Chamber Observation Room**. The player will be able to speed up the shattering of the glass by shooting or hitting the glass while the Cartwheeler bashes against it, though the thick, bulletproof glass will be unbreakable from the player's attacks alone. While escaping into the **Gas Chamber Observation Room**, the player will simultaneously need to deal with fighting the Cartwheeler.

DH34. In the **Gas Camber Observation Room**, the player finds several corpses, which have been propped up in the observation chairs, as if to watch the execution. The corpses include one guard and several prisoners, some of whom have been beheaded. The guard is still clutching the prison-issue **Stun Stick**, which the player can pick up.

DH35. From the **Gas Chamber Observation Room**, the player sees a wall that has been bashed through, apparently by the **Cartwheeler**. It looks like the wall was made to cover up an old, abandoned door that leads down into the darkness of the **Basement**.

Area: Death House, Basement

DH36. Traveling down the stairs, the player finds himself in the pitch-black **Basement**. Old pieces of prison equipment such as shackles, a pillory, and various torture devices are found here. The player finds several gates, which are locked for the time being. The player must navigate the musty, abandoned, and initially totally dark basement, where the player will have to fight numerous **Cartwheelers**. The player will be able to turn on the gas-powered lights that are in the basement if he finds the **Gas Control Switch**. But only some of the lights work, so this will provide only partial illumination of the basement, but will make fighting the Cartwheelers considerably easier.

DH37. If the player searches the **Basement**, he will find one tile on the tiled stone floor that makes a different, hollow sound when walked on. This panel is partially covered by a heavy piece of furniture, which the player can push and pull. When the object is pushed off the floor tile, it springs open, revealing a cache of **Revolvers** and **Revolver Ammo**.

DH38. The only obvious way out of the **Basement** leads up some stairs, but these stairs are behind a closed gate the player cannot open. However, in the Basement the player finds a **Metal Lever** sticking out of a long horizontal slot in the wall. The Metal Lever does not rotate, but the player is able to push and pull this Metal Lever along the slot in the wall. Though not immediately obvious, if the player is at all observant he will notice that moving the Metal Lever moves a corresponding part of the wall opposite the Metal Lever. When the Lever is positioned just so, the wall opens to reveal a passage the player can enter.

Area: Death House, First Floor

DH39. Traveling through the passage, the player reaches the stairs on the other side of the closed iron gate. The stairs lead up through another wall, similar to the one leading out of the **Gas Chamber Observation Room**, which has recently been smashed through, apparently by the Cartwheelers. Now back on the first floor of the prison, the player sees a locked **Door to the Outside** and another passageway that leads into the **Lethal Injection Observation Room**.

DH40. In the **Lethal Injection Observation Room**, the player sees a glass wall facing into the **Lethal Injection Room**, along with a number of chairs where the witnesses would sit. In these chairs are more dead prisoners and guards, propped up in the chairs, some decapitated. Among them is a guard who is clutching his **Revolver**, which the player can pick up to allow him to use two Revolvers simultaneously (if he didn't find the hidden ones in the basement). There is also a **Security Monitor**, which the player can walk up to and use to get a televised view of the **Lethal Injection Room**.

DH41. Looking into the **Lethal Injection Room**, the player sees a **Lethal Injection Victim** strapped to the gurney in the room, struggling in the straps that hold him down. If the player uses the **Security Monitor**, he sees a view of the man on the table, but now **Killjoy** (the doctor boss eventually fought in the Asylum) is there, hooking up the IV, bloody amputation cleaver in his free hand. If the player continues to watch, Killjoy looks into the security camera, straight at the player. If the player stops using the Security Monitor and looks back into the Lethal Injection Room through the window, Killjoy is not there. Eventually the Lethal Injection Victim dies, whether the player looks at him over the Security Monitor or not.

DH42. The player hears a knocking coming from behind him, from the **Door to the Outside**, followed by a voice on the other side of the door asking, "Is there anybody there?" The player hears keys rattling, and the Door to the Outside opens, revealing **Dallas**, a friendly prisoner who is eager to talk to the player. He quickly explains what he thinks is causing these monsters to appear: they have been doing experiments on the inmates and something went horribly wrong. (Of course this is not actually true, but Dallas believes it wholeheartedly.) He explains that he has just come from the **North Cellblock Building**, and that there are lots of Cartwheelers in there, so he's looking for another way out. This end of the **Death House** only leads to dead ends, so Dallas suggests he saw another way out through the Death House, and tells the player to follow him. If the player kills Dallas at any time, the prisoner drops his Ring of Keys, which the player can pick up.

Area: Courtyard Outside Death House

CY43. **Dallas** leads the player through the **Courtyard**, which is to the northeast of the **Death House**. Here the player sees the bodies of a number of guards and prisoners strewn about, with a few dead **Cartwheelers** as well. Many of the guards will have dropped their **Revolvers** when they died, and the player will be able to collect them for their ammo. The player also sees assorted hypodermic needles lying scattered around the yard. Dallas leads the player to where there is a large hole in the wall, apparently caused by the earthquake. The hole leads back into the Death House, and the Friendly Player leads the player back into the building.

Area: Death House, First Floor

DH44. The player and **Dallas** enter the **Lethal Injection Room** through the hole in the wall. Here Dallas is stunned to see the **Lethal Injection Victim** on the table, and tells the player that it was an old buddy of his. The Lethal Injection Victim lies dead on the table as the player had seen him from the **Lethal Injection Observation Room**, except now he is stuck with thirty or more hypodermic needles, making him resemble an acupuncture patient. "What the hell is this?" questions Dallas. The door out of the Lethal Injection Room is unopenable, however, and so Dallas admits that they won't be able to get out through the **Death House**. As a result, Dallas, leads the player back out into the **Courtyard**.

Area: Courtyard Outside Death House

CY45: Returning to the **Courtyard**, there are now a number of **Cartwheelers** that the player must fight. **Dallas** is defenseless, and the player must try to keep the Cartwheelers away from him to keep him alive.

CY46: With the Cartwheelers killed, **Dallas** leads the player to a door that leads into the **North Cellblock Building**, which is located across the **Courtyard** from the **Death House**. Dallas unlocks the door, heading into the building.

CY47. If the player killed **Dallas**, or Dallas was killed by one of the **Cartwheelers**, the player will have to pick up the **Ring of Keys** that he drops. If the player then tries to open the door to the **North Cellblock Building**, the player will automatically use the keys and be able to open the door. Also, as soon as Dallas is killed, the Cartwheelers start appearing in the **Courtyard**, if they have not already shown up.

Area: North Cellblock Building

CB1. Inside the door of the **North Cellblock Building**, the player and Dallas stop in the **Entryway**. Dallas warns the player that there are a number of Cartwheelers ahead. He suggests that the player should lead the way now, since he's armed and more of a bad-ass, besides.

CB2. From the **Entryway**, the player hears sounds coming from around the corner. First is the distinctive blade clattering noise of the Cartwheeler, followed by a new sound of the squirting of fluid through a hypodermic needle (made by the **Mainliner**, though the player does not realize this yet). The sounds seem to indicate something in a fight with the **Cartwheeler**. After that, only the sound of the Mainliner is left, and then everything is quiet.
[…]

The Quarry

[…]

Transition to Asylum

[...]

Asylum

[...]

The Woods

[...]

The Beach

[...]

Return to Prison

[...]

Bluff

[...]

Caverns to Lighthouse

[...]

Lighthouse

[...]

Surrounding Area Outside Lighthouse

[...]

Return to Lighthouse

[...]

Road to Docks

[...]

The Docks

[...]

Section VII: Maps

Island Overview

Prison

Death House
Second Floor

First Floor

Basement

Courtyard Outside Death House

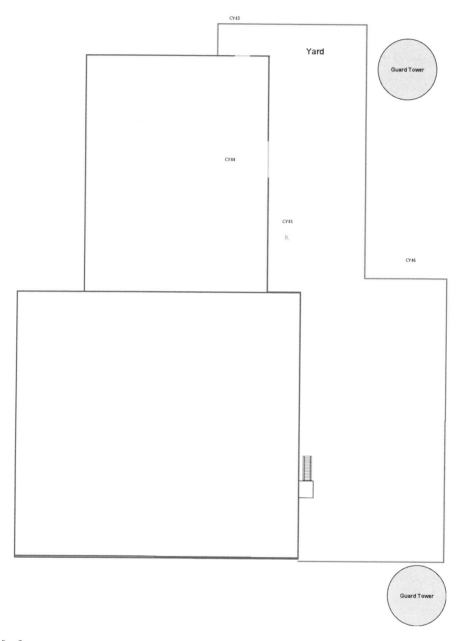

[...]

The Quarry

[…]

Asylum

[…]

The Woods

[…]

The Beach

[…]

Escape Tunnel

[…]

Return to Prison

[…]

Bluff

[…]

Lighthouse

[…]

Road to Docks & Docks

[…]

Section VIII: Menus

All menus (except the Main Menus and the Save Game Screen) can be accessed when no game is running as well as while a game is paused in the background. When no game is running, a custom-build 3D prison environment will be displayed behind the menus, while when the game is paused the game-world will be shown behind the current screen.

Main Menu Screen (No Saved Game Available)

New Game -> Immediately starts a new game
Options -> Goes to the Options Screen

Main Menu Screen (Saved Game Available)

Continue -> Immediately loads the last created/used saved game
Load -> Goes to the Load Game Screen
New Game -> Immediately starts a new game

Options -> Goes to the Options Screen
The Archives -> Goes to the Archives Screen

Game Paused Menu Screen

Resume -> Unpauses the game and closes the menu
Save -> Goes to the Saved Game Screen
Revert -> Goes to Confirm Dialog, then ends current game and loads last used save-game
Load -> Goes to the Load Game Screen
Options -> Goes to the Options Screen
Quit -> Goes to Confirm Dialog, then ends current game and goes to the Main Menu

Load Game Screen

Lists all currently saved games. If the player selects one, that game is loaded and the game is started. Player is also able to delete old saved games.

Save Game Screen

Shows all available save slots, including those with saves already in them. If the player selects one, the current game state is saved there and gameplay is resumed.

Options Screen

Controller Settings -> Goes to the Controller Settings Screen
Screen Alignment Settings -> Goes to the Screen Alignment Settings Screen
Audio Settings -> Goes to the Audio Settings Screen
Return to Main Menu -> Goes to the Main Menu

Controller Settings Screen

Controller Configuration Selection (Player selects from three presets)
Customize Controller -> Goes to the Customize Buttons Screen
Checkpoint Save -> Save to Memory/Prompt/Save to Memory Card
Help Text On/Off
Look Sensitivity Slider
Invert Pitch Toggle Box
Vibration On/Off Toggle Box
AutoTargeting On/Off Toggle Box
Auto Pitch Correction On/Off
Return to the Options Screen -> Goes to the Options Screen

Customize Controller Screen

Allows player to remap functionality of buttons as they desire, including analog sticks.

Screen Alignment Settings Screen

Player is able to adjust the alignment of the screen to fit their display device.
Return to the Options Screen -> Goes to the Options Screen

Audio Settings Screen

Sound Effects Volume Slider
Dialog Volume Slider

Music Volume Slider
Stereo On/Off Toggle Box
Return to the Options Screen -> Goes to the Options Screen

The Archives Screen

Selection for Creature Archive/Clem's Diary
Selection for Location Archive/Consuela's Scrapbook

The Archives

The Archives is a unique feature of *Unspeakable* that allows players to learn more about the game-world without intruding unduly on the game experience itself. The Archives is accessible only from the Main Menu of the game. As the player uncovers each creature or special environment in the game, the game will unlock another section of the Archives, allowing the player to read an informative text section accompanied by an illustration/image. Before the player plays the game, the Archive will be empty, except for an overview of Carnate Island. The player will always be able tell how many elements he has yet to uncover (for example, blank entries will appear in the notebook), which will encourage the player to keep playing to unlock more information or to go back and replay to unlock elements he may have missed. A player may successfully complete the game without unlocking all the elements in the Archive.

Creature Archive/Clem's Journal

For each creature the player encounters, the player will unlock a new page in Clem's Journal. This is a diary-like book with yellowed and worn pages that was written by Clem, the prisoner that the player will meet in the game. Clem writes in an educated manner, almost as if a naturalist writing about new species he discovers. Clem's knowledge of Carnate's past will play into the descriptions he writes of the characters, allowing him to reveal facts only hinted at in the game itself. Accompanying Clem's text will be an illustration of the creature in question that he appears to have drawn himself. Fortunately, Clem is an accomplished illustrator. All seven of the main creatures in the game will be featured, in addition to the four bosses, and interesting sections on prisoners and C.O.s.

Location Archive/Consuela's Scrapbook

For each historically relevant location on the island the player uncovers, the player will unlock a new page out of Consuela's Scrapbook. Consuela is the wife of Ernesto, the ornery guard who leads the player in at the beginning of the game and who the player will battle alongside later on. Consuela lived on the island in the town area, and filled her ample free time by researching the history of the island, exploring its terrain, and taking photographs of various locations. Thus her scrapbook will include a page on numerous key locations she has found, including the prison itself, the prison cemetery, the quarry, the quarry cave-in, the asylum, the native village, the shipwreck, the airplane crash, the execution site on the bluff, the lighthouse, the witch cemetery and burning site, the town, and the docks. Since the player may not find all these locations when playing through the game, the Scrapbook section may contain several empty pages when the player finishes the game. Consuela's book looks much like a well-maintained photo album, with black corner picture holders and little typed-up sheets describing each image.

Interface

Main Menu

From the main menu, the player is given the option of going to the Archives menu.

Archives Selection Menu

This screen comes up from the main menu, and the player is presented with a picture of two books on the left and right of the screen. On the left is Clem's Journal, and on the right is Consuela's Scrapbook. They appear on top of a table in the style of *Medal of Honor: Frontline*. The player is able to select them by pressing left and right to select the one he wants. When selected, an item glows and pulsates to indicate it is selected. When the player presses the Select button on either of these texts, he is taken to one of the two Book screens.

Book Screens

Both Clem's Journal and Consuela's Scrapbook function identically, though they look somewhat different. Both present an open book to the player, viewed from a top-down view, with only the right page visible. The player can then flip through the pages using the left and right buttons. On each page an image appears in the upper right, with text wrapping around it. For both books, each page will at first appear blank, with a "To Be Discovered" text appearing at the bottom of the page. Then, as the player unlocks a given creature or location, the page text and image will show up. A text message will appear in the game indicating that some piece of content has been unlocked, so players will know to go to look for it.

Clem's Journal

Clem's Journal appears to be a worn leather book with various pieces of paper and odd scraps stuck into it. It is very much a journal Clem was able to keep with him through his adventures around the island, scribbling in it with his pen whenever he had a chance. After a brief introduction, each page of Clem's Journal shows a different creature on the island and presents an uncolored illustration of the creature in question, with text that wraps around the illustration. The text in Clem's journal is a readable handwriting, in longhand. The text describes, in a few sentences, what Clem has seen of the creature and how it is tied into the execution theme (something Clem will remark on with curiosity). The text is simultaneously read aloud in Clem's voice.

Consuela's Scrapbook

In contrast to Clem's Journal, Consuela's Scrapbook looks significantly nicer, the product of an intelligent and skilled woman with a lot of time on her hands. Following an introductory page, each page of her scrapbook features a photo of a given location, with text that wraps around it. This text appears to have been created with a typewriter and then cut out and pasted into the scrapbook. The pictures are of 3D renderings of the various locations, and are in black and white, and are held into the book by black photo corners. The text describes the area that is seen in the picture and its historical relevance, and while on the page the player will hear Consuela reading the text aloud.

Glossary

This section includes brief definitions of a number of the terms referred to in this book, and should be of particular use to readers less familiar with the jargon of the computer and video game industry. Some of the definitions veer close to talking about programming, and in these cases I provide only enough information to give the reader a general idea of what the term means. Those looking for more complete definitions are advised to pick up a book about computer game development from a programming standpoint, of which there are many.

A*:   The most popular pathfinding algorithm used by computer games, which finds short and effective paths consistently and quickly, though it is far from perfect. The basis of the A* algorithm is to search for a path by expanding valid nodes that are closest to the target location first in order to try to find the shortest path possible without searching too extensively. Of course, this can be found described in more detail in almost any book about programming games. *See also* Pathfinding.

Agent: *See* AI Agent.

AI: *See* Artificial Intelligence.

AI Agent: The entity that the artificial intelligence controls in a game; the agent of its actions. In a computer game, the AI agents include the monsters the player fights and the NPCs to which he talks. Many people make the mistake of referring to those creatures themselves as "AIs," but this has always bothered me. Just as you would not say that a person walking down the street is an "intelligence," you should not refer to the agents in a game as the "AIs." See Chapter 9, "Artificial Intelligence."

Algorithm: In the land of game development this refers to a usually short piece of code designed to solve a particular problem, typically mathematical in nature. For instance, you might have an algorithm that determines whether one character in a 3D environment can see another one or not. Or you could say that the code that finds a walkable path from the first character to the second one is an algorithm. Or, in a game like *SimCity*, algorithms are used to calculate the population density in a given location based on the choices the player has made in building the city.

A-Life: *See* Artificial Life.

Alpha: Customarily describes a game that is not yet close to being complete but is playable all the way through. At this point, the design and content is largely done, and bug-fixing, refining, and balancing are all that remain to be done on the title. This is often used by publishers to define the state of a project they have in development and is typically followed by the Beta state. Other developers may define Alpha differently, such as using it to mean any game that is in a playable state. *See also* Beta *and* Release Candidate.

Arcade Game: Strictly speaking, a computer game that is found in an arcade environment. It may also refer to home conversions of the same games. More broadly, arcade game describes any game featuring the short and intense gameplay typical of these games. See Chapter 4, which contains an analysis of the arcade game *Centipede* and an exploration of the nature of the arcade game as a genre.

Art: In the context of game development, this is most often used to describe the graphical content of a game. It can also mean what all game developers engage in, the creation of computer games themselves, which qualify as art. The author's favorite definition of art comes from Chapter 7 of Scott McCloud's excellent book *Understanding Comics*: "Art, as I see it, is any human activity which doesn't grow out of either of our species' two basic instincts: survival and reproduction." Some game developers spend endless time debating whether or not computer games qualify as art, but these arguments are seldom productive or useful.

Art Bible: A document used in game development that includes concept sketches of game art assets and possibly some descriptive text. The art bible is used by a game's art team as a reference tool in the development of the game's graphical content, usually in order to maintain consistency.

Artificial Intelligence: The artificial intelligence in a game controls all of the entities or agents in the game that have the ability to react to the player or otherwise provide an unpredictable challenge for the player. Artificial intelligence in a single-player game typically fulfills the role that human intelligence provides in a multi-player game. Thoroughly defined in Chapter 9, "Artificial Intelligence."

Artificial Life: A system for artificial intelligence that tries to imitate biological life by assigning AI agents base behaviors and desires, which cause them to perform specific actions by their "nature." This is the opposite of the type of AI typically used in most games, though artificial life was famously used in the computer game *Creatures*.

Assets: The content of a game; customarily used to refer to the art, sound effects, music, and possibly the levels. Code itself is seldom referred to as an asset.

Avatar: The same as a game-world surrogate, the player's avatar is whatever character represents him in the game-world. It may also be an icon used in chat-room-like situations. "The Avatar" is also the name of the character the player controls in the *Ultima* series of games.

Beta: The state games reach after passing through Alpha, and the last step before a game is published or otherwise released to the public. In Beta, changes made to a game are supposed to be strictly limited to bug fixes. Some developers define Beta to be when they first have what they consider to be a release candidate. *See also* Alpha *and* Release Candidate.

Bible: Used in the gaming industry to refer to various reference materials used during a game's development. *See* Art Bible *and* Story Bible.

Blind-Play: In multi-player gaming, this refers to each player being able to make his moves without the other players being able to see them; the other players are "blind" to their actions. In non-computer games, this is typically accomplished via a physical "screen" of some type that is placed between different players, or between a Game Master and his players. In computer gaming, blind-play is most common in online gaming, where each player has his own computer system and thereby cannot always see what the other players are doing.

Boss Monster: An enemy in a game, though not necessarily a "monster" per se, that is much larger or simply more difficult to defeat than the other opponents in the game. Typically boss monsters are placed at the end of levels and provide a climax for that level's gameplay.

'Bot: Short for "robot," this refers to artificial intelligence agents that are designed to appear to play similarly to humans, typically designed to work in first-person shooter death-match games. *Quake III Arena* and *Unreal Tournament* both feature 'bots as the player's only opposition in the single-player game.

BSP: Short for Binary Space Partition. A method for storing and rendering 3D space that involves dividing the world into a tree of space partitions, most famously used in id Software's games *Doom* and *Quake*.

Builder Games: One term used to describe games in which the player is responsible for building lasting structures in the game-world. In a sense, in builder games, the players are responsible for the level design. Examples of this type of game are *SimCity*, *Civilization*, *RollerCoaster Tycoon*, and *The Sims*.

Burn Rate: The amount of money a company, typically a developer, spends in a month to keep itself in business. This typically includes all of the employees' salaries, rent, utilities, and other persistent expenses. Sometimes publishers will try to fund a developer only to the extent of its burn rate, so that the developer does not have any spare cash and remains forever beholden to the publisher.

Candidate: *See* Release Candidate.

Canned: Another term for "scripted," though "canned" is typically used more derisively. *See* Scripted.

Capture the Flag: A game involving two teams, both of which have a flag. The flag is kept at a specific location and possibly guarded, while the players on both teams try to grab the other team's flag through stealth or brute force. In computer games, this is often a game variant offered in first-person shooter multi-player cooperative games, such as *Quake* or *Unreal*.

Choke-Point: A point in a game past which a player can progress only by passing through a particular area, completing a particular puzzle, or defeating a particular monster. Often the areas preceding and following a choke-point allow the player more freedom of play, while the choke-point presents a task the player absolutely must accomplish before proceeding.

Classic Arcade Game: This does not necessarily mean a game that is a classic, but any game that was released during the early period of arcade games or that exhibits the traits typical of those games. Classic arcade games include simple, single-screen-player games such as *Space Invaders, Centipede, Robotron: 2084*, or *Pac-Man*. Classic arcade game is defined more fully in Chapter 4. *See also* Arcade Game.

Code: When used in reference to games, code is the lines of text that programmers enter into the computer and which the computer then compiles into the functional game. A talented programmer is sometimes referred to as a code-jockey.

Color: Beyond the obvious definition, in terms of game design this may also refer to the specific content and setting of a game. *Monopoly*, for instance, includes the street names of Atlantic City and a Depression era real-estate mogul theme as a means of providing color. Color is separate from the gameplay itself.

Concept Document: Also known as a pitch document. This is a short document that includes text and concept sketches and that is used to initially sell the idea of a project to a publisher or other financier. A concept document gives the reader an idea of what the game will involve without including sufficient detail to actually develop the game. If accepted, the concept document is usually expanded into the design document.

Concept Sketch: A sketch of a particular game art asset that is used to show someone what the art will look like, approximately, before that graphic or model is actually created. May also be a sketch of a scene from the game as it will appear once the game is functional.

Creative Services: A deceptively titled wing of the publisher that is typically in charge of creating the box art and other advertisements and logos for a game.

Critical Path: The path that the player is expected and encouraged to follow when moving through a game or a particular level. Somewhat reminiscent of the yellow brick road in *The Wizard of Oz*.

CRPG: A computer version of a role-playing game. *See also* Role-Playing Game.

CTF: Typically refers to capture the flag multi-player games, though it may also refer to Valve Software's *Classic Team Fortress* game. *See* Capture the Flag.

Cut-Scene: A non-interactive portion of a game typically used to communicate to the player information about the game's story line, sometimes involving pre-rendered or live action full-motion video, other times using the game's real-time graphics engine. Cut-scenes often come between levels in a game, and are sometimes used as rewards for the player having finished a particularly challenging portion of the game.

Death March: When a development team, particularly the programmers, works every waking moment on a project for a long period of time, typically trying to make an unachievable deadline of some sort. Often the death march is entered into thinking it will be over soon enough, but it then drags on long beyond what anyone thought possible.

Death-Match: A multi-player game in which the players' only goals are to kill each other. Usually refers to games of that sort in first-person shooters such as *Half-Life*, *Unreal*, or *Halo*.

Decision Tree: A type of chart that shows how various player decisions will lead to different outcomes. Referred to as a tree, since each fork produces two branches that move away from the previous decision, making it look like a tree.

Design Document: The textual reference used in developing a game that attempts to describe in detail every important aspect of the game's design. Sometimes referred to as the functional specification. Described more completely in Chapter 19, "The Design Document."

Designer's Story: This is the story written by the designer or someone on the development team that the game follows. This story is completely predetermined, even if it has a number of different paths for the player to explore.

DM: *Depending on the context, see* Dungeon Master *or* Death-Match.

Dungeon Master: The term for the Game Master used in conjunction with *Dungeons & Dragons* games. *See* Game Master.

Emergence: In terms of a game, emergence is when unanticipated behaviors and results emerge out of the various game systems interacting with each other and with the player's input. In short, emergence is when the game experience takes a direction the designer never anticipated. Some emergent behaviors may turn into player exploits, which are generally viewed as a negative form of emergence, while other emergent behaviors just mean players are able to author their own experience without ruining it. Some designers view any amount of emergence as a negative, though most would agree emergence is one of the most exciting parts of game design.

Emoticons: Somewhat odious slang expression referring to the sideways smiley faces and other characters made out of the ASCII character set, for example, :-P. These are often used in e-mail, ICQ, or other messaging systems, or when chatting in online gaming experiences.

Engine: The core code that handles the most basic functionality of the game, but not including the code that governs specific gameplay functionality. Sometimes the engine is split up into the rendering engine, the sound engine, the behavior engine, and so forth. Each of these components can be considered to be part of the game's engine as a whole. Engines are typically more general than a particular game, which allows them to be reused for multiple different projects. However, some developers use the term engine to refer to the entirety of a game's source code. For example, id Software has licensed their *Quake* engine for use in a broad range of games, from *Half-Life* to *Soldier of Fortune* to *Medal of Honor: Allied Assault*.

Exploit: An exploit is a technique a player may use in a game to become more successful more quickly than the designers had intended. Exploits are viewed by developers as bugs, and are typically fixed by patches when possible. It is important to differentiate an exploit, which gives a player unfair advancement, from an emergent behavior, which the designer may not have anticipated but which does not ruin the player's experience. Exploits should be fixed, while emergent solutions should be embraced.

Finite State Machine: *See* State-Based AI.

First-Person Shooter: The type of game exemplified by *Doom*, *Half-Life*, *Unreal*, *Marathon*, *Halo*, and *Medal of Honor*. In first-person shooters, the player's perspective of the world is from the first person and his objective is to shoot everything in sight, though some first-person shooters offer some subtle variations on this goal.

Flight Simulator: Often shortened to flight sim, this is a type of game that attempts to model the flight of a real-world aircraft. The amount of realism involved varies from game to game; some games are extremely realistic and difficult, while others prevent the player from crashing entirely. Examples include *Microsoft Flight Simulator, F-15 Strike Eagle*, *Flight Unlimited*, and *Hellcats Over the Pacific*.

FMV: *See* Full-Motion Video.

Focus: A brief, three- to five-sentence description of the most important concepts guiding a game's development. Described in detail in Chapter 5, "Focus."

FPS: Depending on the context, this may refer to the first-person shooter genre of games or to the frames per second that the game's engine is currently rendering. *See* First-Person Shooter.

FSM: Stands for finite state machine. *See* State-Based AI.

Full-Motion Video: Any non-real-time graphics in a game that are displayed quickly in a sequential order to create a movie-like effect. Full-motion video can be of live actors, computer-generated environments, or a combination of the two.

Functional Specification: The sister document to the technical specification, in that it describes how the game will function from the user's perspective, as opposed to how the programmer will implement that functionality. In game development, typically referred to as the design document. *See also* Design Document.

Fuzzy Logic: A type of AI that introduces some degree of randomness into the decision making process. This means that, given the exact same inputs, an AI agent will make different decisions based on chance.

Game: *The Oxford Universal Dictionary* includes a number of definitions for "game." The definition we are most interested in for this book reads as follows: "A diversion of the nature of a contest, played according to rules, and decided by superior skill, strength, or good fortune." To rephrase, a game presents an entertaining challenge to the player or players, a challenge which the player or players can understand and may be able to succeed at using their wits, dexterity, luck, or some combination thereof. To expand, in order for that challenge to be meaningful, the player must be presented with a number of interesting choices for how to succeed at the game, and those choices must be non-trivial. And in order for the challenge to be truly meaningful, the game must define the criterion for success. This excludes "software toys" such as *SimCity* from being games. Of course, one could write an entire book about the nature of a game at its purest level, but this is not that book.

Game Design: The game design establishes the shape and form of the gameplay in a game. The game design may be communicated through a design document, or it may only exist in the head of the implementors of the game. *See also* Gameplay.

Game Designer: The game designer is the person on a project who is responsible for establishing the form of the gameplay through the game design. *See also* Gameplay *and* Game Design.

Game Engine: *See* Engine.

Game Flow: The chain of events that make up the playing of a given game. A game can be said to flow between its action, exploration, puzzle-solving, and storytelling components. The proportional amount of time spent in each of these components and the pace at which the game takes place contributes to its overall flow.

Game Master: In a pen and paper role-playing game, the Game Master is the player who governs the actions of all of the other players in the game-world. The Game Master often has also dreamt up the adventures that the players are going on, and continues to dynamically create this story as the players navigate through it.

Game Mechanic: A specific way in which a part of the gameplay is implemented. For instance, the mechanic for doing an attack-jump in *Crash Bandicoot* is to hold down the "down" or "crouch" button while in mid-jump. The mechanic for sending a unit to a new location in *WarCraft* is to click on the unit in question with the left mouse button, move the pointer to the desired position on the map, and then click there with the right mouse button. The gameplay as a whole is made up of a number of different game mechanics combined together.

Game Minute: A narrative description of how gameplay will proceed in a given situation in a game. These prose narratives are typically written before development on the game has begun, to give the development team an idea of how the game will play when it is complete. You will find a detailed discussion of game minutes in Chapter 17, "Game Development Documentation."

Gameplay: The gameplay is the component that distinguishes games from all other artistic mediums. The gameplay defines how players are able to interact with the game-world and how that game-world will react to their actions. One could consider the gameplay to be the degree and nature of a game's interactivity. Of course many different people have different definitions for gameplay, but as far as this book is concerned, gameplay does not include the game's story, graphics, sound, or music. This is easy to understand if one recalls that gameplay is what separates games from other artistic mediums; each of these components is found in literature, film, or theater. Gameplay also does not include the code used to make the game run, the game's engine, though that engine does necessarily implement the gameplay. The gameplay, however, could be implemented using a completely different engine while remaining identical.

Game-World: This is the space in which a game takes place. In a board game such as *The Settlers of Catan*, the game-world is represented by the board the game takes place on. For a sports game, the game-world is the real-world but is limited to the extent of the field the game is played on. For a role-playing game, the game-world is maintained within the imaginations of the Game Master and the players. For a computer game, this is a "virtual" space that is stored in the computer's memory and that the players can view via the computer screen. The actions the player makes in a game are limited to the game-world, as are the reactions of either the game itself or the other players.

GM: *Depending on the context, see* Gold Master *or* Game Master.

Go Live: Term used for when a massively multi-player game is launched and players start playing it. *See* Live.

Going Gold: The time when a team completes a game and is thereby able to create the gold master, which is sent to the duplicators. *See also* Gold Master.

Gold Candidate: *See* Release Candidate.

Gold Master: The version of the game, typically recorded onto gold CDs, that is going to be used by the duplicator to create copies of the actual shipping game. In other words, the final version of the game.

Graphical User Interface: This is any communications method the player has of interacting with the computer that is primarily graphical in nature. For instance, the Macintosh has always had a graphical user interface, as opposed to the text-oriented one available in MS-DOS or UNIX. Games use GUIs for starting up new games, loading saved games, and choosing other options from the main menu, but also for communicating information to the player not readily apparent from their view of the game-world: the player character's health, currently equipped weapon, amount of ammo, number of lives, score, and so forth.

Griefing: In a multi-player game, especially a massively multi-player online game, griefing is when players go out of their way to ruin the play experience of other gamers. This may be as simple as blocking a doorway so other players cannot travel through it, or it may be as mean-spirited as actually killing them. Griefing is different from simple competition, since "griefers" have little to gain by their actions beyond sadistic satisfaction.

GUI: *See* Graphical User Interface.

Heads Up Display: A type of graphical user interface that is overlaid on top of the player's game-world view. This may include the player character's health, a mini-map of the area, or radar of some sort, and typically communicates vital information to which the player must always have easy access. Heads up displays take their name from the displays used by jet fighter pilots, which constantly convey crucial flying information to those pilots while they are navigating the plane. *See also* Graphical User Interface.

High Concept: The most primitive form of a game idea, high concept describes a game in the simplest terms. Unfortunately, high concept ideas have a bad reputation because of their tendency to describe games that are best not developed. For example, a high concept might attempt to merge disparate types of gameplay or setting into one game, without regard to whether those different ideas will work well together. An example might be making a first-person shooter with a turn-based strategy game, or a wargame that includes a golf simulator. In these unfortunate cases, a high concept is often synonymous with a "bad concept."

HUD: *See* Heads Up Display.

IF: *See* Interactive Fiction.

IK: *See* Inverse Kinematics.

Immersive: When discussed in the context of games, an immersive game is one that tries to suck players into the world, making it as believable and consistent as possible, while giving the players as many choices as possible. Typical of an immersive game is a first-person viewpoint and a lack of "gamey" elements, such as blinking power-ups or obtrusive GUIs and HUDs.

Input/Output: Often shortened to I/O, this refers to the systems a computer uses to allow the player to input information (typically a keyboard and a mouse) in combination with how it communicates information back out to the user (typically the monitor). In terms of computer games, the I/O refers to the controls with which the player manipulates the game and the way the game then communicates to the player the current nature of the game-world.

Interactive: An interaction is when two systems, be they a human and a human, a human and a computer, or a computer and a computer, are mutually active in a given process. For instance, a television show is not interactive, since the television only outputs data and completely ignores whatever the user/audience does. A conversation between two people is interactive, however, since both parties listen to what the other has to say and will then say something related or in response to that. As another example, a strict lecture is not interactive since the lecturer reads a prepared speech without any input from the audience. A discussion group, however, is interactive, since the professor or leader of the discussion will answer the students' questions and listen to and evaluate their ideas. Games are interactive since they allow both the player and the computer to determine the shape of that particular game. Computer games are not being especially interactive when they play long cut-scenes over which the player has no control.

Interactive Fiction: A term originally coined by Infocom, interactive fiction is an alternate name for text adventures. Some people use interactive fiction to describe any games that use text to describe scenes and include a text parser, even if graphics are also included. *See also* Text Adventure.

Interactive Movie: A term coined by those working in games who wish to call their profession something more glamorous than what it is. This is similar to how the comic book industry sometimes attempts to call some of its longer and more sophisticated works "graphic novels." Typically, interactive movies involve more and longer cut-scenes than your average game. Unfortunately, the makers of so-called "interactive movies" typically add more movie than they do interactivity, resulting in works that are almost always not very good movies and lack the interactivity to be good games.

Inverse Kinematics: An animation technique whereby a joint in a character's skeleton is moved to a desired location and the joints that depend on or are influenced by that joint are automatically moved to the correct location. For example, if animating a humanoid, the hand could be moved toward a door handle and the elbow and shoulder would automatically move to reasonable positions. *See also* Skeletal Animation.

I/O: *See* Input/Output.

Isometric: Isometric is defined to mean "equality of measure," particularly in reference to drawing objects. If one were isometrically drawing a cube from a distance with one of the points of the cube pointing directly toward the viewer, the lines of the cube would all be of the same length and would not use any foreshortening. Games such as *Civilization II*, *SimCity 3000*, and *StarCraft* are drawn isometrically. This allows a game to be drawn from a somewhat 3D overhead view, which can then be scrolled around in all directions, without actually needing to involve a 3D rendering engine. The perspective on the world is technically wrong, but players do not seem to mind. Also referred to as a "three-quarters" view of the game world. *See also* Three-Quarters View.

LAN: An acronym for a Local Area Network. These networks typically consist of a small number of computers in a specific area networked to each other but not necessarily to the Internet or other networks.

LAN Party: Held when a bunch of friends get together, bring their computers to one central location, and play multi-player games over them. Typically the fast "ping" times allow players to have much faster and more lag-free games than are available over the Internet or other long-distance networks.

Linear: When the only way to get from point A to point B is via the line segment that connects them, we say that the movement is linear. Linear implies a lack of choice outside of a single dimension: forward or backward. In gaming, a linear game is one that does not give players much choice in what they do. For some games, linear may mean no choice at all, since backward is often not even an option.

Live: A term used for when a multi-player online game is up and running, with users from the world at large playing it. The expression "go live" means the time when the game is released for the general public to start playing. The "live team" consists of the developers responsible for keeping the game running and updating its content once it has launched. Any MMP developer will tell you that the act of keeping a game live and working smoothly is as much work as developing it prior to launch.

Lone Wolf: Term used to describe game developers who do practically everything themselves in the development of a game: the design, programming, art, sound, and writing. At the very least, a lone wolf developer must do all of the game's design and programming himself. A lone wolf does not typically develop commercially released software any more, though there are exceptions. For example, Chris Sawyer designed and programmed all of *RollerCoaster Tycoon* by himself, with a contractor completing the art to his specifications. Though he did not do the art himself, Sawyer can still be described as a lone wolf developer.

Massively Multi-Player: Strictly defined, a multi-player game involving a very large number of people playing it at once, at least 100 or more. Typically such games are also persistent and played over the Internet. *Ultima Online* and *EverQuest* are examples of massively multi-player games. *See also* Multi-Player *and* Persistent.

Media: Go out and buy Marshall McLuhan's *Understanding Media*. Read it. Come back only when you fully understand it.

Metagame: According to Richard Garfield, creator of *Magic: The Gathering*, the metagame is "how a game interfaces with life." This means what players take to and bring away from a particular playing of a game and how that impacts their subsequent playings of that game. This is particularly applicable to multi-player games. Take, for example, a game of *Unreal Tournament* on the Internet. If one player is known to play unethically through camping and other undesirable tactics, players will be likely to make a special effort to eliminate him in subsequent games. This means that the player may end up losing subsequent games because of his behavior in previous games. This interaction between the players from game to game is not part of the playing of the game itself, but is part of the metagame that the playing creates. For another example, in *Magic: The Gathering* the time a player spends preparing his deck before a game, though not part of the game itself, is part of the metagame.

Milestones: A term often used in contracts between publishers and developers. A milestone is an agreement of how much work on a project will be done at a specific date, with the publisher only paying the developer when that milestone (usually in the form of a current build of the game) is delivered to the publisher.

MMOG: Stands for Massively Multi-Player Online Game. *See* Massively Multi-Player.

MMORPG: Short for Massively Multi-Player Online Role-Playing Game, such as *Dark Age of Camelot*, *EverQuest*, or *Ultima Online*. *See* Massively Multi-Player.

MMP: *See* Massively Multi-Player.

Mod: Short for "modification," mods are user-created add-ons or changes to an existing game. Mods were popularized by id Software's open-architecture policy, which allowed players to make their own levels for *Doom*. Beyond levels, mods also often include new AI, new weapons, new art, or some combination of all three, potentially creating a radically altered gameplay experience from what was found in the original game.

MOO: Stands for MUD, Object Oriented. *See* MUD.

MUD: Originally stood for Multi-User Dungeon, but now can also stand for Multi-User Domain or Multi-User Dimension. MUDs resemble a text adventure with heavy RPG elements in their central play mechanics, with the important difference being that they take place in persistent, massively multi-player worlds. MUDs were set up and run by college students starting in the 1980s. Players of the games, when they reached a high enough experience level or rank, would become the creators of the games' content for other, less experienced players to explore. The primary interest many players have in MUDs is the social component, preferring to chat with people they have never seen before to going on *Dungeons & Dragons* style adventures. In many ways, *Ultima Online* and subsequent MMORPGs are carefully regulated graphical MUDs. Another popular variant are MOOs, which stands for MUD, Object Oriented. MOOs are architected such that players are able to easily expand the game-world themselves. There are also MUSHes, which are Multi-User Shared Hallucinations. MUSHes tend to forgo typical MUD gameplay, which centers around accumulating stats and weapons, in favor of a more social, role-playing oriented experience. There are lots of other acronyms for MUD variants, such as MUCKs and MUVEs, which I encourage readers to search out on the Internet if they are so inclined.

Multi-Player: A game that involves more than one player. Today, this typically also means "networked multi-player" where each player has his own computer and competes with the other players over a network, such as the Internet.

MUSH: Stands for Multi-User Shared Hallucination. *See* MUD.

Newbie: Slang for someone who is new to something. In games, this means novice players who have just started playing a particular game. Often used to refer to players who have just joined an online game, such as a massively multi-player RPG. Newbies are often at an extreme disadvantage to the players who have been playing longer.

Non-Linear: Obviously, the opposite of linear. In terms of gaming, this means that players are not locked into achieving different goals in a specific order or in achieving all of the goals they are presented with. Instead, players are able to move through the game in a variety of paths and can be successful in a variety of ways. Non-linearity leaves players with more choices to play the game their own way. *See also* Linear *and* On a Rail.

Non-Player Character: Any character in a computer game that is not controlled by the player. Typically this refers to game-world characters that are not hostile to the player, such as townspeople in an RPG.

NPC: *See* Non-Player Character.

NURBS: Stands for non-uniform rational B-splines. A 3D graphics technique for creating curved surfaces, a detailed explanation of which should be sought out in a 3D graphics programming book.

On a Rail *or* **On Rails:**   A game is said to be on a rail when players are forced to move through the game in a very specific, carefully controlled way, as if they were locked onto a rail that ran through the game. Games that are said to be "on a rail" or "on rails" are very linear games. A specific type of game called a "rail shooter" is on rails to such an extent that the flight path of the player's vehicle is completely predetermined, and players are only able to shoot at targets as they pass by. *Rebel Assault* is an example of a rail shooter. *See also* Linear.

180 Degree Rule: A film technique for cutting a scene that says that the camera must always stay on one side of a line that extends between the two centers of attention in the frame. If the camera never rotates anywhere outside of those 180 degrees, the audience will not become confused by the scene's cuts from character to character.

Online: A game that is played online is run over any sort of a network, whether a LAN or the Internet. Typically online games are multi-player, and, since each player has his own machine and display, allows each player to have a blind-play experience, where other users cannot see what tactics he is using. This makes online games play significantly different than single system multi-player games.

Parser: In gaming, often refers to the input method used by text adventures. A parser takes natural language words or sentences the player enters and translates them into commands that the game logic can understand. Parsers can become quite sophisticated while still failing to understand many of the sentences that players attempt to use as commands. Natural language processing is a major field of AI research, one that is still far from perfect, so it is no wonder that parsers have as much trouble as they do. A more modern usage of the term parser is in reference to the interpreter for a game's scripting language. *See also* Text Adventure.

Pathfinding: This is the portion of the AI code that allows an agent to figure out how to get from one location to another in the game-world. Ideally, pathfinding allows the AI agent to avoid getting stuck on obstacles or other agents, yet pathfinding in many games is less than perfect. There are various algorithms, such as A*, that can be used for pathfinding, which may have different results in terms of efficiency and the quality of the paths generated, though that is a topic better explored in a book about programming. *See also* A*.

PC: May refer either to a game's player character or to the Intel-based personal computer originally popularized by IBM and powered by MS-DOS. *See also* Player Character.

Persistent: A persistent game is one that continues running and maintaining the state of the game-world regardless of whether a particular player is actively playing it or not. Often persistent games are also massively multi-player, and vice versa. MUDs were one of the first persistent games, while commercial products such as *Ultima Online* and *EverQuest* have made persistent games quite popular to mainstream gamers. *See also* MUD.

Pitch Document: *See* Concept Document.

PK, PKing: *See* Player Killer.

Place-Holder: Typically refers to sound or art used in a game while it is in development but which the development team plans to replace before the game is released to the public.

Platform: Often used to describe the different systems a game can be developed for. Popular gaming platforms past and present include the Apple II, Atari 800, Commodore 64, IBM PC, Commodore Amiga, Macintosh, Atari 2600, Nintendo Entertainment System, Sega Genesis, and Sony PlayStation.

Player Character: This is the character the player controls in the game, such as Mario in *Super Mario 64*, Lara Croft in *Tomb Raider*, or the space marine in *Doom*. This term is a holdover from pencil and paper RPGs such as *Dungeons & Dragons*.

Player Killer: In multi-player games, players who go out of their way to ruthlessly kill other players. These are particularly problematic in games that are supposed to be more collaborative in nature, such as massively multi-player online RPGs.

Player Surrogate: *See* Surrogate.

Player's Story: This is the story the players create through their actions in playing the game. This will involve the clever techniques they used for succeeding at the game's challenges, whether it was where they positioned themselves to shoot and kill their enemies, how they laid the streets down to build up a city, or which plays they chose to win a football game. Some would be hesitant to call this a story, as it can often more resemble a simple chronology of events. However, the player's story is unique to that player's game experience, and is what he is most likely to remember and talk about with his friends.

Playtesting: A term referring to the process of testing the gameplay of the game to see how well it plays. Playtesting is different from bug fixing or quality assurance in general since playtesting focuses on the performance of gameplay itself instead of general bug fixing. See Chapter 25, "Playtesting."

Port/Porting: The process of converting a game from one gaming platform to another, such as from the PC to the Macintosh, or from the Sony PlayStation to the Nintendo 64. Typically, games that are ported are completed on one system first, and only then brought over to the other system.

Power-Up: A generic term that refers to any item in the game-world players may acquire to improve their abilities, either briefly or long-term. Typically used in action/adventure type games, a power-up may include a weapon, ammo, a key, a health pack, a jet pack, or money. Power-ups are often used to draw the player to explore certain locations, with the abilities granted by their acquisition conferring a generally positive reward on the player.

PR: *See* Public Relations.

Pre-Rendered: 3D graphics that are rendered into 2D sprites or images before the player plays the game. *Myst* features pre-rendered 3D graphics, while *Unreal* features real-time 3D graphics. *See also* Real-Time 3D.

Proposal: *See* Concept Document.

PSX: An abbreviation for Sony's PlayStation console. Actually based on an early name for the system, the PlayStation X. Nonetheless, the abbreviation stuck. However, Sony does not like you calling their newer system the PSX2.

Public Relations: A wing of the marketing department whose primary job is to hype a company's upcoming games in the press by readying press releases, screenshots, and other information. They also can be quite helpful in granting permission to use screenshots in books such as this one.

QA: *See* Quality Assurance.

Quality Assurance: This is the process of testing a game to make sure that it is bug-free and plays reasonably well. The quality assurance cycle or period is the time when a nearly complete project is extensively tested just prior to release. In large companies, the quality assurance department or team performs that testing.

Rail, On a: *See* On a Rail.

Real-Time: Anything that is computed or rendered for players while they wait, such as graphics and pathfinding. This differentiates something from being pre-computed before the actual gameplay is taking place. Can also differentiate a game from being turn-based. *See also* Turn-Based.

Real-Time Strategy: A currently popular genre of games, including such titles as *Command & Conquer, WarCraft, Total Annihilation*, and *Myth: The Fallen Lords*. This term is typically emphasized to differentiate these RTS games from turn-based strategy games such as *Civilization, X-Com: UFO Defense*, and *Alpha Centauri*.

Real-Time 3D: Describes 3D graphics that are rendered while the player is looking at them, so that as the player moves around the world, many different views of objects and configurations of the game-world can be generated on the fly. *Unreal* uses real-time 3D graphics while *Myst* uses pre-rendered 3D graphics. *See also* Pre-Rendered.

Release Candidate: A build of the game the development team believes may be the one that can be shipped. A release candidate is generally tested for at least a few days, optimally a week or two, to determine if it is bug-free enough to be acceptable to the publisher. It is not uncommon for a particular product to go through five or more release candidates. *See also* Alpha *and* Beta.

Role-Playing Game: Games based on the type of gameplay established by pencil and paper role-playing games such as *Dungeons & Dragons*. Those original non-computer games were so titled because in them players took on the roles of characters of their own creation and guided them through a fantasy world. Much of the gameplay in RPGs depends on the players role-playing these characters who often had personalities different from their own. Ironically, most computer role-playing games often contain very little of the role-playing aspect of traditional RPGs, instead choosing to concentrate on the combat mechanics and fantasy setting.

RPG: *See* Role-Playing Game.

RT3D: *See* Real-Time 3D.

RTS: *See* Real-Time Strategy.

Scripted: In terms of a game, scripted typically refers to AI behaviors that are planned in advance to allow the AI agents to look clever in specific situations in a level.

Scripted events play the same way every time a player plays a level. *Half-Life* used scripted events, sometimes combined with dynamic AI, to produce very impressive gameplay effects that gave the illusion of a very smart AI system.

Sim: Short for simulator or simulation. *See* Simulation.

Simulation: Typically, in games that are described as simulations, the primary goal of the game's designer is to model a real-life system accurately and realistically, instead of simply making the game as fun as possible. This system could be anything, such as an aircraft of some kind, a race car, or a city. Simulation can also refer to a type of game programming where, instead of hard-coding different outcomes to player input, various systems are created out of which responses emerge. For example, *System Shock* and *Deus Ex* are systems- or simulation-based action/RPGs.

Simulator: *See* Simulation.

Skeletal Animation: An alternative to vertex deformation for 3D animations. With a skeletal animation system, the game keeps track of an animating character's skeleton. The animation then controls this skeleton, moving the animating character's mesh to match the skeleton properly. A skeletal animation system has the advantage of causing animations to take up much less space than when they are animated using a technique such as vertex deformation, and often leads to superior looking animations. Furthermore, the skeleton can be controlled procedurally for inverse kinematics effects of various types. *See also* Vertex Deformation *and* Inverse Kinematics.

Skin: In gaming, skin refers to the texture set being used on a 3D player character in a game like *Quake III Arena, Unreal Tournament*, or *The Sims*. Players will get to choose what skin they play the game with, either from the default collection that comes with the game or by making their own and importing it into the game.

SKU: Stands for stock keeping unit or shelf keeping unit. It is the unique number associated with every bar code and used by stores to track their inventory. Each unique version of a game is sometimes referred to as a different SKU. If one game ships for different platforms, say Macintosh and PC, then each version is a separate SKU. Similarly, *Thief* and *Thief Gold* are two different SKUs, though they are practically the same game.

Software Toy: A term coined by Will Wright of Maxis to describe that company's first product, *SimCity*. A software toy is quite similar to a game, except that it defines no criterion for success. Players are just left to play with the game as they wish without ever "winning" or "losing." Yet players may make a software toy into a game by defining their own personal conditions for success. *See also* Game.

Split-Screen: A technique whereby multiple players are allowed to play and/or compete on a single computer or console because the screen is split into (typically) two or four sections. Each section then displays the portion of the game-world relevant to each player playing the game. The disadvantage to split-screen gaming over online gaming is that all the players can see the screens of the other players. The advantage to split-screen gaming is that all the players play in close proximity to each other, allowing for a significantly more social experience.

State-Based AI: A type of AI that uses states for each of its agents. States include actions such as idle, walking, attacking, and so forth. The AI then switches the agent from one state to another depending on the conditions of the game-world. May also be referred to as a finite state machine or FSM.

State Machine: *See* State-Based AI.

Story Bible: A document that contains all the information available about the story elements of the game-world. Story bibles can be quite large, especially when working with properties with established histories, such as the *Star Trek* or *Ultima* universes. These documents are usually used as reference works for the developers during the game's creation. Described in detail in Chapter 17, "Game Development Documentation."

Surrogate: A term used to describe the entity that the player controls in the game, also known as the player character or the player's avatar. *See also* Avatar *and* Player Character.

Suspension of Disbelief: A mental state that players achieve when they are fully immersed in the game-world and briefly forget that they are playing a game at all. Naturally players will disbelieve what is happening on the screen, since it is projected on a flat screen, it does not look exactly like the real world, and players control their actions in it with a keyboard and mouse or a controller instead of their normal body movements. However, as with movies, the time comes when players make the subconscious decision to forget the inherent fake-ness of the presentation, to suspend their disbelief, and to start to believe that they really are great heroes or they really are in outer space or what have you. Maintaining players in that state for as long as possible is one of the primary goals of immersive games.

TDD: *See* Technical Design Document.

Technical Design Document: This document takes the gameplay as described in the design document and explains how that gameplay will be implemented in more technical, code-centered terms. As a result, this document is often used primarily by the programming team. This can take the form of one massive document that covers the whole project, or it can be a number of smaller documents about specific features. Described in detail in Chapter 17, "Game Development Documentation."

Technical Specification: Another name for the technical design document. *See* Technical Design Document.

Text Adventure: Text adventures are devoid of graphics and describe the game-world to the player exclusively through text. Players are then able to interact with the game-world by typing in natural language sentences in the imperative form, stating what they want their character to do next. The form was made extremely popular by Infocom in the early 1980s. *See also* Interactive Fiction.

Three-Quarters View: Typically refers to games that have an isometric viewpoint. This view can be in any rendering system with an overhead view of the ground where the camera is oriented at a 45-degree angle from the plane of the ground. *See also* Isometric.

Turn-Based: Any game where the computer waits for the player to act before proceeding with its own actions. *Civilization*, for instance, is a turn-based strategy game, while *WarCraft* is a real-time strategy game. For some non-computer game examples, chess is a turn-based game while football (soccer) is real-time. American football is a bizarre hybrid of real-time and turn-based gameplay.

Turn-Based Strategy: *See* Turn-Based.

Vertex Deformation: A 3D animation system where the individual vertices of a model are moved one by one to new positions for each frame of the animation. This is the simplest 3D animation method to code for, but has many disadvantages over a skeletal animation system. Sometimes also called keyframe animation. *See also* Skeletal Animation.

Virtual Reality: Technically, virtual reality, or VR, refers to advanced world-simulation systems at a minimum involving the user wearing a set of goggles with a small monitor or display device in each eyepiece. This allows players to get a truly 3D, stereo-vision experience. Also, the VR headset allows the players to turn their heads and have their view of the virtual world change accordingly to match the new location at which they are "looking." VR systems may also involve wearing gloves or full-body suits that detect the user's motion and translate that into motion in the virtual world. Because of this, VR allows for some of the most immersive virtual environments possible. Virtual reality is one of the most commonly misused terms in all of computer game parlance. Many game developers with inflated senses of what they are doing will refer to their RT3D first-person games as VR when, since they do not involve headsets, they are really nothing of the kind. Marketing people are particularly fond of misusing and abusing this term.

VR: *See* Virtual Reality.

Wargame: When used in reference to computer games, wargame typically refers to strategy-oriented games that employ gameplay based on pen and paper or board wargames such as those made by Avalon Hill. Computer wargames almost always simulate historic battles, typically feature hexagon-based play-fields, and use turn-based gameplay. Games that are set in historical wars but are not strategic in nature are not generally referred to as wargames. Classic examples of computer wargames include *Kampfgruppe* and *Eastern Front (1941),* while more modern examples include *Panzer General* and *Close Combat.*

Selected Bibliography

The following references have been a great help to me in solidifying my ideas about computer games. I list them here as a sort of "recommended reading" list for those who wish to continue to learn about game design outside the confines of this book.

Books

Bogdanovich, Peter. *Who The Devil Made It*. New York: Knopf, 1997.

A fascinating collection of interviews with classic film directors. Bogdanovich's interview style was my model for the interviews conducted in this book.

Campbell, Joseph. *The Hero with a Thousand Faces*. New York: Bollingen Foundation Inc., 1949; reprint Princeton: Princeton University Press, 1972.

Campbell's book is the definitive text on understanding the nature of myths, legends, and heroic stories from throughout the ages.

Crawford, Chris. *The Art of Computer Game Design*. Berkeley, CA: Osborne/McGraw-Hill, 1984.
_____. *The Art of Interactive Design: A Euphonious Guide to Building Successful Software*. San Francisco, CA: No Starch Press, 2002.
_____. *Chris Crawford on Game Design*. Boston, MA: New Riders Publishing, 2003.

Crawford's seminal *The Art of Computer Game Design* was the first book about computer game design and was the inspiration for this book. Despite its age in computer game industry terms, it remains largely relevant today. Long out of print, it can currently be read in a number of locations on the Internet, including www.erasmatazz.com. Recently, Crawford has published two new books that will be of interest to game designers. Originally self-published as *Understanding Interactivity*, Crawford's *The Art of Interactive Design* deals not specifically with games but with interactive design in general. A reworking of sorts of *The Art of Computer Game Design*, *Chris Crawford on Game Design* sees Crawford focusing once again specifically on games, with his unique style and acerbic wit sure to entertain as it enlightens.

DeMaria, Rusel and Johnny L. Wilson. *High Score! The Illustrated History of Electronic Games*. Berkeley, CA: Osborne/McGraw-Hill, 2002.

Long-time game journalists, DeMaria and Wilson's book is a deluxe package, with more gorgeous images of gaming's history than one would have thought existed. The facts and first-hand accounts of computer and video game history are also

672

fantastic. Though not specifically about game design, the book will be a joy to read for anyone who wants to learn more about the fascinating history of computer games.

Kent, Stephen L. *The Ultimate History of Video Games*. Roseville, CA: Prima Publishing, 2001.

> This is the most exhaustive and definitive book about the history of video and computer games written to date. Though it is lighter on images than *High Score!*, it goes into much more detail about the history of computer gaming, both creatively and from a business standpoint. It is not specifically about game design issues, but its insights into game history are riveting for anyone interested in the form.

McCloud, Scott. *Understanding Comics*. Northampton, MA: Kitchen Sink Press, Inc., 1993.

_____. *Reinventing Comics*. New York: Paradox Press, 2000.

> Though these books are technically about comics, they both provide tremendous insight about media and art of all kinds. It is fair to say that *Understanding Comics* fundamentally changed the way I think about art.

McLuhan, Marshall. *Understanding Media*. New York: McGraw-Hill Book Co., 1964. reprint Cambridge, MA: MIT Press, 1994.

> The definitive book on media of all kinds, a work that takes on new meaning in the age of the Internet. McLuhan may be a bit obtuse in his writing style, but his insights are without peer.

Strunk, William and E.B. White. *The Elements of Style*. New York: Macmillan Publishing, 1959; reprint 4th Ed. Boston: Allyn and Bacon, 2000.

> *The Elements of Style* remains the last word on clear and concise writing. It is a book that anyone writing a design document, script, or book about game design would do well to read.

Periodicals

Computer Gaming World (Ziff Davis Media)

> Still the best monthly magazine about computer games.

Develop (MCV Media)

> The UK counterpart to *Game Developer, Develop* has a more sarcastic take on the game industry and is somewhat more business-oriented, while still covering real development issues from all angles.

Edge (Future Publishing, Inc.)

> This unique magazine is equally interested in reviewing games and looking under the hood of how they are developed. In many ways, this was the UK counterpart to *Next Generation*, and with that magazine's demise is now the only magazine of its class.

Game Developer (CMP Media, Inc.)

> The closest the gaming industry has to a trade magazine, *Game Developer* covers all aspects of game development, including articles on game design.

Next Generation (Imagine Media, Inc.)

Sadly no longer being published, *Next Generation* was a unique hybrid computer/console game magazine with an emphasis on cutting-edge game technology and, sometimes, the theory and people behind the games. Back issues are worth attempting to track down.

Surge (Bedford Communications, Inc.)

In many ways *Surge* is staking claim to some of the space left by the demise of *Next Generation*, looking deeper into the world of games than any of the other non-development gaming magazines.

Web Sites

www.anticlockwise.com/dani

A tribute page to the late Dani Bunten Berry, the tremendously gifted designer of the classic *M.U.L.E.* and *Seven Cities of Gold*, and one of the pioneers of multi-player gaming. Includes many of Berry's writings about game design and reflections on her career. Note: the URL for this site has changed numerous times since the first edition of this book came out. If the above link does not work, do a Google search for "Dani Bunten Berry" to find the most up-to-date location.

www.costik.com

Greg Costikyan is best known for his pencil and paper game designs, including the classic games *Toon* and *Paranoia*, though he has also done a number of computer games. His web site includes an array of articles he has written, including the very interesting screed, "I Have No Words & I Must Design."

www.dadgum.com/halcyon

Originally published as an e-book, James Hague's book is now available for free on the Internet and is an invaluable source of information about what it was like to work in the gaming industry just as it was starting to establish itself. All information comes straight from the source through a series of interviews with a broad range of subjects, including many whose work is discussed in this book: Eugene Jarvis, Dani Bunten Berry, Dan Gorlin, Brian Moriarty, Ed Rotberg, Chris Crawford, and so on.

www.8kindsoffun.com

One-time Looking Glass Studios programmer Marc LeBlanc understands the more fundamental concepts of game design better than most game designers, as is evidenced by his numerous lectures on game design at the Game Developers Conference and other venues. Most of his works are collected here.

www.erasmatazz.com

Chris Crawford's current home on the web, centered on his interactive storytelling engine, the Erasmatron. Also includes a vast library of Crawford's writings about game design, including everything he ever wrote for the *Journal of Computer Game Design* and links to the full text of *The Art of Computer Game Design*. Required reading.

www.gamasutra.com

Gamasutra is the sister web site of *Game Developer* magazine. The site runs original content as well as some reprints from the magazine. Within its pages, a vast wealth of information is archived and searchable.

www.gamedev.net

One of the definitive sites about game development on the web and one of Gamasutra's primary rivals. GameDev.net is a much more active site in general, with a broad wealth of knowledge that will be a boon to professionals and hobbyists alike.

www.legendmud.org/raph

Raph Koster's home page on the web, with tons of articles about MMP game design issues. Before becoming lead designer on the original *Ultima Underworld*, Koster had been involved with the MUD community for some time, and his writings reflect his diverse knowledge of the subject.

www.ludix.com/moriarty

A collection of Brian Moriarty's lectures on games. Moriarty is surely one of the most inspirational speakers the community has ever had, and though his lectures may not tell you specific things to do on your next game project, they will force you to reflect on the nature of games and their often challenging development.

www.mobygames.com

This massive site serves the game industry much like the Internet Movie Database does the film industry; though not quite complete, it contains a searchable index of games released for most of the major systems over the last twenty years. Want to know what else the lead designer of your current favorite game worked on previously? Look it up on MobyGames.

www.theinspiracy.com

The home page for Noah Falstein's game consulting company, The Inspiracy. In addition to being kind enough to comment on and write the foreword for this book, Falstein is the game design columnist for *Game Developer* magazine, where he has been working on what he calls "The 400 Project," an effort to record some 400 rules that apply to game design. The site includes a discussion of The 400 Project, as well as other writings by Falstein and transcripts of some of his talks at the Game Developers Conference.

Index

Page numbers in **bold** indicate an image of that particular game.

POWERVR

Visionary IP

PC

Arcade

In-car

Digital TV

Handheld

Internet
Appliance

Set-top/
Console

Get **Deep** into 3D!

Search, View, Translate, Animate, Render and Publish!

Deep Exploration™ provides easy navigation tools that let you search and view your 2D graphics and 3D models. It gives artists everywhere a production edge, including the ability to quickly translate 2D and 3D file formats with animation included. Deep Exploration creates high quality fast renderings of 3D objects and scenes for use in many graphic applications. It is also a powerful web publication tool, ideal for creating interactive 3D content for web-based presentations.

3D Painting and Texturing

Deep Paint 3D® provides artists with an intuitive, easy to use tool to paint and texture 3D models interactively in 3D! It uses textures or natural media paints which can be brushed directly or projected onto 3D models and scenes. This creative environment supports an integrated workflow with 3ds max®, Maya®, SoftImage® and LightWave 3D®. Deep Paint 3D comes complete with a bi-directional interface to Photoshop® and special support for the Wacom® Intuos™ pressure sensitive tablet.

Ultimate UV Mapping

Deep UV™ is a superior set of tools for the creation and modification of UV mapping for polygonal and sub-division surface models within an interactive 2D and 3D UV mapping environment. Deep UV includes fast and easy to use tools such as soft selection, relax and 3D UV selection. Whether you're a beginner or a professional 3D artist, you'll have the most efficient UV mapping possible with both automatic and advanced features. Deep UV can be used standalone, or with Deep Paint 3D.

RIGHT (HEMISPHERE.

www.righthemisphere.com